TABLE OF CONTENTS

Market Trends	1
History of Clocks	3
Identification and Dating	9
Building a Collection	17
Condition	21
Types of Clocks	22
Replicas, Reproductions, and Fakes	28
Display	30
Restoration	32
Suppliers	37
Publications	41
Museums	42
Calendar of Events	46
Glossary	47
Recommended Reading	68
How to Use this Book	76
Ansonia Clock Company	77
Advertising	78
Alarm/Drum	78
Fancy	80
Cabinet	83
Calendar	87
Carriage	91
China or Porcelain	
Large Case	93
Small Case	96
Connecticut Shelf	
Beehive	96
O.G.	97
Round Top	97
Split Top	98
Steeple	99
Crystal Palace	100
Crystal Regulator	100
Crystal Regulator Porcelain	106
Gallery	107
Grandfather	108
Kitchen	109
Kitchen/Ebony	117
Hanging	118
Mantel	120
Mirror Sides	120
Tear Drop	121
Mantel/Black Iron	122
Black Wood	124
Bronze	125
Mahogany	126
Marble	126
Metal Regency	127
Onyx	127
Plush	128
Novelty/Animated	129
Art Nouveau	129
Bisque	131
Brass	131
China	133
Fancy	133
Gilt	133
Iron	135
Night Light	137
Plush	137
Wall	138
Office Ink	138
Regulator	
Astronomical	141
Figure Eight	142
Octagon Top, Long Drop	142
Octagon Top, Short Drop	143
Open Swinging	145
Parlor Shelf	146
Parlor Wall	146
Round Top, Long Drop	151
Seconds Bit	152
Store	153
Sweep Second	154
Statue/Over 17″	155
Under 17″	158
Swing Arm	160
Boardman-Hubbell	161
Calendar	161
E. Burwell-L.F. and W.W. Carter	161
Calendar	161
Clinton and Mood	162
Calendar	162
Davis Clock Company	162
Calendar	162
Empire Calendar Clock Company	163
Calendar	163
C.W. Feishtinger	163
Calendar	163
Franklin-Morse	163
Calendar	163
D.J. Gale	163
Calendar	163
W.L. Gilbert Clock Co.	164
Alarm/Drum	164
Fancy	166
Cabinet	168
Calendar	168
Carriage	172
Connecticut Shelf	
Beehive	174
Column	174
Cottage	175
Octagon Top	176
O.G.	176
Round Top	177
Split Top	178
Steeple	178
Crystal Regulator	179
Gallery	180
Kitchen	180
Hanging	189
Series	190
Tear Drop	190
Mantel/Onyx	190
Round Top	191
Novelty/Gilt	191
Wall	195
Office Ink	196
Regulator/Octagon Top, Long Drop	196
Octagon Top, Short Drop	196
Parlor Wall	197
Round Top, Long Drop	200
Seconds Bit	200
Sweep Second	201
Statue/Over 17″	202
Part Onyx	203
Porcelain	203
Under 17″	204
Gilbert Dial	206
Calendar	206
Gilbert-Maranville	206
Calendar	206
Gilbert-McCabe	206
Calendar	206
E. Howard Clock Co.	207
Astronomical	208
Dial, Standing	209
Dial, Wall	210
Regulator	210
Banjo	211
Figure Eight	212
Electric Gallery	213
Grandfather	213
Hanging Regulator	215
Marble Dial	216
Regulator/Round Top	218
Square Top	218
Wall	220
Watchmakers Regulator Standing	220
Wall, Arch Top	220
Wall Round Top	221
Wall, Square Top	222
Watchmens Clock	222
E. Ingraham Company	224
Alarm	224
Banjo/Spring	224
Spring Lever	225
Spring Pendulum	226
Cabinet	226
Calendar	227
Connecticut Shelf	
Cottage	233
Octagon Top	233
O.G.	234

Round Top 234	Musical 321	Round 382
Split Top 235	Novelty/Brass 322	Automobile Clock 383
Gallery 236	Plush 325	Banjo 383
Kitchen 236	Window 329	Cabinet 383
Series 240	Miscellaneous 329	Cabinet/Westminster
Mantel/Black Wood ... 240	Porcelene 330	Chimes 387
Mahogany Case 241	Regulator	Calendar 388
Round Top 242	Astronomical 334	Carriage 398
Tambour 242	Drop Octagon 334	China/Large 400
Mirror Side 243	Round Top,	Small 401
Regulator/Figure Eight . 243	Long Drop 334	Connecticut Shelf
Octagon Top,	Ionic 335	Arch Top 402
Long Drop 244	Parlor Wall 335	Bee Hive 402
Octagon Top,	Seconds Bit 338	Cottage 403
Short Drop 245	Sweep Second 340	Octagon Top 403
Parlor Wall 247	Rotary 343	O.G. and O.O.G. 404
Round Top,	Statue 345	Round Top 404
Short Drop 248	**Lux and Keebler** 346	Split Top 405
Square Top 248	Alarm 346	Steeple 406
Store 249	Animated 348	Crystal Regulator 407
Ithaca Calendar Clock	Art 349	Gallery 408
Company 250	Cuckoo	Marble 408
Calendar 250	Chain and Weight ... 351	Grandfather 409
Jerome & Company 258	Electric 352	Kitchen 409
Calendar 259	Heartbeat 352	Series 417
Connecticut Shelf	Pendulum and	Tear Drop 419
Beehive 260	Pendulette 353	Wall 419
Cottage 260	Miscellaneous 357	Mantel/Black Iron 420
Empire and Column . 262	**Macomb Calendar Co.** . 359	Black Wood 421
Mantel Lever 262	Calendar 359	Brass Finish 422
O.G. and O.O.G. 263	**G. Maranville** 359	Mahogany Case 422
Papier Mache 264	Calendar 359	Onyx 422
Pearl Inlaid 266	**Monarch Calendar Clock**	Tambour 423
Steeple 266	**Company** 359	Mirror Sides 423
Gallery 267	Calendar 359	Mission 424
Gallery/Octagon,	**Mozart, Beach &**	Cabinet 424
Short Drop 268	**Hubbell** 360	Grandfather 425
Octagon Lever 269	Calendar 360	Kitchen 425
Keyless Auto Clock	**Mueller & Son** 360	Kitchen, Hanging ... 425
Company 270	Character 360	Novelty 425
F. Kroeber 272	Etruscan 361	Octagon, Drop 426
Alarm/Animated 273	Flora and Fauna 362	Novelty/Fancy 426
Drum 274	Floral Painted 364	Gilt 428
Fancy 276	Gothic 365	French Gilt 436
Animated 280	Iron and Bronze 366	Office Ink 436
Cabinet 281	Novelty/Animated 367	Regulator/Figure Eight . 436
Mirror Sides 286	Parlor 368	Octagon Top,
Calendar 287	Statue 369	Long Drop 437
Double Dial 287	**Nicholas Muller's Sons** . 374	Octagon Top,
Carriage 288	Alarm/Fancy 374	Short Drop 438
Connecticut Shelf ... 290	Cabinet 374	Open Swinging 439
Cuckoo/Mantel 294	Mantel/Bronze 374	Parlor Shelf 439
Wall 295	Marble 376	Parlor Teardrop 440
Gallery 297	Novelty 379	Parlor Wall 440
Kitchen 298	Office Ink 379	Round Top 443
Mirror Sides 310	Statue 380	Seconds Bit 444
Teardrop 310	**National Calendar Clock**	Square Top 447
Lever/Wall 312	**Company** 380	Sweep Second 448
Mantel/Black Iron 313	Calendar 380	Statue/Large 451
Black Iron with	**New Haven Clock Co.** . 381	Small 452
Figure 315	Alarm 381	Watch 454
Brass 319	Fancy 381	**G.B. Owen** 455

Calendar 455	Parlor Wall 485	Regulator/Figure Eight . 522
J.I. Peatfield 455	Parlor Wall Chime ... 486	Octagon Top,
Calendar 455	Precision 486	Long Drop 522
Prentiss Improvement Clock	Round Top 486	Octagon Top,
Company 455	Seconds Bit 487	Short Drop 523
Calendar 455	Square Top 489	Open Swinging 524
Russell & Jones Clock	Store 489	Parlor Shelf 525
Company 456	Sweep Seconds 490	Parlor Wall 525
Calendar 456	Statue/Over 18" 490	Round Top,
Joseph K. Seem Dial	Art Nouveau,	Long Drop 528
Company 456	Over 18" 491	Round Top,
Calendar 456	Under 18" 492	Short Drop 528
Seem Calendar 456	Art Nouveau,	Seconds Bit 529
Calendar 456	Under 18" 492	Sweep Seconds 530
Sessions Clock Co. 457	Street 492	Statue/Over 18" 532
Calendar 457	**Southern Calendar Clock**	Under 18" 532
Seth Thomas Clock	**Company** 493	**E.N. Welch Manufacturing**
Company 457	Calendar 493	**Company** 533
Alarm/Fancy 459	**Southern Clock Co.** 493	Alarm/Fancy 533
Round 460	Calendar 493	Round 533
Cabinet 461	**Standard Calendar Clock**	Cabinet 534
Calendar 462	**Company-O.G. Clock**	Calendar 534
Carriage 466	**Company** 493	Welch, Spring and
Connecticut Shelf	Calendar 493	Company 536
Arch Top 466	**Terry Clock Co.** 493	Carriage 537
Column 466	Calendar 494	Connecticut Shelf
Cottage 467	Connecticut Shelf	Beehive 537
Empire 468	Chapel 494	Column 538
Octagon Top 468	Column 494	Cottage 538
O.G. and O.O.G. 468	Cottage 495	Empire 539
Reproductions of Early	Gothic and Mantel .. 495	Octagon Top 539
Models 469	Novelty 495	O.G. and O.O.G. 539
Round Top 469	O.G., O.O.G. and	Round Top 540
Split Top 469	Reverse O.G. 496	Split Top 540
Steeple 469	Round Top 496	Steeple 540
Crystal Regulator 469	Regulator 498	Gallery/Wall Lever 541
Gallery/Wall Lever 472	**Waltham** 499	Kitchen 541
Grandfather 473	Banjo 500	Series 543
Kitchen 473	Library 501	Tear Drop 544
Series 476	**W.A. Terry-Ansonia** ... 502	Mantel/Black Iron 544
Tear Drop 477	Calendar 502	Black Wood 544
Mantel/Brass Finish ... 478	**W.A. Terry-Atkins** 502	Novelty/Fancy 545
Bronze 478	Calendar 502	Iron 545
Decorated Metal 478	**Waterbury Clock Co.** .. 502	Patti Movements 546
Mahogany 478	Alarm/Calendar 503	Regulator/Figure Eight . 546
Metal Regency 479	Round 503	Octagon Top,
Round Top 479	Cabinet 504	Long Drop 546
Westminster Chimes . 479	Calendar 504	Octagon Top,
Mission 480	Carriage 509	Short Drop 547
Novelty/Art Nouveau .. 480	Connecticut Shelf	Parlor Shelf 547
China 482	Cottage 510	Parlor Wall 547
Gilt 483	O.G. 510	Round Top,
Iron 484	Crystal Regulator 510	Long Drop 548
Wall 484	Gallery/Wall Lever 514	Round Top,
Regulator/Figure Eight . 484	Grandfather 514	Short Drop 548
Octagon Top,	Kitchen 515	Seconds Bit 548
Long Drop 484	Wall 517	Sweep Second 548
Octagon Top,	Mantel/Metal Regency . 519	Rotary 548
Short Drop 484	Mission 520	Watches 548
Open Swinging 485	Novelty/Art Nouveau .. 520	About the Author 549
Parlor Shelf 485	Iron 521	

DEDICATION

The values shown in this book have been supplied by collectors and dealers from all over the United States. I'd like to take this opportunity to say thanks for the help they have given me.

Gene Anderson, St. Louis, MO; Bill Andrus, Bossier City, LA; Fred Andrus, Augusta, ME; Don and Sharon Bass, Sandusky, OH; Dr. Douglas Beck, Baton Rouge, LA; Steve and Marsha Berger, Buffalo Grove, IL; Marion Blevins, Bettendorf, IA; Jane A. Brinkmeyer, Manchester, MO; Clyde and Betty Brown, Akron, OH; Mrs. W. Charles Bruer, (deceased), Kansas City, MO; George Collard, Portland, ME; Bob Coonfield, Oklahoma City, OK; Stewart Dow (deceased), Akron, OH; Jerry Faier, Overland Park, KS; Eldon Falke, Kansas City, MO; Judy Ehrhardt, Kansas City, MO; Michael "Mike" Ehrhardt, Kansas City, MO; Sherry L. Ehrhardt, Grandview, MO; Ed Getman, Newton, MA; Jonathan Giunchedi, Lake Forest, IL; Roy Good, Memphis, TN; Luther and Vivian Grinder, Owensboro, KY; Fred Hansen, Montgomery, NY; Robert and Gert Hansen, New Hampton, NY; Russel and Connie Henschel, Fairview Heights, IL; Spencer Hodgson, Arlington Heights, IL; Howard Klein, St. Louis, MO; Jerome Levin, Creve Coeur, MO; Mrs. L. McCormack, Portland, OR; Wiley McNeil, Greensboro, NC; Bill Mather, Randolph Center, VT; William "Bill" Meggers, Jr., Ridgecrest, CA; R. T. "Rod" Minter, Lombard, IL; Paul J. Morrissey, Waterbury, CT; Harry Neames, Baton Rouge, LA; Mr. and Mrs. E. H. Parkhurst, Jr., Lancaster, PA; Daryl Penniston, Lake Charles, LA; Theral and Thelma Pritts, Decatur, IL; Gregg Reddick, Dubuque, IA; Roger Rees, Rockford, IL; Shirley Shelley, Belton, MO; Dr. Sam Simmons, Atlanta, GA; Phil Sommers, Raytown, MO; H. A. Soper (deceased), Harrison, AR; Ron Starnes, Tulsa, OK; Douglas Thomas, Tullhoma, TN; Larry Thompson, Green Lawn, NY; Thomas Tognetti, San Rafael, CA; Col. George Townsend (deceased), Alma, MI; David M. Warner, Manchester, MO; Bobby Webber, Hampton, NH; Ralph Whitmer, Springfield, VA; Col. Henry Williamson, Topeka, KS; Stacy B.C. Wood, Curator NAWCC, Inc. Museum, Columbia, PA; Richard "Dick" Ziebell, Ipswich, MA.

Special Recognition to Malvern (Red) Rabeneck, Clock Historian, a long-time collector and researcher of American clocks. Red has worked closely with me on each of my clock books, spending many hours in consultations and pricing sessions. He is the contributor of the historical text and of the glossary.

Contributors to the Lux Section. John Adams, Jr., Springfield, IL; Dr. Warner Bundens, Woodbury, NJ; Jo Burt, Bloomfield Hills, MI; Patrick Cullen, Natick, MA; Rene Desjardins, Hollywood, CA; Roger and Alice Dankert, Aurora, CO; James Eller, Greensboro, NC; Fred Linker, Fort Wayne, IN; Tom Maker, North Andover, MA; May A. Ong, Union, NJ; Sal Provenzano, Bronx, NY; Royce Shepard, Battle Creek, MI; James B. West, Houston, TX.

NOTE TO READERS

All advertisements appearing in this book have been accepted in good faith, but the publisher assumes no responsibility in any transactions that occur between readers and advertisers.

MARKET TRENDS

The price trends of recent months may be summed up in one sentence, "Now is the time to buy." If you are reading this later than 1984 you may have missed your best opportunities, and, of course, it naturally follows that if you feel you must sell some clocks now (during the first half of 1984) you may not readily get the top price.

Prices rose steadily from 1979 until 1981 when sales slowed. The slowing of sales continued in 1982, with prices weakening and showing some decrease in parts of the country. Antique shops particularly reported very slow sales, due largely to poor specimens at high prices. The marts at the NAWCC Regionals, from the fall of 1982 through the fall of 1983, showed falling prices. I believe the collectors in general where showing more selectivity in their purchases, since during this period certain clocks seemed to sell very readily but more common clocks were carted back home by the owners.

Two major auctions of H.A. "Dutch" Soper were held in late 1982 and June of 1983 that showed the feelings of the nation's top collectors. "Best quality brought top prices when offered through an honest and unreserved auction."

Normally, auctions are a rather poor indicator of values when considering prices for a clock price book, and have been almost disregarded in the past because the transactions will not fit our definition of retail value: the price that will be paid in an arm's length transaction when a knowledgeable collector, investor, dealer, or housewife who wants the clock and has the money, buys from a seller who knows the value. Auctions can generally be put into two classifications: honest and otherwise. Honest, true auctions are those in which the auction bill gives an accurate description of the clock and its condition; the bidders are given ample time to check and examine the clock; there is NO reserve, minimum bid, or bidders for the auctioneer or owner; and the auctioneer does not try to run the bidder up by faking an opposing bidder. With a little thought, you can easily see why (usually) most auctions of the honest sort are estate auctions when the heirs are disinterested and the auctioneer is scrupulously honest.

In late 1982, at a time of dwindling sales and lowering prices due to the economic conditions, a noteworth auction was held in Harrison, Arkansas when, due to failing health, long-time collector H.A. "Dutch" Soper sold all the clocks from his clock shop and a portion of his collection, resulting in a two-day sale of 450 clocks that ran the gamut from poor condition to excellent; from old wood-works to modern; from American to English, French, and German; from common to rare. Although "Dutch" was alive at that time, his condition was such that he was unable to lift a clock, required oxygen to be available at all times, and traveled in a wheelchair. Therefore, his desire was to sell the clocks with no sale restrictions whatsoever.

The auctioneer was the well-known "Col." Glen LaRue of Sweet Springs, Missouri, who has a spotless reputation and refuses to take an auction that is not completely honest, and consequently has such a following that he has been known to have 400-500 registered buyers at what would otherwise have been a routine farm sale. His larger antique auctions normally and routinely draw dealers from as many as 15 to 20 states.

2 / MARKET TRENDS

This, then, was the background of "Dutch" Soper's auction, which drew an assortment of registered buyers from 27 states. These bidders and buyers represented every category of persons interested in clocks: from housewives to large and small dealers; from specialized collectors to general collectors; from newcomers to old timers; from those looking for a bargain to those determined to get one certain clock; and included both NAWCC members and non-members. So, this became a good indicator of present prices, since the buyers had more time to examine the clocks than they would normally have in a mart. The buyers were generally of the type who would not overbid from emotion; the good clocks were in a price range that would preclude careless, reckless, or emotional bidding, and there were no dishonest factors involved to run up the bidding.

In a very few cases where specialized collectors were after one particular clock, I was able to sound out the collectors involved to find out how high they were willing to go for the clocks.

For all these reasons, this auction was a unique and accurate indicator of the prices at a time when sales at the marts had decreased to the point that prices on many clocks were difficult to determine. Auctions of this type are beneficial to the hobby, and "Dutch" Soper is to be commended for having the courage to have an honest auction. The "win some, lose some" auction resulted in satisfaction to both buyer and seller.

The prices paid indicated that collectors were still ready and able to pay the high retail value for the very rare and more desirable clocks. The auction was well-planned and efficiently managed, with few complaints, and a good time was had by all.

"Dutch" passed away on April 28, 1983, and the final auction of his personal clocks that he called "My Museum" was held in June 1983. This was more or less a repeat performance of the first only with a better quality and more rare clocks. With the experience of the first auction, no one doubted that this truly was an unreserved auction and that all clocks would be sold to the highest bidder.

The clocks that are selling well include:

1) Clocks that are mostly in the $25 to $75 range that are, or will be, "collector items." This does not include clocks in this price range that are more expensive but in poor condition.

2) The pretty decorator clocks that collectors enjoy in their home.

3) Most popular during the year were Lux, Sangamo, and battery wound clocks that have collector appeal and were not overpriced.

4) Clocks that are priced below my price guides (considered to be the normal market prices).

5) New reproductions are selling good because they are pretty and lower priced than the originals.

On the other hand, clocks that are moving slowly include:

1) Clocks with a value of over $2,000.

2) Hardly anyone is buying expensive clocks for investment, mainly because they can do better by opening a high interest savings account at the savings and loan companies. The top and middle line clocks are now being bought only by collectors or decorators who really like the clocks and want them, and these buyers are demanding lower prices.

3) Middle range clocks in the $200 to $1,000 range have not been moving unless they are completely original and are priced 10% to 25% below the market of 18 months ago.

4) The old historically important clocks are not selling unless they are priced 25% to 50% below the traditionally recognized prices, and then are being bought only by collectors who have a special place to keep them outside of the regular home furnishings. Now is the time to put together a collection of clocks worthy of a museum.

5) The CORPSES and TROJAN HORSES with parts added of recent construction, marriages, and so-called built-up clocks are becoming more and more hard to sell because of a new awareness among collectors. (The public "stop and swap" places and flea markets are used to unload these built-ups and fakes).

HISTORY OF CLOCKS

INDUSTRIAL REVOLUTION: An Englishman, named Thomas Harland is credited with making the first clocks in America, in quantity, from interchangeable parts. Eli Terry, at the age of fourteen was apprenticed to a man who had picked up Harland's skill. Terry was subsequently the recipient of the first clock patent issued by that United States Office in the late eighteenth century. The patent concerned an equation clock, with two minute hands having a center in common, each of dissimilar hue and form, one showing mean time of day and the other apparent or sundial time.

Terry's first factory in 1802 was little more than a small workshop built over a running stream, with a water-wheel to operate the machinery.

After four years, he was making two hundred clocks a year.

Eventually many old and respected clockmakers were put out of business by machine made clocks, but there was obviously no turning back. The conversion of fossil fuels into energy further hurried along the principles of automation, as did mass production.

Today, the field of electronics comprise the "new" industrial revolution, replacing more than man's muscles (as the first did) but also his brain power, skills, and decision making process. An example reflecting this shift in the public's imagination, are the popular quartz watches, as accurate as the best precision clocks of the previous century.

This trend has resulted in a fluctuating international watch market, with the Americans, Swiss and Japanese, as the main manufacturers. The newest technological discoveries have been, and will continue to be applied to the watch and clock industry.

A convenient and easy to remember classification of the periods in clock production are as follows:

COLONIAL – up to 1800: Tall case and hangups or wags on the wall.

EMPIRE – 1800 to 1840: Mostly wood works, shelf and tall case, 8 Day and 30 Hour.

VICTORIAN – 1840 to 1890: Period of greatest production and greatest variety.

MODERN – 1890 to 1940: Period of change to electric clocks operated by synchronous motors.

CONTEMPORARY – World War II to present: Period of change to electronic timekeepers.

4 / HISTORY OF CLOCKS

An American Clock Price Guide should properly start about 1850. Clocks made before that time, i.e. the tall case, the Pillar and Scroll, the wood movement clocks, etc., not made in extremely large quantities, survive in small quantities, and are usually called museum pieces. After 1800, Eli Terry started the development of mass production techniques in making clock works, and clock works became the first CIVILIAN product to be mass produced. These techniques were further refined and developed by Chauncey Jerome to produce both the works and the cases; however, production before 1850 was still small compared to that indicated by Henry Terry's estimate in 1870 of one to one and half million annually. Therefore, prices paid for these early clocks are a highly individual matter, depending on the buyer's desire and finances. If you find a tall case by Daniel Burnap, whose production during his lifetime was said to be 51 clocks, or a Pillar and Scroll by Eli Terry, Jr., you are not likely to have another opportunity to purchase one of these. The same may be said of many other clocks made before 1850.

After 1840, many changes came about that resulted in the later great production of clocks. Wood works were abandoned, the 30 hours brass works lowered the prices of clocks dramatically, then the development of the spring works paved the way for a variety of new case designs. The development of the Balance Wheel movement allowed a still greater variation in case design, and the clock industry saw the development of novelties, marines, regulators, calendars, and "Parlor Clocks", which were designed to compete with French clocks. The variety of designs became so profuse that in 1892 Hiram Camp wrote that the dealers had become amazed and bewildered to such an extent as to paralyze the trade, the expectation of something new preventing the sale of the old. After 1840 the character of the manufacturers also began to change.

Before this time the manufacturers were mostly individual clockmakers, or family companies. In 1840 the largest factory was the Jerome Company, which was owned by Chauncey Jerome. In 1842 export of clocks to England by Jerome started the exportation of clocks to all parts of the world. In 1844 he built a new factory in New Haven, but lost his factory in Bristol by fire in 1845. In 1855 the Jerome Manufacturing Company, as it was known then, failed. One of the first to be a corporation with a group of unrelated (by blood) stockholders. This company bought Jerome's property after the failure, and became one of the larger companies. C. Jerome was said to have influenced the organizing of the Ansonia Clock Company and the Waterbury Clock Company. These three companies, plus Seth Thomas, E. N. Welch, Ingraham Clock Company, and Gilbert Clock Company became the major producers.

Around 1850 Jerome began issuing catalogs. This practice was adopted by all clock manufacturers, and gave us some of our best records of the clocks produced. The great number of clocks produced in the great variety of designs after 1850, resulting in the survival of sufficient quantities for extensive collector trading, makes these clocks the proper subject for a price guide to help a collector identify and price the clocks that he finds in his searches.

The Victorian period in clock production may be said to encompass the years 1840-1890. Millions of clocks were produced in this period, but the survival rate is small. In 1851 there were 31 clock factories in operation. In 1853 and 1854, Jerome Mfg. Co. produced about 444,000 per year,

HISTORY OF CLOCKS / 5

while J. C. Brown produced 100,000, and a little later Ansonia Clock Company was producing 150,000. The attrition rate of the factories was high. In the ten years ending in 1856, four factories burned, nine failed and five closed because of low prices, leaving 13 factories with an annual production of 143,000. In 1867 New Haven Clock Company was the largest factory, with Seth Thomas second in size. New Haven was producing 200,000 annually, while Seth Thomas, William L. Gilbert, E. N. Welch and Benedict & Burham combined, had a production of 300,000.

The case styles of clocks produced during the Victorian period and the approximate period of greatest production by the entire industry is indicated by the following table:

O.G., Brass Works 1838–1918
Steeple 1843–on
Acorn 1847–1850
Banjo 1842–on
Gallery 1845–on
Iron Front 1850–1870
Connecticut Shelf 1860–1890

These were 30 Hour and 8 Day spring driven brass works in wood cases 10 to 20 inches high with 5 to 6 inch dials, Moon, Spade, or Maltese Hands, with tablet printed or mirrored, usually time and strike, sometimes with alarm.

Cottage 1875–1890
Walnut Parlor 1875–1900

Includes both those called shelf clocks and kitchen clocks.

Oak Kitchen 1880–1915
Black Mantel 1880–1920
Round or Drum Alarms 1880–present
Novelties 1875–1900
Drop Octagon 1875–on
Regulators 1860–present

Parlor Regulators: Usually dead beat escapement, small wood pendulum rod, sometimes covered with gold leaf, with retaining power. Good time keepers.

Jewelers Regulators: Often with Swiss or other imported pin wheel movements, usually mercurial or gridiron compensating pendulums. These were often elaborate, probably because the jeweler considered them good advertising fixtures.

Balance Wheel Clocks 1850–present

Earliest patent to Ely Terry in 1845. Earliest produced were in wood Octagon cases, later in round brass cases, and by 1885 the brass cases were often nickel plated.

Papier-mache Clocks .... 1850–prob. 1858?

Also used during WWII as alarm clock cases.

Calendars 1862–present
  Simple Calendar.
  Double Dial in both Simple and Perpetual.

It will be noted that many of the above styles were produced long after the Victorian period. The period after the Victorian may be called the "new" or perhaps even the modern period. It has seen the introduction of the following styles:

Art Nouveau 1890-1910
Mission 1900-1930

This plain, black-finished style is felt by some to have been a reaction to the elaborate styles of the Victorian period.

China or Porcelain 1890-present
Imitation French 1890-1920

Swinging, Statues, Cast. Usually gold or silver plated, as best exemplified by the Jennings Bros. Manufacturing Company's clocks.

Tambours (Humpbacks) 1900-present
Electric 1916-present

Many collectors use common construction features to determine quickly if a clock is likely to be old. An example is the lantern pinion pioneered by Chauncey Jerome, and once described by Henry Terry as a cheap wire pinion. It had become almost standard by 1870, and a clock with these pinions was almost certain to have been made after 1850. Another is the plate posts, with many collectors using the date of 1885 as the cutoff date for the use of pins to retain the plates. Therefore, if the works have pinned plates, it was most likely made before 1885. Hand nuts are also watched by some, believing that their use was rare in the Victorian period, and became common after the turn of the century. The style of the hands and dial would be an indication of the age if they could be depended on to be the originals. An original tablet can give an indication, as the reverse paintings of the early Empire period gave way to decals and etched glass tablets in the Victorian period.

Nickel plating was well established by 1875 but was not often used before approximately 1870, and bells were rarely used after the turn of the century, with wire gongs as the standard. Until about 1850, American clocks struck hours only.

While the construction features and the type and style of the clock will give you an idea of the probable age of the clock, the label will usually be the one thing that will determine the age and maker faster and easier than any other feature; therefore, it follows that the condition of the label has a definite effect upon the value of the clock.

The plates of the brass works usually have some identifying mark, symbol, or name stamped on them, and if this does not agree with the label it is important to ask "Why?" Was the maker on the label a case maker who purchased his movements, as did Florence Kroeber? Is the name on the label a sales agent? Have the works been changed, destroying the originality of the clock? Is it a fake?

THE VICTORIAN PERIOD OF CLOCK PRODUCTION: Clocks produced by the craftsmen of the Colonial Period are now so rare and expensive that the average collector will see one only in a museum. The same is rapidly becoming true with the Empire Period, which stretched roughly from 1800 to 1840. These periods are not absolute and clear cut, but have

HISTORY OF CLOCKS / 7

a tendency to overlap into the years that we have selected as the beginning and end of certain periods.

The Empire Period actually represents a type of transition in which the production of clocks was developed from the work of the individual craftsman (who built not only his product but also his tools to make that product) to mass production. During the Empire Period, Eli Terry and Chauncey Jerome developed the mass production method that was used and improved upon during the Victorian Period.

The period immediately before and during the Victorian Period was probably one of the most inventive times of human history, not in terms of world-shaking inventions but rather in terms of small inventions, that had a profound effect upon human life.

To reach a true understanding of the Victorian Period it is necessary to take a look and see what else was going on around the country and the world.

We begin our discussion of the events leading up to the Victorian Period by first mentioning a little about some of the early clock makers, i.e., Thomas Harland, who apprenticed Daniel Burnap, who apprenticed Eli Terry, who apprenticed Seth Thomas; happening from around 1780 to perhaps 1795. Around 1812 we find Chauncey Jerome working for Eli Terry, and just before that, Terry, Thomas and Hoadley working together.

Here is a rough presentation of some of the important events that led up to the beginning of the Victorian Period of clock production.

1780 Daniel Burnap.
1790 First U.S. Patent issued.
1793 Eli Whitney Cotton Gin.
1800 COLONIAL PERIOD ENDS.
EMPIRE PERIOD BEGINS.
1807 Fulton's Steamboat.
Eli Terry mass produces clocks.
1810 Hartford Fire Insurance Company.
1812 War of 1812.
Eli Terry – Chauncey Jerome.
1813 Seth Thomas at Plymouth Hollow.
1825 Erie Canal opens.
Iron frames for pianos.
1826 John Stevens' RR Locomotive Run.
1830 Spring Balance (Weighing) invented.
Mass Production of firearms.
1836 Fall of the Alamo.
Samuel Colt patents revolver.
1837 Panic (Depression).
1839 Insurance Company of North America.
First Daguerreotypes.

1840 EMPIRE PERIOD ENDS.
VICTORIAN PERIOD BEGINS.
1841 Mercantile Agency started.
1842 Howard & Davis making clocks.
1844 New York Life Insurance founded.
Morse sent telegraph message.
1845 Mexican War started.
Elias Howe's sewing machine.
1849 California Gold Rush.
1850 Ansonia Clock Company begins.
1851 Wm. L. Gilbert Clock Company.
1853 New Haven Clock Company begins.
Seth Thomas Clock Company begins.
1856 Western Union.
Bessemer Process for steel.
1857 Glass photograph negative.
757 River Steamboats.
Waterbury Clock Company begins.
Ingraham Clock Company begins.

8 / HISTORY OF CLOCKS

1858 First Atlantic cable.
  Mason fruit jar patented.
1859 Massachusetts Institute of Technology founded.
  Oil well, Titusville, Pa.
1861 Civil War begins.
1864 E. N. Welch Clock Company.
1865 Civil War ends.
1865 Chicago Union Stockyards.
1867 Buffalo Bill hired by Union Pacific RR.
  Typewriter invented.
1869 Golden Spike driven at Promontory Point.
1870 Celluloid invented.
1871 Chicago Fire.
1872 First Montgomery Ward Catalog.
  Boston Fire.
  Gatling gun patented.
1873 Panic (Depression).
1876 General Custer killed.
  Alexander Graham Bell patents the telephone.
1882 Thomas Edison's Pearl St. Station.
1883 Brooklyn Bridge opens.
1890 VICTORIAN PERIOD ENDS. MODERN PERIOD BEGINS.
1892 Oklahoma Sooners – Cherokee Strip.
1893 Moving Pictures patented.
1900 4,000 Automobiles.
1901 Marconi sends wireless message.
1903 Wright Bros. airplane flight.
  E.N. Welch becomes Sessions.
  Ford Motor Company organized.
1906 San Francisco Earthquake & Fire.
1907 Panic (Depression).
  Federal Reserve Act.
1912 Titanic sinks.
1914 Panama Canal opens.
1917 U.S. into World War I.
1918 End of World War I.
1920 First U.S. Radio Broadcast.
1927 Lindbergh flies Atlantic.
1929 Stock Market Crash.
  Ansonia Clock Co. sold to Russia.
  First television transmission.
1932 Banks close.
1937 Zepplin Hindenburg crash.
1938 Dupont markets nylon.
1939 Depression ending.
1940 MODERN PERIOD ENDS. CONTEMPORARY PERIOD BEGINS.
1941 U.S. enters World War II.
1944 Waterbury Clock Company fails.
1945 World War II ends.
1964 Gilbert-Spartus Corporation.
1967 Ingraham — McGraw-Edison.
1970 Sessions failed.
  Seth Thomas — Talley Industries.

All during this time and for the rest of the Victorian Period the seven giants of the clock industry were putting out their hundreds and thousands of clocks in all sizes, shapes, kinds and colors. The Modern Period started about 1890.

The Stock Market Crash came in 1929, and in that same year we saw the failure of the first of the seven giants. The Ansonia Clock Company discontinued operations, and the factory and all the equipment was sold and shipped to Russia. In 1930 the old Seth Thomas Clock Company became a division of the General Time Instrument Company, again foretelling the end of the seven giants.

The Contemporary Period stretches from about 1940 until the present. During this time we have seen the end of the Sessions Company, the successors to E. N. Welch, and the end of the New Haven Clock Company. Of the seven giants of the clock industry, only three can be said to exist today. All three of these are now divisions of larger companies or conglomerates. Seth Thomas is a division of Talley Industries, the Ingraham Company a division of McGraw-Edison, and Gilbert has been supplanted by the Sparta Corporation. We can still see some imported spring-driven clocks with the name of some of these seven giants in our stores today. No spring-driven clocks or watches are currently being mass produced in the United States.

IDENTIFICATION AND DATING

For proper identification and dating of clocks it is necessary to know something of the different names used by the companies. When a company purchased another company or factory they often used cases, movements, and lables acquired. It is necessary to know the lines of succession of the companies, especially those resulting in formation of our largest companies. The early clockmakers worked alone at times, but also made and dissolved partnerships seemingly at the drop of a hat. Factory buildings and equipment were rarely abandoned or destroyed (except by the disastrous fires that occurred so often), and when one company quit business by failure or otherwise, either a new company was formed or an existing one absorbed the remaining physical assets of the former one.

The accompanying charts in many cases will date the clocks simply by the form of the company name. You will find this same information from many sources, sometimes with slight variations in dates, but the chart form is easiest to use. For practical purposes, i.e. dating and pricing, we need not worry about the arguments over very precise dates. Some of the gaps in the dates are due to the factory laying idle or the particular clockmaker taking some time off, or getting involved in another enterprise.

In many cases, the only connections of succeeding companies with preceding ones, was the purchase of factories, either real estate or equipment or both.

Some of the companies formed to be sales outlets are shown to help identify the actual maker of the clock. There are many more sales companies that are not shown. Many, were actually assembly plants, usually for tax purposes, and assembled the finished clocks from parts shipped to them.

These charts show the development of a few companies, but to keep perspective, remember that the 1850 census showed the following numbers of clockmakers in various states:

Connecticut	582	In the same census, the number of Clock Peddlers were:	New York	3883
New York	173		Pennsylvania	1317
Pennsylvania	105		Ohio	1155
Ohio	46		Connecticut	336
Illinois	13		Indiana	209
Kentucky	9		Illinois	194
Virginia	8		Virginia	150

To further illustrate the development of the clock industry consider this; in the Colonial period a clockmaker made all his own tools and all parts of the clock. By the beginning of the Empire period, in 1800, all clockmakers' tools could be bought and clock dealing was a separate

10 / IDENTIFICATION AND DATING

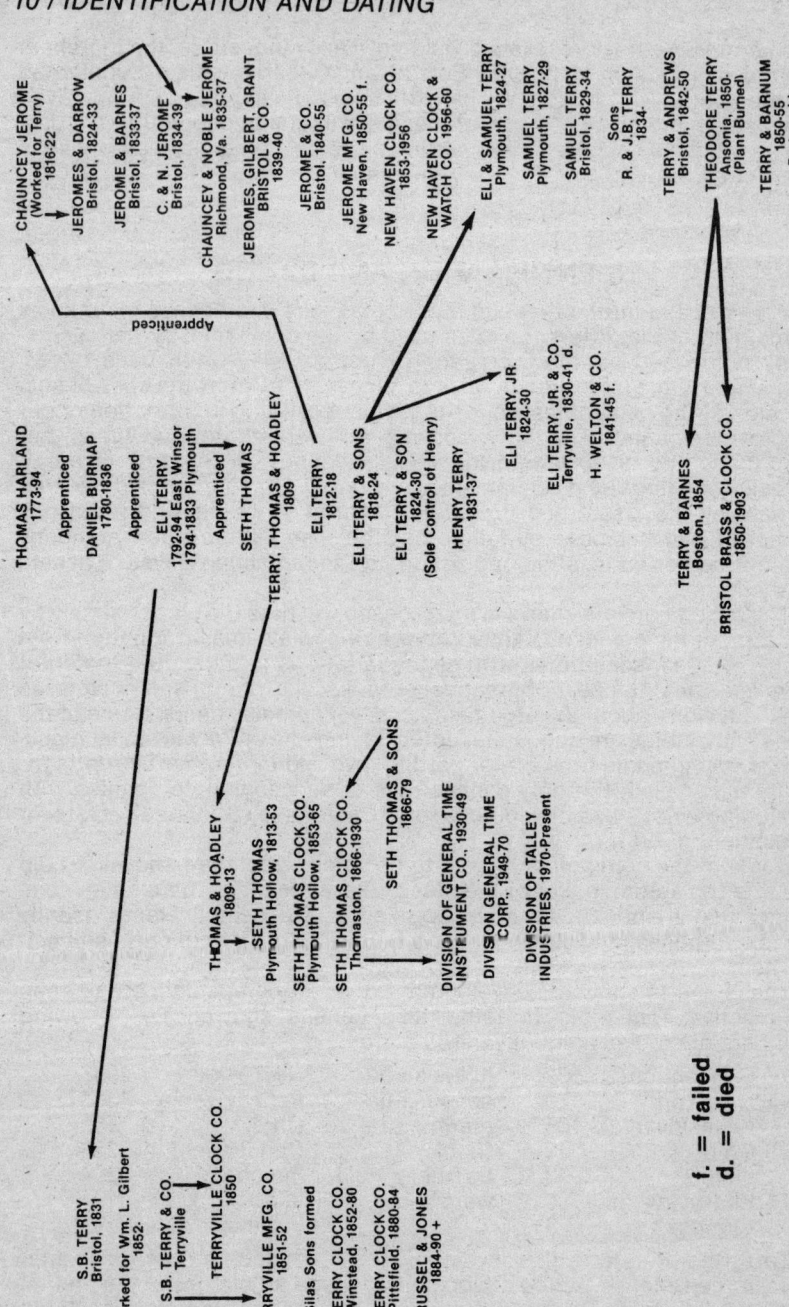

IDENTIFICATION AND DATING / 11

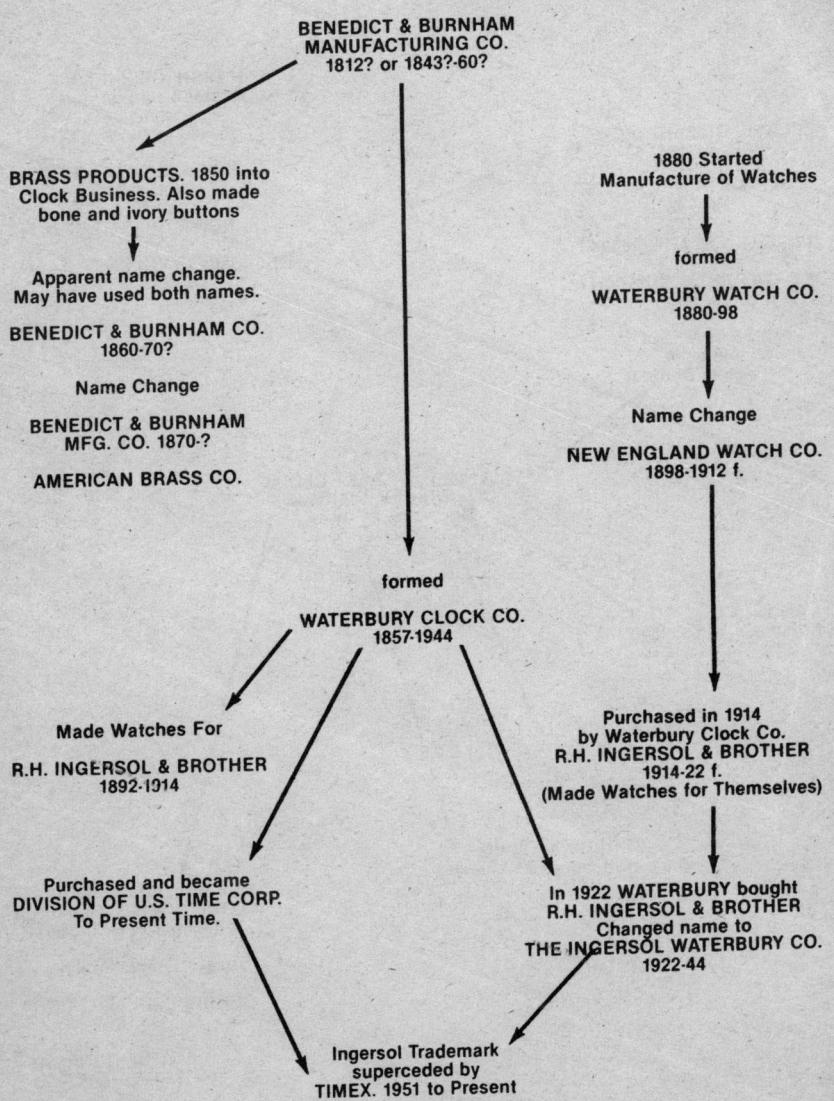

12 / IDENTIFICATION AND DATING

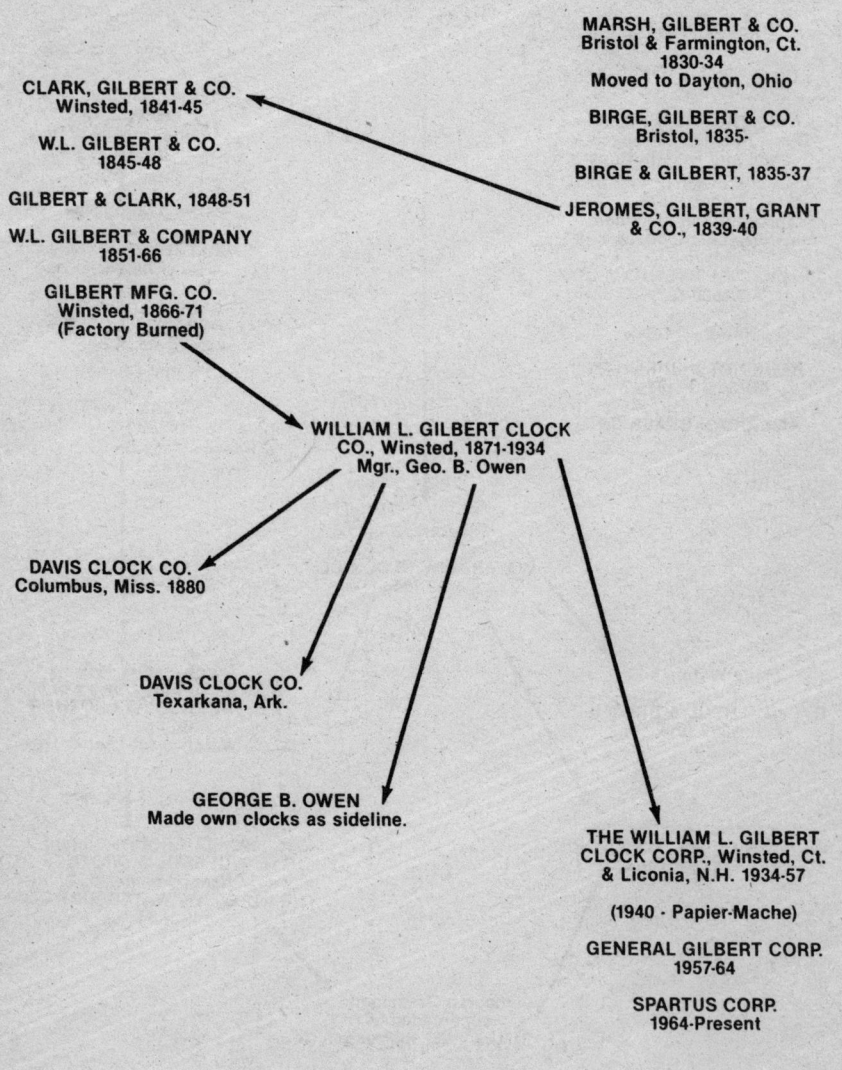

IDENTIFICATION AND DATING / 13

INGRAHAM & BARTHOLOMEW
Bristol, 1831-32

BARTHOLOMEW, BROWN & CO.

INGRAHAM & GOODRICH
Bristol, 1832-33

ELIAS INGRAHAM
Bristol, 1835-40

RAY & INGRAHAM
Bristol, 1841-44

BREWSTER & INGRAHAM
Bristol, 1844-52

E. & A. INGRAHAM
Bristol, 1852-55
Ansonia, Ct., 1855-56

INGRAHAMS & STEDMAN
1855-56 (Sales)

ELIAS INGRAHAM & CO.
1857-60

E. INGRAHAM & CO.
Bristol, 1861-80

THE E. INGRAHAM & CO.
Bristol, 1880-84

THE E. INGRAHAM CO.
Bristol, 1884-1958

THE INGRAHAM CO.
1958-67

DIVISION, MCGRAW EDISON
1967-Present

Name now used as TRADEMARK.

ELIAS INGRAHAM & WILLIAM G. BARTHOLOMEW, 1831-32
(Made Cases)

BARTHOLOMEW, BROWN & CO., 1832-35

FORRESTVILLE MFG. CO.
Bristol, 1835-39

HILLS, BROWN & CO.
Bristol, 1840-42

J.C. BROWN & CO. 1842-49
Also used labels:
The Forrestville Mfg. Co.
J.C. Brown, Bristol, Conn.

FORRESTVILLE CLOCK MANUFACTORY, J.C. BROWN
Prop., 1850-55

FORRESTVILLE HARDWARE & CLOCK CO., 1853-55

BARNES & WELCH
1831-34

FORRESTVILLE MFG. CO.
1841-45

F.S. OTIS, 1853-56

S.C. SPRING & CO.
Bristol, 1864-68

F. & C. H. MANROSS
1854-56

WELCH, SPRING & CO.
Forrestville, Bristol, 1868-84

E.N. WELCH MANUFACTURING CO., BRISTOL, CONN. 1864-1903

BRISTOL BRASS & CLOCK CO.
1850-1903

BRISTOL BRASS CO.
(No Clocks)

SESSIONS CLOCK CO.
Bristol & Forrestville, 1903-56

THE SESSIONS CLOCK CO.
1956-68
The Sessions Company Plant Closed in 1970. Name now used as TRADEMARK.

14 / IDENTIFICATION AND DATING

ANSONIA BRASS CO.
Ansonia, Ct. Anson G. Phelps
Importer of tin, brass, copper.
Built rolling mill for sheet brass.

ANSONIA CLOCK CO.
Ansonia, Ct., 1850-54
(Factory Burned)

Stockholders
Phelps
Theodore Terry
F.C. Andrews
Samual Steele Terry

**ANSONIA CLOCK CO., Ansonia
ANSONIA BRASS & COPPER
COMPANY, 1854-78**

ANSONIA CLOCK CO.
Ansonia, 1878-79

ANSONIA CLOCK CO.
Brooklyn, N.Y., 1879-1929
(Burned 1880)

Sold and moved factory
to Russia.

HOWARD & DAVIS
1842-59

BOSTON WATCH CO.
Roxbury, Ma. 1853-57

E. HOWARD & CO.
1859-61

**THE HOWARD LOCK &
WATCH CO., 1861-63**

OFFICERS
Edward Howard
George P. Reed
David P. Davis
Aaron L. Dennison
Horatio Adams

**THE HOWARD WATCH &
CLOCK CO., 1863-81**

**E. HOWARD WATCH &
CLOCK CO., 1881-1903**

E. HOWARD & CO.

E. HOWARD CLOCK CO.
1903-34

E. HOWARD & CO.
Roxbury, Ma. 1857-61

**HOWARD CLOCK PRODUCTS
INC., 1934-Present**

Sold Watch Company
to
KEYSTONE WATCH CASE CO.

NOTE: E. HOWARD & CO. used
on clocks from 1850 to present.
Most movements numbered.

trade. By 1870, in the Victorian period, almost all clocks were produced by mass production. Dials, bells, keys, mainsprings and other fittings were made by separate and independent factories. By the beginning of the Modern period the major producers had shrunk to slightly over a half-dozen giant corporations and a few smaller companies. At the end of the Victorian period, giants of the clock industry were: Seth Thomas Clock Company, New Haven Clock Company, Ansonia Clock Company, Waterbury Clock Company, E. Ingraham Company, William L. Gilbert Clock Company and E. N. Welch Mfg. Company.
The following are short histories of some major clock companies.

The Daniel Pratt Clock Companies. Daniel Pratt was born in 1797 in Redding, MA and eventually was putting out wooden works clocks. The label usually reads, "Extra Clocks manufactured and sold by Daniel Pratt, Jr." Most of these clocks have manufacturing dates on them. He used brass movements after 1838, and from 1846 to 1871 had a store at 49 Union St., Boston. He died in 1871. Many of his clocks are still around and can occasionally be seen in the Marts.

His business was continued after his death as "Daniel Pratts Sons", and you will find a few clocks with this label from the period 1871-1880. These labels are rare.

It has been reported that the business was continued under other names from 1880-1895, but after 1895 became known as "Daniel Pratt, Son, 339 Washington St., Boston", operated by Frank W. B. Pratt. The business was discontinued in 1915 with the death of Frank Pratt. After being in operation for well over three-quarters of a century, the clocks the business produced should have been better known by collectors.

Bristol Company, Waterbury, CT. Organized about 1892 and operated by the Bristol family, exists today as the Bristol-Babcock Company. Made recording temperature and pressure gauges and some electrical recording instruments. Bought Seth Thomas movements until the flood of 1955 put Seth Thomas out of business, then used German movements and some Lux movements. Also used some electric drives.

NOTE: This company is included because it is often confused with the Bristol Brass and Clock Company, Bristol, CT, and has been thought (by some collectors) to be a branch of one of the seven giant companies.

Boston Clock Company. Formed in 1880 by Joseph H. Eastman, who had learned the clock trade from E. Howard. Best known for making mantel clocks with Eastman's singlewind mechanism. In 1897 the company became the Chelsea Clock Company. Today, Boston Clock Company is shown as a division of Chelsea.

Chelsea Clock Company, 284 Everett Ave., Chelsea, MA. 1897 to present. Famous for high grade marine and ship's bell clocks. It was once said that Chelsea was recognized internationally and in military and scientific circles, but not as well recognized by collectors. This has changed, as evidenced by the prices of Chelsea clocks shown in this book.

Derry Clock Company. Incorporated in Maine in 1908. Closed in 1910. Charter suspended in 1911 for non-payment of fees. Dissolved in 1912. All machinery and equipment sold to Herchede Hall Clock Company.

Herchede. Herchede was first organized in 1885 and made cases, while importing movements and hall clocks. Their first catalog was issued about 1886 to 1890. Their first tubular chime clocks were made in the 1890's, with either the movements or complete clocks obtained through Durfee, made by J.J. Elliot, London. In 1902, a court decision ended Durfee's monopoly in this country on tubular chimes, and the Herchede Hall Clock Company was incorporated. In 1903, Frank Herchede sold all his clock material to the corporation. In 1904, Herchede won a silver medal at the St. Louis World's Fair for their tubular chime clocks. In 1909, the company obtained a building for a movement factory, and in 1910 made the first 100 movements and issued a catalog showing " Crown Hall Clocks" with their own movements. In 1911, 180 to 200 hall clocks were sold, and in 1912 they bought the machinery and stock of the Derry Clock Company. The Canterbury Chimes were introduced in 1913, and in 1914 the company started recording each sale. They entered all known information on previous sales in a ledger.*

In 1915, awards were won by their clocks at the Panama Pacific International Exposition. The company became so prosperous after this that in 1919 they paid a 20% dividend to the common stockholders. In the 20's, as electric clocks became ever more popular, the Herchede Company decided to go into the electric clock business. In 1926, they organized the Revere Clock Company to make electric clocks, but did not publicize the connection for fear of hurting their reputation for high grade clocks. In 1927, they contracted with G.E. to make a line of electric clocks for G.E. These had a red alert dot in the face to show power interruption. In 1929, Herchede announced electrically wound movements with a chime mechanism operated by an electric motor.

As electric clocks became accepted, Revere was absorbed by the company and all production was in one building. In 1960, the company moved to Starkville, Mississippi, and today they are still making high grade clocks at this location.

NOTE: No.6 and No.7 were sold to Daniel Pratt.

Howard. Edward Howard, born 1813, learned clockmaking as an apprentice to Aaron Willard, Jr. In 1842, formed the company of Stephenson, Howard & Davis. They made scales, balances, and clocks. Some references say they made church clocks. In 1847 or 1848, the company became Howard & Davis, still making scales, balances, and high grade clocks. About 1856 to 1858 (according to which reference you use), the company became E. Howard & Company. Some writers claim that wall clocks were made under this name from 1842 to 1858. In 1860, "E. Howard & Company" became their official trademark. In 1903, the company was reorganized under the name of E. Howard Clock Company. They were then making tower clocks, electric time systems, parts, and continuing to make high grade clocks. In the late 20's, the company began to look into synchronous clocks, moved into the Howard Watch Building in the 30's, and reorganized in 1934 as Howard Clock Products, Inc. The company then made precision parts, electrical instruments, aircraft instruments, and other instruments; and also produced a few high grade synchronous electric clocks and slave systems. In 1958, clock production ceased, except that the tower clocks were made until 1964. In the 50's and 60's, 80% of the company's output was for government contracts. In 1975, the company started making a few models of classic clocks and at present are making seven models. All models are given serial numbers. Howard clocks have always been among the most respected by collectors and this respect is shown by the high prices in this book.

NOTE: References to Howard watches have been purposely omitted.

Revere Clock Company. Organized by Herchede as a marketing company for electric clocks. They made electric clocks with an auxiliary 36-hour spring mechanism that would keep the clock running when the electric power went off and start the synchronous motor when power returned.

Warren Telechron Company, Ashland, MA. Organized about 1916 when Warren devised the synchronous electric clock motor. Warren was the first to adapt the synchronous motor to clocks but it was not self-starting. In 1927, Telechron introduced the self-starting synchronous motor. In 1946, Telechron was purchased by G.E.

The following charts will help with the identification and dating of clocks.

BUILDING A COLLECTION

New and young collectors are necessary for the survival of our hobby, so we would like to offer a few hints to them to help make the hobby profitable as well as interesting and enjoyable. As one old collector remarked, "more profit means more enjoyment". Young collectors appear to become discouraged at the marts at the high prices for clocks, especially when they hear the old-timers tell of how cheap the prices were only a few (ten or twenty) years ago. If you fall in this category, take heart and read on. You have the greatest opportunity of all if you are young, for you have time in your favor. The law of supply and demand cannot be repealed, as much as some politicians would like to try. In our case, the supply is decreasing due to attrition (attrition in this case means destruction, both by forces beyond our control, such as fire, and also by the hand of man as when an unskilled person attempts a repair, or by poor storage, etc.). The demand is constantly increasing with the increase in our population, due both to new collectors and to the desire of housewives to have an antique clock in the furnishings of the house. Therefore, the value of a collector's clock MUST increase with time — and will. So, all the new collector has to do is buy wisely and wait. It is true that you make money when you buy, not when you sell. If you do not buy wisely the profit is gone, and the hobby has no room for a con man who will try to recoup profits by getting others to repeat his mistakes.

The young collector should remember that as anything becomes rare it becomes collectible. As it gets older it becomes more collectible. After an item reaches the age of 100 it is considered a "real antique".

History tells you which clocks will be the collector's clocks of the future. Novelty items will probably increase in value first, then stabilize for the long haul. Clocks that are true art with great beauty will always be in demand and will probably be fairly stable in price at first, then show a steady increase for the long haul, with the greatest increase in value at the age of 100 or more. Any clock that shows movement has always been liked by collectors, therefore, good animated clocks will definitely be collector's items in the future. Visible pendulums, visible escapements, and visible balance wheels in the movements are always preferred over clocks with invisible works hidden in the case. Even a seconds hand helps. High quality does not change with time. If a clock is of high quality today it will be high quality in the future, and it will command a higher price, both today and in the future.

Rarity will always win in the end. The extreme high prices that have been paid for some antiques and works of art are always for the rare ones. So the greatest increase in value will be for the rare clock that has other desired features, such as high quality, a desired maker, beauty, motion or animation, and novelty.

So, as a young collector if you do not have much money to spend, analyze the low priced clock that you find in the flea markets from the 20's, 30's and 40's. If it has several desired features, buy it, take it home and wait; and while you wait, document the clock. Write down when and where it was purchased, from whom, and all of the history of the clock that you can get. Add to this information the history of the company that made the clock and any production estimates you can obtain. (In less than 50 years, this information will be impossible to get.) Put this documentation with the clock and in 50 years it will increase the value of the clock considerably at no cost to you.

Some desirable features to look for in a clock include: (1) motion of some kind; (2) unusual shape; (3) unusual or special case material; (4) special or unusual strike; (5) special or unusual name (of clock maker). To explain:

(1) Motion — A pendulum clock is usually more sought after than a balance wheel clock. An animated clock is the most sought after of all. If the motion is interesting enough, the clock is sought after even if it is faulty as a timekeeper. Witness the popularity of the "Ignatz", the "Dickory-Dickory Dock", the "Foliots", and the bouncing and swinging dolls.

(2) Unusual Shape — An ususual shape that is still appealing is much sought after. Witness the "acorn" clocks, the "banjos", the "figure eights", and others.

(3) Unusual or special case materials — In this category we must include the marbles, onyx, marquetry, exotic veneers, the metal cases (iron, brass, bronze, zinc, pewter, etc.), and others such as the so-called "plush cases".

(4) Special or unusual strike — This category includes the quarter-hour strikes, the various chimes, the musical clocks, the coo-coos, and many others you will think of immediately.

(5) Special or unusual name — This category is more elusive, as it can be attributed to both snob appeal and historical interest. Some names, such as Howard, fall into both categories, and in addition are high grade clocks. The names of makers were more important in the clocks of the individual makers, before 1850, but most collectors today develop preferences among the seven giants of the industry, and the names of some of the smaller clockmakers (such as George B. Owen, Florence T. Kroeber, the Mullers, Jennings Brothers, Bailey, Banks & Biddle) tend to raise the price of a clock, even though they were all primarily case modifiers, importers, and sales agents, not movement manufacturers, and so are not always considered true clockmakers. Waltham, Boston, Chelsea and Howard were all true manufacturers of complete, high grade clocks, and all have very loyal followers among the collectors.

We will now take a brief look at clocks that are not at present greatly sought out by collectors, but seem to have great short-term potential for the next 20 years. These are general classes of clocks that seem to be overlooked by collectors at present, but have features for collectors that make them seem underpriced today. Admittedly, this is guessing, and investing in these types of clocks for short-term profit is risky; but these are probably the most interesting risk investments you will ever make as these are interesting clocks.

The first class of clocks that must be mentioned here are the old handmade American clocks produced before 1850. The transition wood-works and the triple deckers of the 1830-50 era have been fairly stable in price for the last five or ten years, going (in many cases) for $300 to $500 in the marts. Many have carved columns and splats and are grossly underpriced in today's market. The wood-works, O.G.'s and 8-Day O.G.'s are in the same category, with prices from $135 to $250 in the marts. All of these clocks are historically important, with many interesting labels but with styles that are not favored today for home furnishings. Housewives do not want them in the house. This, along with the present intense interest in Victorian clocks, has caused their prices to be depressed. Many of these should now be museum pieces. The low prices give you the opportunity to build your own museum.

The next large class of clocks that show the promise of great opportunity for collectors are the electric clocks. Interest in electrics has been slowly building for years. At present, the greatest interest is in the spring-operated, electrically wound clocks — the so-called "self-winding clocks". There are a number of makers of these clocks. Most collectors are only familiar with the "Self-winding Clock Co." Many collectors do not realize that the early Sangamo electric clocks were high grade, jeweled, spring movements, wound by electric motors. Other companies, such as Herchede, also produced this type of clock. Low prices give great opportunities in this area.

Do not overlook the synchronous electric clocks, ignored and sneered at by many collectors. Many of these have all the qualities that will make them great collector items in the future. From the early hand-started models (historically important) to the late quartz movements, low prices and opportunities are numerous. Already, some of the quartz chronometers are being seen in the marts. Clocks of beauty are plentiful in electrics, since the small works allowed flexibility in design. Novelty and animation (or motion) are also available. United electric clocks have animated designs such as the "Ballerina", the "Fisherman", and other clocks that have a clock section combined with a lighted animated section. These can be bought for a range of $15 to $150 today and will definitely be the collector's items of tomorrow. Many are shown in this book.

The last class to be mentioned here is the small clocks: the bedroom or boudoir clocks, the travel clocks, the car clocks, and the alarms. Many of these are high quality clocks, but a look at the prices in this book will show low prices. Waltham made many high quality clocks called "travel", "bedroom", and "car" clocks, but while collectors have snatched up the small banjos and pillar and scroll models (and driven the prices up accordingly), they have largely ignored the other small clocks made by Waltham. This will not be true in the future. Waltham, Boston, Chelsea, the Rimwind companies, and most of the seven giants of the clock industry all made high quality car clocks. Westclox and others made low quality car clocks. Keywinds, stemwinds, backwinds, rimwinds, and pullwind models all seem to abound at low prices. But, at the auto swap meets the supplies have dried up and prices are rising. The same will be true in the marts.

Most collectors tend to ignore currently produced clocks as not being worthy of attention. However, past experience teaches us that if the clock is rare enough, or interesting enough, or beautiful enough, it will be a collector's item before waiting a century — some in only five or ten years. Certainly, no collector would turn down the chance to own one of the reproductions (replicas in some cases) put out by Howard, Chelsea, and the Boston Division of Chelsea. If the price is right, they change hands readily and quickly. However, there are other clocks that may be in great demand a few years in the future, such as Edward Cielascyk's decimal clock put out in 1979 by Westclox, and Hamilton Clock Co.'s cube clock put out in 1980, called the "Forecast Q" (which was a cube that swiveled on a base and had time, temperature, humidity, and barometric pressure on the four sides of the cube), should also make collector status some day. A man named Chipley of Prescott, Arizona, supposedly during the last three years has been making wooden geared clocks in different case styles with a production goal of 50 clocks. These should be rare enough to attain collector status. And last but not least, the Atmos clock, produced currently and in production since 1925, has already attained collector status due to the interesting perpetual motion drive used by the clock.

A ship's chronometer is another article of interest to clock collectors. These timepieces are collected by both watch and clock collectors, since they have some of the characteristics of both. Watch collectors in general call the movement a watch movement but the faces (dials) are as large as a small clock. The ship's chronometers are too large to be carried on your person as a watch, and when mounted on the gimbals in a box becomes an armful for carrying, but they do present a nice appearance on a shelf. With their extreme accuracy, undisturbed by being moved around (because of the gimbal mounting), the ship's chronometer is very suitable for a clock collector to carry around as a time standard for setting his clocks accurately.

In this country, Waltham, Elgin, and Hamilton made many chronometers, with Waltham using their 8-Day lever movemnt; Elgin and Hamilton using a detent escapement. Elgin made about 200 of these but according to reports these were never used by the Navy.

Ship's chronometers can serve to educate clock collectors to the fact that serial numbers allow production dates and production totals to be closely estimated, thus age and rarity can be determined. With clocks in general, age and rarity are usually determined by guesswork tempered by wishful thinking.

CONDITION

As the price of a clock increases, the number of ready buyers decreases. In simpler terms, there are many times as many buyers for $100.00 clocks as there are $1,000.00 clocks. About $300.00 to $400.00 is a level where this is most apparent. It seems here is where a lot of people choke off. If you take the original cost of a clock, which is a direct indication of the quality of the materials and workmanship, and the number of man hours it cost to produce it, you will find, for example, the cheap kitchen clocks bringing 50 times what they sold for new. On the other hand, a Jeweler's or Parlor Regulator may not bring more than 10 times its original cost. Some clocks that have not come to the attention of collectors hardly bring their original cost, an example being car clocks. As a buyer becomes more knowledgeable he usually advances to the better clocks.

Factors such as choking level, dollar depreciation, and nostalgia, coupled with buyers becoming more knowledgeable, will surely cause the higher quality clocks to increase in value rapidly.

Another thing to keep in mind is that there are (and the number is increasing every day) more buyers than there are clocks. Market pressure or demand is what sets the price of any clock more than anything else, and with a steadily decreasing supply, there is nowhere to go but up. Since we have been working on this book, some of the clocks have doubled in price in a relatively short period of time. I would say that you can buy a clock or clocks at the current market value, keep and enjoy them as long as you like, and then resell them at a profit, or hand them down as family heirlooms.

CONDITION: Mint original condition — 100%.

Paper dial replacing painted dial — deduct 10%. New paper dial replacing original paper dial or old paper dial in poor condition — deduct 5%.

Replacement hands or pendulum ball, if reproductions of original — deduct 2%. If not reproductions of original — deduct 5%.

Old and original works not of correct type for particular model of clock — deduct 20%.

New calendar works, reproduction of original — deduct 20%

New time works, reproduction of original — deduct 30%. New works, not reproduction of original — deduct 50-80%, or figure value of case only plus value of works.

LABELS: Clocks that were originally produced with labels should have legible labels in fair condition. For a mint original label, add 10%. Always make sure that the label, the works and the case are consistent, matching and original. If the label is a replacement, but is a duplicate of the original that should be there, deduct 10%. No label, deduct 15-20% except on kitchen clocks, where it doesn't make as much difference.

If the works, label and the case are not consistent and matching, it is usually not a collector's item. Remember — in clocks, condition, originality and rarity are most important.

CASE: Refinished like original, or original finish fair — deduct 5%. Good refinish, not like original, or original in poor condition — deduct 15%. Poor refinish, not of original type — deduct 25%.

Missing minor unnoticeable parts, or minor damage — deduct 5%. Missing noticeable small parts, or noticeable damage — deduct 10%.

Missing part of base or top, or more major damage — deduct 25%. Missing most of top or base, or more major damage — deduct 50-75%.

Many clocks were originally offered with alarm, strike, and driving power options. Some collectors feel these options enhance the value of a clock as follows:

Operating Alarm — add $10.00-$20.00. If weight operated — add $50.00-$75.00.

Hour strike — add $5.00. Hour and one-half hour strike — add $10.00; Gong — $5.00.

Beware — Many times these options are added to a clock of a model that did not have them offered as an option originally. In this case, they detract from the value of a clock.

If a clock is a rare model, these options do not affect the value nearly as much as on the common models.

TYPES OF CLOCKS

ALARM CLOCK: About five years ago, alarms suddenly jumped in price from the $2.00 to $5.00 range to the $15.00 range. Since then they have slowly crept up to the $20.00 to $25.00 range. They are a good bet for investment, since beginning clock collectors are likely to start with alarms. They are readily salable to most antique dealers. They are easier to work on than watches. The loud tick of the old ones, the names on most models, and the varied case designs all seem to attract collectors.

Considering the millions produced, not a very great percentage survived. This percentage will decrease as they become popular, as many will be dismantled for parts. Yet, there are undoubtedly many thousands lying around in attics, basements, and packed in old trunks waiting to be discovered, probably at reasonable prices.

Remember the following points that affect the value of alarms.

Condition is everything. Prices are predicated on mint condition. Deduct for flaws in condition. New, old stock in original boxes will usually double the value. Finding any in the original box increases value.

Prices given are for the particular make and model. Any variation changes the value.

Eight day models are the most sought after.

Other features collectors look for: calendars, striking models, solid brass cases, external bells on top, fancy cases, sweep second hands, second hands, well-known model names, beveled glass, jeweled works, single spring alarms, extra large or extra small cases, automated dials (especially popular), unusual sound, shape, size, or type of bell, bezel winding (or other unusual winding) combinations of several of these features.

Most collectors avoid foreign alarms (unless they are automated or very unusual), primarily because it is almost impossible to determine their age. If you cannot identify an alarm as American, be warned.

American alarms are more desirable if the maker's name is on the dial, but in the case of certain well-known model names, it is not necessary. Beware of any alarm that does not have the original dial.

The old alarms manufactured before 1900 bring a higher price than the later models. Some model names were used continuously over many years, such as the Waterbury Sunrise, but may be identified by the catalog pictures.

Many model names such as Sentry, were used by several manufacturers on very different types. Even the same manufacturers used the same model name for very different alarms over the years. It takes careful checking to know exactly what you have.

ANSONIA SWING CLOCK: The Swing Clocks were originally designed as "attention getters" for store window displays. Today, they are very desirable collector pieces. The clocks with square gilt and nickel cases were of an early make, probably originating around the late 19th century. The round cases were made later. Beautifully made, these exquisite decorator or conversation pieces, are either in collections, destroyed, or lost, because you will seldom see one for sale.

The French also made swingers, but they weres usually bigger, and more expensive.

Be careful of a reproduction of the German Junghans, a small swinger. They are not worth very much, and any time a clock is reproduced, it hurts the value of the original model.

BANJO CLOCK: Similar to a banjo in shape, the clock's sloping sides and rectangular base offer symmetrical and visually pleasing lines. An American clock maker, Simon Willard, created the banjo design around 1800, calling it his "improved clock." Extremely American in its' design, it was made in large numbers and became popular with railway companies as station timekeepers.

Willard's design was copied by several other clockmakers, not all of them licensed, and the situation became worse after his patent ran out. The Banjo Clock is much sought after by collectors today, but buyers must be cautioned of discrepancies in determining the actual origin of the manufacturer.

BLACK ONYX: These clocks should go much higher in price. They are sleepers and are sold low because most collectors do not know what it is. Imitation marble should go lower, but sells well. Marble has always had a following but black onyx clocks are just starting to be collected. Look for sharp upward price trends here. Black wood will have its day later.

CALENDAR CLOCK: A Calendar Clock shows the date, occasionally the month, and even the day of the week. Many have to be adjusted at the end of the months with fewer than 31 days. The perpetual calendar clock will make this correction itself. At midnight, every 24 hours, a pin on a wheel turns once, putting the mechanism into operation.

CAR CLOCK: Car clocks probably present one of the greatest short-term investment opportunities that the clock collector can find today. Consider the following:

1. Car clocks are collected by clock collectors.
2. Car clocks are collected by watch collectors.
3. Car clocks are collected by antique car buffs.

Considering this, how long will the present bountiful supply last? Car clocks were produced by both the clock companies and the watch companies. They represent most of the 8-day movements produced by the watch companies, and these all have serial numbers. Most car clocks

24 / TYPES OF CLOCKS

produced by watch companies were jeweled movements, from 4 to 15 jewels. Some clock companies produced both jeweled and non-jeweled movements. There seems to have been no serious research to determine the types or quantities manufactured; therefore, you must rely on experience and price books to help recognize the rare models.

Car clocks are priced at probably the lowest multiple of original price of any clock available today. In this category the Swiss movements are selling at prices comparable to the American, but will probably not increase as much in the future unless they have a well-known American name on the dial, such as Bailey, Banks & Biddle.

The antique car buffs particularly look for the car clocks that have auto names on the dial, such as Hudson, Oldsmobile, Ford, etc. Therefore, these original dials often double or triple the value. These collectors also desire the large, heavy, brass cases, and the mounting accessories. They also look for the bezel wind and the pull cord wind, and also the mirror mounted clocks.

The watch collectors seem to prefer the higher jeweled and short run movements. The clock collectors seem to prefer the models produced by the well-known clock manufacturers, such as Seth Thomas, Waterbury, New Haven, Ingraham, etc.

All collectors seem to prefer the 8-Day models. Features such as alarms, winding indicators, sweep second hands and small second hands, unusual winding, setting or mounting, or other unusual features, all seem to increase the value.

A winding indicator is rare and will double or triple the value.

CARRIAGE CLOCK: Carriage clocks have become extremely collectible. The value of these clocks depend on so many intricate details it would be impossible to include them in this section of the book. For example, a Grand Sonnerie (full quarter striking and repeating) carriage clock in a very simple case would be priced between $1400.00 to $1800.00, but the very same movement in a very ornate case with enamel work or porcelain panels could sell for $3000.00 to $6000.00. There are also miniature carriage clocks that sell for $300.00 for a simple timepiece up to several thousand dollars for a miniature ornate repeater.

When purchasing carriage clocks, you should seek the advice of dealers who specialize not only in the sale of such clocks but are also experts in the repair and restoration because they will be able to judge the authenticity of the item. It should also be noted that there are excellent reproductions being reproduced in Europe including repeaters, and miniatures. I have also come across old carriage clocks with reproduction porcelain panels that are very well done and could fool the average collector.

CRYSTAL REGULATOR: If glass is not beveled, subtract $50.00 to $75.00. If the glass is not mint and matched in color and thickness, the value is reduced accordingly.

For original real mercury pendulum, add $20.00 to $25.00.

If priced with visible escapement, subtract $50.00 if without. If priced without visible escapement, add $50.00 if the clock has this feature.

Dials must be mint. Reduce value if porcelain is cracked, chipped, or numbers faded.

Note gold plating on many models. Value is reduced if plating is worn or peeling.

Many of these were supplied with jewelers' or sales company names on the dial. Some of these companies became as famous and well-known as the manufacturers, and their names increase the value of the clock. This is especially true with imported clocks that have an American name on the dial. (Example: Bailey, Banks & Biddle.)

Unusual wood, stone, or pewter trim adds considerably to the value.

There are a few rare crystal regulators in existence that were manufactured by companies that were in business only a short time. These command premium prices from the collectors when they appear. (Example: Jennings Bros.)

CUCKOO CLOCK: The imported cuckoo clocks have not been extremely popular due to the difficulty of identifying and determining the age of these clocks. These prices are based on the approximate age as shown by the date of the catalog.

American clocks are approximately twice the value of the imported ones, and are much desired by collectors.

The very small, so-called cuckoo clocks without the bellows, do not sell well, and usually go under $10.00. The 3-Weight clocks are the most desired by collectors, and the fancier the animation the higher the price. The quarter-hour strike and the musical clocks are also much desired, and go at higher prices.

The 8-Day versions are rare, but are easily identified by the large weights. These are the most sought after. An 8-Day, 3-Weight, fancy carving with animation brings a high price.

Remember, many of these models are still made today. If you cannot verify the age of the clock, reduce the price accordingly.

Modern cuckoo clocks can be purchased at discount houses from $30.00 to $150.00 and used ones are worth somewhat less. If you cannot verify that it is more than 50 years old, buy or sell it as a used modern clock.

If you find an early cuckoo made before 1800, it is a real collector's item (maybe a museum piece), and will be valued accordingly.

Age and complexity are the greatest value-producing elements in that order, with fancy carvings and size being the next most important elements.

DECORATOR CLOCK (Housewife): Clocks offered for sale by the antique shops will usually be priced higher and will bring more money here than they will anywhere else. Buyers of these clocks are not usually collectors but only want one or two for use as decorator items and conversation pieces and will pay according to their desire. Some of the most common (and a lot of times very recently made clocks) will bring very high prices. Almost no type of clock escapes this kind of buyer. This is one of the reasons the beautiful statue clocks of French and American make are now bringing in so much money.

DECORATOR CLOCK (Office or Museum): Beautiful hanging wall or standing clocks will occasionally bring enormous prices, far exceeding the ones shown in this book. Here are some of the reasons. An important businessman may want a certain clock for his home or office. His time being very important to him, he will not want to wait and search for a good buy. The purchase price usually can be written off his taxes, therefore allowing him to pay much more than a collector would pay.

Museums, who charge admissions and whose purchases are tax deductible can pay more for the same reasons. Examples would be most of the E. Howard Banjos and Regulators and the more ornate Jeweler's and Parlor Regulators of all makes. Dealers and collectors should be watching for these situations because a few extra dollars can be picked up this way.

DECORATED PORCELAIN CLOCK: Must be mint and original. Value is reduced if porcelain is cracked, chipped, or retouched. Beware of reproductions.

Three piece sets consisting of clock and candelabrum or vases command the highest prices. Some of the vases were reverse painted from the inside. These are rare and good collector items.

Most dials were porcelain. Subtract $25.00 to $50.00 normally if dial is paper. Reduce the value if dial is cracked, chipped, or faded. If priced with plain porcelain dial, add $50.00 for visible escapement or $15.00 for fancy dial.

Porcelain clocks designated as Royal Bonn usually command somewhat higher prices. Subtract $15.00 if bezel does not have beveled glass.

DRUM CLOCK: Used in several French clocks, the movement came outfitted in a brass container that was drum shaped. It was then placed in the clock case.

GRANDFATHER CLOCK: Once called "Long, Tall Case," or even "Coffin Clocks," the Grandfather Clock is probably the most well known of timekeeping collectibles. Invented in London around 1660, the Long Case or Grandfather Clock was the first household item to be successfully mass produced by an American clockmaker, (Eli Terry). The earliest surviving model, however, was made by Abel Cottey in the early 18th century.

It is reputed that the name "grandfather" originated for the tall case clock from a song written by Henry Clay in 1876 which began with the lyrics, "My grandfather's clock was too tall for the shelf ..." Grandmother clocks are of similar design, but stand under six feet in height.

HOWARD HALL CLOCK: These clocks are very scarce, if not downright rare. For this reason there are not enough sales to establish any kind of a price range. A good rule of thumb, in determining the value of a Howard Hall Clock, is to multiply their original cost 10 to 12 times.

The clocks of this type, are rarely shown publicly, because of the difficulty in transporting them, and also because they are rarely for sale. The clocks were, for the most part, custom made with variants as to case, style, wood, dial, and most importantly, movement. I have never talked to anyone who has seen any hall clocks of an identical, or even very similar make.

Due to their size, not many modern houses will accommodate them, and this factor limits the market somewhat. On the other hand, they are so desirable to many collectors that, if given a chance to buy one, they would — putting it in storage until they could alter their home or office.

IRON CLOCK: The first generally known household timekeepers, iron clocks were originally made by blacksmiths and locksmiths. In some geographic areas it became popular to fit unusual wooded cases around the clocks, and to place them on wooden wall fixtures.

LANTERN CLOCK: A weight driven clock, with a lantern shaped brass case, the lantern clock originated in England, and was made for about 100 years after the early part of the 17th century. The name of the clock may originate from a mispronunciation of "latten" meaning brass, although the earliest clocks of this design sold during or before 1600 were made of iron.

LIGHTHOUSE CLOCK: The American inventor of the popular Banjo Clock, Simon Willard, is also responsible for the ornate, tall, table clock shaped like a lighthouse with a wooden base and glass shade on top. Some of these lighthouse or "lamphouse" clocks were made in France during the 19th century. Willards' version was unique in that he designed his as an alarm, where a special device tapped the top of the wooden case, instead of ringing an alarm. Sales were not too successful at the time.

The French have some models with a clock dial that turns underneath the rounded glass arch.

MANTEL CLOCK: It is said that the smaller "grandmother" clock, inspired the trend towards the handy, easily transportable mantel clocks. As their name implies, they are intended for the mantelpiece.

MUSICAL CLOCK: A revolving pin barrel operates the bell hammers, affecting this magnificent clock to play tunes at the hour, or at any one time. One of the earliest late 16th century British designs had 13 bells. In the 18th century, David Rittenhouse made a musical clock in Philadelphia that played ten tunes on 15 bells. It sold at the time for under $700.00.

REGULATOR CLOCK: Generally refers to a very precise, plain cased clock, with a long pendulum and no strike. A regulator made in the mid 18th century was utilized by Captain Cook on two of his sea voyages, but was used on land with other instruments to check their current longitude.

SCHOOL HOUSE, ROUND DROP, DROP OCTAGON: Prices have accelerated over the years rather rapidly until they exceed the amount people are willing to pay. Clock dealers are not quite ready to reduce to a point where they will sell readily. At the present time not many of these clocks are moving among knowledgeable buyers at the values shown in this book.

Two other factors causing the value to drop, may be the importing of old Japanese clocks and prolific current reproduction.

STATUE CLOCK: Production figures for statue clocks are unknown; therefore, the only criterion for rarity is experience, which varies with each collector. The price collectors will pay for a certain statue will sometimes vary considerably, however, certain preferences are evident. The double statue clocks are the most desired. Standing statue clocks are sought ahead of the sitting statue. The visible escapement and fancy dials certainly increase the value. Generally, the larger the size the greater the price. Condition is everything. Prices given are for mint clocks. Broken or missing parts of trim or statues drop the price drastically.

Certain Ansonia statues are very well-known, and although not as rare as others, command higher prices since every collector wants one.

Some collectors desire the three piece sets and will pay a premium for the complete set.

The price trend for all statues has been a sharp rise for the last four years.

REPLICAS, REPRODUCTIONS, AND FAKES

A clock collector (and probably any collector of a valuable item) does not pursue the hobby for long, before he has an encounter with a seemingly desirable item that is not exactly what it seems. He may be lucky and have a fellow collector or an honest dealer point out the disturbing features that indicate that the clock is not what it appears to be. He may also be unlucky and purchase and carry home what he felt was a real sleeper, only to find that he was the sleeper. That rude awakening is the beginning of a rather intensive and extensive education. The acquisition of this book is one of the steps in that education.

To properly discuss the subject of clocks as related to their value, the following definitions are necessary and desirable.

ORIGINAL: A clock that is exactly as it was made, with no changes, alterations or restorations; may show all the results of age and use.

MINT ORIGINAL: An original clock that is in perfect condition, with no great signs of wear and tear except yellowing of dial and label. If the finish is dull it can be brought out by a good lemon oil or tung oil polish. If the clock originally had a label, it must still be complete and perfect except for the yellowing or browning of age. If the clock is mint original, its condition can make you imagine that it was stored since manufacture.

RESTORED: A clock that with replacement of parts and repair has been brought back to as near original as possible.

MINT RESTORED: A clock in perfect condition that has been restored to exactly original condition. This means that the restoration would be considered minor, such as refinished case, dial restored to original, or minor parts of case replaced.

REPLICA: An exact copy of an older clock. Replicas are usually manufactured by the same company that made the original, and the label will so indicate. Occasionally, a replica will be produced by another company, but again the label will so state. More on this later.

REPRODUCTION: A clock that is made to reproduce as closely as possible, the appearance of an antique clock. Reproductions fall into several classes:
   a. Old clocks that have had such an extensive restoration that over 50% of the clock has been replaced with new parts.
   b. New clocks that have been made from old wood.
   c. New clocks made from new wood.

FAKE: Any clock that is made to appear to be older than its actual age, or original when it is not, or otherwise contrived to fool the purchaser. Fakes have only one purpose — to cause the purchaser to pay a higher price.

Very experienced collectors will tell you that they can detect a fake by sight, feel and smell. They say that the smell of old age is detectable and distinctive, and cannot be duplicated or faked. The main factors in detecting fakes (which they modestly may not mention), are experience and knowledge. Knowledge of the original design and appearance of a clock is necessary to detect any deviation. Experience tells you what to look for when inspecting a possible fake.

Knowledge of clocks is obtained through visits to NAWCC marts, to museums, to collectors, and through study of books that show original pictures of the clocks. A detailed study of the pictures in this book and in catalog reprints, will allow you to detect the slight deviations that occur in many fakes. The experience that you obtain from examining many clocks and talking to many collectors is necessary to detect the fakes.

Logically, the more valuable a clock, the more likely it is to be faked. It has been said that the most faked clocks in America are the Weight Banjos and the Pillar and Scrolls. The fact that several of the major companies reproduced the Willard Banjo in the Victorian period has made it easy for the unscrupulous to represent some of these as original, either with or without some judicious faking. It has been cynically remarked that there are more Willard Banjos and Eli Terry Pillar & Scrolls existing today than ever came out of the makers' shops. The same has been said of Howard Banjos. To be more accurate, we should not call a clock, but rather the one who misrepresents the clock a fake. All clocks have value. A clock has value based on its own merits, regardless of whether we call it a fake, or a "fake dealer" calls it something else.

Since replicas are represented to be such, no discussion of these are necessary, except to advise the beginning collector that they are considered collectible and there is a market for them. Many collectors feel if they can't afford an original, the replica or a reproduction is the next best thing.

Reproductions do warrant some discussion, since there is a considerable variation in opinion among collectors as to the standing of reproductions. Reproductions made from new materials, represented as such, and exact copies of the original are sometimes collected exactly as the replicas. Reproductions made from old wood are more exact copies of the original as the original appears today, and are more desired by some collectors. Any reproduction becomes a fake when it is represented as original, and the beginning collector will gain valuable knowledge by spending time studying reproductions so that he can recognize them later when they may not be shown as such.

It is in the area of restorations that the most divergent opinions exist among collectors. How far may you go in bringing a clock to a mint restored condition? Everyone seems to agree that the works should be restored to running order, and as long as the works are original, considerable restoration may be done. Replacement trim parts on the case, such as finials, moulding parts and metal parts, lower the value of the clock but are generally accepted. All collectors do not agree with the 50% replacement figure that transforms the object of a repair job from a restoration to a reproduction. Some feel the figure should be higher and some feel it should be lower. Most collectors simply adjust the price for which they will buy or sell the clock, to reflect the originality and condition.

For the beginning collector the best advice is to examine a clock carefully before you buy. It is not always prudent to refuse to buy a clock that is not mint — simply adjust the price accordingly.

WORKS: When you are restoring a clock, however, and particularly when buying a clock that has been restored, make sure it has the original works for that clock. Just having an old works is not enough. It must be a works that was used in the particular case you have. A clock case with a non-original works becomes a compromise (if it's an old works or misrepresented) and so loses a great part of its antique value. If the clock does not have the original works, it cannot be considered a *mint, original* clock in the sense in which that definition is used in this book. Look for extra screw holes that have been filled, mounting brackets or blocks that have been added or moved to identify tampering with the works.

REPLICAS: A phase that has been growing in popularity is the collection of replicas of famous expensive clocks. A look at any of the NAWCC Marts will show you that this has become quite an important phase of the hobby. Some of these replicas are even put out by the same company that put out the original. They are reported to be limited in production, usually to how many they can sell. The price is very reasonable compared to the original. While you can't say this is collecting antique clocks, it's still collecting clocks.

The collector who cannot afford an original clock because it sells for thousands of dollars, feels as though it is very worthwhile to collect an exact replica that is selling for hundreds of dollars. This type of collecting cannot be criticized because it still educates the collector and the public as to what the original clocks were like. In the future this will probably become even more important. It is possible to have an entire collection of clocks with nothing but replicas.

Looking back at the history of clocks we find that in the late 1800's there were many replicas (sometimes called outright fakes) of the earlier clocks sold at that time. Those replicas sold in 1890 are now sold as antiques, hence, the replicas that are being sold today will in 50 years or so, be considered antiques. It is certainly a part of the hobby for each collector to keep himself posted on the replicas so he can recognize when they are offered for sale, whether they are represented to be replicas or not.

ESCAPEMENTS: The concept of the escapement is believed to be attributed to an ancient Eastern monk, who was trying to control the rate of a water clock.

The earliest mechanical escapement device was the verge and the foliot, originating somewhere around the 14th century. The verge is a straight supporting bar, with the two escapement pawls and the balance wheel on top. It is called a verge, because it is like the pole that was carried in church processions by the verger.

The foliot is a French derivitive, from the word "folier," meaning to dance about wildly.

Many thousands of escapements have been invented since then, although the early clockmakers gave up the original verge only with the greatest persuasion. The most common escapement devices we are familiar with are: the lever for clocks and watches with balances, the anchor for pendulum clocks, and the detent escapement for marine chronometers. Some other escapement devices are illustrated on the escapement chart.

DISPLAY

There are three basic places to stand a group of antique clocks: on the wall, in a cabinet, or on top of furniture. Sometimes, as in the case of Grandfather or Grandmother clocks, the antique IS the furniture, and must be displayed appropriately as befits its value. This means appropriating a space or corner, that is not cluttered with knickknacks or other memorabilia; where the fine lines, workmanship, and grace of your antique can be fully appreciated. This holds true for the smaller pieces as well. Let your clocks command the focal point in the interior design of your home. They are well able to carry it off.

A very effective way to show a small sized series is to display a grouping of clocks; preferably in a glass paneled cabinet that is kept dust free so as not to distract from the impact of your collection. In this manner you have a distinct advantage over an open display; the clocks themselves will take much longer to collect dust. Novelty clocks in particular tend to accumulate dust and grit within the elaborate grooves and scrollwork that embellish the design.

Metal or wooden stands can also be used to place specimens on top of tables, mantles, or any flat surface. They can be very decorative and add to the style of the clock, or plain to avoid detracting from it. Displayed in this manner they are, however, susceptible to damage from children or accidents. This holds true for direct placement on television surfaces, bureaus, bookshelves, and coffee tables.

When displaying wall clocks, the question is not so much how to display as where. You must use your own judgement and the overall design of your home to decide the most appropriate room for your antique clock. A pendulum clock may be a bit to "weighty" for the kitchen — then again if you have a breakfast nook or overall dark wooded ambiance, it may be just the thing. Check the manufacturers label in a catalogue for your hanging clocks; often this ascertains exactly where it was intended to be placed. Parlor Wall, or Kitchen Hanging is self explanatory. You are not bound by these designations, but they may provide a clue in the right direction of the room your clock will serve its decorative and functional purpose best.

A topical arrangement can also work, if not carried to excess. Cherubs, gold filigree, a particular type of wood, can be carefully matched in one grouping. Beware of allowing the items to overlap or merge together; a walnut cased clock against a wood paneled wall can lose its effect. The eye must follow an interesting variation of like items, and not pass over it entirely.

If you have tried to specialize in a particular clock manufacturer, by all means try a grouping of this nature, perhaps sequencing the arrangement from earliest models to latest jeweled and non-jeweled variations, etc. This can result in an eclectic display, that will delight you, and fellow collectors.

If you only have two or three clocks instead of a substantial quantity, (as many beginners do) the style, period and condition of these items will determine whether or not you choose to group them together for a certain impact, or allow them to grace a solitary position in your home. Owners of large collections may choose a scattered tactic also, providing they have the space. Some antique clocks do best when displayed in their unique glory; you will also avoid a cluttered appearance as can happen with a group display of too many elaborate pieces.

RESTORATION

"Mint, Original Condition" is a phrase used constantly in connection with antiques. The term is defined in detail earlier in this text, but the implications of the term go somewhat deeper than a cursory perusal of the definitions would lead you to believe.

In antique furniture and violins, with pieces that have reached astronomical values, chemical analyses to determine if the finishes and glues are original are not unknown. In the future, as antique clock prices soar, such analyses may be used with a subsequent greater value being placed on original.

Due in part to the fact that many antique clock collections are considered as part of the furnishings of the home of the collector, some collectors have been more concerned with a "nice" appearance than with originality. This attitude may change as the hobby becomes more sophisticated, with much greater values being placed on originality and rarity.

The original factory catalogs show the pictures of the clocks as they were produced, and are the best means of checking a clock for originality. Actual photos of clocks as they exist today may show some alterations that the clock has accumulated over the years, and collectors should view such photos with caution until they are compared with the original catalog picture and description.

To give a more practical understanding of the term, "restored to mint, original condition", herewith is presented a brief discussion of some of the facets of this term as applied to clock cases.

When acquiring a new clock, my personal preference is to leave it as I get it, and simply protect it to keep it in the same condition. However, quite often the only chance you have to acquire a particular model, is in less than ideal condition. If it has been stored in an attic or shed, it is usually covered with dirt and must be carefully cleaned before you can determine its condition. Here is a reprint of the instructions for cleaning, taken from a 1926 Furniture Dealers Reference Book. (It goes without saying that the works should be removed before working on the case.)

HOW TO KEEP CLOCKS CLEAN: When wood furniture or clocks are finger marked, a trifle oiled, smoky, or carrying a bit of gloom due to the rubbing oil, try asking your druggist for a pound of USP Green soap. Take no substitute. This will come in a tin can or a jar, and looks very much like vaseline. Then pick out the oiliest and dirtiest table top or clock. On a 6-foot table top, put a heaping tablespoonful of this soap, then take a few yards of absolutely clean, soft cheese cloth, soak it in water and wring it out. Begin spreading soap over the entire piece. Have enough in the cloth so that it spreads with a smear, and then add a little more water until you can freely rub with the grain and the sliding is easy. Then rinse out the cloth and follow each stroke with the grain, until you know you are wiping it with absolutely clear water. This may take several rinsings of the cheese cloth, and it must be continued until you are absolutely positive that every bit of soap has been removed. What has happened? We all know that the evaporation of any liquid causes a reduction of temperature. Besides this, the process contracts and hardens the finished film so that it is forced to exude any small particles of oil that may remain there. When the top is absolutely clean, take a clean piece of cheese cloth and wipe up the surface until it is absolutely dry and clear. It will be found that a surface of this kind can be kept in condition for months without a repetition of the process. The dust that may settle will not stick, and when the dust becomes noticeable pass over the article with a vacuum cleaner. Avoid dusters. They often scratch the fine finishes, which the vacuum will not do. The same process may be employed on enamels.

In a case where Green Soap is not obtainable, obtain a cake of Ivory Soap or Ivory Chips, and melt them by heating with sufficient water to obtain a consistency of vaseline. This will also do the trick.

In repair work, when it becomes necessary to give a coat of varnish or shellac or wood lacquer, (which is best applied by the spray or a brushing lacquer), try this: Reduce the soap with water to the consistency of rubbing oil. Use the finest pumice stone that can be obtained, and proceed to rub just as though it were oil. You will immediately notice that the pumice stone "bites" or cuts quicker than when rubbing with oil and, therefore, the process may be likened very much to steel wooling. You take the gloss off quickly being careful not to cut through, and you have the advantage that after you have cleaned off the pumice stone your piece is ready for delivery.

MARBLE AND ONYX CASES: Before starting to repair an onyx or marble case, be sure that you understand the composition of these, particularly if you need to replace a portion of the case.

MARBLE: Technically speaking, the term SHOULD only be applied to metamorphosed, recystallized limestones and dolomites. Practically speaking, the term is used to designate any limestone that is hard enough to take a polish. As a trade term, it is generally used for ANY crystalline calcium carbonate rock of pleasing pattern and color when cut and polished. All marble is composed of crystals of the minerals calcite ($CaCO_3$) and/or dolomite ($CaMg(CO_3)_2$) usually mixed with other minerals that give it the great variety of colors.

ONYX: Technically speaking, the term should only be applied to a striped agate in which white layers alternate with either black or darker layers of other colors. Practically speaking, (and for our purposes as clock collectors) it is generally applied to a quartz agate that is dyed black. As a trade term, it is loosely applied to both banded agate and banded marble.

ONXY MARBLE: For our purposes, any marble that is called "Onyx", e.g. "Mexican Onyx." Usually marble that is striped in more or less parallel layers that somewhat resemble true onyx.

Both marble and agate have been known and used since ancient times, and the terms "onyx" and "onyx marble" were also used in ancient times. The Germans developed a method of dying agate black, and now most commercial agate is artificially dyed in many different colors. The method used for coloring onyx black consisted of soaking the onyx in either oil (olive) or a sugar solution for a long period, then "carburizing" the onyx with sulphuric acid. The acid left the carbon from the oil or sugar in the onyx and thus colored it black. If some of the layers were particularly hard and impermeable, they would not absorb as much sugar or oil, and thus the color would not be as deep, so that the bands could still be distinguished after the coloring.

Black marble is found near Shoreham, Vermont and Glen Falls, New York. Marble can also be artificially colored black, but whether this was done by the nineteenth century clock factories, I do not know.

34 / RESTORATION

The "imitation black marble" clocks were generally iron cases finished with a very hard Japanned black finish and can, of course, be detected with a magnet. We have also found some black mantels in what appears to be slate, but so far I have been unable to find references to this in the old catalogs.

How do you distinguish black onyx from black marble? In appearance, black onyx is usually more translucent than marble, but this cannot be used as a positive test to determine of which material a specimen is composed, since the characteristics of different speciments vary so greatly. Qualitative chemical analysis cannot be used due to the heterogeneous composition of the minerals. Quantitative tests of a large portion would be indicative. Acid will attack and destroy marble, although the harder dolomites will resist diluted sulphuric acid, while agate or onyx will resist acid. So, sulphuric acid, or preferably, hydrochloric acid, may be used to determine if a rock or clock case is marble or true onyx.

The easiest practical test is a hardness test. In a scale of hardness from 1 to 10, with talc as 1 and diamond as 10, marble has a hardness of 3 to 4, while true onyx has a hardness of 6 to 7. Since iron or mild steel has a hardness of 4 to 5, you can use a scratch test with a nail, and it should scratch marble but will not touch onyx.

This is about the extent of the tests available to check the composition of a case. Any test will be somewhat damaging to a clock case.

Once, while on vacation, I had a lot of fun asking antique dealers if they could tell me the difference between black marble and black onyx. The most common answer was that you just know from experience. One practical dealer said, "I just ask the customer what he thinks it is, and that's what it is." Another practical dealer said, "I just look it up in the book, and if it says "onyx", that's what it is." I have not yet determined if the old catalogs are always accurate when they show black onyx clock cases, but from the original prices as compared to the original prices of the black marble, I suspect that they are usually referring to true onyx. In the case of the green onyx cases, they are not accurate as these are marble, or, if you prefer, marble onyx.

VENEERED WOODEN CASES: Probably a majority of wooden clock cases are veneered, since this allowed the maker to get any grain desired at a much lower price. Even in the Victorian Period, solid walnut was not cheap. A 1902 book reports that a very large walnut tree would bring as much as $5,000. Convert that to today's prices and you will see that the trees will not bring that much today. Veneer was used by the Greeks and Romans, and the use of veneer has seemed to vary with the degree of civilization. The greater the degree of civilization, the greater the use of veneer. There was little veneer used during the dark ages. In the early 1800's, veneer was still made by hand methods. During the mid-1800's, more and more sophisticated saws were developed for sawing thin sheets from logs to make veneer, and eventually very thin saws were capable of cutting sheets that were less than $1/16$" thickness, so that some sanding to finish the surface was all that was left to do after the sawing.

In the last 25 years of the 19th Century, the techniques of slicing, rolling, and "reverse rolling" came to be common techniques for making veneer, although sawing was still used for ebony, rose olive, and quarter-sawed oak and sycamore. Surprisingly, at the turn of the century New York was the greatest veneer producing center ahead of Boston, Grand Rapids, Cincinnati, and Chicago, in that order.

Razor-sharp knives were used for slicing a log into thin sheets. It is easy to see that both sawing and slicing could be used in a variety of ways to produce the desired grain effects. Logs could be sawed, or sliced lengthwise or crosswise, or the log could be cut into quarters, halves, or sections, and the veneer taken from these to get the desired figure.

To make veneer by rolling, the log was first boiled in large vats which were covered and heated by steam pipes. When thoroughly cooked the log was hoisted out (with a big cloud of steam) and put into a lathe large enough to take up to a 16 foot log. Then a razor-sharp knife as long as the log was fed into the log. As soon as the log was perfectly round the knife was adjusted to slice off exactly the thickness of veneer needed, which could be as thin as $\frac{1}{32}$" and as thick as $\frac{1}{4}$" or more. It is easy to see that this does not produce much figure or pattern in the grain, so this method is usually used to make plywood layers.

"Reverse Rolling" to make veneer is a variation of rolling in which the log is sawed lengthwise in halves and the centers of the lathe are set near the bark side so that as the log is rolled, the knife is shaving the veneer off across the grain, which gives a much more figured veneer than plain rolling.

This discussion of how veneer is made is designed to make the collector aware of the different types of grain and figure that he might see on a clock. And, if you are attempting to replace a missing piece of veneer, it is easy to see you must obtain a replacement piece made by the same method as the original if you desire a close match.

TO REPAIR VENEER: When possible, always glue the old veneer back in place, preferably without cracking it. The joints and cracks will leave lines in the surface that will show through the finish. Use slick shellac to fill the cracks and joints. If it is necessary to replace some of the veneer, you must use material of the same color, grain and thickness. An old piece of veneer from an old piece of furniture will usually be easiest to match.

When cutting a piece of veneer for a patch, trim the edges with a bevel slanting somewhat inward on the bottom so that the top edges are tight when it is pushed into place and clamped. Veneer always darkens with age, which is why new material must be stained to match old. Stain a patch before trimming, as the stain may expand the veneer. After trimming, sand the edges of the patch lightly until smooth, then stain the edges. Use a sharp, thin-pointed blade of a knife or a suitable carving chisel to remove all dirt and old glue from the area under the patch, as new glue will not stick properly to old. Neither will the patch lay properly in place if the surface is not clean and smooth.

Cover the hole and the bottom of the patch with a thin layer of glue, then lay the patch in place. Cover the area with waxed paper or a piece of plastic film from the kitchen to keep the glue from sticking to your blocks, weights, or clamps. If you used slightly too much glue so that it will be oozing up around the patch, a little wax on the wood around the patch will keep it from sticking so tight and reduce the sanding you must do later. A small patch on a flat area will require only a block and a weight or clamp to hold it in place until dry. A larger patch may require a sandbag or several clamps, or a press to hold it, and a curved surface may require that you make a mold beforehand so that it will properly hold the patch in place.

Let the glue dry for at least 24 hours, then remove the weights, clamps, waxed paper or plastic, and any excess glue not stuck to the clock, then finish sanding with 8/0 or 6/0 sandpaper until smooth.

If you have a loose edge, and when you lift it slightly adequate glue remains under the veneer, spray a little water on the glue (an atomizer works very well), then use an almost hot thin metal spatula to slide under the glue. Then lay a sheet of foil over the veneer and weight it down with a very warm, old fashioned flat iron for 24 hours. If you are careful enough and lucky enough not to break or crack the veneer, you will have a perfect repair. Do not use this method if there is dirt or inadequate glue under the veneer. In this case, carefully scrape the dirt and glue from under the veneer, put new glue on a spatula blade, and carefully spread the new glue under the veneer with the spatula blade. Then press the veneer down, roll it with a roller (roll toward the edge) if necessary to squeeze out all excess glue, wipe off the excess with a damp cloth, cover the area with a piece of plastic film, then a block and a weight for 24 hours.

If you have a blister or wave in the veneer (a place where the veneer has raised from the surface), read the following methods of repair and choose the one that fits the conditions:

(a) If the veneer is not cracked or broken, cover the blister with a piece of smooth foil and very gently place a moderately hot old-fashioned flat iron on the blister. Be gentle — do not crack the veneer. The iron should not be hot enough to ruin the finish. Leave the iron in place for 24 hours. If the condition of the old glue is satisfactory and there is enough moisture in the wood below the veneer, the heat should draw out sufficient moisture from the wood to soften the old glue and make it stick.

(b) If the veneer is broken or cracked at the blister, lay a damp blotter over the blister and put the moderately hot flat iron over the blotter and blister. Leave for 24 hours, then if you had a broken piece that had fallen out or had been removed, glue it in place as in patching, put the weight on it and let set 24 hours.

Another method for a blister with cracked or broken veneer: Put vinegar in the blister and allow to stand for 8-12 hours to soften the glue, then pour out any remaining vinegar from the blister and place a dry blotter and the hot flat iron over the blister. The blotter will absorb the moisture and the heat should shrink the veneer back to the flat position. If any edges remain unglued, carefully raise the loose veneer and reglue as described for repairing loose edges.

(c) If the veneer over the blister is cracked and there is dirt under the veneer, take a razor blade knife and cut down the crack to open it to the edges of the blister, then make a similar cut at right angles to the crack so that you now have an X crossing the blister. Carefully lift the points of the flaps at the center of the X, clean out all dirt from underneath, then glue down by one of the above methods or by inserting new glue.

If there is too much dirt or old glue, to easily remove as above cut a "barn door" flat instead of the X. This is done by making two cuts with the grain and one across the grain to make a square or rectangular flap which you can lift higher for heavy duty cleaning.

(d) If all the above methods are inadequate, cut out the blister and patch with an inlay. Always cut two sides of the veneer along the grain. Use a straight edge to cut out the veneer so that the edges of the patch are easier to fit. After cutting out the veneer, lay a piece of paper over the recess and rub your finger or a pencil lead around the edge of the recess so that it makes a line on the paper. Carefully lay the paper on a piece of veneer so that the grain runs correctly for the patch and cut out the patch with a large pair of scissors. Glue in place as described at the first of this section.

NOTE: An eye dropper and a large hypodermic needle (veterinarian style) are almost indispensible tools for applying glue when repairing veneer or loose glued joints. They save enough time to be worth the cleaning it takes later.

To get a stock of old veneer for use in repairing clock cases, go around the junk stores and secondhand furniture stores and buy some pieces of veneered furniture. Get the flat surfaces for easier working. Remove the finish from the old veneer and sand with 3/0 or finer sandpaper to open the grain. Soak the surface with a wet cloth for 12 hours, moistening the cloth frequently. Start at an edge, lift the veneer with a knife and remove. If it does not come off easily, continue soaking until it does. After removing the veneer, place it on a flat surface (while still wet) with the underside up. Use a scraper to remove all the remaining old glue. When dry, sand carefully with 3/0 or finer sandpaper until thoroughly clean and ready to use. Store in a dry place pressed between two flat surfaces with sufficient weight to keep the veneer from wrinkling and curling. Note that you will rarely need a piece of old veneer larger than this page. The above techniques are passed on to you in memory of my dad, A. F. Rabeneck, a true artist who spent 40 years restoring antique furniture, and could make patches and repairs in veneer that were practically invisible.

SUPPLIERS

Most of the following suppliers have catalogs available illustrating their complete line of clock parts and supplies. Some are free and some make a small charge that is refunded on the first order.

To assure getting a response to any type of inquiry from any service or supply company, it is absolutely necessary to include a SASE (Self-addressed, stamped envelope). Do not write to anyone requesting information without enclosing a SASE if you expect a response.

*Note: Displays large assortments of clock parts and supplies at the NAWCC Regionals.

Antique Clocks
Briscoe Road
Rt. 1, Box 242-C
Swan Lake, NY 12783
(914) 292-7287

Aguilar Jewelers' Supply
520-C "E" Street
Robinson Bldg., Room 408
San Diego, CA 92101
(714) 232-2993

M. Beresh, Inc.
21700-C Greenfield Suite No.353
Oak Park, MI 48237
(313) 968-2930

Otto Frei – Jules Borel
Box 796-C
Oakland, CA 94604
(415) 832-0355

38 / SUPPLIERS

Borel & Frei
315-C West 5th St.
Los Angeles, CA 90013
(213) 689-4630

Jules Borel & Co.
121-C S.E. First St.
Miami, FL 33131
(816) 421-6100

Jules Borel & Co.,
1110-C Grand
Kansas City, MO 64106
(816) 421-6110

D.R.S. Borel
15-C West 57th St.
New York, NY 10036
(212) 757-7370

Colmans-Borel
648-C Huron Road
Cleveland, OH 44115
(216) 771-2342

California Time Service, Inc.,
3210-C Airport Way
Long Beach, CA 90806
(213) 595-5415

The Cas-Ker Company
P.O. Box 2347-C
128 E. 6th Street
Cincinnati, OH 45201
(513) 241-7076

*Bernard Edwards Dial Co.
Specializing in Clock Dials Only
1331-C Southwind Drive
Northbrook, IL 60062
(312) 272-2563

Empire Clock Inc.
1295-C Rice Street
St. Paul, MN 55117
(612) 487-2885

Esslinger & Co.
1165-C Medallion Drive
St. Paul, MN 55120
(612) 452-7180

Ewing Bros.
P.O. Box 445-C
Tucker, GA 30084
(404) 938-0115

Florida Watch & Jewelers Supply, Inc.
P.O. Box 14533-C
2828 Central Avenue
St. Petersburg, FL 33712
(813) 327-1100

Fried & Field Company
Watch Materials — Tools
657-C Mission St.
San Francisco, CA 94105

The Gould Co.
13750-C Neutron Rd.
Dallas, TX 75234
(214) 233-7725

Herr & Kline Inc.
1914-C Granby St.
Norfolk, VA 23517
(804) 623-0714
(800) 446-8094

Kilb & Company
219-C N. Milwaukee St.
P.O. Drawer 8-A
Milwaukee, WI 53201
(414) 272-6250

Langert Bros.
P.O. Box 27487-C
1620 W. Camelback Rd.
Phoenix, AZ 85061
(602) 264-1620

*S. LaRose, Inc.
234-C Commerce Place
Greensboro, NC 27420

Livesay's Inc.
2942-C W. Columbus Drive
Suite 203
Tampa, FL 33607

Marshall-Swartchild Co.,
2040-C N. Milwaukee Ave.
Chicago, IL 60647
(312) 278-2300
IL (800) 972-3776
Other (800) 621-4767

Mason and Sullivan Co.
39-C Blossom Ave.
Osterville, MA 02655
(617) 428-6993
(617) 428-5726

Mayer Bros., Inc.
P.O. Box 750
4th & Pike Bldg.
Seattle, WA 98111
(206) 682-1525

Merritt's Antiques, Inc.
RD 2-C
Douglasville, PA 19518
(800) 345-4101

Michigan Jewelers Supply Co.
Troy Commerce Center
1116-C E. Big Beaver Rd.
P.O. Box 412
Troy, MI 48084
(313) 689-9100

The Nest Co.
915-C Olive St.
St. Louis, MO 63101
(314) 241-0770

*Southwest Clock Supply
2442-C Walnut Ridge
Dallas, TX 75229
(214) 241-3570

E & J Swigart Co.
34-West Sixth St.
Cincinnati, OH 45202
(513) 721-1427

Tani Engineering
6226 Waterloo
Box 338-C
Atwater, OH 44201
(216) 947-2268

Roland V. Tapp Imports
13525 Alondra Blvd.
Santa Fe Springs, CA 90670
(213) 921-5611
(714) 521-2354

Tec Specialties (Ed Collum)
P.O. Box 909
Smyrna, GA 30081

*Timesavers (Steve Berger)
P.O. Box 171-C
Wheeling, IL 6000
(312) 394-4818

Tiny Clock Shop
1378-C Old Northern Blvd.
Roslyn, NY 11576

Turncraft Clock Imports Co.
611-615-C Winnetka Avenue No.
Golden Valley, MN 55427
(612) 544-1711

The following clock dealers offer new clocks for sale with emphasis on reproduction of American antique clocks. Some issue catalogs and are free for the asking. Be sure to send a self-addressed, stamped envelope (SASE) when writing an inquiry or requesting a catalog.

*Note: Displays large assortments of new clocks at the NAWCC Regionals.

Alpine Import & Export
230-C Fifth Avenue
New York, NY 10001
(212) 686-4646

*Aubrey A. Aramaki
331-C N.W. Gilman Blvd.
Issaquah, WA 98027
(206) 392-5200

Clocks, Ltd.
P.O. Box 66106-C
5256 North Rose St.
Rosemont, IL 60018
(312) 678-0988

Empire Clock, Inc.
1295-C Rice Street
St. Paul, MN 55117
(612) 487-2885

*Foster Campos
213-C Schoosett St., Route 139
Pembroke, MA 02359
(617) 826-8577

Houseman & Spong Clocks
11829-C Rockinghorse Road
Rockville, MD 20852

*Ken Kyckelhahn
252-C California Ave.
Oakdale, CA 95361
(209) 847-1337

40 / SUPPLIERS

*S. Larose, Inc.
234-C Commerce Place
Greensboro, NC 27420
(919) 275-0462

Mason & Sullivan Co.
39-C Blossom Ave.
Osterville, MA 02655
(617) 428-6993

*Merritt's Antiques, Inc.
RD 2-C
Douglassville, PA 19518
(800) 345-4101

*Timesavers
P.O. Box 171-C
Wheeling, IL 60090
(312) 394-4818

Turncraft Clock Imports Co.
611-C Winnetaka Ave.
Golden Valley, MN 55427
(612) 544-1711

The following companies issue catalogs of horological books and literature. Call or write for catalog.
   *Note: Visa and Master Card telephone orders are accepted.

*Adams Brown Company
P.O. Box 357
Cranbury, NJ 08512
(800) 257-5378
In New Jersey
(609) 799-2125

*American Reprints
111 W. Dent
Ironton, MO 63650
Bob Spence
(314) 546-7251

Arlington Book Company
2025 Eye St., NW
Suite 102
Washington, DC 20006
Tran Du Ly
(202) 296-6750
(202) 524-1931

Books of All Time
P.O. Box 604
Brockville, Ontario
Canada 56V 5V8
Marion Parker
(613) 345-2702

*Heart of America Press
P.O. Box 9808
10101 Blue Ridge
Kansas City, MO 64134
Shirley Shelley
(816) 761-0080

*S. Larose, Inc.
234 Commerce Place
Greensboro, NC 27420
(919) 275-0462

Movements In Time
*Specializing in out-of-print
   horological books*
Box 6629, Station A
Toronto M5W 1X4 Canada
Carol Hayter
(416) 883-1924
(416) 895-1439

PUBLICATIONS

To find local dealers check the yellow pages under "Antiques." You may also visit antiques shows, flea markets, auctions and conventions, or you can enjoy the thrill of detection by attending yard or tag sales, and by going to thrift and second-hand stores.

PUBLICATIONS / 41

The following publications not only are sources of information on the history of various antiques and collectibles and trends in the field, they also contain dealer ads and ads of private individuals who either want to sell or want to buy. You can place your own want ads in many of them for a reasonable fee.

AMERICAN ART AND ANTIQUES
1515 Broadway
NYC, NY 10036

AMERICAN COLLECTOR
P.O. Box A
Reno, NV 89506

THE MAGAZINE ANTIQUES
551 Fifth Avenue
NYC, NY 10017

ANTIQUES AND THE ARTS WEEKLY
Newtown Bee
Bee Publishing Co.
Newtown, CT 06470

ANTIQUES AND COLLECTIBLES
525 N. Barry Ave.
Mamaroneck, NY 10543

ANTIQUE COLLECTING
(American Antique Collector)
P.O. Box 327
Ephrata, PA 17522

ANTIQUE COLLECTOR
Chestergate House
Vauxhall Bridge Road
London SW1V 1HF

ANTIQUES JOURNAL
P.O. Box 1046
Dubuque, IA 52001

ANTIQUE MONTHLY
P.O. Drawer 2
Tuscaloosa, AL 35401

ANTIQUE TRADER
P.O. Box 1050
Dubuque, IA 52001

ANTIQUES WORLD
P.O. Box 990
Farmingdale, NY 11737

BULLETIN OF THE NATIONAL ASSOCIATION OF WATCH AND CLOCK COLLECTORS, INC.
514 Poplar St.
Columbia, PA 17512
(Bi-monthly publication.
Membership in The
NAWCC required.)

**THE CLARION
AMERICA'S FOLK ART MAGAZINE**
49 West 53rd St.
NYC, NY 10019

CLOCKS
Wolsey House, Wolsey Road
Hemel Hempstead
Herts, England HP 2-4SS

CLOCKWISE MAGAZINE
1235 E. Main Street
Ventura, CA 93001

COLLECTIBLES MONTHLY
P.O. Box 2023
York, PA 17405

COLLECTOR EDITIONS QUARTERLY
170 Fifth Ave.
NYC, NY 10010

HOBBIES
1006 S. Michigan Avenue
Chicago, IL 60605

HOROLOGICAL TIMES
P.O. Box 11011
Cincinnati, OH 45211

MAINE ANTIQUES DIGEST
P.O. Box 358
Waldoboro, ME 04572

42 / MUSEUMS

THE MART OF THE NATIONAL ASSOCIATION OF WATCH AND CLOCK COLLECTORS, INC.
514 Poplar St.
Columbia, PA 17512
(Bi-Monthly publication. Membership in the NAWCC required)

MODERN JEWELER MAGAZINE
15 W. 10th St.
Kansas City, MO 64105

NATIONAL ANTIQUES COURIER
P.O. Box 500
Warwick, MD 21912

THE NEW YORK-PENNSYLVANIA COLLECTOR
c/o Wolfe Publications
4 S. Main Street
Pittsford, NY 14534

NINETEENTH CENTURY (FORBES)
60 Fifth Avenue
NYC, NY 10011

OHIO ANTIQUE REVIEW
72 North St.
P.O. Box 538
Worthington, OH 43085

POLITICAL COLLECTOR
503 Madison Avenue
York, PA 17404

JOEL SATER'S ANTIQUES NEWS
P.O. Box B
Marietta, PA 17547

SPINNING WHEEL
Fame Avenue
Hanover, PA 17331

THE TICK-TOCK TIMES
P.O. Box 7443
Salem, OR 97303

TRI-STATE TRADER
P.O. Box 90-CS
Knightstown, IN 46148

WATCH AND CLOCK REVIEW
2403 Champa St.
Denver, CO 80205

Y-NOT
P.O. Box 8561
Ft. Lauderdale, FL 33310

MUSEUMS

This list includes only museums who have a substantial collection of clocks or watches, or both. Some museums, because of limited space, do not always have their clocks and watches on display. An asterisk (*) indicates that these museums will always have a good exhibit of clocks or watches.

ARIZONA
Arizona Pioneers Historical Society
949 E. Second St.
Tucson
(602) 628-5774

CALIFORNIA
California Academy of Science
Golden Gate Park
San Francisco
(415) 752-8268

Los Angeles County Museum
900 Exposition Blvd.
Los Angeles
(213) 744-3411

Oakland Public Museum
1426 Oak St.
Oakland
(415) 834-2413

MUSEUMS / 43

CONNECTICUT
*American Clock & Watch Museum
100 Maple Street
Bristol
(203) 583-6070

P.T. Barnum Museum
804 Main Street
Bridgeport
(203) 576-7320

The Marine Historical Association, Inc.
Mystic Seaport
Mystic
(203) 536-2631

Wethersfield Historical Society
150 Main St.
Wethersfield
(203) 529-7656

DELAWARE
*Henry Francis DuPont Winterthur Museum
Winterthur
(302) 656-8591

DISTRICT OF COLUMBIA
*Smithsonian Institution
National Museum of American History
Washington
(202) 357-1300

United States Naval Observatory
Massachusetts Ave. at 34th St. NW
Washington
(202) 254-4569

FLORIDA
Lightner Museum of Hobbies
St. Augustine
(904) 824-2874 or
(904) 829-9677

Martin County Historical Society
Box 1497
Stuart
(305) 225-1961

HAWAII
Bernice P. Bishop Musuem
1355 Kalihi St.
Honolulu
(808) 847-1443

ILLINOIS
Chicago Museum of Science & Industry
5700 S. Lakeshore Dr.
Chicago
(312) 684-1414

Illinois State Museum of Natural History & Art
Spring & Edwards Sts.
Springfield
(217) 782-7386

*Time Museum
7801 E. State St.
Rockford
(815) 398-6000

INDIANA
Bartholomew County Historical Society
Court House - Washington St.
Columbus
(812) 372-3541

IOWA
*The Bily Clock Exhibit Horology Museum
Spillville
(319) 562-3569

KANSAS
Wichita Historical Museum
3751 E. Douglas Ave.
Wichita
(316) 265-9314

MAINE
Jonathan Fisher Memorial Museum
Blue Hill
(207) 374-2454

Portland Museum of Art
Portland
(207) 775-6148

MARYLAND
Maryland Historical Society
210 W. Monument St.
Baltimore
(301) 685-3750

The Walters Art Gallery
N. Charles at Centre Sts.
Baltimore
(301) 547-9000

MASSACHUSETTS

Brandeis University Library
Waltham
(617) 647-2000

Essex Institute
132 Essex St.
Salem
(617) 744-3390

Harvard University, Fogg Art Museum
Quincy St.
Cambridge
(617) 495-2387

Museum of Fine Arts
Boston
(617) 267-9300

Old Colony Historical Society
66 Church Green
Tauton
(617) 822-1622

Old Deerfield
Deerfield
(413) 774-5581

*Old Sturbridge Village
Sturbridge
(617) 347-3362

*Willard House
Grafton
(617) 839-3500

MICHIGAN

*Henry Ford Museum and Greenfield Village
Dearborn
(313) 271-1620

Michigan State University Museum
East Lansing
(517) 355-2370

MINNESOTA

Lake County Historical Society
Two Harbors
(218) 834-4898

MISSISSIPPI

Old Spanish Fort Museum
200 Fort St.
Pascagoula
(601) 769-1505

Russel C. Davis Plantation
201 E. Pascagoula St.
Jackson
(601) 960-1550

MONTANA

Montana State University Museum
M.S.U. Campus Fine Arts Bldg.
Missoula
(406) 243-0211

NEVADA

Nevada Historical Society
P.O. Box 1129
Reno
(702) 784-6397

NEW YORK

The Brooklyn Museum
Brooklyn
(212) 638-5000

Buffalo & Erie County Historical Society
25 Nottingham Court
Buffalo
(716) 873-9644

Buffalo Museum of Science
Humboldt Park
Buffalo
(716) 896-5200

*Hoffman Foundation
Newark Public Library
Newark
(315) 331-4370

Metropolitan Museum
New York
(212) 535-7710

New York State Historical Association
Cooperstown
(607) 547-2533

*New York University Museum of Clocks & Watches
Albany
(518) 457-3300

*New York University Museum of Clocks & Watches
University Ave. at 181st St.
Bronx
(212) 295-1630

Franklin D. Roosevelt Library
Hyde Park
(914) 229-8114

The Shaker Museum
Old Chatham
(518) 794-9100

NORTH CAROLINA
*Greensboro Clock Museum
300 Bellemeade St.
Greensboro
(919) 275-0462

*Old Salem, Inc.
614 Main St.
Winston-Salem
(919) 723-3688

OHIO
Cleveland Museum of Art
11150 East Blvd.
Cleveland
(216) 421-7340

Licking County Historical Society
6th Street Park
Newark
(614) 345-4898

Warren County Museum
S. Broadway
Lebanon
(513) 932-1817

Western Reserve Historical Society
10825 East Blvd.
Cleveland
(216) 721-5722

PENNSYLVANIA
Museum of Art Carnegie Institute
4400 Forbes Ave.
Pittsburgh
(412) 622-3270

The Ephrata Colister
632 W. Main
Ephrata
(717) 733-6600

Franklin Institute Museum
Ben Franklin Pkwy.
Philadelphia
(215) 448-1000

Hershey Museum
Park Avenue & Derry Road
Hershey
(717) 534-3439

Heritage Center of Lancaster County
Center Square
Box 997
Lancaster
(717) 299-6440

*National Museum of Clocks & Watches
514 Poplar St.
Box 33
Columbia
(717) 684-8261
Note: Headquarters of the National Association of Watch and Clock Collectors. Write for membership application.)

Old Economy Village
Ambridge
(412) 266-4500

Philadelphia Museum of Art
Philadelphia
(215) 763-8100

William Penn Memorial Museum
3rd & North Streets
Harrisburg
(717) 787-4980

SOUTH DAKOTA
South Dakota Historical Society
Memorial Bldg.
Pierre
(605) 773-3615

TEXAS
Bosque Memorial Museum
Avenue Q
Clifton
(817) 675-3845

*Old Clock Museum
929 E. Preston
Pharr
(512) 787-1923

VIRGINIA
**Colonial Williamsburg
 Foundation**
Williamsburg
(804) 229-1000

The Mariner's Museum
Newport News
(804) 595-0368

WASHINGTON
Bellingham Public Museum
121 Prospect St.
Bellingham
(206) 676-6981

Seattle Art Museum
Seattle
(206) 447-4670

CANADA
Fort George Restoration
Niagara-on-the-Lake, Ontario
(416) 468-4257

Huron County Pioneer Museum
Central Public School
North Street
Goderich, Ontario
(519) 524-9610

Robert Phillip Museum of Time
RR 1
Cookstown, Ontario
(705) 458-9221

CALENDAR OF EVENTS

*February 16-19	Florida Mid-Winter Regional, Sheraton-Twin Towers, Orlando, FL, Kathryn Mosley 904-782-3989
*February 23-26	Pacific-Northwest Regional, Red Lion Motor Inn, Portland, OR, Betty Chisum 503-761-6469
*March 1-3	Lone Star Regional, North Park Inn, Dallas, TX, Robert Wingate 214-620-9520
*March 8-10	Southern Regional, Coliseum Ramada Inn, Jackson, MS, Fred Ingram 601-981-6692
*March 10-11	Strongsville, Ohio Annual Meeting & Auction, Holiday Inn, Strongsville, (Rt. 82 and I-71), OH, Don Bass 419-625-1405
★ March 17-18	Wichita Antique Watch & Clock Club, Public School, Wichita, KS, E.W. Ferguson 316-683-7629
*April 13-14	Southern Ohio Regional, Drawbridge Motor Inn, Ft. Mitchell, KY, L. Harold Wehling 513-871-3896
*April 26-29	Greater New York Regional, Travelodge International Hotel, JFK International Airport, NY, Henry Richman
*May 10-13	Southwest California Regional, Hanalei Hotel, San Diego, CA, Loren L. Schmitz 714-469-7324
*May 18-19	Great Plains Regional, Holiday Inn, Omaha, NE, Richard Svehla 402-391-3453
*May 25-27	St. Louis Regional, Concourse Hotel, St. Louis, MO, Robert E. Webb 314-723-2037
*June 1-2	Kansas City Antique Watch & Clock Club, Ramada Inn Southeast, 87th & I-435 South, Kansas City, MO, Roy Ehrhardt 816-761-0080
*June 6-10	NAWCC National Convention, Indiana Convention Center/Hyatt Regency, Indianapolis, IN
*July 13-14	Midwest Regional, Ramada O'Hare, Des Plains, IL, Steve Berger 312-394-8877

*August 3-5	Missouri Regional, Ramada Inn, Columbia, MO, Jere A. De Vilbiss 314-442-8993
*August 10-11	Rocky Mountain Regional, Sheraton-Denver Tech Center, Denver, CO, Roger Dankert 303-755-0871
*August 24-26	Eastern States Regional, Sheraton Inn, Liverpool, NY, G. Russell Oechsle 315-662-7912
*August 31-September 1	Great Lakes Regional, Hyatt Regency, Dearborn, MI, George Hedges 313-626-3494
*September 14-15	Kentucky Blue-Grass Regional, Holiday Inn Louisville-South, Louisville, KY, John R. Buschermohle 502-267-5070
*September 20-23	Western Regional, San Jose Convention Center/Holiday Inn, San Jose, CA, Dorothea M. Sanderson 415-937-6272
*October 18-21	Mid-South Regional, Sheraton/Nashville Hotel, Nashville, TN, Dr. Cullen R. Merritt 615-327-0404
*October 26-27	NAWCC Seminar #5, Sheraton Civic Center Plaza, Hartford, CT 717-684-8261
*November 2-3	Mid-Eastern Regional, Raddison Hotel, Charlotte, NC, Jarvis Warren 704-366-1530
★ November 23-24	Kansas City Antique Watch & Clock Club, Ramada Inn Southeast, 87th Street & I-435 South, Kansas City, MO, Roy Ehrhardt 816-761-0080

MONTHLY SHOWS

★ Tampa Time Traders, 2nd Monday evening of each month, American Legion Seminole Post 3111, 6918 N. Florida Ave., Tampa, FL, Stanley Henry 816-839-1193.

★ Kansas City Antique Watch & Clock Club, 1st Tuesday evening of each month, Ramada Inn Southeast, 87th St. & I-435 South, Kansas City, MO, Roy Ehrhardt 816-761-0080.

★ Fox Valley Watch & Clock Club, 2nd Wednesday evening of each month, Community Center, Aurora, IL, Scott Williams 815-768-8729.

NAWCC members only. Detailed information may be obtained from the bi-monthly publication, The Mart. Educational programs are available at all meetings.

★ *Open to the public. No membership required. Educational programs are a part of each meeting.*

GLOSSARY
Courtesy of Malvern "Red" Rabeneck

ABRASIVE: A substance used for grinding and polishing. These are generally oilstone, emery, carborundum, lavigated aluminum oxide; any substance gritty enough to wear the surface of another material.

ACETONE: A chemical liquid used to dissolve celluloids; used in crystal cement and as a dehydrator after cleaning watch parts although not well recommended as a rinse because of its violent inflammability.

ACORN CLOCK: Called this because of the shape of the case.

ADJUSTED: Term applied to watch movements and some small clock movements to indicate that they have been corrected for various errors, such as isochronism, temperature, and positions.

ADVERTISING CLOCK: Any clock used with advertising. This advertising could be on the clock dial, tablet, or case, or the clock could be part of the advertising.

ALARM: An attachment to a clock whereby, at a predetermined time, a bell is sounded.

AMERICAN DIAL: Black or white Paper Dial

AMERICAN RED GUM: Hard, not quite as dense as Walnut and Chestnut. Reddish brown in color with some dark streaks. Good grain figure.

This covers most of the woods used in clock cases during and after the Victorian Period. It seems that a majority of the wood clock cases were veneered.

AMERICAN RED OAK: Redder in color than the white.

AMERICAN WHITE OAK: Hard and dense. color varies from pale yellow to pale reddish-brown. Very well known wood.

AMMONIA: A sharp smelling liquid used in practically all watch and clock cleaning solutions.

ANIMATED CLOCK: A clock with a visible life-like motion imitating, among many other things, a pecking bird, dancing ballerina, spinning wheel, etc.

ANNIVERSARY CLOCK: So called because it needs winding only once a year on the "anniversary" of the previous winding. Also known as a 400 day clock.

ANCHOR ESCAPEMENT: Resembles a ship's anchor in appearance. Invented about 1671, and enabled the clockmaker to use a long pendulum. Also called recoil escapement.

ANCHOR (VERGE): A device that regulates the speed of rotation of the escape wheel.

APPARENT SOLAR DAY: The interval between successive sun crossings of the local meridian by the sun as indicated by a sundial.

APRON: The decorative piece below the base of a case; can be between the legs of a shelf or floor clock, or on the bottom of the case of a shelf clock.

ARABIC FIGURES: Figures on a dial, such as 1, 2, 3, as opposed to *Roman Numerals,* such as I, II, V, IX.

ARBOR: The axle of a wheel (gear) or a shaft that turns in a bearing; commonly referred to as the barrel arbor, pallet arbor, winding arbor, etc.

ARC: The angle through which the balance wheel or pendulum swings.

ARCH: The curved part of any clock case that resembles a door arch.

ARKANSAS STONE: A white marble-like silicon stone used in various shapes and sizes as a grinding stone to sharpen gravers and tools. Used in powdered form as an abrasive with grinding laps. So called because the highest grade stones were found in Arkansas.

ATMOS CLOCK: A clock operated by a bellows-like mechanism that operates the clock because of changes in atmospheric temperature and pressure. Changes in temperature provide most of the power. The first Atmos clock used a tube of mercury rather than an aneroid. All use a torsion pendulum.

AUTO CLOCK: A timepiece designed to be mounted in an automobile, usually on the instrument panel, but may be mounted in other places.

BACK PLATE: The arbors of a clock train are supported by two plates; the one farthest from the dial is known as the back plate. Also called Top Plate and Upper Plate.

BALANCE: The oscillating wheel of a clock or watch, which in conjunction with the hairspring (balance spring) regulates the speed of a clock or watch. May be made of bi-metal to compensate for temperature changes and may be studded with screws for regulation.

BALANCE COCK: The support for the upper pivot of the balance staff.

BALANCE SPRING: A long fine spring that regulates the vibration of the balance. Also known as a hairspring.

BALANCE STAFF: The axis of the balance. (Axle shaft)

BALANCE WHEEL: Coloquial term for the balance.

BALLOON CLOCK: Shaped like hot-air balloons of the late 18th century; these were bracket (table or shelf) clocks.

BANDING: Strip of veneer around a panel or door, strictly for decoration.

BARN CLOCK: Very early electric clock.

BARREL: The round container or housing that holds the mainspring. This was eliminated on most American clocks.

BARREL ARBOR: The axle of the barrel around which the mainspring is coiled.

BARREL HOOK: A hook or slot in the inside of the barrel wall upon which the end of the last coil of mainspring is attached.

BEAT: The sound of the ticking of a clock, caused by the teeth of the escape wheel striking the pallets or arms of the escapement. A clock is said to be "in beat" if the ticks are very evenly spaced.

BEARING: The support for a pivot or arbor. Jeweled bearings are used where there is danger of rapid wear on the pivots of fast moving parts such as the balance staff and also train wheel pivots. In clocks, the bearings are usually brass, but wood, ivory and various jewels have also been used.

BEEHIVE CLOCK: Clock with a rounded Gothic case.

BEESWAX: A tough, yellowish-brown wax used as a temporary adhesive by watchmakers. Also was often used to polish the wooden clock cases.

BEETLE HAND: The hour hand, shaped like a stag beetle, frequently found on early Massachusetts shelf clocks and other early clocks. Generally used with a poker or straight minute hand.

BELL TOP: the rounded top of a bracket clock, resembling a bell, popular in England in the late 17th century.

BENZENE: A coal tar product used as a cleaner and rinse in watch and clock cleaning. Highly volatile and inflammable. (Benzol) (C_6H_6). More expensive than *benzine*.

50 / GLOSSARY

BERYLLIUM: A metal used in minute quantities with nickel and steel to produce nonmagnetic, noncorrosive balances and springs capable of good temperature adjustments.

BEZEL: The metal or wood ring that holds the glass over the dial.

BIMETALLIC: Made up of two metals. In watchmaking, this refers to the split balance having a brass rim and steel frame.

BLACK FOREST CLOCK: Term now used to mean any clock made in the Black Forest area of Germany.

BLACK MANTEL CLOCK: Shelf clock with a case, generally a horizontal rectangle in shape, but made in all possible variations of shape and trim but predominantly black in color. Very popular from 1890 to 1930.

BLACK WALNUT OR AMERICAN WALNUT: Probably the most common case wood, and certainly its beauty leaves nothing to be desired. Familiar to everyone. Cherry is similar.

BLIND MAN'S CLOCK: Colloquial usage — applies the term to a braille clock which has the numbers in braille; and also applies the term to a quarter-hour repeater in which the strike may be activated at will.

BLINKING EYE (WINKER): Iron statue clock with winking eye.

BLOWPIPE: A thin, tapered tube made of copper, used to force a jet of blown air through a flame and directed at an object. The jet of air directs the flame to a point and raises the heat of the flame. Usually the blowpipe is held in the mouth.

BLUING: To change the color of polished steel by heating it to approximately 540°F.

BOB: The weighted end of a pendulum. Usually held on the threaded rod by a nut, thus enabling it to be raised or lowered for time adjustment.

BOSS: The round disk applied to the arch of a dial on which is usually recorded the maker's name. Usually used on early brass dials.

BOX REGULATOR: A very plain rectangular wall clock, usually with trim on the top and bottom but none on the sides, sometimes with advertising on the tablet.

BRACE: The hook or connection attached to the outer end of the mainspring.

BRACKET CLOCK: Term used by British to indicate a shelf clock.

BRASS WORKS: Clock works with brass plates and brass wheels.

BREGUET: A horological genius of the late 18th and early 19th century. The name applied to the type of hairspring which has its last outer coil raised above the body of the spring and curved inwards.

BRIDGE: Upper plates in a plate watch for the support of the wheels. Always has at least two feet or supports.

BROACH: A tapered steel tool, with flat cutting edges used to enlarge holes already drilled.

BROCOT ESCAPEMENT: Trade term for visible escapement (wheel and pallets) on the clock dial.

BROKEN ARCH: An arch that has a short, horizontal, straight section outward from each bottom end of the arch.

BUSHING: The bearing that supports the end or pivot of the arbor. Called a bushing because it is usually made of a brass bushing or tube inserted into a hole in the plate. May be bradded in place. (Term not in common usage except by clockmakers and watchmakers.) In a watch, bushings are known as jewels.

BUTTING: The action of two wheels or a wheel and pinion improperly matched or distorted wherein their teeth butt each other instead of enmeshing perfectly.

CABINET CLOCK: Trade term for a small 12" to 24" shelf or table clock without visible pendulum (a vague term).

CAMEL BACK: Trade term for clock resembling the shape of Napoleon's hat; also called Hump Back or Tambour.

CAM: A small flat piece used to transfer circular motion into back-and-forth motion to a lever or other contacted piece.

CANNON PINION: A thin, steel tube with pinion leaves at its lower end and carrying the minute hand on its upper end.

CANNON TUBES: A misnomer applied to the hour pipe which carries the hour hand.

CAP JEWEL: The flat solid jewel upon which rests the pivot end. Also called the *endstone*.

CAPITAL: The trim terminating the top of a column.

CARRIAGE CLOCK: Small portable clock, usually with a brass case with glass sides and top. Spring driven with a balance wheel escapement.

CASE: That which contains the clock or watch; the housing or containment for the works.

CASTLE WHEEL: The clutch wheel.

CENTER OF GRAVITY: That point in a body around which the mass is evenly balanced.

CENTER-SECONDS HAND: Sometimes called sweep-seconds hand. Mounted on the center post of clocks and watches.

CENTER WHEEL: The wheel in a watch the axis of which usually carries the minute hand.

CHAIN (FUSEE): A miniature "bicycle" chain connecting the barrel and fusee of English watches and chronometers.

CHAMFER: To remove a sharp edge from a hole or drilled surface.

CHAPTER RING: The circle on the dial that contains the numbers for the hours and minutes. So called because in early clocks it was a separate ring attached to the dial.

CHESTNUT: Hard and dense. When finished light, chestnut becomes similar to Oak in appearance, but sometimes slightly redder and closer grained. When finished darker, it is sometimes mistaken for Walnut. When highly polished, resembles Sycamore. Watch for this wood! You will find some cases made of it that will usually be mistakenly indicated as Oak or Walnut.

CHRONOGRAPH: A watch that has a center-seconds hand driven from the fourth wheel which can be started, stopped, and caused to fly back to zero by pressing on a knob or lever.

CHRONOMETER: A clock which has passed strict observatory tests; a very accurate timekeeper; term also used for watches, particularly mounted, boxed watches with spring detent escapements, for use on ships at sea.

CHRONOMETER ESCAPEMENT: A detent escapement used in chronometers.

CHINA OR PORCELAIN CLOCK: Entire case of glazed porcelain. (Very fragile and easily broken.)

52 / GLOSSARY

CIRCULAR ESCAPEMENT: The lever escapement wherein the center of the pallets lifting surface is planted on a circle whose center is the pallet arbor. Found mostly in American watches.

CIRCULAR PITCH: The pitch circle divided into as many spaces as there are teeth on the wheel or pinion.

CLEPSAMMIA: An hour glass filled with sand; also called a "sand thief."

CLEPSYDRA: A form of clock using water, instead of sand, that falls from one container to another at a given rate.

CLICK: A spring-tensioned pawl holding the ratchet wheel against the tension of the mainspring, enabling the spring to be wound, usually making the clicking noise as the clock is wound.

CLOCK: A machine that records the passing of time and also strikes at least the hours — differing from a "timepiece," which keeps time only.

CLOCKWISE: The direction of circular motion going in the same direction as the hands of a clock, circling from horizontal left, upward around and down toward lower right.

CLUB-TOOTH WHEEL: That type of wheel which has a lifting face off the end of the teeth.

CLUTCH PINION: The pinion surrounding the square of the stem. Serves alternately to wind and set the watch.

COCK: An overhanging support for a bearing such as the balance cock; a bridge having a support at one end only.

COLLET: A collar, usually brass, that holds a wheel on an arbor.

COMPENSATING BALANCE: A balance with a bi-metallic rim made of brass and steel. The diameter increases or decreases with changes in temperature to compensate for these changes.

COMPENSATING PENDULUM: A pendulum that maintains a constant distance between the center of gravity of the pendulum and the suspension point, thus compensating for changes in temperature and keeping much more accurate time. The two principle forms are the Harrison or grid pendulum and the Graham or mercury pendulum.

CONICAL PIVOT: A pivot which curves back into the main body of its arbor, such as those used with cap jewels. (Balance staff pivots.)

CONNECTICUT SHELF: Any shelf clock manufactured in Connecticut. Some common styles are: Beehive, Column, Cottage, Octagon Top, OG & OOG, Round Top (Venetian), Split Top, Steeple.

CORDLESS CLOCK: Slang term for a battery-operated clock.

CORNICE: Topmost moulding of a case.

COUNT WHEEL: The clock wheel that regulates the "count" of the striking by means of slots on the circumference.

CROWN: A grooved circular piece fastened to the stem for winding the watch. (Slang winding knob or button)

CROWN WHEEL: A wheel that drives the ratchet wheel.

CROWN WHEEL ESCAPEMENT: So called because of its resemblance to a crown. Another name for verge escapement.

CRUTCH: The arm from the pallet arbor which connects the escapement to the pendulum, thus regulating the escapement with the motion of the pendulum and giving the pendulum the impulse or power to keep it swinging.

CRUTCH WIRE: A wire that carries the impulse from the escapement to the pendulum.

CRYSTAL REGULATOR (FOUR GLASS REGULATOR): Shelf clock with glass panels on each side, completely exposing the interior.

CRYSTAL PALACE CLOCK: Made by Ansonia.

CURB PINS: The two regulator pins almost pinching the hairspring.

CYANIDE (POTASSIUM): A poisonous, white crystalline substance dissolved in water to brighten tarnished metals. Very, very poisonous. Can kill by inhalation of fumes, absorption through the skin, or by ingestion. Not recommended for use.

CYLINDER ESCAPEMENT: A frictional escapement patented by Thomas Tompion 1695.

DATE DIAL: An accessory dial marked with the dates of the month. Usually moved twice every 24 hours.

DEAD BEAT ESCAPEMENT: So called because when the pallets engage the escape wheel, there is no further movement of the escapement — the mechanism was "dead." Generally considered to be the most accurate type.

DEDENDUM: The portion of a wheel tooth or pinion leaf that is below the pitch circle. In a watch wheel (train) the dedendum would be the portion of the tooth that is below the curved top of the tooth.

DENNISON GAUGE: A mainspring gauge composed of a thick strip of brass with numbered and graduated notches or slots used to designate the width of a mainspring. The system uses the millimeter as its unit. 1.00 mm equals No. 1 Dennison; 1.10 mm equal No. 2 Dennison, etc.

DEPTHING TOOL: A tool which will accommodate two wheels or a wheel and pinion between their centers and, by means of a screw, bring them into correct pitch; this distance may then be transferred to the plates for comparison or verification.

DETENT: The setting lever. Also that part of the chronometer escapement that locks the escape wheel. A detainer or pawl.

DIAL: The face of a clock.

DIAL TRAIN: The train of wheels under the dial which moves the hands. The cannon pinion, hour wheel, minute wheel and pinion.

DIAL ARCH: The arched portion at the top of some dials. It usually contains a Boss, moon dial or fancy decoration.

DIAL FOOT: A post or pillar on the back of a dial for attaching the dial to the front or false plate.

DIE: A plate with cutting edges normally used to thread screws and stems. A steel plate used to shape objects forced into them.

DISCHARGING PALLET: The exit pallet jewel. The pallet jewel from which an escape tooth drops as it leaves the pallet.

DOLLAR WATCH: A practical timepiece with a non-jeweled movement. The case and movement an integral unit with a dial of paper on brass or other inexpensive material. Ingersoll sold his first Dollar watch for $1.00 in 1892. (Taken from *The Watch That Made the Dollar Famous* by George E. Townsend.)

DOUBLE-ROLLER ESCAPEMENT: A form of lever escapement in which a separate roller is used for the safety action.

DOUBLE WIND: Nickname for a clock with two springs (therefore two winding arbors) geared together to drive the time train. Used in many 15 day and 30 day clocks.

DOUBLE DIAL CALENDAR: Calendar dial is usually round and is separate, and usually under the time dial.

DOWEL: A wooden peg used to hold two pieces together, or to reinforce a joint.

DRAW: The force which keeps the pallet against the banking pins. The result of the combined angles of the escape teeth and the pallet locking surface.

DROP: The free, unrestrained motion of the escape wheel as it leaves one pallet jewel before it drops upon the locking surface of another pallet jewel.

DROP LOCK: The extent of the lock on the pallets after an escapement has been banked to the drop.

DRUM: In a weight-driven clock, the round barrel on which the weight gut or cord is wound.

DUMB REPEATER: Where the hammer strikes a fixed metal block instead of a bell or gong.

DUPLEX ESCAPEMENT: A watch escapement in which the escape wheel has two sets of teeth. One set locks the wheel by pressing on the balance staff. The other set gives impulse to the balance. The balance receives impulse at every other vibration.

EBAUCHE: A term used by Swiss watch manufacturers to denote the raw movement without jewels, escapement, plating, engraving. The ebauche manufacturers supply their ebauches to trade name importers in the U.S.A. and other countries who have them finished, jeweled, dialed, cased, etc., and engraved with their own (advertised) name brands.

EIGHT DAY CLOCK: Will run eight days on one winding.

ELECTRIC CLOCK: General term for clock powered by electricity. In this country, usually used to indicate a clock powered by AC.

ELINVAR: A nonrusting, nonmagnetizing alloy containing iron, nickel, chromium, tungsten, silicon and carbon. Used for balance and balance spring. (Hamilton)

ENGINE CLOCK: A small, usually round metal cased, balance wheel clock that could be used in any position without affecting its rate. (A slang term for any clock that could have been used in the engine room of a ship.)

ENAMEL (SOFT): A soluble paint used in dials.

ENAMEL (HARD): A porcelain-like paint, acid-resisting and durable. A baked enamel.

ENDSHAKE: The free up and down space of pivoted wheels or arbors in their bearings. (End play.)

ENTRANCE JEWEL: The jewel first contacted by an escape tooth before it enters between the pallets. Also called the *right jewel.* Also called *stone.*

EPICYCLOID: A curve generated by a point in the circumference of a circle as it rolls upon another circle. It forms the kind of tooth used in watch wheels.

EQUATION CLOCK: A type of clock that shows the difference between solar time and mean time.

EQUIDISTANT ESCAPEMENT: The lever escapement whose pallet jewels have their entrance corners equally distant from the center of the pallet. Used more often in Swiss watches.

EPHEMERIS TIME (ET): Is based on the revolution of the earth around the sun. The ephemeris second is defined as 1/31,556,925.9747 of the tropical year for 1900.
ESCAPE: The method of regulating the release of power.
ESCAPE WHEEL: Regulator of the running of the clock.
ESCAPEMENT: A means by which the pendulum allows the going train to operate at a regular interval, thus controlling the passage of time. It usually consists of anchor and escape wheel.
ESCUTCHEON: The trim around a keyhole.
EUREKA CLOCK: A clock whose movement has a large balance wheel, driven by a battery-powered electromagnet. Invented 1906.
FALSE PLATE: A plate between the front plate of the movement and the dial on some clocks to make it easier to fit the dial to the movement.
FINIAL: The spires, or turnings, or finishing points, on top of a clock case. May be wood or metal. Various types, according to their shapes and appearance, are called "ball and spike", "urn", "acorn", "pineapple", "flower basket", "eagle", etc. Sometimes removable.
FLASHPOINT: The point at which the vapor of heated oil will explode or ignite at the approach of a spark or flame.
FLAT HAIRSPRING: A hairspring whose spirals develop on a flat surface. As opposed to the overcoil (Breguet) hairspring.
FLAT OGEE: A clock whose appearance closely resembles an Ogee, except that the front surface is flat rather than having the S-curve of a typical Ogee.
FLOATING BARREL: A barrel whose arbor has only one bearing surface. One attached only to the barrel bridge with no support from the lower plate.
FLUTED COLUMNS: Columns with grooves running the length of the turning.
FLY: A fan or type of air brake used to regulate or slow the speed of a strike train. Usually a thin, flat plate set in a slot in the arbor so that it provides maximum air resistance when rotating.
FLYING PENDULUM CLOCK (Also called Ignatz): Novelty clock invented in 1883 with a small ball on a thread hung from an arm which swings in a horizontal circle, regulated by twisting and untwisting a round vertical rod. Famous for lack of accuracy. Reproduced in 1959.
FOLIOT: An early type of pendulum used in verge escapements; later used on the Columbus clock. It has two arms with adjustable weights on the ends and swings in a horizontal plane.
FORK: A two-pronged rod sometimes used to engage the verge or pallet with the pendulum; the end of the pallet containing the slot, horns and guard finger.
FOUR HUNDRED DAY CLOCK: See Anniversary Clock.
FOURTH WHEEL: Usually the wheel which carries the second hand and drives the escape wheel; it is the fourth wheel from the great wheel in the going train of a clock.
FREE PENDULUM CLOCK: Most accurate pendulum clock ever made.
FRET: Lattice-type or other fancy decoration across the top of some wood tall cases or mantel clocks, usually between finials.
FRICTION ROLLER: As a bearing for pivots, it needs no lubrication.

FRONT PLATE: Two plates hold the arbor's of a clock train; the front plate is nearest to the dial, also called Pillar Plate, Dial Plate and Lower Plate.

FRONT WIND: Clock wound through the dial.

FULL PLATE: Top plate of a watch in full round diameter. Clocks are also referred to as "full plate" when the plates are not pierced or otherwise cut out.

FUZEE: A grooved, cone-shaped pulley with a spiral track cut around it, which the mainspring barrel drives by a chain or cord (usually gut). As the spring runs down, it preserves, more or less, a constant torque on the train as long as the clock is running. The word "fuzee" means thread.

GALLERY CLOCK: Usually 8" dial or larger, either eight day or electric, with a simple case of various configuration for use on walls of public places; i.e. in galleries.

GATHERING PALLET: A part of the rack-and-snail strike train. A small metal bar that rotates once for each strike and gathers one tooth of the rack until the striking is completed.

GILT: As applied to clock cases, meant gold-leafed. In modern times the term is sometimes used to mean gold-colored.

GIMBAL: A device, similar to a universal joint, that keeps a clock level. Usually used in ships' chronometers.

GINGERBREAD: Nickname for a kitchen clock with very elaborate designs pressed into the wood of the case.

GIRANDOLE CLOCK: A variant of the banjo clock. Invented by Lemuel Curtis and, as far as can be determined, made only by him in Concord, Massachusetts. Usually considered to be the most beautiful wall clock ever built. (Many reproductions)

GOLD FILLED: Another name for rolled gold.

GOLD PLATED: Electro-plated a few thousandths of an inch thick with pure or alloyed gold.

GOLD LEAF: Very, very thin sheet of solid gold. Was applied to clock cases, columns, and tablets for decoration; the term "Gold Leaf" was also used to mean the act of applying the gold.

GOTHIC CASE: Case that resembles Gothic architecture, having a pointed top like the end of a gabled roof.

GRANDE SONNIERIE: A quarter hour repeater; a type of striking in which the last hour struck is repeated at each quarter. Present day usage sometimes applies the term to a quarter hour repeater which can be made to strike at will.

GRANDMOTHER CLOCK: Popular name for the dwarf or miniature tall case clock. Today the height is usually 66" plus or minus 6".

GRANDDAUGHTER CLOCK: Popular name for the dwarf or miniature tall case clock. Today the height is usually 48" plus or minus 6".

GRAVITY CLOCK: A clock driven by its own weight.

GRAVITY ESCAPEMENT: A type of escapement used on tower clocks. The impulse is given to the pendulum directly by a small falling weight that is raised by the going train after each beat of the pendulum.

GREAT WHEEL: The first wheel in the train. On the drum, it is weight-driven; on the going barrel or on the fuzee, it is spring-driven, depending upon which type is used.

GREENWICH CIVIL TIME: Also called Universal Time (UT). It is Local mean time as measured at Greenwich, England.

GLOSSARY / 57

GRIDIRON PENDULUM: A series of steel and brass rods in the pendulum to counteract the heat and cold to which it is subjected. By this means the pendulum length is kept constant. Invented by John Harrison of London.

GROANER MOVEMENT: A wood works with a distinctive appearance, so called because of the distinctive noise usually made by these movements.

GUARD PIN: A thin finger emerging from a boss below the slot in the pallet fork and working in conjunction with the safety roller to aid in preventing "over-banking."

HAIRSPRING: The spiraled spring attached to the balance to govern the speed of the balance oscillations.

HALLMARK: A mark or design stamped on gold, silver or platinum objects, such as watch and clock cases, to indicate the quality of the objects. Marks were used to indicate the assayor, the location purity of metal, the maker, and the date.

HAMMER: The part of a clock that strikes the bell, gong, rod, tube, etc. in striking, chiming and alarm mechanisms.

HANDS: Used to mark hours, minutes, or seconds on a clock dial.

HAND SET CLOCKS: A clock which is set by pushing against the hands to move them.

HANGING BARREL: Same as floating barrel.

HEEL OF TOOTH: Letting-off corner of a tooth of the escape wheel.

HELICAL HAIRSPRING: The spiraled cylindrical spring used in marine chronometer balances.

HOLLOW-COLUMN CLOCKS: A type of shelf clock in which the weights fall through a hollow column situated on either side of the case.

HOOD: The top part of a tall clock that covers the dial and works.

HOOK (Pendulum hook): The hook at the top of the pendulum which engages the suspension spring. Not used in all clocks.

HOROLOGY: The science of measuring time, or the principles and art of constructing instruments for measuring and indicating portions of time.

HOURGLASS: An early form of timekeeper in which sand falls at a given rate from one container to another through a slender glass neck.

HOUR WHEEL: A flat, brass, toothed wheel mounted on a tube which fits over the cannon pinion and supports the hour hand.

HUMP BACK: See Camel Back.

HYPOCYCLOIDAL: A path or curve generated by a point on the circumference of a circle rolling within another circle. Generally, flanks of pinion leaves have this form.

IMPULSE CLOCK: A slave clock driven by electrical impulses from the master clock.

IMPULSE PIN: Roller jewel.

IMPULSE AND LOCKING: Dead-beat escapements have two actions: impulse is the period during which the train imparts impulse to the balance or pendulum; during the rest of the time the train is locked.

INCABLOC: Trade name for a shock-resisting arrangement of balance jewels and staff design. Mostly used in watches.

INCLINED PLANE CLOCK: A form of gravity clock consisting of a drum clock which was powered by a weight attached to the center wheel arbor which turned the arbor as the clock rolled down the inclined plane.

58 / GLOSSARY

INDEX: The regulator scale. Used to help in adjusting the regulation. Some pendulums had indexes. Many later mantel clocks that adjusted regulator through a hole in the dial with the small end of the key had indexes. Most balance wheel clocks and watches had indexes.

INVAR: A steel alloy containing about 36 percent nickel that remains the same length at different temperatures. Used in the making of balance wheels. Also used for pendulum rods in clocks for temperature compensation. Similar to Elinvar.

INVOLUTE: A curve traced by the end of a string as it is unwound from a spool. The shape of wheel teeth used in gears where great strength is needed.

IRON-FRONT CLOCK: Connecticut Shelf Clock with cast-iron front.

ISOCHRONISM: Quality of keeping equal time during the normal run of the mainspring, usually the qualitites of a well-formed overcoil hairspring.

JACK: A moving figure turned by a clock mechanism. In very clocks, the Jack struck the bell.

JACOT TOOL: A tool used for burnishing or polishing pivots.

JAPANNING: Refers to finishing a decorative wood object with colored or black lacquer. Often used as a finish for clocks.

JEWEL: Synthetic or semiprecious stones used for bearings in watches and precision clocks.

JEWELER'S REGULATOR CLOCK: A high grade, accurate, compensated clock used by a jeweler as a time standard for regulating timepeices.

KEY, BENCH: A tool with varied size prongs capable of fitting into all sizes of winding arbors.

KIDNEY DIAL: So called because of its shape. Usually used on the Massachusetts shelf clock.

LACQUER: The sap of a tree cultivated in China and Japan. This resin has been in use in China since legendary times and in Japan since the 6th Century.

LUNETTE: The halt circle above the dial. Usually contains a phase of the moon or ornamentation.

LYRE CLOCK: A variation of the banjo, usually attributed to Aaron Willard, Jr., of Boston.

MAHOGANY: Probably the second most common case wood. However, recognition is complicated by three distinct varieties of mahogany: (a) Cuban Mahogany, the original mahogany. The hardest and most dense of the mahoganies, it is close grained and figured; (b) Honduras or Central American Mahogany, lighter and softer than the Cuban variety, with a great variety of color and figure; (c) Phillipine Mahogany, the softest, lightest, cheapest variety, with practically no figure. Commonly seen today as the cheapest plywood and almost caused mahogany to lose its standing as a fine wood.

MAINSPRING: The flat, ribbon-like tempered steel spring wound inside the barrel and used to drive the train wheels. Most American clocks eliminated the barrel.

MAINTAINING POWER: A device in a clock that provides sufficient power to keep it going while being wound.

MAIN TRAIN: The toothed wheels in a watch that connect the barrel with the escapement.
MAIN WHEEL: An ambiguous term applied occasionally to the crown wheel, the center wheel, and sometimes to the barrel.
MALTESE CROSS: The cross-like part of the stop works attached to the barrels of fine watches.
MARINE CHRONOMETER: A boxed watch clock set in gimbals utilizing the spring detent escapement; used on shipboard to determine longitude.
MARQUETRY: A type of decoration on wood made by inlaying wood veneer in elaborate designs.
MASK: A face used as a decoration.
MASSACHUSETTS SHELF CLOCK: Style of clock sometimes called Half Clock, or Box on Box Clock.
MASTER CLOCK: A clock which can control slave clocks by various methods.
MEAN SOLAR TIME: The time used in everyday life, the time shown by clocks, obtained by averaging solar time into equal periods (hours, days).
MEAN TIME: Where all days and hours are of equal length. This is opposed to Solar Time where all days are not of equal length.
MEANTIME SCREWS: The adjustable screws in a better grade balance used to bring the watch to close time without the use of the regulator. Sometimes called *timing screws*.
MEDALLION: On American clocks, usually refers to a small, flat turning, glued to the surface of the case for decoration.
MIDDLE-TEMPERATURE ERROR: The temperature error between the extremes of heat and cold characteristic of a compensating balance and steel balance spring.
MILLIMETERS: The smallest unit in the metric linear system. One millimeter equals 0.03937 of an inch.
MINUTE REPEATER: A striking watch that will ring the time to the minute by a series of gongs activated by a plunger or push piece. A watch striking the hours, quarter hours, and additional minutes.
MINUTE WHEEL: The wheel in the dial train that connects the cannon pinion with the hour wheel.
MISSION STYLE: A trade term used for an American clock case of very plain design, usually of dark oak. Became popular in 1900 to 1930, usually as a reaction to the earlier Victorian style.
MOON DIAL: Usually at the top in the arch portion of a clock dial that indicates the phases of the moon.
MOTION TRAIN: A series of wheels and pinions that allows the rotation of the hour and minute hands.
MOVEMENT: The assembly of gears between two plates in such a fashion as to provide the transmitting of power from either the weights or the springs. Sometimes called "works."
MOVING EYE CLOCK: A clock with a case shaped like a figure of man or animal, with the eyeballs connected to the escapement, giving them movement.
MUSICAL ALARM: An alarm that activates a music box instead of a bell.
MYSTERY CLOCK: A clock which appears to work without any power or wheels.

NEW HAMPSHIRE MIRROR CLOCK: A type of clock thought to have originated in New Hampshire and attributed to Benjamin Morrill of Boscawen.

NONMAGNETIC: A balance and spring composed of alloys that will not retain magnetism after being put through a magnetic field.

NOVELTY CLOCK: Trade term for a variety of small clocks, usually in the shape of a familiar object or idea, sometimes animated. A vague term used for many variants of clocks.

OG Or Ogee: A wave-like molding, one side convex, the other concave, shaped like the letter "S." From 1825 to 1915, six or more sizes were used.

OILSTONE: Generally, the Arkansas white stone used with oil.

ONE DAY CLOCK OR WATCH: Will run usually 30 hours on one winding.

OPEN FACE: A watch dial with the figure "12" at the winding stem.

ORMOULU: Sometimes mistakenly spelled "Ormolu." Refers to brass castings that have gilt or gold plating for clock cases or parts of cases.

ORRERY: A machine in a planetarium that shows the relative positions of the planets.

OIL SINK: An indentation at the pivot hole of a clock used for the retention of oil.

OVERBANKING: The malfunction of the pallet fork in which it shifts from one banking pin to another without being released by the roller jewel.

OVERCOIL: The last coil of the Breguet spring that is bent up and over the body of the spring.

OVER-COMPENSATION: When the temperature rises, a clock pendulum becomes longer due to expansion and the clock slows down and loses time. The compensation pendulum was developed to correct this defect. Then, if a clock gained time with increasing temperature, it was said to have "over-compensation."

PATTI MOVEMENT: Made by E.N. Welsh and Co., is a good collector piece and has a distinctive plate design and enclosed mainsprings.

PALLET: The part through which the escape wheel gives the impulse to the pendulum or balance wheel. The jeweled lever working in conjunction with the escape wheel; the frame containing the pallet jewels.

PALLET ARMS: The metal body which contains the pallet stones.

PALLET ARBOR: The axis of the pallets.

PALLETS: The two projections from the ends of the anchor that engage with the escape wheel teeth and allow one tooth to pass with each swing of the pendulum.

PALLET STONES: Jewels or stones inserted in the pallet arms.

PATINA: The distinctive appearance of old wood after years of TLC. Constant polishing for many years enhances this appearance.

PEDIMENT: Used to indicate the decorative top of a case; that structure above the cornice.

PEDOMETER: A watch with a delicately tripped pendulum and ratchet attached used to tell walking-distances covered by the wearer. The jogging motion moves the pendulum which advances a set of gears attached to an indicator. Later this principle was used to wind a watch called the "self-winding watch."

PEGWOOD: Small wood stick about $1/8$" thick and 6" long whose sharpened end is used to clean or "peg" jewel holes or bushings.

PENDULUM: A weight swinging under the influence of gravity. In clocks, the time controlling element is usually a pendulum, consisting of a pendulum rod (of wood or metal) with a weight (called a "bob") at the bottom end, which swings to time the release of energy from the springs, or falling weights. Since a pendulum swings in a circular arc rather than the desired cycloidal arc, in practice, the shorter the swing the more accurate.

PETITE SONNERIE CLOCK: Strikes the quarters and half hour but does not strike the hours at each quarter as does Grand Sonnerie.

PHILLIPS' SPRING: A balance spring with terminal curves formed on lines laid down by M. Phillips. The term "Phillips' curve" is rarely used.

PILLAR: A rod or post of metal or wood that connects to the front and back plates holds them a fixed distance apart in both clocks and watches.

PILLAR CLOCK: A French clock with a case consisting of a drum clock mounted on two or four pillars standing on a base. The pendulum hangs in the middle of the pillars.

PILLAR PLATE: The lower or dial plate of the watch; also called front plate.

PILLAR AND SCROLL: Shelf clock design attributed to Eli Terry. Has columns on each side of the case and a splat cut in a double scroll design. Usually has three finials.

PINION: The smaller wheel with teeth called leaves, working in connection with a larger wheel. See Lantern Pinion.

PIN PALLET: The lever escapement wherein the pallet has upright pins instead of horizontally set jewels. Used in alarm clocks and nonjeweled watches.

PIN-WHEEL CLOCK: A pendulum-type clock movement using a pin-wheel escapement.

PIN-WHEEL ESCAPEMENT: Where the locking and impulse is affected by pins mounted near the rim of the escape wheel, at right angles to the plane of the wheel. Considered very accurate, usually made by the Swiss, and used in many high-grade Jeweler's Regulator clocks.

PITCH CIRCLE: A circle concentric with the circumference of a toothed wheel and cutting its teeth at such a distance from their points as to touch the corresponding circle of a pinion working with it and having with that circle a common velocity, as in a rolling contact.

PITCH DIAMETER: The diameter of the pitch circle.

PIVOT: The end of a rotating arbor; the ends of the shafts in a clockworks; the tips that run in the jewels or bushings or other bearings.

PLATE: Discs of brass or nickel which form the foundation of a movement. The pillar or lower plate lies next to the dial. The upper pieces supporting one, two, or three wheels are generally referred to as bridges. In the full-plate watch the upper piece is called the top plate or back plate.

PLATES: The front and back of the clock movement, between which the wheels, pinions and arbors are fitted.

PLATFORM ESCAPEMENT: A balance wheel escapement mounted on a separate self-contained plate so that it can be removed and replaced as a unit. Often used on carriage clocks.

PLATO CLOCK: Small carriage size clock with flipping cards or panels to indicate the hours and minutes.

POISING: An operation to adjust the balance so that all weights are counterpoised. In other words, statically balancing a wheel or balance in a clock or watch.

POSITION CLOCK: A regulator.

POSITION REGULATOR: A regulator.

POSITION TIMING: Adjusting a watch so that it keeps precise time when the watch is placed in a given position. Adjusted to three, four, five, or six positions.

POTENCE: Supporting one pivot of an arbor, a cock or bracket fixed to the plate of a clock or watch.

PULL REPEATER: A device whereby the striking mechanism of a clock is set in motion between the hours.

QUAIL CLOCK: Essentially a cuckoo clock, but with bellows that give sounds imitating the call of a quail.

QUARTER REPEATER: A repeater which strikes the hours and quarter hours.

QUARTER SCREWS: Four screws used in timing.

QUARTER STRIKE: A clock that strikes the quarter hours, usually on two bells.

QUARTZ CLOCK: An accurate electronic clock invented in 1929, which has a quartz crystal controlled oscillator followed by frequency dividers controlling a phonic motor that drives the clock.

QUICK TRAIN: A watch movement beating five times per second, or 18,000 per hour.

"R-A" REGULATOR: Slang term for wall regulator with "R-A" on pendulum, which probably actually means: R = retard by turning the adjusting nut toward R to lower the pendulum; A = advance by turning the adjusting nut toward A to raise the pendulum.

RACK CLOCK: A gravity clock consisting of a rack or straight toothed bar mounted vertically so that the clock slides down the rack with a pinion engaging the rack to drive the clock.

RACK AND SNAIL: The rack is a bar with teeth on one edge; the snail is a snail-shaped cam. Simply, a striking mechanism which allows the strike to be repeated, by setting itself for correct striking shortly before striking begins.

RATCHET: A wheel usually placed over a mainspring arbor and working with a retaining click or pawl.

RATCHET TOOTH WHEEL: The name given to the English type escape wheel which has pointed teeth.

RATE: A "good rate" is a good timekeeper; if it gains or loses, it is said to have a gaining or losing rate.

R.C.: Rounded corners.

RECEIVING PALLET: The pallet stone over which a tooth of the escape wheel slides in order to enter between the pallet stones.

RECOIL CLICK: A click designed so that it will not permit the mainspring to be wound dead tight, recoiling a bit after any winding.

RECOIL ESCAPEMENT: An escapement whose escape wheel recoils when the pallets become more deeply locked or push back the escape wheel during the unlocking action. Results in the second hand backing up slightly before advancing.

REGULATOR: Part of the balance bridge which resembles a racquette (racket) and contains vertical pins which straddle the hairspring. When the regulator moves towards the stud, the effective length of the hairspring is made longer and the balance slows in speed; when the pins are moved farther from the stud, the hairspring is made shorter and the watch goes faster.

REGULATOR CLOCK TRADE AND SLANG TERMS
- A. **Octagon Top Long Drop:** eight, ten, 12" dial with case, approximately 36" high.
- B. **Octagon Top Short Drop:** Same as above except 25" high.
- C. **Round Top Long Drop:** eight, ten, 12" dial with case approximately 36" high.
- D. **Round Top Short Drop:** Same as above except approximately 25" high.
- E. **Square Top:** Same as above.
- F. **Wall Seconds Bit:** Usually 40" to 84" long with seconds bit.
- G. **Parlor (Shelf):** Usually 26" to 34" high.
- H. **Parlor (Wall Hanging):** Usually 30" to 60".
- J. **Jewelers (Sweep second):** Largest type, up to eight feet long.

REPEATER: In clock parlance, a clock that can be triggered to repeat the last strike. A watch that strikes, having two hammers and two gongs. A lever is provided to set the striking mechanism into action. A quarter repeater strikes the hour and the last quarter hour. A minute repeater, in addition, strikes the number of minutes since the last quarter.

REPEATER ALARM: An alarm that rings in short bursts and keeps repeating the ringing at regular intervals.

REVERSE PAINTING: Painting of a picture or design on glass, painted on the back side of the glass. Since the painting is done in reverse order of a normal painting (background is put on last), this gives it the name. Used on clock tablets since the painting is protected, being inside the case, and it can also be painted over with a layer of protective paint.

RIGHT-ANGLED ESCAPEMENT: An escapement in which the line of centers of the escape wheel and pallets are at right angles to pallets and balance.

RIPPLE FRONT: The wavy part of the clock case, usually applied. Commonly used on the beehive and steeple cases.

ROCOCO: A term used in several ways to indicate ornamentation in clocks, sometimes used to mean an over-supply of ornamentation.

ROLLED GOLD: A metal plate formed by bonding a thin sheet of gold to one or both sides of a backing metal. Made by rolling the sandwich until the gold is at the desired thinness.

ROLLER JEWEL: A long, thin jewel inserted in the roller table; sometimes called impulse pin.

ROLLER TABLE: A circular disc attached to the balance staff in which is fitted the roller jewel.

ROLLING CLOCK: See Inclined Plane Clock.

ROMAN STRIKE: Instead of one bell, two-bells of different tone were used for striking the hours, a "one" bell and a "five" bell. Hours one, two, and three were struck on the "one" bell. Six was struck by one strike on the "five" bell, and one on the "one", thus following the Roman numerals which appear on the clock dial as VI. Four was struck by one strike on the "one" bell and one on the "five" bell, since "four" appears on these dials as IV, instead of the usual IIII.

ROSEWOOD: A hard wood, much heavier than American Walnut. Has a distinctive grain structure that finishes into a dark brown, chesnut color with darker, almost black streaks of grain. Takes a good polish; used solid or as veneer. Sometimes faked with mahogany by the casemakers, as mahogany was cheaper

ROSKOPF WATCH: A watch with the barrel encroaching upon the center of the movement; hence no center wheel. The dial train is activated through the minute wheel which is set clutch tight on the barrel cover. Usually employing the pin pallet escapement. (First dollar watch)

ROUND TOP: Nickname for a clock case with a top in the shape of a full semi-circle. (Venetian)

RUBY PIN: The upright roller jewel set into the impulse roller.

RUN: A term applied to the action of slide caused by draw. The action of the pallet toward the banking pin after lock takes place.

SAFETY ROLLER: The small, crescented roller disc planted above the impulse roller. The upper part of the double roller.

SCREWPLATE: A steel plate with holes of many sizes threaded with cutting edges for the forming of watch screws.

SEAT BOARD: Short board board upon which movement is mounted.

SECONDS PENDULUM: A pendulum that has a one-second swing. Theoretically has to be 39.14″ long.

SELF WINDING CLOCK: A spring driven clock with a mechanism for automatic winding, usually powered by batteries.

SETTING LEVER: The detent which fits into the slot of the stem and pushes down the clutch lever.

SHAKE: The distance the escape wheel can be moved backward (manually) before the back of a tooth contacts a pallet jewel when the opposite jewel is at the very moment of unlocking. Shake is always less than drop.

SHEEP'S-HEAD CLOCK: A lantern clock in which the chapter ring is wider than the rest of the clock.

SHELF CLOCK: A type of case designed to sit on a shelf as opposite to a tall clock.

SHELLAC: A resinous secretion (or excretion) of the lac insect. When dissolved in acetone or alcohol, sometimes called shellac varnish. The natural orange shellac is bleached to form white shellac.

SHIP'S BELL CLOCK: A clock that strikes on the ship's bell system.

SIDEREAL DAY: Duration of the earth's rotation with respect to the stars. The calculated relation between sidereal time and mean time is tabulated for each day in the Nautical Almanac. Mean sidereal day is twenty-three hours, fifty-six minutes, 4.091 seconds of mean solar time.

SIMPLE CALENDAR: Trade term for days of the month indicated by an extra hand pointing to the day of the month number around the outside of the chapter ring.

SINGLE ROLLER ESCAPEMENT: A form of lever escapement in which one roller performs the functions of both impulse and safety actions.

SKELETON CLOCK: Clock that had the plates cut out so that only a "skeleton" remained. This allowed a good view of the wheel, and the clock was usually placed under a glass dome for better viewing.

SLAVE CLOCK: A clock that did not keep time on its own, but was slaved to a master clock.
SLIDE: The opening of the banking pins beyond that of drop lock.
SOLAR TIME: Time as indicated by a sundial.
SONORA CHIME CLOCK: A Seth Thomas clock that used turned cupped bells to play the Westminster chimes.
SPANDREL: The four corners of a square clock dial in which designs are painted or fancy metalwork is applied.
SPLAT: The decorator piece at the top of a clock case.
SPIRIT LEVEL: A small sealed disc with a liquid bubble used on poising tools to determine when the jaws are level.
SPRING BARREL: The barrel containing the mainspring.
SPRING CLOCK: Springs rather than weights are the motive power.
SPRINGING: The act of co-ordinating a hairspring with a balance so that the vibrations will equal a given number per hour; also called vibrating.
STAFF: A pivoted arbor or axle usually referred to the axle of the balance; as the "balance staff".
STAR WHEEL: A steel wheel used in chronographs to lift levers.
STEADY PINS: Pins used to secure the perfect alignment of two pieces of metal.
STEEPLE CLOCK: Clock with a sharp gothic case with finials on each side.
STEM: The squared shaft going through the winding pinion and clutch wheel.
STENCILED: Decoration applied to splats, columns, and other areas of the clock cases.
STOPWATCH: A simple form of chronograph with controlled starting and stopping of the hands; sometimes also stopping the balance wheel. A timer in pocket watch form.
STOPWORK: The mechanism on a barrel of a watch or clock that permits only the central portion of the mainspring to be wound, thus utilizing that portion of the spring whose power is less erratic.
STORE CLOCK: Nickname for the box reguator.
STRAIGHT LINE ESCAPEMENT: An escapement in which the centers of the escape wheel, pallets, and balance are planted in a straight line.
STRIKE LEVER: The lever that strikes the gong, bell, or chimes.
STRIKE TRAIN: The added gears used to operate the striking mechanism of a clock.
STUD: The metal piece anchored to the balance bridge into which the outer end of the hairspring is attached.
SUNK SECONDS: The small second dial which is depressed to avoid the second hand from interfering with the progress of the hour and minute hand.
SUSPENSION SPRING: The straight, flat spring at the top of the pendulum, from which the pendulum hangs and which allows the pendulum to swing.
SWEEP SECONDS: Mounted in the center of the clock dial, this hand sweeps the full area of the dial. Also called "center seconds".

SWINGING ARM: Clock takes the form of a pendulum, usually supported by an arm of a statue. Most common seen are made by Ansonia, German Junghams and French. (The Japanese are now reproducing the German version.)

SYNCHRONOUS CLOCK: A clock driven by an alternating current (AC) synchronous electric motor whose speed was regulated by the frequency of the AC. The name was derived from the speed of the motor being sychronized with the frequency of the alternating current. Naturally, the accuracy of the clock was dependent on the accuracy of the frequency of the AC.

TABLET: The front lower glass of a clock case.

TALL CLOCK: Long-case, floor or hall clock, nicknamed Grandfather.

TAMBOUR: See Camel Back.

TAPE CLOCK: A round clock that lay horizontally on a table, with the hours and fractions of hours shown on a "tape" dial wrapped around the case. This portion of the case revolved with a single pointer showing the time. This rather rare clock was usually operated by an alarm clock type movement, and sometimes had an alarm.

TAVERN CLOCK: Also generally known as an Act of Parliament Clock; usually an English clock.

TEAR DROP: A shelf clock with rounded top and hanging finials, usually out of walnut.

THIRD WHEEL: The wheel of a watch that drives the fourth pinion.

TIME AND STRIKE: Any clock that strikes as well as telling the time.

TIMEPIECE: Any clock that does not strike or chime.

TIMER: A timepiece that does not show the time of day, but shows elapsed time, used to time any event or operation, hence the name. See Stop Watch.

TIME RECORDER: A clock that, by imprinting or punching paper, records the time it is activated.

TIME STAMP: A date stamp which incorporates a timepiece to also stamp the time.

TIMING SCREWS: Screws used to bring a watch to time, sometimes called the mean-time screws.

TOE OF TOOTH: Locking corner of a tooth of the escape wheel.

TORSION PENDULUM: A pendulum that hangs from a suspension spring and rotates in a horizontal plane, twisting and untwisting the suspension spring. Very roughly analogous to the operation of a balance wheel. Has a very long period, therefore, generally used in 400-day clocks.

TOTAL LOCK: The distance of lock upon the pallet jewel after slide when the pallet rests against the banking pin.

TOURBILLION: A watch in which the escapement, mounted on a cage attached to the fourth pinion, revolves around the mounted and stationary fourth wheel.

TOWER OR TURRET CLOCK: A steeple, church or public clock in a tower.

TRAIN: A combination of two or more wheels and pinions, geared together and transmitting power from one part of a mechanism to another, usually from the power source (weight or spring) to the escapement.

TRIPPING: A malfunction caused by the failure of the escape tooth to lock upon the locking surface of the pallet jewel. Instead, the tooth enters directly upon the lifting surface with the result that the pallet may have an action like an alarm clock hammer.

TROPICAL YEAR (or Mean Solar Year): The time it takes the earth to revolve about the sun, as reckoned from the vernal equinox, or first point of Aries.

UNIVERSAL TIME (UT): This is also known as Greenwich Civil Time. A corrected value of Universal Time (UT) to account for observed motion of the geographic poles and for the projected annual variation in the earth's rate of rotation is called UT-2.

UP-AND-DOWN INDICATOR: The semi-circular dial on chronometers that tells how much the mainspring has been unwound and thus indicates when the spring should be wound.

VENETIAN: Trade name of a clock case with the top in the shape of a full semi-circle.

VERGE: A recoil frictional escapement with a crown escape wheel and pallets set at right angles to the axis of the escape wheel.

VERGE STAFF: The arbor upon which the pendulum, crutch or balance is mounted is the verge or verge staff.

VISIBLE ESCAPEMENT: Trade term when wheel and pallet are visible on the clock dial.

V.P.: Trade abbreviation for Visible Pendulum.

WAGON-THE-WALL-CLOCK: Slang name for a wall clock on which the weights and pendulum are exposed.

WAGON SPRING CLOCK: A clock whose spring is a flat-leaved arched semi-elliptical spring, resembling a wagon spring (or early auto spring). Invented by J. Ives, it is now a rare clock because of the tendency to self-destruct if the cable connecting the spring to the winding drum would break.

WARNING: In striking clocks, the strike train is set in motion to strike a few minutes before the hour but is stopped short until released by the minute hand.

WATCHMAN'S CLOCK: A portable time recorder, usually in a carrying case, with provisions for a key to be inserted and turned which prints the time. Thus, the keys were placed at points on a watchman's rounds so that it would show the time he passed each station.

WEIGHTS: A source of power for the movement in clocks, as opposed to springs.

WHEEL: Any circular piece of metal on the periphery of which teeth may be cut of various forms and numbers.

WINDING DRUM (Barrel): The cylinder onto which the wire or cord supporting the weight is wound.

WINDING PINION: The first winding wheel through which the stem enters. A wheel with two sets of teeth. One is set radial to its center and the other is set upright, crown style with ratchet teeth. The wheel above the clutch wheel.

WINDING SQUARE: The square end of the arbor on which the key is placed for winding the clock.

WINKER (Blinking Eye): Iron statue clock with moving eyes.

Recommended Reading . . .

The Official Price Guide to Antique Clocks is designed as a basic introductory course for the beginning collector and flea market shopper, as well as a handy, tote-along reference book for the more seasoned hobbyist.

This guide offers the beginner a general overview of collecting techniques, tips, and prices for the collectibles most commonly bought and sold on the market today.

You can slip this price guide into a pocket or a purse and take along your own "official" expert on your next shopping excursion.

As your interest and your collection grows, you may want to start a reference library of your favorite areas. For the collector who needs a more extensive coverage of the collectibles market, The House of Collectibles publishes a complete line of comprehensive companion guides to the pocket-sized books. These larger price guides, which are itemized at the back of this book, contain full coverage on buying, selling, and caring of valuable articles, plus listings with thousands of prices for rare, unusual, and common antiques and collectibles.

$9.95-3rd Edition, 672 pgs., Order #401-1

The House of Collectibles recommends **The Official Price Guide to Antiques Jewelry,** third edition as the companion to this pocket book.

- **THOUSANDS OF CURRENT VALUES** for antique and collectible jewelry from 1750 to 1930.
- **HANDY, EASY-TO-USE** — Each item is illustrated and listed alphabetically by type of article: Bracelets • Brooches • Buckles • Chains • Charms, Fobs and Seals • Chatelaines • Earrings • Hair Combs, Hatpins and Barrettes • Lockets • Nutmeg Graters, Snuff Boxes and Scent Bottles • Watches.
- **SPECIAL SECTION** on pocket watches and wrist watches including gentlemen's and ladies vintage timepieces.
- **COMPLETE DESCRIPTION** of styles, patterns, identifying features and date of manufacturer.
- **COMPARE THE CURRENT MARKET VALUE WITH LAST YEAR'S AVERAGE SELLING PRICE** — A special price column indicates which items have increased in value . . . offering the best investment potential.
- **IMPORTANT COLLECTOR'S ADVICE** — How to Evaluate Collectible Jewelry, Where to Collect, Buying From Dealers, Mail-Bids, Selling, and Cleaning.

Available from your local dealer or order direct from:
THE HOUSE OF COLLECTIBLES, see order blank

RECOMMENDED READING / 69

Most of these books cannot be found in your local book store and must be ordered from one of the horological book dealers listed under *Sources of Horological Books and Literature*, or go to your local library.

Abbot, Henry G. (pseud. for Hazlitt, George Henry A.,) *The American Watchmaker and Jeweler*, Chicago, Hazlitt and Walter, 1910.

Abbot, Henry George (pseud.), *Antique Watches and How to Establish Their Age*, Chicago, G. K. Hazlitt, 1897.

Allix, Charles, *Carriage Clocks, Their History and Development*, Woodbridge, Suffolk, Baron, Antique Collectors Club, 1974.

American Waltham Watch Company, Bristol, CT; London, Ken Roberts, 1972.

Asprey And Co., *The Cockwork of the Heavens*, London, Asprey.

Avery, Amos Geer, *New England Clocks at Old Sturbridge Villa, the Cheney Wills collection*, second edition Sturbridge, MA 1966.

A.W.I. (Baier, Tigner and Whitney,) *Question And Answers Of And For The Clockmaking Profession*, 1981.

A.W.I. *The Watchmakers And Clockmakers Buying Guide*, a where-to-buy-it directory for watch and clock repairmen, collectors, users and suppliers, edition of 1980.

Bailey, Chris H., comp., *Seth Thomas Clock Company*, reprint, Bristol CT, Ken Roberts, 1973.

200 Years of American Clocks and Watches, Englewood Cliffs, NJ, Prentice-Hall, 1975.

Bailey, Roy Rutherford, *Romance and History of Time*, Chicago, Elgin National Watch Co., 2 vol., 1922.

Baillie, G.H., *Watchmakers And Clockmakers Of The World*, 36,000 makers, necessary for the collector, Vol. 1.

Balm Alexander, *Short History of Electric Clocks*, London, Turner and Devereux, 1973.

Barr, Lockwood Anderson, *Eli Terry Pillar and Scroll Shelf Clocks*, National Association of Watch and Clock Collectors, 1952; reprint, Exeter, NH, Adams Brown, 1956.

Barr, Lockwood Anderson, *The Origin of the Clock Lable*, reprint form the *Bulletin of the National Association of Watch and Clock Collectors*, December 1955, Vol.7, No.61, Columbia, PA, 1955.

Basserman-Jordon, Ernst Von, *The Book of Old Clocks and Watches*, London, Allen and Unwin; New York, Crown, 1964, (Essential, standard work.)

Beckett, Sir Edmund, *Clock and Watch Work*, from the 8th edition of the *Encyclopaedia Britannica*, Edinburgh, A. and C. Black, 1855.

Beckman, E. D., *Cincinnati Silversmiths, Jewelers, Watch and Clock Makers*, Harrison, NY, R. A. Green, 1975.

Bloomfield, Jo Burt, *Fun And Fancy, The Nawll Bulletin*, Hills, Michigan, August 1981, whole number 213, volume No. XXIII, No. 4.

Booth, Mary Louise, comp., *New and Complete Watchmaker's Manual with an Appendix Containing a History of Clock and Watch Making in America*, New York, J. Wiley, 1860, 1863, 1869, 1872, 1889.

Borland, Kathryn Kilby, and Helen Ross Speicher, *Clocks, from Shadow to Atom*, Chicago, Follett, 1969.

Boston Clock Company, Illustrated Catalogue, 1881, reprint, Exeter, NH, Adams Brown, 1970's.

Brearley, Harry Chase, *Time Telling Through the Ages*, New York, Doubleday, Page, for Robert H. Ingersoll Co., 1919.

RECOMMENDED READING

Britten, F.J., *Old Clocks And Watches And their Makers*, contains comprehensive list of former clock and watchmakers. Republished from 1932 edition. Contains 12,000 names. 1977 printing.

Britten, F.J., *The Watch And Clockmakers' Handbook Dictionary And Guide*, 11th edition, definitions, illustrations, if the practical horologist, to say nothing of the collector or dealer were allowed one book, this would be the one, contains wealth of now almost forgotten information some of which was omitted from later revised editions, indexed.

Camp, Hiram, 1811-1893. *A Sketch of the Clock Making Business, 1792-1892*, New Haven, CT.

Carlisle, Lilian Baker, *Vermont Clock and Watchmakers, Silversmiths, and Jewelers, 1778-1878*. Shelburne, VT, Shelburne Museum, 1970, Burlington, VT.

Catalogue of Timepieces, Exeter, NH, Adams Brown, 1969, (tools, music boxes, clocks, watches, barometers), reprint.

Chamberlain, Paul Mellen, *It's About Time*, New York, Richard R. Smith, 1941; reprint. London, Holland Pr, 1964.

Chandlee, Edward E. *Six Quaker Clockmakers*, Philadelphia The Historical Society of Pennsylvania, 1943.

Cipolla, Carlo Maria, *Clocks and Culture, 1300-1700*, London, Collins; New York, Walker, 1967.

Clock Makers of Concord, Massachusetts, as gathered at the Concord Antiquarian Museu, April-May 1966, Concord, MA, 1966.

Clocks and Watches, Garden City, NY, Doubleday, 1968.

Collectors Guide to Clocks, Price Guide, Gas City, IN, L. W. Promotions, 1973. (Schiller, Welch, Ansonia, Gilbert, Lasallita, Seth Thomas, Tiger, Waterbury, Ironclad, Ingraham, Ithaca.)

Conrad, Henry Clay, *Duncan Beard, Clockmaker; an address delivered at Old Drawyers Meeting House, in St. George's Hundred, New Castle County, Delaware*, June, 3 1928.

Old Delaware Clock-Makers. Wilmington, DE, The Historical Society, 1898. Primarily biographies.

Crossman, Charles S. *A Complete History of Watch and Clock Making in America*, Exeter, NH, Adams Brown, 1970.

Cumhail, P. W., *Investing in Clocks and Watches*, New York, Potter, 1967; London, Corgi, 1971. –

Cumming, Alexander, 1733-1814. *The Elements of Clock and Watch Work*, adapted to practice, in two essays, London, Author, 1766.

Cunynghame, Sir Henry Hardinge Samuel, *Time and Clocks*, ancient and modern methods of measuring time, Detroit, Singing Tree Pr, 1970.

De Carle, Donald, *Clocks and Their Value, Illustrated guide to ancient and modern clocks with a unique chart of all known Tompion clocks*, London, N. A. G. Pr, 1968, second edition 1971.

Desjardins, Rene, *Clocks with Personality*, 1976, available from Clock Book, 5151 Clinton, Hollywood, CA 90004.

De Carle, *D. Practical Clock Repairing*, 1977, deals with the most common repair problems, tools and equipment discussed and construction of parts.

Dent, Edward John, 1790-1835, *On the Construction and Management of Chronometers, clocks and watches*, 1951, reprint of 1844 edition Exeter, NH, Adams Brown, 1970's.

RECOMMENDED READING / 71

Desjardins, Rene, *Clocks with Personality*, 1976, available from Clock Book, 5151 Clinton, Hollywood, CA 90004.

Drepperd, Carl William, *American Clocks and Clockmakers*, Bailey and Swinfen, 1958.

Drost, William E., *Clocks and Watches of New Jersey*, Elizabeth, NJ, Engineering Pub, 1966, (last 250 years.)

Dworetsky, Lester, and Robert Dickstein, *Horology Americana*, Roslyn Heights, NY, Horology Americana, 1972.

Eckhardt, George H. *Early Pennsylvania Clocks*, Lancaster, North Museum Commission, 1938.

Pennsylvania Clocks and Clockmakers; an epic on early Americana Science, industry and craftmanship, New York, Devin-Adair, Bonanza, 1955.

United States Clock and Watch Patents, 1790-1890; the Record of a century of American horology and enterprise, New York, 1960.

Edwardes, Ernest Lawrence, *Weight-Driven Chamber Clocks of the Middle Ages and Renaissance 1350-1680; with some observations concerning certain larger clocks of medieval time*, Vol. 1, of *Old Weight-Driven Chamber Clocks, 1350-1850 series*, Altrincham, Eng. J. Sherratt, 1965.

Ehrhardt, Roy, *Clock Identification And Price Guide, Book 2*, carefully selected actual pages from original factory sales catalogs, factory advertisements, supply house catalogs and sales brochures. Covers American and imported clocks from 1850 to the 1940's. Notes year clock offered for sale. Original prices, 1979 retail value, 3,080 clock pictured or described.

Ehrhardt, Roy, *Clock Identification And Price Guide, Book 3*, a continuation of Book 1 shown above, with an additional 3,257 clocks pictured or described showing 1979 retail values.

Ehrhardt, Roy, *Clock Identification And Price Guide, Book 3*, a continuation of books 1 and 2, all new and different with 1966 illustrations, showing 1983 retail values.

Ehrhardt, Roy Kroeber, *F. Clock Company, Identification And Price Guide* uses the same format as Books 1, 2, and 3 with 292 clocks illustrated.

Ehrhardt, Roy, *The Pocket Watch Guide*, Kansas City, Heart of America Pr, 1972; *Book 2*, 1974, (2,600 watches and prices.)

The Timekeeper, Kansas City, Heart of America Pr, 1972.

Trade Marks on Watch Cases, Pocket Watches, Gold Rings, Kansas City, Heart of America Pr, 1975.

Electric Clocks and Chimes; a practical handbook giving complete instructions for the making of successful electrical timepieces, syncronised clock systems, and chiming mechanisms, London, P. Marshall, 1921; rev. ed. 1929.

Fenelly, Catherine, *New England Clocks, The J. Cheney Wells Collection*, Sturbridge, MA, Old Sturbridge Village, 1955.

Ferguson, James, 1710-1776, *Select Mechanical Exercises: shewing how to construct different clocks, orreries, and sun-dials, on plain and easy principles . . . with tables . . .* London, printed for W. Strahan; and T. Cadell, 1773; second edition London, 1778; third edition London, for Strahan and Cadeli (?), 1790.

Fleet Simon, *Clocks*, London, Weidenfeld and Nicolson; New York, Putnam, 1961; London, Octopus, 1972.

Fredyma, James P. *A Directory of Maine Silversmiths and Watch and Clock Makers*, Hanover, NH, Marie-Louise Antiques, 1972.

72 / RECOMMENDED READING

Fredyma, John J., *A Directory of Connecticut Silversmiths and Watch and Clock Makers*, Hanover, NH, P.J. and M-L Fredyma, 1973.

Fredyma, Paul J., and Marie-Louise Fredyma, *A Directory of Boston Silversmiths and Watch and Clock Makers*, Hanover, NH, M-L Fredyma, 1975.

A Directory of Vermont Silversmiths and Watch and Clock Makers, Hanover, NH, M-L Fredyma, 1975.

Fried, H.B., *Bench Practices For Watch and Clockmakers*, revised in 1974.

Fried, Henry B, *Calvacade of Time; a visual history of watches. From the private collection of the Zale Corporation*, Dallas, 1968.

The James W. Packard Collection of Unusual and Complicated Watches, owned and presented by the Horological Institute of America, Indianapolis?, the Institute, 1959.

Gazeley, William John, *Clock and Watch Escapements*, London, Heywood, 1956.

Gibbs, James W., *Buckeye Horology. A Review of Ohio clock and watchmakers*, Columbia, PA, Art Crafters, 1971.

Gilbert, (William L.,) Clock Company, Illustrated Catalogue 1901-02, reprint, Exeter, NH, Adams Brown, 1970's.

Goodrich, Ward L., *The Modern Clock. A Study of time keeping mechanism; its construction, regulation and repair*, 9th printing, Chicago, 1970.

Hagans, Orville, (compiler,) *The Best Of J.E. Coleman, 1979*, from his "Question and Answers" and "Clockwise and Otherwise" columns over the past 40 years. One of America's foremost horological authorities.

Hagans, Orville Roberts, *Horological Collection, Clock Manor Museum, Evergreen, Colorado*, Denver, Golden Bell Pr, 1964.

Hatton, Thomas, watchmaker, *An Introduction to the Mechanical Part of Clock and Watch Work*... London, T. Longman and G. Robinson, P. Law, and Co., 1773.

Hering, Daniel Webster, *Key to the Watches in the James Arthur Collection of Clocks and Watches. Addendum to the Lure of the Clock*, New York, NY U. Pr, 1934.

The Lure of the Clock; an account of the James Arthur Collection of Clocks and Watches at New York University, New York, Crown, 1963.

Hoopes, Penrose Robinson, *Connecticut Clockmakers of the 18th Century*, New York, Dodd Mead, Hartford, CT, E. V. Mitchell, 1930.

Early Clockmaking in Connecticut, New Haven, Tercentenary Commission, 1934.

Shop Records of Daniel Burnap, clockmaker, Hartford, Connecticut Historical Society, 1958.

Howard, (Edward), and Co. *Illustrated Catalogue of Clocks Manufactured by the Howard Watch and Clock Company, Boston, 1874*, facsim., reprint, Bristol, CT; London, Ken Roberts.

Howard And Davis, reprint, the earliest known trade catalog 1858 showing their line of clocks, scales and watches.

1889 Catalogue of Fine Regulators, bank and office clocks, reprint, Exeter, NH, Adams Brown, 1966.

Ingraham, (E.), and Co. *Illustrated Catalogue and Price List of Clocks Manufactured by E. Ingraham and Co., Bristol, Connecticut, 1880. Introductory historical sketch of Elias Ingraham*... Bristol; London, Ken Roberts, 1972.

James, Arthur Edwin, *Chester County Clocks and their Makers*, West Chester, PA, Chester County Historical Society, 1947.

RECOMMENDED READING / 73

Jerome, Chauncey, *History of the American Clock Business for the Past 60 Years, and life of Chauncey Jerome, written by himself,* New Haven, CT, F. C. Dayton, Jr., 1860; reprint, Exeter, NH, Adams Bron, 1970's.

Jerome And Co., Philadelphia, *manufacturers and wholesale clock dealers,* catalogue, Philadelphia, Young and Duross, 1852; reprint, Bristol, CT, American Clock and Watch Museum, 1964.

Johnson, Chester, *Clocks and Watches,* New York, Odyssey Pr, 1964; London, Hamlyn, 1965.

Johnson, Marilyn Ann, *Clockmakers and Cabinetmakers of Elizabethtown, New Jersey, in the Federal Period,* 1963.

Kendal, James Francis, *A History of Watches and Other Timekeepers,* London, C. Lockwood, 1892.

Lloyd, Herbert Alan, *Chats on Old Clocks,* First written by Arthur Hayden in 1917, London, Benn. 1951; second edition New York, Wyn, 1952; second edition rev. and reset as *Old Clocks,* London, Benn, 1958; Fair Lawn, NJ, Essential Books, 1959; third edition rev. London, 1964; four edition rev. and enl. London, Benn; New York, Dover 1970.

The Collector's Dictionay of Clocks, London Country Life, 1964; South Brunswick, NJ; A.S. Barnes, 1965.

The Complete Book of Old Clocks, New York, Putnam, 1965.

Some Outstanding Clocks Over 700 Years. 1250-1950, London, L. Hill, 1958.

Loomes, Brian, *The White Dial Clock,* New York, Drake 1975.

Lyon and Scott, *Evolution of the Timepiece,* Ottumwa, Iowa, Lyon and Scott, 1895.

Maloney, Terry, *The Story of Clocks,* N.Y., Sterling, 1960; London, Oak Tree Pr, 1962, (Juvenile Literature.)

Marshall, P. *Electric Clocks and Chimes,* complete instructions for making successful electric timepieces, a practical handbook, synchronized clock systems, and chiming mechanism.

Maust, Don, comp. *Early American Clocks. A collection of essays on early American clocks and their makers, a practical reference,* 2 vol. Uniontown, PA, E.G. Warman, 1971, 1973.

Milham, Willis Isbister, *The Columbus Clock,* Williamstown, MA, 1945.

Milham, Willis I., *Time and Timekeepers, including the history, construction, care, and accuracy of clocks and watches,* New York, Macmillan, 1923, reprint.

Miller, Robert, *Clock Guide Identification With Prices,* 1981, new price update, 146 pages, 65 full page illustrations, 16 pp in color, also has 17 pages of clocks listed with prices, no illustrated, glossary of terms, soft cover.

Miller, R. *Clock Identification With Prices   2,* clocks and prices in addition to Book #1, more foreign clocks, German, Japanese, French and English, collectible and rare clocks.

Naylot, Arthur Henry, *The Study Book of Time and Clocks,* London, Bodley Head, 1959, 1965, (Juvenile Literature.)

Nelthropp, Henry Leonard, *Treatise on Watchwork, past and present,* London; New York, E. and F. N. Spon, 1873.

New Haven Clock Company, 1886 Catalog, reprint with 1887 price list supplement, Bloomsburg, PA, G. and G.

1889-90 Catalogue, reprint, Exeter, NH, Adams Brown, 1974.

Nicholls, Andrew, *Clocks in Color,* New York, Macmilla, 1976.

Nicholson, Don and Alice, *Novelty and Antimated Pendulette Wall Clocks,* 1977, available from the authors, P.O. Box 401012, Garland, TX 75040.

Nutting, Wallace, *The Clock Book; being a description of foreign and American clocks,* Framingham, MA, Old America Co., 1924; expanded edition as *The Complete Clock Book,* by William B. Jacobs, Jr., and John E. Edwards, Stratford, CT, Edmund-Bradley, 1970's; facsim. reprint, Greens Farms, CT, Modern Farms and Crafts, 1975.

Overton, George Leonard, *Clocks and Watches,* London; New York, Pitman, 1922.

Palmer, Brooks *The Book Of American Clocks,* 12th printing, 318 pages, 310 illustrations, extensive list of American clockmakers, good for identification.

Palmer, Brooks, *The Romance of Time,* New Haven, C. Schaffner Advertising Agency, 1954.

Palmer, Brooks, *A Treasury Of American Clocks,* 9th printing.

Pertuch, Walter Albert Richard, and Emerson W. Hilker, comps., *Horological Books and Pamphlets in the Franklin Institute Library,* Philadelphia, the Institute, 1956; second edition Philadelphia, 1968.

Pocket Timepieces of New York Chapter Members, New York, National Association of Watch and Clock Collectors, 1968.

Prentiss Clock Improvement Company, 1897 catalogue, reprint, St. Louis, American Reprints, 1969; 1972.

Proctor, (Frederick T.), *Collection of Antique Watches and Table Clocks,* Utica, NY, 1913.

Richardson, Albert Deane, 1833-69, *Ancient and Modern Time-Keepers, containing... notice of works of the National Watch Company, Elgin, Illinois,* reprint from Harper's Monthly Magazine, 1869, New York, 1870.

Roberts, Kenneth D., *Contributions of Joseph Ives to Connecticut Clock Technology, 1810-62,* Bristol, CT, Ken Roberts, 1970.

Eli Terry and the Connecticut Self Clock, Bristol, CT, Ken Roberts, 1973.

Robertson, John Drummond, 1857, *The Evolution of Clockwork, with a special section on the clocks of Japan. With a comprehensive bibliography of horology,* London, Cassell, 1931; facsim. reprint, Wakefield, Eng. S.R.

Royer-Collard, Frederick Bernard, *Skeleton Clocks,* London, N.A.G. Pr, 1969.

Sanderson, R. L., *Waltham Industries,* Waltham MA, 1957, American Waltham Watch Co., U.S.

Sands, Anna B., *Time Pieces of Old and New Connecticut,* Hartford, CT, Manufacturers Association, 1926.

Schwartz, Marvin D., *Collector's Guide to Antique American Clocks, history, style, identification,* Garden City, NY, Doubleday, 1975.

Seth Thomas Clock Co. Illustrated Catalogue of Clocks, 1892-93, reprint, Exeter, NH, Adams Brown, 1970's.

Factory List of Seth Thomas Clock Movements, 1907 Catalogue, reprint, Exeter, NH, Adams Brown, 1970's.

Smith, Alan, *Clocks and Watches,* London, Connoisseur, 1975; New York, Hearst, 1976.

Smith, Eric, *Repairing Antique Clocks: a guide for amateurs,* Newton Abbot, David and Charles, 1973.

Sobol, Ken, *The Clock Museum,* New York, McGraw-Hill, 1967.

RECOMMENDED READING / 75

St. Louis Clock and Silver Ware Co., 1904 catalog, St. Louis, American Reprints, 1975, (Ansonia, Sempire, Waterbury, Gilbert, Ingraham, Newman.)

The Story of Edward Howard and the First American Watch, Boston, E. Howard Watch Works, 1910.

Terwilliger, Charles, *The Horolovar Collection, a comprehensive history and catalogue of 400-day clocks, 1880-1912,* Bronxville, NY, Horolovar Co., 1962.

Thomson, Richard, *Antique American Clocks and Watches,* Princeton, NJ; London, Van Nostrand, 1968.

Tyler, Eric John, *The Craft of the Clockmaker,* London, Ward Lock, 1973; New York, Crown, 1974, (14th century to present, includes tools.)

Ullyett, Kenneth, *Clocks and Watches,* Feltham, Hamlyn, 1971.

The Plain Man's Guide to Antique Clocks, by W. J. Bentley; London, M. Josepth, 1963.

In Quest of Clocks, Feltham, Spring Books, 1968.

Vulliamy, Benjamin Lewis, 1780-1854, *On the Construction and Regulation of Clocks for Railway Stations,* London, W. Clowes, 1845.

Some Considerations on Public Clocks, Particularly Church Clocks, London, priv. printed, 1831.

Ward, Francis Alan Burnett, *Clocks and Watches, Vol.I.*

Warman, Edwin G. *Early American Clocks,* 3 vol., Uniontwon, PA, Warman Pub. Co., 1970's.

Watch-making in America. Embodying the history of watchmaking as an invention, and as an industry, reprint from Appleton's Journal, July, 2, 1870, Boston, Appleton, 1870.

Waterbury Clock Company, 1867 Catalog, reprint, St. Louis, American Reprints, 1973.

Way, Robert Barnard, and Noel D. Green, *Time and Its Reckoning,* New York, Chemical Pub. Co., 1940.

Weight-Driven Clocks; Vol. II. Spring-Driven Clocks, 2 vol., London, Science Museum, 1973, 1972.

Welch, (E. N.), Manufacturing Co. Catalogue 1885, reprint, Exeter, NH, Adams Brown, 1970, (regulators, calendars, alarms, ship bell, cottage, etc.)

Welch, Kenneth Frederick, *Time Measurement: An Introductory History,* London, David and Charles, 1972; as *The History of Clocks and Watches,* New York, Drake, 1972.

Wells, Joel Cheney, *1874, New England Clocks at Old Sturbridge Village, the J. Cheney Wells Collection,* Sturbridge Village, MA, 1955.

Willard, John Ware, *A History of Simon Willard, inventor and clockmaker, together with some account of his sons — his apprentices — and the workmen associated with him,* Boston, E. O. Cockayne, 1911; reprint, New York, 1968.

Willsberger, Johann, *Clocks and Watches,* New York, Dial Pr, 1975.

Wood, Edward J., *Curiositics of Clocks and Watches from the Earliest Times,* London, Richard Bentley, 1866, reprint of 1866 edition, Detroit, Gale, 1975.

Wright, Lawrence, *Clockwork Man: the story of time, its origins, its uses, its tyranny,* New York, Horizon, 1969.

Wyatt, Sir Matthew Digby, 1820-77, *The History of the Manufacture of Clocks,* reprints from the *Clerkenwell News,* London, 1870's.

HOW TO USE THIS BOOK

The Official 1984 Price Guide to Antique Clocks is arranged in alphabetical order. Headings refer to manufacturers and clocks designs. Within the printed listing you will find technical information, further designed to help in identifying YOUR particular clock. Information listed will include: the name of the clock (if it was not named by the manufacturer, then the name it most commonly goes under in horological circles), metal, wood (these are broken into specific listings and corresponding price differences), color, parts of the movement (pendulums, spring wound, etc.), any other visual characteristics, dimensions in inches, approximate date (if known), and individual characteristics such as day, strike, alarm, calendar, etc. A glossary of terms is provided for identification of these features.

You will also find a price RANGE beside each listing description. These listings are current and as accurate as possible. Remember that these price ranges listed do *not* represent the highest and lowest prices the clock has ever sold for. Rather, it represents an average RANGE for that particular clock value.

The information contained in parenthesis after each listing, refers to additional references. The (E) picture references alluded to in parenthesis, refer to CLOCK BOOK I, II, III and (K) by the author of this book, Roy Ehrhardt. The (K) reference refers to a book on F. Kroeber. The (M) picture references refer to Survey of *American Calendar Clocks,* by Andrew and Dalia Miller, 1972.

These five books are also listed in the bibliography. They can easily be ordered through one or more of the preceeding horological book sources. Inquire by phone or mail. As with most of the pictures in this book, (and since there are over one thousand illustrations you may very well find what you're looking for right here), the Ehrhardt and Miller volumes, feature line drawings culled from the pages of old clock manufacturers catalogues. Wide and subtle differences are apparent. You could not ask for a more accurate representation of your antique clock.

Once you have located a picture and/or printed listing that seems to resemble the clock YOU own, you must deduce the following items of information by examining your clock thusly: First, look for the name of the manufacturer if the clock is all original. The name can be found in a number of places; on the dial (sometimes out near the edge under the bezel), on the back of the movement; on a paper label inside; on the back or bottom of the clock; and sometimes, though rarely on large clocks, underneath the dial. Second, measure both the height, and width, and dial size of the clock you are trying to identify. Compare your clock's size, with the size in the listings. Third, check the movement to see whether it has a calendar, alarm, etc. This information will also be included in the listings.

If you cannot find a picture of your clock in the section under the manufacturer, look under the other manufacturers as well. Clocks that were good sellers (shelf, mantle, kitchen, etc.) were sold by all of the major makers with only slight variations. Fortunately in most instances, the makers name will not affect the actual value of your antique clock. What it DOES do is make the identification of a clock much easier to ascertain. There should be enough information in *The Official Price Guide to Antique Clocks,* to make up the missing pieces in your clock identification puzzle.

78 / ANSONIA CLOCK COMPANY

inside the cast. The Ansonia Company produced a similar non jeweled model. They sold millions of these inexpensive watches in the two and a half decades before they went out of business; an interesting comparison to the scrolled elaborate clockwork the Ansonia collector is familiar with.

ADVERTISING

☐ **Correct Time.** dial 10", spring, c. 1890, 8 Day (E2-29).
235.00   260.00   (250.00)

☐ **Our Advertiser.** Silver or Gold Plate, height 7½", dial 2", spring, c. 1890, 1 Day (E2-31).
100.00   125.00   (115.00)

☐ **Window Clock,** dial 20", spring, c. 1890, 8 Day, Standard Time (E2-29).
325.00   360.00   (330.00)

☐ **Window Clock,** plate glass, embossed gilt figures, dial 20", spring, c. 1890, 8 Day (E2-29).
350.00   385.00   (360.00)

Our Advertiser

Window Clock, standard

ALARM/DRUM

☐ **The Ansonia Watch,** Roman or Arabic dial, small seconds dial at bottom, stem wind, nickel plated, spring, c. 1898, 1 Day (E1-161).
35.00   50.00   (42.00)

☐ **Bee,** nickel, dial 2", spring, c. 1898, 1 Day (E1-161).
40.00   50.00   (45.00)

☐ **Bee,** nickel, dial 2", spring, c. 1898, 1 Day, alarm (E1-161).
55.00   65.00   (60.00)

☐ **Bee,** nickel, dial 2", winds without key, spring, c. 1890, 1 Day (E2-10).
40.00   50.00   (45.00)

☐ **Bee,** nickel, stem-winding alarm, no key for winding, dial 2", spring, c. 1890, 1 Day (E2-10).
45.00   55.00   (50.00)

☐ **Bee Time,** nickel, dial 2", spring, c. 1917, (E1-179).
50.00   60.00   (55.00)

☐ **Dandy,** nickel, dial 3", spring, c. 1890, 1 Day, (E2-10).
25.00   35.00   (30.00)

☐ **As above,** 1 Day, alarm.
30.00   40.00   (35.00)

☐ **Electric clock,** dry cell battery enclosed in polished oak case, 10" x 8¾", c. 1898, 1 Day, alarm (E1-161).
95.00   115.00   (100.00)

ANSONIA CLOCK COMPANY

The Ansonia Company was best known for its decorative imitation gold, and ornate novelty clocks. Petulant cupids and angels, deep thinkers, athletes, babies, and languid ladies drape and adorn the ornamental designs, that characterize the name and products of Ansonia.

Anson Phelps founded the Company in Derby, Connecticut. An importer of tin, brass, and copper in the Eastern section of the states, he already owned a copper mill (hence the ormolu). Phelps maintained considerable financial backing, as well as contacts and knowledgeable business associates in his venture. From such formidable beginnings he suffered two serious setbacks. In 1854 the factory burned at a loss of several thousand dollars. At this time the Ansonia Clock Company became the Ansonia Brass and Copper Company, as Phelps had little choice but to move the clock facilities into the standing copper mill. By 1879, or thereabouts, the clock company was reformed, and manufacturing operations were moved to the Brooklyn section of New York. Unfortunately this factory also burned, after a scant few months in its new location of operation.

By the late 19th and early 20th century, Phelps had reestablished his name in the clock industry as one of the major manufacturers. The factory was rebuilt and expanded. Ansonia sales officers and agents could be found all over the world. It was during this time, also, that many different designs of clocks were included in the manufacturing process: alarms, cabinet, carriage, crystal regulators, galley, kitchen, mantel or shelf, onyx and marble, porcelain and china, statue, etc. Ansonia was in its heyday, at the height of its productivity, fame, and power.

Any type of business enterprise is vulnerable to some extent or another; changing tides in the publics' imagination, world events and crisis, new inventions, world leaders, even literature and art can spell success or eventual failure in a business or industry. The events leading up to these financial difficulties are not always completely fair insofar as the amount of effort or expertise expended by the company, may be completely professional.

We have already discussed some of the elemental threats to business in those days. Fire was the greatest hazard. Ansonia had already weathered two severe setbacks for this reason, and recovered admirably. Their next major problem was not as obvious although just as dehabilitating.

Just before World War I Ansonia's strongest selling point, the novelty clock, became subject to fierce competition. Rather than maintain competitive realistic prices for their clocks, they attempted to cut their losses, offering clocks at, "old pricing." This tactic failed, and Ansonia began a downward spiral in the clock industry, that resulted in heavy losses. By 1929 the majority of the timekeeping machinery and some tools and dies, were sold to the Russian government and shipped out of the country. This formulated the basis (along with the remains of a watch company purchased a year later) of the clock and watch industry in Moscow.

None of the major clock industries survived the Depression and subsequent Second World War, intact. Ansonia was the first to go under. In 1904 the company had attempted to jump on "the dollar watch" bandwagon, perhaps as an ineffectual guard against the first hints of potential financial difficulties. (Ansonia clocks were not cheap.)

The idea behind the dollar watch was to make it in the same manner as a cheap clock. This concept bore little resemblance to the traditional, intricate style that went into the handcrafted watch. It did not pan out. Instead designers turned to the tourbillon watch, concocted by the French genius Breguet.

Watches are difficult timekeepers due to the unstable positions they are likely to fall into. Breguet's watch had a turning escapement which minimized these errors in accuracy. American designers went one step further, allowing the entire movement to rotate

ANSONIA CLOCK COMPANY / 79

Dandy

☐ **Improved Bee,** *seamless brass case, nickel plated, dial 2", spring, c. 1917, 1 Day, alarm (E1-179).*
   55.00   65.00   (60.00)

☐ **Midget,** *nickel, dial 8", spring, c. 1883, 1 Day, alarm (E2-9).*
   75.00   85.00   (80.00)
☐ **As above,** *dial 8", 8 Day.*
   65.00   75.00   (70.00)
☐ **As above,** *dial 12", 1 Day, alarm.*
   110.00   125.00   (115.00)
☐ **As above,** *dial 12", 8 Day.*
   100.00   110.00   (105.00)

☐ **Peep-O-Day,** *nickel, sunken center, dial 6", spring, c. 1883, 1 Day, alarm (E2-9).*
   25.00   30.00   (27.00)

☐ **Peep-O-Day,** *nickel, dial 4", spring, c. 1883, 1 Day, alarm (E2-9).*
   25.00   30.00   (27.00)
☐ **As above,** *1 Day, alarm, calendar.*
   65.00   75.00   (70.00)
☐ **As above,** *1 Day, strike.*
   70.00   85.00   (75.00)

☐ **Peep-O-Day,** *nickel, dial 5", spring, c. 1898, 1 Day, alarm (E1-161).*
   40.00   50.00   (45.00)

☐ **Peep-O-Day,** *nickel, dial 6", spring, c. 1898, 1 Day, alarm (E1-161).*
   40.00   50.00   (45.00)

☐ **Peep-O-Day,** *nickel, dial 4", repeating strike, spring, c. 1890, 1 Day (E2-10).*
   85.00   95.00   (90.00)

☐ **Pirate,** *nickel, dial 4", spring, c. 1890, 1 Day, alarm (E2-10).*
   40.00   50.00   (45.00)

☐ **Planet,** *nickel, dial 4", spring, c. 1883, 1 Day (E2-9).*
   110.00   115.00   (113.00)

☐ **Princess,** *nickel, spring, c. 1883, 1 Day (E2-9).*
   30.00   40.00   (35.00)
☐ **As above,** *dial 5", 8 Day.*
   45.00   55.00   (50.00)
☐ **As above,** *dial 6", 1 Day.*
   35.00   45.00   (40.00)

☐ **Racket,** *nickel, dial 5", spring, c. 1898, 1 Day, strike, alarm (E1-161).*
   45.00   55.00   (50.00)

☐ **Simplex,** *seamless brass case, nickel plated, spring, c. 1917, 8 Day, alarm (E1-179).*
   45.00   55.00   (50.00)

☐ **Six-Inch Peep-O-Day,** *fancy, nickel, dial 6", spring, c. 1890, 1 Day, alarm (E2-10).*
   45.00   55.00   (50.00)

Midget

80 / ANSONIA CLOCK COMPANY

Peep-O-Day

Pirate

- [ ] **Standard,** nickel, dial 4", spring, c. 1890, 1 Day (E2-10).
  40.00   50.00   (45.00)

ALARM/FANCY

- [ ] **Bee,** nickel, leather case, height 4", spring, c. 1890, 1 Day, alarm (E2-10).
  50.00   60.00   (55.00)

Bella

- [ ] **Bella,** height 9", dial 4", spring, c. 1890, 1 Day (E2-30).
  90.00   110.00   (95.00)
- [ ] **As above,** 1 Day, alarm.
  100.00   120.00   (110.00)
- [ ] **Charmer,** bronze finish, height 15", dial 4", spring, c. 1883, 1 Day, alarm (E2-8).
  90.00   110.00   (95.00)
- [ ] **Cupid's Dart,** bronze and nickel finish, height 16", dial 4", spring, c. 1883, 1 Day, alarm, (E2-9).
  135.00   155.00   (140.00)
- [ ] **As above,** 8 Day, alarm.
  155.00   175.00   (160.00)
- [ ] **Dauntless,** bronze and nickel finish, height 18", dial 4", spring, c. 1883, 1 Day, alarm.
  150.00   170.00   (160.00)
- [ ] **As above,** dial 4", 8 Day.
  170.00   190.00   (175.00)
- [ ] **As above,** dial 5", 8 Day, alarm.
  150.00   170.00   (160.00)
- [ ] **As above,** dial 5", 8 Day.
  170.00   190.00   (175.00)

ANSONIA CLOCK COMPANY / 81

Charmer

Dauntless

Domestic

☐ **Domestic,** *bronze and nickel finish, height 15", dial 6", spring, c. 1883, 1 Day, alarm (E2-9).*
    130.00   150.00   (140.00)
☐ **As above,** *8 Day, strike.*
    150.00   170.00   (160.00)

☐ **Echo,** *bronze and nickel finish, hand moves automatically and rings bell, height 7½", dial 4", spring, c. 1883, 1 Day, alarm (E2-9).*
    165.00   185.00   (170.00)
☐ **As above,** *1 Day, strike.*
    170.00   205.00   (180.00)

☐ **Good Luck,** *bronze finish, dial 4", spring, c. 1883, 1 Day (E2-9).*
    60.00   70.00   (65.00)
☐ **As above,** *1 Day, alarm.*
    80.00   90.00   (85.00)

☐ **Grandfather,** *bronze and nickel finish, height 8", dial 4", spring, c. 1883, 1 Day, calendar (E2-8).*
    170.00   200.00   (175.00)

☐ **Jewel Case,** *bronze finish, height 16", dial 4", spring, c. 1883, 1 Day, alarm (E2-8).*
    130.00   150.00   (145.00)
☐ **As above,** *8 Day, alarm.*
    150.00   170.00   (160.00)

82 / ANSONIA CLOCK COMPANY

Echo

Jewel Case

Little Dorrit

- **Little Dorrit,** *black enamel case, height 12", dial 4", spring, c. 1883, 1 Day, alarm (E2-9).*
  150.00   170.00   (160.00)

- **Nightingale,** *bronze and nickel finish, height 10", dial 4", spring, c. 1883, 1 Day, alarm (E2-8).*
  80.00   90.00   (85.00)

- **As above,** *8 Day, alarm.*
  90.00   110.00   (95.00)

- **Octagon Peep-O-Day,** *nickel, dial 4", spring, c. 1890, 1 Day (E2-10).*
  25.00   35.00   (30.00)

- **Octagon Peep-O-Day,** *nickel, dial 4", spring, c. 1890, 1 Day, alarm, calendar (E2-10).*
  90.00   110.00   (95.00)

- **Octagon Princess,** *nickel, dial 4", spring, c. 1890, 1 Day (E2-10).*
  25.00   35.00   (30.00)

- **Pagoda,** *bronze and nickel finish, height 15", dial 4", spring, c. 1883, 1 Day, alarm (E2-9).*
  155.00   175.00   (145.00)
- **As above,** *dial 4", 8 Day.*
  175.00   195.00   (170.00)
- **As above,** *dial 5", 1 Day, alarm.*
  165.00   185.00   (170.00)
- **As above,** *dial 5", 8 Day.*
  185.00   210.00   (180.00)

ANSONIA CLOCK COMPANY / 83

Pagoda

Woodbine

☐ **Pride,** *bronze and nickel finish, height 10", dial 4", spring, c. 1883, 1 Day, alarm (E2-8).*
90.00   110.00   (95.00)

☐ **Tally-Ho,** *bronze and nickel finish, height 10", dial 4", c. 1883, 1 Day, alarm (E2-9).*
80.00   100.00   (85.00)
☐ **As above,** *8 Day.*
80.00   110.00   (90.00)

☐ **Twins No.1,** *bronze and nickel finish, height 12", dial 4", spring, c. 1883, 1 Day (E2-8).*
115.00   135.00   (120.00)
☐ **As above,** *1 Day, alarm.*
125.00   145.00   (130.00)

☐ **Twins No. 2,** *bronze and nickel finish, height 10", dial 4", spring, c. 1883, 1 Day (E2-8).*
130.00   150.00   (135.00)
☐ **As above,** *1 Day, alarm.*
150.00   170.00   (160.00)

☐ **Woodbine,** *bronze finish, height 13", dial 4", spring, c. 1883, 1 Day, alarm (E2-8).*
115.00   135.00   (120.00)
☐ **As above,** *8 Day, alarm.*
125.00   145.00   (130.00)

CABINET

☐ **Cabinet Antique,** *polished oak or mahogany, with antique brass trimmings, French sash, porcelain dial, ½ hour old English bell strike, bell on top, 18¾" x 11½", dial 4¾", spring, c. 1896, 8 Day (E2-13).*
700.00   950.00   (750.00)

☐ **Cabinet Antique,** *polished mahogany or oak, with antique brass trimmings, French sash, porcelain dial, ½ hour gong strike, 20" x 9¼", dial 4¾" spring, c. 1896, 8 Day (E2-13).*
600.00   850.00   (650.00)

☐ **Cabinet A,** *antique oak, with antique brass lacquered trimmings, 19" x 10¼", sash and dial 5¾", ½ hour slow strike movement, cathedral gongs on sounding boards, French sash and metal dials, spring, c. 1896, 8 Day (E2-13).*
230.00   260.00   (245.00)

84 / ANSONIA CLOCK COMPANY

Cabinet Antique, 18¾" x 11½"

☐ **Cabinet B,** *antique oak, with antique brass lacquered trimmings, 18" x 11½", sash and dial 5¾", ½ hour slow strike movement, cathedral gongs on sounding boards, French sash and metal dial, spring, c. 1896, 8 Day (E2-13).*
    225.00   250.00   (240.00)

☐ **Cabinet C,** *antique oak, with antique brass lacquered trimmings, 18½" x 11½", sash and dial 5¾", ½ hour slow strike movement, cathedral gongs on sounding boards, French sash and metal dial, spring, c. 1896, 8 Day (E2-13).*
    240.00   270.00   (245.00)

Cabinet Antique, 20" x 9¼"

☐ **Cabinet E,** *antique oak, with antique brass lacquered trimmings, 18" x 12", sash and dial 5¾", ½ hour slow strike movement, cathedral gongs on sounding boards, French sash and metal dial, spring, c. 1896, 8 Day (E2-13).*
    225.00   250.00   (235.00)

☐ **Idaho,** *oak, 15½" x 11¼", dial 6", spring, c. 1910, 8 Day, strike (E2-12).*
    105.00   125.00   (115.00)

☐ **Ilion,** *oak, 13" x 9½", dial 6", spring, c. 1910, 8 Day, strike (E2-12).*
    100.00   120.00   (115.00)

☐ **Inca,** *oak, 13" x 9½", dial 6", spring, c. 1910, 8 Day, strike (E2-12).*
    95.00   115.00   (100.00)

☐ **India,** *oak, 15¾" x 11¼", dial 6", spring, c. 1910, 8 Day, strike (E2-12).*
    105.00   125.00   (120.00)

ANSONIA CLOCK COMPANY / 85

Cabinet C

Leeds

Idaho

Plymouth

☐ **Ipswich,** *oak, 15¼" x 11¾", dial 6", spring, c. 1910, 8 Day, strike (E2-12).*
      105.00   125.00   (115.00)

☐ **Leeds,** *oak, 11½" x 8⅓", dial 4¼", c. 1883, 8 Day, strike (E2-11).*
      130.00   150.00   (145.00)

☐ **Island,** *oak, 13" x 9½", dial 6", spring, c. 1910, 8 Day, strike (E2-12).*
      100.00   120.00   (105.00)

86 / ANSONIA CLOCK COMPANY

Rialto

☐ **Plymouth,** oak, 10½" x 8½", dial 4¼", spring, c. 1883, 8 Day, strike (E2-11).
130.00   150.00   (140.00)

☐ **Ramsgate,** oak, 16¼" x 11¾", dial 6", spring, c. 1910, 8 Day, strike (E2-12).
125.00   145.00   (140.00)

☐ **Rialto,** oak, 16" x 10¼", dial 6", c. 1910, 8 Day, strike (E2-12).
125.00   145.00   (140.00)

☐ **Riverdale,** oak, 16½" x 11½", dial 6", c. 1910, 8 Day, strike (E2-12).
125.00   145.00   (135.00)

☐ **Rockland,** oak, 16¼" x 10¾", dial 6", spring, c. 1910, 8 Day, strike (E2-12).
125.00   145.00   (135.00)

☐ **Rockwood,** oak, 16" x 10¾", dial 6", c. 1910, 8 Day, strike (E2-12).
125.00   145.00   (140.00)

☐ **Roxbury,** oak, 16¼" x 10¾", dial 6", spring, c. 1910, 8 Day, strike (E2-12).
125.00   145.00   (135.00)

Summit

☐ **Salem,** oak, 14¾" x 10¾", dial 5", spring, c. 1883, 8 Day, strike (E2-11).
145.00   165.00   (155.00)

☐ **Summit,** oak, 14¾" x 10¾", dial 5", spring, c. 1883, 8 Day, strike (E2-11).
150.00   170.00   (155.00)

☐ **Tivoli,** oak, 15" x 11½", dial 5", spring, c. 1883, 8 Day, strike (E2-11).
140.00   160.00   (145.00)

☐ **As above,** walnut.
160.00   180.00   (165.00)

☐ **As above,** mahogany.
160.00   180.00   (165.00)

☐ **Toronto,** oak, 16¾" x 11¼", dial 5", spring, c. 1883, 8 Day, strike (E2-11).
140.00   160.00   (150.00)

☐ **As above,** mahogany.
165.00   185.00   (180.00)

☐ **Trieste,** oak, 14¾" x 11½", dial 5", spring, c. 1883, 8 Day, strike (E2-11).
130.00   150.00   (200.00)

☐ **As above,** mahogany.
165.00   185.00   (180.00)

ANSONIA CLOCK COMPANY / 87

Toronto

Tunis

☐ **Troy,** oak, height 15¼", base 10¾", dial 5", spring, ½ hour gong, c. 1890, 8 Day, strike (E2-21).
90.00   110.00   (95.00)
☐ **As above,** walnut.
110.00   135.00   (115.00)
☐ **As above,** mahogany.
110.00   135.00   (115.00)

☐ **Tunis,** oak, height 14", base 11½", dial 5", spring, ½ hour gong, c. 1890, 8 Day, strike (E2-21).
85.00   105.00   (110.00)
☐ **As above,** walnut.
110.00   125.00   (115.00)
☐ **As above,** mahogany.
110.00   120.00   (115.00)

☐ **Turkey,** oak, 15¾" x 10", dial 5", spring, c. 1883, 8 Day, strike (E2-11).
135.00   160.00   (136.00)
☐ **As above,** walnut.
160.00   180.00   (165.00)
☐ **As above,** mahogany
160.00   180.00   (195.00)

CALENDAR

☐ **Adelaide,** walnut parlor, height 24", dial 6", spring, 8 Day, strike, simple calendar (E2-25).
250.00   275.00   (260.00)

☐ **Bankers Ink Stand,** height 12", dial 4", 1 Day, simple calendar (E2-8).
210.00   240.00   (220.00)

☐ **Carlos,** walnut parlor, height 24½", dial 6", spring, 8 Day, strike, simple calendar (E2-25).
225.00   260.00   (240.00)

☐ **Gem Ink,** height 8¾", dial 4", spring, 1 Day, simple calendar (E2-8, M258-88).
230.00   275.00   (235.00)

☐ **Grandfather,** height 8", dial 4", spring, 1 Day, simple calendar (E2-8).
160.00   180.00   (170.00)

☐ **Lily Ink,** height 7", dial 4", spring, 1 Day, simple calendar (E2-8, M256-87).
220.00   270.00   (230.00)

88 / ANSONIA CLOCK COMPANY

Carlos

Gem Ink

Grandfather

☐ **Novelty Calendar,** Ansonia Brass and Copper Co., Connecticut, height 26", dial 10½", spring, 8 Day (M263-90).
    700.00   900.00   (800.00)

☐ **Octagon Peep-O-Day,** dial 4", spring, 1 Day, alarm, simple calendar (E2-10, M260-88).
    90.00   115.00   (95.00)

☐ **Octagon Top,** gilt short drop, 19½" x 12", dial 8", spring, 8 Day, strike, simple calendar (E1-177, E2-39, M253-86).
    215.00   235.00   (220.00)

☐ **Octagon Top,** gilt short drop, height 21½", dial 10", spring, 8 Day, strike, simple calendar (E2-39).
    215.00   235.00   (220.00)

☐ **Octagon Top,** gilt short drop, height 24", dial 12", spring, 8 Day, strike, simple calendar (E2-39).
    250.00   275.00   (260.00)

☐ **Octagon Top,** long drop, height 32", dial 12", spring, 8 Day, strike, simple calendar (M247-85).
    325.00   375.00   (340.00)

☐ **Octagon Top,** long drop, regulator A, height 32", dial 12", spring, 8 Day, strike, simple calendar (E1-177, E2-39, M248-85).
    375.00   400.00   (390.00)

ANSONIA CLOCK COMPANY / 89

- **Office Ink Stand,** *height 13", dial 4", 1 Day, simple calendar (E2-8).*
  225.00   275.00   (250.00)

- **Para Parlor,** *wall regulator, height 39", dial 8", spring, 8 Day, strike, simple calendar (E2-40).*
  550.00   625.00   (600.00)

- **Parlor Ink Stand No.2,** *height 8", dial 2", 1 Day, simple calendar (E2-27).*
  225.00   275.00   (240.00)

- **Peep-O-Day,** *round alarm, dial 4", spring, 1 Day, alarm, simple calendar (E2-9).*
  75.00   100.00   (80.00)

- **Planet,** *round alarm, dial 4", spring, 1 Day, simple calendar (E2-9).*
  100.00   125.00   (110.00)

- **R.C. Octagon Top,** *short drop, height 19½", dial 8", spring, 8 Day, strike, simple calendar (E2-39).*
  225.00   250.00   (230.00)

- **R.C. Octagon Top,** *short drop, height 21½", dial 10", spring, 8 Day, strike, simple calendar (E2-39).*
  250.00   275.00   (260.00)

- **R.C. Octagon Top,** *short drop, height 24", dial 12", spring, 8 Day, strike, simple calendar (E2-39).*
  275.00   300.00   (290.00)

Octagon Peep-O-Day

Office Ink Stand

Lily Ink

90 / ANSONIA CLOCK COMPANY

Peep-O-Day, round

Para Parlor

Rio Parlor

Parlor Ink Stand No. 2

☐ **Regulator Octagon Top,** *height 32", dial 12", spring, 8 Day, strike, simple calendar (E2-39).*
    400.00   450.00   (425.00)

☐ **Rio Parlor,** *wall regulator, height 39", dial 8", spring, 8 Day, strike, simple calendar (E2-40).*
    550.00   625.00   (600.00)

ANSONIA CLOCK COMPANY / 91

- ☐ **Round Alarm,** *lion's head on each side, dial 4", spring, 1 Day, strike, simple calendar (M254-87).*
  75.00   100.00   (80.00)

- ☐ **Round Top,** *long drop, height 32", dial 12", spring, 8 Day, strike, simple calendar (E2-39).*
  350.00   400.00   375.00

- ☐ **Study Ink Stand,** *height 9½", dial 4", 1 Day, simple calendar (E2-27).*
  225.00   270.00   260.00

- ☐ **Victorian Kitchen,** *23" x 14½", barometer and thermometer, dial 5", spring, 8 Day, strike, simple calendar (M251-86).*
  135.00   150.00   140.00

CARRIAGE

- ☐ **Bee Carriage,** *brass finish, height 6", spring, c. 1890, 8 Day (E2-22).*
  105.00   125.00   (115.00)

- ☐ **Bonnibel,** *polished brass, height 15", dial 1½", spring, c. 1910, 8 Day (E2-36).*
  140.00   160.00   (150.00)

- ☐ **Brilliant,** *nickel, height 7½", dial 2½", spring, c. 1883, 1 Day (E2-8).*
  105.00   125.00   (115.00)

- ☐ **Comet,** *silver plated, height 7⅞", dial 2½", spring, c. 1910, 1 Day, strike, alarm (E2-36).*
  180.00   200.00   (190.00)

- ☐ **Companion,** *nickel, height 8", dial 2", spring, c. 1883, 1 Day, alarm (E2-8).*
  105.00   125.00   (110.00)

- ☐ **Dora,** *black enameled case, hand painted decorations, French sash, gilt finish, height 10", dial 4", spring, c. 1883, 1 Day, strike (E2-9).*
  105.00   125.00   (115.00)
- ☐ **As above,** *8 Day, strike.*
  130.00   150.00   (125.00)

- ☐ **Elliptical Carriage,** *nickel, height 6", spring, c. 1883, 1 Day, alarm (E2-8).*
  105.00   125.00   (115.00)

Comet

Oriole

92 / ANSONIA CLOCK COMPANY

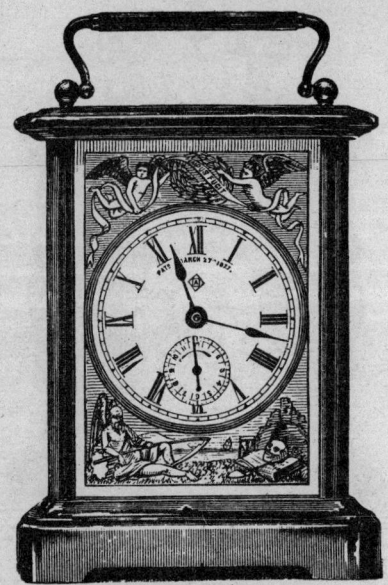

Peep-O-Day Carriage

☐ **Gem,** *rich burnished silver or gold, fancy, height 4½", dial 1½", spring, c. 1898, 1 Day (E1-161).*
    55.00   75.00   (60.00)

☐ **Oriole,** *brass finish, enameled in fancy colors, height 7", dial 3", spring, c. 1890, 1 Day, alarm (E2-10).*
    80.00   100.00   (85.00)
☐ **As above,** *1 Day, strike.*
    105.00   125.00   (115.00)
☐ **As above,** *1 Day, musical alarm.*
    130.00   150.00   (135.00)

☐ **Ornamental Carriage,** *black enameled panels, embossed with gilt ornamentation, height 7", dial 3", spring, c. 1890, 1 Day, alarm (E2-10).*
    135.00   155.00   (140.00)

☐ **Pearl,** *rich burnished gold, fancy, height 5", dial 1½", c. 1898, 1 Day (E1-161).*
    70.00   90.00   (75.00)

☐ **Peep-O-Day Carriage,** *nickel, height 7", dial 3", spring, c. 1890, 1 Day, alarm (E2-10).*
    115.00   135.00   (120.00)

☐ **Peep-O-Day,** *nickel, black enameled panels, hand painted decorations, height 7", dial 3", spring, c. 1883, 1 Day, alarm (E2-8).*
    130.00   150.00   (140.00)

☐ **Pert,** *nickel, height 5", dial 5¾", spring, c. 1910, 1 Day, alarm (E2-36).*
    115.00   135.00   (125.00)

☐ **Pert,** *nickel, height 5", dial 1¾", spring, c. 1898, 1 Day, alarm (E1-161).*
    95.00   115.00   (100.00)

☐ **Satellite,** *rich gold, height 5⅝", dial 1½", spring, c. 1910, 8 Day (E2-36).*
    200.00   220.00   (205.00)

☐ **Tally-Ho Carriage,** *nickel, repeating strike, height 8½", dial 3", spring, c. 1883, 8 Day, strike (E2-8).*
    260.00   300.00   (275.00)

☐ **Tourist,** *nickel, height 7⅛", dial 2½", spring, c. 1910, 1 Day, strike, alarm (E2-36).*
    115.00   135.00   (120.00)

☐ **Vida,** *rich burnished gold, fancy, height 5¼", dial 2", spring, c. 1898, 1 Day (E1-161).*
    50.00   70.00   (55.00)

Pert

ANSONIA CLOCK COMPANY / 93

CHINA OR PORCELAIN
LARGE CASE

☐ **Accomac,** *painted and decorated porcelain, 11½" x 9¾", spring, c. 1898, 8 Day, strike with gong (E1-157).*
    165.00   185.00   (170.00)

☐ **Chemung,** *hand painted and gold decorated cases, ½ hour strike, cathedral gong on sounding board, round polished brass escapement movement, ruby pallets, rack strike, with patent regulator and striking parts, cream porcelain dial, Rococo sash, 10½" x 8", spring, c. 1898, 8 Day (E1-158).*
    160.00   180.00   (160.00)

☐ **Kennebeck,** *hand painted and gold decorated cases, ½ hour strike, cathedral gong on sounding board, round polised brass escapement movement, ruby pallets, rack strike, with patent regulator and striking parts, cream porcelain dial, Rococo sash, 11" x 10½", spring, c. 1898, 8 Day (E1-158).*
    245.00   275.00   (260.00)

☐ **La Bretagne,** *15" x 12½", spring, c. 1910, 8 Day, strike (E2-38).*
    310.00   350.00   (315.00)

La Charny

La Flandre

☐ **La Calle,** *hand painted and gold decorated cases, ½ hour strike, cathedral gong on sounding board, round polished brass escapement movement, ruby pallets, rack strike, with patent regulator and striking parts, cream porcelain dial, Rococo sash, 14½" x 10", spring, c. 1898, 8 Day (E1-158).*
    270.00   300.00   (290.00)

☐ **La Cannes,** *11¾" x 11¼", dial 4", spring, c. 1890, 8 Day, strike (E2-37).*
    270.00   300.00   (290.00)

☐ **La Cette,** *12" x 12", dial 4", spring, c. 1890, 8 Day, strike (E2-37).*
    270.00   300.00   (290.00)

☐ **La Chapelle,** *12" x 12", dial 4", spring, c. 1890, 8 Day, strike (E2-37).*
    295.00   325.00   (300.00)

☐ **La Charny,** *11½" x 11", dial 4", spring, c. 1890, 8 Day, strike (E2-37).*
    270.00   300.00   (290.00)

☐ **La Chartres,** *11¾" x 11¼", dial 4", spring, c. 1890, 8 Day, strike (E2-37).*
    270.00   300.00   (275.00)

94 / ANSONIA CLOCK COMPANY

☐ **La Clair,** *hand painted and gold decorated cases, ½ hour strike, cathedral gong on sounding board, round polished brass escapement movement, ruby pallets, rack strike, with patent regulator and striking parts, cream porcelain dial, Rococo sash, 13" x 9¾", spring, c. 1898, 8 Day (E1-158).*
    270.00   300.00   (275.00)

☐ **La Clairmont,** *11¾" x 10¾", dial 4", spring, c. 1890, 8 Day, strike (E2-37).*
    250.00   280.00   (275.00)

☐ **La Cruz,** *11½" x 8½", dial 4", spring, c. 1910, 8 Day, strike (E2-36).*
    230.00   260.00   (250.00)

☐ **La Flandre,** *14¾" x 12½", dial 4", c. 1910, 8 day, strike (E2-38).*
    310.00   350.00   (320.00)

☐ **La Fleur,** *14" x 12¾", dial 4", spring, c. 1890, 8 Day, strike (E2-37).*
    295.00   325.00   (300.00)

☐ **La Floride,** *14½" x 12½", dial 4", spring, c. 1910, 8 Day, strike (E2-38).*
    260.00   300.00   (275.00)

☐ **La Formose,** *12¾" x 13½", dial 4", spring, c. 1890, 8 Day, strike (E2-37).*
    310.00   350.00   (315.00)

☐ **La France,** *12¾" x 9½", dial 4", spring, c. 1890, 8 Day, strike (E2-37).*
    260.00   300.00   (275.00)

☐ **La Friese,** *10¾" x 12½", dial 4", spring, c. 1890, 8 Day, strike (E2-37).*
    260.00   300.00   (265.00)

☐ **La Gironde,** *13¾" x 11", dial 4", spring, c. 1910, 8 Day, strike (E2-38).*
    250.00   280.00   (265.00)

☐ **La Isere,** *11¾" x 12½", dial 4", spring, c. 1910, 8 Day, strike (E2-38).*
    295.00   325.00   (300.00)

La Formose

☐ **La Layon,** *14½" x 15", dial 4", spring, c. 1910, 8 Day, strike (E2-38).*
    345.00   375.00   (350.00)

☐ **La Manche,** *13¾" x 14", dial 4", spring, c. 1890, 8 Day, strike (E2-37).*
    295.00   325.00   (300.00)

☐ **La Mayenne,** *13½" x 9½", dial 4", spring, c. 1890, 8 Day, strike (E2-37).*
    240.00   280.00   (250.00)

☐ **La Meuse,** *14" x 10½", dial 4", c. 1910, 8 day, strike (E2-38).*
    240.00   280.00   (250.00)

☐ **La Mine,** *14½" x 11¼", dial 4", spring, c. 1910, 8 Day, strike (E2-38).*
    295.00   325.00   (300.00)

☐ **La Moselle,** *14½" x 9", dial 4", spring, c. 1910, 8 Day, strike (E2-38).*
    240.00   280.00   (260.00)

☐ **La Nord,** *11¾" x 14½", dial 4", spring, c. 1910, 8 Day, strike (E2-38).*
    295.00   325.00   (300.00)

☐ **La Orb,** *13" x 14½", dial 4", c. 1890, 8 Day, strike (E2-37).*
    310.00   350.00   (325.00)

☐ **La Palma,** *11⅞" x 14¼", dial 4", spring, c. 1910, 8 Day, strike (E2-38).*
    310.00   350.00   (325.00)

ANSONIA CLOCK COMPANY / 95

- ☐ **La Plaine,** *11½" x 8½", dial 4", spring, c. 1910, 8 Day, strike (E2-36).*
  210.00   240.00   (220.00)

- ☐ **La Plata,** *13" x 14", dial 4", spring, c. 1890, 8 Day, strike (E2-37).*
  310.00   350.00   (340.00)

- ☐ **La Rambla,** *12" x 10", dial 4", spring, c. 1890, 8 Day, strike (E2-37).*
  300.00   315.00   (310.00)

- ☐ **La Riviere,** *12½" x 14½", dial 4", spring, c. 1910, 8 Day, strike (E2-38).*
  295.00   325.00   (300.00)

- ☐ **La Savoie,** *11¼" x 9", dial 4", spring, c. 1910, 8 Day, strike (E2-36).*
  230.00   260.00   (240.00)

- ☐ **La Scarpe,** *11¼" x 9¼", dial 4", spring, c. 1910, 8 Day, strike (E2-36).*
  230.00   260.00   (240.00)

- ☐ **La Sedan,** *11¼" x 9¼", dial 4", spring, c. 1910, 8 Day, strike (E2-36).*
  230.00   260.00   (240.00)

- ☐ **La Seine,** *11½" x 9¾", dial 4", spring, c. 1910, 8 Day, strike (E2-36).*
  230.00   260.00   (240.00)

- ☐ **La Tosca,** *14½" x 10", dial 4", spring, c. 1910, 8 Day, strike (E2-38).*
  310.00   350.00   (325.00)

- ☐ **La Vendee,** *hand painted and gold decorated cases, ½ hour strike, cathedral gong on sounding board, round polished brass escapement movement, ruby pallets, rack strike, with patent regulator and striking parts, cream porcelain dial, Rococo sash, 14½" x 13", spring, c. 1898, 8 Day (E1-158).*
  345.00   375.00   (350.00)

- ☐ **La Verdon,** *hand painted and gold decorated cases, ½ hour strike, cathedral gong on sounding board, round polished brass escapement movement, ruby pallets, rack strike, with patent regulator and striking parts, cream porcelain dial, Rococo sash, 14½" x 13½", spring, c. 1898, 8 Day (E1-158).*
  300.00   340.00   (325.00)

- ☐ **La Vergne,** *11¾" x 14¼", dial 4", c. 1910, 8 day, strike (E2-38).*
  310.00   350.00   (330.00)

La France

La Friese

96 / ANSONIA CLOCK COMPANY

La Orb

☐ **La Vogue,** *hand painted and gold decorated cases, ½ hour strike, cathedral gong on sounding board, round polished brass escapement movement, ruby pallets, rack strike, with patent regulator and striking parts, cream porcelain dial, Rococo sash, 12¾" x 11¼", spring, c. 1898, 8 Day (E1-158).*
    310.00   350.00   (330.00)

☐ **Osceola,** *hand painted and gold decorated cases, ½ hour strike, cathedral gong on sounding board, round polished brass escapement movement, ruby pallets, rack strike, with patent regulator and striking parts, cream porcelain dial, Rococo sash, 11¾" x 13½", spring, c. 1898, 8 Day (E1-158).*
    310.00   350.00   (330.00)

☐ **Ossipee,** *decorated porcelain, 11¾" x 12½", spring, c. 1898, 8 Day, strike (E1-137).*
    240.00   280.00   (250.00)

CHINA OR PORCELAIN
SMALL CASE

☐ **Acme,** *decorated porcelain, height 4½", dial 2", spring, c. 1898, 1 Day, strike (E1-156).*
    35.00   40.00   (37.50)

☐ **Crescent,** *decorated porcelain, height 5¼", dial 2", spring, c. 1898, 1 Day (E1-157).*
    35.00   40.00   (37.50)

☐ **Cuckoo,** *decorated porcelain, height 6", dial 2", spring, c. 1898, 1 Day (E1-157).*
    35.00   40.00   (37.50)

☐ **Flora,** *decorated porcelain, height 4½", dial 2", spring, c. 1898, 1 Day (E1-157).*
    30.00   35.00   (32.50)

☐ **Gannet,** *decorated or delft porcelain, height 6⅞", spring, c. 1898, 1 Day, strike (E1-155).*
    65.00   75.00   (70.00)

☐ **Helena,** *decorated porcelain, height 5¼", dial 2", spring, c. 1898, 1 Day, strike (E1-157).*
    35.00   40.00   (37.50)

CONNECTICUT SHELF
BEE HIVE

☐ **Tudor, V.P.,** *veneered wood, height 19", dial 6", spring, c. 1890, 1 Day, strike (E2-15).*
    115.00   150.00   (130.00)

☐ **As above,** *8 Day, strike.*
    165.00   185.00   (175.00)

Tudor, V.P.

ANSONIA CLOCK COMPANY / 97

CONNECTICUT SHELF/O.G.

- ☐ **O.G.** *weight, veneered, height 26",
  c. 1890, 1 Day (E2-20).*
  135.00   155.00   (140.00)
- ☐ **As above,** *1 Day, alarm.*
  180.00   200.00   (190.00)

- ☐ **O.G.,** *weight, polished and
  veneered oak, height 30", dial 9",
  c. 1898, 1 Day, strike, with weights
  (E1-155).*
  195.00   225.00   (200.00)
- ☐ **As above,** *1 Day, strike, spring.*
  135.00   155.00   (140.00)

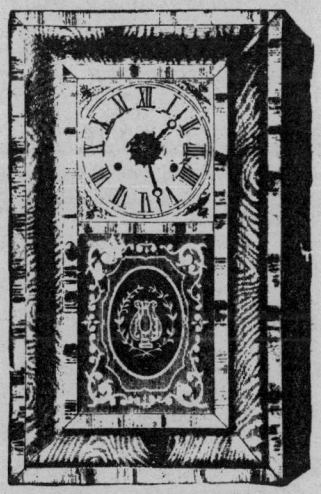

O.G., 1 Day strike

CONNECTICUT/ROUND TOP

- ☐ **Arab,** *veneered wood, height 14",
  spring, c. 1890, 1 Day (E2-15).*
  65.00   85.00   (70.00)
- ☐ **As above,** *1 Day, strike.*
  85.00   105.00   (95.00)
- ☐ **As above,** *8 Day, strike.*
  130.00   150.00   (135.00)

- ☐ **Arcadian,** *veneered wood, height
  18", dial 6", spring, c. 1890, 1 Day,
  strike (E2-15).*
  125.00   145.00   (130.00)
- ☐ **As above,** *8 Day, strike.*
  165.00   185.00   (170.00)

Arcadian

- ☐ **Cottage,** *polished and veneered
  oak, height 12", dial 5", spring,
  c. 1898, 1 Day (E1-155).*
  50.00   70.00   (55.00)
- ☐ **As above,** *1 Day, strike.*
  70.00   90.00   (95.00)

- ☐ **Cottage,** *veneered, height 12",
  spring, c. 1890, 1 Day (E2-20).*
  70.00   90.00   (80.00)
- ☐ **As above,** *1 Day, alarm.*
  90.00   110.00   (95.00)

- ☐ **Cottage Extra,** *polished and
  veneered oak, height 12", dial 6",
  spring, c. 1898, 1 Day, strike
  (E-155).*
  60.00   80.00   (70.00)
- ☐ **As above,** *8 Day, strike.*
  80.00   100.00   (90.00)

- ☐ **Cottage Extra,** *veneered, height
  13", spring, c. 1890, 1 Day, strike
  (E2-20).*
  70.00   90.00   (80.00)
- ☐ **As above,** *1 Day, strike, alarm.*
  90.00   110.00   (100.00)

98 / ANSONIA CLOCK COMPANY

Flint

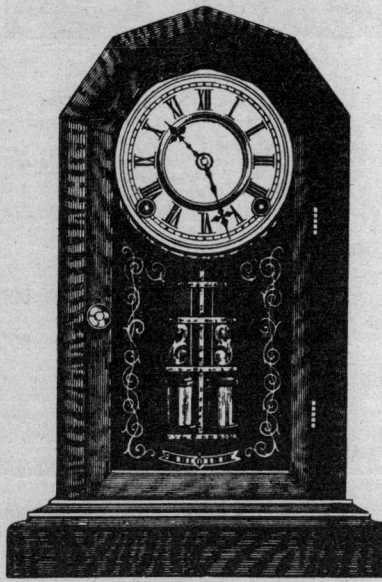

Theban

☐ **Flint,** *wood, height 19½", dial 5½", spring, c. 1890, 1 Day, strike (E2-15).*
    115.00   135.00   (120.00)
☐ **As above,** *8 Day, strike.*
    165.00   185.00   (170.00)

☐ **Standard,** *veneered wood, height 18½", dial 6", spring, c. 1890, 1 Day, strike (E2-15).*
    115.00   135.00   (120.00)
☐ **As above,** *8 Day, strike.*
    165.00   185.00   (175.00)

☐ **Theban,** *veneered wood, height 18½", dial 6", spring, c. 1890, 1 Day, strike (E2-15).*
    115.00   135.00   (120.00)
☐ **As above,** *8 Day, strike.*
    165.00   185.00   (170.00)

CONNECTICUT/SPLIT TOP

☐ **Maud,** *veneered wood, height 19", dial 6", spring, c. 1890, 1 Day, strike (E2-15).*
    105.00   125.00   (110.00)
☐ **As above,** *8 Day, strike.*
    155.00   175.00   (160.00)

☐ **Neptune,** *veneered wood, height 15", dial 5", c. 1890, 1 Day, strike (E2-15).*
    115.00   135.00   (120.00)
☐ **As above,** *8 Day, strike.*
    145.00   165.00   (150.00)

☐ **Neptune,** *walnut, height 15", spring, c. 1890, 1 Day, strike or alarm (E2-20).*
    115.00   135.00   (120.00)

☐ **Pansy,** *wood, height 15", dial 5", spring, c. 1890, 1 Day, strike (E2-15).*
    115.00   135.00   (120.00)
☐ **As above,** *8 Day, strike.*
    145.00   165.00   (150.00)

☐ **Spartan,** *walnut veneered, height 18½", dial 6", spring, c. 1891, 1 Day, strike (E2-21).*
    110.00   130.00   (115.00)
☐ **As above,** *1 Day, strike, alarm.*
    130.00   150.00   (135.00)

ANSONIA CLOCK COMPANY / 99

Spartan

☐ **Sharp Gothic,** V.P., *veneered wood, height 19½", dial 6", spring, c. 1890, 1 Day, strike (E2-15).*
    130.00   150.00   (140.00)
☐ **As above,** *8 Day, strike*
    180.00   200.00   (190.00)

☐ **Small Sharp Gothic,** *veneered wood, height 15", dial 4½", spring, c. 1890, 1 Day (E2-15).*
    105.00   135.00   (115.00)
☐ **As above,** *1 Day, alarm.*
    105.00   135.00   (115.00)
☐ **As above,** *1 Day, strike.*
    145.00   165.00   (150.00)

☐ **Small Sharp Gothic,** *polished and veneered oak, height 16", dial 4½", spring, c. 1898, 1 Day (E1-155).*
    80.00   100.00   (85.00)
☐ **As above,** *1 Day, strike.*
    100.00   120.00   (110.00)

☐ **Spartan,** *veneered wood, height 18½", dial 6", spring, c. 1890, 1 Day, strike (E2-15).*
    95.00   125.00   (100.00)
☐ **As above,** *8 Day, strike.*
    145.00   165.00   (150.00)

CONNECTICUT SHELF/STEEPLE

☐ **Decorated Gothic,** *veneered wood, bronze ornaments, height 20", dial 6", spring, c. 1890, 1 Day, strike (E2-15).*
    130.00   150.00   (140.00)
☐ **As above,** *8 Day, strike.*
    180.00   200.00   (190.00)

☐ **Sharp Gothic,** V. P., *polished and veneered oak, height 19½", dial 6", spring, c. 1898, 1 Day, strike (E1-155).*
    130.00   150.00   (135.00)
☐ **As above,** *8 Day, strike.*
    180.00   200.00   (190.00)

☐ **Sharp Gothic,** V.P., *veneered, spring, c. 1890, 1 Day, strike, or 1 Day, alarm (E2-20).*
    130.00   150.00   (135.00)

Sharp Gothic

100 / ANSONIA CLOCK COMPANY

CRYSTAL PALACE

- **Crystal Palace No.1,** *extra, glass covered, height 18½", spring, c. 1890, 8 Day, strike (E2-22).*
  575.00   650.00   (600.00)
- **As above,** *without dome.*
  375.00   450.00   (400.00)

- **Crystal Palace No.2,** *extra, glass covered, height 20", dial 6", spring, c. 1896, 8 Day, hour and ½ hour strike, cathedral gong movement (E2-14).*
  100.00   600.00   (650.00)
- **As above,** *without dome.*
  500.00   550.00   (525.00)

CRYSTAL REGULATOR

- **Acme,** *porcelain dial, white beveled plate glass front, back and sides, 10¾" x 6⅞", dial 4", c. 1910, 8 Day, strike, polished brass (E1-134).*
  165.00   190.00   (170.00)
- **As above,** *gold plated.*
  195.00   215.00   (200.00)

- **Admiral,** *visible escapement, porcelain dial, white beveled plate glass front, back and sides, green onyx top and base, 18" x 10", dial 4", c. 1910, 8 Day, strike (E1-133).*
  950.00   1200.00   (1000.00)

- **Ambassador,** *visible escapement, porcelain dial, white beveled plate glass front, back and sides, green onyx top and base, 11½" x 7¼", dial 4", c. 1910, 8 Day, strike (E1-133).*
  310.00   350.00   (400.00)

- **Apex,** *rich gold, visible escapement, porcelain dial, white beveled plate glass front, back and sides, 18½" x 10½", dial 4", c. 1910, 8 Day, strike (E1-138).*
  2350.00   2500.00   (2400.00)

- **Aquitaine,** *rich gold plated, beveled white plate glass back door, pendulum visible through beveled white plate glass panel, 11¾" x 6¼", dial 4", c. 1917, 8 Day, strike (E1-180).*
  265.00   305.00   (275.00)

Crystal Palace No. 1

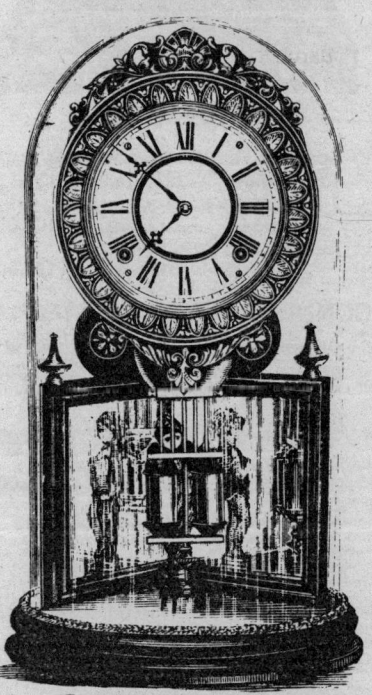

Crystal Palace No. 2

ANSONIA CLOCK COMPANY / 101

Claudius

☐ **Baronet,** *polished brass, rich gold ornaments, visible escapement, porcelain dial, white beveled plate glass front, back and sides, 12½" x 7½", dial 4", c. 1910, 8 Day, strike (E1-138).*
360.00   400.00   (375.00)

☐ **Blazon,** *visible escapement, porcelain dial, white beveled plate glass front, back and sides, green onyx top and base, 13¼" x 8", dial 4", c. 1910, 8 Day, strike (E1-133).*
460.00   520.00   (475.00)

☐ **Carlton,** *visible escapement, porcelain dial, white beveled plate glass front, back and sides, 10½" x 7", dial 4", c. 1910, 8 Day, strike, polished brass (E1-134).*
160.00   185.00   (165.00)
☐ **As above,** *gold plated.*
190.00   210.00   (195.00)

☐ **Cavalier,** *visible escapement, porcelain dial, white beveled plate glass front, back and sides, green onyx top and base, 12" x 8", dial 4", c. 1910, 8 Day, strike (E1-135).*
410.00   460.00   (425.00)

☐ **Cetus,** *visible escapement, porcelain dial, white beveled plate glass front, back and sides, 11" x 6⅝", dial 4", c. 1910, 8 Day, strike, polished brass (E1-134).*
190.00   210.00   (200.00)
☐ **As above,** *gold plated.*
205.00   235.00   (215.00)

☐ **Chancellor,** *visible escapement, porcelain dial, white beveled plate glass front, back and sides, green onyx top and base, 13" x 7½", dial 4", c. 1910, 8 Day, strike (E1-133).*
425.00   475.00   (430.00)

☐ **Claudius,** *porcelain dial, white beveled plate glass front, back and sides, 11¼" x 7", dial 4", c. 1910, 8 Day, strike, gold plated (E1-134).*
190.00   210.00   (200.00)

☐ **Clifton,** *visible escapement, porcelain dial, white beleved plate glass front, back and sides, 10¼" x 6½", dial 4", c. 1910, 8 Day, strike, polished brass (E1-134).*
190.00   210.00   (200.00)
☐ **As above,** *gold plated.*
205.00   235.00   (215.00)

☐ **Colby,** *porcelain dial, white beveled plate glass front, back and sides, 10¾" x 6¾", dial 4", c. 1910, 8 Day, strike, polished brass (E1-134).*
195.00   225.00   (200.00)
☐ **As above,** *gold plated.*
220.00   250.00   (240.00)

☐ **Consort,** *visible escapement, porcelain dial, white beveled plate glass front, back and sides, green onyx top and base, 16" x 8", dial 4", c. 1910, 8 Day, strike (E1-133).*
540.00   600.00   (575.00)

☐ **Consul,** *visible escapement, porcelain dial, white beveled plate glass front, back and sides, green onyx top and base, 13" x 7¾", dial 4", c. 1910, 8 Day, strike, polished brass (E1-138).*
270.00   310.00   (280.00)

Excelsior

☐ **Coral,** *porcelain dial, white beveled plate glass front, back and sides, 9¾" x 6⅜", dial 2", c. 1910, 8 Day, strike, polished brass (E1-134).*
140.00   165.00   (145.00)
☐ **As above,** *gold plated.*
165.00   190.00   (175.00)

☐ **Corona,** *visible escapement, porcelain dial, white beveled plate glass front, back and sides, 11½" x 6⅞", dial 4", c. 1910, 8 Day, strike, polished brass (E1-134).*
175.00   205.00   (180.00)
☐ **As above,** *gold plated.*
200.00   230.00   (215.00)

☐ **Cosmo,** *visible escapement, porcelain dial, white beveled plate glass front, back and sides, green onyx top and base, 15¼" x 8", dial 4", c. 1910, 8 Day, strike (E1-135).*
610.00   685.00   (630.00)

Marchioness

☐ **Count,** *visible escapement, porcelain dial, white beveled plate glass front, back and sides, 16½" x 8", dial 4", c. 1910, 8 Day, strike (E1-133).*
515.00   575.00   (550.00)

☐ **Danube,** *rich gold plate, beveled plate glass front, back and sides, porcelain dial, 9" x 7¾", dial 3", c. 1917, 8 Day, strike (E1-180).*
190.00   210.00   (200.00)

☐ **Dawson,** *porcelain dial, white beveled plate glass front, back and sides, 9¼" x 5⅞", dial 3", c. 1910, 8 Day, strike, polished brass (E1-135).*
145.00   170.00   (150.00)
☐ **As above,** *gold plated.*
165.00   190.00   (180.00)

☐ **Delta,** *porcelain dial, white beveled plate glass front, back and sides, 9¼" x 5⅝", dial 3", c. 1910, 8 Day, strike, polished brass (E1-135).*
135.00   160.00   (160.00)
☐ **As above,** *gold plated.*
155.00   180.00   (140.00)

ANSONIA CLOCK COMPANY / 103

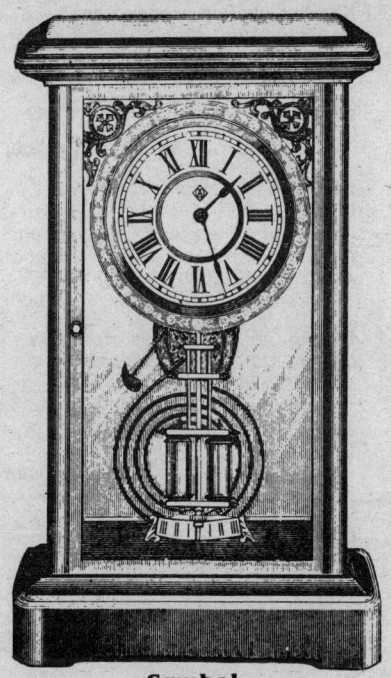

Symbol

☐ **Deputy**, *visible escapement, porcelain dial, white beveled plate glass front, back and sides, green onyx top and base, 13¼" x 7¾", dial 4", c. 1910, 8 Day, strike (E1-133).*
490.00   550.00   (500.00)

☐ **Diplomat**, *polished brass, rich gold ornaments, visible escapement, porcelain dial, white beveled plate glass front, back and sides, 18¼" x 7¾", dial 4½", c. 1910, 8 Day, strike (E1-138).*
450.00   500.00   (600.00)

☐ **Dolphin**, *porcelain dial, white beveled plate glass front, back and sides, 9¼" x 5⅝", dial 3", c. 1910, 8 Day, strike, polished brass (E1-133).*
135.00   160.00   (140.00)
☐ **As above**, *gold plated.*
155.00   180.00   (160.00)

Symbol No. 2

☐ **Doria**, *rich gold plate, convex glass front, beveled plate glass sides and back, plain porcelain dial, 8⅞" x 6", dial 3", c. 1917, 8 Day, strike (E1-180).*
165.00   190.00   (185.00)

☐ **Dorval**, *porcelain dial, white beveled plate glass front, back and sides, 8⅞" x 5⅝", dial 3", c. 1910, 8 Day, strike, polished brass (E1-135).*
130.00   155.00   (140.00)
☐ **As above**, *gold plated.*
150.00   175.00   (160.00)
☐ **Duchess**, *visible escapement, porcelain dial, white beveled plate glass front, back and sides, green onyx top and base, 11" x 7¼", dial 4", c. 1910, 8 Day, strike (E1-133).*
310.00   350.00   (325.00)

104 / ANSONIA CLOCK COMPANY

- **Dunbar,** *porcelain dial, white beveled plate glass front, back and sides, 9⅛" x 5⅝", dial 3", c. 1910, 8 Day, strike, polished brass (E1-135).*
  135.00   160.00   (145.00)
- **As above,** *gold plated.*
  155.00   180.00   (160.00)
- **Envoy,** *polished brass, rich gold ornaments, visible escapement, porcelain dial, white beveled plate glass front, back and sides, 19" x 9¾", dial 4", c. 1910, 8 Day, strike (E1-138).*
  535.00   610.00   (550.00)
- **Escutcheon,** *visible escapement, porcelain dial, white beveled plate glass front, back and sides, green onyx top and base, 13¾" x 8⅛", dial 4", c. 1910, 8 Day, strike (E1-133).*
  400.00   450.00   (425.00)
- **Eulogy,** *rich gold, visible escapement, porcelain dial, white beveled plate glass front, back and sides, 19½" x 9¼", dial 4", c. 1910, 8 Day, strike (E1-138).*
  675.00   750.00   (700.00)
- **Excelsior,** *gilt or silver finish, height 20½", dial 5½", hour and ½ hour strike, cathedral gong movement, c. 1896, 8 Day (E2-14).*
  850.00   1100.00   (900.00)
- **Floral,** *rich gold, visible escapement, porcelain dial, white beveled plate glass front, back and sides, 16½" x 8¾", dial 4", c. 1910, 8 Day, strike (E1-138).*
  900.00   1000.00   (950.00)
- **Gardant,** *visible escapement, porcelain dial, white beveled plate glass front, back and sides, green onyx top and base, 16¼" x 9", dial 4", c. 1910, 8 Day, strike (E1-133).*
  625.00   700.00   (650.00)
- **Griffin,** *visible escapement, porcelain dial, white beveled plate glass front, back and sides, green onyx top and base, 13" x 8¾", dial 4", c. 1910, 8 Day, strike (E1-135).*
  450.00   500.00   (475.00)

- **Khedive,** *visible escapement, porcelain dial, white beveled plate glass front, back and sides, green onyx top and base, 14¼" x 8⅛", dial 4", c. 1910, 8 Day, strike (E1-135).*
  565.00   640.00   (600.00)
- **Laureate,** *visible escapement, porcelain dial, white beveled plate glass front, back and sides, green onyx top and base, 16" x 8", dial 4", c. 1910, 8 Day, strike (E1-135).*
  625.00   700.00   (650.00)
- **Legate,** *polished brass, rich gold ornaments, visible escapement, porcelain dial, white beveled plate glass front, back and sides, 14¼" x 9¾", dial 4½", c. 1910, 8 Day, strike (E1-138).*
  425.00   475.00   (450.00)
- **Marchioness,** *polished brass, rich gold ornaments, visible escapement, porcelain dial, white beveled plate glass front, back and sides, 15¾" x 8¼", dial 4", c. 1910, 8 Day, strike (E1-136).*
  725.00   800.00   (750.00)
- **Marquis,** *polished brass, rich gold ornaments, visible escapement, porcelain dial, white beveled plate glass front, back and sides, 15½" x 7½", dial 4", c. 1910, 8 Day, strike (E1-136).*
  625.00   700.00   (650.00)
- **Octavia,** *porcelain dial, white beveled plate glass front, back and sides, 12¼" x 7⅝", dial 4", c. 1910, 8 Day, strike, gold plated (E1-138).*
  295.00   335.00   (300.00)
- **Oriel,** *visible escapement, porcelain dial, white beveled plate glass front, back and sides, 13¾" x 6⅞", dial 4", c. 1910, 8 Day, strike, polished brass (E1-134).*
  210.00   240.00   (225.00)
- **As above,** *gold plated.*
  235.00   265.00   (240.00)

ANSONIA CLOCK COMPANY / 105

☐ **Premier,** *visible escapement, porcelain dial, white beveled plate glass front, back and sides, green onyx top and base, 13¾" x 8", dial 4", c. 1910, 8 Day, strike (E1-133).*
    440.00   490.00   (450.00)

☐ **Prince,** *visible escapement, porcelain dial, white beveled plate glass front, back and sides, green onyx top and base, 15" x 8½", dial 4", c. 1910, 8 Day, strike (E1-135).*
    635.00   710.00   (650.00)

☐ **Prism,** *visible escapement, porcelain dial, white beveled plate glass front, back and sides, green onyx top and base, 10¾" x 6⅜", dial 4", c. 1910, 8 Day, strike, polished brass (E1-134).*
    160.00   185.00   (175.00)
☐ **As above,** *gold plated.*
    180.00   210.00   (185.00)

☐ **Provence,** *visible escapement, porcelain dial, white beveled plate glass front, back and sides, 11" x 6½", dial 4", c. 1910, 8 Day, strike, polished brass (E1-134).*
    195.00   225.00   (200.00)
☐ **As above,** *gold plated.*
    220.00   250.00   (225.00)

☐ **Queen,** *visible escapement, porcelain dial, white beveled plate glass front, back and sides, green onyx top and base, 13½" x 8⅛", dial 4", c. 1910, 8 Day, strike (E1-135).*
    430.00   480.00   (450.00)

☐ **Radiant,** *visible escapement, porcelain dial, white beveled plate glass front, back and sides, green onyx top and base, 17" x 9¼", dial 4", c. 1910, 8 Day, strike (E1-133).*
    645.00   720.00   (650.00)

☐ **Rampant,** *visible escapement, porcelain dial, white beveled plate glass front, back and sides, 13¾" x 9", dial 4", c. 1910, 8 Day, strike (E1-135).*
    540.00   600.00   (550.00)

Vulcan

☐ **Regis,** *visible escapement, porcelain dial, white beveled plate glass front, back and sides, 11½" x 8", dial 4", convex front and sides, c. 1910, 8 Day, strike, gold plated (E1-138).*
    270.00   310.00   (290.00)

☐ **Renaissance,** *visible escapement, porcelain dial, white beveled plate glass front, back and sides, 16½" x 8", dial 4", c. 1910, 8 Day, strike, rich gold (E1-138).*
    665.00   740.00   (700.00)

☐ **Rouen,** *porcelain dial, white beveled plate glass front, back and sides, 11" x 6¾", dial 4", c. 1910, 8 Day, strike, polished brass (E1-134).*
    190.00   220.00   (200.00)
☐ **As above,** *gold plated.*
    215.00   245.00   (225.00)

☐ **Roy,** *porcelain dial, white beveled plate glass front, back and sides, convex front, 11⅛" x 7¼", dial 4", c. 1910, 8 Day, strike, polished brass (E1-134).*
    195.00   225.00   (200.00)
☐ **As above,** *gold plated.*
    220.00   250.00   (235.00)

106 / ANSONIA CLOCK COMPANY

- **Sirius,** *visible escapement, porcelain dial, white beveled plate glass front, back and sides, 13" x 9", dial 4", polished brass, rich gold ornaments, c. 1910, 8 Day, strike (E1-138).*
  900.00   1000.00   (950.00)

- **Symbol,** *gilt or silver finish, height 20", dial 6", hour and ½ hour strike, cathedral gong movement, c. 1896, 8 Day (E2-14).*
  400.00   450.00   (425.00)

- **Symbol Extra,** *gilt or silver finish, height 15¼", dial 5½", hour and ½ hour strike, cathedral gong movement, c. 1896, 8 Day (E2-14).*
  465.00   525.00   (485.00)

- **Symbol No.1,** *gilt or silver finish, height 22", dial 6", hour and ½ hour strike, cathedral gong movement, c. 1896, 8 Day (E2-14).*
  465.00   525.00   (475.00)

- **Symbol No.2,** *gilt or silver finish, height 15½", dial 5", hour and ½ hour strike, cathedral gong movement, c. 1896, 8 Day (E2-14).*
  425.00   475.00   (450.00)

- **Touraine,** *rich gold plated, beveled white plate glass back door, pendulum visible through beveled white plate glass panel, 11" x 6¼", dial 4", c. 1917, 8 Day, strike (E1-180).*
  260.00   295.00   (275.00)

- **Viceroy,** *polished brass, rich gold ornaments, visible escapement, porcelain dial, white beveled plate glass front, back and sides, 16" x 8¼", dial 4", c. 1910, 8 Day, strike (E1-136).*
  625.00   700.00   (650.00)

- **Viscount,** *polished brass, rich gold ornaments, visible escapement, porcelain dial, white beveled plate glass front, back and sides, 16" x 8¼", dial 4", c. 1910, 8 Day, strike (E1-136).*
  645.00   720.00   (675.00)

- **Vulcan,** *porcelain dial, white beveled plate glass front, back and sides, 12¼" x 7½", dial 4", c. 1910, 8 Day, strike, rich gold (E1-134).*
  205.00   235.00   (215.00)

- **Wanda,** *visible escapement, porcelain dial, white beveled plate glass front, back and sides, 11¼" x 6⅝", dial 4", c. 1910, 8 Day, strike, polished brass (E1-134).*
  180.00   210.00   (185.00)

- **As above,** *gold plated.*
  205.00   235.00   (215.00)

CRYSTAL REGULATOR PORCELAIN

- **Porcelain Regulator No.1,** *visible escapement, porcelain dial, white beveled plate glass front, back and sides, Bonn decorated top and bases, 17½" x 9", dial 4", spring, c. 1910, 8 Day, strike (E1-136).*
  1250.00   1550.00   (1400.00)

Porcelain Regulator No. 3

ANSONIA CLOCK COMPANY / 107

☐ **Porcelain Regulator No.2,** *visible escapement, porcelain dial, white beveled plate glass front, back and sides, Bonn decorated top and bases, 17½" x 9¼", dial 4", spring, c. 1910, 8 Day, strike (E1-136).*
    1175.00   1425.00   (1300.00)

☐ **Porcelain Regulator No.3,** *visible escapement, porcelain dial, white beveled plate glass front, back and sides, Bonn decorated top and base, 18¼" x 9¼", dial 4", spring, c. 1910, 8 Day, strike (E1-136).*
    1250.00   1500.00   (1300.00)

☐ **Porcelain Regulator No.4,** *visible escapement, porcelain dial, white beveled plate glass front, back and sides, Bonn decorated top and base, 17¾" x 9½", dial 4", spring, c. 1910, 8 Day, strike (E1-136).*
    1150.00   1400.00   (1250.00)

☐ **Porcelain Regulator No.5,** *visible escapement, porcelain dial, white beveled plate glass front, back and sides, Bonn decorated top and base, 17½" x 8½", dial 4", spring, c. 1910, 8 Day, strike (E1-136).*
    1160.00   1410.00   (1250.00)

☐ **Porcelain Regulator No.6,** *visible escapement, porcelain dial, white beveled plate glass front, back and sides, Bonn decorated top and base, 17½" x 9", dial 4", spring, c. 1910, 8 Day, strike (E1-136).*
    1185.00   1435.00   (1250.00)

GALLERY

☐ **Ansonia Lever,** *walnut, dial 12", spring, c. 1900, 8 Day (E2-24).*
    135.00   160.00   (140.00)
☐ **As above,** *8 Day, strike.*
    155.00   180.00   (160.00)

☐ **Foyer No.1,** *antique oak or oak, height 39", dial 18", pendulum, c. 1890, 8 Day (E2-28).*
    220.00   250.00   (230.00)
☐ **As above,** *8 Day, strike.*
    245.00   275.00   (250.00)
☐ **As above,** *30 Day.*
    360.00   400.00   (375.00)

Porcelain Regulator No. 5

Foyer No. 4

108 / ANSONIA CLOCK COMPANY

☐ **Foyer No.2,** *antique oak or oak, height 32½", dial 14", pendulum, c. 1890, 8 Day (E2-28).*
  175.00 200.00 (195.00)
☐ **As above,** *8 Day, strike.*
  195.00 225.00 (200.00)
☐ **As above,** *30 Day.*
  270.00 300.00 (275.00)

☐ **Foyer No.3,** *antique oak or oak, height 25½", dial 12", pendulum, c. 1890, 8 Day (E2-28).*
  155.00 180.00 (160.00)
☐ **As above,** *8 Day, strike.*
  175.00 200.00 (180.00)

☐ **Foyer No.4,** *dark wood, oak, height 23", dial 12", pendulum, c. 1890, 8 Day (E2-28).*
  150.00 175.00 (160.00)
☐ **As above,** *8 Day, strike.*
  175.00 200.00 (195.00)

GRANDFATHER

☐ **Antique Standing,** *mahogany, oak, antique brass trimming, weight, height 94", gilt and silvered dial 10", c. 1910, 8 Day, strike (E2-42).*
  5400.00 6000.00 (5800.00)

☐ **Antique Standing No.2,** *mahogany, oak, heavy brass, with raised numerals on raised silvered circle, gilt center, pierced corners, moon disk, showing moon changes, weight, antique brass trimmings, height 104", dial 12", c. 1910, 8 Day, strike (E2-42).*
  5000.00 5500.00 (5250.00)

☐ **Antique Standing No.3,** *mahogany, oak, heavy brass, with raised numerals on raised silvered circle, gilt center, pierced corners, moon disk, showing moon changes, antique brass trimmings, weight, height 100", dial 12", c. 1910, 8 Day, strike (E2-42).*
  5000.00 5500.00 (5250.00)

☐ **Antique Standing No.5,** *mahogany, oak, brass ornaments, weight, height 93", gilt and silvered dial 12", c. 1910, 8 Day, strike (E2-42).*
  3150.00 3500.00 (3400.00)

Antique Standing

ANSONIA CLOCK COMPANY / 109

KITCHEN

Antique Standing No. 3

- **Aspen,** walnut, 22" x 14¼", dial 6", spring wound, c. 1900, 8 Day, strike (E2-24).
  150.00   175.00   (160.00)
- As above, Arlington.
  150.00   175.00   (160.00)
- As above, Arden.
  150.00   175.00   (160.00)
- As above, Antler.
  150.00   175.00   (160.00)
- As above, Arctic.
  150.00   175.00   (160.00)
- As above, Andes.
  150.00   175.00   (160.00)

- **Aspen,** oak, 22" x 14¼", dial 6", spring wound, c. 1900, 8 Day, strike (E2-24).
  125.00   150.00   (140.00)
- As above, Arlington.
  125.00   150.00   (140.00)
- As above, Arden.
  125.00   150.00   (140.00)
- As above, Antler.
  125.00   150.00   (140.00)
- As above, Arctic.
  125.00   150.00   (140.00)
- As above, Andes.
  125.00   150.00   (140.00)

- **Ada,** dark wood or oak, height 22½", dial 5", c. 1890, 8 Day hour and ½ hour strike (E2-16).
  175.00   200.00   (185.00)

- **Adelaide,** dark wood or oak, height 24", dial 6", spring wound, c. 1900, 8 Day, strike, calendar (E2-25).
  250.00   280.00   (265.00)

- **Aden,** walnut, height 21", dial 6", spring wound, c. 1890, 8 Day, strike, spring alarm (E2-20).
  150.00   175.00   (160.00)

- **Africa,** walnut, height 21", dial 6", spring wound, c. 1890, 8 Day, strike, spring alarm (E2-20).
  145.00   170.00   (160.00)

- **Agnes,** dark wood or oak, height 21", dial 5", spring wound, c. 1890, 8 Day, hour and ½ hour strike (E2-16).
  175.00   200.00   (185.00)

110 / ANSONIA CLOCK COMPANY

Aspen

☐ **Alaska,** walnut, height 21", dial 6", spring wound, c. 1890, 8 Day, strike, spring, alarm (E2-20).
    145.00   175.00   (155.00)

☐ **Amazon,** antique oak, height 19", spring wound, c. 1890, 8 Day, strike (E2-22).
    115.00   140.00   (125.00)

☐ **As above,** 8 Day, strike, spring alarm.
    135.00   160.00   (140.00)

☐ **America,** walnut, height 21", dial 6", spring wound, c. 1890, 8 Day, strike, spring alarm (E2-20).
    160.00   185.00   (175.00)

☐ **Amy,** dark wood or oak, height 21½", dial 5", spring wound, c. 1890, 8 Day, hour and ½ hour strike (E2-16).
    160.00   185.00   (165.00)

☐ **Arabia,** walnut, height 21", dial 6", spring wound, c. 1890, 8 Day, strike (E2-19).
    150.00   175.00   (170.00)

☐ **Atlas,** walnut, height 21", dial 6", spring wound, c. 1890, 8 Day, strike (E2-19).
    165.00   190.00   (170.00)

☐ **Aurania,** walnut, height 20", dial 6", spring wound, c. 1890, 8 Day, strike (E2-19).
    115.00   140.00   (125.00)

☐ **Austria,** walnut, height 21", dial 6", spring wound, c. 1890, 8 Day, strike, alarm (E2-20).
    150.00   175.00   (160.00)

☐ **Australia,** dark wood or oak, height 21", dial 6", spring wound, c. 1890, 8 Day, strike (E2-18).
    150.00   175.00   (160.00)

☐ **Baltic,** walnut, height 19", dial 6", spring wound, c. 1890, 1 Day, strike (E2-19).
    110.00   135.00   (120.00)

☐ **Blackbird,** ebonized case, spring wound, c. 1890, 1 Day, strike, spring, and 8 Day, strike (E2-17).
    165.00   190.00   (175.00)

Ada

☐ **Blanche,** *dark wood or oak, height 23", dial 6", spring wound, c. 1890, 8 Day, hour and ½ hour strike (E2-16).*
    175.00   200.00   (185.00)

☐ **Britannic,** *walnut, height 20", dial 6", spring wound, c. 1890, 1 Day, strike, spring (E2-21).*
    105.00   130.00   (120.00)

☐ **As above,** *1 Day, strike, alarm.*
    125.00   150.00   (130.00)

☐ **Belgrade,** *dark wood or oak, height 24", dial 6", spring wound, c. 1900, 8 Day, hour and ½ hour strike (E2-25).*
    230.00   260.00   (240.00)

☐ **Canada,** *walnut, height 21", dial 5½", spring wound, c. 1891, 1 Day, strike, spring (E2-21).*
    105.00   130.00   (115.00)

☐ **As above,** *1 Day, strike, spring, alarm.*
    125.00   150.00   (135.00)

☐ **Carlos,** *dark wood or oak, height 24½", dial 6", spring wound, c. 1900, 8 Day, strike, calendar (E2-25).*
    250.00   280.00   (275.00)

☐ **Celtic,** *walnut, height 19", dial 6", spring wound, c. 1890, 1 Day, strike (E2-19).*
    110.00   135.00   (125.00)

☐ **Chicago,** *antique oak, height 21¼", spring wound, c. 1890, 8 Day, strike, spring (E2-22).*
    165.00   190.00   (185.00)

☐ **As above,** *8 Day, strike, spring alarm.*
    180.00   210.00   (200.00)

☐ **Clara,** *dark wood or oak, height 23", dial 6", spring wound, c. 1890, 8 Day, hour and ½ hour strike (E2-17).*
    160.00   185.00   (165.00)

☐ **Colon,** *walnut, height 24", dial 6", spring wound, c. 1890, 8 Day, strike (E2-19).*
    190.00   220.00   (200.00)

Adelaide

Africa

☐ **Colorado,** *walnut, height 25", dial 6", spring wound, c. 1890, 8 Day, strike (E2-22).*
    165.00   180.00   (175.00)

☐ **As above,** *8 Day, strike, alarm.*
    180.00   210.00   (190.00)

112 / ANSONIA CLOCK COMPANY

Agnes

☐ **Cuba,** *black walnut, height 24½", dial 6", spring wound, c. 1890, 8 Day, strike (E2-17).*
175.00   200.00   (185.00)

☐ **Epsom,** *dark wood or oak, height 19", dial 5", spring wound, c. 1890, 8 Day, hour and ½ hour strike (E2-17).*
165.00   190.00   (180.00)

☐ **Ranger,** *dark wood or oak, height 19", dial 5", spring wound, c. 1890, 8 Day, hour and ½ hour strike (E2-17).*
160.00   185.00   (170.00)

☐ **Embossed,** *dark wood or oak, height 21", dial 5", spring wound, c. 1890, 8 Day, hour and ½ hour strike (E2-17).*
160.00   185.00   (165.00)

☐ **Express,** *walnut, height 21", dial 6", spring wound, c. 1890, 8 Day, strike (E2-18).*
165.00   190.00   (175.00)

☐ **Farragut,** *dark wood or oak, height 22", dial 6", spring wound, c. 1890, 8 Day, strike (E2-18).*
155.00   180.00   (175.00)

☐ **Fulda,** *walnut, height 21", dial 6", spring wound, c. 1890, 1 Day, strike (E2-19).*
115.00   140.00   (125.00)

☐ **Fulda,** *walnut, height 21", dial 6", spring wound, c. 1891, 8 Day, strike, spring (E2-21).*
105.00   130.00   (115.00)

☐ **As above,** *1 Day, strike, spring, alarm.*
125.00   150.00   (130.00)

☐ **Fulton,** *walnut, height 21", dial 6", spring wound, c. 1890, 8 Day, strike (E2-18).*
165.00   190.00   (175.00)

☐ **Galena,** *walnut, height 21", dial 6", spring wound, c. 1890, 8 Day, strike (E2-18).*
165.00   190.00   (175.00)

☐ **Gallant,** *black walnut, height 22½", dial 6", spring wound, c. 1890, 8 Day, strike (E2-18).*
155.00   180.00   (160.00)

☐ **Globe,** *walnut, height 19", dial 6", spring wound, c. 1890, 1 Day, strike (E2-18).*
155.00   180.00   (160.00)

☐ **As above,** *8 Day, strike.*
200.00   230.00   (225.00)

☐ **Hampshire,** *walnut, height 23", dial 6", spring wound, c. 1890, 8 Day, strike (E2-21).*
145.00   170.00   (150.00)

☐ **As above,** *8 Day, strike, alarm.*
165.00   190.00   (170.00)

☐ **Herald,** *hand painted decoration, height 16½", dial 5", spring wound, c. 1890, 1 Day, strike and 8 Day, strike (E2-19).*
125.00   150.00   (130.00)

☐ **Hudson,** *antique oak, height 21½", spring wound, c. 1890, 8 Day, strike, spring (E2-22).*
125.00   150.00   (130.00)

☐ **As above,** *8 Day, strike, spring, alarm.*
145.00   170.00   (150.00)

ANSONIA CLOCK COMPANY / 113

- ☐ **Idaho,** *walnut, height 22¼", dial 6", spring wound, c. 1890, 8 Day, strike (E2-22).*
  135.00   160.00   (140.00)
- ☐ **As above,** *8 Day, strike, alarm.*
  155.00   180.00   (160.00)

- ☐ **Illinois,** *walnut, height 22", dial 6", spring wound, c. 1890, 8 Day, strike (E2-22).*
  135.00   155.00   (145.00)
- ☐ **As above,** *8 Day, strike, alarm.*
  155.00   180.00   (170.00)

- ☐ **Ingomar,** *walnut, height 22", dial 6", spring wound, c. 1890, 8 Day, strike (E2-18).*
  170.00   195.00   (180.00)
- ☐ **As above,** *ash.*
  220.00   245.00   (230.00)

- ☐ **Iowa,** *walnut, height 22¼", dial 6", spring wound, c. 1890, 8 Day, strike (E2-22).*
  135.00   160.00   (150.00)
- ☐ **As above,** *8 Day, strike, alarm.*
  155.00   180.00   (160.00)

- ☐ **Japan,** *walnut, height 19", dial 6", spring wound, c. 1890, 1 Day, strike and 8 Day, strike (E2-19).*
  115.00   140.00   (125.00)

Blackbird

Amy

Clara

114 / ANSONIA CLOCK COMPANY

☐ **Julia,** *dark wood, height 19", dial 5", spring wound, c. 1890, 8 Day, hour and ½ hour strike (E2-16).*
    160.00   185.00   (170.00)

☐ **"K" Assortment,** *Kenmore, oak, height 22½" x 14½", dial 6", spring wound, c. 1900, 8 Day, strike (E2-24).*
    145.00   170.00   (160.00)
☐ **As above,** *Kinsico.*
    145.00   170.00   (160.00)
☐ **As above,** *Kirkwood.*
    145.00   170.00   (160.00)

☐ **Kentucky,** *black walnut, with rosewood trimmings, height 22", dial 6", spring wound, c. 1890, 8 Day, strike (E2-18).*
    160.00   185.00   (175.00)
☐ **As above,** *ash.*
    210.00   235.00   (220.00)

☐ **Lima,** *black walnut, height 24", dial 6", spring wound, c. 1890, 8 Day, strike (E2-18).*
    170.00   195.00   (175.00)

☐ **Louise,** *dark wood or oak, height 21", dial 5", c. 1890, 8 Day hour and ½ hour strike (E2-16).*
    160.00   185.00   (165.00)

Embossed

Colorado

Express

ANSONIA CLOCK COMPANY / 115

Idaho

Iowa

☐ **Lowell,** *black walnut with rosewood trimmings, height 23½", dial 6", c. 1890, 8 Day, strike (E2-18).*
    155.00   180.00   (160.00)
☐ **As above,** *ash.*
    180.00   205.00   (185.00)

☐ **Madison,** *black walnut, rosewood trimmings, height 22½", dial 6", spring wound, c. 1890, 8 Day, strike (E2-18).*
    165.00   190.00   (175.00)
☐ **As above,** *ash.*
    185.00   210.00   (200.00)

☐ **Maryland,** *walnut, height 23", dial 6", spring wound, c. 1890, 8 Day, strike (E2-21).*
    135.00   160.00   (140.00)
☐ **As above,** *8 Day, strike, alarm.*
    155.00   180.00   (160.00)

☐ **Metropolis,** *walnut, height 24", dial 6", spring wound, c. 1890, 8 Day, gong, strike (E2-22).*
    165.00   190.00   (180.00)
☐ **As above,** *8 Day, strike, alarm.*
    180.00   210.00   (190.00)

☐ **Louisiana,** *walnut, height 22¾", dial 6", c. 1890, 8 Day, strike (E2-21).*
    135.00   160.00   (140.00)
☐ **As above,** *8 Day, strike, alarm.*
    155.00   180.00   (160.00)

Julia

116 / ANSONIA CLOCK COMPANY

"K" Assortment

- **Michigan,** walnut, height 24", dial 6", spring wound, c. 1890, 8 Day, gong, strike (E2-22).
  165.00   190.00   (180.00)
- **As above,** 8 Day, strike, alarm.
  180.00   210.00   (190.00)

- **Mobile,** walnut, height 20", dial 6", spring wound, c. 1890, 8 Day, strike (E2-19).
  170.00   195.00   (175.00)
- **As above,** ash.
  200.00   225.00   (215.00)

- **Mosel,** walnut, height 23", dial 6", spring wound, c. 1891, 1 Day, strike (E2-21).
  105.00   130.00   (115.00)
- **As above,** 1 Day, strike, alarm.
  125.00   150.00   (130.00)

- **Oder,** walnut, height 19", dial 6", spring wound, c. 1890, 1 Day, strike (E2-19).
  110.00   135.00   (120.00)

- **Oder,** walnut, height 19", dial 6", spring wound, c. 1891, 1 Day, strike, spring (E2-21).
  105.00   130.00   (120.00)
- **As above,** 1 Day, strike, spring, alarm.
  125.00   150.00   (130.00)

- **Ohio,** walnut, height 22", dial 6", spring wound, c. 1890, 8 Day, strike (E2-21).
  135.00   160.00   (140.00)
- **As above,** 8 Day, strike, alarm.
  155.00   180.00   (160.00)

- **Oregon,** walnut, height 19", dial 6", spring wound, c. 1890, 1 Day, strike (E2-19).
  110.00   135.00   (120.00)

- **Pauline,** dark wood or oak, height 22", dial 5", spring wound, c. 1890, 8 Day, hour and ½ hour strike (E2-17).
  160.00   185.00   (175.00)

- **Peru,** walnut, height 21¼", dial 6", spring wound, c. 1890, 8 Day, strike (E2-19).
  160.00   185.00   (175.00)

- **Plebeian,** dark wood or oak, height 20½", dial 6", spring wound, c. 1890, 8 Day, hour and ½ hour strike (E2-17).
  140.00   165.00   (145.00)

- **Post,** walnut, height 20", dial 6", spring wound, c. 1890, 1 Day, strike (E2-18).
  155.00   180.00   (160.00)

Mosel

ANSONIA CLOCK COMPANY / 117

☐ **Primrose,** *dark wood or oak, height 16", dial 4", spring wound, c. 1890, 8 Day, strike (E2-17).*
    155.00   180.00   (160.00)

☐ **Quality,** *dark wood or oak, height 17", dial 5", spring wound, c. 1890, 8 Day, hour and ½ hour strike (E2-17).*
    155.00   180.00   (160.00)

☐ **Quebec,** *antique oak, height 21¼", spring wound, c. 1890, 8 Day, strike, spring (E2-22).*
    145.00   170.00   (150.00)
☐ **As above,** *8 Day, strike, spring, alarm.*
    165.00   190.00   (170.00)

☐ **Ranger,** *walnut, height 20", dial 5", spring wound, c. 1890, 8 Day, strike (E2-19).*
    170.00   195.00   (180.00)

☐ **Ringgold,** *dark wood or oak, height 24¾", dial 6", spring wound, c. 1890, 8 Day, strike (E2-17).*
    155.00   180.00   (160.00)

☐ **Steel,** *bronze ornaments, height 16½", dial 6", spring wound, c. 1890, 1 Day, strike (E2-19).*
    110.00   135.00   (115.00)
☐ **As above,** *8 Day, strike.*
    140.00   165.00   (145.00)

☐ **Sun,** *hand painted decoration, height 16", dial 6", spring wound, c. 1890, 1 Day, strike and 8 Day, strike (E2-19).*
    130.00   155.00   (145.00)

☐ **Sydney,** *ash with black trimmings, height 22", dial 6", spring wound, c. 1890, 8 Day, strike (E2-19).*
    165.00   190.00   (185.00)

☐ **Tantivy,** *walnut, height 23", dial 6", spring wound, c. 1890, 8 Day, strike (E2-19).*
    170.00   195.00   (180.00)

Tribune

☐ **Tribune,** *hand painted decoration, height 18", dial 6", spring wound, c. 1890, 1 Day, strike (E2-18).*
    110.00   135.00   (115.00)
☐ **As above,** *8 Day, strike.*
    165.00   190.00   (170.00)

☐ **Umbria,** *walnut, height 22", dial 6", spring wound, c. 1891, 1 Day, strike (E2-21).*
    105.00   130.00   (110.00)
☐ **As above,** *1 Day, strike, alarm.*
    125.00   150.00   (130.00)

☐ **Werra,** *walnut, height 20", dial 5", spring wound, c. 1891, 1 Day, strike, spring (E2-21).*
    105.00   130.00   (115.00)
☐ **As above,** *1 Day, strike, spring, alarm.*
    125.00   150.00   (130.00)

KITCHEN/EBONY

☐ **Greek,** *walnut, ebonized case, height 17", dial 5", spring wound, c. 1900, 1 Day, strike, spring (E2-24).*
    165.00   190.00   (175.00)
☐ **As above,** *1 Day, strike, spring.*
    210.00   240.00   (225.00)

118 / ANSONIA CLOCK COMPANY

Greek

Carlos No. 1

KITCHEN/HANGING

☐ **Carlos No.1,** *oak and dark wood, height 24½", dial 6", spring wound, c. 1910, 8 Day, strike (E2-41).*
    375.00   425.00   (400.00)
☐ **As above,** *No.2.*
    375.00   425.00   (400.00)
☐ **As above,** *No.3.*
    375.00   425.00   (400.00)
☐ **As above,** *No.4.*
    375.00   425.00   (400.00)
☐ **As above,** *No.5.*
    375.00   425.00   (400.00)
☐ **As above,** *No.6.*
    375.00   425.00   (400.00)

☐ **Gomez,** *oak, , height 24", dial 6½", spring wound, c. 1910, 8 Day, strike (E2-41).*
    310.00   350.00   (335.00)
☐ **As above,** *mahogany.*
    335.00   375.00   (350.00)
☐ **As above,** *walnut.*
    360.00   400.00   (375.00)

Habana

ANSONIA CLOCK COMPANY / 119

Hanging Assortment No. 4

Habana, *dark wood or oak, height 25",
dial 6", spring wound, c. 1890, 8 day,
hour and ½ hour strike (E2-16).*
  230.00   260.00   (250.00)

☐ **Hanging Assortment No.3-A,**
*walnut, height 26", dial 6", spring
wound, c. 1900, 8 Day, hour and
½ hour strike (E2-23).*
  210.00   240.00   (225.00)
☐ **As above,** *No.3-B.*
  210.00   240.00   (225.00)
☐ **As above,** *No.3-C.*
  210.00   240.00   (225.00)
☐ **As above,** *No.3-D.*
  210.00   240.00   (225.00)
☐ **As above,** *No.3-E.*
  210.00   240.00   (225.00)
☐ **As above,** *No.3-F.*
  210.00   240.00   (225.00)

☐ **Hanging Assortment No.4,**
*Cardenas, walnut, height 26", dial
6", spring wound, c. 1900, 8 Day,
strike (E2-24).*
  260.00   290.00   (275.00)
☐ **As above,** *Canada.*
  260.00   290.00   (275.00)
☐ **As above,** *Colon.*
  260.00   290.00   (275.00)
☐ **As above,** *Chile.*
  260.00   290.00   (275.00)

Trinidad

☐ **Hanging Assortment No.4,**
*Cardenas, oak, height 26", dial 6",
spring wound, c. 1900, 8 Day,
strike (E2-24).*
  210.00   240.00   (225.00)
☐ **As above,** *Canada.*
  210.00   240.00   (225.00)
☐ **As above,** *Colon.*
  210.00   240.00   (225.00)
☐ **As above,** *Chile.*
  210.00   240.00   (225.00)
☐ **As above,** *Caldera.*
  210.00   240.00   (225.00)
☐ **As above,** *Cuba.*
  210.00   240.00   (225.00)

☐ **Matanzas,** *oak, height 27½", dial
6", spring wound, c. 1898, 8 Day,
alarm. (E1-155).*
  195.00   225.00   (200.00)

120 / ANSONIA CLOCK COMPANY

- **Mexico,** walnut, height 27¼", dial 6", spring wound, c. 1898, 8 Day, alarm (E1-155).
  245.00   275.00   (250.00)

- **Trinidad,** walnut, height 27¼", dial 6", spring, c. 1898, 8 Day, alarm (E1-155).
  195.00   225.00   (200.00)

- **Trinidad,** dark wood or oak, height 27½", dial 6", spring wound, c. 1890, 8 Day, strike (E2-16).
  230.00   260.00   (240.00)

KITCHEN/MANTEL

- **Albion Oak,** height 24", dial 6", spring wound, c. 1898, 8 Day, strike (E1-155).
  115.00   140.00   (120.00)

- **Chicago Calendar,** oak, barometer and thermometer, height 23", dial 6", spring wound, c. 1898, 8 Day, strike (E1-155).
  175.00   200.00   (180.00)

- **Topaz Calendar,** oak, barometer and thermometer, height 23", dial 6", spring wound, c. 1898, 8 Day, strike (E1-155).
  175.00   200.00   (180.00)

Topaz Calendar

KITCHEN/MIRROR SIDES

- **Reflector,** ebony or mahogany, height 35", dial 6", spring wound, c. 1910, 8 Day, strike (E2-40).
  550.00   625.00   (575.00)

Chicago Calendar

Triumph

ANSONIA CLOCK COMPANY / 121

☐ **Triumph,** *dark wood or oak, silver cupid, plate glass mirrors, bronze ornaments, height 24½", dial 6", spring wound, c. 1900, 8 Day (E2-25).*
    285.00   325.00   (300.00)

☐ **Triumph,** *walnut, silver cupids, plate glass mirrors, bronze ornaments, height 24½", dial 6", spring wound, c. 1890, 8 Day gong, strike (E2-22).*
    335.00   375.00   (350.00)
☐ **As above,** *8 Day, strike, alarm.*
    355.00   395.00   (375.00)

☐ **Windsor,** *dark wood or oak, silver cupids, plate glass mirrors, bronze ornaments, height 21½", dial 5", spring wound, c. 1900, 8 Day, strike (E2-25).*
    250.00   280.00   (260.00)

KITCHEN/TEAR DROP

☐ **King,** *dark wood or oak, height 24", dial 6", spring wound, c. 1900, 8 Day, strike (E2-25).*
    250.00   280.00   (260.00)

Parisian

☐ **King,** *walnut, height 24", dial 6", spring, c. 1890, 8 Day, strike, bell (E2-21).*
    240.00   260.00   (250.00)
☐ **As above,** *8 Day, strike, alarm, bell.*
    260.00   280.00   (270.00)
☐ **As above,** *8 Day, strike, gong.*
    240.00   260.00   (250.00)
☐ **As above,** *8 Day, strike, alarm, gong.*
    260.00   280.00   (275.00)

☐ **Parisian,** *dark wood or oak, height 23½", dial 6", spring wound, c. 1900, 8 Day, strike (E2-25).*
    260.00   280.00   (275.00)

Windsor

122 / ANSONIA CLOCK COMPANY

- **Parisian,** walnut, height 24", dial 6", spring wound, c. 1890, 8 Day, strike, bell (E2-21).
  260.00   280.00   (275.00)
- **As above,** 8 Day, strike, alarm, bell.
  280.00   300.00   (285.00)
- **As above,** 8 Day, strike, gong.
  260.00   280.00   (275.00)
- **As above,** 8 Day, strike, alarm, gong.
  280.00   300.00   (295.00)

- **Remus,** dark wood or oak, height 23", dial 5", spring wound, c. 1890, 8 Day, hour and ½ hour strike (E2-16).
  190.00   220.00   (200.00)

MANTEL/BLACK IRON

- **Angelo,** 12½" x 14", dial 5", spring, c. 1890, 8 Day, strike (E2-26).
  115.00   140.00   (120.00)
- **Cardiff,** black Japanned, gilt engraved, 9½" x 11½", dial 5", spring, c. 1898, 8 Day, strike (E1-157).
  60.00   75.00   (65.00)
- **Egypt,** 10¾" x 16", dial 4½", spring, c. 1890, 8 Day, strike (E2-26).
  210.00   240.00   (220.00)
- **Euclid, With Figure No.1042,** bust included, 16" x 10", dial 5", spring, c. 1890, 8 Day, strike (E2-26).
  165.00   190.00   (175.00)

- **Grenada,** black Japanned with bronze ornaments, 8½" x 14¾", dial 5", spring, c. 1898, 8 Day, strike (E1-157).
  60.00   75.00   (65.00)
- **Nero,** 12¾" x 10¾", dial 4½", spring, c. 1890, 8 Day, strike (E2-26).
  175.00   200.00   (185.00)

Egypt

Euclid

Angelo

ANSONIA CLOCK COMPANY / 123

Grenada

Nile

Nero

Pompeii

Rosalind

☐ **Nile,** *urn included, 18" x 13¼",
dial 4½", spring, c. 1890, 8 Day,
strike (E2-26).*
      150.00   175.00   (160.00)

☐ **Parma, Figure No. 1069,** *11" x 22",
dial 4½", spring, c. 1890, 8 Day,
strike (E2-26).*
      245.00   275.00   (260.00)

☐ **Pompeii,** *10¾" x 15", dial 4½",
spring, c. 1890, 8 Day, strike
(E2-26).*
      165.00   180.00   (175.00)

124 / ANSONIA CLOCK COMPANY

- **Rembrandt,** *20" x 11", dial 5", spring, c. 1890, 8 Day, strike (E2-26).*
  140.00   160.00   (150.00)

- **Rosalind,** *12¼" x 15¼", dial 5", spring, c. 1890, 8 Day, strike (E2-26).*
  200.00   230.00   (220.00)

- **Saint Clair,** *11¼" x 10½", dial 4½", spring, c. 1890, 8 Day, strike (E2-26).*
  170.00   190.00   (180.00)

- **Timbrell,** *13" x 11", dial 4½", spring, c. 1890, 8 Day, strike (E2-26).*
  125.00   150.00   (135.00)

- **Unique,** *10½" x 9½", dial 5", spring, c. 1890, 8 Day, strike (E2-26).*
  95.00   115.00   (100.00)

- **Vendome,** *black Japanned, gilt ornaments, French rococo sash, cream porcelain dial, 11" x 12¾", dial 4⅛", spring, c. 1898 (E1-157).*
  60.00   75.00   (65.00)

Timbrell

Unique

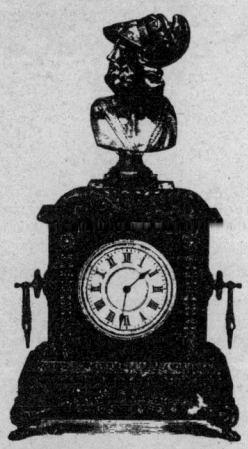

Saint Clair

MANTLE/BLACK WOOD

- **Boston Extra,** *enameled iron, bronze columns, French sash, beveled glass, porcelain dial, 11" x 15", dial 4", spring, c. 1917, 8 Day, strike (E1-178).*
  60.00   75.00   (65.00)

- **Savoy,** *black Japanned, oak, gilt trimmings, 9½" x 9", dial 5", spring, c. 1898, 8 Day, strike (E1-157).*
  65.00   85.00   (75.00)

- **As above,** *mahogany.*
  80.00   110.00   (90.00)

ANSONIA CLOCK COMPANY / 125

Boston Extra

Savoy

Franconia

Lydia

MANTLE/BRONZE

☐ **Emporia,** *height 18", base 11", spring, c. 1891, 8 Day, strike (E2-32).*
    440.00   500.00   (475.00)

☐ **Eureka,** *black enameled, silver finish, gilt dial, height 9", base 20", spring, c. 1891, 8 Day, strike (E2-32).*
    900.00   1000.00   (950.00)

☐ **Franconia,** *height 18", spring, c. 1891, 8 Day, strike (E2-32).*
    400.00   450.00   (425.00)

☐ **Lydia,** *height 19½", spring, c. 1891, 8 Day, strike (E2-32).*
    1150.00   1350.00   (1250.00)

☐ **Senator,** *antique oak and brass, height 22", base 19½", spring, c. 1891, 8 Day, strike (E2-32).*
    1250.00   1500.00   (1400.00)

MANTLE/MAGOHANY

- **Fairfax,** *mahogany case, fancy panels, 10⅞" x 15¼", spring, c. 1917, 8 Day, strike (E1-178).*
  55.00   70.00   (60.00)
- **Fairmont,** *mahogany, 10¾" x 15¾", spring, c. 1917, 8 Day, strike (E1-178).*
  55.00   70.00   (60.00)
- **Fenton,** *mahogany, bronze columns, 10¼" x 16", dial 4", spring, c. 1917, 8 Day, strike (E1-178).*
  55.00   70.00   (60.00)
- **Flanders,** *mahogany, bronze columns, 12¾" x 14", dial 4", spring, c. 1917, 8 Day, strike (E1-178).*
  55.00   70.00   (60.00)
- **Fowler,** *mahogany, bronze columns, 12⅝" x 16", dial 4", spring, c. 1917, 8 Day, strike (E1-178).*
  55.00   70.00   (60.00)
- **Fraser,** *mahogany, bronze columns, 12¼" x 13¼", dial 4", spring, c. 1917 (E1-178).*
  55.00   70.00   (60.00)

Fraser

MANTLE/MARBLE

- **Dorothy,** *black marble, 9½" x 13¾", porcelain dial 5", spring, c. 1898, 8 Day, strike (E1-157).*
  115.00   140.00   (125.00)
- **El Limon,** *black marble, 15½" x 14¼", porcelain dial 5", spring, c. 1898, 8 Day, strike (E1-157).*
  105.00   130.00   (115.00)
- **El Tule,** *black marble, 12" x 11¼", porcelain dial 5", spring, c. 1898, 8 Day, strike (E1-157).*
  105.00   125.00   (115.00)
- **Pinafore,** *black marble, 9½" x 14½", porcelain dial 5", spring, c. 1898, 8 Day, strike (E1-157).*
  125.00   150.00   (135.00)

Flanders

Dorothy

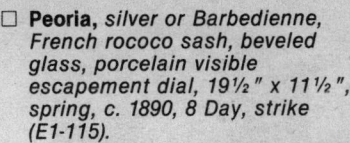

Pinafore

MANTLE/METAL REGENCY

☐ **Amphion,** *rich gold, decorated porcelain panels, French rococo sash, beveled glass, porcelain dial 4¼", 15" x 10", spring, c. 1890, 8 Day, strike (E1-116).*
    335.00   375.00   (350.00)

☐ **Lucania,** *gold bronze, French rococo sash, beveled glass, porcelain visible escapement dial, 13¾" x 7½", spring, c. 1890, 8 Day, strike (E1-115).*
    310.00   350.00   (340.00)

☐ **Orienta,** *rich gold, French rococo sash, beveled glass, porcelain visible escapement dial, 16¾" x 9¾", spring, c. 1890, 8 Day, strike (E1-116).*
    285.00   325.00   (300.00)

☐ **Peoria,** *silver or Barbedienne, French rococo sash, beveled glass, porcelain visible escapement dial, 19½" x 11½", spring, c. 1890, 8 Day, strike (E1-115).*
    360.00   400.00   (375.00)

☐ **Rococo,** *Syrian bronze, French rococo sash, beveled glass, porcelain visible escapement dial, 15½" x 11, dial 5½", spring, c. 1890, 8 Day, strike (E1-115).*
    335.00   375.00   (350.00)

☐ **Versailles,** *rich gold, decorated porcelain panel, French rococo sash, beveled glass, porcelain, 15" x 8", dial 4¼", spring, c. 1890, 8 Day, strike (E1-116).*
    310.00   350.00   (325.00)

MANTLE/ONYX

☐ **Warren,** *Brazilian green onyx case, bronze trimmings, rococo sash, cream porcelain dial 5", 12" x 13", spring, c. 1898, 8 Day, strike (E1-157).*
    195.00   225.00   (210.00)

☐ **Winthrop,** *Brazilian green onyx case, bronze trimmings, rococo sash, cream porcelain dial 5", 11¼" x 11", spring, c. 1898, 8 Day, strike (E1-157).*
    115.00   140.00   (120.00)

Orienta

Warren

128 / ANSONIA CLOCK COMPANY

Winthrop

MANTLE/PLUSH

- **Florentine No.1,** *height 15½", dial 5½", spring, c. 1890, 8 Day (E2-31).*
  285.00   325.00   (300.00)

- **Florentine No.2,** *height 14", dial 5½", spring, c. 1890, 8 Day (E2-31).*
  190.00   220.00   (200.00)

- **Florentine No.3,** *with or without figure, height 13½", dial 5½", spring, c. 1890, 8 Day (E2-31).*
  190.00   220.00   (200.00)

- **Florentine No.4,** *silver or brass antique finish, height 15", dial 5½", spring, c. 1890, 8 Day (E2-31).*
  250.00   280.00   (260.00)

- **Florentine No.5,** *silver or brass antique finish, height 14", dial 4½", spring, c. 1890, 8 Day (E2-31).*
  190.00   220.00   (200.00)

- **Florentine No.6,** *height 16", dial 6¾", spring, c. 1890, 8 Day (E2-31).*
  210.00   240.00   (225.00)

Florentine No. 1

Florentine No. 2

ANSONIA CLOCK COMPANY / 129

NOVELTY/ANIMATED

☐ **Automatic Swing No.2,** *bronze and nickel finish, height 8", dial 4", spring, c. 1896, 1 Day (E2-14).*
      360.00   420.00   (375.00)

Florentine No. 3

Alameda

NOVELTY/ART NOUVEAU

☐ **Alameda,** *gold finish, height 8¼", dial 2", spring, c. 1910, 8 Day (E2-33).*
      95.00   115.00   (100.00)

☐ **Argyle,** *gold finish, height 8¾", dial 2", spring, c. 1910, 8 Day (E2-33).*
      90.00   110.00   (100.00)

☐ **Arverne,** *gold finish, height 9", dial 2", spring, c. 1910, 8 Day (E2-33).*
      95.00   115.00   (100.00)

☐ **Cherry,** *gold finish, height 6½", dial 2", spring, c. 1910, 1 Day (E2-33).*
      50.00   65.00   (60.00)
☐ **As above,** *8 Day.*
      90.00   110.00   (95.00)

Florentine No. 4

130 / ANSONIA CLOCK COMPANY

Argyle

Arverne

Harmony

- ☐ **Chic,** *gold finish, height 8¾", dial 2", spring, c. 1910, 1 Day (E2-33).*
  50.00   65.00   (55.00)
- ☐ **As above,** *8 Day.*
  90.00   110.00   (95.00)
- ☐ **Cora,** *mahogany or oak with gilt trimmings, height 7⅛", fancy dial 2", spring, c. 1898, 1 Day (E1-161).*
  50.00   65.00   (55.00)
- ☐ **Flora,** *gilt center, height 7⅜", cream porcelain dial 2", spring, c. 1898, 1 Day (E1-161).*
  65.00   85.00   (70.00)
- ☐ **Harmony,** *gold finish, height 9", dial 2", spring, c. 1910, 1 Day (E2-33).*
  60.00   75.00   (65.00)
- ☐ **As above,** *8 Day.*
  105.00   125.00   (110.00)
- ☐ **Norwood,** *antique silver, height 5¾", fancy dial 2", spring, c. 1898, 1 Day (E1-161).*
  30.00   40.00   (35.00)
- ☐ **Olga,** *gold finish, height 8¾", dial 2", spring, c. 1910, 1 Day (E2-33).*
  50.00   65.00   (55.00)
- ☐ **As above,** *8 Day.*
  90.00   110.00   (95.00)

NOVELTY/BISQUE

- **Contemplation,** bisque, height 5½", dial 2", spring, c. 1890, 1 Day (E2-28).
  75.00   90.00   (80.00)

- **Friends,** bisque, height 5½", dial 2", spring, c. 1890, 1 Day (E2-28).
  80.00   100.00   (85.00)

- **Poodle,** bisque, height 6", dial 2", spring, c. 1890, 1 Day (E2-28).
  70.00   90.00   (80.00)

- **Restful,** bisque, height 5½", dial 2", spring, c. 1890, 1 Day (E2-28).
  70.00   90.00   (80.00)

- **Wildlife,** bisque, height 7", dial 2", spring, c. 1890, 1 Day (E2-28).
  70.00   90.00   (80.00)

- **Worker,** bisque, height 7", dial 2", spring, c. 1890, 1 Day (E2-28).
  100.00   120.00   (110.00)

Worker

NOVELTY/BRASS

- **Armour No.25,** brass or steel finish, height 11", dial 2", spring, c. 1890, 1 Day (E2-30).
  130.00   155.00   (140.00)

- **Easel No.1,** height 11", dial 2", spring, c. 1890, 1 Day (E2-27).
  80.00   100.00   (90.00)
- **As above,** No.2, painted or plain.
  80.00   100.00   (90.00)
- **As above,** No.3.
  80.00   100.00   (90.00)
- **As above,** No.5.
  80.00   100.00   (90.00)

Poodle

Armour No. 25

132 / ANSONIA CLOCK COMPANY

- **Empire,** *antique brass or rich gold, height 9½", fancy dial 1½", spring, c. 1898, 1 Day (E1-158).*

  60.00   75.00   (65.00)

- **Etruscan,** *brass or silver, height 14½", spring, c. 1890, 8 Day (E2-29).*

  360.00   400.00   (375.00)

- **Renaissance,** *brass, silver or brass antique, c. 1890, 8 Day, strike (E2-29).*

  465.00   525.00   (475.00)

Easel No. 3

Easel No. 1

Easel No. 5

ANSONIA CLOCK COMPANY / 133

Renaissance

Snap

Pilgrim

NOVELTY/CHINA

☐ **Pilgrim,** height 7", dial 2", spring, c. 1890, 1 Day (E2-30).
    40.00   55.00   (50.00)

NOVELTY/FANCY

☐ **Baby,** rich burnished silver or gold, height 5¼", fancy dial 1½", spring, c. 1898, 1 Day (E1-161).
    60.00   85.00   (70.00)

☐ **Snap,** bronze finish, height 11", dial 4", spring, c. 1883, 8 Day (E2-9).
    65.00   80.00   (75.00)

☐ **Twilight,** rich burnished silver or gold, height 4¾", fancy dial 1¹¹/₁₆", spring, c. 1898, 1 Day (E1-161).
    40.00   55.00   (45.00)

NOVELTY/GILT

☐ **Amigos,** gold finish, jeweled, height 5¾", dial 2", spring, c. 1910, 1 Day (E2-33).
    70.00   85.00   (75.00)

☐ **Cantor,** gold finish, height 9¼", dial 2", spring, c. 1910, 1 Day (E2-33).
    70.00   90.00   (80.00)

☐ **Ensign,** rich burnished silver or gold, height 4¼", fancy dial 1½", spring, c. 1898, 1 Day (E1-161).
    40.00   50.00   (45.00)

☐ **Eveline,** antique brass, rich gold, cream porcelain, gilt center, height 8¼", dial 2", spring, c. 1898, 1 Day (E1-161).
    40.00   55.00   (45.00)

134 / ANSONIA CLOCK COMPANY

Amigos

- [ ] **Modern,** *gold finish, height 4¼", dial 2", spring, c. 1910, 1 Day (E2-33).*
  35.00   45.00   (40.00)
- [ ] **As above,** *8 Day.*
  60.00   75.00   (65.00)
- [ ] **Orchestra,** *rich burnished gold, height 4¼", fancy dial 2", spring, c. 1898, 1 Day (E1-161).*
  30.00   40.00   (35.00)
- [ ] **Pepa,** *mirror, gold finish, height 8", dial 2", spring, c.1910, 8 Day (E2-33).*
  105.00   125.00   (115.00)
- [ ] **Phyllis,** *silver and gold plate, gilt trimmings, cream porcelain dial, gilt centers, height 7", fancy dial 2", spring, c. 1898, 1 Day (E1-161).*
  45.00   60.00   (50.00)
- [ ] **Play,** *gold finish, height 9¼", dial 2", spring, c. 1910, 1 Day (E2-33).*
  60.00   75.00   (65.00)
- [ ] **As above,** *8 Day.*
  105.00   125.00   (115.00)

La Belle

Republic

- [ ] **Gladys,** *rich burnished silver or gold, height 5½", fancy dial 2", spring, c. 1898, 1 Day (E1-161).*
  70.00   85.00   (75.00)
- [ ] **La Belle,** *gold finish, height 6¼", dial 2", spring, c. 1910, 1 Day (E2-33).*
  40.00   55.00   (45.00)

ANSONIA CLOCK COMPANY / 135

Rita

Carpenter

- **Republic,** *rich burnished silver or gold, height 8¼", fancy dial 2", spring, c. 1898, 1 Day (E1-161)*
  55.00   70.00   (60.00)

- **Rita,** *gold finish, height 7", dial 2", spring, c. 1910, 8 Day (E2-33).*
  95.00   115.00   (100.00)

NOVELTY/IRON

- **Barrow,** *height 4", dial 2, spring, c. 1890, 1 Day (E2-30).*
  40.00   50.00   (45.00)

- **Beating Time,** *height 5", dial 2", spring, c. 1890, 1 Day (E2-30).*
  55.00   70.00   (60.00)

- **Cadet,** *bronze, pendulum, height 4½", dial 2", spring, c. 1890, 1 Day (E2-30).*
  50.00   65.00   (55.00)

- **Carpenter,** *silver or gold plate, height 7¼", dial 2", spring, c. 1890, 1 Day (E2-31).*
  40.00   55.00   (45.00)

- **Chef,** *Japanese bronze or silver, height 5½", fancy metal dial 1½", spring, c. 1898, 1 Day (E1-158).*
  45.00   60.00   (50.00)

- **Cherub,** *silver or bronze finish, height 4½", dial 2", spring, c. 1890, 1 Day (E2-30).*
  45.00   60.00   (50.00)

Dawn

- **Cupid Wreath,** *silver or bronze, height 5", dial 2", spring, c. 1890, 1 Day (E2-30).*
  60.00   75.00   (65.00)

- **Dawn,** *old silver and gilt finish, c. 1890, 8 Day (E2-22).*
  60.00   75.00   (65.00)

- **Duet,** *height 5½", dial 2", spring, c. 1890, 1 Day (E2-30).*
  45.00   60.00   (50.00)

136 / ANSONIA CLOCK COMPANY

☐ **Engine,** *gilt and old silver finish, height 8", spring, c. 1891, 1 Day (E2-32).*
    60.00   75.00   (65.00)

☐ **Eva,** *gold finish, beveled mirror, height 9¼", dial 2", spring, c. 1910, 1 Day (E2-34).*
    60.00   85.00   (65.00)

☐ **As above,** *8 Day.*
    105.00   125.00   (115.00)

☐ **Fan,** *finished in silver and old silver, height 7¾", spring, c. 1891, 1 Day (E2-32).*
    60.00   85.00   (65.00)

☐ **Fly,** *nickel, pendulum, height 4½", dial 2", spring, c. 1890, 1 Day (E2-30).*
    50.00   65.00   (55.00)

☐ **Good Luck No.2,** *silver or gold plate, height 4½", dial 2", spring, c. 1890, 1 Day (E2-31).*
    45.00   60.00   (50.00)

☐ **Good Luck No.3,** *silver or gold plate, height 4¾", dial 2", spring, c. 1890, 1 Day (E2-31).*
    40.00   50.00   (45.00)

☐ **Hummingbird,** *silver or gold plate, height 7½", dial 2", spring, c. 1890, 1 Day (E2-31).*
    55.00   70.00   (60.00)

☐ **Lock,** *height 6", dial 2", spring, c. 1891, 1 Day (E2-32).*
    60.00   75.00   (65.00)

☐ **Navy,** *gilt finish, silver or old silver, height 12½", dial 2½", spring, c. 1891, 8 Day (E2-32).*
    80.00   100.00   (90.00)

☐ **Navy,** *gold finish, height 12½", dial 2", spring, c. 1910, 1 Day (E2-34).*
    85.00   105.00   (95.00)

☐ **Novelty, No.44,** *height 7¾", dial 2", spring, c. 1890, 1 Day (E2-30).*
    60.00   75.00   (65.00)

☐ **Oriental Fan,** *silver or gold plate, height 6½", dial 2", spring, c. 1890, 1 Day (E2-31).*
    55.00   70.00   (60.00)

☐ **Pearl,** *bronze finish, dial 4", spring, c. 1883, 1 Day (E2-9).*
    40.00   50.00   (45.00)

Hummingbird

Novelty No. 44

ANSONIA CLOCK COMPANY / 137

Oriental Fan

- **Photo,** *gold finish, height 12½", dial 2", spring, c. 1910, 8 Day (E2-34).*
  115.00   140.00   (125.00)

- **Saw,** *height 4½", dial 2", spring, c. 1890, 1 Day (E2-30).*
  40.00   50.00   (45.00)

- **Ship,** *old silver finish, height 14½", dial 3", spring, c. 1891, 1 Day (E2-32).*
  70.00   90.00   (80.00)

- **Temple,** *old silver, height 9¾", c. 1891, 8 Day (E2-32).*
  95.00   115.00   (100.00)

- **Trotter,** *old silver, height 6", dial 2½", spring, c. 1891, 8 Day (E2-32).*
  60.00   75.00   (65.00)

NOVELTY/NIGHT LIGHT

- **Aladdin Night Light,** *bronze and nickel finish, extra, dial 4", spring, battery, c. 1883, 1 Day (E2-9).*
  120.00   145.00   (125.00)

Aladdin Night Light

NOVELTY/PLUSH

- **Brass Antique or Silver Antique,** *diameter 15", spring, c. 1890, 8 Day (E2-29).*
  130.00   155.00   (140.00)

- **Pluribus,** *blue or red plush, bronze, silver and gilt finish, 18½" x 15", spring, c. 1890, 8 Day (E2-29).*
  170.00   195.00   (180.00)

Brass Antique

138 / ANSONIA CLOCK COMPANY

Pluribus

☐ **Richelieu,** *brass with plush, 16" x 18½", spring, c. 1890, 8 Day (E2-29).*
      170.00   195.00   (190.00)

☐ **Round Plush Plaque,** *diameter 16", spring, c. 1890, 8 Day (E2-29).*
      150.00   175.00   (160.00)

☐ **Square Plush Plaque,** *16" square, spring, c. 1890, 8 Day (E2-29).*
      155.00   180.00   (165.00)

NOVELTY/WALL

☐ **What-Not, No.1,** *wood, height 26", dial 8", spring, c. 1896, 8 Day (E2-14).*
      450.00   525.00   (460.00)

What-Not No. 1

OFFICE INK

☐ **Banker's Inkstand,** *bronze finish, height 12", dial 4", spring, c. 1883, 1 Day, calendar (E2-8).*
      240.00   280.00   (260.00)

☐ **Bee Ink,** *solid brass, height 7¼", dial 2½", spring, c. 1890, 8 Day (E2-22).*
      70.00   90.00   (80.00)

☐ **Boudoir Ink,** *gold, height 6½", dial 2", spring, c. 1910, 1 Day (E2-34).*
      70.00   90.00   (80.00)
☐ **As above,** *8 Day.*
      100.00   120.00   (110.00)

ANSONIA CLOCK COMPANY / 139

Banker's Inkstand

Butterfly Ink

Bee Ink

Ladies' Ink

☐ **Butterfly Ink,** *silver with nickel finish, colored enameled bottles and thermometer, height 10½", dial 4", spring, c. 1890, 1 Day, calendar (E2-27).*
    280.00   320.00   (300.00)

☐ **Ladies' Ink,** *cut glass, blue or ruby, height 8", dial 2", spring, c. 1890, 1 Day (E2-27).*
    150.00   175.00   (160.00)

☐ **Marguerite,** *black enameled case, hand painted decorations, clock and mirror, height 13", dial 4", c. 1883, 1 Day, alarm (E2-8).*
    135.00   160.00   (140.00)

☐ **Office Inkstand,** *bronze finish, height 13", dial 4", spring, c. 1883, 1 Day, calendar (E2-8).*
    220.00   240.00   (240.00)

☐ **Parlor Ink, No.1,** *solid brass, bee movement, height 9", dial 2", spring, c. 1890, 1 Day, perpetual calendar (E2-27).*
    120.00   230.00   (200.00)

140 / ANSONIA CLOCK COMPANY

Marguerite

☐ **Parlor Ink, No.3,** *brass, height 11",
dial 4", spring, c. 1890, 1 Day,
calendar (E2-27).*
    270.00   320.00   (280.00)

☐ **Studio Ink,** *gold, height 6", dial 2",
spring, c. 1910, 1 Day (E2-34).*
    70.00   85.00   (75.00)

☐ **As above,** *8 Day.*
    105.00   125.00   (110.00)

☐ **As above,** *calendar.*
    180.00   220.00   (190.00)

Office Inkstand

Parlor Ink No. 3

Studio Ink

ANSONIA CLOCK COMPANY / 141

REGULATOR/ASTRONOMICAL

- **Regulator No.8,** *wood, 105" x 36", dial 16", c. 1910, 8 Day, weight (E2-42).*
    8000.00   9000.00   (8500.00)

- **Regulator No.9,** *wood, 96" x 33", dial 16", c. 1910, 8 Day, weight (E2-42).*
    10000.00   12000.00   (1100.00)

Regulator No. 9

Regulator No. 8

142 / ANSONIA CLOCK COMPANY

REGULATOR/FIGURE EIGHT

- **Brooklyn,** *solid brass case and glass pendulum, height 34", dial 12", spring, c. 1910, 8 Day (E2-40).*
  2800.00   3000.00   (2900.00)
- **As above,** *8 Day, strike.*
  2900.00   3100.00   (3000.00)
- **Hiogo,** *black enamel finish, height 28", dial 10", spring, c. 1890, 8 Day (E2-39).*
  325.00   350.00   (335.00)
- **As above,** *8 Day, strike.*
  350.00   375.00   (360.00)
- **Kobe,** *walnut, height 21½", dial 10", spring, c. 1890, 8 Day (E2-39).*
  325.00   350.00   (340.00)
- **As above,** *8 Day, strike.*
  350.00   375.00   (360.00)
- **Kobe,** *oak, height 21½", dial 10", spring, c. 1890, 8 Day (E2-39).*
  275.00   300.00   (300.00)
- **As above,** *8 Day, strike.*
  300.00   325.00   (315.00)

Kobe

Brooklyn

REGULATOR/OCTAGON TOP, LONG DROP

- **Office Regulator,** *ash, duplex movement, retaining power, height 32", dial 12", spring, c. 1890, 8 Day (E2-39).*
  300.00   330.00   (315.00)
- **As above,** *8 Day, strike.*
  330.00   355.00   (340.00)
- **As above,** *8 Day, calendar.*
  355.00   380.00   (360.00)
- **As above,** *8 Day, strike, calendar.*
  380.00   405.00   (390.00)
- **Office Regulator,** *black walnut, duplex movement, retaining power, height 32", dial 12", spring, c. 1890, 8 Day (E2-39).*
  270.00   300.00   (285.00)
- **As above,** *8 Day, strike.*
  285.00   325.00   (295.00)
- **As above,** *8 Day, calendar.*
  310.00   350.00   (325.00)
- **As above,** *8 Day, strike, calendar.*
  335.00   375.00   (340.00)

ANSONIA CLOCK COMPANY / 143

☐ **Regulator,** oak, height 32", dial 12", spring, c. 1890, 8 Day (E2-39).
335.00   375.00   (340.00)
☐ **As above,** 8 Day, strike.
360.00   400.00   (375.00)
☐ **As above,** 8 Day, calendar.
375.00   425.00   (385.00)
☐ **As above,** 8 Day, strike, calendar.
400.00   450.00   (425.00)

Regulator "A", ash

☐ **Regulator "A",** ash, height 32", dial 12", spring, c. 1890, 8 Day (E2-39).
370.00   395.00   (380.00)
☐ **As above,** 8 Day, strike.
395.00   405.00   (400.00)
☐ **As above,** 8 Day, calendar.
405.00   435.00   (415.00)
☐ **As above,** 8 Day, strike, calendar.
435.00   470.00   (445.00)

☐ **Regulator "A",** black walnut, height 32", dial 12", spring, c. 1890, 8 Day (E2-39).
325.00   350.00   (340.00)
☐ **As above,** 8 Day, strike.
350.00   375.00   (360.00)
☐ **As above,** 8 Day, calendar.
375.00   400.00   (385.00)
☐ **As above,** 8 Day, strike, calendar.
400.00   425.00   (415.00)

Regulator, oak

REGULATOR/OCTAGON TOP, SHORT DROP

☐ **8" Drop Octagon, R.C.,** oak veneer, height 19½", dial 12", spring, c. 1890, 8 Day (E2-39).
150.00   175.00   (160.00)
☐ **As above,** 8 Day, strike.
175.00   200.00   (180.00)
☐ **As above,** 8 Day, calendar.
195.00   225.00   (200.00)
☐ **As above,** 8 Day, strike, calendar.
220.00   250.00   (225.00)

144 / ANSONIA CLOCK COMPANY

☐ **8" Drop Octagon, R.C.,** *rosewood veneer, height 19½", dial 12", spring, c. . 1890, 8 Day (E2-39).*
    200.00   225.00   (215.00)
☐ **As above,** *8 Day, strike.*
    225.00   250.00   (235.00)
☐ **As above,** *8 Day, calendar.*
    245.00   275.00   (250.00)
☐ **As above,** *8 Day, strike, calendar.*
    270.00   300.00   (285.00)

☐ **8" Drop Octagon,** *gilt rosewood veneer with gilt moulding, height 19½", dial 12", spring, c. 1890, 8 Day (E2-39).*
    150.00   175.00   (160.00)
☐ **As above,** *8 Day, strike.*
    175.00   200.00   (185.00)
☐ **As above,** *8 Day, calendar.*
    195.00   225.00   (200.00)
☐ **As above,** *8 Day, strike, calendar.*
    220.00   250.00   (225.00)

☐ **10" Drop Octagon, R.C.,** *oak, height 21½", dial 12", spring, c. 1890, 8 Day (E2-39).*
    175.00   200.00   (185.00)
☐ **As above,** *8 Day, strike.*
    195.00   225.00   (200.00)
☐ **As above,** *8 Day, calendar.*
    220.00   250.00   (230.00)
☐ **As above,** *8 Day, strike, calendar.*
    245.00   275.00   (250.00)

☐ **10" Drop Octagon, R.C.,** *rosewood veneer, height 21½", dial 12", spring, c. 1890, 8 Day (E2-39).*
    225.00   250.00   (235.00)
☐ **As above,** *8 Day, strike.*
    245.00   275.00   (250.00)
☐ **As above,** *8 Day, calendar.*
    270.00   300.00   (290.00)
☐ **As above,** *8 Day, strike, calendar.*
    295.00   325.00   (300.00)

☐ **10" Drop Octagon,** *gilt rosewood veneer with gilt moulding, height 21½", dial 12", spring, c. 1890, 8 Day (E2-39).*
    175.00   200.00   (190.00)
☐ **As above,** *8 Day, strike.*
    195.00   225.00   (200.00)
☐ **As above,** *8 Day, calendar.*
    220.00   250.00   (230.00)
☐ **As above,** *8 Day, strike, calendar.*
    245.00   275.00   (250.00)

☐ **12" Drop Octagon, R.C.,** *oak, height 24", dial 12", spring, c. 1890, 8 Day (E2-39).*
    195.00   225.00   (200.00)
☐ **As above,** *8 Day, strike.*
    220.00   250.00   (225.00)
☐ **As above,** *8 Day, calendar.*
    245.00   275.00   (250.00)
☐ **As above,** *8 Day, strike, calendar.*
    270.00   300.00   (280.00)

☐ **12" Drop Octagon, R.C.,** *rosewood veneer, height 24", dial 12", spring, c. 1890, 8 Day (E2-39).*
    245.00   275.00   (260.00)
☐ **As above,** *8 Day, strike.*
    270.00   300.00   (280.00)
☐ **As above,** *8 Day, calendar.*
    295.00   325.00   (300.00)
☐ **As above,** *8 Day, strike, calendar.*
    320.00   350.00   (340.00)

12" Drop Octagon, R.C. oak

ANSONIA CLOCK COMPANY / 145

12" Drop Octagon, gilt

☐ **12" Drop Octagon,** *gilt rosewood veneer with gilt moulding, height 24", dial 12", spring, c. 1890, 8 Day (E2-39).*
    195.00   225.00   (215.00)

☐ **As above,** *8 Day, strike.*
    220.00   250.00   (225.00)

☐ **As above,** *8 Day, calendar.*
    245.00   275.00   (250.00)

☐ **As above,** *8 Day, strike, calendar.*
    270.00   300.00   (280.00)

☐ **Office, No.2,** *walnut, height 26", dial 12", spring, c. 1900, 8 Day, strike (E2-24).*
    285.00   325.00   (300.00)

REGULATOR/OPEN SWINGING

☐ **Antique Hanging,** *mahogany, oak, antique brass trimmings, gilt and silvered dial 9½", height 46½", c. 1910, 8 Day, weight, strike (E2-42).*
    3800.00   4800.00   (4200.00)

Antique Hanging

☐ **Niobe,** *oak, antique brass trimmings, height 45", silvered dial 10", weight, c. 1910, 8 Day, strike (E2-40).*
    1200.00   1400.00   (1300.00)

146 / ANSONIA CLOCK COMPANY

Niobe

REGULATOR/PARLOR SHELF

- **Broadway,** *dark wood or oak, height 24½", dial 6", spring, c. 1900, 8 Day, hour and ½ hour strike (E2-25).*
  310.00   350.00   (325.00)

- **Monarch,** *dark wood or oak, bronze ornaments, French sash, height 24½", dial 6", spring, c. 1900, 8 Day, gong (E2-25).*
  350.00   375.00   (360.00)
- **As above,** *8 Day, gong alarm.*
  360.00   385.00   (375.00)

Monarch

- **Monarch,** *walnut, bronze ornaments, French sash, height 24½", dial 6", spring, c. 1890, 8 Day, gong strike (E2-22).*
  335.00   375.00   (350.00)
- **As above,** *8 Day, strike, alarm.*
  355.00   395.00   (365.00)

REGULATOR/PARLOR WALL

- **Argentina,** *walnut, height 33", dial 6½", spring, c. 1910, 8 Day, strike (E2-41).*
  460.00   500.00   (475.00)
- **As above,** *mahogany.*
  435.00   475.00   (445.00)
- **As above,** *oak.*
  360.00   400.00   (375.00)

- **Bagdad,** *walnut, height 50½", dial 8", spring, c. 1896, 8 Day (E1-153).*
  725.00   800.00   (750.00)
- **As above,** *8 Day, strike, spring.*
  775.00   850.00   (800.00)
- **As above,** *8 Day, weight.*
  950.00   1050.00   (1000.00)

ANSONIA CLOCK COMPANY / 147

☐ **Bagdad,** ash, height 50½", dial 8", spring, c. 1896, 8 Day (E1-153).
  775.00   850.00   (800.00)
☐ **As above,** 8 Day, strike, spring.
  825.00   900.00   (875.00)
☐ **As above,** 8 Day, weight.
  1000.00   1150.00   (1050.00)

☐ **Bagdad,** mahogany, height 50½", dial 8", spring, c. 1896, 8 Day (E1-153).
  700.00   775.00   (750.00)
☐ **As above,** 8 Day, strike, spring.
  725.00   825.00   (775.00)
☐ **As above,** 8 Day, weight.
  925.00   1025.00   (1000.00)

☐ **Bagdad,** oak, height 50½", dial 8", spring, c. 1896, 8 Day (E1-153).
  625.00   700.00   (650.00)
☐ **As above,** 8 Day, strike, spring.
  675.00   750.00   (700.00)
☐ **As above,** 8 Day, weight.
  850.00   950.00   (900.00)

☐ **Barcelona,** walnut, 31½" x 14¼", dial 8", spring, c. 1920, 8 Day (E1-185).
  370.00   400.00   (390.00)
☐ **As above,** oak.
  270.00   300.00   (290.00)
☐ **As above,** mahogany.
  370.00   400.00   (390.00)

☐ **Brazil,** walnut, 32" x 15", dial 8", spring, c. 1920, 8 Day (E1-185).
  370.00   400.00   (390.00)
☐ **As above,** mahogany.
  345.00   375.00   (350.00)
☐ **As above,** oak.
  270.00   300.00   (290.00)

☐ **Capital,** walnut, height 54", dial 8", spring, c. 1896, 8 Day (E1-153).
  675.00   750.00   (700.00)
☐ **As above,** 8 Day, strike
  725.00   800.00   (775.00)
☐ **As above,** 8 Day, weight.
  850.00   950.00   (900.00)

Argentina

Dispatch

148 / ANSONIA CLOCK COMPANY

Major

- Commerce, *wood, 41" x 15", dial 8", spring, c. 1910, 8 Day (E2-43).*
  425.00   475.00   (450.00)
- Forrest, *black walnut, height 41", dial 8", spring, c. 1910, 8 Day (E2-40).*
  490.00   550.00   (525.00)
- As above, *8 Day, strike.*
  540.00   600.00   (560.00)

- Lisboa, *walnut, 37" x 18¾", dial 8", spring, c. 1920, 8 Day (E1-185).*
  370.00   400.00   (375.00)
- As above, *mahogany.*
  345.00   375.00   (350.00)
- As above, *oak.*
  270.00   300.00   (275.00)

- Major, *wood, 30" x 14", dial 6", spring, c. 1910, 8 Day (E2-43).*
  425.00   475.00   (450.00)
- As above, *8 Day, strike.*
  450.00   500.00   (475.00)

- Capital, *ash, height 54", dial 8", spring, c. 1896, 8 Day (E1-153).*
  725.00   800.00   (775.00)
- As above, *8 Day, strike.*
  775.00   850.00   (800.00)
- As above, *8 Day, weight.*
  900.00   1000.00   (950.00)

- Capital, *mahogany, height 54", dial 8", spring, c. 1896, 8 Day (E1-153).*
  640.00   725.00   (660.00)
- As above, *8 Day, strike.*
  700.00   775.00   (750.00)
- As above, *8 Day, weight.*
  825.00   925.00   (850.00)

- Capital, *oak, height 54", dial 8", spring, c. 1896, 8 Day (E1-153).*
  575.00   650.00   (600.00)
- As above, *8 Day, strike.*
  625.00   700.00   (650.00)
- As above, *8 Day, weight.*
  750.00   850.00   (800.00)

Mississippi

- **Mississippi,** wood, 27" x 12", dial 6", spring, c. 1910, 8 Day (E2-43).
  360.00   400.00   (375.00)
- **As above,** 8 Day, strike.
  375.00   425.00   (395.00)

- **Pampa,** walnut, height 36", dial 8", spring, c. 1910, 8 Day, strike (E2-41).
  475.00   525.00   (500.00)
- **As above,** mahogany.
  450.00   500.00   (475.00)
- **As above,** oak.
  375.00   425.00   (400.00)

- **Para,** black walnut, height 39", dial 8", spring, c. 1910, 8 Day (E2-40).
  490.00   550.00   (500.00)
- **As above,** 8 Day, strike.
  515.00   575.00   (550.00)
- **As above,** 8 Day, calendar.
  540.00   600.00   (565.00)
- **As above,** 8 Day, strike, calendar.
  550.00   625.00   (575.00)

- **Ponderosa,** walnut, height 32", dial 7", spring, c. 1910, 8 Day, strike (E2-41).
  475.00   525.00   (485.00)
- **As above,** mahogany.
  450.00   500.00   (475.00)
- **As above,** oak.
  375.00   425.00   (400.00)

Ponderosa

Queen Isabella

- **Prompt,** walnut, height 50", dial 8", spring, c. 1896, 8 Day (E1-153).
  725.00   800.00   (750.00)
- **As above,** 8 Day, strike, spring.
  775.00   850.00   (800.00)
- **As above,** 8 Day, weight.
  950.00   1050.00   (1000.00)

- **Prompt,** ash, height 50", dial 8", spring, c. 1896, 8 Day (E1-153).
  775.00   850.00   (800.00)
- **As above,** 8 Day, strike, spring.
  825.00   900.00   (850.00)
- **As above,** 8 Day, weight.
  1000.00   1100.00   (1050.00)

- **Prompt,** mahogany, height 50", dial 8", spring, c. 1896, 8 Day (E1-153).
  700.00   775.00   (750.00)
- **As above,** 8 Day, strike, spring.
  750.00   825.00   (775.00)
- **As above,** 8 Day, weight.
  925.00   1025.00   (1000.00)

150 / ANSONIA CLOCK COMPANY

- **Prompt,** *oak, height 50", dial 8", spring, c. 1896, 8 Day (E1-153).*
  655.00   725.00   (675.00)
- **As above,** *8 Day, strike, spring.*
  700.00   775.00   (750.00)
- **As above,** *8 Day, weight.*
  875.00   975.00   (900.00)

- **Queen Anne,** *oak, height 40½", dial 8", spring, c. 1898, 8 Day (E1-155).*
  555.00   615.00   (575.00)
- **As above,** *8 Day, strike, spring.*
  590.00   665.00   (575.00)

- **Queen Charlotte,** *oak, height 40", dial 8", spring, c. 1898, 8 Day, (E1-155).*
  580.00   665.00   (590.00)
- **As above,** *8 Day, strike, spring.*
  640.00   715.00   (650.00)

- **Queen Elizabeth,** *walnut, height 37", dial 8", spring, c. 1896, 8 Day (E1-153).*
  590.00   650.00   (625.00)
- **As above,** *8 Day, strike, spring.*
  640.00   700.00   (650.00)

- **Queen Elizabeth,** *mahogany, height 37", dial 8", spring, c. 1896, 8 Day (E1-153).*
  565.00   625.00   (585.00)
- **As above,** *8 Day, strike, spring.*
  615.00   675.00   (625.00)

- **Queen Elizabeth,** *oak, height 37", dial 8", spring, c. 1896, 8 Day (E1-153).*
  490.00   550.00   (500.00)
- **As above,** *8 Day, strike, spring.*
  540.00   600.00   (575.00)

- **Queen Isabella,** *dark wood or oak, height 38½", dial 8", spring, c. 1910, 8 Day (E2-41).*
  415.00   465.00   (430.00)
- **As above,** *8 Day, strike.*
  440.00   480.00   (460.00)

- **Queen Jane,** *oak, height 41", dial 8", spring, c. 1898, 8 Day (E1-155).*
  540.00   600.00   (555.00)
- **As above,** *8 Day, strike, spring.*
  575.00   650.00   (600.00)

Queen Mab

- **Queen Mab,** *dark wood or oak, height 36½", dial 8", spring, c. 1910, 8 Day (E2-41).*
  400.00   450.00   (425.00)
- **As above,** *8 Day, strike.*
  425.00   475.00   (450.00)

- **Queen Mary,** *walnut, height 42", dial 8", spring, c. 1896, 8 Day (E1-153).*
  590.00   650.00   (600.00)
- **As above,** *8 Day, strike, spring.*
  675.00   750.00   (725.00)

- **Queen Mary,** *oak, height 42", dial 8", spring, c. 1896, 8 Day (E1-153).*
  490.00   550.00   (525.00)
- **As above,** *8 Day, strike, spring.*
  575.00   650.00   (600.00)

ANSONIA CLOCK COMPANY / 151

Rio

- **Rio,** oak, height 39", dial 8", spring, c. 1910, 8 Day (E2-40).
  490.00   550.00   (500.00)
- **As above,** 8 Day, strike.
  515.00   575.00   (530.00)
- **As above,** 8 Day, calendar.
  540.00   600.00   (575.00)
- **As above,** 8 Day, strike, calendar.
  550.00   625.00   (580.00)

- **Rosario,** walnut, 32" x 14½", dial 8", spring, c. 1920, 8 Day (E1-185).
  350.00   380.00   (375.00)
- **As above,** mahogany.
  325.00   355.00   (340.00)
- **As above,** oak.
  260.00   290.00   (275.00)

- **San Luis,** walnut, height 28", dial 6½", spring, c. 1910, 8 Day, strike (E2-41).
  410.00   450.00   (425.00)

- **Uruguay,** walnut, height 30", dial 7", spring, c. 1910, 8 Day, strike (E2-41).
  410.00   450.00   (425.00)
- **As above,** mahogany.
  385.00   425.00   (400.00)
- **As above,** oak.
  310.00   350.00   (325.00)

- **Victoria,** oak, 36" x 14½", dial 8", spring, c. 1920, 8 Day (E1-185).
  310.00   350.00   (325.00)
- **As above,** mahogany.
  385.00   425.00   (400.00)

REGULATOR
ROUND TOP, LONG DROP

- **English Drop,** black walnut, height 32", dial 12", spring, c. 1910, 8 Day (E2-40).
  310.00   350.00   (340.00)
- **As above,** 8 Day, strike.
  335.00   375.00   (350.00)
- **As above,** 8 Day, calendar.
  360.00   400.00   (375.00)
- **As above,** 8 Day, strike, calendar.
  375.00   425.00   (400.00)

- **English Drop,** ash, height 32", dial 12", spring, c. 1910, 8 Day (E2-40).
  360.00   400.00   (375.00)
- **As above,** 8 Day, strike.
  385.00   425.00   (400.00)
- **As above,** 8 Day, calendar.
  410.00   450.00   (425.00)
- **As above,** 8 Day, strike, calendar.
  425.00   475.00   (430.00)

- **Regulator,** black walnut, height 32", dial 12", spring, c. 1890, 8 Day (E2-39).
  310.00   350.00   (330.00)
- **As above,** 8 Day, strike.
  335.00   375.00   (345.00)
- **As above,** 8 Day, calendar.
  360.00   400.00   (375.00)
- **As above,** 8 Day, strike, calendar.
  385.00   425.00   (390.00)

- **Regulator,** oak, height 32", dial 12", spring, c. 1890, 8 Day (E2-39).
  285.00   325.00   (300.00)
- **As above,** 8 Day, strike.
  310.00   350.00   (340.00)
- **As above,** 8 Day, calendar.
  335.00   375.00   (345.00)
- **As above,** 8 Day, strike, calendar.
  360.00   400.00   (365.00)

152 / ANSONIA CLOCK COMPANY

English Drop

☐ **Regulator,** *rosewood, height 32",
dial 12", spring, c. 1890, 8 Day
(E2-39).*
      335.00   375.00   (350.00)
☐ **As above,** *8 Day, strike.*
      360.00   400.00   (375.00)
☐ **As above,** *8 Day, calendar.*
      385.00   425.00   (400.00)
☐ **As above,** *8 Day, strike, calendar.*
      410.00   450.00   (425.00)

☐ **Regulator M.,** *walnut, 32" x 16¾",
dial 12", spring, c. 1920, 8 Day
(E1-185).*
      310.00   350.00   (325.00)

REGULATOR/SECONDS BIT

☐ **Colonel,** *walnut, height 61", dial
18", c. 1910, 8 Day, weight (E2-43).*
      1650.00   1950.00   (1750.00)
☐ **As above,** *mahogany.*
      1600.00   1900.00   (1800.00)
☐ **As above,** *oak.*
      1450.00   1750.00   (1500.00)

Mecca

☐ **General,** *walnut, height 68", dial
18", c. 1910, 8 Day, weight (E2-43).*
      2400.00   2700.00   (2600.00)
☐ **As above,** *mahogany.*
      2350.00   2650.00   (2400.00)
☐ **Mecca,** *black walnut, weight,
height 58", porcelain dial 8", c.
1910, 8 Day (E2-40).*
      1000.00   1100.00   (1050.00)
☐ **As above,** *mahogany.*
      850.00   950.00   (875.00)

ANSONIA CLOCK COMPANY / 153

- **York,** *oak, height 46¼", dial 8", spring, c. 1910, 8 Day, strike (E2-43).*
  950.00   1200.00   (1000.00)
- **As above,** *8 Day, strike, spring.*
  1000.00   1250.00   (1100.00)
- **As above,** *8 Day, weight.*
  1050.00   1300.00   (1100.00)

REGULATOR/STORE

- **Ledger No.1,** *dark wood or oak, height 25", dial 6", c. 1890, 8 Day, strike (E2-16).*
  280.00   310.00   (290.00)
- **As above,** *8 Day.*
  230.00   260.00   (250.00)

York

Ledger No. 1

- **Medina,** *black walnut, height 52", porcelain dial 8", weight, c. 1910, 8 Day (E2-40).*
  1000.00   1250.00   (1100.00)
- **As above,** *mahogany.*
  850.00   1100.00   (900.00)

REGULATOR/SWEEP SECOND

☐ **Regulator, No.4,** *wood, height 84", dial 12", c. 1910, 8 Day, weight (E2-42).*
    3500.00   4500.00   (4000.00)
☐ **As above,** *8 Day, weight, strike.*
    4000.00   5000.00   (4500.00)

☐ **Regulator No.11,** *wood, height 105", dial 14", c. 1910, 8 Day, weight, Mercury pendulum (E2-43).*
    7500.00   8500.00   (8000.00)
☐ **As above,** *8 Day, weight, Gridiron pendulum.*
    8000.00   9000.00   (8500.00)

☐ **Regulator No.14,** *wood, height 84", dial 12", c. 1910, 8 Day, weight (E2-42).*
    5500.00   6500.00   (6000.00)

Regulator No. 11

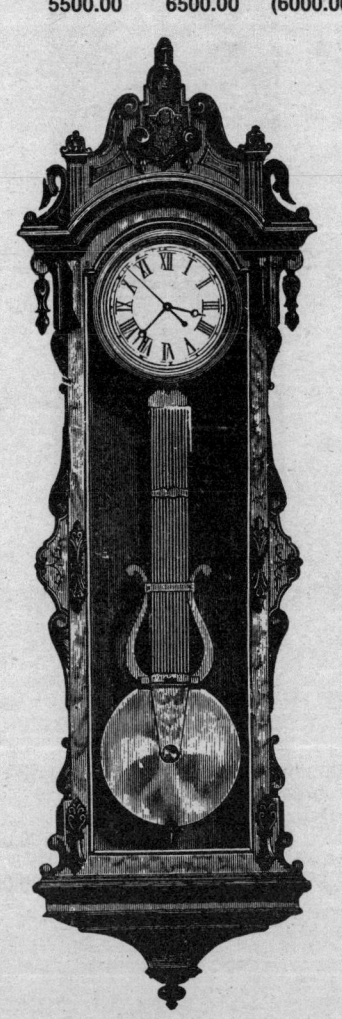

Regulator No. 14

STATUE/OVER 17"

☐ **Alpha,** violet bronze, French rococo sash, beveled glass, porcelain dial, 24¼" x 11¾", dial 4¼", spring, c. 1890, 8 Day, strike (E1-113).
    490.00   550.00   (525.00)

☐ **Art and Commerce,** Japanese bronze, French rococo sash, beveled glass, porcelain visible escapement dial, 20½" x 25½", spring, c. 1890, 8 Day, strike (E1-114).
    750.00   850.00   (800.00)

☐ **Attila,** Japanese or Syrian bronze, French rococo sash, beveled glass, porcelain visible escapement dial, 21½" x 19½", spring, c. 1890, 8 Day, strike (E1-115).
    490.00   550.00   (525.00)

☐ **Combatants,** Japanese bronze, French rococo sash, beveled glass, porcelain visible escapement dial, 21" x 19", spring, c. 1890, 8 Day, strike (E1-114).
    625.00   750.00   (650.00)

☐ **Cortez,** Japanese or Syrian bronze, French rococo sash, beveled glass, porcelain visible escapement dial, 21¾" x 19½", spring, c. 1890, 8 Day, strike (E1-115).
    450.00   500.00   (475.00)

☐ **Fisher,** bronze finish, French sash, beveled glass, porcelain dial, visible escapement, 22" x 15", dial 5½", spring, c. 1910, 8 Day, hour and ½ hour strike (E2-44).
    465.00   525.00   (500.00)

Combatants

Cortez

Fisher

156 / ANSONIA CLOCK COMPANY

Mars

Muses

Music And Poetry

☐ **Fisher,** Japanese, Barbedienne or Syrian bronze, French rococo sash, beveled glass, porcelain visible escapement dial, 22" x 15", dial 5½", spring, c. 1890, 8 Day, strike (E1-114).
    540.00   600.00   (560.00)

☐ **Fisher and Hunter,** Japanese bronze, iron base, 21½" x 19", dial 5½", spring, c. 1898, 8 Day, strike (E1-155).
    750.00   850.00   (775.00)

☐ **Mars,** Japanese or Syrian bronze, French rococo sash, beveled glass, porcelain visible escapement dial, 21½" x 19½", spring, c. 1890 (E1-115).
    450.00   500.00   (475.00)

☐ **Muses,** Japanese bronze, French rococo sash, beveled glass, porcelain visible escapement dial, 21½" x 19", spring, c. 1890, 8 Day, strike (E1-114).
    750.00   850.00   (800.00)

☐ **Music,** Japanese bronze, black iron base, 21¾" x 19½", spring, c. 1898, 8 Day, strike (E1-155).
    490.00   550.00   (525.00)

☐ **Music and Poetry,** Japanese bronze, French rococo sash, beveled glass, porcelain visible escapement dial, 20¾" x 20½", spring, c. 1890, 8 Day, strike (E1-114).
    800.00   900.00   (850.00)

☐ **Olympia,** Syrian bronze, rich gold trimmings or rich gold, French rococo sash, beveled glass, porcelain dial 4¾", 24¾" x 15½", spring, c. 1890, 8 Day, strike (E1-113).
    700.00   750.00   (725.00)

☐ **Patricia,** violet bronze, French rococo sash, beveled glass, porcelain dial, 24½" x 9", dial 4¾", spring, c. 1890, 8 Day, strike (E1-113).
    450.00   500.00   (475.00)

ANSONIA CLOCK COMPANY / 157

☐ **Pizarro,** Japanese or Syrian bronze, French rococo sash, beveled glass, porcelain visible escapement dial, 21¾" x 19½", spring, c. 1890, 8 Day, strike (E1-115).
450.00   500.00   (475.00)

☐ **Pizarro and Cortez,** Japanese bronze, French rococo sash, beveled glass, porcelain visible escapement dial, 20½" x 25¾", spring, c. 1890, 8 Day, strike (E1-114).
700.00   800.00   (750.00)

☐ **Provocation,** Japanese or Syrian bronze, French rococo sash, beveled glass, porcelain visible escapement dial, 21¾" x 21", spring, c. 1890, 8 Day, strike (E1-115).
450.00   500.00   (465.00)

☐ **Reflection,** Syrian bronze, French rococo sash, beveled glass, porcelain visible escapement dial, 25" x 24½", dial 5½", spring, c. 1890, 8 Day, strike (E1-114).
1000.00   1100.00   (1050.00)

☐ **Sappho,** Barbedienne or Verde bronze, French rococo sash, cream porcelain dial 4¼", 25" x 9¼", spring, c. 1898, 8 Day, strike (E1-156).
500.00   550.00   (525.00)

☐ **Sibyl and Gloria,** Barbedienne or Verde Clair bronze, French rococo sash, cream porcelain dial 4¾", 27½" x 10¾", spring, c. 1898, 8 Day, strike (E1-156).
600.00   650.00   (625.00)

☐ **Sibyl and Melody,** Barbedienne or Verde bronze, French rococo sash, cream porcelain dial 4¼", 25¼" x 10¾", spring, c. 1898 (E1-156).
550.00   600.00   (575.00)

☐ **Spring,** Syrian bronze, French rococo sash, beveled glass, porcelain visible escapement, 35" x 12¼", dial 5½", spring, c. 1890, 8 Day, strike (E1-113).
1000.00   1250.00   (1100.00)

☐ **Superba and La Source,** Art Nouveau, Syrian bronze, Brazilian onyx inlay, French rococo sash, beveled glass, porcelain dial, 28" x 15", dial 4", spring, c. 1890, 8 Day, strike (E1-113).
800.00   900.00   (850.00)

Pizarro and Cortez

Sappho

158 / ANSONIA CLOCK COMPANY

☐ **Tasso,** Japanese or Syrian bronze, French rococo sash, beveled glass, porcelain visible escapement dial, 20½" x 25¾", spring, c. 1890, 8 Day, strike (E1-115).
      400.00   450.00   (425.00)

☐ **Teresa,** violet bronze, French rococo sash, beveled glass, porcelain dial, 24" x 9", spring, c. 1890, 8 Day, strike (E1-113).
      450.00   500.00   (475.00)

☐ **Vocalists,** Syrian bronze, French rococo sash, beveled glass, porcelain visible escapement dial 5½", 22" x 24", spring, c. 1890, 8 Day, strike (E1-114).
      800.00   1000.00   (850.00)

Tasso

Superba and La Source

STATUE/UNDER 17"

☐ **No.1011,** bronze finish, height 17", dial 4", spring, c. 1883, 1 Day (E2-9).
      205.00   235.00   (215.00)

☐ **Alcazar,** gold, height 10¾", dial 2", spring, c. 1910, 1 Day (E2-34).
      60.00   75.00   (65.00)
☐ **As above,** 8 Day.
      95.00   115.00   (100.00)

☐ **Arion,** bronze finish, French rococo sash, beveled glass, porcelain dial, visible escapement, 15" x 17½", dial 4½", spring, c. 1910, 8 Day, hour and ½ hour strike (E2-44).
      250.00   280.00   (270.00)

☐ **Armour,** gold, height 8¼", dial 2", spring, c. 1910, 1 Day (E2-34).
      65.00   80.00   (70.00)
☐ **As above,** 8 Day.
      100.00   120.00   (105.00)

☐ **Artist,** Japanese bronze, 11" x 14", dial 4¼", spring, c. 1898, 8 Day, strike (E1-155).
      150.00   175.00   (160.00)

☐ **Boar Hunter,** Japanese bronze, French rococo sash, porcelain visible escapement dial, dial 5½", 15¾" x 26", spring, c. 1890, 8 Day, strike (E1-116).
      575.00   650.00   (600.00)

☐ **Cincinnatus,** bronze finish, French rococo sash, beveled glass, porcelain dial, visible escapement, 16½" x 19", dial 4½", spring, c. 1910, 8 Day, hour and ½ hour strike (E2-44).
      250.00   280.00   (260.00)

ANSONIA CLOCK COMPANY / 159

Cincinnatus

☐ **Dagobert,** *bronze finish, French rococo sash, beveled glass, porcelain dial, visible escapement, 15¾" x 19", dial 5½", spring, c. 1910, 8 Day (E2-44).*
335.00 375.00 (350.00)

☐ **Denis Papin,** *Japanese or Syrian bronze, French rococo sash, beveled glass, porcelain dial, 16¼" x 19", spring, c. 1890, 8 Day, strike (E1-116).*
285.00 325.00 (300.00)

☐ **Don Juan,** *Japanese or Syrian bronze, French rococo sash, beveled glass, porcelain visible escapement dial, 22" x 19½", dial 5½", spring, c. 1890, 8 Day, strike (E1-115).*
490.00 550.00 (525.00)

☐ **Egyptian,** *Japanese bronze, black iron base, 17" x 15", dial 5½", spring, c. 1898, 8 Day, strike (E1-155).*
335.00 375.00 (350.00)

☐ **Fantasy,** *bronze finish, French rococo sash, beveled glass, porcelain dial, visible escapement, 15" x 17½", dial 4½", spring, c. 1910, 8 Day, hour and ½ hour strike (E2-44).*
250.00 280.00 (260.00)

☐ **Hector,** *Venetian bronze, French rococo sash, beveled glass, porcelain visible escapement dial, 18" x 9¼", dial 4½", spring, c. 1890, 8 Day, strike (E1-113).*
270.00 300.00 (285.00)

☐ **Industry,** *Grecian or Venetian bronze, French rococo sash, beveled glass, porcelain dial, 19¼" x 10¾", dial 4¼", spring, c. 1890, 8 Day, strike (E1-115).*
360.00 400.00 (375.00)

☐ **Knight,** *Japanese bronze, 11½" x 16", dial 5", spring, c. 1898, 8 Day, strike (E1-158).*
335.00 375.00 (350.00)

☐ **Newton,** *Japanese or Syrian bronze, French rococo sash, beveled glass, porcelain visible escapement dial, 15" x 17½", dial 5½", spring, c. 1890, 8 Day, strike (E1-116).*
310.00 350.00 (325.00)

Dagobert

Knight

ANSONIA CLOCK COMPANY

☐ **Opera,** *Japanese or Syrian bronze, French rococo sash, beveled glass, porcelain visible escapement dial, 16¼" x 21", spring, c. 1890, 8 Day, strike (E1-116).*
    310.00   350.00   (325.00)

☐ **Philosopher,** *Japanese or Syrian bronze, French rococo sash, beveled glass, porcelain visible escapement dial, 15" x 17½", spring, c. 1890, 8 Day, strike (E1-116).*
    285.00   325.00   (300.00)

☐ **Reubens,** *Japanese bronze, French rococo sash, beveled glass, porcelain visible escapement dial, 16¼" x 21", spring, c. 1890, 8 Day, strike (E1-116).*
    360.00   400.00   (375.00)

☐ **Rex,** *bronze finish, French rococo sash, porcelain dial, visible escapement, 11½" x 16", dial 4", spring, c. 1910, 8 Day, hour and ½ hour strike (E2-44).*
    250.00   280.00   (275.00)

☐ **Shakespeare,** *Japanese or Syrian bronze, French rococo sash, beveled glass, porcelain visible escapement dial, 15" x 17½", dial 5½", spring, c. 1890, 8 Day, strike (E1-116).*
    310.00   350.00   (325.00)

☐ **Siren,** *Japanese or Syrian bronze, French rococo sash, beveled glass, porcelain visible escapement dial, 11½" x 16", dial 5", spring, c. 1890, 8 Day, strike (E1-116).*
    310.00   350.00   (325.00)

☐ **Trilby,** *Japanese bronze, 11" x 14", dial 4¼", spring, c. 1898, 8 Day, strike (E1-156).*
    150.00   175.00   (165.00)

☐ **Victory,** *bronze finish, French rococo sash, beveled glass, porcelain dial, visible escapement, 15" x 17½", dial 4½", spring, c. 1910, 8 Day, hour and ½ hour strike (E2-44).*
    250.00   280.00   (260.00)

SWING ARM

☐ **Arcadia Ball Swing,** *bronze and nickel finish, height 31½", c. 1890, 8 Day (E1-113).*
    2400.00   2800.00   (2500.00)

☐ **Juno Swing,** *Syrian bronze, clock and pendulum ball cobalt blue enameled, raised gold plated numerals and ornamentations, c. 1890, 8 Day (E1-113).*
    2000.00   2400.00   (2200.00)

Juno Swing

BOARDMAN-HUBBELL

Chauncey Boardman is best known for his uncased movements, and for continuing to produce the wooden tall clocks five years after most clock makers had virtually abandoned this style. Boardman did get into shelf clock production, though he never acquired a license or patent from Eli Terry, the original manufacturer of the design.

Boardman, and others (Hoadley, Leavenworth, and Ives) got around this sticky situation by producing clock movements of a unique style. Boardman's movement was of an overhead striking shelf clock. The clocks were similiar to Terry's, but not close enough to warrant legal action.

Boardman made movements for Chauncey Jerome at various times, went into partnership with J. Wells, and continued with his business in Bristol, and various other clockmaking ventures, until bankruptcy forced him out entirely.

Laporte Hubbell is associated primarily with the manufacture of marine clocks, and calendar clocks with a marine movement. Marine clocks are not necessarily found on seagoing vessels, but do have the advantage of running fairly accurately despite unstable positions. The marine clock movement evolved into the alarm clock.

Hubbel worked primarily with Hendrick, Clark and Barnes, and Levi Beach. He was associated with Chauncey Jerome in an unsuccessful business venture, and at one time formed a partnership with D.J. Mozart.

Foremost a mechanic, Hubbell, supplied countless marine movements to the trade for a great number of years.

CALENDAR

☐ **Shelf Model,** *8 Day lever, double spring, 16½" x 12½", dial 5½", calendar in aperture in bottom of door (M156-56).*
    2100.00   2500.00   (2200.00)

☐ **Wall Model,** *8 Day lever, double spring, 25" x 18", dial 11½", month-date strip made of sized linen, calendar in aperture in bottom door (M158-57).*
    3700.00   4000.00   (3750.00)

E. BURWELL-L.F. AND W.W. CARTER

A Bristol firm, Elias Burwell-Luther and William Carter prospered from an invention by Benjamin Bennett Lewis which featured a calendar clock.

Most of the wooden longcase clocks used a calendar device, and clockmakers considered it important that they remain relatively accurate. This meant they must account for irregularities such as leap year and 30 or 31 days in the month.

Although shelf clocks largely displaced the calendar mechanism, another famous clock company (Seth Thomas) revived them after purchasing an improved calendar patent from James and Eugene Mix. It was used for many years.

Lewis's mechanism was patented in 1862 and subsequently improved in the 80's. This calendar device was utilized not only by Burwell and Carter, but by other prominent manufacturers as well: E. Ingraham Company and the E.N. Welch Manufacturing Company.

CALENDAR

☐ **Italian-Type Shelf,** *8 Day, spring, strike, calendar mechanism (M179A-64).*
    800.00   900.00   (850.00)

☐ **Lewis No. 2,** *8 Day, double weight retaining power, rolling pinions, year calendar mechanism, 31" x 15½", 12" time and 8" calendar dial (E1-22, M172-62).*
    1000.00   1200.00   (1100.00)

☐ **Lewis No. 3,** *8 Day, double weight retaining power, rolling pinions, year calendar mechanism, 43" x 18", 14" time and 10" calendar dial (M174-63).*
    1300.00   1400.00   (1350.00)

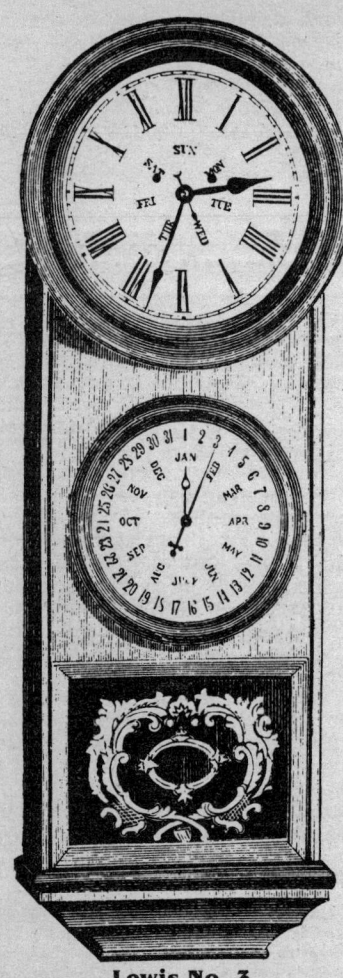

Lewis No. 3

☐ **Lewis No. 6,** 8 Day, double spring, lever, jeweled balace, year calendar mechanism 28" x 12¾", 5½" time and 7½" calendar dial (E1-22, M178-64).
    2600.00   2800.00   (2700.00)

☐ **Lewis No. 8,** 8 Day, double weight solid plates, rolling pinions, year calendar mechanism, 36" x 21", 8" time and 12" calendar dial (E1-22, M180-65).
    1000.00   1150.00   (1050.00)

☐ **Round Drop Wall,** 8 Day, double weight retaining power, year calendar mechanism, 57" x 21", 15" time and 10" calendar dial (M176-63).
    2200.00   2600.00   (2300.00)

☐ **Round Drop Wall,** 8 Day, double weight retaining power, year calendar mechanism, height 55", 18" time and 12" calendar dial (E1-22, M175-63).
    1600.00   1800.00   (1700.00)

☐ **Round Drop Wall,** 8 Day, time spring, strike, year calendar mechanism 26" x 13½", 9" time and 5½" calendar dial (M171-62).
    950.00   1100.00   (1000.00)

☐ **Round Drop Wall,** 8 Day, spring, year calendar mechanism, 27½" x 15", 11" time and 5½" calendar dial (M173-62).
    1250.00   1500.00   (1300.00)

☐ **Shelf,** manufactured by B.B. Lewis for L.F. and W.W. Carter, Bristol, CT, 8 Day, spring, strike, year calendar mechanism, 21" x 13½", dials 6" (M183-65).
    800.00   1100.00   (900.00)

☐ **Shelf,** 8 Day, spring, strike, year calendar mechanism, 22" x 13½", dials 6" (M182-65).
    875.00   1075.00   (900.00)

CLINTON AND MOOD
CALENDAR

☐ **1873 Patent Calendar Mechanism,** 8 Day, double spring, pendulum, glass sided wood top and bottom case (M161-58).
    4000.00   4500.00   (4250.00)

DAVIS CLOCK COMPANY
CALENDAR

☐ **Column Flat Top,** shelf, Columbus, MI, 8 Day, strike, simple calendar, 25" x 15¼", dial, 7" (M448-139).
    400.00   450.00   (425.00)

☐ **Shelf Clock,** *Texarkana, AR, 8 Day, strike, simple calendar, 27" x 15½", dial, 7" (M450-139).*
500.00   575.00   (550.00)

☐ **Shelf Clock,** *Texarkana, AR, 8 Day, strike, simple calendar, 27½" x 15½", dial, 7" (M451-139).*
475.00   575.00   (500.00)

EMPIRE CALENDAR CLOCK COMPANY

CALENDAR

☐ **Victorian Kitchen,** *8 Day, strike, simple calendar, 20½" x 12", dial, 6" (M470-145).*
500.00   600.00   (550.00)

☐ **Victorian Kitchen,** *8 Day, strike, simple calendar, 22" x 12½", dial, 6" (M471-145).*
700.00   800.00   (750.00)

C.W. FEISHTINGER

CALENDAR

☐ **Victorian Kitchen,** *8 Day, strike, 22" x 13½", dials, 5" (M477-146).*
700.00   800.00   (750.00)

☐ **Victorian Kitchen,** *8 Day, strike, 22" x 13½", dials, 5" (M479-147).*
725.00   825.00   (760.00)

☐ **Victorian Kitchen,** *8 Day, strike, 22" x 13½", dials, 5" (M480-147).*
700.00   800.00   (750.00)

☐ **Victorian Kitchen,** *8 Day, strike, 22" x 13½", dials, 5" (M481-147).*
700.00   800.00   (750.00)

FRANKLIN-MORSE

CALENDAR

☐ **Franklin-Morse Calendar,** *8 Day, strike, 22½" x 16", (M489-150).*
500.00   600.00   (550.00)

D.J. GALE

Also associated exclusively with the calendar clock, D.J. Gale, developed an intricate operational mechanism, that was patented in the last quarter of the 19th century. The rights were purchased by a Bristol company that was fairly prominent: Welch, Spring and Company.

A Wisconsin native, Gale's invention is much sought after by modern clock enthusiasts.

CALENDAR

☐ **Arditi,** *E.N., Welch Manufacturing Company, 8 Day, strike, 27½" x 17½", dials, 8" (E1-163, M505-155).*
1250.00   1500.00   (1300.00)

Arditi

☐ **Astronomical,** *Welch, Spring and Company, 8 Day, lever, dial, 24", 1877 patent calendar mechanism (E1-22, M498-153).*
4000.00   4500.00   (4250.00)

164 / W.L. GILBERT CLOCK COMPANY

Astronomical

Damrosch

☐ **Damrosch,** E.N. Welch Manufacturing Company, 8 Day, strike, height 41", dials, 8" (E1-163, M508-155).
    2100.00   2400.00   (2250.00)

☐ **Gale Drop,** Welch, Spring and Company, 8 Day, strike, height 30", dial 12" (E1-32, M501-154).
    3000.00   3500.00   (3300.00)

W.L. GILBERT CLOCK COMPANY

A product of the age of manufacturing, William Lewis Gilbert was once the employer of Silas Terry in Winsted. Terry moved to Waterbury before the entire factory burned. Gilbert, alas, did not.

Gilbert began his clockmaking career in the first quarter of the 19th century at a small clock shop which he owned in conjunction with a relative by marriage, named George Marsh. Gilbert also was in partnership with a John Birge in Bristol, and later with Chanucey and Noble Jerome.

After the Winsted factory burned, large brick buildings housed the facilities of the manufacturer. Eventually a corporation, Gilbert continued clock manufacturing until after World War II, when a decline that had been spiraling downward for years, caused it to be absorbed by a computing machines company.

Gilbert is best known for manufacturing inexpensive brass and alarm clocks.

ALARM/DRUM

☐ **Artistic,** nickel, long alarm, gilt perforated dial, height 6¾" dial 4½", c. 1896, 1 Day, alarm (E2-45).
    75.00   85.00   (80.00)

☐ **Basket Alarm,** basket work sides of brass, fancy brass matting and nickel trimmings, height 6¼", dial 4", c. 1896, 1 Day, alarm (E2-45).
    50.00   65.00   (55.00)

☐ **Blossom Alarm,** floral decorations on sides, assorted colors, nickel trimmings, height 6¼" dial 4", 1 Day (E2-45).
    45.00   55.00   (50.00)

☐ **Drum,** nickel, intermitting alarm, height 6¾", gilt perforated dial 4½", c. 1896, 1 Day, alarm (E2-45).
    75.00   85.00   (80.00)

Artistic

Basket Alarm

Blossom Alarm

Drum

166 / W.L. GILBERT CLOCK COMPANY

Ossa

☐ **Pet,** nickel, long alarm, height 6¾", dial 4½", c. 1896, 1 Day, alarm (E2-45).
    30.00   45.00   (35.00)

☐ **Reveille,** intermitting alarm, nickel, height 6¾", dial 4⅛", c. 1896, 1 Day, alarm (E2-45).
    45.00   55.00   (50.00)

☐ **Rob Roy Alarm,** marbleized, assorted colors, height 6¼", dial 4", c. 1896, 1 Day, alarm (E2-45).
    30.00   40.00   (35.00)

☐ **Spy,** nickel, dial 4", c. 1896, 1 Day, (E2-45).
    20.00   30.00   (25.00)

☐ **Wake-Up,** nickel, dial 4", c. 1896, 1 Day, alarm (E2-45).
    25.00   35.00   (30.00)

ALARM/FANCY

☐ **Cannon,** long alarm, marbleized wood case, gilt ornaments, gilt perforated dial, height 12", width 5", c. 1896, 1 Day, alarm (E2-46).
    100.00   120.00   (110.00)

☐ **Dewey Long Alarm,** nickel or gilt finish, ivory porcelain dial, height 8¾", base 9", dial 4", c. 1896 (E2-46).
    105.00   125.00   (115.00)

Reveille

☐ **Ossa,** height 6", dial 4½", c. 1896, 1 Day, (E2-45).
    15.00   25.00   (20.00)
☐ **As above,** 1 Day, alarm.
    20.00   30.00   (25.00)
☐ **As above,** 1 Day, calendar.
    60.00   80.00   (70.00)
☐ **As above,** 1 Day, alarm, calendar.
    70.00   85.00   (75.00)

Dewey Long Alarm

W.L. GILBERT CLOCK COMPANY / 167

Lighter Time

☐ **Singal Long Alarm,** *bronze or gilt, height 9¼", width 8¼", dial 4", c. 1896, 1 Day, alarm (E2-46).*
    65.00   80.00   (70.00)

Salute Long Alarm

Singal Long Alarm

☐ **Liberty Alarm,** *antique oak, brass pillars, height 9", dial 3", c. 1896, 1 Day, alarm (E2-46).*
    70.00   85.00   (75.00)

☐ **Lighter Time,** *red enamel clock case, oak battery box, height 6¼", width 5", c. 1896, 1 Day, (E2-45).*
    75.00   90.00   (80.00)

☐ **Salute Long Alarm,** *gilt clock and ornaments, marbleized base, height 9¼", dial 4", base 9", c. 1896, 1 Day, alarm (E2-46).*
    80.00   95.00   (85.00)

Sunlight Alarm

168 / W.L. GILBERT CLOCK COMPANY

☐ **Sunlight Alarm,** *nickel, oak battery box, height 8¼", width 5", c. 1896, 1 Day, alarm (E2-45).*
      90.00   110.00   (95.00)

CABINET

☐ **Champion No. 1,** *oak, height 17", dial 5½", c. 1899, 8 Day, strike, (E2-60).*
      135.00   160.00   (140.00)

☐ **Champion No. 2,** *oak, height 17", dial 5½", c. 1899, 8 Day, strike, (E2-60).*
      135.00   160.00   (150.00)

☐ **Champion No. 3,** *oak, height 17", dial 5½", c. 1899, 8 Day, strike, (E2-60).*
      135.00   160.00   (150.00)

☐ **Excelsior No. 1,** *oak, height 16½", dial 5½", c. 1899, 8 Day, strike, (E2-60).*
      145.00   165.00   (150.00)

☐ **Excelsior No. 2,** *oak, height 16½", dial 5½", c. 1899, 8 Day, strike, (E2-60).*
      145.00   165.00   (150.00)

Excelsior No. 1

☐ **Excelsior No. 3,** *oak, height 16½", dial 5½", c. 1899, 8 Day, strike, (E2-60).*
      145.00   165.00   (150.00)

☐ **Excelsior No. 4,** *oak, height 16½", dial 5½", c. 1899, 8 Day, strike, (E2-60).*
      145.00   165.00   (150.00)

CALENDAR

☐ **Alpine,** *gallery type, height 24", dial 12", 8 Day, strike, simple calendar (E2-63).*
      225.00   250.00   (230.00)

☐ **Benworth,** *27" x 15", dial 8", 8 Day, strike, simple calendar (E1-152, E2-61).*
      700.00   800.00   (750.00)

☐ **Columbia,** *oak wall, height 37½", dial 8", 8 Day, strike, simple calendar (E2-58).*
      550.00   625.00   (560.00)

☐ **Concord (Kitchen),** *thermometer and barometer, height 23½", dial 6", 8 Day, strike, simple calendar (E2-57).*
      175.00   200.00   (190.00)

☐ **Concord,** *23½" x 14½", 8 Day, strike, simple calendar (M442-137).*
      160.00   185.00   (165.00)

Champion No. 1

W.L. GILBERT CLOCK COMPANY / 169

Alpine

Columbia

Benworth

Janeiro-Figure 8

170 / W.L. GILBERT CLOCK COMPANY

Longbranch

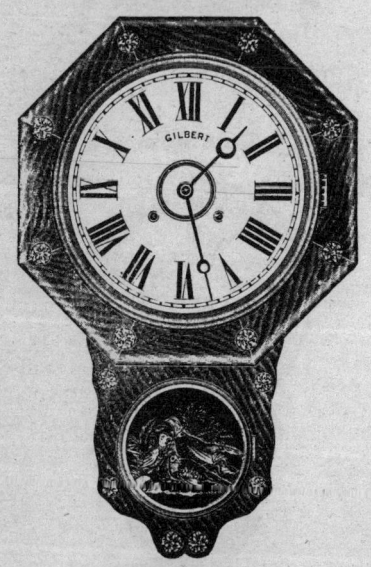

Mountauk

☐ **Consort Octagon Top,** *height 31", dial 12", 8 Day, strike, simple calendar (E2-63).*
325.00   375.00   (350.00)

☐ **Eureka,** *29" x 15½", 8 Day, strike, simple calendar, spring (M443-137).*
350.00   400.00   (375.00)

☐ **Excelsior,** *27½" x 15½", 8 Day, strike, simple calendar, spring (M444-138).*
350.00   400.00   (360.00)

☐ **Janeiro-Figure 8,** *height 22", dial 10", 8 Day, strike, simple calendar (E2-63).*
325.00   375.00   (340.00)

☐ **Longbranch,** *28" x 16", dial 8", 8 Day, strike, simple calendar, spring (E2-61, M447-138).*
425.00   475.00   (450.00)

☐ **Mountauk Octagon Top,** *short drop, height 26", dial 12", 8 Day, strike, simple calendar (E2-63).*
325.00   375.00   (350.00)

☐ **National,** *thermometer and barometer, 27½" x 16", dial 8", 8 Day, strike, simple calendar, spring (M446-138).*
450.00   500.00   (475.00)

☐ **Octagon Top,** *short drop, height 22½", dial 12", 8 Day, strike, simple calendar (M439-136).*
300.00   350.00   (335.00)

☐ **Octagon Top,** *short drop gilt, height 20½", dial 8", 8 Day, strike, simple calendar (E2-63).*
225.00   250.00   (230.00)

☐ **Octagon Top,** *short drop gilt, height 23½", dial 10", 8 Day, strike, simple calendar (E2-63).*
250.00   275.00   (260.00)

☐ **Octagon Top,** *short drop gilt, height 25½", dial 12", 8 Day, strike, simple calendar (E2-63).*
250.00   300.00   (275.00)

☐ **Ossa,** *round alarm, height 6", dial 1½", 1 Day, alarm, simple calendar (E2-45).*
65.00   85.00   (75.00)

W.L. GILBERT CLOCK COMPANY / 171

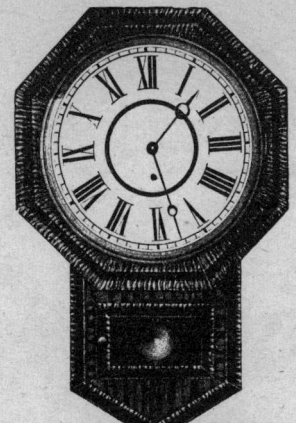

Octagon Top

Ossa

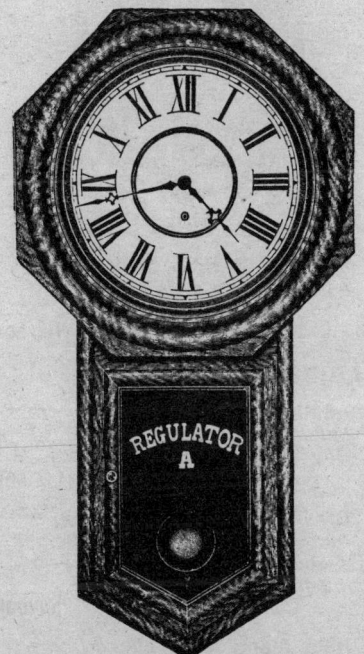

Regulator A

Saratoga

172 / W.L. GILBERT CLOCK COMPANY

☐ **Regulator A-Long Drop,** *height 31",
dial 12", 8 Day, strike, simple
calendar (E2-63).*
    325.00   375.00   (350.00)

☐ **Regulator B Octagon Top,** *height
29", dial 12", 8 Day, strike, simple
calendar (E2-63).*
    325.00   375.00   (350.00)

☐ **Riverside Octagon Top,** *short drop,
height 23", dial 10", 8 Day, strike,
simple calendar (E2-63).*
    325.00   375.00   (350.00)

☐ **Saratoga Wall Regulator,** *height
39", dial 8", 8 Day, strike, simple
calendar (E2-64).*
    450.00   500.00   (475.00)

Star

☐ **Victorian Shelf No. 28,** *19½" x 12",
8 day, strike, simple calendar
(M440-137).*
    150.00   175.00   (160.00)

CARRIAGE

☐ **All Right,** *oxidized copper or brass,
height 10", dial 2¾", c. 1896, 1
Day, alarm (E2-46).*
    100.00   120.00   (115.00)

☐ **Graduate Alarm,** *nickel-plated
frame and sides, gilt front, height
9", dial 3", c. 1896, 1 Day, alarm
(E2-46).*
    85.00   105.00   (90.00)

☐ **Hello Alarm,** *nickel-plated frame,
leatherette, glass sides, height 9",
dial 2¾", c. 1896, 1 Day, alarm
(E2-46).*
    90.00   110.00   (95.00)

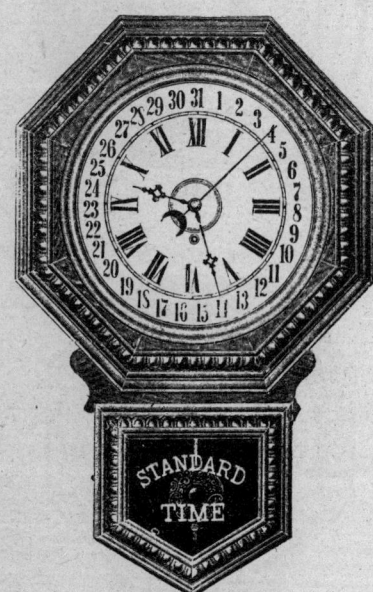

Standard Admiral

☐ **Standard Admiral Octagon Top,**
*short drop, height 24", dial 12", 8
Day, strike, simple calendar (E2-63,
M437-136).*
    300.00   325.00   (315.00)

☐ **Star Octagon Top,** *long drop, height
32½", dial 12" 8 Day, strike, simple
calendar (E2-62).*
    450.00   500.00   (475.00)

W.L. GILBERT CLOCK COMPANY / 173

All Right

☐ **Hello Long Alarm,** *nickel-plated frame, glass sides, height 9", dial 2¾", c. 1896, 1 Day, alarm (E2-46).*
      90.00   **110.00**   **(95.00)**

☐ **Interval,** *intermitting alarm, nickel-plated frame, glass sides, height 9", dial 2¾", c. 1896, 1 Day, alarm (E2-46).*
      95.00   **115.00**   **(100.00)**

Interval

Graduate Alarm

☐ **'76 Alarm, Rolling Bell,** *nickel-plated frame and sides, height 9", dial 3", c. 1896, 1 Day, alarm (E2-46).*
      90.00   **110.00**   **(95.00)**

☐ **Turnout,** *nickle-plated frame and sides, height 9", dial 3", c. 1896, 1 Day, alarm (E2-46).*
      80.00   **100.00**   **(85.00)**

174 / W.L. GILBERT CLOCK COMPANY

CONNECTICUT SHELF
BEE HIVE
- **Round Gothic,** *walnut, height 19",
c. 1875, 1 Day, strike (E1-18).*
  90.00   110.00   (95.00)
- **As above,** *8 day, strike*
  110.00   135.00   (115.00)

Round Gothic

CONNECTICUT SHELF
COLUMN
- **Column Spring,** *dark wood, rose,
shell and gilt columns, spring, 15" x
10⅝", c. 1875, 1 Day, strike (E2-52).*
  105.00   130.00   (115.00)
- **As above,** *8 day, strike*
  140.00   165.00   (145.00)
- **Column Spring,** *rosewood, shell or
gilt columns, height 15", c. 1875, 1
Day, strike, (E1-61).*
  175.00   200.00   (195.00)
- **As above,** *8 day, strike*
  195.00   225.00   (200.00)
- **Column Weight,** *dark wood, weight,
rose, shell and gilt columns, 25" x
15⅛", c. 1875, 1 Day, strike (E2-52).*
  150.00   170.00   (165.00)

Column Weight

- **Extra Rolling Pinion,** *rosewood,
rose shell or gilt column, height
30½", c. 1875, 8 Day, weight, strike
(E1-19).*
  285.00   325.00   (300.00)
- **Gilt And Shell Column,** *rosewood,
mahogany and zebra, height weight
clocks, 25", spring clocks, 18", c.
1875, 1 Day, strike, mahogany
(E1-19).*
  125.00   150.00   (140.00)
- **As above,** *8 Day, strike, mahogany*
  150.00   175.00   (165.00)
- **As above,** *1 Day, strike, rosewood*
  150.00   175.00   (165.00)
- **As above,** *8 Day, strike, rosewood*
  150.00   175.00   (165.00)
- **As above,** *1 Day, strike, zebra*
  160.00   185.00   (175.00)
- **As above,** *8 Day, strike, zebra*
  185.00   210.00   (200.00)
- **London Mantel,** *rosewood, rose and
gilt pillars, height 17½", c. 1875, 8
Day, simple spring (E1-19).*
  175.00   200.00   (195.00)

W.L. GILBERT CLOCK COMPANY / 175

Paragon

- ☐ **Paragon,** *dark wood, rose or gilt ornaments, spring, 15" x 10⅝", c. 1875, 1 Day, strike (E2-52).*
  105.00   125.00   (115.00)
- ☐ **As above,** *8 Day, strike*
  140.00   165.00   (145.00)
- ☐ **Paragon Spring,** *rosewood or gilt ornamented, height 15", c. 1875, 1 day, strike (E1-61).*
  140.00   165.00   (145.00)
- ☐ **As above,** *8 Day, strike*
  165.00   190.00   (175.00)

CONNECTICUT SHELF
COTTAGE

- ☐ **Cottage,** *walnut, height 11" to 13", c. 1875, 1 Day, simple spring (E1-18).*
  65.00   80.00   (75.00)
- ☐ **No. 2 Cottage Time,** *dark wood, 12" x 8", c. 1875, 1 Day (E2-52).*
  70.00   90.00   (80.00)
- ☐ **Coupon,** *dark wood, spring, 13¼" x 10⅝", c. 1875, 1 Day, strike (E2-53).*
  70.00   90.00   (80.00)
- ☐ **As above,** *8 Day, strike*
  105.00   125.00   (115.00)
- ☐ **Coupon,** *walnut veneer, 14" x 11" spring, c. 1875, 1 Day (E2-53).*
  70.00   90.00   (75.00)
- ☐ **As above,** *8 Day*
  105.00   125.00   (115.00)
- ☐ **As above,** *8 Day, strike*
  110.00   135.00   (120.00)
- ☐ **Favorite,** *dark wood, spring, height 13½", weight 11⅛", c. 1875, 1 Day, strike (E2-51).*
  65.00   80.00   (75.00)
- ☐ **As above,** *8 Day, strike*
  90.00   110.00   (95.00)

Favorite

- ☐ **Rose Cottage Time,** *rose sash, dark wood, 9⅞" x 7¾", c. 1875, 1 Day (E2-52).*
  70.00   85.00   (75.00)
- ☐ **Rose Gilt,** *rosewood, height 9½", c. 1875, 1 Day, spring (E1-18).*
  70.00   85.00   (75.00)
- ☐ **Rose Gilt Time,** *gilt sash, dark wood, 9⅞" x 7¾", c. 1875, 1 Day.*
  70.00   85.00   (75.00)

176 / W.L. GILBERT CLOCK COMPANY

- ☐ **Rose Mantel,** *rosewood, height 12", c. 1875, 1 Day, simple spring (E1-18).*
  80.00   100.00   (85.00)
- ☐ **As above,** *8 Day, simple spring*
  105.00   125.00   (115.00)
- ☐ **Victoria,** *walnut, height 14½", c. 1875, 8 Day, simple spring (E1-18).*
  150.00   175.00   (160.00)
- ☐ **Waverly,** *dark wood, spring, 13¼" x 10⅝", c. 1875, 1 Day, strike (E2-52).*
  80.00   100.00   (85.00)
- ☐ **As above,** *8 Day, strike*
  110.00   135.00   (115.00)

CONNECTICUT SHELF
OCTAGON TOP

- ☐ **Comet,** *walnut veneer, 14" x 11", spring, c. 1875, 1 Day (E2-53).*
  65.00   80.00   (70.00)
- ☐ **As above,** *1 Day, strike*
  70.00   90.00   (75.00)
- ☐ **As above,** *8 Day*
  80.00   100.00   (85.00)
- ☐ **As above,** *8 Day, strike*
  90.00   110.00   (95.00)
- ☐ **Comet,** *dark wood, spring, height 14¾", weight 10⅝", c. 1875, 1 Day, strike (E2-53).*
  60.00   75.00   (65.00)
- ☐ **As above,** *8 Day, strike*
  75.00   90.00   (80.00)
- ☐ **Comet Time,** *walnut veneer, width 11", weight 9", spring, c. 1875, 1 Day, (E2-53).*
  80.00   100.00   (90.00)
- ☐ **Octagon Top,** *walnut, height 10", c. 1875, 1 Day, spring (E1-19).*
  70.00   85.00   (75.00)
- ☐ **Octagon Top,** *walnut, height 13½", c. 1875, 1 Day, simple spring (E1-19).*
  70.00   85.00   (75.00)
- ☐ **As above,** *8 Day, simple spring*
  85.00   105.00   (90.00)

CONNECTICUT SHELF/O.G.

- ☐ **O.O.G. Spring,** *dark wood, spring, 18⅜" x 11¾", c. 1875, 1 Day, strike (E2-51).*
  80.00   100.00   (90.00)

Comet

O.O.G. Spring

W.L. GILBERT CLOCK COMPANY / 177

☐ **O.G. Weight,** *dark wood, 25⅞" x 15⅜", c. 1875, 1 Day, strike (E2-51).*
    100.00   120.00   (110.00)
☐ **As above,** *8 Day, strike*
    135.00   160.00   (140.00)

CONNECTICUT SHELF/ROUND TOP

☐ **Carved Walnut,** *walnut, height 19", c. 1875, 8 Day, simple spring (E1-19).*
    95.00   115.00   (100.00)

☐ **Keystone,** *polished rosewood, height 17¾", c. 1875, 1 Day, simple spring (E1-58).*
    150.00   175.00   (160.00)
☐ **As above,** *8 Day, simple spring*
    175.00   200.00   (195.00)

☐ **Key-Stone,** *dark wood, spring, 17¾" x 12⅝", c. 1875, 1 Day, strike, (E2-51).*
    150.00   175.00   (160.00)
☐ **As above,** *8 Day, strike*
    175.00   200.00   (180.00)

☐ **Round Top,** *dark wood, spring, 13⅜" x 10⅜", c. 1875, 1 Day, strike (E2-51).*
    70.00   90.00   (80.00)
☐ **As above,** *8 Day, strike*
    110.00   135.00   (125.00)

☐ **Round Top Time,** *dark wood, 11" x 8⅛", c. 1875, 1 Day, strike (E2-51).*
    80.00   100.00   (85.00)
☐ **As above,** *8 Day, strike*
    105.00   125.00   (115.00)

☐ **Star Round Top,** *dark wood, spring, 16¾" x 11⅝", c. 1875, 1 Day, strike (E2-53).*
    90.00   110.00   (95.00)
☐ **As above,** *8 Day, strike*
    120.00   145.00   (125.00)

Star Round Top Extra

☐ **Star Round Top Extra,** *dark wood, spring, 16¾" x 11¾", c. 1875, 1 Day, strike (E2-53).*
    90.00   110.00   (95.00)
☐ **As above,** *8 Day, strike*
    120.00   145.00   (125.00)

☐ **Venetian,** *rosewood, rose and gilt, height 15", c. 1875, 1 Day, simple spring (E1-19).*
    95.00   115.00   (100.00)
☐ **As above,** *height 18", 8 Day, simple spring*
    115.00   140.00   (125.00)

☐ **Walnut Arch Top,** *walnut, height 13½", c. 1875, 8 Day, simple spring (E1-18).*
    125.00   150.00   (140.00)

Round Top

178 / W.L. GILBERT CLOCK COMPANY

- ☐ **Walnut Crown,** *spring, 21" x 11", c. 1875, 8 Day, strike (E2-53).*
  150.00   175.00   (160.00)

- ☐ **Walnut Round Gothic,** *walnut, height 13", c. 1875, 1 Day, simple spring (E1-18).*
  65.00   85.00   (75.00)

- ☐ **Walnut Round Top,** *walnut, height 10", c. 1875, 1 Day, simple spring (E1-19).*
  75.00   90.00   (80.00)

CONNETICUT SHELF
SPLIT TOP

- ☐ **Gilbert Gem,** *dark wood, spring, 17¼" x 10¾", c. 1875, 1 Day, strike (E2-52).*
  105.00   125.00   (115.00)
- ☐ **As above,** *8 Day, strike*
  125.00   150.00   (140.00)

- ☐ **Rocket,** *dark wood, spring, 15½" x 11⅛", c. 1875, 1 Day, strike (E2-52).*
  75.00   95.00   (80.00)
- ☐ **As above,** *8 Day, strike*
  95.00   105.00   (100.00)

Rocket

- ☐ **Rose Doric,** *rosewood, height 16", c. 1875, 1 Day, simple spring (E1-19).*
  105.00   125.00   (115.00)

- ☐ **Walnut Gothic,** *walnut, height 14½", c. 1875, 8 Day, simple spring (E1-19).*
  70.00   85.00   (75.00)

- ☐ **Walnut Gothic Pillar,** *walnut, height 15", c. 1875, 8 Day, simple spring (E1-19).*
  105.00   125.00   (115.00)

CONNECTICUT SHELF
STEEPLE

- ☐ **Sharp Gothic,** *walnut, height 20", c. 1875, 1 Day, simple spring (E1-19).*
  95.00   115.00   (100.00)

- ☐ **Sharp Gothic,** *dark wood, spring, 19½" x 11¼", c. 1875, 1 Day, strike (E2-51).*
  95.00   115.00   (100.00)
- ☐ **As above,** *8 Day, strike*
  125.00   150.00   (135.00)

Gilbert Gem

W.L. GILBERT CLOCK COMPANY / 179

Sharp Gothic

☐ **Terese,** rich ormolu gold finish, mercurial pendulum, ivory porcelain dial, visible escapement, white beveled plate glass front, back and sides, 17" x 8¾", c. 1910 (E1-125).
    540.00   600.00   (575.00)

☐ **Trinity,** rich ormolu gold finish, fancy visible pendulum, four fancy columns, ivory porcelain dial, visible escapement, 16½" x 10½", c. 1910 (E1-125).
    625.00   700.00   (640.00)

☐ **Tunis,** rich ormolu gold finish, mercurial pendulum, ivory porcelain dial, visible escapement, white beveled plate glass front, back and sides, 10½" x 8¾", c. 1910 (E1-125).
    425.00   475.00   (450.00)

☐ **Tuscan,** Brazilian green onyx columns, onyx cap and base, mercurial pendulum, rich ormolu gold finish, porcelain dial, visible escapement, 19" x 11½", c. 1910, (E1-125).
    675.00   750.00   (700.00)

☐ **Small Gothic,** walnut, height 14½", c. 1875, 1 Day, simple spring (E1-18).
    100.00   120.00   (110.00)

☐ **Small Sharp Gothic,** dark wood, 14¾" x 8⅞", c. 1875, 1 Day (E2-51).
    80.00   100.00   (85.00)

☐ **As above,** 1 Day, strike
    100.00   120.00   (110.00)

☐ **Winstead Gothic Extra,** dark wood, 17¼" x 10½", c. 1875, 1 Day, strike (E2-51).
    80.00   100.00   (85.00)

☐ **As above,** 8 Day, strike
    110.00   135.00   (115.00)

CRYSTAL REGULATOR

☐ **Tarsus,** onyx base, rich ormolu gold finish, fancy visible pendulum, ivory porcelain dial, visible escapement, 16¾" x 11", c. 1910 (E1-125).
    575.00   650.00   (600.00)

Trinity

180 / W.L. GILBERT CLOCK COMPANY

☐ **Valerie,** polished brass finish, mercurial pendulum, ivory porcelain dial, visible escapement, white beveled plate glass front, back and sides, 9¼" x 6⅜", c. 1910 (E1-125).
205.00   235.00   (225.00)

☐ **Venice,** rich ormolu gold finish, mercurial pendulum, ivory porcelain dial, visible escapement, white beveled plate glass front, back and sides, 16" x 7¾", c. 1910 (E1-125).
490.00   550.00   (500.00)

☐ **Verdi,** rich ormolu gold finish, mercurial pendulum, ivory porcelain dial, visible escapement, white beveled plate glass front, back and sides, 15" x 8¾", c. 1910 (E1-125).
800.00   900.00   (850.00)

☐ **Vista,** polished brass finish, mercurial pendulum, porcelain dial, visible escapement, white beveled plate glass front, back and sides, 10¾" x 6⅜", c. 1910 (E1-125).
245.00   275.00   (260.00)

GALLERY

☐ **Brass Lever,** brass, dial, 5", c. 1875, 1 Day (E1-18).
105.00   125.00   (115.00)

☐ **Bronze Lever,** bronze, dial, 4", c. 1875, 1 Day (E1-18).
60.00   75.00   (65.00)

☐ **Corridor,** varnished oak finish, 24" x 15½", c. 1920, 8 Day (E1-184).
1 05.00   125.00   (115.00)

☐ **Octagon Lever,** oak, 4" dial, c. 1875, 1 Day (E2-54).
45.00   60.00   (50.00)
☐ As above, 6" dial, 1 Day.
65.00   80.00   (70.00)
☐ As above, 6" dial, 1 Day, alarm.
75.00   90.00   (80.00)
☐ As above, 6" dial, 1 Day, strike.
80.00   100.00   (85.00)
☐ As above, 8" dial, 1 Day.
105.00   125.00   (115.00)
☐ As above, 8" dial, 1 Day, alarm.
110.00   135.00   (120.00)
☐ As above, 8" dial, 1 Day, strike.
125.00   150.00   (130.00)

Octagon Lever

☐ **Plain Gilt Gallery,** pendulum, spring, 12", c. 1875, 8 Day, strike (E1-18).
335.00   375.00   (350.00)
☐ As above, 10", 8 Day, strike.
285.00   325.00   (300.00)
☐ As above, 8", 8 Day, strike.
245.00   275.00   (260.00)

KITCHEN

☐ **Abyla,** walnut, walnut trimmed, height 20", dial 6", c. 1888, 8 Day, strike, spring wound (E1-30).
125.00   150.00   (140.00)
☐ As above, ash.
175.00   200.00   (190.00)

☐ **Albany No. 44,** oak, height 22½", dial 6", c. 1900, 8 Day, strike, spring wound (E2-56).
135.00   160.00   (145.00)

☐ **Alpine,** walnut, height 19½", dial 6", c. 1888, 1 Day, strike, spring wound (E1-30).
120.00   145.00   (130.00)
☐ As above, ash.
170.00   195.00   (180.00)

☐ **Austin No. 45,** oak, height 22½", dial 6", c. 1900, 8 Day, strike, spring wound, (E2-56).
135.00   160.00   (140.00)

☐ **Britannic No. 47,** oak, height 25", dial 6", c. 1900, 8 Day, strike, spring wound (E2-56).
155.00   180.00   (160.00)

W.L. GILBERT CLOCK COMPANY / 181

Abyla

Britannic No. 47

Austin No. 45

Calpe

182 / W.L. GILBERT CLOCK COMPANY

Concord

- **Cairo,** oak, height 23", dial 6", c. 1905, 8 Day, strike, spring wound (E2-55).
  150.00   175.00   (155.00)

- **Calla,** walnut, height 20", dial 6", c. 1888, 8 Day, strike, spring wound (E1-30).
  115.00   140.00   (125.00)

- **Calpe,** ash, walnut trimmed, height 20", dial 6", spring wound, c. 1888 (E1-30).
  120.00   145.00   (130.00)

- **Calypso,** walnut, height 20½", dial 6", c. 1888, 8 Day, strike, spring wound (E1-30).
  115.00   140.00   (125.00)

- **Clay,** oak, height 24", dial 6", c. 1900, 8 Day, strike, spring wound (E2-55).
  150.00   175.00   (160.00)

- **Concord,** oak, height 23½", dial 6", c. 1903, 8 Day, strike, spring wound (E2-57).
  150.00   175.00   (160.00)

- **Concord Calendar,** oak, height 23½", dial 6", c. 1903, 8 Day, strike, spring wound (E2-57).
  175.00   200.00   (180.00)

- **Crius,** walnut, height 19½", dial 6", c. 1888, 1 Day, strike, spring wound (E1-30).
  110.00   135.00   (120.00)
- **As above,** ash.
  160.00   185.00   (175.00)

- **Dio,** walnut, height 20", dial 6", c. 1888, 8 Day, strike, spring wound (E1-30).
  115.00   140.00   (120.00)

- **Dove,** oak, height 22", dial 6", c. 1896, 8 Day, strike, spring wound (E2-59).
  145.00   170.00   (150.00)
- **As above,** walnut
  170.00   195.00   (175.00)

- **Eagle,** oak, height 22", dial 6", c. 1896, 8 Day, strike, spring wound (E2-59).
  145.00   170.00   (160.00)
- **As above,** walnut
  170.00   195.00   (180.00)

- **Eclipse,** oak, height 25", dial 6", c. 1903, 8 Day, strike, spring wound (E2-57).
  160.00   185.00   (175.00)

- **Edina,** walnut, height 18¾", dial 5", c. 1888, 1 Day, strike, spring wound (E1-30).

- **Egypt,** oak, height 23", dial 6", c. 1905, 8 Day, strike, spring wound (E2-55).
  150.00   175.00   (160.00)

- **Erie,** oak, height 22½", dial 6", c. 1896, 8 Day, strike, spring wound (E2-59).
  140.00   165.00   (165.00)
- **As above,** walnut
  165.00   190.00   (190.00)

- **Eros,** walnut, height 19½", dial 6", c. 1888, 8 Day, strike, spring wound (E1-30).
  115.00   140.00   (120.00)

Dove

Eclipse

Eagle

Fruit

184 / W.L. GILBERT CLOCK COMPANY

Geranium

- [ ] **Ersa**, walnut, height 19½", dial 6", c. 1888, 8 Day, strike, spring wound (E1-30).
  115.00   130.00   (120.00)
- [ ] **As above**, ash
  165.00   180.00   (175.00)
- [ ] **Flora**, walnut with ash trimmings, height 17", dial 5", c. 1888, 1 Day, strike, spring wound ((E1-30).
  110.00   135.00   (125.00)
- [ ] **Fruit**, oak, height 24½", dial 6", c. 1903, 8 Day, strike, spring wound (E2-57).
  160.00   185.00   (175.00)
- [ ] **As above**, walnut
  185.00   210.00   (200.00)
- [ ] **Geranium**, oak, height 24", dial 6", c. 1903, 8 Day, strike, spring wound (E2-57).
  150.00   175.00   (160.00)
- [ ] **Hawk**, oak, height 22", dial 6", c.1896, 8 Day, strike, spring wound (E2-59).
  150.00   170.00   (160.00)
- [ ] **As above**, walnut
  175.00   195.00   (180.00)
- [ ] **Hestia**, walnut, height 20½", dial 6", c. 1888, 1 Day, strike, spring wound (E1-30).
  110.00   135.00   (120.00)

- [ ] **Huron**, oak, height 22½", dial 6", c. 1896, 8 Day, strike, spring wound (E2-59).
  145.00   170.00   (150.00)
- [ ] **As above**, walnut
  170.00   195.00   (180.00)
- [ ] **Indiana No. 25**, oak, height 24", dial 6", c. 1900, 8 Day, strike, spring wound (E2-56).
  155.00   180.00   (160.00)
- [ ] **Iowa No. 23**, height 24", dial 6", c. 1900, 8 Day, strike, spring wound (E2-56).
  155.00   180.00   (165.00)
- [ ] **Laurel, Thermometer And Barometer**, oak, height 24", dial 6", c. 1903, 8 Day, strike, spring wound (E2-57).
  160.00   185.00   (175.00)
- [ ] **Lesbia**, walnut, height 16½", dial 5", c. 1888, 1 Day, strike, spring wound (E1-30).
  105.00   125.00   (115.00)
- [ ] **Lincoln**, oak, height 23", dial 6", c. 1900, 8 Day, strike, spring wound (E2-55).
  150.00   175.00   (160.00)
- [ ] **Mahuta**, walnut, height 18½", dial 6", c. 1888, 1 Day, strike, spring wound (E1-30).
  110.00   135.00   (120.00)
- [ ] **Michigan**, oak, height 22½", dial 6", c. 1896, 8 Day, strike, spring wound (E2-59).
  140.00   165.00   (145.00)
- [ ] **As above**, walnut
  165.00   190.00   (175.00)
- [ ] **Missouri No. 26**, oak, height 24", dial 6", c. 1900, 8 Day, strike, spring wound (E2-56).
  155.00   180.00   (160.00)
- [ ] **Mogul**, oak, height 23, dial 6", c. 1900, 8 Day, strike, spring wound (E2-55).
  150.00   175.00   (165.00)
- [ ] **Ontario**, oak, height 22½", dial 6", c. 1896, 8 Day, strike, spring wound (E2-59).
  145.00   170.00   (150.00)
- [ ] **As above**, walnut
  170.00   195.00   (188.00)

W.L. GILBERT CLOCK COMPANY / 185

Hawk

Iowa No. 23

Huron

Laurel

186 / W.L. GILBERT CLOCK COMPANY

Lincoln

Michigan

☐ **Oregon No. 24,** *oak, height 24", dial 6", c. 1900, 8 Day, strike, spring wound (E2-56).*
    155.00   180.00   (160.00)

☐ **Owl,** *oak, height 22", dial 6", c. 1896, 8 Day, strike, spring wound (E2-59).*
    145.00   170.00   (150.00)

☐ **As above,** *walnut*
    170.00   195.00   (190.00)

☐ **Pasha,** *oak, height 23", dial 6", c. 1905, 8 Day, strike, spring wound (E2-55).*
    150.00   175.00   (160.00)

☐ **Perfect,** *oak, height 23½", dial 6", c. 1903, 8 Day, strike, spring wound (E2-57).*
    145.00   170.00   (150.00)

☐ **Perfect, Thermometer And Barometer,** *oak, height 23½", dial 6", c. 1903, 8 Day, strike, spring wound (E2-57).*
    155.00   180.00   (160.00)

☐ **Peto,** *walnut, height 20", dial 6", c. 1888, 8 Day, strike, spring wound (E1-30).*
    115.00   140.00   (125.00)

☐ **Petrel No. 28,** *oak, height 24", dial 6", c. 1900, 8 Day, strike, spring wound (E2-56).*
    155.00   180.00   (160.00)

☐ **Pharaoh,** *oak, height 23", dial 6", c. 1905, 8 Day, strike, spring wound (E2-55).*
    150.00   175.00   (160.00)

☐ **Polk,** *oak, height 23", dial 6", c. 1900, 8 Day, strike, spring wound (E2-55).*
    150.00   175.00   (160.00)

☐ **Prince,** *walnut, height 20½", dial 6", c. 1888, 8 Day, strike, spring wound (E1-30).*
    115.00   140.00   (125.00)

☐ **Pyramid,** *oak, height 23", dial 6", c. 1905, 8 Day, strike, spring wound (E2-55).*
    150.00   175.00   (160.00)

Peto

Prince

Pharaoh

Pyramid

188 / W.L. GILBERT CLOCK COMPANY

Superior

Trenton No. 43

Teutonic No. 46

Winnipeg

W.L. GILBERT CLOCK COMPANY / 189

- **Quail,** *oak, height 22", dial 6", c. 1896, 8 Day, strike, spring wound (E2-59).*
  145.00   170.00   (150.00)
- **As above,** *walnut*
  170.00   195.00   (175.00)
- **Superior,** *oak, height 22½", dial 6", c. 1896, 8 Day, strike, spring wound (E2-59).*
  145.00   170.00   (150.00)
- **As above,** *walnut*
  170.00   195.00   (175.00)
- **Swan,** *oak, height 22", dial 6", c. 1896, 8 Day, strike, spring wound (E2-59).*
  145.00   170.00   (150.00)
- **As above,** *walnut*
  170.00   195.00   (175.00)
- **Teutonic No. 46,** *oak, height 25", dial 6", c. 1900, 8 Day, strike, spring wound (E2-56).*
  155.00   180.00   (160.00)
- **Trenton No. 43,** *oak, height 22½", dial 6", c. 1900, 8 Day, strike, spring wound (E2-56).*
  135.00   160.00   (140.00)
- **Walnut Enterprise,** *21¾" x 12", c. 1875, 8 Day, strike, spring wound (E2-51).*
  145.00   170.00   (150.00)
- **Washington,** *oak, height 23", dial 6", c. 1900, 8 Day, strike, spring wound (E2-55).*
  150.00   175.00   (160.00)
- **Winnipeg,** *oak, height 22½", dial 6", c. 1896, 8 Day, strike, spring wound (E2-59).*
  145.00   170.00   (150.00)
- **As above,** *walnut*
  170.00   195.00   (175.00)

KITCHEN/HANGING

- **Cambridge,** *oak, height 29", dial 6", c. 1903, 8 Day, strike, spring wound (E2-58).*
  250.00   280.00   (260.00)
- **As above,** *walnut*
  300.00   330.00   (315.00)
- **Drexel,** *oak, height 24", dial 6", c. 1903, 8 Day, strike, spring wound (E2-58).*
  210.00   240.00   (225.00)

Cambridge

- **Dundee,** *oak, height 24", dial 6", c. 1903, 8 Day, strike, spring wound (E2-58).*
  210.00   240.00   (225.00)
- **Durham,** *oak, height 24", dial 6", c. 1903, 8 Day, strike, spring wound (E2-58).*
  210.00   240.00   (225.00)
- **Girard,** *oak or walnut, height 29", dial 6", c. 1903, 8 Day, strike, spring wound (E2-58).*
  250.00   280.00   (260.00)
- **Oxford,** *oak, height 28", dial 6", c. 1903, 8 Day, strike, spring wound (E2-58).*
  230.00   260.00   (240.00)
- **As above,** *walnut*
  280.00   310.00   (290.00)

190 / W.L. GILBERT CLOCK COMPANY

Drexel

KITCHEN/TEAR DROP

☐ **Walnut Shell,** *dark wood, 21" x 13", c. 1875, 8 Day, strike, spring wound (E2-51).*
      150.00   175.00   (160.00)

Walnut Shell

KITCHEN/SERIES

☐ **Bird Set (6),** *oak, height 22", dial 6", c. 1896, spring wound (E2-59).*
      145.00   170.00   (160.00)

☐ **As above,** *walnut.*
      135.00   160.00   (150.00)

☐ **Capitol Set (3),** *oak only, height 22½", dial 6", c. 1900, 8 Day, strike, spring wound (E2-56).*
      135.00   160.00   (160.00)

☐ **Citizen Set (6),** *oak, c. 1900, 8 Day, strike, spring wound (E2-55).*
      150.00   175.00   (160.00)

☐ **Egyptian Set (6),** *oak, c. 1905, 8 Day, strike, spring wound (E2-55).*
      150.00   175.00   (160.00)

MANTEL/ONYX

☐ **Onyx No. 1,** *green onyx, gilt metal trimmings, 17½", x 9½", porcelain dial 4½", c. 1910, 8 Day, strike (E2-47).*
      200.00   240.00   (225.00)

☐ **Onyx No. 2,** *green onyx, gilt metal trimmings, 15" x 8", porcelain dial 4½", c. 1910, 8 Day, strike (E2-47).*
      210.00   240.00   (225.00)

☐ **Onyx No. 3,** *green onyx, gilt metal trimmings, 16¼" x 8", porcelain dial 4½", c. 1910, 8 Day, strike (E2-47).*
      190.00   220.00   (200.00)

W.L. GILBERT CLOCK COMPANY / 191

Onyx No. 1

MANTLE/ROUND TOP
☐ **Medal,** *walnut, pendulum, 9" x 8", c. 1875, 8 Day (E2-53).*
    125.00   140.00   (135.00)

Medal

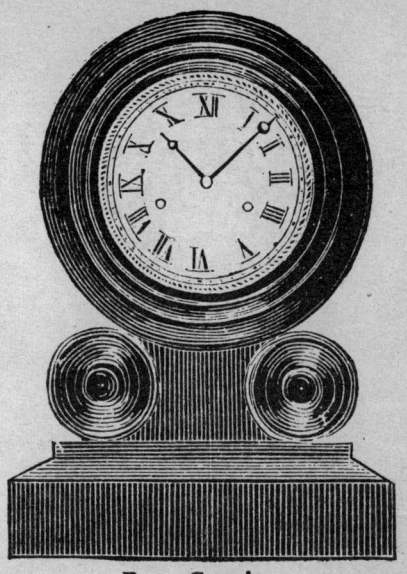

Rose Grecian

☐ **Rose Grecian,** *rosewood, height 13½", c. 1875, 1 Day, simple spring (E1-18).*
    175.00   200.00   (188.00)

NOVELTY/GILT
☐ **Amarna,** *metal gold ormolu, plain sash or Venetian green and gold, 11" x 5¼", dial 2", c. 1910, 1 Day (E2-47).*
    80.00   100.00   (90.00)

☐ **Amon,** *metal gold ormolu, plain sash or Venetian green or gold, 14¾" x 5¾", dial 2", c. 1910, 1 Day (E2-47).*
    100.00   120.00   (110.00)

☐ **Apsu,** *ormulu gold, Venetian bronze and barbedienne, French sash, 11" x 9", dial 2¾", c. 1910, 1 Day (E2-50).*
    50.00   65.00   (55.00)

☐ **Arch Altar,** *metal gold ormolu, plain sash, 8¼" x 5", dial 2", c. 1910, 1 Day (E2-48).*
    85.00   105.00   (90.00)

192 / W.L. GILBERT CLOCK COMPANY

Apsu

☐ **Chariot No. 1,** *metal gold ormolu, plain sash, 6¼" x 9", dial 2", c. 1910, 1 Day (E2-48).*
    50.00   65.00   (55.00)

☐ **Chariot No. 2,** *metal gold ormolu, plain sash, 8" x 8", dial 2", c. 1910, 1 Day (E2-48).*
    65.00   80.00   (70.00)

☐ **Cheri,** *gilt, plain or jeweled sash, 7" x 3½", dial 2", c. 1910, 1 Day (E2-49).*
    40.00   55.00   (45.00)

Castle

Darius

☐ **Balli,** *metal gold ormolu, plain sash, 9" x 6", dial 2", c. 1910, 1 Day (E2-49).*
    45.00   60.00   (50.00)

☐ **Castle,** *ormolu gold, Venetian bronze and barbedienne, French sash, 13¾" x 7", ivory dial 4", c. 1910, 8 Day, strike (E2-50).*
    100.00   120.00   (120.00)

Father Time

W.L. GILBERT CLOCK COMPANY / 193

- **Clarence,** *ormolu gold, Venetian bronze and barbedienne, French sash, 12" x 7", ivory dial 4", c. 1910, 8 Day, strike (E2-50).*
  105.00   130.00   (115.00)

- **Clyde,** *ormolu gold, Venetian bronze and barbedienne, French sash, 13½" x 9½", ivory dial 4", c. 1910, 8 Day, strike (E2-50).*
  105.00   125.00   (115.00)

- **Comforter,** *metal gold ormolu, plain gold or jeweled sash, 10½" x 5¼", dial 2", c. 1910, 1 Day (E2-47).*
  55.00   70.00   (60.00)

- **Content,** *metal gold ormolu, plain or jeweled sash, 10¼" x 5¼", dial 2", c. 1910, 1 Day (E2-47).*
  55.00   70.00   (60.00)

- **Cortige,** *gilt, plain or jeweled sash, 6½" x 4", dial 2", c. 1910, 1 Day (E2-49).*
  50.00   65.00   (55.00)

- **Darius,** *metal gold ormolu, plain or jeweled sash, 9¾" x 5¼", dial 2", c. 1910, 1 Day (E2-47).*
  60.00   75.00   (65.00)

- **Duo,** *metal gold ormolu, plain sash, 10¾" x 5¾", dial 2", c. 1910, 1 Day (E2-47).*
  65.00   80.00   (70.00)

- **Fairy,** *ormolu gold, Venetian bronze and barbedienne, French sash, 15½" x 7½", ivory dial 4", c. 1910, 8 Day, strike (E2-50).*
  105.00   130.00   (115.00)

- **Father Time,** *metal gold ormolu, 10¼" x 9¾", dial 2¾", c. 1910, 1 Day (E2-49).*
  65.00   80.00   (70.00)

- **Fedora,** *ormolu gold, Venetian bronze and barbedienne, French sash, 15" x 6", ivory dial 4", c. 1910, 8 Day, strike (E2-50).*
  95.00   115.00   (100.00)

- **Fidelity,** *ormolu gold, Venetian bronze and barbedienne, French sash, onyx base, 14½" x 7", ivory dial 4", c. 1910, 8 Day, strike (E2-50).*
  105.00   130.00   (115.00)

- **Florence,** *metal gold ormolu, plain sash or Venetian green, 12¾" x 6¾", dial 2", c. 1910, 1 Day (E2-48).*
  95.00   115.00   (100.00)

- **Floss,** *ormolu gold, Venetian bronze and barbedienne, French sash, 14" x 7½", ivory dial 4", c. 1910, 8 Day, strike (E2-50).*
  125.00   140.00   (130.00)

- **Freedom,** *metal gold ormolu, plain sash or Venetian green, 10" x 3¾", dial 2", c. 1910, 1 Day (E2-47).*
  85.00   105.00   (90.00)

- **Good Luck,** *metal gold ormolu, enameled, 3¾" x 3¾", dial 2", c. 1910, 1 Day (E2-48).*
  30.00   40.00   (35.00)

- **Gold Pillar,** *metal gold ormolu, plain sash, 9½" x 4½", dial 2", c. 1910, 1 Day (E2-48).*
  85.00   105.00   (90.00)

- **Hester,** *ormolu gold, Venetian bronze and barbedienne, French sash, 13¾" x 7½", ivory dial 4", c. 1910, 8 Day, strike (E2-50).*
  105.00   130.00   (115.00)

- **Huny,** *metal gold ormulu, plain or jeweled sash, 8" x 6½", dial 2", c. 1910, 1 Day (E2-48).*
  50.00   65.00   (55.00)

- **Innocence,** *metal gold ormolu, plain sash, 11" x 5", dial 2", c. 1910, 1 Day (E2-48).*
  55.00   70.00   (60.00)

- **Joy,** *metal gold ormolu, plain or jeweled sash, 10" x 5", dial 2", c. 1910, 1 Day (E2-47).*
  55.00   70.00   (60.00)

- **Lacanada,** *metal gold ormolu, plain or jeweled sash, 10" x 6", dial 2", c. 1910, 1 Day (E2-49).*
  90.00   110.00   (95.00)

- **Lasanada,** *metal gold ormolu, plain or jeweled sash, 10" x 6", dial 2", c. 1910, 1 Day (E2-49).*
  55.00   70.00   (60.00)

- **Localla,** *gilt finish, plain or jeweled sash, 8½" x 4½", dial 2", c. 1910, 1 Day (E2-49).*
  55.00   70.00   (60.00)

194 / W.L. GILBERT CLOCK COMPANY

Lacanada

Playful

☐ **Pami,** *metal gold ormolu, plain or jeweled sash, 9¼" x 3¾", dial 2", c. 1910, 1 Day (E2-47).*
    55.00   70.00   (60.00)

☐ **Playful,** *metal gold ormolu, plain sash, 9¾" x 5¼", dial 2", c. 1910, 1 Day (E2-48).*
    55.00   70.00   (60.00)

☐ **Ramese,** *metal gold ormolu, plain sash, 8½" x 4½", dial 2", c. 1910, 1 Day (E2-47).*
    45.00   60.00   (50.00)

☐ **Ramone,** *metal gold ormolu, plain sash, 9¾" x 4½", dial 2", c. 1910, 1 Day (E2-47).*
    55.00   70.00   (60.00)

☐ **Reason,** *metal gold ormolu, plain sash, 11" x 4¾", dial 2", c. 1910, 1 Day (E2-48).*
    60.00   75.00   (65.00)

☐ **Restful,** *metal gold ormolu, plain sash, 10" x 5", dial 2", c. 1910, 1 Day (E2-48).*
    60.00   75.00   (65.00)

☐ **Rococo No. 1,** *gilt finish, enameled circle around dial in blue and pink, 9" x 7", dial 2¾", c. 1910, 1 Day (E2-49).*
    40.00   50.00   (45.00)

Rococo No. 1

☐ **Menes,** *metal gold ormolu, plain or jeweled sash, 10" x 6½", dial 2", c. 1910, 1 Day (E2-48).*
    60.00   75.00   (65.00)

☐ **Nefer,** *metal gold ormolu, plain or jeweled sash, 10¾" x 4", dial 2", c. 1910, 1 Day (E2-48).*
    65.00   80.00   (70.00)

W.L. GILBERT CLOCK COMPANY / 195

☐ **Rococo No. 2**, *gilt finish, enameled circle around dial in blue and pink, 9" x 7½", dial 2¾", c. 1910, 1 Day (E2-49).*
    40.00   55.00   (45.00)

☐ **Rococo No. 3**, *gilt finish, enameled circle around dial in blue and pink, 7¾" x 7", dial 2¾", c. 1910, 1 Day (E2-49).*
    40.00   50.00   (45.00)

☐ **Rose No. 1**, *gold ormolu with metal leaves (dark green) and roses, natural color, 9" x 7", dial 2", c. 1910, 1 Day (E2-49).*
    70.00   85.00   (75.00)

☐ **Rose No. 2**, *gold ormolu with metal leaves (dark green) and roses, natural color, 9½" x 6", dial 2", c. 1910, 1 Day (E2-49).*
    65.00   80.00   (70.00)

☐ **Rose No. 3**, *gold ormolu with metal leaves (dark green) and roses, natural color, 8" x 5½", dial 2", c. 1910, 1 Day (E2-49).*
    60.00   75.00   (65.00)

☐ **Rose No. 4**, *gold ormolu with metal leaves (dark green) and roses, natural color, 10½" x 5½", dial 2", c. 1910, 1 Day (E2-49).*
    70.00   85.00   (75.00)

☐ **Rose No. 5**, *gold ormolu with metal leaves (dark green) and roses, natural color, 11" x 6", dial 2", c. 1910, 1 Day (E2-49).*
    70.00   85.00   (75.00)

☐ **Rose No. 6**, *gold ormolu with metal leaves (dark green) and roses, natural color, 9" x 5½", dial 2", c. 1910, 1 Day (E2-49).*
    65.00   80.00   (70.00)

☐ **Tahar**, *metal gold ormolu, plain or jeweled sash, onyx base, 9½" x 4", dial 2", c. 1910, 1 Day (E2-47).*
    50.00   65.00   (55.00)

☐ **Teti**, *metal gold ormolu, plain or jeweled sash, 11½" x 5¼", dial 2", c. 1910, 1 Day (E2-48).*
    65.00   80.00   (70.00)

☐ **Trumpeter**, *metal gold ormolu, plain sash, 9" x 7", dial 2", c. 1910, 1 Day (E2-47).*
    70.00   85.00   (75.00)

☐ **Trumpeter**, *metal gold ormolu, plain sash or Venetian green, 12½" x 7", dial 2", c. 1910, 1 Day (E2-48).*
    105.00   130.00   (115.00)

☐ **Yawn**, *metal gold ormolu, plain sash, 11¼" x 4½", dial 2", c. 1910, 1 Day (E2-48).*
    60.00   75.00   (65.00)

NOVELTY/WALL

☐ **Masonic Lever**, *walnut, height 14½", dial 4", c. 1875, 1 Day (E2-54).*
    65.00   80.00   (70.00)

☐ **Walnut Parachute**, *height 15¼", c. 1875, 8 Day (E2-53).*
    85.00   105.00   (90.00)

Masonic Lever

Walnut Parachute

OFFICE INK

☐ **Parlor Ink,** *metal gold ormolu, jeweled sash, 6½" x 10", dial 2", c. 1910, 1 Day (E2-48).*
    75.00   90.00   (80.00)

REGULATOR/OCTAGON TOP, LONG DROP

☐ **Consort,** *varnished oak finish, 32" x 18", c. 1920, 8 Day (E1-184).*
    270.00   300.00   (275.00)

☐ **Regulator B.,** *oak, height 29", dial 12", c. 1896, 8 Day (E1-149).*
    325.00   375.00   (350.00)

☐ **Regulator No. 2,** *oak, height 33½", c. 1875, 8 Day, weight (E2-54).*
    875.00   975.00   (900.00)

Regulator No. 2

REGULATOR/OCTAGON TOP, SHORT DROP

☐ **Admiral,** *varnished oak finish, 27½" x 18", 8 Day, c. 1920 (E1-184).*
    175.00   200.00   (190.00)

☐ **Armiral,** *oak, height 26¾", dial 12", c. 1896, 8 Day, (E1-149).*
    195.00   225.00   (200.00)

☐ **As above,** *8 Day, strike.*
    220.00   250.00   (225.00)

☐ **As above,** *8 Day, calendar.*
    245.00   275.00   (250.00)

☐ **As above,** *8 Day, strike, calendar.*
    270.00   300.00   (280.00)

W.L. GILBERT CLOCK COMPANY / 197

Regulator

- **Hampton,** *light or dark finish, height 23", dial 10", c. 1896, 8 Day (E1-149).*
  175.00   200.00   (190.00)
- **As above,** *8 Day, strike.*
  195.00   225.00   (200.00)
- **Regulator,** *walnut, spring, 22½" x 15½", c. 1875, 8 Day (E2-54).*
  245.00   275.00   (250.00)
- **As above,** *8 Day, strike.*
  270.00   300.00   (280.00)
- **As above,** *8 Day, strike, calendar.*
  285.00   325.00   (300.00)

REGULATOR/PARLOR WALL

- **Asbury,** *oak, height 37", dial 8", c. 1896, 8 Day, (E1-149).*
  540.00   600.00   (550.00)
- **As above,** *8 Day, gong, cathedral.*
  575.00   650.00   (600.00)
- **As above,** *walnut, 8 Day.*
  640.00   700.00   (650.00)
- **As above,** *walnut, 8 Day, gong cathedral.*
  675.00   750.00   (700.00)

Asbury

- **Berkshire,** *oak, height 38", dial 8", c. 1896, 8 Day, calendar (E1-149).*
  1050.00   1350.00   (1100.00)
- **As above,** *walnut, 8 Day, calendar.*
  1150.00   1450.00   (1200.00)
- **Bonita,** *mahogany flat finish, 33" x 13", c. 1920, 8 Day (E1-183).*
  230.00   260.00   (240.00)
- **Brighton,** *oak, height 38", dial 8", c. 1896, 8 Day (E1-149).*
  540.00   600.00   (550.00)
- **As above,** *8 Day, gong, cathedral.*
  575.00   650.00   (600.00)
- **As above,** *walnut, 8 Day.*
  640.00   700.00   (650.00)
- **As above,** *8 Day, gong, cathedral.*
  675.00   750.00   (700.00)

198 / W.L. GILBERT CLOCK COMPANY

Brighton

Columbia

☐ **Columbia,** *oak, height 37½", dial 8", c. 1903, 8 Day (E2-58).*
   425.00   475.00   (450.00)
☐ **As above,** *8 Day, strike.*
   465.00   525.00   (475.00)
☐ **As above,** *8 Day, calendar.*
   515.00   575.00   (550.00)
☐ **As above,** *8 Day, strike, calendar.*
   550.00   625.00   (560.00)
☐ **Defender,** *oak, dial 12", c. 1896, 8 Day (E1-153).*
   725.00   800.00   (750.00)
☐ **As above,** *8 Day, cathedral.*
   750.00   850.00   (775.00)
☐ **Defender,** *oak, 49½" x 20", dial 12", c. 1903, 8 Day (E2-58).*
   725.00   800.00   (750.00)
☐ **As above,** *8 Day, gong, cathedral.*
   750.00   850.00   (775.00)

☐ **Habana,** *mahogany flat finish, 37" x 13½", c. 1920, 8 Day (E1-184).*
   190.00   220.00   (200.00)
☐ **Hanging Weight,** *walnut, height 47", c. 1875, 1 Day, strike, weight (E2-54).*
   675.00   750.00   (700.00)
☐ **Leeds,** *mahogany flat finish, 31½" x 14½", c. 1920, 8 Day (E1-183).*
   190.00   220.00   (200.00)
☐ **Observatory,** *varnished oak finish, 36" x 15½", c. 1920, 8 Day (E1 181).*
   245.00   275.00   (250.00)

W.L. GILBERT CLOCK COMPANY / 199

Defender **Regulator No. 4**

☐ **Oldham,** *fumed oak finish, 31½" x 14¾", c. 1920, 8 Day (E1-183).*
200.00   240.00   (225.00)

☐ **Regulator No. 4,** *walnut, glass sides, dead beat escapement, height 51", dial 8", c. 1888, 8 Day, weight (E1-24).*
900.00   1100.00   (950.00)

☐ **Regulator No. 9,** *hanging, walnut, dead beat escapement, sweep center second, 6'6" x 1'10½", dial (porcelain) 12", c. 1896 (E1-153).*
2100.00   2400.00   (2200.00)
☐ **As above,** *oak.*
2000.00   2300.00   (2200.00)
☐ **As above,** *cherry.*
2150.00   2450.00   (2300.00)
☐ **As above,** *ash.*
2150.00   2450.00   (2300.00)

REGULATOR/ROUND TOP, LONG DROP

☐ **Regulator No. 1,** *dark wood, dead beat escapement, height 33½", c. 1875, 8 Day (E2-54).*
    700.00   800.00   (750.00)

Regulator No. 1

REGULATOR/SECONDS BIT

☐ **Regulator No. 10,** *walnut, glass sides, dead beat escapement, height 53", dial 10", c. 1888, 8 Day, weight (E1-24).*
    1000.00   1200.00   (1100.00)

Regulator No. 10

☐ **Regulator No. 11,** *walnut, glass sides, height 50", dial 8", c. 1888, 8 Day, weight (E1-24).*
    1000.00   1200.00   (1100.00)
☐ **As above,** *8 Day, weight, strike.*
    1100.00   1350.00   (1100.00)
☐ **As above,** *ash, 8 Day, weight, strike.*
    1300.00   1500.00   (1400.00)
☐ **As above,** *ash, 8 Day, weight.*
    1250.00   1450.00   (1300.00)

☐ **Regulator No. 14,** *oak only, dead beat escapement, retaining power, 50" x 20", dial 12", 8 Day, weight (E2-64).*
    1000.00   1100.00   (1050.00)

REGULATOR/ SWEEP SECOND
(Note: Any of these sweep second regulators may have American, French, or Swiss pinwheel escapements and the prices are based on a pinwheel movement. Deduct at least $500.00 if not.)

Regulator No. 18

Regulator No. 20

☐ **Regulator No. 9,** *walnut, glass sides, dead beat escapement, sweep second, height 78", porcelain dial 12", c. 1888, 8 Day, weight (E1-24).*
    2200.00   2500.00   (2300.00)
☐ **As above,** *mahogany.*
    2000.00   2300.00   (2300.00)
☐ **As above,** *ash.*
    2250.00   2550.00   (2400.00)

202 / W.L. GILBERT CLOCK COMPANY

☐ **Regulator No. 9,** *walnut, dead beat escapement, height 6'6", dial 12", c. 1903 (E2-65).*
    2450.00   2950.00   (2600.00)
☐ **As above,** *oak.*
    2250.00   2750.00   (2400.00)
☐ **As above,** *cherry.*
    2500.00   3000.00   (2650.00)

☐ **Regulator No. 12,** *standing, walnut, Swiss movement, dead beat escapement, retaining power, 8'6" x 2'6", dial 12", c. 1903 (E2-65).*
    4050.00   4450.00   (4200.00)
☐ **As above,** *oak.*
    3850.00   4250.00   (4000.00)

☐ **Regulator No. 12,** *hanging, walnut, 7' x 2'6", c. 1903 (E2-65).*
    3950.00   4200.00   (4000.00)
☐ **As above,** *oak.*
    3750.00   4000.00   (4000.00)

☐ **Regulator No. 18,** *oak, retaining power, dead beat escapement, 7'7" x 2'1", dial 12", c. 1903 (E2-65).*
    2600.00   3000.00   (2750.00)
☐ **As above,** *cherry.*
    2850.00   3250.00   (3000.00)
☐ **As above,** *walnut.*
    2800.00   3200.00   (2900.00)

☐ **Regulator No. 20,** *fine quartered oak, dead beat escapement, retaining power, 6'11" x 20½", dial 12", c. 1903 (E2-65).*
    2750.00   3250.00   (2800.00)

STATUE/OVER 17"

☐ **Angel,** *extra gold finish, ivory porcelain dial, French sash, beveled glass, 24" x 9", dial 4½", c. 1910, 8 Day, strike (E2-69).*
    270.00   300.00   (275.00)

☐ **Archer,** *barbedienne finish, gold trimmings, ivory porcelain dial, French sash, beveled glass, 32" x 12", dial 4", c. 1910, 8 Day, strike (E2-68).*
    490.00   550.00   (500.00)

☐ **Cinderella,** *imperial green, gold trimmings, ivory porcelain dial, French sash, beveled glass, 23" x 12", dial 4", c. 1910, 8 Day, strike (E2-68).*
    335.00   375.00   (350.00)

☐ **Dandy,** *gold and imperial green finish, ivory porcelain dial, French sash, fancy gilt center, beveled glass, 22½" x 9½", dial 4½", c. 1910, 8 Day, strike, (E2-67).*
    175.00   200.00   (180.00)

☐ **Mildred,** *gold finish, ivory porcelain dial, French sash, fancy gilt center, beveled glass, 30" x 9", dial 4½", c. 1910, 8 Day, strike (E2-67).*
    210.00   240.00   (220.00)

Angel

W.L. GILBERT CLOCK COMPANY / 203

☐ **Philip,** *gold finish, ivory porcelain dial, French sash, fancy gilt center, beveled glass, 21¾" x 9", dial 4½", c. 1910, 8 Day, strike (E2-67).*
    155.00   180.00   (160.00)

☐ **Princess,** *gold finish, ivory porcelain dial, French sash, fancy gilt center, beveled glass, 27" x 10¾", dial 4½", c. 1910, 8 Day, strike (E2-67).*
    230.00   260.00   (240.00)

☐ **Sandy,** *gold and barbedienne finish, ivory porcelain dial, French sash, fancy gilt center, beveled glass, 23¾" x 9", dial 4½", c. 1910, 8 Day, strike (E2-67).*
    170.00   195.00   (180.00)

☐ **Torch-Bearer,** *barbedienne finish, gold trimmings, ivory porcelain dial, French sash, beveled glass, 29" x 12", c. 1910, 8 Day, strike (E2-68).*
    425.00   475.00   (440.00)

STATUE/PART ONYX

☐ **Cherub,** *gold finish, onyx pedestal, ivory porcelain dial, visible escapement, rococo sash, beveled glass, 22½" x 12¾", dial 4", c. 1910, 8 Day, strike (E2-66).*
    465.00   525.00   (475.00)

☐ **Tease,** *rich gold finish, onyx inlay, ivory porcelain dial, French sash, beveled glass, 22" x 15½", c. 1910, 8 Day, strike (E2-69).*
    625.00   750.00   (650.00)

☐ **Tiamut,** *marble inlay, ivory porcelain dial, French sash, beveled glass, 25½" x 17½", dial 4½", c. 1910, 8 Day, strike (E2-69).*
    490.00   550.00   (500.00)

STATUE/PORCELAIN

☐ **Claribel,** *gold finish, china inlay, ivory porcelain dial, French sash, beveled glass, 13" x 7", 4" dial, c. 1910, 8 Day, strike (E2-68).*
    300.00   330.00   (315.00)

Forever

☐ **Estelle,** *rich ormolu gold finish, china inlay, ivory porcelain dial, French sash, beveled glass, 14" x 8½", dial 4", c. 1910, 8 Day, strike (E2-68).*
    340.00   380.00   (350.00)

Gabriel

204 / W.L. GILBERT CLOCK COMPANY

☐ **Forever,** French gold finish, porcelain inlay, ivory porcelain dial, French sash, beveled glass, 16" x 13¾", dial 4½", c. 1910, 8 Day, strike (E2-69).
    375.00   425.00   (400.00)

☐ **Gabriel,** rich ormolu gold finish, china egg and inlay, ivory porcelain dial, French sash, beveled glass, 14" x 7½", dial 4", c. 1910, 8 Day, strike (E2-68).
    350.00   390.00   (365.00)

☐ **Kingston,** gold finish, porcelain inlay, ivory porcelain dial, French sash, beveled glass, 14½" x 8½", dial 4", c. 1910, 8 Day, strike (E2-68).
    360.00   400.00   (375.00)

☐ **Marlboro,** gold finish, decorated porcelain inlay, onyx top, ivory porcelain dial, visible escapement, rococo sash, beveled glass, 10¾" x 17", dial 4", c. 1910, 8 Day, strike (E2-66).
    335.00   370.00   (340.00)

☐ **Marquess,** gold finish, decorated porcelain inlay, ivory porcelain dial, visible escapement, rococo sash, beveled glass, 14½" x 19", dial 4", c. 1910, 8 Day, strike (E2-66).
    600.00   650.00   (625.00)

☐ **Maybell,** rich ormolu gold finish, decorated china inlay, ivory porcelain dial, French sash, beveled glass, dial 4", c. 1910, 8 Day, strike (E2-68).
    550.00   650.00   (575.00)

☐ **Muriel,** rich ormolu gold finish, decorated china egg and inlay, ivory porcelain dial, French sash, beveled glass, 14" x 10", dial 4", c. 1910, 8 Day, strike (E2-68).
    550.00   650.00   (575.00)

☐ **Violinist,** decorated porcelain inlay, onyx pedestal, French sash, ivory porcelain dial, visible escapement, rococo sash, beveled glass, 23" x 13", dial 4", c. 1910, 8 Day, strike (E2-66).
    650.00   750.00   (675.00)

Kingston

Maybell

STATUE/UNDER 17"

☐ **Airondack,** gold and bronze finish, marbleized base, ivory porcelain dial, French sash, fancy gilt center, beveled glass, 12" x 14½", dial 4½", c. 1910 (E2-67).
    190.00   220.00   (200.00)

W.L. GILBERT CLOCK COMPANY / 205

☐ **Belmar,** *gold or Venetian green finish, ivory porcelain dial, French sash, fancy gilt center, beveled glass, 12" x 14½", dial 4½", c. 1910, 8 Day, strike (E2-69).*
    170.00   195.00   (185.00)

☐ **Bramble,** *ormolu gold finish, ivory porcelain dial, visible escapement, rococo sash, beveled glass, 13½" x 12", dial 4", c. 1910, 8 Day, strike (E2-66).*
    210.00   240.00   (225.00)

☐ **Charger,** *gold or Venetian green finish, ivory porcelain dial, French sash, fancy gilt center, beveled glass, 12" x 14½", dial 4½", c. 1910, 8 Day, strike (E2-69).*
    170.00   195.00   (175.00)

☐ **Edward,** *gold finish, ivory porcelain dial, French sash, fancy gilt center, beveled glass, 13½" x 14", dial 4½", c. 1910, 8 Day, strike (E2-67).*
    190.00   220.00   (200.00)

☐ **Elenor,** *gilt or Venetian green finish, ivory porcelain dial, French sash, beveled glass, 12" x 8½", dial 4½", c. 1910, 8 Day, strike (E2-69).*
    160.00   185.00   (165.00)

☐ **Frolic,** *ormolu gold, ivory porcelain dial, visible escapement, rococo sash, beveled glass, 16" x 13", dial 4", c. 1910, 8 Day, strike (E2-66).*
    250.00   280.00   (265.00)

☐ **Grace,** *ormolu gold, ivory porcelain dial, visible escapement, rococo sash, beveled glass, 15½" x 11½", dial 4", c. 1910, 8 Day, strike (E2-66).*
    190.00   220.00   (200.00)

☐ **Grecian,** *gold or Venetian green finish, ivory porcelain dial, French sash, fancy gilt center, beveled glass, 12" x 14½", dial 4½", c. 1910, 8 Day, strike (E2-67).*
    170.00   195.00   (175.00)

Bramble

Grace

☐ **Hercules,** *gold finish, ivory porcelain dial, visible escapement, rococo sash, beveled glass, 16½" x 14½", dial 4", c. 1910, 8 Day, strike (E2-66).*
    250.00   280.00   (260.00)

206 / GILBERT DIAL

- [ ] **Holland,** *barbedienne or gilt finish, ivory porcelain dial, visible escapement, rococo sash, beveled glass, 12" x 14½", dial 4", c. 1910, 8 Day, strike (E2-66).*
  230.00   260.00   (240.00)

- [ ] **Mignon,** *gold or bronze finish, marbleized base, ivory porcelain dial, French sash, beveled glass, 12" x 14½", dial 4½", c. 1910, 8 Day, strike (E2-69).*
  165.00   190.00   (175.00)

- [ ] **Republic,** *rich ormolu gold finish, onyx base and back, fancy visible pendulum, ivory porcelain dial, French sash, beveled glass, 15" x 9½", dial 4", c. 1910, 8 Day, strike (E2-68).*
  550.00   625.00   (600.00)

- [ ] **Salvator,** *gold or Venetian green finish, ivory porcelain dial, French sash, beveled glass, 12" x 14½", c. 1910, 8 Day, strike, (E2-69).*
  170.00   195.00   (175.00)

- [ ] **Serenade,** *gold or Venetian green finish, ivory porcelain dial, French sash, fancy gilt center, beveled glass, 12" x 14½", dial 4½", c. 1910, 8 Day, strike (E2-67).*
  170.00   195.00   (175.00)

- [ ] **Sportsman,** *gold or bronze finish, ivory porcelain dial, French sash, beveled glass, 13½ x 14", dial 4½", c. 1910, 8 Day, strike (E2-69).*
  170.00   195.00   (175.00)

GILBERT DIAL

CALENDAR

- [ ] **Victorian Kitchen,** *spring, 20" x 11½", dial 5", 8 Day, strike (M432-135).*
  225.00   275.00   (250.00)

- [ ] **Victorian Kitchen,** *dial 5", 8 Day, strike (M433-135).*
  250.00   295.00   (260.00)

GILBERT-MARANVILLE

CALENDAR

- [ ] **Round Drop Wall,** *spring, 33" x 18½", dial 14", 8 Day (E2-62, M424-133).*
  750.00   800.00   (775.00)

- [ ] **Round Drop Wall,** *spring, 34½" x 18½", dial 14", 8 Day, simple calendar (E2-62, M427-133).*
  500.00   600.00   (550.00)

GILBERT-MCCABE

CALENDAR

- [ ] **Bershire,** *spring, 39" x 14", dial 8", 8 Day (E2-62, E1-149, M461-142).*
  1800.00   2100.00   (1900.00)

- [ ] **Elberon,** *spring, 30½ x 15", dial 8", 8 Day, strike, perpetual calendar (E2-61).*
  1400.00   1750.00   (1500.00)

- [ ] **Lenox,** *spring, 35½" x 15", dial 8", 8 Day (E1-149, M462-142).*
  1800.00   2050.00   (2000.00)

- [ ] **Maine,** *spring, 49" x 18", dial 12", 8 Day, strike, (E2-62, M466-143).*
  2200.00   2400.00   (2300.00)

- [ ] **Oriental,** *spring, 30" x 15½", dial 8", 8 Day, strike, perpetual calendar (E1-152, E2-61).*
  1500.00   1850.00   (1600.00)

- [ ] **Sharon,** *spring, 38" x 14½", dial 8", 8 Day (E1-149, M463-142).*
  1850.00   2100.00   (1900.00)

- [ ] **Sharon,** *spring, 38" x 14½", dial 8", 8 Day (E1-149, M464-142).*
  1850.00   2100.00   (1900.00)

E. HOWARD CLOCK COMPANY

David Porter Davis is NOT associated with the first immigrant clockmaker, William Davis of Boston, although the surname does lend a good auspice to his career, and his association with Edward Howard.

D.P. Davis, a former apprentice of the prestigious Willard brothers, was in partnership with Howard for a time in a company known as Howard and Davis. Howard was trained in Boston and apprenticed (as was Davis) under Aaron Willard. A Luther Stephenson entered into the two men's company partnership for a time, but he lasted only five seasons. Interestingly enough Howard and Davis produced items for other fields besides horology, and even received awards for the fine manufacturing insured in all their wares.

Howard and Davis were the recipients of two of the first 28 day watches manufactured by Aaron Dennison. They had financed the ingenious inventor, and these particular watches are angraved with their names.

Davis eventually left the partnership because of severe financial problems within the firm. Howard perserved through the difficulties, and ended up retiring with a fortune.

Howard is also associated with the manufacture of tower clocks, in which the Seth Thomas Company was his primary rival.

Howard clocks are considered by some collectors to be the most desirable of all. This is the main reason the prices are at such a high level. Seldom do you see any Howards on the market except for some of the small regulators. I'm sure some of the bigger clocks occasionally change hands but not often in public because old time collectors and dealers know where they are and when they are sold it usually is done privately.

Howard Regulators No. 1, 2, 3, 4 and 5 were being copied even in the 1860's, or maybe a better explanation is that a number of companies were making similar clocks with Howard being the surviving maker. Out of the No. 1 to No. 10 Regulator series, two or three models have been reproduced at one time or another, and currently the No. 1 is being made and offered for sale as an original. The Howard Company is presently making limited editions of some of its old model, small regulators.

With all the above in mind, before a prospective buyer will lay down the high dollar that is now being asked, "he will frequently ask for the original dust." Howard clocks should never be refinished unless it is an absolute must. Refinishing almost always reduces the value.

The clocks on this page came out of an 1858 company catalog, this being the successor to Howard and Davis Clock Company in 1857. The company continued to make some of these clocks for many years. I have no way of knowing how many of each model was made. I know that there are not enough for every collector to have one. I have indicated which of the small regulators that collectors consider scarce or rare. Only the most serious collectors will pay much for some models, especially the marble, marble dial and watchmen's clock.

All of the Howard section of this book was selected from original factory catalogs and the general catalogs of some of their dealers. A few models appear in all catalogs and some only one time, which would tend to indicate some models were not successful and were made only for a short time. It would take a book on the Howard Company alone to discuss it thoroughly.

I offer the values and these short comments in an effort to help you as much as I can in the limited space available. On the clocks not priced, I just can't get a handle on what they may be worth. Most of these sales will be what the seller can get the buyer to pay, but more often (and this is where you come in), the seller will not have the knowledge or the guts to ask you the true value and you will be able to get a fine clock for very little money.

I can remember a day less than ten years ago, being called down to a local hospital that had closed to look at an old clock. They were selling the odds and ends that were left and he asked me $750.00 for the clock. I looked all over for a name and all I could find was a name I recognized as a high-class jewelry firm in New York City. Not having the knowledge to know what the clock was, I turned it down. A short time later, while looking through a Howard catalog, I realized the clock was a No. 46 Regulator. As you can guess, I have thought about that mistake many times.

I think many of the larger Howard clocks were pretty much custom made as to case wood, size, and movement. Movements are very important. For instance, if any clock I have priced has a "No. 1 Dennison's Gravity Escapement" add $150.00 to the value of the clock.

In short, with Howard clocks being so scarce, plenty of buyers with money around, and money not being worth what it used to be, it's just about impossible to put a value on one. I think the beauty of the clock, the desire of the buyer and his ability to pay (coupled with the seller's knowledge or lack of same), will determine the actual value for that point in time.

Good luck in your search for a Howard clock for your home, office or collection.

ASTRONOMICAL

☐ **No. 74,** *four jar mercury pendulum, made in three grades, 60" x 19", rare.*

     15000.00   20000.00 (16500.00)

Note: The No. 74 Astronomical clock was manufactured in three grades for the principal observatories in the United States. According to a Howard catalog issued around 1915, at least 75 of these clocks were made.

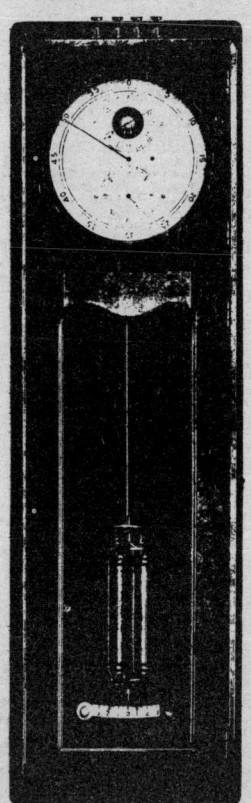

No. 74 Astronomical

E. HOWARD CLOCK COMPANY / 209

ASTRONOMICAL/DIAL, STANDING

☐ **Regular No. 43,** walnut, Graham dead beat escapement, height 8'8", dial 14" (E1-91).
  12500.00   15000.00   (1400.00)

☐ **No. 45 Regulator,** walnut, Graham dead beat escapement, height 8'2", dial 14" (E1-91).
  15000.00   17500.00   (16500.00)

No. 45 Regulator

☐ **No. 46 Regulator,** walnut, Graham dead beat escapement, height 10'6", dial 18" (E1-91).
  12000.00   15000.00   (1300.00)

☐ **No. 48 Regulator,** walnut, Graham dead beat escapement, height 9'6", dial 14" (E1-91).
  12000.00   15000.00   (13500.00)

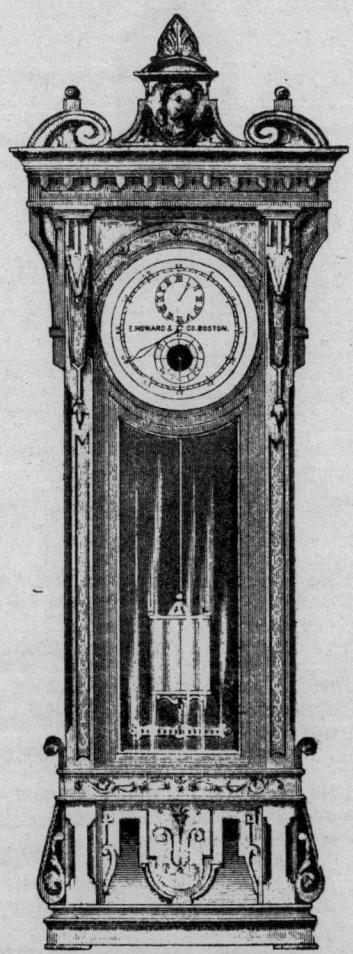

No. 43 Regulator

210 / E. HOWARD CLOCK COMPANY

ASTRONOMICAL/DIAL, WALL

☐ **No. 49 Regulator,** *walnut, Graham dead beat escapement, height 7'6", dial 14" (E1-92).*
    14500.00   16000.00   (1500.00)

☐ **No. 67 Regulator,** *walnut, Graham dead beat escapement, height 10'3", dial 16" (E1-94).*
    12000.00   14000.00   (13000.00)
☐ **As above,** *height 9'3".*
    10000.00   12000.00   (11000.00)
☐ **As above,** *height 8'9", dial 14".*
    9000.00   11000.00   (9500.00)
☐ **As above,** *height 7'9", dial 14".*
    8000.00   10000.00   (8500.00)

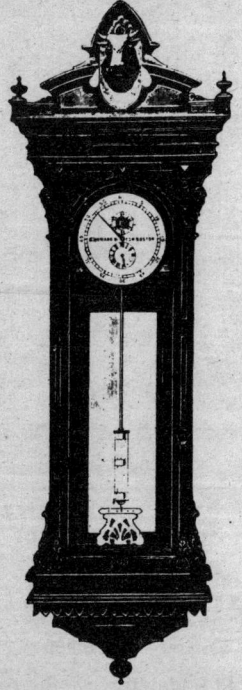

No. 67 Regulator

ASTRONOMICAL/REGULATOR

☐ **No. 22 Regulator,** *walnut, Graham dead beat escapement, height 8'9", dial 16" (E1-91).*
    9000.00   12000.00   (9500.00)

No. 23 Regulator

☐ **No. 23 Regulator,** *walnut, Graham dead beat escapement, height 7'3", dial 16" (E1-91).*
    10000.00   12000.00   (10500.00)

☐ **No. 24 Regulator,** *walnut, Graham dead beat escapement, height 8', dial 14" (E1-91).*
    10000.00   12500.00   (11000.00)

☐ **No. 25 Regulator,** *walnut, Graham dead beat escapement, height 6'9", dial 14" (E1-91).*
    9000.00   11000.00   (9500.00)

☐ **No. 47 Regulator,** *walnut, Graham dead beat escapement, height 9'6", dial 14" (E1-94).*
    14000.00   18000.00   (16000.00)

E. HOWARD CLOCK COMPANY / 211

No. 24 Regulator

No. 1 Regulator

No. 2 Regulator

BANJO

☐ **No. 1 Regulator**, *stained rosewood or cherry, dead beat escapement, height 4'2", dial 12" (E1-90).*
    6000.00   7000.00   (6500.00)

☐ **No. 2 Regulator**, *stained rosewood, recoil escapement, height 3'8", dial 9" (E1-90).*
    5000.00   6000.00   (5500.00)

☐ **No. 3 Regulator**, *stained rosewood, recoil escapement, height 3'2", dial 9" (E1-90).*
    4000.00   4500.00   (4250.00)

212 / E. HOWARD CLOCK COMPANY

No. 3 Regulator

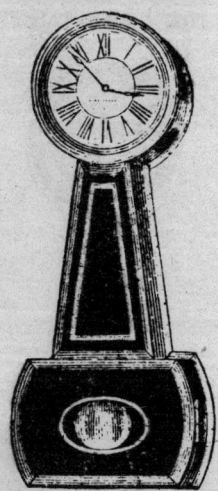

No. 4 Regulator

☐ **No. 4 Regulator,** *imitation rosewood, recoil escapement, height 2'8", dial 8" (E1-90).*
    2000.00   2500.00   (2250.00)

☐ **No. 5 Regulator,** *imitation rosewood, recoil escapement, height 2'5", dial 7" (E1-90).*
    1500.00   1800.00   (1600.00)

☐ **No. 5 Regulator,** *imitation rosewood, recoil escapement, height 2'5", square, rare bottom, dial 7" (E1-90).*
    3000.00   5000.00   (3500.00)

BANJO/FIGURE EIGHT

☐ **No. 6 Regulator,** *walnut, Graham dead beat escapement, height 4'10", dial 14" (E1-93).*
    10500.00   12000.00   (11000.00)

☐ **No. 7 Regulator,** *walnut, oak or cherry, recoil escapement, height 4'2", dial 12" (E1-93).*
    6500.00   8500.00   (7500.00)

☐ **No. 8 Regulator,** *walnut, oak or cherry, recoil escapement, height 3'8", dial 11" (E1-93).*
    4000.00   5500.00   (4550.00)

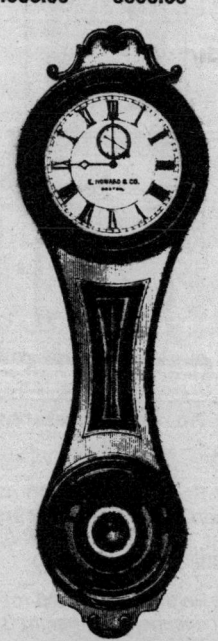

No. 6 Regulator

E. HOWARD CLOCK COMPANY / 213

GRANDFATHER

☐ **No. 77,** *dark mahogany, beveled French plate, wire gong, hour strike, Graham dead beat escapement, height 8'10".*
    4750.00   5000.00   (4950.00)

☐ **No. 79,** *mahogany, Westminster chimes on wire gongs, Cambridge chimes on saucer gongs, Graham dead beat escapement, height 10'2".*
    17500.00   18000.00   (17750.00)

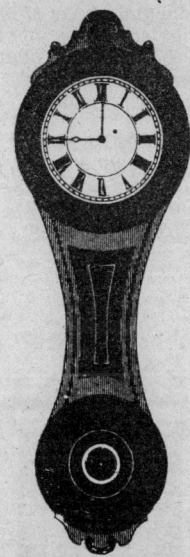

No. 7 Regulator

ELECTRIC GALLERY

☐ **No. 66-1,** *height 17" square, walnut case, height 17" square, dial 12" (E1-93).*
    125.00   150.00   (130.00)

☐ **No. 66-2,** *height 23" square, dial 16".*
    155.00   180.00   (165.00)

☐ **No. 66-3,** *height 28" square, dial 20".*
    175.00   200.00   (185.00)

No. 66-1 Square

No. 77 Grandfather

214 / E. HOWARD CLOCK COMPANY

No. 80 Grandfather

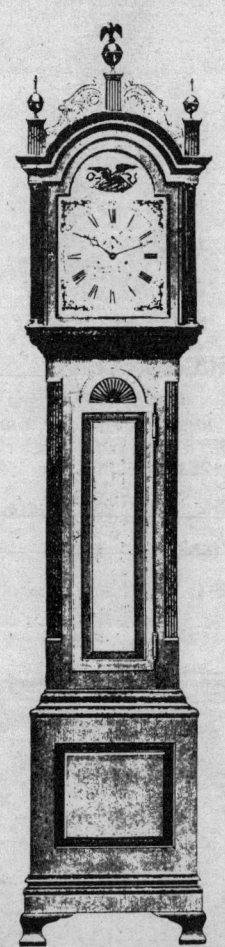

☐ **No. 82-15,** *mahogany or oak, Westminster chimes on saucer gongs, Graham dead beat escapement, height 9'3".*
   15750.00   16500.00   (16000.00)

☐ **No. 83,** *mahogany, brass ornaments, saucer gong, hour strike, Graham dead beat escapement, height 7'9½".*
   3125.00   3400.00   (3250.00)

☐ **No. 80,** *mahogany, rich carvings, beveled French plate, cathedral gong, hour strike, Westminster chimes on wire gongs, Cambridge chimes on saucer gongs, Graham dead beat escapement, height 8'11".*
   11500.00   13500.00   (12000.00)

☐ **No. 82-13,** *mahogany, beveled French plate, Graham dead beat escapement, cathedral gong, hour and half hour strike, height 8'3".*
   6800.00   7200.00   (7000.00)

No. 83 Grandfather

E. HOWARD CLOCK COMPANY / 215

☐ **No. 84,** *dark mahogany, beveled French plate, wire gong, hour strike, Graham dead beat escapement, height 8'4".*
    4000.00   5000.00   (4500.00)

☐ **No. 87,** *mahogany or oak, beveled French plate, cathedral gong, hour and half hour strike, Graham dead beat escapement, height 8'7".*
    6000.00   7000.00   (6500.00)

No. 87 Grandfather

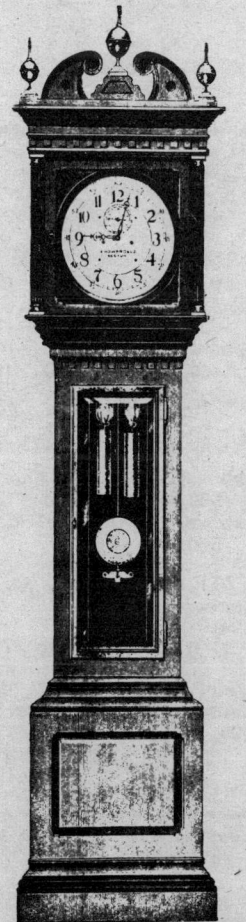

No. 84 Grandfather

☐ **No. 88,** *mahogany or oak, beveled French plate, cathedral gong, hour and half hour strike, Graham dead beat escapement, height 8'10".*
    4500.00   5500.00   (4750.00)

HANGING REGULATOR

☐ **No. 14 Regulator,** *walnut, recoil escapement, no seconds bit, height 3' 6", dial 10" (E1-92).*
    2400.00   2800.00   (2500.00)

216 / E. HOWARD CLOCK COMPANY

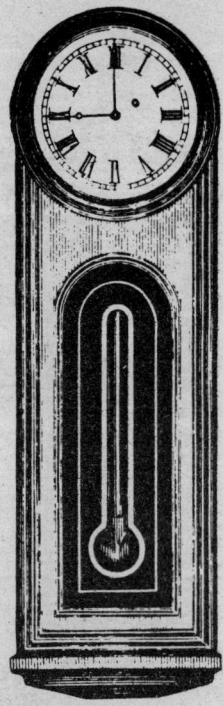

No. 14 Regulator

MARBLE DIAL

☐ **No. 16 Round Top Drop,** *recoil escapement, Italian marble, height 4' 3", dial 30" (E1-93).*
   1500.00   2000.00   (1600.00)

☐ **No. 15-1 Round Top Drop,** *Italian marble, recoil escapement, height 4' 9", dial 36" (E1-93).*
   1800.00   2000.00   (1900.00)

☐ **No. 15-2 Round Top Drop,** *Italian marble, recoil escapement, height 4', dial 30".*
   2000.00   2200.00   (2100.00)

☐ **No. 15-3 Round Top Drop,** *Italian marble, recoil escapement, height 3' 6", dial 24"*
   1600.00   1800.00   (1700.00)

☐ **No. 20-1 Square,** *recoil escapement, Italian marble, height 2', dial 24" (E1-94).*
   650.00   700.00   (675.00)

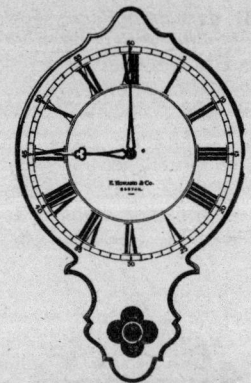

No. 15-1 Round Top Drop

☐ **No. 20-2,** *As above, height 1' 10", dial 22".*
   650.00   700.00   (675.00)

☐ **No. 27 Round,** *top drop, Italian marble, height 2' 11", dial 18" (E1-94).*
   1650.00   1850.00   (1700.00)
☐ **As above,** *height 2' 4", dial 14"*
   1450.00   1650.00   (1500.00)

☐ **No. 21 Round,** *Italian marble, height 2', dial 24" (E1-94).*
   500.00   600.00   (550.00)
☐ **As above,** *height 2' 6", dial 30"*
   500.00   600.00   (550.00)
☐ **As above,** *height 3', dial 36"*
   500.00   600.00   (550.00)

☐ **No. 29 Round,** *walnut case, recoil escapement, 3' 2" x 5' 3", dial 24" (E1-94).*
   1250.00   1500.00   (1300.00)

☐ **No. 30 Round,** *pine case, recoil escapement, height 2', dial 24" (E1-94).*
   1250.00   1500.00   (1300.00)

☐ **No. 33 Round,** *walnut case, recoil escapement, 4' 2" x 5'9", dial 24" (E1-92).*
   4250.00   4800.00   (4500.00)

☐ **No. 35 Round,** *walnut case, recoil escapement, 4' x 3'4", dial 24" (E1-92).*
   4250.00   4500.00   (4400.00)

E. HOWARD CLOCK COMPANY / 217

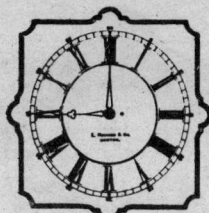

No. 20-1 Square

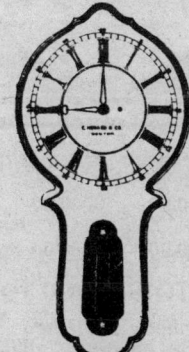

No. 27 Round

No. 33 Round

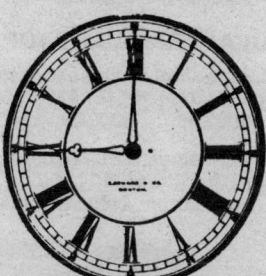

No. 21 Round

No. 35 Round

- **No. 52 Round,** *walnut case, recoil escapement, height 3' 11", dial 20" (E1-94).*
      3800.00   4200.00   (4000.00)
- **As above,** *height 3', dial 16"*
      3750.00   3850.00   (3800.00)
- **No. 63 Round,** *walnut case, recoil escapement, 5'2" x 3', dial 24", (E1-94).*
      4000.00   4500.00   (4250.00)

- **No. 65 Round,** *walnut case, height 5' 3", dial 24" (E1-94).*
      4000.00   4500.00   (4250.00)
- **As above,** *height 4' 5", dial 20"*
      3500.00   4000.00   (3750.00)

218 / E. HOWARD CLOCK COMPANY

No. 52 Round

No. 73 French Glass

- ☐ **NO. 73 French Glass,** *walnut case, height 3', dial 30" (E1-93).*
  2500.00   3000.00   (2750.00)
- ☐ **As above,** *height 2' 6", dial 24"*
  2000.00   2500.00   (2250.00)

REGULATOR/ROUND TOP

- ☐ **No. 11,** *cherry or stained rosewood, height 31", dial 11" (E1-93).*
  2500.00   3000.00   (2750.00)

REGULATOR/SQUARE TOP

- ☐ **No. 39,** *walnut, recoil escapement, height 5', dial 12" (E1-92).*
  4000.00   5000.00   (4250.00)
- ☐ **No. 40,** *walnut, recoil escapement, height 4' 6", dial 11" (E1-92).*
  3100.00   4100.00   (3400.00)

No. 63 Round

No. 65 Round

No. 11 Round Top

E. HOWARD CLOCK COMPANY / 219

No. 39 Square Top

No. 40 Square Top

☐ **No. 41,** *walnut, recoil escapement, height 4', dial 9" (E1-92).*
　　　3000.00　　3500.00　　(3400.00)

☐ **No. 42,** *walnut, recoil escapement, height 3' 8", dial 8" (E1-92).*
　　　2500.00　　3000.00　　(2750.00)

No. 41 Square Top

220 / E. HOWARD CLOCK COMPANY

REGULATOR/WALL

☐ **No. 58,** *walnut, recoil escapement, height 5' 4", dial 12" (E1-93).*
    4000.00   4500.00   (4250.00)
☐ **As above,** *height 4' 3", dial 10"*
    3000.00   3500.00   (3250.00)
☐ **As above,** *height 3' 5", dial 8"*
    2000.00   2500.00   (2250.00)

☐ **No. 59,** *walnut, recoil escapement, height 5' 10", dial 12" (E1-93).*
    5000.00   6000.00   (5500.00)
☐ **As above,** *height 4' 8", dial 10"*
    4500.00   5000.00   (4750.00)
☐ **As above,** *height 3' 10", dial 8"*
    3500.00   4500.00   (3600.00)
☐ **As above,** *height 3', dial 6"*
    3500.00   4000.00   (3750.00)

No. 70 Wall

☐ **No. 70,** *walnut, oak or cherry, recoil escapement, height 4' 8", dial 24" (E1-93).*
    3500.00   4000.00   (3750.00)
☐ **As above,** *height 4", dial 20"*
    3000.00   3500.00   (3250.00)
☐ **As above,** *height 3" 5", dial 16"*
    2000.00   2500.00   (2250.00)

WATCHMAKERS REGULATOR
STANDING

☐ **No. 61,** *walnut, Graham dead beat escapement, height 7' 10", dial 14" (E1-94).*
    6000.00   7000.00   (6500.00)

☐ **No. 75,** *walnut, mahogany or oak, recoil escapement, height 5', dial 14" (E1-93).*
    5000.00   6500.00   (5600.00)
☐ **As above,** *height 2'10", dial 12".*
    3500.00   4000.00   (3850.00)

WATCHMANS REGULATOR
WALL, ARCH TOP

☐ **No. 71,** *walnut, Graham dead beat escapement, height 5'10", dial 12" (E1-94).*
    6000.00   8000.00   (6500.00)

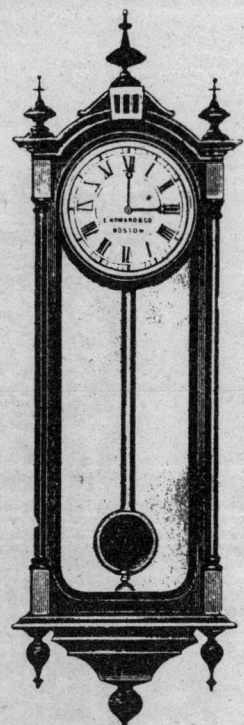

No. 59 Wall

E. HOWARD CLOCK COMPANY / 221

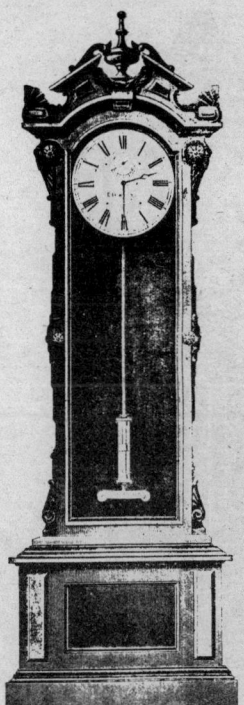

No. 75 Wall

No. 71 Arch Top

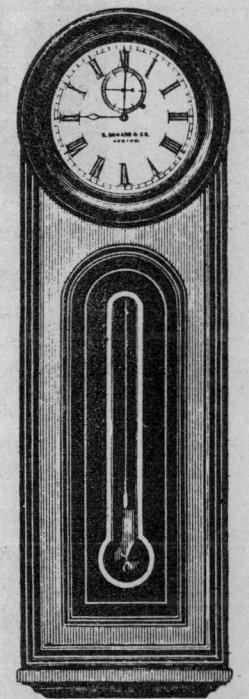

No. 13 Round Top

WATCHMANS REGULATOR
WALL, ROUND TOP

☐ **No. 13,** *walnut, beats seconds, dead beat escapement, height 4' 8", dial 12" (E1-92).*
    3000.00   3500.00   (3250.00)

☐ **No. 36,** *walnut, Graham dead beat escapement, height 6', dial 14" (E1-94).*
    6000.00   8000.00   (6250.00)

222 / E. HOWARD CLOCK COMPANY

No. 36 Round Top

No. 38 Square Top

WATCHMANS REGULATOR
WALL, SQUARE TOP
- ☐ **No. 38,** *walnut, Graham dead beat escapement, height 6', dial 14" (E1-92).*
  5500.00   7000.00   (5600.00)
- ☐ **No. 57,** *walnut, Graham dead beat escapement, height 6' 2", dial 14" (E1-93).*
  6500.00   7500.00   (7200.00)
- ☐ **No. 86,** *walnut, Graham dead beat escapement, height 6' 4", dial 14" (E1-94).*
  6500.00   7500.00   (7000.00)
- ☐ **No. 72,** *walnut, Graham dead beat escapement, height 5' 5", dial 14" (E1-94).*
  3500.00   4000.00   (3750.00)
- ☐ **As above,** *height 5' 4", dial 12".*
  3000.00   3500.00   (3250.00)
- ☐ **No. 85,** *mahogany, Graham dead beat escapement, height 5', dial 14" (E1-94).*
  5000.00   6000.00   (5500.00)
- ☐ **No. 89,** *walnut, Graham dead beat escapement, height 5' 5", dial 12" (E1-94).*
  2300.00   2800.00   (2400.00)

WATCHMENS CLOCK
- ☐ **No. 26 Regulator,** *walnut, height 4', dial 9" (E1-92).*
  800.00   1000.00   (850.00)

E. HOWARD CLOCK COMPANY / 223

No. 57 Square Top

No. 85 Square Top

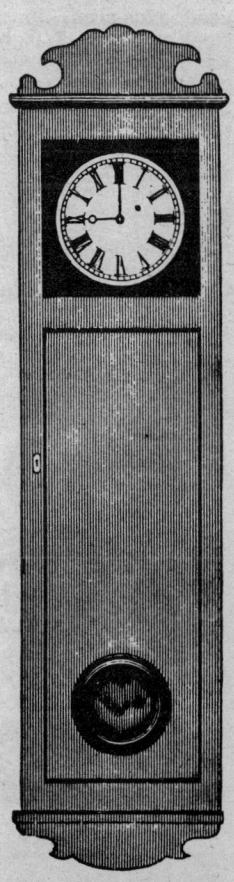

No. 26 Regulator

E. INGRAHAM COMPANY

Elias Ingraham a former cabinet maker, originally worked for a merchant named George Mitchell in Bristol. Mitchell set him to the task of case making, where he did exceptionally well, inventing a carved model of mahogany, occasionally embellished with bronze.

After two years Ingraham began working for C. and L.C. Ives, where he invented a case called the triple-decker. He also designed the steeple case.

After going through several transitions, including a cabinet making shop used exclusively for the making of clock cases, the E. Ingraham Company was formed, which eventually became simply The Ingraham Company. New plants were opened in Canada, Kentucky, and North Carolina. In the latter location electric and battery clocks were made.

ALARM

☐ **Ace,** *solid brass, nickeled, height 6", c. 1917, 8 Day, alarm (E1-173).*
    35.00   45.00   (40.00)

☐ **Autocrat Intermittent,** *nickel and brass, height 7¼", c. 1917, 1 Day, alarm (E1-173).*
    20.00   30.00   (25.00)

Ace

Autocrat

☐ **Cinch Intermittent,** *solid brass, nickeled, height 6", c. 1917, 1 Day, alarm (E1-173).*
    15.00   25.00   (20.00)

☐ **Ideal Intermittent,** *nickel, height 6", c. 1917, 1 Day, alarm (E1-173).*
    15.00   25.00   (20.00)

☐ **Indian,** *nickel, height 6", c. 1917, 1 Day, alarm (E1-173).*
    20.00   30.00   (25.00)

☐ **Premier Intermittent,** *solid brass, nickeled, height 7½", c. 1917, 8 Day, alarm (E1-173).*
    35.00   45.00   (37.50)

☐ **Sentry,** *nickel, height 6", c. 1917, 1 Day, alarm (E1-173).*
    20.00   30.00   (25.00)

BANJO/SPRING

☐ **Nile,** *mahogany finish, 39" x 10", iveroid or silver dial 8", c. 1900, 8 Day, (E2-77).*
    250.00   300.00   (275.00)

☐ **As above,** *8 Day, strike*
    300.00   350.00   (325.00)

☐ **Nyanza,** *mahogany, convex glass, 39" x 10", dial 8", c. 1917, 8 Day, strike (E1-172).*
    310.00   350.00   (335.00)

E. INGRAHAM COMPANY / 225

Nile

Nyanza

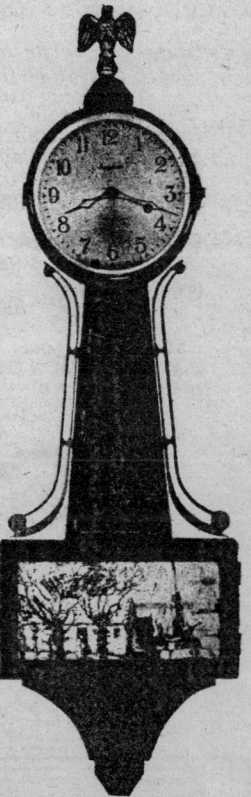

Nurse

BANJO/SPRING LEVER

☐ **Neptune,** *mahogany finish, green, rose or blue in crackle finish, circular silver plated dial, height 26", c. 1932, 8 Day, marine (E1-108).*
      80.00   100.00   (85.00)

226 / E. INGRAHAM COMPANY

☐ **Norway**, red or green finished, circular finish silver plated dial, height 26", c. 1932, 8 Day, marine (E1-108).
 75.00   90.00   (80.00)

☐ **Nurse**, mahogany or green finish, circular finish silver plated dial, height 26", c. 1932, 8 Day, marine (E1-108).
 80.00   100.00   (40.00)

BANJO/SPRING PENDULUM

☐ **Treasure**, mahogany finish, height 39", dial 8", c. 1932, 8 Day (E1-108).
 310.00   350.00   (330.00)

CABINET

☐ **Acme**, oak, height 17", dial 5", c. 1898, 8 Day, strike (E1-160).
 115.00   140.00   (125.00)

☐ **Bazar**, oak, height 18½", dial 5", c. 1898, 8 Day, strike (E1-160).
 130.00   150.00   (135.00)

☐ **Bismarck**, oak, fancy gilt, 15" x 10½", dial 6", 8 Day, strike (E1-144).
 80.00   100.00   (85.00)

☐ **Cabinet No. 1**, oak, height 15½", dial 5", c. 1894, 8 Day, strike (E1-139).
 80.00   100.00   (90.00)

☐ **Cabinet No. 2**, oak, height 15½", dial 5", c. 1894, 8 Day, strike (E1-139).
 80.00   100.00   (90.00)

Cabinet No. 4

☐ **Cabinet No. 3**, oak, height 15½", dial 5", c. 1894, 8 Day, strike (E1-139).
 80.00   100.00   (90.00)

☐ **Cabinet No. 4**, oak, height 15½", dial 5", c. 1894, 8 Day, strike (E1-139).
 80.00   100.00   (90.00)

☐ **Cabinet No. 5**, oak, height 15½", dial 5", c. 1894, 8 Day, strike (E1-144).
 80.00   100.00   (90.00)

☐ **Cabinet No. 6**, oak, height 15½", dial 5", c. 1894, 8 Day, strike (E1-144).
 80.00   100.00   (90.00)

☐ **Cabinet No. 7**, oak, height 15½", dial 5", c. 1894, 8 Day, strike (E1-141).
 80.00   100.00   (90.00)

☐ **Cabinet No. 8**, oak, height 15½", dial 5", c. 1894, 8 Day, strike (E1-141).
 80.00   100.00   (90.00)

☐ **Cabinet No. 9**, oak, height 15½", dial 5", c. 1894, 8 Day, strike (E1-141).
 80.00   100.00   (90.00)

☐ **Cabinet No. 10**, oak, height 15½", dial 5", c. 1894, 8 Day, strike (E1-141).
 80.00   100.00   (90.00)

Cabinet No. 3

E. INGRAHAM COMPANY / 227

☐ **Cabinet No. 11,** *oak, height 15½", dial 5", c. 1894, 8 Day, strike (E1-141).*
      80.00   100.00   (90.00)

☐ **Cabinet No. 12,** *oak, height 15½", dial 5", c. 1894, 8 Day, strike (E1-141).*
      80.00   100.00   (90.00)

☐ **Gladstone,** *oak, fancy gilt, 15" x 10½", dial 6", 8 Day, strike (E1-144).*
      80.00   100.00   (90.00)

☐ **Tablet,** *walnut, cathedral bell, patent regulator, height 15", dial 5", c. 1894, 8 Day, strike (E1-143).*
      80.00   100.00   (90.00)

☐ **Target,** *walnut, cathedral bell, patent regulator, height 16", dial 5", c. 1894, 8 Day, strike (E1-143).*
      80.00   100.00   (90.00)

☐ **Thistle,** *light wood, black ornaments, cathedral bell, patent regulator, height 16½", dial 5", c. 1894, 8 Day, strike (E1-143).*
      80.00   100.00   (90.00)

☐ **Thorn,** *oak, cathedral bell, patent regulator, height 12", dial 5", c. 1894, 8 Day, strike (E1-143).*
      80.00   100.00   (90.00)

☐ **Verona,** *oak, marbleized column, height 15¾", dial 5", 8 Day, strike (E1-160).*
      125.00   150.00   (135.00)

CALENDAR

☐ **Aliance Square Top,** *38½" x 16", dial 12", 8 Day, strike, simple calendar, spring wound (E2-76, M224-77).*
      450.00   500.00   (475.00)

☐ **Artic,** *office wall regulator, 37", dial 8", 8 Day, strike, simple calendar, spring wound (E1-154).*
      600.00   650.00   (625.00)

☐ **Aurora,** *Victorian kitchen, thermometer and barometer, height 25", dial 6", 8 Day, strike, simple claendar, spring wound (E2-74).*
      200.00   225.00   (212.00)

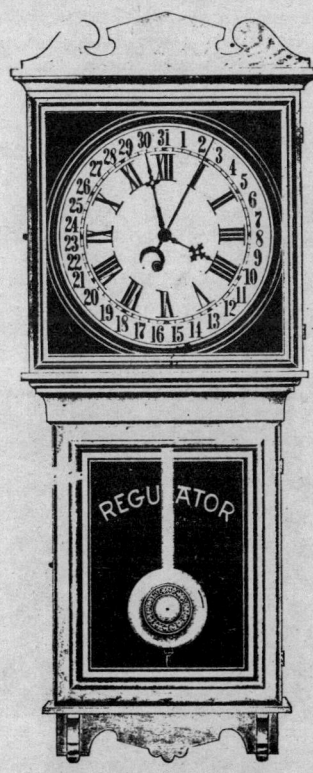

Aliance Square Top

☐ **Boston 12" Octagon Top,** *long drop, oak, height 32", 8 Day, strike, simple claendar (E2-78).*
      325.00   375.00   (350.00)

☐ **8" Bristol Octagon Top,** *short drop, oak, height 19", 8 Day, strike, simple calendar (E2-78).*
      225.00   250.00   (230.00)

☐ **10" Bristol Octagon Top,** *short drop, oak, height 21", 8 Day, strike, simple calendar (E2-78).*
      250.00   275.00   (265.00)

☐ **12" Bristol Octagon Top,** *short drop, oak, height 25", 8 Day, strike, simple calendar (E2-78).*
      250.00   300.00   (265.00)

228 / E. INGRAHAM COMPANY

Artic

Aurora

Boston, 12"

- ☐ **Chicago,** *Victorian kitchen, thermometer and barometer, height 23", dial 6", 8 Day, strike, simple calendar, spring wound (E2-75).*
        200.00   225.00   (210.00)

- ☐ **Commercial Octagon Top,** *long drop, oak, height 32", dial 12", 8 Day, strike, simple calendar (E2-78).*
        325.00   375.00   (340.00)

- ☐ **Dew Drop Octagon,** *24" x 16", dial 11", 8 Day, strike, simple calendar, spring wound (E1-156, M225-77).*
        300.00   350.00   (325.00)

E. INGRAHAM COMPANY / 229

Chicago

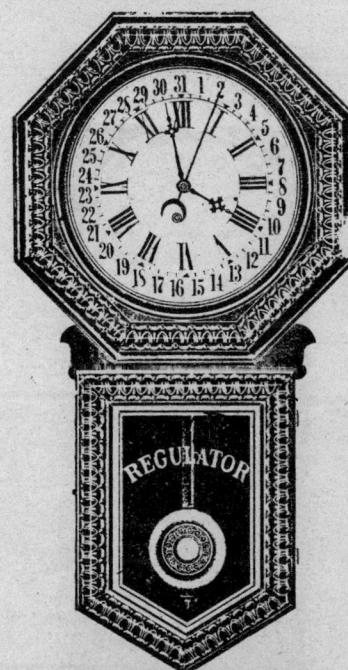

Hartford

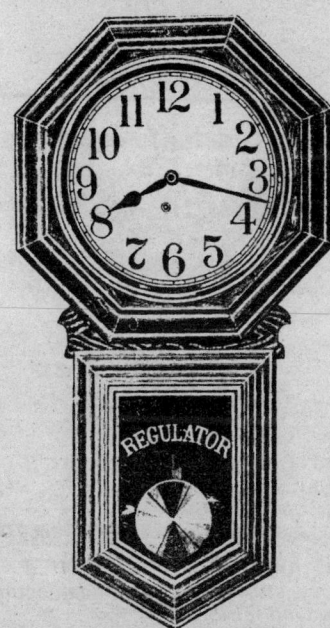

Commercial Octagon Top

☐ **Figure 8 (Wall),** *B.B. Lewis V calendar mechanism, 22" x 13½", 9" time and 5½" calendar dial, 8 Day, strike, double dial (M217-75).*
    1600.00   1800.00   (1700.00)

☐ **Gila,** *barometer left of door, thermometer right of door, 23", dial 6", 8 Day, strike, simple calendar, spring wound (M221-76).*
    225.00   250.00   (240.00)

☐ **Hartford 12" Octagon Top,** *long drop, oak, height 32", 8 Day, strike, simple calendar (E2-75).*
    350.00   400.00   (375.00)

☐ **Landau,** *wall regulator, oak, 38¼", dial 10", 8 Day, strike, simple calendar (E2-78).*
    300.00   350.00   (325.00)

☐ **Lyric Octagon Top,** *short drop, height 27", dial 12", 8 Day, strike, simple calendar (E2-75).*
    250.00   300.00   (275.00)

230 / E. INGRAHAM COMPANY

Landau

Minerva

Misay Octagon

☐ **Minerva,** Victorian kitchen, thermometer and barometer, height 25", dial 6", 8 Day, strike, simple calendar (E2-74).
    200.00   225.00   (215.00)

☐ **Misay Octagon,** short drop, 24", dial 12", 8 Day, strike, simple calendar, spring wound (E1-156).
    300.00   350.00   (325.00)

☐ **Mosaic Figure 8,** B.B. Lewis V calendar mechanism, 29 " x 16", 11" time and 10" calendar dial, 8 Day, double dial, spring wound (M218-75).
    850.00   1050.00   (900.00)

☐ **8" Octagon,** short drop, 19", 8 Day, strike, simple calendar, spring wound (E1-156).
    300.00   350.00   (325.00)

☐ **10" Octagon,** short drop, 21", 8 Day, strike, simple calendar, spring wound (E1-156).
    350.00   375.00   (360.00)

☐ **12" Octagon,** short drop, 24", 8 Day, strike, simple calendar, spring wound (E1-156).
    350.00   400.00   (375.00)

E. INGRAHAM COMPANY / 231

8" Octagon

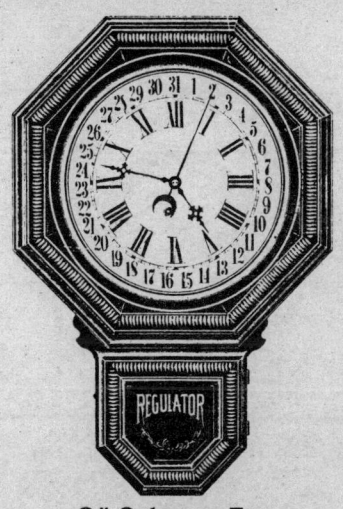

8" Octagon Top

12" Octagon

- [ ] **8" Octagon Top,** *short drop, oak, height 19", 8 Day, strike, simple calendar (E2-75).*
  225.00   250.00   (230.00)

- [ ] **10" Octagon Top,** *short drop, oak, height 21", 8 Day, strike, simple calendar (E2-75).*
  250.00   275.00   (260.00)

- [ ] **12" Octagon Top,** *short drop, oak, height 24", 8 Day, strike, simple calendar (E2-75).*
  250.00   300.00   (275.00)

- [ ] **8" Octagon,** *short drop, oak, height 19", 8 Day, strike, simple calendar (E2-78).*
  225.00   250.00   (240.00)

- [ ] **10" Octagon,** *short drop, oak, height 21", 8 Day, strike, simple calendar (E2-78).*
  250.00   275.00   (260.00)

- [ ] **12" Octagon,** *short drop, oak, height 25", 8 Day, strike, simple calendar (E2-78).*
  250.00   300.00   (260.00)

- [ ] **Ormond,** *round top long drop regulator, 35½", dial 12", 8 Day, simple calendar, spring wound (E1-175).*
  350.00   400.00   (375.00)

- [ ] **Parlor Shelf,** *B.B. Lewis V calendar mechanism, 22" x 12", 5" time and 7" calendar dial, 8 Day, double dial (E1-141, M216-75).*
  1400.00   1600.00   (1500.00)

- [ ] **Round Drop,** *wall, 24" x 16", dial 11", 8 Day, strike, simple calendar, spring wound (M222-77).*
  300.00   350.00   (325.00)

- [ ] **Topaz,** *Victorian kitchen, thermometer and barometer, height 23", dial 6", 8 Day, strike, simple calendar, spring wound (E2-75).*
  200.00   225.00   (210.00)

232 / E. INGRAHAM COMPANY

Topaz

Urania

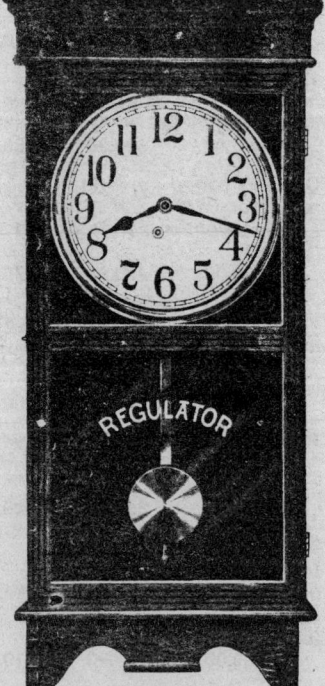

Trenton

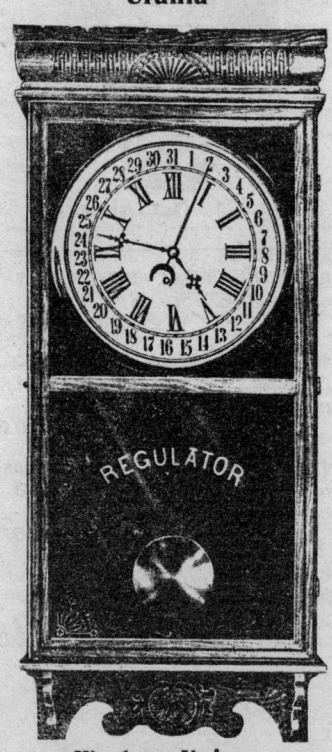

Western Union

E. INGRAHAM COMPANY / 233

☐ **Trenton,** *wall box regulator, oak, or mahogany, height 38", dial 12", 8 Day, strike, simple calendar (E2-78).*
      300.00   350.00   (325.00)

☐ **Urania,** *Victorian kitchen, thermometer and barometer, height 25", dial 6", 8 Day, strike, simple calendar, spring wound (E2-74).*
      200.00   225.00   (210.00)

☐ **Western Union,** *box wall regulator, oak, height 36", dial 12", 8 Day, strike, simple calendar (E2-78).*
      300.00   350.00   (325.00)

CONNECTICUT SHELF
COTTAGE

☐ **Cottage Extra,** *polished, veneered, height 12¾", dial 6", c. 1894, 1 Day, strike (E1-140).*
      70.00   85.00   (75.00)
☐ **As above,** *8 Day, strike*
      80.00   100.00   (85.00)

CONNECTICUT SHELF
OCTAGON TOP

☐ **Britannic,** *wood, height 16", c. 1880, 1 Day, strike (E2-72).*
      115.00   140.00   (125.00)

☐ **Crystal,** *wood, height 15½", c. 1880, 1 Day, strike (E2-70).*
      75.00   90.00   (80.00)
☐ **As above,** *8 Day, strike*
      95.00   115.00   (100.00)

☐ **Era,** *wood, height 15¼", c. 1880, 1 Day, strike (E2-70).*
      80.00   100.00   (85.00)
☐ **As above,** *8 Day, strike*
      105.00   125.00   (115.00)

☐ **Octagon Doric,** *wood, height 16", c. 1880, 1 Day, strike (E2-70).*
      80.00   100.00   (85.00)
☐ **As above,** *8 Day, strike*
      105.00   125.00   (115.00)

☐ **Octagon Doric,** *extra, wood, height 16", c. 1880, 1 Day, strike (E2-72).*
      80.00   100.00   (85.00)
☐ **As above,** *8 Day, strike*
      105.00   125.00   (115.00)

Cottage Extra

Crystal

☐ **Octagon Doric,** *gilt column, wood, height 16", c. 1880, 1 Day, strike (E2-70).*
      80.00   100.00   (85.00)

☐ **Octagon Doric,** *mosaic, wood, height 16", c. 1880, 1 Day, strike (E2-70).*
      80.00   100.00   (85.00)
☐ **As above,** *8 Day, strike*
      105.00   125.00   (115.00)

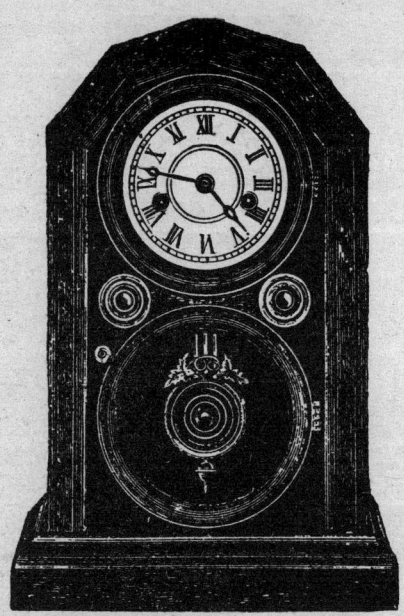

Octagon Doric

O.G. Weight

Empire

CONNECTICUT SHELF/O.G.

- ☐ **O.G. Weight,** *polished, veneered, height 26", dial 8", c. 1894, 1 Day, strike (E1-140).*
  130.00   155.00   (140.00)
- ☐ **As above,** *8 Day, strike*
  175.00   200.00   (180.00)

CONNECTICUT SHELF
ROUND TOP

- ☐ **Baltic,** *wood, height 16", c. 1880, 1 Day, strike (E2-72).*
  115.00   140.00   (125.00)
- ☐ **As above,** *8 Day, strike*
  140.00   165.00   (160.00)
- ☐ **Empire,** *wood, height 18", c. 1880, 8 Day, strike (E2-72).*
  175.00   200.00   (185.00)
- ☐ **Idaho,** *wood, gilt columns, height 18", c. 1880, 8 Day, strike (E2-72).*
  140.00   165.00   (145.00)
- ☐ **Venetian No. 2,** *wood, gilt columns, height 18", c. 1880, 8 Day, strike (E2-71).*
  150.00   175.00   (160.00)

E. INGRAHAM COMPANY / 235

☐ **Venetian No. 2,** *extra, wood, gilt columns, height 18", c. 1880, 8 Day, strike (E2-71).*
    155.00   180.00   (160.00)

☐ **Venetian No. 2,** *mosaic, wood, height 18", c. 1880, 1 Day, strike (E2-71).*
    130.00   155.00   (145.00)
☐ **As above,** *8 Day, strike*
    155.00   180.00   (165.00)

☐ **Venetian No. 3,** *wood, height 16", c. 1880, 1 Day, strike.*
    115.00   140.00   (125.00)
☐ **As above,** *8 Day, strike.*
    140.00   165.00   (165.00)

☐ **Venetian No. 3,** *extra, wood, height 16", c. 1880, 1 Day, strike (E2-71).*
    130.00   150.00   (140.00)

☐ **Venetian No. 3,** *mosaic, wood, height 16", c. 1880, 1 Day, strike (E2-71).*
    130.00   150.00   (140.00)
☐ **As above,** *8 Day, strike*
    150.00   175.00   (160.00)

CONNECTICUT SHELF
SPLIT TOP

☐ **Arctic,** *wood, height 16", c. 1880, 1 Day, strike (E2-71).*
    75.00   90.00   (80.00)
☐ **As above,** *8 Day, strike*
    95.00   115.00   (100.00)

☐ **Doric,** *wood, height 16", c. 1880, 1 Day, strike (E2-70).*
    75.00   90.00   (80.00)
☐ **As above,** *8 Day, strike*
    105.00   125.00   (115.00)

☐ **Doric,** *extra, wood, height 16", c. 1880, 1 Day, strike (E2-72).*
    80.00   100.00   (85.00)
☐ **As above,** *8 Day, strike*
    105.00   125.00   (115.00)

☐ **Doric,** *gilt column, wood, height 16", c. 1880, 1 Day, strike (E2-70).*
    80.00   100.00   (85.00)
☐ **As above,** *8 Day, strike*
    105.00   125.00   (115.00)

☐ **Doric,** *extra, gilt columns, wood, height 16", c. 1880, 1 Day, strike (E2-70).*
    90.00   110.00   (95.00)

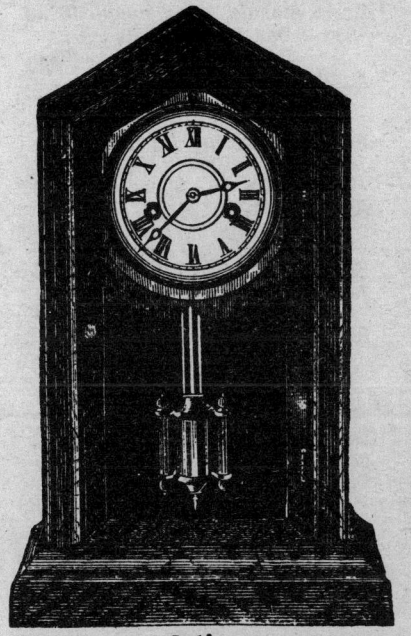

Artic

Doric

236 / E. INGRAHAM COMPANY

☐ **Doric,** mosaic, wood, height 16", c. 1880, 1 Day, strike (E2-70).
      80.00   100.00   (85.00)
☐ **As above,** 8 Day, strike
     105.00   125.00   (125.00)

☐ **Pony,** extra, wood, height 14", c. 1880, 1 Day, strike (E2-72).
      75.00   90.00   (80.00)
☐ **As above,** 8 Day, strike
      95.00   115.00   (100.00)

☐ **Ricarda,** wood, height 16", c. 1880, 1 Day, strike (E2-71).
      75.00   90.00   (80.00)
☐ **As above,** 8 Day, strike
      95.00   115.00   (100.00)

GALLERY

☐ **Gallery,** corrugated walnut, chestnut and gilt, 10" c. 1880, 8 Day and 8 Day, gilt (E2-72).
     175.00   200.00   (185.00)
☐ **As above,** 12"
     200.00   230.00   (210.00)
☐ **As above,** 14"
     220.00   250.00   (225.00)
☐ **As above,** 18"
     250.00   275.00   (260.00)
☐ **As above,** 20"
     250.00   275.00   (260.00)
☐ **As above,** 24"
     250.00   275.00   (260.00)

☐ **Gallery,** walnut, chestnut and gilt, 10" c. 1880, 8 Day and 8 Day, gilt (E2-73).
     155.00   180.00   (165.00)
☐ **As above,** 12"
     175.00   200.00   (180.00)
☐ **As above,** 14"
     195.00   245.00   (200.00)
☐ **As above,** 18"
     225.00   250.00   (230.00)
☐ **As above,** 20"
     225.00   250.00   (220.00)

☐ **Maxim,** solid oak, dial 10", c. 1900, 8 Day (E2-78).
     175.00   200.00   (185.00)

☐ **Milford,** oak, dial 12", c. 1900, 8 Day (E2-78).
     160.00   180.00   (175.00)
☐ **As above,** 8 Day, strike
     175.00   195.00   (180.00)
☐ **As above,** walnut, 8 Day
     200.00   225.00   (210.00)

Maxim

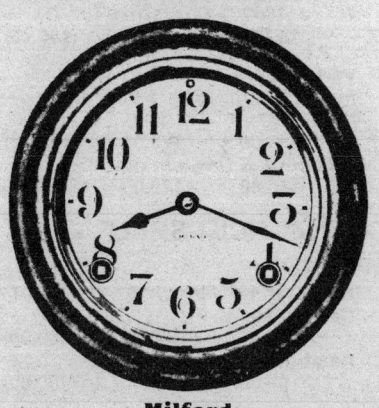

Milford

KITCHEN

☐ **Albion,** oak, height 24", dial 6", c. 1894, 8 Day, strike, spring wound (E1-142).
     115.00   140.00   (120.00)

☐ **Antler,** oak, walnut trimmings, height 24", dial 6", c. 1894, 8 Day, strike, spring wound (E1-143).
     125.00   150.00   (130.00)

☐ **Astra,** oak, height 22", dial 6", c. 1898, 8 Day, strike, spring wound (E1-160).
     140.00   165.00   (145.00)

☐ **Aurora Calendar,** oak, barometer and thermometer, height 25", dial 6", c. 1905, 8 Day, strike, calendar, spring wound (E2-74).
     190.00   220.00   (200.00)

E. INGRAHAM COMPANY / 237

☐ **Aztec,** *oak, height 24", dial 6", c. 1894, 8 Day, strike, spring wound (E1-142).*
    125.00   150.00   )130.00)

☐ **Bazar,** *oak, cathedral gong, height 18½", dial 5", c. 1894, 8 Day, strike, spring wound (E1-144).*
    160.00   185.00   (165.00)

☐ **Brazos,** *oak, height 23", dial 6", c. 1905, 8 Day, strike, spring wound (E2-76).*
    145.00   170.00   (150.00)

☐ **Bullion,** *walnut, gilt trimmings, height 24", dial 6", c. 1894, 8 Day, strike, spring wound (E1-140).*
    140.00   165.00   (160.00)

☐ **Capitol,** *oak, height 22", dial 6", c. 1905, 8 Day, strike, spring wound (E2-75).*
    210.00   240.00   (220.00)

☐ **Carmen,** *light wood, black trimmings, cathedral bell, height 18", dial 5", c. 1894, 8 Day, strike, spring wound (E1-144).*
    195.00   225.00   (200.00)

☐ **Cayuga,** *oak, height 22", dial 6", c. 1905, 8 Day, strike, spring wound (E2-74).*
    150.00   175.00   (160.00)

☐ **Chicago Combination,** *oak, thermometer and barometer, height 23", dial 6", c. 1905, 8 Day, strike, calendar, spring wound (E2-75).*
    190.00   220.00   (200.00)

☐ **Contest,** *walnut, height 16", dial 6", c. 1894, 1 Day, strike, spring wound (E1-141).*
    70.00   85.00   (75.00)

☐ **Dahlia,** *oak, height 22", dial 6", c. 1894, 8 Day, strike, spring wound (E1-142).*
    110.00   135.00   (115.00)

☐ **Delaware,** *oak, height 23", dial 6", c. 1905, 8 Day, strike, spring wound (E2-76).*
    145.00   170.00   (150.00)

☐ **Diana,** *oak, thermometer and barometer, height 25", dial 6", c. 1905, 8 Day, strike, spring wound (E2-74).*
    155.00   185.00   (165.00)

Chicago Combination

☐ **Divan,** *walnut, cathedral bell, height 16½", dial 5", c. 1894, 8 Day, strike, spring wound (E1-144).*
    195.00   225.00   (200.00)

☐ **Ducat,** *oak, height 24", dial 6", c. 1894, 8 Day, strike, spring wound (E1-140).*
    135.00   160.00   (140.00)

☐ **Easton,** *walnut, height 19", dial 6", c. 1894, 1 Day, strike, spring wound (E1-141).*
    100.00   120.00   (110.00)

☐ **Gila,** *oak, height 23", dial 6", c. 1905, 8 Day, strike, spring wound (E2-76).*
    145.00   170.00   (150.00)

☐ **Globe,** *oak, height 23", dial 6", c. 1894, 1 Day, spring wound (E1-140).*
    95.00   115.00   (100.00)

☐ **As above,** *8 Day, spring wound.*
    115.00   140.00   (120.00)

☐ **Globe, Calendar,** *oak, height 23", dial 6", c. 1894, 8 Day, strike, calendar, spring wound (E1-142).*
    125.00   150.00   (130.00)

238 / E. INGRAHAM COMPANY

☐ **Globe, Extra,** oak, thermometer and barometer, height 23", dial 6", c. 1894, 8 Day, strike, spring wound (E1-142).
150.00   175.00   (160.00)

☐ **As above,** walnut.
175.00   200.00   (180.00)

☐ **Ingot,** walnut, height 24", dial 6", c. 1894, 8 Day, strike, spring wound (E1-140).
140.00   165.00   (150.00)

☐ **Itasca,** oak, height 22", dial 6", c. 1905, 8 Day, strike, spring wound (E2-74).
150.00   175.00   (160.00)

☐ **Jasper,** oak, dial 6", c. 1898, 8 Day, strike, spring wound (E1-160).
135.00   160.00   (150.00)

☐ **Juno,** oak, height 22", dial 6", c. 1898, 8 Day, strike, spring wound (E1-160).
140.00   165.00   (160.00)

☐ **Lilac,** walnut, height 23", dial 6", c. 1894, 8 Day, strike, spring wound (E1-142).
115.00   140.00   (120.00)

☐ **Lily,** oak, height 22", dial 6", c. 1894, 8 Day, strike, spring wound (E1-141).
110.00   135.00   (120.00)

☐ **Lion,** oak, height 22", dial 6", c. 1905, 8 Day, strike, spring wound (E2-75).
170.00   195.00   (180.00)

☐ **Maine,** oak, height 23", dial 6", c. 1905, 8 Day, strike, spring wound (E2-75).
190.00   210.00   (200.00)

☐ **Mars,** oak, walnut trimmings, height 22", dial 6", c. 1898, 8 Day, strike, spring wound (E1-160).
140.00   165.00   (145.00)

☐ **McKinley,** oak, height 23", dial 6", c. 1905, 8 Day, strike, spring wound (E2-75).
200.00   220.00   (210.00)

☐ **Minerva Calendar,** oak, barometer and thermometer, height 25", dial 6", c. 1905, 8 Day, strike, calendar, spring wound (E2-74).
190.00   220.00   (200.00)

Kitchen No. 2

☐ **Mt. Vernon,** oak, height 22", dial 6", c. 1905, 8 Day, strike, spring wound (E2-75).
185.00   200.00   (190.00)

☐ **Niagara,** oak, height 23", dial 6", c. 1905, 8 Day, strike, spring wound (E2-76).
145.00   170.00   (150.00)

☐ **No. 2,** oak, height 22", dial 6", c. 1905, 8 Day, strike, spring wound (E2-74).
145.00   170.00   (165.00)

☐ **No. 4,** oak, height 22", dial 6", c. 1905, 8 Day, strike, spring wound (E2-74).
140.00   165.00   (145.00)

☐ **No. 6,** oak, walnut trimmings, height 22", dial 6", c. 1905, 8 Day, strike, spring wound (E2-74).
140.00   165.00   (145. 00)

☐ **Oneida,** oak, height 22", dial 6", c. 1905, 8 Day, strike, spring wound (E2-74).
150.00   175.00   (160.00)

E. INGRAHAM COMPANY / 239

☐ **Onyx,** *oak, walnut trimmings, dial 6", c. 1898, 8 Day, strike, spring wound (E1-160).*
    135.00   160.00   (145.00)

☐ **Opal,** *oak, height 22", dial 6", c. 1905, 8 Day, strike, spring wound (E2-75).*
    150.00   175.00   (165.00)

☐ **Orion,** *walnut, height 22", dial 6", c. 1898, 8 Day, strike, spring wound (E1-160).*
    140.00   165.00   (150.00)

☐ **Peace,** *oak, height 22", dial 6", c. 1905, 8 Day, strike, spring wound (E2-75).*
    170.00   195.00   (175.00)

☐ **Post,** *oak, height 23", dial 6", c. 1894, 1 Day, spring wound (E1-140).*
    95.00   115.00   (100.00)
☐ **As above,** *8 Day, spring wound.*
    115.00   140.00   (120.00)

☐ **Press,** *walnut, height 23", dial 6", c. 1894, 1 Day, spring wound (E1-140).*
    95.00   115.00   (100.00)
☐ **As above,** *8 Day, spring wound.*
    115.00   140.00   (120.00)

☐ **Press, Calendar,** *walnut, height 23", dial 6", c. 1894, 8 Day, strike, spring wound (E1-142).*
    115.00   140.00   (120.00)
☐ **As above,** *gong, 8 Day, strike, calendar, spring wound.*
    150.00   175.00   (165.00)

☐ **Press, Extra, Calendar,** *oak, thermometer and barometer, height 23", dial 6", c. 1894, 8 Day, strike, spring wound (E1-142).*
    150.00   175.00   (160.00)
☐ **As above,** *walnut, spring wound.*
    165.00   205.00   (170.00)

☐ **Puck,** *oak, height 24", dial 6", c. 1894, 8 Day, strike, spring wound (E1-140).*
    125.00   150.00   (130.00)

☐ **Rondo,** *walnut, height 18½", dial 5", c. 1898, 8 Day, strike, spring wound (E1-160).*
    140.00   165.00   (150.00)

☐ **Rose,** *walnut, height 22", dial 6", c. 1894, 8 Day, strike, spring wound (E1-141).*
    110.00   135.00   (120.00)

☐ **Ruby,** *walnut, dial 6", c. 1898, 8 Day, strike, spring wound (E1-160).*
    135.00   160.00   (140.00)

☐ **Sapphire,** *oak, dial 6", c. 1898, 8 Day, strike, spring wound (E1-160).*
    135.00   160.00   (140.00)

☐ **Saturn,** *oak, height 22", dial 6", c. 1898, 8 Day, strike, spring wound (E1-160).*
    140.00   165.00   (145.00)

☐ **Semi-Cabinet,** *oak, height 19", dial 6", c. 1905, 8 Day, strike, spring wound (E2-76).*
    75.00   90.00   (80.00)
☐ **As above,** *8 Day, strike, alarm, spring wound.*
    85.00   100.00   (90.00)
☐ **As above,** *mahogany, 8 Day, strike, spring wound.*
    100.00   115.00   (110.00)
☐ **As above,** *8 Day, strike, alarm, spring wound.*
    110.00   125.00   (120.00)

☐ **Shekel,** *oak, height 24", dial 6", c. 1894, 8 Day, strike, spring wound (E1-142).*
    125.00   150.00   (130.00)

☐ **Sun,** *walnut, height 23", dial 6", c. 1894, 1 Day, spring wound (E1-140).*
    95.00   115.00   (100.00)
☐ **As above,** *8 Day, spring wound.*
    115.00   140.00   (125.00)

☐ **Suwanee,** *oak, height 23", dial 6", c. 1905, 8 Day, strike, spring wound (E2-76).*
    145.00   170.00   (150.00)

☐ **Thalia,** *oak, thermometer and barometer, height 25", dial 6", c. 1905, 8 Day, strike, spring wound (E2-74).*
    160.00   185.00   (165.00)

☐ **Times,** *walnut, height 23", dial 6", c. 1894, 1 Day (E1-140).*
    90.00   110.00   (100.00)

Thalia

- **Topaz,** oak, dial 6", c. 1898, 8 Day, strike (E1-160).
  135.00   160.00   (140.00)

- **Topaz Combination,** oak, thermometer and barometer, height 23", dial 6", c. 1905, 8 Day, strike, calendar (E2-75).
  190.00   220.00   (195.00)

- **Tulip,** walnut, height 23", dial 6", c. 1894, 8 Day, strike (E1-142).
  115.00   140.00   (120.00)

- **Urania Calendar,** oak, thermometer and barometer, height 25", dial 6", c. 1905, 8 Day, strike, calendar (E2-74).
  190.00   220.00   (200.00)

- **Venus,** oak, height 22", dial 6", c. 1898, 8 Day, strike (E1-160).
  140.00   165.00   (145.00)

- **Vesta,** oak, thermometer and barometer, height 25", dial 6", c. 1905, 8 Day, strike (E2-74).
  160.00   185.00   (165.00)

- **Violet,** oak, height 22", dial 6", c. 1894, 8 Day, strike (E1-142).
  110.00   135.00   (115.00)

- **Wabash,** oak, height 23", dial 6", c. 1905, 8 Day, strike (E2-76).
  145.00   170.00   (150.00)

- **Warwick,** walnut, cathedral bell, height 18", dial 5", c. 1894, 8 Day, strike (E1-144).
  175.00   200.00   (180.00)

- **World,** oak, height 23", dial 6", c. 1894, 1 Day (E1-140).
  90.00   110.00   (95.00)
- **As above,** 8 Day.
  115.00   140.00   (120.00)

KITCHEN SERIES

- **Jewel,** oak, dial 6", c. 1898 (E1-160).
  135.00   160.00   (145.00)
- **As above,** walnut.
  160.00   185.00   (165.00)

- **Planet (6),** oak, height 22", dial 6", c. 1898, 8 Day, strike (E1-160).
  140.00   165.00   (145.00)
- **As above,** walnut.
  165.00   190.00   (175.00)

MANTEL/BLACK WOOD

- **Adrian,** enameled wood case, green marbleized mouldings and columns, gilt trimmings, cathedral gong, height 11", base 17½", iveroid dial 5½", c. 1900, 8 Day, strike (E2-77).
  90.00   110.00   (95.00)

- **Desoto,** enameled wood case, mahogany finished panels, inlaid silver and gilt, imitation onyx columns, gilt trimmings, cathedral gong, height 10½", base 20", iveroid dial 5½", c. 1900, 8 Day, strike (E2-77).
  100.00   120.00   (110.00)

- **Majestic,** enameled wood case, green marbleized mouldings, imitation onyx columns, gilt trimmings, cathedral gong, height 12½", base 17", iveroid dial 5½", c. 1900, 8 Day, strike (E2-77).
  90.00   110.00   (95.00)

- **Palace,** enameled wood case, cathedral glass window effect, green metal columns, gilt trimmings, cathedral gong, height 11", base 20½", iveroid dial 5½", c. 1900, 8 Day, strike (E2-77).
  100.00   120.00   (110.00)

E. INGRAHAM COMPANY / 241

☐ **Sigma,** *enameled wood case, cathedral glass window effect, green metal columns, gilt trimmings, cathedral gong, height 10¼", base 16¾", iveroid dial 5½", c. 1900, 8 Day, strike (E2-77).*
    75.00   90.00   (80.00)

☐ **Stanford,** *enameled wood case, green metal columns, green mouldings, gilt trimmings, cathedral gong, height 12", base 17", iveroid dial 5½", c. 1900, 8 Day, strike (E2-77).*
    80.00   100.00   (85.00)

Adrian

☐ **Stratford,** *enameled wood case, imitation onyx columns, green marbleized mouldings and panel, gilt trimmings, cathedral gong, height 11", base 17", iveroid dial 5½", c. 1900, 8 Day, strike (E2-77).*
    85.00   105.00   (90.00)

Palace

MANTLE/MAHOGANY CASE

☐ **Belmont,** *mahogany finish, 12" x 9", iveroid dial 5", c. 1917, 8 Day, strike (E1-173).*
    40.00   50.00   (45.00)

☐ **Berlin,** *mahogany finish, 12¼" x 9", iveroid dial 5", c. 1917, 8 Day, strike (E1-173).*
    40.00   50.00   (45.00)

☐ **Burgundy,** *mahogany finish, 10½" x 11", iveroid dial 5", c. 1917, 8 Day, strike (E1-173).*
    45.00   60.00   (50.00)

Berlin

☐ **Elegant,** *mahogany, scratched brass sash, convex glass, 11" x 15", dial 8", c. 1917 (E1-172).*
    40.00   50.00   (45.00)

☐ **Empire,** *mahogany, scratched brass sash, convex glass, 12" x 14", dial 8", c. 1917 (E1-172).*
    60.00   75.00   (65.00)

☐ **Hampton,** *mahogany, 11" x 14", dial 5", c. 1917 (E1-172).*
    40.00   50.00   (45.00)

☐ **Hanover,** *mahogany, 10" x 14", dial 5", c. 1917 (E1-172).*
    40.00   50.00   (45.00)

Lander

242 / E. INGRAHAM COMPANY

- **Howard,** mahogany, 10" x 16", dial 5", c. 1917 (E1-172).
  40.00   50.00   (45.00)

- **Lander,** mahogany finish, 11" x 19", iveroid dial 5", c. 1917, 8 Day, strike (E1-173).
  65.00   70.00   (70.00)

- **Saturn,** mahogany, porcelain dial, 7" x 6", c. 1917, 8 Day, alarm (E1-172).
  30.00   40.00   (35.00)

- **Seville,** mahogany, porcelain dial, 7" x 6", c. 1917, 8 Day, alarm (E1-172).
  30.00   40.00   (35.00)

- **Sibyl,** mahogany, porcelain dial, 8" x 6", c. 1917, 8 Day, alarm (E1-172).
  30.00   40.00   (35.00)

MANTLE/ROUND TOP

- **Dakota,** wood, height 15¾", c. 1905, 8 Day, strike (E2-73).
  210.00   240.00   (225.00)

- **Grecian,** wood, height 15", c. 1880, 1 Day, strike (E2-73).
  175.00   200.00   (190.00)

- **As above,** 8 Day, strike.
  195.00   225.00   (200.00)

Huron

- **Grecian,** mosaic, wood, height 15", c. 1880, 1 Day, strike (E2-73).
  175.00   200.00   (190.00)

- **Huron,** wood, height 15¾", c. 1905, 8 Day, strike (E2-73).
  210.00   240.00   (220.00)

MANTLE/TAMBOUR

- **Grinnell,** mahogany finish, inaloid decoration, 10" x 19", iveroid dial 5", c. 1917, 8 Day, strike (E1-173).
  40.00   50.00   (45.00)

- **Hammond,** mahogany, 11" x 19", dial 5", c. 1917 (E1-172).
  35.00   45.00   (40.00)

- **Nomad,** mahogany finish, 10" x 19¼", iveroid dial 5", c. 1917, 8 Day, strike (E1-173).
  40.00   50.00   (45.00)

- **Sage,** mahogany, porcelain dial, 6" x 8", c. 1917, 8 Day, alarm (E1-172).
  30.00   40.00   (35.00)

- **Sancho,** mahogany, porcelain dial, 6" x 11", c. 1917, 8 Day, alarm (E1-172).
  35.00   45.00   (40.00)

Grecian

E. INGRAHAM COMPANY / 243

Hammond

Occidental

12" Ionic

Reflector

☐ **Sorrento,** *mahogany, paper dial, lever, 8" x 15", dial 5", c. 1917, 8 Day (E1-172).*
      35.00   45.00   (40.00)

MIRROR SIDE
☐ **Occidental,** *walnut, height 24", dial 6", c. 1894, 8 Day, strike (E1-140).*
    285.00   325.00   (300.00)
☐ **As above,** *oak.*
    250.00   280.00   (275.00)

REGULATOR/FIGURE EIGHT
☐ **12" Ionic,** *wood, height 22", c. 1905, 8 Day (E2-73).*
    285.00   325.00   (300.00)
☐ **As above,** *8 Day, strike.*
    310.00   350.00   (315.00)
☐ **As above,** *8 Day, calendar.*
    335.00   375.00   (340.00)
☐ **As above,** *8 Day, strike, calendar.*
    360.00   400.00   (375.00)

☐ **12" Ionic,** *mosaic, wood, height 22", c. 1880, 8 Day (E2-73).*
    285.00   325.00   (290.00)
☐ **As above,** *8 Day, strike.*
    310.00   350.00   (325.00)
☐ **As above,** *8 Day, calendar.*
    335.00   375.00   (340.00)
☐ **Reflector,** *rosewood, height 29½", dial 12", c. 1898, 8 Day (E1-156).*
    310.00   350.00   (315.00)

244 / E. INGRAHAM COMPANY

REGULATOR/OCTAGON TOP, LONG DROP

☐ **Boston,** *solid oak, height 32", dial 12", c. 1900, 8 Day (E2-78).*
    270.00   300.00   (275.00)
☐ **As above,** *8 Day, strike*
    285.00   325.00   (295.00)
☐ **As above,** *8 Day, calendar*
    310.00   350.00   (315.00)
☐ **As above,** *8 Day, strike, calendar*
    335.00   375.00   (340.00)

☐ **Commercial,** *solid oak, height 32", dial 12", c. 1900, 8 Day (E2-78).*
    270.00   300.00   (290.00)
☐ **As above,** *8 Day, strike*
    285.00   325.00   (300.00)
☐ **As above,** *8 Day, calendar*
    310.00   350.00   (315.00)
☐ **As above,** *8 Day, strike, calendar*
    335.00   375.00   (340.00)

Hartford

☐ **Hartford,** *oak, height 32", dial 12", c. 1905, 8 Day (E2-76).*
    285.00   325.00   (300.00)
☐ **As above,** *8 Day, strike*
    310.00   350.00   (315.00)
☐ **As above,** *8 Day, calendar*
    335.00   375.00   (340.00)
☐ **As above,** *8 Day, strike, calendar*
    360.00   400.00   (370.00)

☐ **Reflector No. 2,** *wood, height 32", c. 1905, 8 Day (E2-73).*
    310.00   350.00   (325.00)
☐ **As above,** *8 Day, strike*
    335.00   375.00   (350.00)

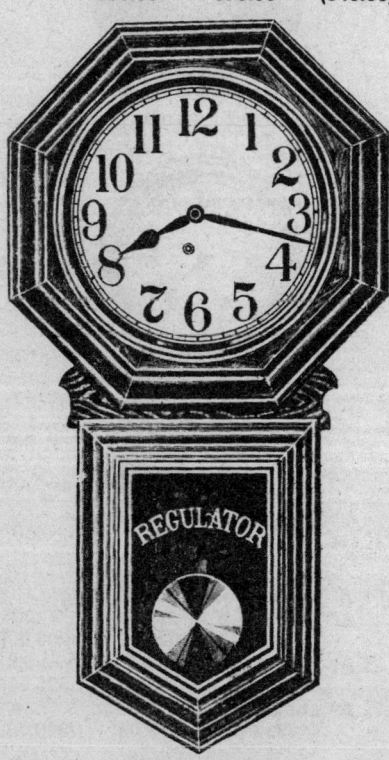

Commercial

REGULATOR
OCTAGON TOP, SHORT DROP

☐ **Bristol,** *solid oak, height 19", dial 8", c. 1900, 8 Day (E2-78).*
　　150.00　　175.00　　(160.00)
☐ **As above,** *8 Day, strike*
　　175.00　　200.00　　(180.00)
☐ **As above,** *8 Day, calendar*
　　195.00　　225.00　　(200.00)
☐ **As above,** *8 Day, strike, calendar*
　　220.00　　250.00　　(225.00)

☐ **Bristol,** *solid oak, height 21", dial 10", c. 1900, 8 Day (E2-78).*
　　175.00　　200.00　　(180.00)
☐ **As above,** *8 Day, strike*
　　195.00　　225.00　　(200.00)
☐ **As above,** *8 Day, calendar*
　　220.00　　250.00　　(240.00)
☐ **As above,** *8 Day, strike, calendar*
　　245.00　　275.00　　(250.00)

☐ **Bristol,** *solid oak, height 25", dial 12", c. 1900, 8 Day (E2-78).*
　　195.00　　225.00　　(200.00)
☐ **As above,** *8 Day, strike*
　　220.00　　250.00　　(225.00)
☐ **As above,** *8 Day, calendar*
　　245.00　　275.00　　(260.00)

Bristol

Drop Octagon

☐ **Drop Octagon,** *oak, height 19", dial 12", c. 1905, 8 Day (E2-75).*
　　195.00　　225.00　　(200.00)
☐ **As above,** *8 Day, strike*
　　220.00　　250.00　　(230.00)
☐ **As above,** *8 Day, calendar*
　　245.00　　275.00　　(250.00)
☐ **As above,** *8 Day, strike, calendar*
　　270.00　　300.00　　(290.00)

☐ **Drop Octagon,** *oak, height 19", dial 10", c. 1905, 8 Day (E2-75).*
　　175.00　　200.00　　(185.00)
☐ **As above,** *8 Day, strike*
　　195.00　　225.00　　(200.00)
☐ **As above,** *8 Day, calendar*
　　220.00　　250.00　　(225.00)
☐ **As above,** *8 Day, strike, calendar*
　　245.00　　275.00　　(250.00)

☐ **Drop Octagon,** *oak, height 19", dial 8", c. 1905, 8 Day (E2-75).*
　　150.00　　175.00　　(165.00)
☐ **As above,** *8 Day, strike*
　　175.00　　200.00　　(180.00)
☐ **As above,** *8 Day, calendar*
　　195.00　　225.00　　(200.00)
☐ **As above,** *8 Day, strike, calendar*
　　220.00　　250.00　　(235.00)

246 / E. INGRAHAM COMPANY

- **Drop Octagon**, solid oak, height 19", dial 8", c. 1900, 8 Day (E2-78).
  150.00   175.00   (160.00)
- **As above**, 8 Day, strike
  175.00   200.00   (185.00)
- **As above**, 8 Day, calendar
  195.00   225.00   (200.00)
- **As above**, 8 Day, strike, calendar
  220.00   250.00   (230.00)

- **Drop Octagon**, solid oak, height 21", dial 10", c. 1900, 8 Day (E2-78).
  175.00   200.00   (180.00)
- **As above**, 8 Day, strike
  195.00   225.00   (200.00)
- **As above**, 8 Day, calendar
  220.00   250.00   (225.00)
- **As above**, 8 Day, strike, calendar
  245.00   275.00   (250.00)

- **Drop Octagon**, solid oak, height 25", dial 12", c. 1900, 8 Day (E2-78).
  195.00   225.00   (200.00)
- **As above**, 8 Day, strike
  220.00   250.00   (230.00)
- **As above**, 8 Day, calendar
  245.00   275.00   (260.00)
- **As above**, 8 Day, strike, calendar
  270.00   300.00   (275.00)

- **Drop Octagon**, oak, rosewood or walnut, c. 1898 (E1-156)
  Rosewood, height 19", dial 8", 8 Day.
  225.00   250.00   (240.00)
- Rosewood, height 19", dial 8", 8 Day, strike
  245.00   275.00   (265.00)
- Rosewood, height 21", dial 10", 8 Day.
  270.00   300.00   (280.00)
- Rosewood, height 21", dial 10", 8 Day, strike
  295.00   325.00   (300.00)
- Walnut, height 19", dial 8", 8 Day.
  225.00   250.00   (230.00)
- Walnut, height 19", dial 8", 8 Day, strike
  245.00   275.00   (250.00)
- Walnut, height 21", dial 10", 8 Day.
  270.00   300.00   (285.00)
- Walnut, height 21", dial 10", 8 Day, strike
  295.00   325.00   (300.00)
- Oak, height 19", dial 8", 8 Day.
  175.00   200.00   (185.00)

- Oak, height 19", dial 8", 8 Day, strike
  195.00   225.00   (200.00)
- Oak, height 21", dial 10", 8 Day.
  220.00   250.00   (225.00)
- Oak, height 21", dial 10", 8 Day, strike
  245.00   275.00   (265.00)

Lyric

Misay

E. INGRAHAM COMPANY / 247

- ☐ **Drop Octagon,** *oak, height 24", dial 12", c. 1898, 8 Day (E1-156).*
  195.00   225.00   (200.00)
- ☐ **As above,** *8 Day, strike.*
  220.00   250.00   (230.00)
- ☐ **As above,** *8 Day, calendar.*
  245.00   275.00   (260.00)
- ☐ **As above,** *8 Day, strike, calendar.*
  270.00   300.00   (285.00)

- ☐ **Lyric,** *oak, height 27", dial 10", c. 1905, 8 Day (E2-75).*
  175.00   200.00   (180.00)
- ☐ **As above,** *8 Day, strike.*
  195.00   225.00   (215.00)
- ☐ **As above,** *8 Day, calendar.*
  220.00   250.00   (225.00)
- ☐ **As above,** *8 Day, strike, calendar.*
  245.00   275.00   (250.00)

- ☐ **Lyric,** *oak, height 27", dial 12", c. 1905, 8 Day (E2-75).*
  195.00   225.00   (200.00)
- ☐ **As above,** *8 Day, strike.*
  220.00   250.00   (225.00)
- ☐ **As above,** *8 Day, calendar.*
  245.00   275.00   (285.00)
- ☐ **As above,** *8 Day, strike, calendar.*
  270.00   300.00   (295.00)

- ☐ **Lyric,** *oak, height 27", dial 8", c. 1905, 8 Day (E2-75).*
  150.00   175.00   (160.00)
- ☐ **As above,** *8 Day, strike.*
  175.00   200.00   (200.00)
- ☐ **As above,** *8 Day, calendar.*
  195.00   225.00   (225.00)

- ☐ **Misay,** *rosewood, height 21", dial 12", c. 1898, 8 Day (E1-156).*
  245.00   275.00   (250.00)
- ☐ **As above,** *8 Day, strike.*
  270.00   300.00   (285.00)
- ☐ **As above,** *8 Day, calendar.*
  285.00   325.00   (290.00)
- ☐ **As above,** *8 Day, strike, calendar.*
  310.00   350.00   (315.00)

REGULATOR/PARLOR WALL

- ☐ **Arctic,** *oak, height 37", dial 8", c. 1898, 8 Day (E1-154).*
  450.00   500.00   (475.00)
- ☐ **As above,** *8 Day, strike.*
  490.00   550.00   (500.00)
- ☐ **As above,** *8 Day, calendar.*
  540.00   600.00   (560.00)
- ☐ **As above,** *8 Day, strike, calendar.*
  575.00   650.00   (585.00)

Artic

- ☐ **Bartholdi,** *oak, height 44", dial 8", c. 1898, 8 Day (E1-154).*
  450.00   500.00   (475.00)
- ☐ **As above,** *8 Day, strike.*
  490.00   550.00   (525.00)
- ☐ **As above,** *walnut, 8 Day.*
  550.00   600.00   (575.00)

- ☐ **Indus,** *oak, height 29", dial 6", c. 1898, 8 Day (E1-154).*
  335.00   375.00   (340.00)
- ☐ **As above,** *8 Day, strike.*
  360.00   400.00   (375.00)
- ☐ **As above,** *8 Day, calendar.*
  375.00   425.00   (385.00)

248 / E. INGRAHAM COMPANY

Landau

☐ **Landau**, *solid oak, height 38¼", dial 10", c. 1900, 8 Day (E2-78).*
245.00   275.00   (225.00)
☐ **As above**, *8 Day, strike.*
270.00   300.00   (275.00)
☐ **As above**, *8 Day, calendar.*
285.00   325.00   (300.00)
☐ **As above**, *8 Day, strike, calendar.*
310.00   350.00   (325.00)

☐ **Pacific**, *oak, height 37", dial 8", c. 1898, 8 Day (E1-154).*
540.00   600.00   (560.00)
☐ **As above**, *8 Day, strike.*
575.00   650.00   (600.00)
☐ **As above**, *8 Day, calendar.*
625.00   700.00   (650.00)
☐ **As above**, *8 Day, strike, calendar.*
675.00   750.00   (700.00)

REGULATOR
ROUND TOP, SHORT DROP
☐ **Dew Drop**, *oak, height 23½", dial 12", c. 1898, 8 Day (E1-156).*
175.00   200.00   (185.00)
☐ **As above**, *8 Day, strike.*
195.00   225.00   (200.00)
☐ **As above**, *8 Day, calendar.*
220.00   250.00   (230.00)
☐ **As above**, *8 Day, strike, calendar.*
245.00   275.00   (250.00)
☐ **As above**, *rosewood, 8 Day.*
225.00   250.00   (230.00)
☐ **As above**, *8 Day, strike.*
245.00   275.00   (260.00)
☐ **As above**, *8 Day, calendar.*
270.00   300.00   (285.00)
☐ **As above**, *8 Day, strike, calendar.*
295.00   325.00   (310.00)
☐ **As above**, *walnut, 8 Day.*
225.00   250.00   (230.00)
☐ **As above**, *8 Day, strike.*
245.00   275.00   (260.00)
☐ **As above**, *8 Day, calendar.*
270.00   300.00   (290.00)
☐ **As above**, *8 Day, strike, calendar.*
295.00   325.00   (310.00)

REGULATOR/SQUARE TOP
☐ **Aliance**, *oak, 38½" x 16", dial 12", c. 1905, 8 Day (E2-76).*
360.00   400.00   (375.00)
☐ **As above**, *8 Day, strike.*
375.00   425.00   (425.00)
☐ **As above**, *8 Day, calendar.*
400.00   450.00   (425.00)
☐ **As above**, *8 Day, strike, calendar.*
425.00   475.00   (400.00)

E. INGRAHAM COMPANY / 249

Aliance

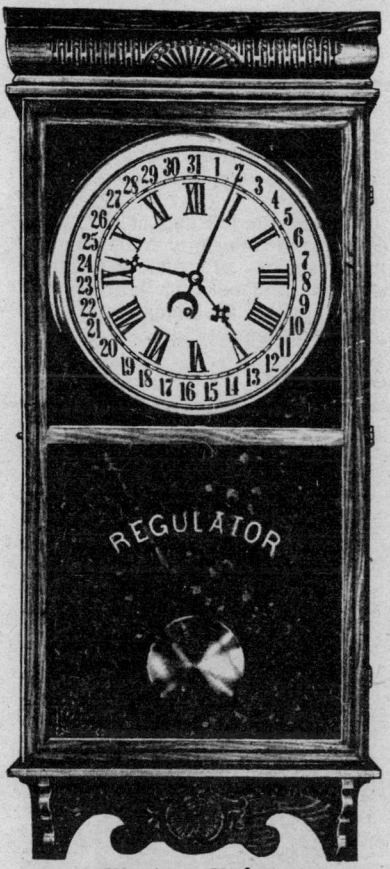

Western Union

REGULATOR/STORE

☐ **Trenton,** *golden oak, height 38",*
dial 12", c. 1900, 8 Day (E2-78).
  245.00   275.00   (260.00)
☐ **As above,** *8 Day, strike.*
  270.00   300.00   (275.00)
☐ **As above,** *8 Day, calendar.*
  285.00   325.00   (300.00)
☐ **As above,** *8 Day, strike, calendar.*
  310.00   350.00   (325.00)
☐ **As above,** *mahogany, 8 Day.*
  265.00   295.00   (275.00)
☐ **As above,** *8 Day, strike.*
  295.00   325.00   (315.00)
☐ **As above,** *8 Day, calendar.*
  310.00   350.00   (325.00)
☐ **As above,** *8 Day, strike, calendar.*
  335.00   375.00   (340.00)

☐ **Western Union,** *solid oak, height*
36", dial 12", c. 1900, 8 Day,
(E2-78).
  245.00   275.00   (260.00)
☐ **As above,** *8 Day, strike.*
  270.00   300.00   (275.00)
☐ **As above,** *8 Day, calendar.*
  285.00   325.00   (300.00)
☐ **As above,** *8 Day, strike, calendar.*
  310.00   350.00   (325.00)

ITHACA CALENDAR CLOCK COMPANY

Solely a calendar clock manufacturing company, Ithaca began due to the business ingenuity of Henry Horton. He invented the calendar mechanism that was used by the company he originated.

The most unique aspect of Ithaca, was not in the movements themselves, but in their area of production output. The cases and calendar mechanisms were produced in Ithaca, New York rather than Connecticut.

CALENDAR

☐ **Bank No. 0,** *double weight, 61" x 20", dials 12", 8 Day (E1-82, M78-31).*
        4300.00   4800.00   (4500.00)

Bank No. 2

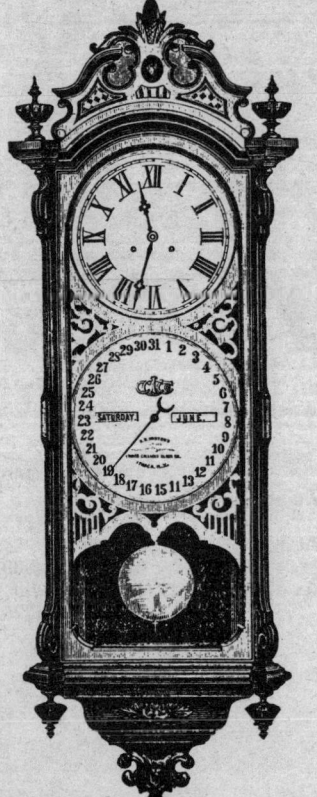

Bank No. 0

☐ **Bank Regulator No. 1,** *sweep second, 72" x 19½", dials 12", 8 Day (E1-82, M79-32).*
        7000.00   8000.00   (7500.00)

☐ **Bank No. 2,** *weight, 61" x 20", dials 12", 8 Day (E1-82, M81-31).*
        2900.00   3250.00   (3100.00)

☐ **Belgrade Hanging No. 5½,** *spring, 37½" x 14", dials 7", 8 Day, strike (E1-26, M99-38).*
        2000.00   2250.00   (2100.00)

☐ **Brisbane No. 2½,** *spring, 40" x 16", both dials 10½", 8 Day, strike (E1-26, M84-33).*
        2250.00   2500.00   (2300.00)

ITHACA CALENDAR CLOCK COMPANY / 251

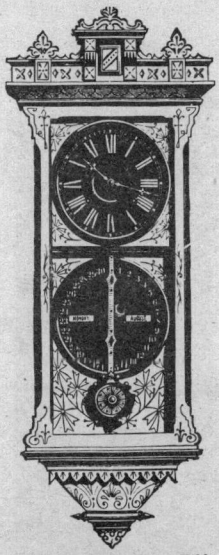

Belgrade No. 5½

Emerald Shelf No. 5

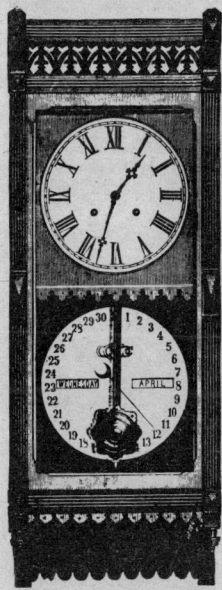

Brisbane No. 2½

- **Chronometer,** *spring, "Chronometer" in gold on glass, height 33", dials 7", 8 Day, strike (M135-50).*
  1250.00   1650.00   (1400.00)

- **Combination Time And Date Dial Shelf Clock,** *spring, open escapement, black enameled wood, 16½" x 12½", 8 Day, strike (M143-52).*
  2200.00   2600.00   (2400.00)

- **Emerald Shelf No. 5,** *spring, 33" x 15", 6½" time and 8" calendar dial, 8 Day, strike (E1-82, M97-37).*
  1500.00   1750.00   (1600.00)

- **Farmers (Old.) No. 10,** *alarm, double spring, 21" x 12", dials 7", 8 Day, strike (E1-80, M119-45).*
  550.00   600.00   (575.00)

- **Farmers With Pillars No. 10,** *alarm, spring, 21½" x 12", dials 7", 8 Day, strike (M120-45).*
  800.00   850.00   (825.00)

252 / ITHACA CALENDAR CLOCK COMPANY

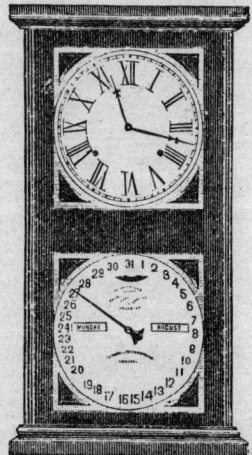

Farmers No. 10

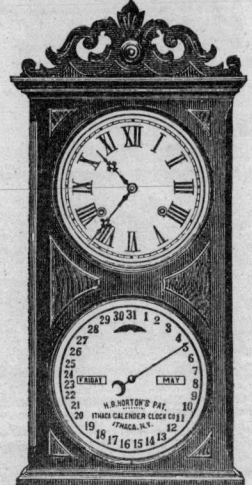

Farmers No. 10, with pillars

Favorite No. 4½

Granger No. 14

☐ **Favorite Shelf No. 4½,** *spring, "Favorite" on door glass in gold, 32" x 13½", dials 7", 8 Day, strike (E1-83, M95-37).*
      1250.00   1500.00   (1300.00)

☐ **Granger No. 14,** *spring, 26" x 12", dials 7", 8 Day, strike (E1-26, M130-48).*
      850.00   950.00   (900.00)

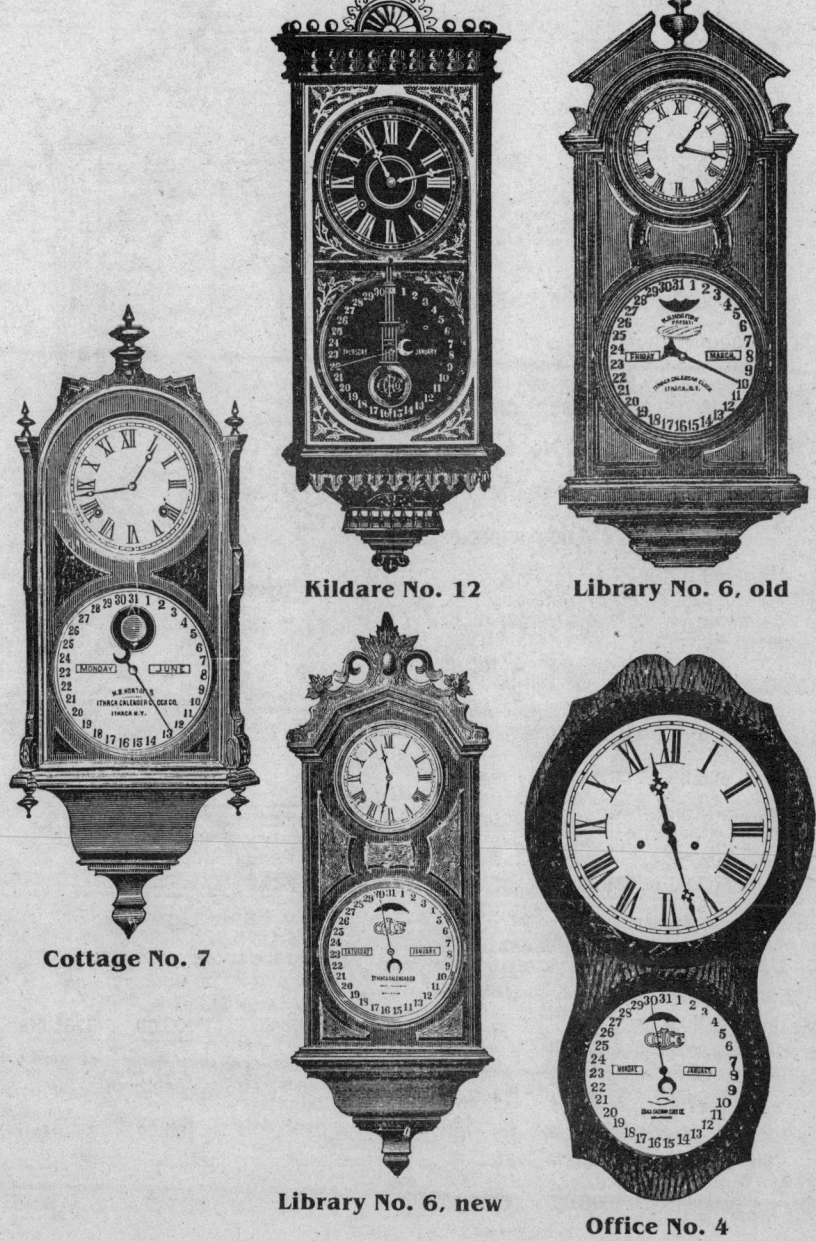

254 / ITHACA CALENDAR CLOCK COMPANY

☐ **Hanging Cottage (Old.) No. 7,** spring, 25" x 12", 5" time and 7" calendar dial, 8 Day, strike (E1-80, M113-43).
925.00   1025.00   (960.00)

☐ **Hanging Cottage (New.) No. 7,** alarm, spring, 29" x 13½", 5" time and 7" calendar dial, 8 Day, strike (E1-83, M116-44).
950.00   1050.00   (975.00)

☐ **Hanging Index No. 16,** spring, 30½" x 15", dials 7", 8 Day, strike (M132-49).
900.00   1000.00   (950.00)

☐ **Hanging Kildare No. 12,** spring, calendar, 33" x 13", dials 8", 8 Day, strike (E1-83, M125-47).
2600.00   2900.00   (2750.00)

☐ **Hanging Library (Old.) No. 6,** double spring, 28" x 12", 6" time and 8" calendar dial, 8 Day (E1-81, M105-40).
900.00   975.00   (950.00)

☐ **Hanging Library (New.) No. 6,** spring, 32" x 12", 5" time and 7" calendar dial, 8 Day, strike (E1-83, M110-42).
950.00   1100.00   (1100.00)

☐ **Hanging Office No. 4,** double spring, 28" x 15½", 12" time and 9" calendar dial, 30 Day (E1-26, M91-36).
925.00   1025.00   (960.00)

☐ **Hanging Regulator No. 0,** double weight, height 52", both dials 12", 8 Day (M71-29).
3000.00   3500.00   (3250.00)

☐ **Hanging Steeple,** spring, 32½" x 12", 7" time and 8" calendar dial, 8 Day, strike (M136-50).
1550.00   1790.00   (1650.00)

☐ **Index Advertising,** spring 36" x 14", dials 7", 8 Day, strike (M134-49).
1000.00   1050.00   (1100.00)

☐ **Index,** spring, "Index" in gold on glass, 33½" x 15", dials 7", 8 Day, time, strike (M138-51).
1250.00   1500.00   (1300.00)

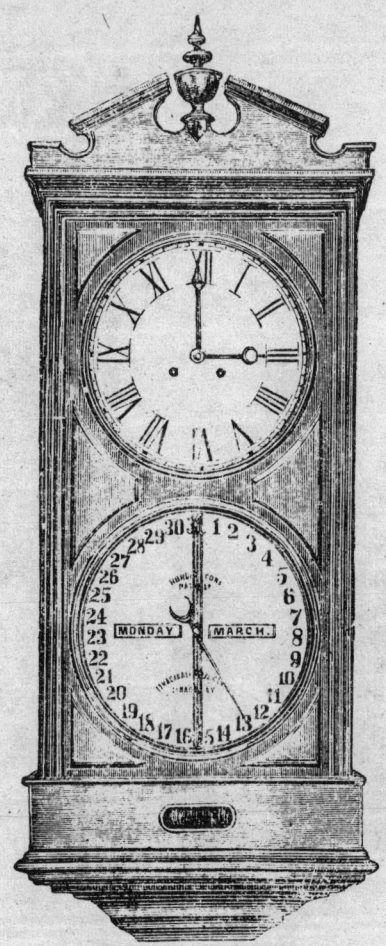

Iron Case, figure 8

☐ **Iron Case,** double spring, 21" x 9", 5" time and 7" calendar dial, 8 Day, strike (M64-26).
3100.00   3400.00   (3250.00)

☐ **Iron Case,** double spring, 21" x 9", 5" time and 7" calendar dial, 30 Day (M68-26).
3200.00   3500.00   (3350.00)

ITHACA CALENDAR CLOCK COMPANY / 255

☐ **Iron Case,** *figure 8 double dial wall calendar, spring, height 19", 5" time and 8" calendar dial, 8 Day (M63-26).*
    3300.00   3550.00   (3400.00)

☐ **Mantel Index No. 17,** *spring, 28½" x 15½", dials 7", 8 Day, strike (E1-83, M133-49).*
    750.00   950.00   (775.00)

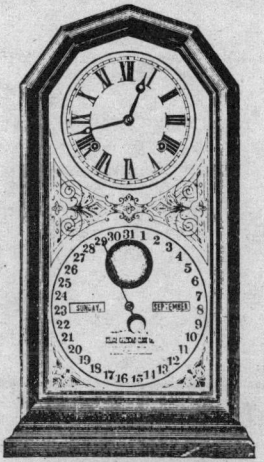

Octagon No. 11

Mantel Index No. 17

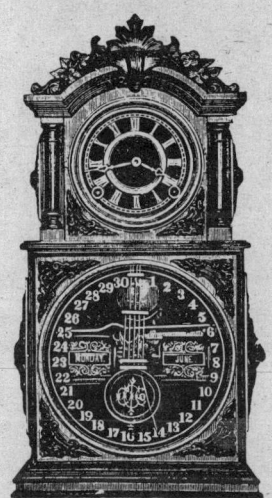

Parlor No. 3½

Melrose No. 15

☐ **Melrose No. 15,** *spring, crystal bob, cherry case, ebony finish, 22" x 12", 6" time and 8" calendar dial (black and gold), 8 Day, strike (E1-83, M131-48).*
    6000.00   7000.00   (6500.00)

☐ **Octagon (New.) No. 11,** *spring, 21" x 11", 7" time and 8" calendar dial, 8 Day, strike (E1-26, M124-46).*
    690.00   750.00   (675.00)

256 / ITHACA CALENDAR CLOCK COMPANY

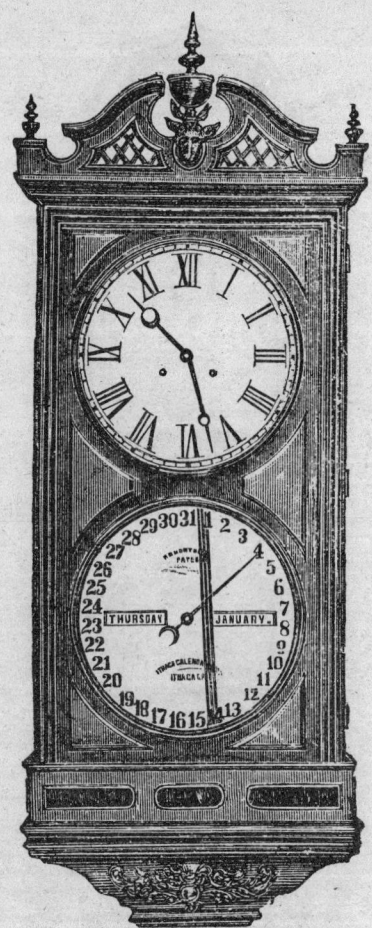

☐ **Regulator Shelf No. 1,** *double weight, 43" x 19", dials 12", 8 Day (M73-29).*
      2600.00   2900.00   (2750.00)

☐ **Regulator Shelf No. 1,** *double weight, 43" x 19", dials 12", 8 Day (M75-30).*
      2200.00   2500.00   (2300.00)

☐ **Regulator Shelf No. 2,** *double weight, 42" x 19", both dials 12", 8 Day (M76A-31).*
      1650.00   1850.00   (1800.00)

☐ **Regulator Hanging No. 3,** *double weight, 45" x 19", both dials 12", 8 Day (M77-31).*
      1450.00   1650.00   (1600.00)

☐ **Regulator Shelf No. 3,** *double weight, 39" x 19", both dials 12", 8 Day (E1-81, M77A-31).*
      1250.00   1300.00   (1275.00)

Regulator No. 1

☐ **Parlor No. 3½,** *1st model, spring, black dials, silvered hands, 20" x 10", 5" time and 8" calendar dial, 8 Day, spring (E1-82, M86-34).*
      2800.00   3400.00   (2950.00)

☐ **Regulator Shelf No. 0,** *double weight, height 52", both dials 12", 8 Day (M71A-29).*
      2000.00   2500.00   (2250.00)

☐ **Regulator No. 1,** *double weight 49" x 19", both dials 12", 8 Day (M72-29).*
      2800.00   3300.00   (2900.00)

Regulator No. 3

ITHACA CALENDAR CLOCK COMPANY / 257

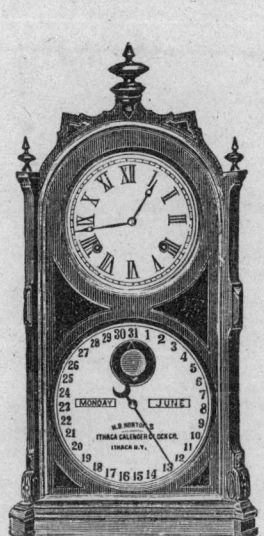

Shelf No. 9, new

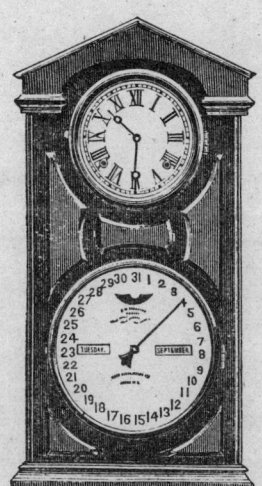

Shelf No. 9, old

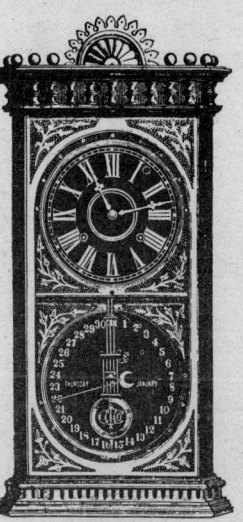

Shelf Library

Shelf No. 8, old

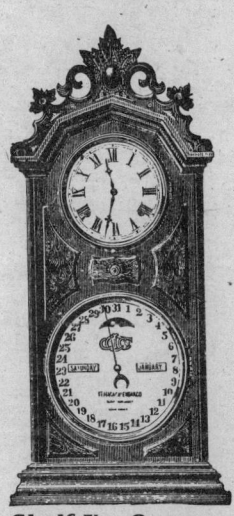

Shelf No. 8, new

258 / JEROME & COMPANY

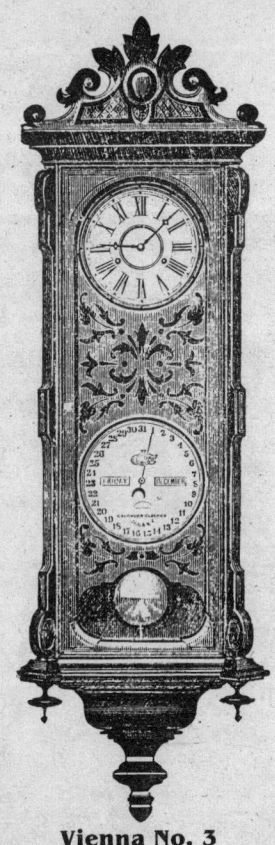

Vienna No. 3

- **Reno,** "Reno" in gold on glass, 8 Day, time, strike (M139-51).
  1100.00   1300.00   (1200.00)

- **Round Top Shelf (Old.) No. 5,** double spring, height 20", 5" time and 7" calendar dial, 8 Day (M101-39).
  650.00   700.00   (675.00)

- **Round Top Shelf (New.) No. 5,** double spring, 22½" x 11", 6" time and 7" calendar dial, 8 Day (M102-39).
  750.00   850.00   (775.00)

- **Round Top Shelf No. 102A,** double spring, 22½" x 11", 7" time and 8" calendar dial, 8 Day (E1-81).
  700.00   800.00   (725.00)

- **Shelf Cottage No. 7,** spring, 25" x 12", 5" time and 7" calendar dials, 8 Day, time, strike (E1-57).
  750.00   850.00   (775.00)

- **Shelf Cottage No. 9,** new, spring, 24" x 12", 5" time and 7" calendar dial, 8 Day, strike (E1-83, M117-44).
  950.00   1050.00   (975.00)

- **Shelf Cottage No. 9,** old, spring, 22" x 12", 5" time and 7" calendar dial, 8 Day, strike (E1-80, M114-43).
  700.00   800.00   (750.00)

- **Shelf Library,** alarm, spring, 31½" x 11½", 6" time and 8" calendar dial, 8 Day, time, strike (M140-51).
  900.00   1050.00   (950.00)

- **Shelf Library No. 8,** old, spring, 25½" x 12", 5" time and 7" calendar dial, 8 Day (M106-40).
  700.00   800.00   (750.00)

- **Shelf Library No. 8,** new, alarm, spring, 26" x 12", 5" time and 7" calendar dial, 8 Day, strike (E1-83, M112-42).
  950.00   1050.00   (1000.00)

- **Shelf Steeple,** spring, 25½" x 12", 6½" time and 7½" calendar dial, 8 Day, time, strike (M137-50).
  1550.00   1800.00   (1600.00)

- **Skeleton,** spring, nickel plated bell, silver cast iron dial and frame, (walnut with ebony trim), 24" x 12", 4½" time and 6½" calendar dial, 8 Day, time, strike (M145-53).
  7000.00   8000.00   (7500.00)

- **Vienna No. 3,** double spring, 52" x 16", dials 8", 30 Day (E1-82, M85-33).
  3250.00   3500.00   (3300.00)

JEROME AND COMPANY

So much has been written about Chauncey Jerome, perhaps it is safe to say he exemplified the image of the clock manufacturers of the time. An imposing looking man, his face was etched with stern lines above the stiff high collars he wore in the fashion of the times. He was bright, creative, ingenious, he formed and dissolved partnerships, had his finger in every clock making "pie," resorted to desperate measures, and eventually failed to provide a sound financial foundation to his clockmaking business.

He began his career in transit; purchasing clock movements and cases in Bristol, and assembling them in Virginia. He and his brother, Noble with whom he was in partnership, eventually moved to Bristol where they succeeded in selling vast quantities of shelf clocks. History was made when Noble obtained the patent for the cheap brass clock movement. Most clocks were still made with wooden movements up until that time — a difficult time consuming task. Noble and Chauncey were responsible for revolutionizing the entire clockmaking industry.

The Jerome brothers were able to sell the brass clocks at extremely low prices. Chauncey is also credited with opening up the market for American clock exports. By this time they were the largest of the clock manufacturing firms.

Chauncey Jerome committed his fatal mistake by entering a partnership with Theodore Terry and the notorious P.T. Barnum. It is rumored that Barnum was not strictly aboveboard in his disposal of company funds. At any rate the trios' combined investment was gone in short order, leaving the Jerome empire bankrupt and Chauncey destitute. It is said he ended his days in a white apron at the watchmakers bench.

Many thousands of clocks were produced by the various Jerome Companies but not too many survive. The values vary considerably according to the type and the period. The period is indicated by the label.

The early clocks by Jeromes and Darrow, C. and N. Jerome, and Jeromes, Gilbert, Grant and Company are rare collector items, and the values are subject to negotiations with the individuals concerned. The early labels used from 1841-44 of Chauncey Jerome and Jeromes and Company have a higher value than the later labels of Jerome Company and Jerome and Company of New Haven.

The name of The Jerome Manufacturing Company was used from 1851-55. After 1855 the New Haven Clock Company often used the label, Chauncey Jerome, which is not as prized by collectors as the earlier labels. The New Haven Clock Company also used the label, Jerome and Company, which is the least desired of all.

A rare variation and highly desirable was used by Chauncy Jerome 1844-45 — "Chauncey Jerome, Clockmaker". These labels were all printed by Benham, 650 Orange St., N.H.

Other labels show sales subsidiaries of Jerome, the southern companies being particularly desirable.

The last label used by C. Jerome in the 1860's is "Chauncey Jerome, Austin", which is rare.

In summary, if it has no label, the value will be decreased considerably, and the label must be considered to establish the period and the value. Every company making clocks during this period made similar clocks. Thus creating various values according to the fame of the maker.

CALENDAR

☐ **Alarm,** *nickel, dial 3¾", 1 Day, alarm, simple calendar (M404-126).*
       100.00   130.00   (110.00)

☐ **Crown,** *spring, calendar mechanism, 34½" x 19½", 8½" depth, dials 7", 8 Day, strike (M395-124).*
       1250.00   1600.00   (1300.00)

☐ **Dneister,** *spring, B.B. Lewis V calendar mechanism, 36¾" x 15", dials 7½", 8 Day (E1-103, M402-126).*
       1000.00   1100.00   (1050.00)

☐ **Register,** *spring, calendar mechanism, 33¾" x 12", dials 7½", 8 Day, strike (E1-104, M399-125).*
       1150.00   1300.00   (1200.00)

☐ **Rokeby Wall,** *weight, B.B. Lewis V calendar mechanism, 64" x 19½", 8 Day (E1-104, M403-126).*
       1405.00   1650.00   (1500.00)

Dneister

☐ **Shelf Clock,** *calendar mechanism, 21½" x 12¾", 5" time and 3½" calendar dial, 8 Day, strike (M390-123).*
    1200.00   1400.00   (1300.00)

☐ **Wall Clock,** *spring, calendar mechanism, 40" x 15", dials 8", 8 Day (M401-125).*
    1750.00   1900.00   (1800.00)

CONNECTICUT SHELF
BEE HIVE

☐ **Tudor Style,** *with and without alarms, mahogany, black walnut, rosewood, height 19", 8 Day (E1-7).*
    160.00   180.00   (175.00)
☐ **As above,** *8 Day, alarm.*
    165.00   185.00   (180.00)
☐ **As above,** *1 Day.*
    140.00   160.00   (150.00)
☐ **As above,** *1 Day, alarm.*
    145.00   165.00   (150.00)

Tudor Style

☐ **Tudor,** *striking, also alarms, mahogany, walnut, zebra and rosewood, height 19", 8 Day (E1-7).*
    160.00   180.00   (165.00)
☐ **As above,** *8 Day, strike.*
    165.00   185.00   (175.00)
☐ **As above,** *8 Day, alarm.*
    170.00   190.00   (175.00)
☐ **As above,** *1 Day.*
    145.00   165.00   (160.00)
☐ **As above,** *1 Day, alarm.*
    150.00   170.00   (160.00)
☐ **Tudor Style,** *30 hour lever, striking, height 14", 1 Day (E1-7).*
    140.00   160.00   (160.00)
☐ **Tudor Style,** *height 14", 8 Day (E1-7).*
    160.00   180.00   (165.00)

CONNECTICUT SHELF
COTTAGE

☐ **Cottage,** *mahogany and black walnut, height 12", 30 hour*
    120.00   130.00   (125.00)
☐ **As above,** *striking.*
    130.00   150.00   (140.00)
☐ **David Crocket,** *mahogany and walnut, time piece, height 12", 30 hour*
    120.00   130.00   (125.00)
☐ **French Style,** *marble, height 13", 8 Day*
    130.00   150.00   (140.00)

Cottage

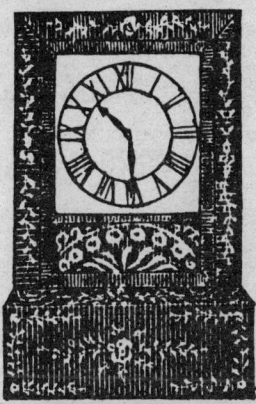

Prince Albert

French Style

- **French Style,** *rosewood, height 13", 8 day*
  110.00   130.00   (120.00)

- **N.E. Company,** *mahogany, walnut, zebra, time piece, height 11", 30 hour*
  110.00   125.00   (120.00)
- **As above,** *with alarms, (E1-8).*
  115.00   130.00   (125.00)

- **Prince Albert,** *mahogany, rosewood, height 15", 8 Day (E1-8)*
  155.00   175.00   (165.00)
- **As above,** *1 Day.*
  135.00   155.00   (140.00)

- **Prince Albert,** *mahogany, height 15", 30 hour, striking (E1-8).*
  130.00   150.00   (140.00)
- **As above,** *rosewood.*
  140.00   160.00   (150.00)
- **As above,** *zebra.*
  150.00   170.00   (160.00)

- **Prince Albert,** *rosewood, height 15", 8 day, striking (E1-8).*
  140.00   160.00   (150.00)

- **S.B.T.,** *time piece, height 10½", 30 hour*
  170.00   190.00   (185.00)

- **Union,** *mahogany, rosewood, height 13", 8 Day, striking*
  120.00   140.00   (125.00)
- **As above,** *with alarms, 1 Day (E1-8).*
  110.00   130.00   (120.00)

- **Union,** *mahogany, rosewood, height 13", 30 hour, striking*
  110.00   130.00   (120.00)
- **As above,** *with alarms (E1-8).*
  115.00   135.00   (125.00)

- **Union,** *mahogany, black walnut, rosewood, height 13", 8 day*
  120.00   140.00   (135.00)
- **As above,** *30 hour (E1-8).*
  110.00   130.00   (115.00)

- **Union,** *rosewood with gilt moldings, height 13", 8 Day, striking (E1-8)*
  120.00   140.00   (130.00)

262 /JEROME & COMPANY

- **Union,** *rosewood with elaborate gilt moldings, height 13", 8 Day (E1-8).*
  130.00   150.00   (140.00)

- **Victoria,** *rosewood, height 15", 30 hour, striking (E1-7).*
  130.00   150.00   (140.00)

CONNECTICUT SHELF
EMPIRE AND COLUMN

- **Column,** *mahogany, rosewood, gilt and rose pillars, 30 hour*
  175.00   225.00   (200.00)

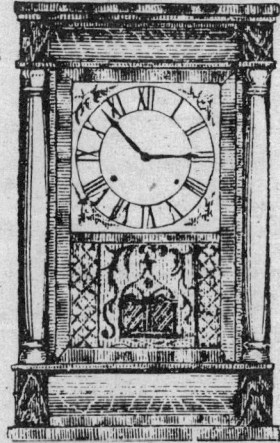

Column

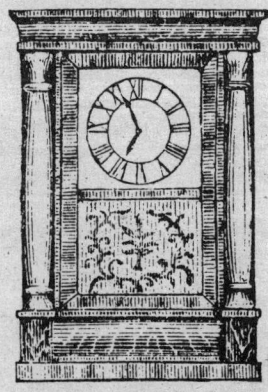

Column Spring Clock

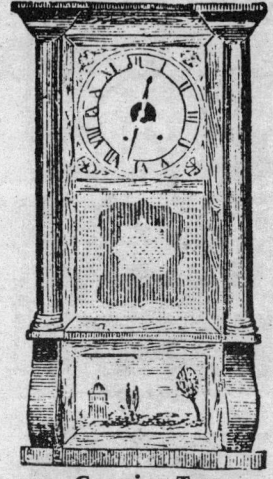

Cornice Top

- **Column Spring Clock,** *mahogany, rosewood, gilt and rose pillars, height 20", 8 Day*
  220.00   240.00   (230.00)
- **As above,** *30 hour*
  155.00   175.00   (160.00)

- **Cornice Top,** *mahogany, extra column, rolling pinion, height 33", 8 Day, with weights (E1-8).*
  385.00   435.00   (390.00)

- **Cornice Top,** *gilt and rose columns, height 24", 8 Day, striking (E1-8).*
  230.00   250.00   (240.00)

- **Extra Column,** *scenic picture on case under dial, height 25", with alarms (E1-6)*
  185.00   235.00   (190.00)

- **Gilt Top And Column,** *mahogany, rolling pinion, 8 Day, with weights*
  525.00   575.00   (550.00)

CONNECTICUT SHELF
MANTEL LEVER

- **Bronze Lever,** *silent, height 9", 1 Day*
  110.00   130.00   (125.00)
- **As above,** *8 Day*
  125.00   145.00   (130.00)

JEROME & COMPANY / 263

☐ **Bronze Lever Time Piece,** *1 Day*
  180.00   200.00   (190.00)
☐ **As above,** *8 Day*
  220.00   240.00   (230.00)

☐ **Bronze Lever Time Piece,** *1 Day*
  180.00   200.00   (190.00)
☐ **As above,** *8 Day*
  200.00   240.00   (225.00)

☐ **Mantel Lever,** *rosewood, carved base, striking, height 12", 1 Day*
  110.00   130.00   (125.00)
☐ **As above,** *1 Day, strike*
  115.00   135.00   (125.00)
☐ **As above,** *8 Day*
  125.00   155.00   (140.00)
☐ **As above,** *8 Day, strike*
  140.00   160.00   (150.00)

CONNECTICUT SHELF
O.G. AND O.O.G.

☐ **Barnum,** *mahogany, walnut, rosewood, zebra, height 15", 30 hour, 1 Day*
  130.00   150.00   (140.00)
☐ **As above,** *1 Day, strike*
  140.00   160.00   (150.00)

☐ **O.G. AND O.O.G.,** *8 Day*
  230.00   250.00   (225.00)
☐ **As above,** *8 Day, strike*
  240.00   260.00   (250.00)

Mantle Lever

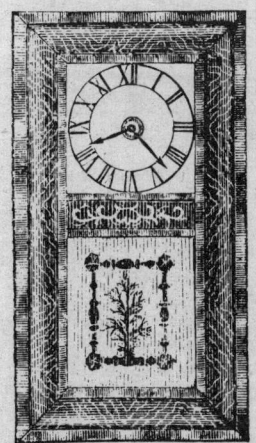

O.G. and O.O.G., 8 Day

☐ **Mantel Lever,** *rosewood and mahogany, silent, height 10", 1 Day*
  110.00   130.00   (120.00)
☐ **As above,** *1 Day, strike*
  115.00   135.00   (125.00)
☐ **As above,** *8 Day*
  125.00   155.00   (130.00)
☐ **As above,** *8 Day, strike*
  140.00   160.00   (150.00)

☐ **Mantel Lever Time Piece,** *rosewood, 1 Day*
  110.00   130.00   (120.00)
☐ **As above,** *1 Day, alarm*
  115.00   135.00   (120.00)
☐ **As above,** *8 Day*
  125.00   155.00   (140.00)
☐ **As above,** *8 Day, alarm*
  130.00   150.00   (125.00)
☐ **As above,** *8 Day, strike, alarm*
  140.00   160.00   (150.00)

O.G. and O.O.G., 1 Day

JEROME & COMPANY

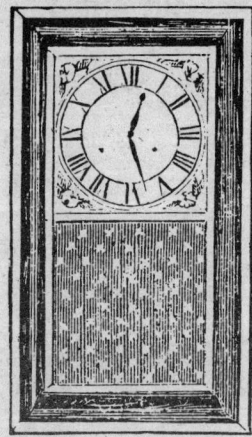

O.O.G., with weights

☐ **O.G. AND O.O.G.** *mahogany and zebra, 30 hour, 1 Day*
    145.00   165.00   (150.00)
☐ **As above,** *1 Day, strike*
    155.00   175.00   (160.00)

☐ **O.O.G.,** *height 18", 1 Day*
    130.00   150.00   (140.00)
☐ **As above,** *1 Day, strike*
    140.00   160.00   (150.00)
☐ **As above,** *1 Day, alarm*
    150.00   170.00   (160.00)

☐ **O.O.G.,** *height 15", 30 hour, 1 Day*
    145.00   165.00   (155.00)

☐ **O.O.G.,** *with weights, height 39", 1 Day*
    120.00   140.00   (130.00)
☐ **As above,** *1 Day, strike*
    130.00   150.00   (140.00)
☐ **As above,** *1 Day, alarm*
    140.00   160.00   (150.00)
☐ **As above,** *8 Day*
    210.00   230.00   (225.00)
☐ **As above,** *8 Day, strike*
    230.00   240.00   (225.00)
☐ **As above,** *8 Day, strike, alarm*
    230.00   250.00   (235.00)

☐ **Reversed O.G.,** *mahogany, walnut, rosewood, zebra, 30 hour, 1 Day*
    160.00   180.00   (165.00)
☐ **As above,** *1 Day, strike*
    170.00   190.00   (175.00)

☐ **Rough And Ready No. 1,** *rosewood, height 16", 30 hour, 1 Day*
    160.00   180.00   (170.00)
☐ **As above,** *1 Day, alarm*
    170.00   190.00   (180.00)
☐ **As above,** *1 Day, strike*
    180.00   190.00   (185.00)
☐ **As above,** *1 Day, strike, alarm*
    190.00   200.00   (195.00)

CONNECTICUT SHELF
PAPIER MÂCHÉ
☐ **French Style,** *height 13", 8 Day.*
    165.00   185.00   (175.00)
☐ **As above,** *30 hour*
    145.00   160.00   (150.00)

Gothic Style

Navy

JEROME & COMPANY / 265

Paris Style, 8 Day

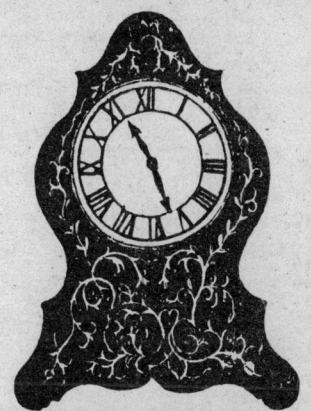

Paris Style, 1 Day

- **Gothic Style,** *lever, height 14", 30 hour, 1 Day*
  140.00   160.00   (150.00)
- **As above,** *8 Day*
  160.00   180.00   (170.00)
- **As above,** *8 Day, strike*
  180.00   200.00   (190.00)
- **Kossuth,** *height 16", 30 hour, 1 Day*
  140.00   160.00   (150.00)
- **Kossuth,** *height 16", 8 Day*
  160.00   180.00   (170.00)
- **As above,** *8 Day, strike*
  180.00   200.00   (190.00)
- **Kossuth Style,** *lever, height 11", 1 Day*
  140.00   160.00   (150.00)
- **As above,** *8 Day*
  160.00   180.00   (170.00)
- **As above,** *8 Day, strike*
  180.00   200.00   (190.00)
- **Mantel Lever,** *height 11", 1 Day*
  135.00   155.00   (140.00)
- **As above,** *1 Day, strike*
  155.00   175.00   (160.00)
- **As above,** *8 Day*
  165.00   185.00   (170.00)
- **As above,** *8 Day, strike*
  175.00   195.00   (180.00)
- **Navy,** *time piece, dial 9", 1 Day.*
  300.00   325.00   (315.00)
- **As above,** *8 Day*
  325.00   375.00   (350.00)
- **As above,** *8 Day, strike*
  350.00   400.00   (375.00)

- **Paris Style,** *height 16", 8 Day*
  160.00   180.00   (175.00)
- **As above,** *8 Day, strike*
  180.00   200.00   (185.00)
- **Paris Style,** *striking lever, height 16", 30 hour, 1 Day*
  140.00   160.00   (150.00)
- **As above,** *1 Day, strike*
  160.00   180.00   (175.00)
- **Paris Style,** *lever, silent, height 10", 1 Day*
  135.00   155.00   (140.00)
- **As above,** *1 Day, strike*
  145.00   165.00   (150.00)
- **As above,** *8 Day, strike*
  165.00   185.00   (175.00)
- **Putnum Style,** *lever, height 10", 1 Day*
  135.00   155.00   (140.00)
- **As above,** *1 Day, strike*
  145.00   165.00   (150.00)
- **As above,** *8 Day*
  155.00   175.00   (160.00)
- **As above,** *8 Day, strike*
  165.00   185.00   (170.00)
- **Union Style,** *1 Day*
  135.00   155.00   (146.00)
- **As above,** *1 Day, strike*
  145.00   165.00   (150.00)
- **As above,** *8 Day*
  155.00   175.00   (160.00)
- **As above,** *8 Day, strike*
  165.00   185.00   (170.00)

- Union Style, *lever, 1 Day*
  140.00   160.00   (150.00)
- As above, *1 Day, strike*
  150.00   170.00   (160.00)
- As above, *8 Day*
  160.00   180.00   (170.00)
- As above, *8 Day, strike*
  170.00   190.00   (175.00)

CONNECTICUT SHELF
PEARL INLAID

- Jenny Lind, *height 15", 30 hour, 1 Day*
  160.00   180.00   (170.00)
- As above, *8 Day*
  170.00   190.00   (180.00)
- As above, *8 Day, strike*
  180.00   200.00   (190.00)

Kossuth

- Kossuth, *height 19", 8 Day*
  180.00   200.00   (190.00)
- As above, *8 Day, strike*
  200.00   220.00   (210.00)
- LaFayette, *height 13", 8 Day*
  140.00   160.00   (150.00)
- As above, *8 Day, strike*
  160.00   180.00   (165.00)
- Mantel, *lever, with alarms, height 11", 30 hour, 1 Day*
  125.00   145.00   (130.00)
- Mantel Lever Time Piece, *striking, height 11", 1 Day*
  130.00   150.00   (140.00)
- Tom Thumb Jr., *lever, metal case, height 8", 30 hour, 1 Day*
  165.00   185.00   (175.00)

- Union, *striking, height 13", 1 Day*
  125.00   145.00   (130.00)
- As above, *8 Day*
  150.00   170.00   (160.00)
- As above, *8 Day, strike*
  160.00   180.00   (165.00)
- Washington, *height 10", 1 Day*
  140.00   160.00   (145.00)
- As above, *8 Day*
  160.00   180.00   (170.00)
- As above, *8 Day, strike*
  180.00   200.00   (190.00)
- Washington, *lever, time piece, height 10½", 1 Day*
  160.00   185.00   (165.00)
- Eight Day Pearl Inlaid, *iron frame, 1 Day*
  140.00   160.00   (150.00)
- As above, *8 Day*
  160.00   180.00   (170.00)
- As above, *8 Day, strike*
  180.00   200.00   (190.00)

CONNECTICUT SHELF
STEEPLE

- Gothic, *mahogany, rosewood, black walnut, height 19", 8 Day.*
  180.00   200.00   (190.00)
- As above, *with alarms.*
  190.00   210.00   (200.00)
- As above, *30 hour.*
  145.00   165.00   (155.00)
- As above, *30 hour, with alarms.*
  155.00   175.00   (160.00)

Gothic

☐ **Gothic,** *mahogany, rosewood, walnut, zebra, height 20", 8 Day, striking.*
190.00   210.00   (200.00)
☐ **As above,** *with alarms.*
200.00   220.00   (210.00)
☐ **As above,** *30 hour.*
155.00   175.00   (160.00)
☐ **As above,** *30 hour, with alarms.*
165.00   185.00   (170.00)

GALLERY

☐ **Gallery,** *diameter 22", 8 Day.*
325.00   345.00   (330.00)
☐ **As above,** *diameter 20".*
300.00   325.00   (315.00)
☐ **As above,** *diameter 18".*
270.00   290.00   (275.00)
☐ **As above,** *diameter 16".*
230.00   250.00   (240.00)
☐ **As above,** *diameter 14".*
210.00   230.00   (220.00)

☐ **Gilt Gallery,** *dial 15", 8 Day.*
240.00   260.00   (250.00)

☐ **Gilt Gallery,** *dial 10", 8 Day, lever.*
180.00   200.00   (190.00)

☐ **Gilt Gallery,** *dial 12", 8 Day.*
180.00   200.00   (190.00)

☐ **Gilt Gallery,** *dial 8", 8 Day, lever.*
160.00   180.00   (170.00)
☐ **As above,** *30 hour, lever.*
140.00   160.00   (150.00)

Gilt Gallery, 15"

Gilt Gallery, 10"

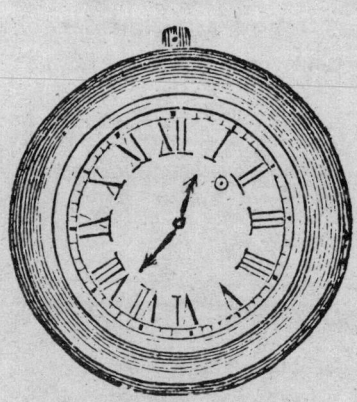
Gallery

Gilt Gallery, 12"

GALLERY/OCTAGON, SHORT DROP

- **Octagon,** *mahogany, rosewood, dial 10", 8 Day (E1-8).*
  220.00   230.00   (225.00)
- **As above,** *striking.*
  230.00   250.00   (240.00)
- **As above,** *dial 12".*
  245.00   265.00   (250.00)
- **As above,** *dial 12", striking.*
  255.00   275.00   (260.00)

Octagon, 12"

Octagon

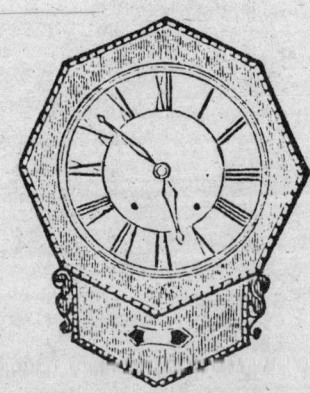

Octagon, 12" timepiece

- **Octagon,** *mahogany, rosewood, time piece 10", dial 12", 8 Day, striking (E1-8).*
  250.00   270.00   (260.00)
- **Octagon,** *mahogany, rosewood, dial 12", 8 Day.*
  245.00   265.00   (250.00)
- **As above,** *striking.*
  255.00   275.00   (260.00)
- **Octagon,** *mahogany, rosewood, time piece 12", dial 12", 8 Day.*
  240.00   260.00   (250.00)
- **As above,** *8 Day, striking.*
  250.00   270.00   (260.00)

Octagon, 10" timepiece

GALLERY/OCTAGON LEVER

- **Detached Lever Time Pieces,** *mahogany, rosewood, walnut, zebra, dial 6", 30 hour.*
  110.00   130.00   (120.00)
- **As above,** *dial 8", 8 Day.*
  130.00   150.00   (140.00)
- **As above,** *8 Day, strike.*
  140.00   160.00   (150.00)
- **As above,** *dial 10", 8 Day.*
  140.00   160.00   (150.00)
- **As above,** *8 Day, strike.*
  150.00   170.00   (160.00)
- **As above,** *dial 9", 8 Day.*
  140.00   160.00   (150.00)
- **As above,** *8 Day, strike.*
  145.00   165.00   (155.00)

- **Octagon 8 Day Bank Clock,** *white and gilt dial 18", 8 Day.*
  230.00   250.00   (240.00)
- **As above,** *8 Day, strike*
  250.00   270.00   (260.00)

- **Octagon Lever,** *mahogany, rosewood, dial 8", 8 Day.*
  135.00   155.00   (145.00)
- **As above,** *8 Day, strike*
  145.00   165.00   (155.00)

- **Octagon Lever,** *papier mâché, dial 10", 8 Day.*
  170.00   180.00   (175.00)
- **As above,** *8 Day, strike*
  190.00   210.00   (200.00)

- **Octagon Lever,** *mahogany, rosewood, dial 10", 8 Day.*
  140.00   160.00   (150.00)
- **As above,** *8 Day, strike*
  150.00   170.00   (170.00)

- **Octagon Papier Mâché Lever,** *dial 8", 8 day.*
  135.00   155.00   (140.00)
- **As above,** *8 Day, strike*
  155.00   175.00   (165.00)

- **Octagon Mâché papier Lever Time Piece,** *dial 6", 1 Day.*
  120.00   140.00   (125.00)
- **As above,** *1 Day, strike*
  140.00   160.00   (145.00)

- **Papier Mâché,** *dial 10", 8 Day.*
  130.00   150.00   (135.00)
- **As above,** *8 Day, strike*
  140.00   160.00   (145.00)

Octagon Bank Clock

Octagon Papier Mâché

Papier Mâché

KEYLESS AUTO CLOCK COMPANY

☐ **Abro,** an offset clock with Best keywinding movement, thief proof, black and nickel finish, dial 2¼", 8 Day.
  35.00 55.00 (45.00)

☐ **Belmont,** keywind, a cowl clock that sets close to the dash, black and nickel finish, dial 2¾", 8 Day.
  35.00 55.00 (45.00)

☐ **Denver Cowl,** keywind, a cowl clock that sits close to the dash, all nickel, or black and nickel case, dial 2¼", 8 Day.
  35.00 55.00 (45.00)

☐ **No. K2N,** keywind, cowl, all nickel case, dial 2½", 1 Day.
  35.00 55.00 (45.00)

☐ **No. K1BN,** keywind, offset model, black and nickel case, dial 2½", 1 Day.
  30.00 45.00 (35.00)

Knockabout Klock, guaranteed for one year, can be adjusted to fit any angle dash, by simple ball joint which can be adjusted and tightened to any angle making it possible to see the face of the clock, regardless of how far it is from the lamp.

☐ **No. KAB,** Black, Japanese finish.
  35.00 55.00 (65.00)

Model L, rim wind-rim set, straight base.

☐ **No. KLN,** all nickel case, height 2¼", dial 2¼".
  45.00 60.00 (50.00)

☐ **No. KLBN,** black and nickel case.
  45.00 60.00 (50.00)

Model M And M Jr., rim wind-rim set, offset model, thief proof, a very reliable timepiece.

☐ **No. KMN,** all nickel, dial 2¾", 8 Day.
  45.00 65.00 (50.00)

☐ **No. KMBN,** black and nickel, dial 2¾", 8 Day.
  45.00 65.00 (50.00)

☐ **No. KMJRN,** all nickel, dial 2¼", 8 Day.
  45.00 65.00 (50.00)

☐ **No. KMJRBN,** black and nickel, dial 2¼", 8 Day.
  45.00 65.00 (50.00)

New Ormond, keywind, an offset clock with the highest grade movement, thief proof locking plate.

☐ **No. NOBN,** black and nickel case, dial 3", 8 Day.
  40.00 55.00 (45.00)

NOJAR, stem wind, for any dash, any make of car, rubber retained clock for dash, drill holes for screws are attached permanently to metal base, embody in rubber, tighten ends, and the clock is ready for use, 1 Day.

☐ **No. FD2,** clock retained in red rubber holder, weight per clock ¾ pounds.
  30.00 45.00 (35.00)

NOJAR, stem wind, for steering wheel on Ford or Dodge cars, rubber retained, no trouble to attach, simply remove nut from top of steering wheel and attach to the clock, may be adjusted at any angle as the rubber holder is movable on the metal base, a good timekeeper, 1 Day.

☐ **No. FN1,** clock retained in red rubber holder, weight per clock ½ pound.
  35.00 45.00 (40.00)

☐ **Rim Wind-Rim Set No. K4RD,** for Ford cars, thief proof, black and nickel case, dial 2¼", 8 Day.
  45.00 60.00 (50.00)

☐ **Rim Wind-Rim Set No. 7N,** a very reliable timepiece, all nickel dial 2¾", 8 Day.
  60.00 70.00 (65.00)

☐ **No. 7BN,** black and nickel, dial 2¾", 8 Day.
  60.00 70.00 (65.00)

☐ **No. 12N,** all nickel, dial 2¼", 8 Day.
  60.00 70.00 (65.00)

☐ **No. 12BN,** black and nickel, dial 2¼", 8 Day.
  60.00 70.00 (65.00)

☐ **Rim Wind-Rim Set *No. K9N,** all nickel, dial 2¾", 8 Day.
   60.00   75.00   (65.00)

☐ ***No. K9BN,** black and nickel, dial 2¾", 8 Day.
   60.00   75.00   (65.00)

☐ ***No. K12BAN,** all nickel, dial 2¼", 8 Day.
   60.00   75.00   (65.00)

☐ ***No. 12BBN,** black and nickel, dial 2¼", 8 Day.
   60.00   70.00   (65.00)

*Note: Model 9 for Cadillac, Hudson, White, Buick, Overland, Cole, Studebaker, Lewis, Austin. Model 12B for Chandler, Paige, Hudson, Hupmobile, Overland, Buick, Dodge, Mercer, Pathfinder.

Nojar

Shasta, keywind, an offset clock of the most approved type, no locking plate, dial 2¼".

☐ **No. KSN,** all nickel case, 8 Day.
   35.00   50.00   (40.00)

☐ **No. KSBN,** black and nickel case, 8 Day.
   35.00   50.00   *(35.00)

☐ **Stem Wind,** Devere, heavy, solid brass case, polished, with offset holding a complete watch, stem wind and set, 3½" x 2⅞", white dial 1⅛", 1 Day.
   45.00   65.00   (45.00)

☐ **Stem Wind,** Duane, light, solid brass case, polished, with offset holding a complete watch, stem wind and set 3½" x 2⅞", white dial 1½", 1 Day.
   45.00   65.00   (45.00)

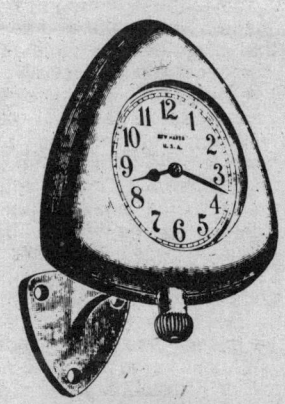

Devere

☐ **No. FIAT,** stem wind, for steering wheel on Ford or Dodge cars, sets on top of steering column, no bolts or screws needed, simply raise the nut on steering column, slide in clock and screw in tight, 1 Day.
   25.00   45.00   (30.00)

☐ **No. PANAMA,** stem wind, black and nickel case, with this clock it is not necessary to cut cowl board, 1 Day.
   25.00   45.00   (30.00)

Duane

F. KROEBER

FLORENCE T. KROEBER, THE MYSTERIOUS CLOCKMAKER

By Red Rabeneck

KROEBER'S CLOCKS FOR THE COLLECTOR AND THEIR PRICES

Florence Kroeber's clocks have long been recognized by some collectors to have that something special that sets them apart from the run-of-the-mill and makes them desirable. Usually at the marts you will find their prices are 10% to 20% above those for comparable clocks made by the major companies. Those that are priced the same as the major company clocks usually sell quickly. Yet, in discussing prices with dealers, some dealers say that Kroeber clocks will bring no more than other comparable clocks. This brings up three possibilities: (1) One or both of the parties involved in a sale are not knowledgeable; (2) The dealer is being out-maneuvered by his customers; (3) There are no Kroeber collectors among the dealer's customers.

This situation, whether one or all of the three possibilities apply, leads to wide fluctuations in the prices reported, with little or no standardization. And some of Kroeber's clocks are so rare that sales rarely occur and become like the sales on old museum pieces — each one a matter of individual negotiation.

Compounding the situation is the evidence pointing to the probability that Kroeber sometimes put his labels on standard mass-produced American and imported clocks. This seems to be particularly true with regard to the labels that said: "F. Kroeber, Agent for the New Haven, Gilbert, Jerome, Atkins, Seth Thomas, and other companies." It is not known whether Kroeber put his labels on all clocks that he sold, or only those that he modified in some way. Regardless, the more information the collector has, the more the prices will tend to standardize and stabilize.

The true Kroeber collector will certainly try to complete his collection to have examples of all the patents and trademarks used by Kroeber. This could lead to a lifetime of searching, as we have no idea how many examples of each might still survive. You can be certain that any museum would welcome a chance to display a collection showing these American patents on actual products.

The collector who looks at a Kroeber clock should look for the features that distinguish it as a Kroeber. If the clock appears identical to a mass-produced model, it should have three items to bring maximum price: A Kroeber label, a Kroeber dial, and a marked Kroeber movement. If any of these are missing, be wary and realize that it probably will not bring the top price listed.

And now the final mystery — three clocks have turned up with the label of "Fuller & Kroeber" with the address of "25 John Street," which was the address given for Kroeber's business in the earliest listing in the city directory. One of these used the George Owen case patent. Fuller has not yet been identified but these are undoubtedly some of the earliest clocks made by Kroeber in the 1863-68 period when it was thought he was merely importing clocks.

DATING F. KROEBER CLOCKS

Therefore, on the labels, if they are "Fuller & Kroeber, 25 John Street" it is an early clock, probably between 1863 and 1868. If they are "F. Kroeber" or "F. Kroeber & Co." with an "8 or 14 Cortlandt Street" address, the clock can most likely be dated before the incorporation in 1887. "F. Kroeber Clock Co., 360 Broadway" probably dates the clock between 1887 and 1899, while a label with "F. Kroeber" or "F. Kroeber & Co." with a "14 Maiden Lane" or "45 Maiden Lane" address probably dates the clock between 1899 and 1904. We say probably because there may be some overlap due to using up supplies of labels.

The catalog reprint shows the dials used. It is doubtful that any mint rubber dials survive. The porcelain dials with visible escapement are the most desirable; the paper "American dials" the least desirable. But the most desirable dial to a collector is the one marked with Kroeber's name or monogram.

The movement should have Kroeber's name stamped on a plate. Everyone knows that Seth Thomas Clock Company made the No. 89 movement especially for Kroeber. The movement lists put out by Seth Thomas shows other movements listed for Kroeber. It is suspected that Kroeber bought movements from still other companies, but if he did he probably had them stamp his name on the plate.

Most new collectors receive their first introduction to Florence Kroeber when they are in a mart or clock shop looking at clocks, and, like most people, noting the type or style of clock, then looking at the price before they look at the clock. A low whistle, pursed lip, or shocked expression at the high price will lead the seller to say, "It's a Kroeber." This is the normal welcome to the world of Kroeber clocks, and the astute collector will soon realize that his collection will not be complete without a Kroeber clock, and it makes no difference if the collector collects only a certain type of clock, as Kroeber put his touch on most types of clocks. So, find your Kroeber before the price goes higher, for the name of Florence T. Kroeber will live for many years to come on his clocks and in the minds of many clock collectors who will be proud to own a clock that is distinctively "Kroeber."

The above articles represents all of the information that I have at my disposal at this time. Anyone with additional information as to original factory catalogs, advertisements in trade magazines of the day, or small articles and bits and pieces, I would appreciate your letting me know about them in some way. Any new information submitted will be used ina future article. Send to me at P.O. Box 11097, Kansas City, Missouri 64119.

ALARM/ANIMATED

☐ **Watermill,** *nickel with moving waterwheel, dial 4", c. 1888, spring, lever (E-3-81).*
      200.00   250.00   (225.00)

☐ **As above,** *with alarm.*
      250.00   300.00   (275.00)

Watermill

Windmill

274 / F. KROEBER

Bell Ringer

- **Windmill,** *nickel with moving windmill, dial 4", c. 1888, spring, lever (E3-81).*
  200.00   250.00   (225.00)
- **As above,** *with alarm.*
  250.00   300.00   (275.00)

- **Bell Ringer,** *Kroeber patent no. 228.202, nickel case, bronze figure with movable arm, ringing bell, height 8¼", dial 3", c. 1888, lever (E3-81).*
  225.00   250.00   (237.00)

ALARM/DRUM

- **Aurora,** *nickel, calendar alarm, dial 4", c. 1888, spring, lever (k-25).*
  125.00   150.00   (137.00)
- **As above,** *alarm only.*
  50.00   60.00   (55.00)
- **As above,** *time only.*
  40.00   50.00   45.00

- **Comtess,** *nickel, spring, no second bit, dial 4", c. 1888, lever (E3-81).*
  45.00   55.00   (50.00)
- **As above,** *center seconds.*
  70.00   90.00   (80.00)
- **As above,** *extra decorated dial.*
  60.00   70.00   65.00
- **As above,** *simple calendar.*
  110.00   130.00   (120.00)

- **Flash,** *nickel, with illuminating dial, center second, no seconds bit, spring, dial 4", c. 1888, lever (K-25).*
  40.00   50.00   (45.00)
- **As above,** *with center seconds.*
  70.00   90.00   (80.00)
- **As above,** *with alarm.*
  50.00   65.00   (58.00)

Aurora

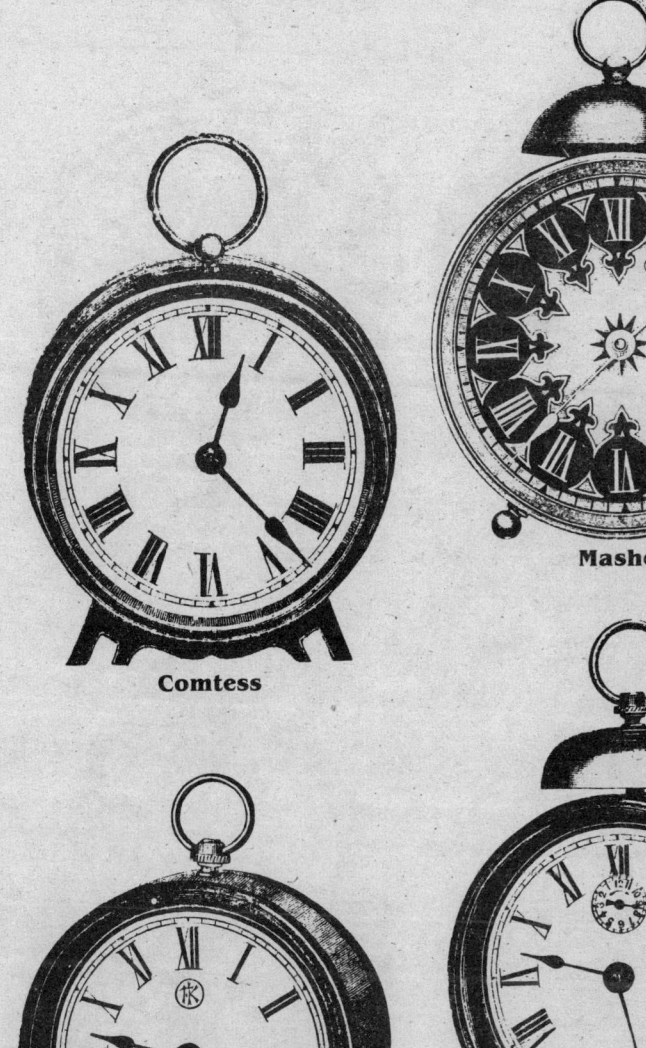

Ticker

Birdie

Brilliant

☐ **Masher,** *nickel, spring, fancy dial, dial 4½", c. 1888, lever (K-26).*
    140.00   160.00   (150.00)
☐ **As above,** *plain dial.*
    100.00   120.00   (110.00)

☐ **Starter,** *nickel, time only, dial 4", c. 1888, spring, lever (K-25).*
    35.00   50.00   (43.00)
☐ **As above,** *with alarm.*
    45.00   60.00   (53.00)

☐ **Ticker,** *nickel, dial 4", c. 1888, spring, lever (E3-81).*
    45.00   55.00   (50.00)

ALARM/FANCY

☐ **Birdie,** *nickel, time only, height 5", c. 1888, spring, lever (K-25).*
    45.00   55.00   (50.00)
☐ **As above,** *with alarm.*
    60.00   75.00   (70.00)

☐ **Brilliant,** *nickel, marbleized iron base, time only, height 6", dial 4", c. 1888, spring, lever (E3-81).*
    80.00   100.00   (90.00)
☐ **As above,** *alarm.*
    100.00   130.00   (115.00)
☐ **As above,** *alarm, simple calendar.*
    175.00   200.00   (187.00)

Cordelia

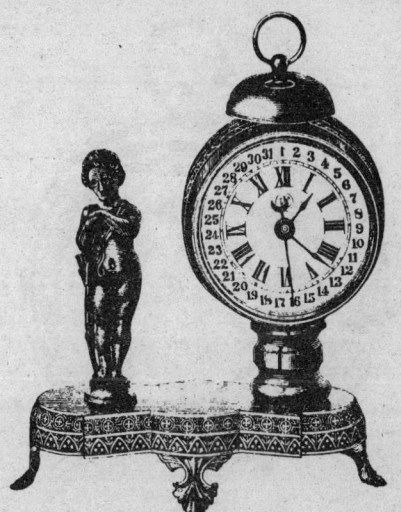

Cupid No. 1

Cupid No. 2

☐ **Cordelia,** *nickel, height 10", dial 4", c. 1888, one day, time only, spring, lever (K-28).*
150.00   175.00   (163.00)
☐ **As above,** *alarm.*
185.00   220.00   (206.00)
☐ **As above,** *strike.*
225.00   260.00   (242.00)

☐ **Cupid No. 1,** *nickel, time only, height 9½", dial 4", c. 1888, spring lever (K-26).*
120.00   150.00   (135.00)
☐ **As above,** *alarm.*
150.00   175.00   (163.00)
☐ **As above,** *alarm, simple calendar.*
225.00   265.00   (245.00)

☐ **Cupid No. 2,** *nickel, gilt figure, time only, height 6½", dial 4", c. 1888, spring, lever (k-26).*
115.00   135.00   (125.00)
☐ **As above,** *alarm.*
135.00   160.00   (143.00)
☐ **As above,** *simple calendar.*
200.00   225.00   (212.00)

☐ **Daisy,** *nickel, time only, height 4½", c. 1888, spring, lever (K-25).*
45.00   55.00   (50.00)
☐ **As above,** *alarm.*
60.00   75.00   (67.00)

Daisy

Inkstand No. 1

Horse Shoe

- **Horse Shoe,** *nickel, time only, height 6½", c. 1888, spring, lever (K-25).*
  80.00 100.00 (90.00)
- **As above,** *alarm.*
  90.00 110.00 (100.00)

- **Inkstand No. 1,** *time only with call bell, cut bottles, height 9", c. 1888, spring, lever.*
  175.00 200.00 (183.00)
- **As above,** *alarm.*
  200.00 225.00 (212.00)
- **As above,** *simple calendar.*
  300.00 340.00 (320.00)

- **Inkstand No. 2,** *time only with call bell, cut glass bottles, height 10", c. 1888, one day, spring, lever (K-28).*
  225.00 275.00 (250.00)
- **As above,** *alarm.*
  250.00 300.00 (275.00)
- **As above,** *simple calendar.*
  300.00 350.00 (325.00)

- **Rover,** *nickel, time only, height 11½", dial 4", c. 1888, spring, lever (K-26).*
  155.00 180.00 (167.00)
- **As above,** *alarm.*
  175.00 200.00 (183.00)
- **As above,** *alarm, simple calendar.*
  250.00 300.00 (275.00)

F. KROEBER / 279

Inkstand No. 2

Schoolboy

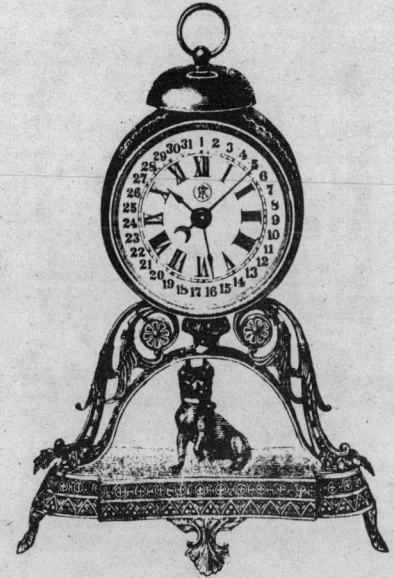

Rover

Thistle

280 / F. KROEBER

Trump

Mechanical Bird

- ☐ **Schoolboy,** *nickel, bronze fugure, time only, height 7", dial 4", c. 1888, spring, lever (K-26).*
  150.00   175.00   (167.00)
- ☐ **As above,** *alarm.*
  175.00   200.00   (187.00)
- ☐ **As above,** *simple calendar.*
  210.00   235.00   (222.00)
- ☐ **Thistle,** *nickel, time only with white or black dial, height 8¼", c. 1888, spring, lever (K-28).*
  175.00   200.00   (183.00)
- ☐ **As above,** *with alarm.*
  185.00   230.00   (210.00)
- ☐ **Trump,** *nickel, time only, seconds bit, white or black dial, height 6½", c. 1888, spring, lever (E3-81).*
  100.00   125.00   (112.00)
- ☐ **As above,** *alarm.*
  120.00   145.00   (137.00)

ANIMATED

- ☐ **Mechanical Bird Clock,** *with glass cover, height 22", c. 1880, spring, pendulum (K-17).*
  2000.00   2500.00   (2250.00)

Mechanical Ship

- ☐ **Mechanical Ship Clock,** *with glass cover and music, height 20", c. 1880, spring, pendulum (K-17).*
  2000.00   2500.00   (2250.00)

CABINET

- **Cabinet No. 3,** *ebony, black or white paper dial, height 12½", dial 5", c. 1880, 8 Day, strike, pendulum (K-11).*
  220.00   260.00   (240.00)

- **Cabinet No. 4,** *ebony, black or white paper dial, height 12½", dial 5", c. 1888, spring, pendulum, 8 Day, strike.*
  190.00   220.00   (205.00)

- **Cabinet No. 8,** *ebony, rubber or American black or white paper dial, height 12¾", dial 5", c. 1888, spring, pendulum, 8 Day, strike (K-11).*
  200.00   235.00   (218.00)

- **Cabinet No. 9,** *ebony, hand painted front, rubber or American black or white paper dial, height 14", dial 5", c. 1888, spring, pendulum, 8 Day, strike (K-11).*
  200.00   230.00   (215.00)

Cabinet No. 4

Cabinet No. 3

Cabinet No. 8

282 / F. KROEBER

Cabinet No. 9

Cabinet No. 12

Cabinet No. 11

☐ **Cabinet No. 11,** *ebony, marbleized front, American black or white paper dial, height 14½", dial 5", c. 1888, spring, pendulum, 8 Day, strike (K-11).*
    270.00   290.00   (280.00)

☐ **Cabinet No. 12,** *ebony or mahogany, American black or white paper dial, height 14", dial 5", c. 1888, spring, pendulum, 8 Day, strike (K-11).*
    240.00   280.00   (260.00)

☐ **Cabinet No. 13,** *mahogany, polished brass panel, height 14½", dial 5", c. 1888, spring, pendulum, 8 Day, strike (E3-76).*
    210.00   240.00   (225.00)

☐ **Cabinet No. 14,** *mahogany, polished brass panel, rubber dial, height 14", dial 5", c. 1880, spring, pendulum, 8 Day, strike (K-10).*
    180.00   220.00   (200.00)

Cabinet No. 13

Cabinet No. 15

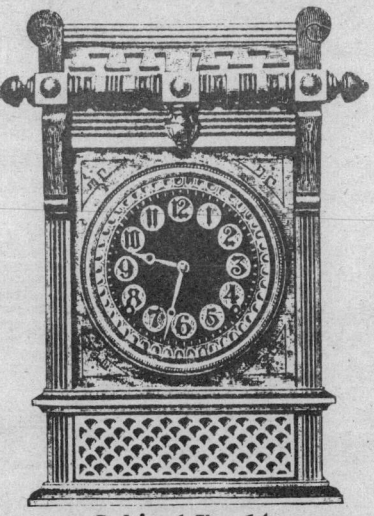

Cabinet No. 14

Cabinet No. 50

Cabinet No. 51

Cabinet No. 52

Cabinet No. 53

☐ **Cabinet No. 15,** *mahogany, carved panels, porcelain dial, height 14½", dial 5", c. 1888, spring, pendulum, 8 Day, strike (K-11).*
    235.00   265.00   (250.00)

☐ **Cabinet No. 50,** *walnut, American white or black paper dial, height 13", dial 4½", c. 1888, spring, pendulum, 8 Day, strike (E3-76).*
    200.00   240.00   (220.00)

☐ **Cabinet No. 51,** *walnut, American black or white paper dial, height 13½", dial 4½", c. 1888, spring, pendulum, 8 Day, strike (E3-76).*
    175.00   200.00   (187.00)
☐ As above, *ash.*
    200.00   225.00   (212.00)

☐ **Cabinet No. 52,** *walnut, American black or white paper dial, height 13", dial 4½", c. 1888, spring, pendulum, 8 Day, strike (K-9).*
    175.00   200.00   (187.00)
☐ As above, *ash.*
    200.00   225.00   (212.00)

☐ **Cabinet No. 53,** *walnut, bronze columns, black dial, height 14", dial 4½", c. 1888, spring, pendulum, 8 Day, strike (E3-76).*
    260.00   280.00   (270.00)

F. KROEBER / 285

Cabinet No. 57

Cabinet No. 58

☐ **Cabinet No. 57,** *walnut, American black or white paper dial, height 18", dial 5", c. 1888, spring, pendulum, 8 Day, gong strike (E3-77).*
    250.00   275.00   (267.00)
☐ **As above,** *ash.*
    275.00   300.00   (287.00)

☐ **Cabinet No. 58,** *ash, American paper dial, height 16", dial 5", c. 1888, spring, pendulum, 8 Day, gong strike (E3-77).*
    275.00   300.00   (287.00)
☐ **As above,** *walnut.*
    250.00   300.00   (275.00)

☐ **Cairo,** *mahogany, American dial, height 13½", dial 5", c. 1888, spring, pendulum, 8 Day, strike (K-11).*
    220.00   255.00   (233.00)

☐ **Calcutta,** *walnut, cabinet finish, porcelain dial, height 15", dial 5", c. 1888, spring, pendulum, 8 Day, strike (K-10).*
    210.00   240.00   (225.00)

Cairo

286 / F. KROEBER

Calcutta

Modena

Delta

☐ **Delta,** *walnut, porcelain dial, height 14", dial 5", c. 1888, spring, pendulum, 8 Day, strike (E3-76).*
      150.00   175.00   (163.00)
☐ **As above,** *ash.*
      175.00   200.00   (187.00)

☐ **Modena,** *mahogany, American dial, height 15½", dial 5", c. 1888, spring, pendulum, 8 Day, strike (K-10).*
      200.00   230.00   (215.00)

CABINET/MIRROR SIDES

☐ **Cabinet No. 59,** *walnut, American dial, mirrored sides, height 16½", dial 5", c. 1888, spring, pendulum, 8 Day, strike (E3-76).*
      275.00   300.00   (287.00)

☐ **Cabinet No. 60,** *walnut, mirrored sides, American dial, height 14½", dial 5", c. 1888, spring, pendulum, 8 Day, strike (E3-76).*
      250.00   300.00   (275.00)

☐ **Cabinet No. 61,** *walnut, American dial, mirrored sides, height 15½", dial 5", c. 1888, spring, pendulum, 8 Day, strike (K-9).*
      275.00   300.00   (287.00)

Cabinet No. 59

Cabinet No. 60

Cabinet No. 61

CALENDAR

☐ **Desk Inkwell,** *patent date May 28, 1878, 1 Day, alarm, simple calendar (M487-149).*
    200.00   250.00   (225.00)

☐ **Galena,** *23½" x 14½", 8 Day, strike (M484-148).*
    350.00   450.00   (400.00)

☐ **Round Alarm,** *patent date May 28, 1878, 1 Day, alarm, simple calendar (M488-149).*
    200.00   225.00   (212.00)

CALENDAR/DOUBLE DIAL

☐ **Ionic,** *height 25½", dial 12", c. 1888, spring, pendulum (K-15).*
☐ **As above,** *8 Day, calendar.*
    1000.00   1100.00   (1050.00)
☐ **As above,** *8 Day, calendar.*
    1100.00   1200.00   (1150.00)

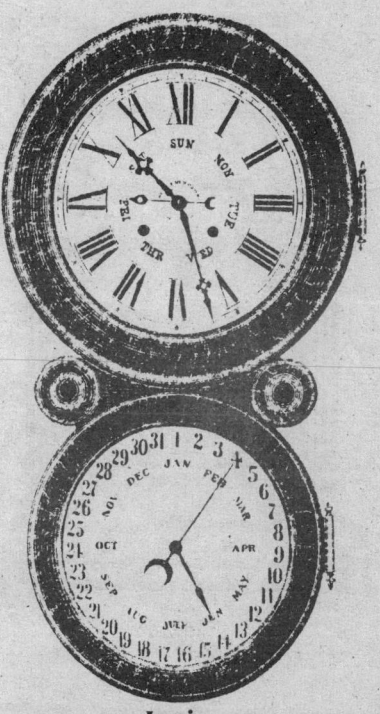

Ionic

CARRIAGE

- **Blaze**, *heavy bell-metal castings in gilt, seconds bit, time only, height 6½", dial 4", c. 1888, spring, lever (K-28).*
      180.00   210.00   (195.00)
- **As above**, *with alarm.*
      210.00   240.00   (225.00)
- **Brass Carriage**, *honey comb decorative pattern on case, seconds bit, time only, height 6", dial 3", c. 1888, spring, lever (K-26).*
      90.00   120.00   (105.00)
- **As above**, *alarm.*
      100.00   135.00   (117.00)
- **Checkmate**, *nickel, embossed gilt front, seconds bit, glass sides, time only, height 6½", dial 3", c. 1888, spring, lever (E3-81).*
      175.00   200.00   (187.00)
- **As above**, *alarm.*
      190.00   215.00   (103.00)
- **As above**, *strike.*
      245.00   265.00   (255.00)

Brass Carriage

Blaze

Checkmate, nickel

☐ **Checkmate,** *extra, nickel, glass sides, time only, seconds bit, height 6½", dial 3", c. 1888, spring, lever (K-30).*
　　175.00　　200.00　　(187.00)
☐ **As above,** *with alarm.*
　　185.00　　218.00　　(200.00)
☐ **As above,** *strike.*
　　245.00　　265.00　　(255.00)

☐ **Eclipse,** *mahogany, time only, height 7½", dial 3", c. 1888, spring, lever, 1 Day (E3-77).*
　　110.00　　130.00　　(120.00)
☐ **As above,** *alarm.*
　　125.00　　150.00　　(137.00)

☐ **Emblem,** *nickel, ornamented black dial and glass sides, seconds bit, time only, height 6½", dial 3", c. 1888, spring, lever (K-30).*
　　180.00　　220.00　　(200.00)
☐ **As above,** *with alarm.*
　　220.00　　260.00　　(240.00)

Eclipse

Checkmate, extra

Emblem

290 / F. KROEBER

Nankin

Superb

- **Nankin,** *nickel, glass sides, front engraved with bugs and flowers, seconds bit, time only, height 6½", c. 1888, spring, lever.*
  210.00   235.00   (222.00)
- **As above,** *alarm.*
  235.00   265.00   (250.00)
- **Rival,** *nickel, ornamented dial and glass sides, seconds bit, time only, height 6½", dial 3", c. 1888, spring, lever (K-30).*
  175.00   200.00   (187.00)
- **As above,** *alarm.*
  210.00   235.00   (222.00)
- **Superb,** *mahogany, time only, height 7½", dial 3", c. 1888, spring, lever, 1 Day (K-28).*
  110.00   140.00   (125.00)
- **As above,** *alarm.*
  140.00   165.00   (152.00)

CONNECTICUT SHELF

- **Cottage,** *polished veneer, height 12", dial 5", 1 Day, spring, pendulum (E3-77).*
  100.00   120.00   (110.00)
- **As above,** *1 Day, strike.*
  125.00   145.00   (135.00)

Rival

Cottage

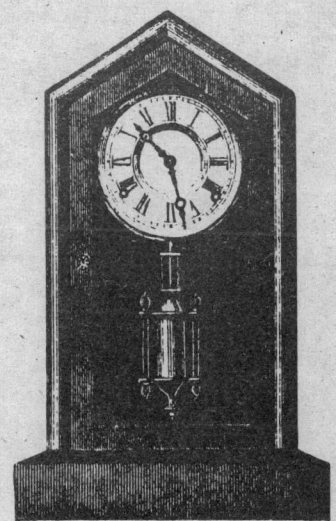

Dictator

Cottage No. 750

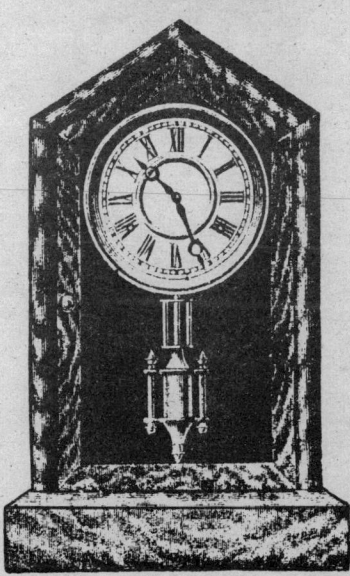

Dictator

292 / F. KROEBER

O.G. No. 2

Octagon Rocket

Octagon Top, V.P.

- ☐ **Cottage No. 750,** *brass ornaments, height 19¼", dial 5", 8 Day, (K-16).*
  140.00   160.00   (150.00)
- ☐ **As above,** *8 Day, strike.*
  170.00   190.00   (180.00)

- ☐ **Dictator,** *V.P., rosewood or walnut, polished veneer, height 17½", dial 6", c. 1888, spring, pendulum, 1 Day (K-16).*
  80.00   100.00   (90.00)
- ☐ **As above,** *1 Day, strike.*
  100.00   120.00   (110.00)

- ☐ **Dictator,** *V.P., rosewood or walnut, polished veneer, height 17½", dial 6", c. 1888, spring, pendulum, 8 Day (K-16).*
  100.00   120.00   (110.00)
- ☐ **As above,** *8 Day, strike.*
  120.00   140.00   (130.00)

- ☐ **O.G.No. 2,** *weight pendulum, height 26", dial 8", c. 1888, 1 Day (K-16).*
  150.00   200.00   (175.00)
- ☐ **As above,** *1 Day, strike.*
  200.00   250.00   (225.00)

Rocket

Small Tuscan

- **Octagon Rocket,** *V.P., polished veneer, height 13", dial 5", c. 1888, spring, pendulum, 1 Day, (K-16).*
  120.00   140.00   (130.00)

- **Octagon top,** *V.P., No. 254, polished veneer, height 14", dial 5", c. 1888, spring, pendulum, 1 Day (K-16).*
  100.00   125.00   (112.00)
- **As above,** *1 Day, strike.*
  125.00   150.00   (137.00)

- **Rocket,** *polished veneer, height 10¾", dial 4", c. 1888, spring, pendulum, 1 Day (K-16).*
  100.00   120.00   (110.00)

- **Small Tuscan, Extra,** *V.P., polished veneer, height 16", dial 5", c. 1888, spring, pendulum, 1 Day (K-16).*
  100.00   130.00   (150.00)
- **As above,** *1 Day, strike.*
  140.00   160.00   (150.00)

- **Steeple,** *V.P. No. 251, polished veneer, height 17¾", dial 5", c. 1888, spring, pendulum, 1 Day, (K-16).*
  150.00   170.00   (160.00)
- **As above,** *1 Day, strike.*
  165.00   190.00   (177.00)

Steeple

CUCKOO/MANTEL

☐ **Cuckoo No. 5029,** *brass movement, height 23½", c. 1888, spring, pendulum, 1 Day (E-80).*
    800.00   900.00   (850.00)

☐ **Cuckoo No. 5041,** *brass movement, height 21½", c. 1888, spring, pendulum, 1 Day (K-17).*
    350.00   400.00   (375.00)

☐ **Cuckoo No. 5043,** *brass movment, height 21", c. 1888, spring, pendulum, 1 Day (K-17).*
    275.00   325.00   (300.00)

☐ **Cuckoo No. 5048,** *brass movment, height 22½", c. 1888, spring, pendulum, 1 Day (K-17).*
    275.00   325.00   (300.00)

☐ **Trumpeter No. 9,** *brass movment, height 25½", c. 1888, spring, pendulum, 1 Day (E3-80).*
    800.00   900.00   (850.00)

Cuckoo No. 5041

Cuckoo No. 5029

Cuckoo No. 5043

CUCKOO/WALL

☐ **Cuckoo B,** *brass movement, 2 weight, height 18", c. 1888, pendulum (K-17).*
    200.00   250.00   (225.00)

☐ **Cuckoo C.,** *brass movement, 2 weight, height 21", c. 1888, pendulum (K-17).*
    225.00   250.00   (237.00)

☐ **Cuckoo D,** *brass movement, 2 weight, height 20", c. 1888, pendulum (K-17).*
    250.00   275.00   (262.00)

☐ **Trumpeter No. 1,** *brass movement, 2 weights, height 24", c. 1888, pendulum, 1 Day (E3-80).*
    600.00   700.00   (650.00)

Cuckoo No. 5048

Trumpeter No. 9

Cuckoo B

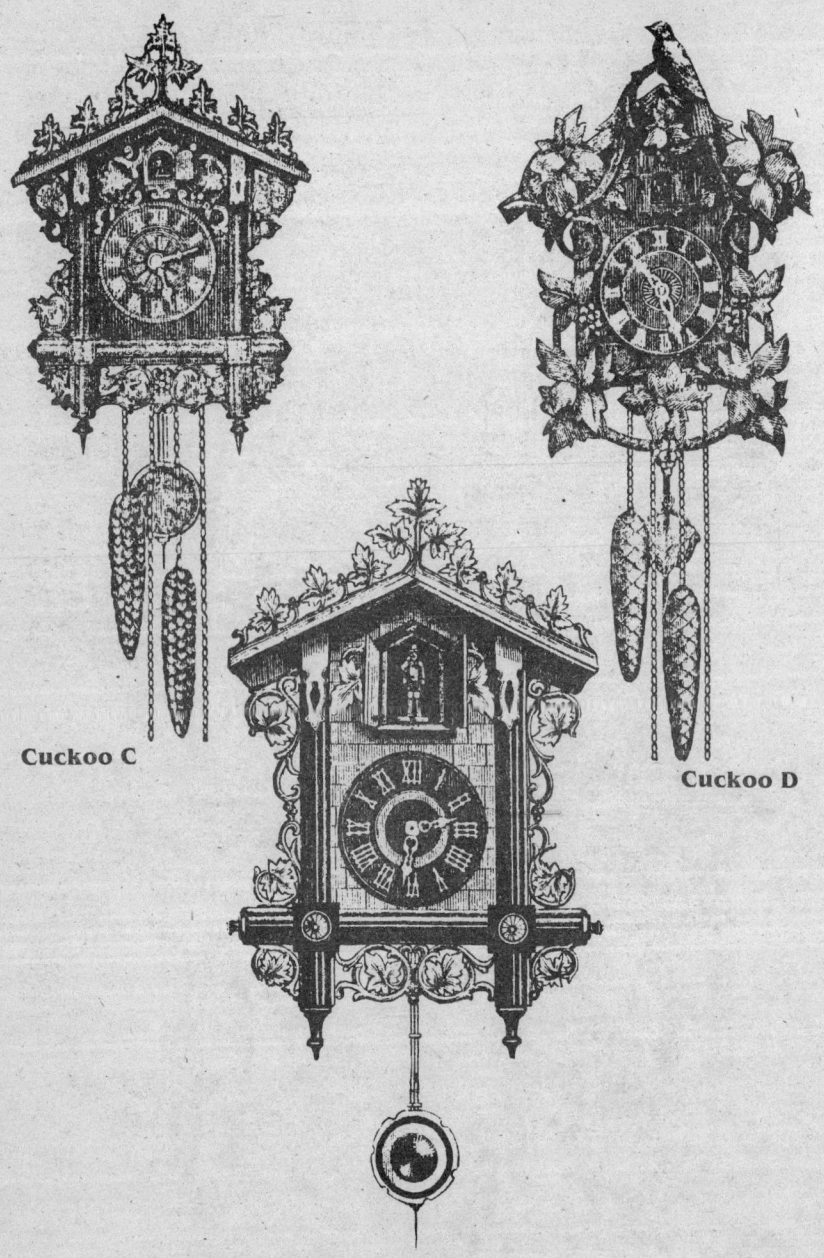

GALLERY

☐ **Gallery,** *walnut, spring, dial 14", c. 1888, pendulum (K-15).*
   300.00   350.00   (325.00)
☐ **As above,** *dial 18".*
   350.00   400.00   (375.00)

☐ **Gallery,** *cabinet, walnut or mahogany, spring, height 35", dial 14", c. 1888, pendulum, 8 Day (E3-77).*
   350.00   400.00   (375.00)
☐ **As above,** *8 Day, strike.*
   400.00   450.00   (425.00)
☐ **As above,** *calendar.*
   400.00   450.00   (425.00)
☐ **As above,** *strike calendar.*
   450.00   550.00   (500.00)

☐ **Maltese Gallery,** *spring, height 27½", dial 14", c. 1888, pendulum, 8 Day (E3-77).*
   400.00   450.00   (425.00)
☐ **As above,** *8 Day, strike.*
   450.00   500.00   (425.00)
☐ **As above,** *calendar.*
   450.00   500.00   (475.00)
☐ **As above,** *strike calendar.*
   500.00   550.00   (525.00)

Gallery Cabinet

Gallery

Maltese Gallery

KITCHEN

Alexandria

- **Adonis,** *walnut, spring, patent pendulum, height 18", dial 5", c. 1888, 8 Day, strike (K-17).*
  180.00 210.00 (195.00)

- **Alexandria,** *mahogany, spring, pendulum, procelain dial, height 18½", dial 5", c. 1888, 8 Day, strike (E3-74).*
  400.00 450.00 (425.00)

- **Bengal,** *walnut, spring, patent pendulum, height 22", dial 5", c. 1888, 8 Day, strike (K-11).*
  260.00 285.00 (277.00)

- **Bermuda,** *walnut, spring, patent pendulum, white or black dial, height 19", dial 6", c. 1888, 8 Day, strike.*
  275.00 325.00 (300.00)
- **As above,** *ash*
  300.00 350.00 (325.00)

Bermuda

Brighton

F. KROEBER / 299

☐ **Brighton,** *walnut, spring, patent pandulum, height 21", dial 6", c. 1888, 8 Day, strike (K-7).*
210.00   245.00   (227.00)

☐ **Buckshot,** *walnut, spring, patent pendulum, height 21½", dial 6", c. 1888, 8 Day, strike (K-7).*
215.00   240.00   (228.00)

☐ **Chief,** *gilt trim, walnut, drawer in bottom, spring, patent pendulum, height 23", dial 6", c. 1888, 8 Day, strike (K-8).*
250.00   285.00   (267.00)

☐ **Congress,** *walnut, spring, pendulum, height 24", dial 6", c. 1888, 8 Day, strike (E3-74).*
300.00   350.00   (325.00)

☐ **Conquest,** *walnut, spring, glass pendulum, height 21½", dial 5", c. 1888, 8 Day, strike (K-11).*
250.00   275.00   (263.00)

Chief

☐ **Corinth,** *mahogany, porcelain dial, spring, pendulum, height 18", dial 6", c. 1888, 8 Day, strike (K-10).*
250.00   295.00   (273.00)

☐ **Dahlia,** *walnut, spring, patent pendulum, height 18", dial 5", c. 1888, 8 Day, strike (K-7).*
175.00   205.00   (190.00)

☐ **Essex,** *walnut, spring, glass pendulum, height 21½", dial 5", c. 1888, 8 Day, strike (E3-74).*
180.00   220.00   (200.00)

☐ **Fearless,** *walnut, spring, pendulum, height 18", dial 5", c. 1888, 8 Day, strike (K-6).*
180.00   210.00   (195.00)

☐ **Florida,** *walnut, spring, patent pendulum, height 19", dial 5", c. 1888, 8 Day, strike (K-7).*
180.00   215.00   (197.00)

Buckshot

Conquest

Dahlia

Corinth

Essex

Fearless

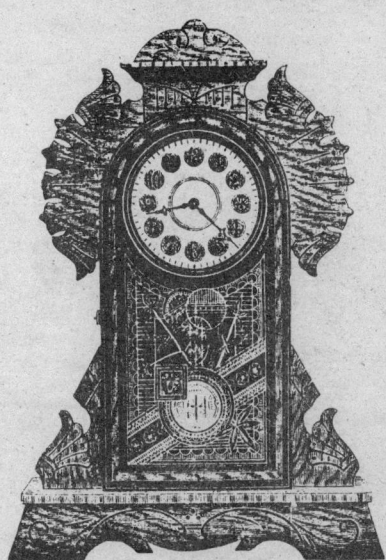

Garnet

Florida

Hector

302 / F. KROEBER

Java

☐ **Fulton,** *walnut, spring pendulum, height 20", dial 5", c. 1888, 8 Day, strike (E3-75).*
250.00   275.00   (263.00)

☐ **Garnet,** *walnut, fancy dial, spring, patent pendulum, height 22½", dial 6", c. 1888, 8 Day, strike (K-6).*
235.00   265.00   (250.00)

☐ **Hector,** *black polished and gilt, spring patent pendulum, height 22", dial 6", c. 1888 (K-9).*
230.00   265.00   (253.00)

☐ **Java,** *walnut, spring, patent pendulum, height 18½", dial 5", c. 1888, 8 Day, strike (K-7).*
180.00   220.00   (200.00)
☐ **As above,** *ash.*
200.00   240.00   (220.00)

☐ **Jefferson,** *walnut, spring, pendulum, height 20", dial 5", c. 1888, 8 Day, strike (E3-74).*
190.00   225.00   (107.00)

☐ **Langtry,** *walnut, white or black paper dial, height 23", dial 6", c. 1888, 8 Day, strike, spring (E3-75).*
450.00   490.00   (470.00)

☐ **Leghorn,** *walnut, height 20", dial 5", c. 1888, 8 Day, strike, spring (E3-74).*
190.00   225.00   (208.00)

☐ **Marigold,** *walnut, height 18", dial 5", c. 1888, 8 Day, strike, spring (K-7).*
180.00   215.00   (197.00)

☐ **Mariposa,** *gilt, walnut, height 21½", dial 6", c. 1888, 8 Day, strike, spring, Kroeber case patent no. 5409 (E3-74).*
350.00   400.00   (375.00)

☐ **Miranda,** *black polished and gilt, height 23", dial 6", c. 1888, 8 Day, strike, spring (K-9).*
245.00   285.00   (265.00)

Jefferson

F. KROEBER / 303

☐ **Nevada,** *walnut, height 23", dial 6", c. 1888, 8 Day, strike, spring (K-8).*
    200.00   235.00   (217.00)

☐ **Newton,** *walnut, height 20½", dial 6", c. 1888, 8 Day, strike, spring (K-6).*
    225.00   245.00   (235.00)

☐ **Patrol,** *walnut, height 21½", dial 6", c. 1888, 8 Day, strike, spring (E-6).*
    200.00   235.00   (217.00)

☐ **Pet,** *walnut, black decorated dial, height 16½", dial 5", c. 1888, 8 Day, strike, spring (E3-77).*
    275.00   300.00   (287.00)
☐ **As above,** *ash.*
    250.00   275.00   (263.00)

Leghorn

Langtry

Marigold

Mariposa

Nevada

Miranda

Newton

Patrol

Pet

Pilgrim

Prism

Pyramid

Rose Dale

Rambler

Solitaire

☐ **Pilgrim,** *walnut, height 22½ ", dial 6", c. 1888, 8 Day, strike, spring (K-11).*
        250.00   275.00   (263.00)

☐ **Polaris,** *walnut, height 20", dial 6", c. 1888, 8 Day, strike, spring, kroeber patent no. 2236 (E3-75).*
        300.00   350.00   (325.00)

☐ **Prism,** *black polished and gilt, height 19", dial 5", c. 1888, 8 Day, strike, spring (K-9).*
        210.00   255.00   (232.00)

☐ **Pyramid,** *mahogany, porcelain dial, height 18", dial 5", c. 1888, 8 Day, strike, spring (E3-75).*
        425.00   475.00   (450.00)

☐ **Rembler,** *walnut, height 20½ ", dial 6", c. 1888, 8 Day, strike, spring (K-7).*
        230.00   260.00   (245.00)

☐ **Rosedale,** *walnut, gilt trim, height 20", dial 5", c. 1888, 8 Day, strike, spring (K-10).*
        270.00   300.00   (285.00)

Thunderer

Texas

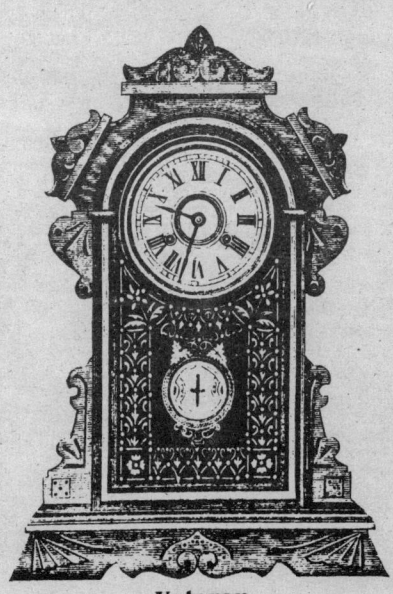

Veteran

308 / F. KROEBER

Virgil

☐ **Virgil,** *walnut, height 24½", dial 6", c. 1888, 8 Day, strike, spring (E3-75).*
    300.00   340.00   (320.00)

☐ **Vixen,** *walnut, height 21", dial 6", c. 1888, 8 Day, strike, spring (E3-75).*
    210.00   255.00   (232.00)

☐ **Vulcan,** *walnut, height 21½", dial 6", c. 1888, 8 Day, strike, spring (K-6).*
    200.00   235.00   (217.00)

☐ **Wanderer,** *walnut, fancy dial, height 23", dial 6", c. 1888, 8 Day, strike, spring (E3-75).*
    250.00   275.00   (262.00)

☐ **Warbler,** *walnut, height 22½", dial 6", c. 1888, 8 Day, strike, spring (K-6).*
    190.00   225.00   (107.00)

☐ **Wasp,** *walnut, height 18½", dial 5", c. 1888, 8 Day, strike, spring (K-6).*
    190.00   220.00   (205.00)

☐ **Saranac,** *walnut, height 22½", dial 6", c. 1888, 8 Day, strike, spring (K-11).*
    240.00   265.00   (252.00)

☐ **Solitaire,** *walnut, height 18", dial 5", c. 1888, 8 Day, strike, spring (K-6).*
    180.00   205.00   (193.00)

☐ **Talisman,** *black polished and gilt, height 21½", dial 6", c. 1888, 8 Day, strike, spring (K-9).*
    235.00   265.00   (250.00)

☐ **Texas,** *walnut, height 24", dial 6", c. 1888, 8 Day, strike, spring (K-8).*
    290.00   330.00   (310.00)

☐ **Thunderer,** *walnut, height 21", dial 6", c. 1888, 8 Day, strike, spring (E3-75).*
    240.00   265.00   (253.00)

☐ **Veteran,** *walnut, height 18", dial 5", c. 1888, 8 Day, strike, spring (K-6).*
    180.00   210.00   (195.00)

Vixen

F. KROEBER / 309

Vulcan

Warbler

Wanderer

Wasp

KITCHEN/MIRROR SIDES

☐ **Headlight,** *walnut, fancy dial, height 23", dial 6", c. 1888, 8 Day, strike, spring (K-6).*
      350.00   400.00   (375.00)

☐ **Occidental,** *walnut, height 23½", dial 6", c. 1888, 8 Day, strike, spring (K-8).*
      450.00   495.00   (472.00)

☐ **Oregon,** *walnut, height 24", dial 6", c. 1888, 8 Day, strike, spring (K-11).*
      400.00   450.00   (425.00)
☐ **As above,** *ash.*
      425.00   475.00   (450.00)

Occidental

Headlight

Oregon

KITCHEN/TEAR DROP

Alaska, *walnut, height 19", dial 5", c. 1888, 8 Day, strike, spring (K-8).*
  260.00   285.00   (273.00)

☐ **Angel Swing No. 2,** *walnut, height 19", dial 5", spring, patent escapement and pendulum no. 184972, Dec. 5, 1876, 8 Day, strike (E3-74).*
  850.00   950.00   (900.00)

☐ **Baltic,** *walnut, height 24", dial 6", c. 1888, 8 Day, strike, spring (K-8).*
  300.00   350.00   (325.00)

☐ **Floretta,** *walnut, height 20", dial 5", c. 1888, 8 Day, strike, spring (E3-74).*
  300.00   340.00   (320.00)

☐ **Parisian,** *walnut, height 23½", dial 6", c. 1888, 8 Day, strike, spring (K-8).*
  280.00   325.00   (303.00)

Angel Swing

Alaska

Baltic

312 / F. KROEBER

Floretta

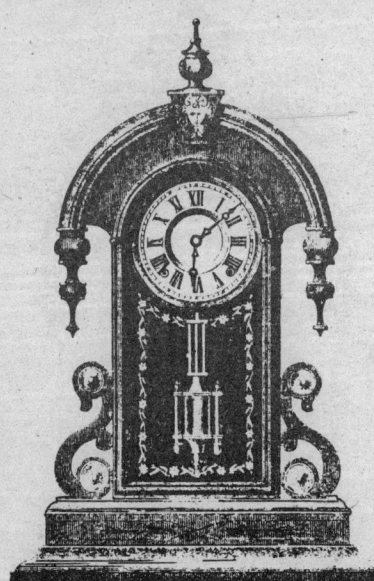

Parisian

LEVER/WALL

☐ **Brass**, *round, locomotives, seconds bit, dial 6", c. 1888, 1 Day, spring (K-15).*
      125.00   150.00   (137.00)

☐ **Nickel**, *round, seconds bit, dial 4", c. 1888, 1 Day, spring (K-15).*
      75.00   100.00   (87.00)
☐ **As above**, *dial 8".*
      125.00   150.00   (137.00)
☐ **Add $25**, *for strike*

Brass

Nickel

MANTLE/BLACK IRON

Octagon, with seconds bit

Octagon

☐ **Algeria**, *enameled iron, marbleized, porcelain dial, height 10", dial 5", 8 Day strike (K-22).*
    170.00   200.00   (185.00)

☐ **Austria**, *enameled iron, marbleized, porcelain arabic dial, height 11", dial 5", 8 Day, strike (K-23).*
    190.00   225.00   (207.00)

☐ **Batavia**, *enameled iron, porcelain dial, height 17", dial 5", c. 1880, 8 Day, strike, spring (K-20).*
    150.00   185.00   (172.00)

☐ **Etruria**, *enameled iron, marbleized, gilt dial, height 10¼", dial 5", c. 1888, 8 Day, strike, spring (K-22).*
    200.00   225.00   (212.00)

☐ **Moravia**, *enameled iron, marbleized, composition dial, c. 1888, 8 Day, strike (K-20).*
    150.00   170.00   (160.00)

☐ **Octagon**, *round corner, walnut, seconds bit, dial 4", c. 1888, 1 Day, time or strike (E-15).*
    100.00   125.00   (112.00)
☐ **As above**, *dial 6".*
    135.00   160.00   (153.00)
☐ **As above**, *dial 10".*
    175.00   200.00   (187.00)
Note: Add $25 to each for strike.

☐ **Octagon**, *round corner, walnut, seconds bit, dial 10", c. 1888, 1 Day, strike, spring (K-15).*
    200.00   225.00   (212.00)

Algeria

Austria

☐ **Portland,** *enameled iron, marbleized, porcelain, height 17½", dial 5", 8 Day, strike, spring (K-20).*
        230.00   260.00   (245.00)

☐ **Ravenna,** *enameled iron, marbleized, porcelain arabic dial, height 14½", dial 5", c. 1880, 8 Day, strike, spring (K-20).*
        150.00   165.00   (157.00)

Batavia

Etruria

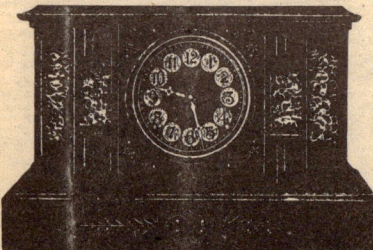

Moravia

Portland

Ravenna

F. KROEBER / 315

Scotia

Verona

☐ **Bolivia,** Milton, enameled iron, marbleized, gilt dial, height 18", dial 5", c. 1880, 8 Day, strike, spring (K-20).
190.00   230.00   (210.00)

☐ **Bombay,** with vase, enameled iron, marbleized, rubber dial, height 17", dial 5", c. 1888, 8 Day, strike, spring (K-22).
195.00   225.00   (210.00)

Armenia

☐ **Scotia,** enameled iron, marbleized, porcelain dial, height 10¼", dial 5", 8 Day, strike, spring (K-22).
160.00   190.00   (175.00)

☐ **Verona,** enameled iron, American dial, height 10½", dial 4½", 8 Day, strike (K-22).
110.00   130.00   (120.00)

MANTLE/BLACK IRON WITH FIGURE

☐ **Armenia,** enameled iron, marbleized, porcelain dial, Rembrandt, height 19¾", dial 5", c. 1880, 8 Day, strike, spring (K-21).
260.00   290.00   (275.00)

Bolivia

Bombay

Cuba

☐ **Cuba, Roman,** *enameled iron, marbleized, procelain dial, height 18½", dial 5", c. 1888, 8 Day, strike, spring (K-21).*
　　235.00　　265.00　　(250.00)

☐ **Livonia,** *figure of a lady, enameled iron, marbleized, black or white paper dial, height 18½", dial 5", c. 1888, 8 Day, strike, spring (K-21).*
　　200.00　　230.00　　(215.00)

☐ **Malvern No. 1006,** *Pandora seated, enameled wood, height 21", dial 5", c. 1888, 8 Day, strike, spring (K-16).*
　　190.00　　220.00　　(205.00)

☐ **Merida,** *harvest figure, enameled iron, porcelain dial, height 18½", dial 5", 8 Day, strike, spring (K-22).*
　　170.00　　200.00　　(185.00)

☐ **Odessa, with Cleopatra,** *enameled iron, marbleized, gilt dial, height 17½", dial 5", c. 1888, 8 Day, strike, spring (K-22).*
　　250.00　　280.00　　(265.00)

Cimbria

☐ **Cimbria,** *Grecian, enameled iron, marbleized, procelain dial, height 18", dial 5", c. 1888, 8 Day, strike, spring (K-22).*
　　250.00　　285.00　　(267.00)

F. KROEBER / 317

Livonia

Merida

Malvern

Odessa

318 / F. KROEBER

Persia

Saxonia

☐ **Saxonia,** with Hamlet, enameled iron, porcelain dial, height 20", dial 5", c. 1888, 8 Day, strike, spring (K-20).
350.00   385.00   (367.00)

☐ **Siberia No. 4,** with Milton, enameled iron, rubber dial, height 22", dial 5", c. 1888, 8 Day, strike, spring (K-21).
360.00   390.00   (375.00)

☐ **Silesia,** with study, enameled iron, marbleized, porcelain dial, height 21", dial 5", c. 1880, 8 Day, strike, spring (K-20).
230.00   265.00   (247.00)

Siberia

Silesia

☐ **Persia No. 2,** with Horse Dexter, enameled iron marbleized, procelain dial, height 21", dial 5", c. 1888, 8 Day, strike, spring (K-21).
210.00   240.00   (225.00)

F. KROEBER / 319

☐ **Syria,** *with urn, enameled iron, marbleized, porcelain dial, height 15½", dial 5", c. 1888, 8 Day, strike, spring (K-23).*
      150.00   180.00   (165.00)

Syria

Valencia

☐ **Umbria,** *with seated sailor boy, enameled iron, marbleized, porcelain dial, height 16½", dial 5", c. 1888, 8 Day, strike, spring (K-21).*
      220.00   240.00   (230.00)

☐ **Valencia,** *with seated lady, enameled iron, marbleized, porcelain dial, height 21", dial 5", c. 1888, 8 Day, strike, spring (K-21).*
      270.00   300.00   (285.00)

MANTLE/BRASS

☐ **America,** *with shepherdess, American dial, height 17", dial 5", c. 1888, 8 Day, strike, spring (K-24).*
      290.00   325.00   (207.00)

☐ **Arabia No. 1,** *porcelain dial, height 13", dial 5", c. 1888, 8 Day, strike, spring (K-24).*
      265.00   295.00   (280.00)

☐ **Arabia No. 2,** *with figure, porcelain dial, height 20½", dial 5", c. 1880, 8 Day, strike, spring (E3-77).*
      360.00   395.00   (372.00)

Umbria

☐ **Asia No. 1,** *porcelain dial, height 12½", dial 5", c. 1888, 8 Day, strike, spring (K-24).*
      200.00   240.00   (220.00)

☐ **Asia No. 2,** *with vase, rubber dial, height 17½", dial 5", c. 1888, 8 Day, strike, spring (K-24).*
      270.00   300.00   (285.00)

America

Arabia No. 2

Arabia No. 1

Asia No. 1

F. KROEBER / 321

Asia No. 2

Musical No. 2

MANTEL/MUSICAL

The following patterns have two-tune music that is wound through a key hole in the dial. They play for eight days, once an hour.

- ☐ **Musical No. 2,** *enameled iron, American dial, height 10", dial 5", c. 1888, 8 Day, spring (K-18).*
  450.00   500.00   (475.00)

- ☐ **Musical No. 3,** *enameled iron, American dial, height 9½", dial 5", c. 1888, 8 Day, spring (K-18).*
  450.00   500.00   (475.00)

Musical No. 3

- ☐ **Musical No. 4,** *enameled iron, American dial, height 12½", dial 5", c. 1888, 8 Day, spring (E3-76).*
  500.00   550.00   (525.00)

- ☐ **Musical No. 5,** *enameled iron, arabic porcelain dial, height 10", dial 5", c. 1888, 8 Day, spring (K-18).*
  475.00   525.00   (500.00)

- ☐ **Musical No. 6,** *enameled iron, porcelain dial, height 10¼", dial 5", 8 Day, spring (K-18).*
  550.00   600.00   (575.00)

Musical No. 4

Musical No. 5

Musical No. 6

Musical No. 7

Musical No. 8

☐ **Musical No. 7,** *with figure, enameled iron, porcelain dial, height 18", dial 5", c. 1888, 8 Day, spring (K-18).*
      700.00   750.00   (525.00)

☐ **Musical No. 8,** *enameled iron, porcelain dial, height 16", dial 5", 8 Day, spring (K-18).*
      600.00   650.00   (625.00)

NOVELTY/BRASS

☐ **Brass Easel No. 1,** *time only, fancy porcelain figures, height 13", c. 1888, 1 Day, spring (K-27).*
      300.00   350.00   (325.00)
☐ **As above,** *with alarm.*
      350.00   385.00   (367.00)

☐ **Brass Owl,** *glass eyes, alarm, height 9¾", dial 3", c. 1888, spring (K-25).*
      175.00   200.00   (187.00)

☐ **Brass Plaque No. 1,** *plush dial, height 9", c. 1888, 1 Day, spring (K-27).*
      125.00   150.00   (137.00)

Brass Easel No. 1

Brass Plaque No. 2

Brass Plaque No. 3

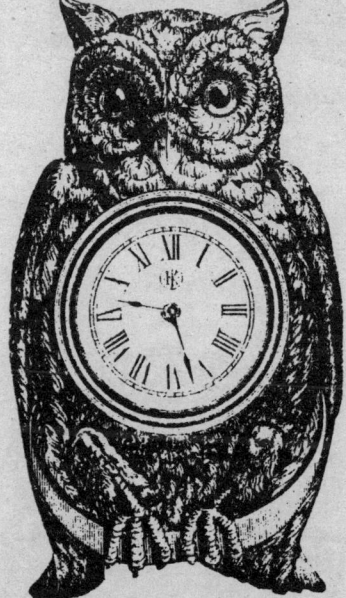

Brass Owl

Brass Plaque No. 4

Hanging Brass Plaque No. 2

Hanging Brass Plaque No. 3

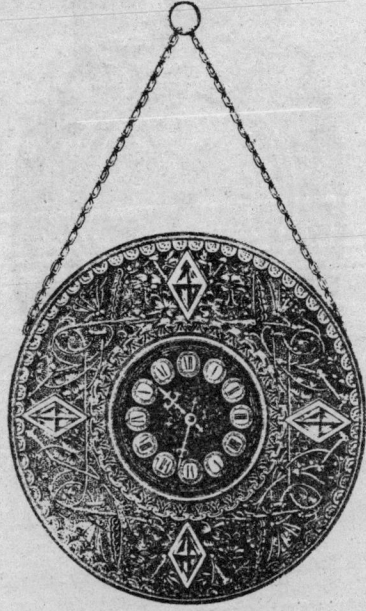

Hanging Brass Plaque No. 4

F. KROEBER / 325

☐ **Knapsack,** *silk plush, height 6½", dial 2", c. 1888, 1 Day, spring (K-29).*
　　140.00　　165.00　　(152.00)

☐ **Lock,** *silk plush, height 7", dial 2", 1 Day, spring (K-29).*
　　125.00　　155.00　　(140.00)

☐ **Organ No. 1,** *music box attached, operated by crank, silk plush, height 4½", dial 2", c. 1888, spring, lever.*
　　300.00　　350.00　　(325.00)

Brass Plaque No. 1

☐ **Brass Plaque No. 2,** *alarm, plush dial, fancy porcelain figures, height 12", c. 1888, 1 Day, spring (K-27).*
　　200.00　　250.00　　(225.00)

☐ **Brass Plaque No. 3,** *plush dial, fancy porcelain figures, height 12", c. 1888, 1 Day, spring (K-27).*
　　130.00　　155.00　　(142.00)

☐ **Brass Plaque No. 4,** *alarm, plush dial, fancy porcelain figures, cut glass jewels, height 12", c. 1888, 1 Day, spring (K-27).*
　　225.00　　250.00　　(237.00)

☐ **Handing Brass Plaque No. 2,** *porcelain figures, diameter 12", c. 1888, 8 Day, lever, spring (K-27).*
　　200.00　　250.00　　(225.00)

☐ **Hanging Brass Plaque No. 3,** *plush dial, porcelain figures, diameter 12", c. 1888, 8 Day, lever, spring (K-27).*
　　150.00　　175.00　　(163.00)

☐ **Hanging Brass Plaque No. 4,** *plush dial, porcelain figures, cut glass jewels, diameter 12", 8 Day, lever (K-27).*
　　225.00　　250.00　　237.00

NOVELTY/PLUSH

☐ **Drum,** *silk plush, seconds bit, height 4½", dial 2", c. 1888, 1 Day, spring (K-29).*
　　100.00　　120.00　　(110.00)

Drum

Knapsack

326 / F. KROEBER

Lock

Organ No. 1

Organ No. 2

Piano

- **Organ No. 2,** *with music box, operated by crank, silk plush, height 7½", c. 1888, spring, lever.*
      350.00   400.00   (375.00)

- **Piano,** *silk plush, height 6½", dial 2", c. 1888, 1 Day, spring, lever (K-29).*
      250.00   280.00   (265.00)

- **Plush No. 2,** *silk plush, height 6¾", dial 2", c. 1888, 1 Day, spring, lever (K-29).*
      100.00   130.00   (115.00)
- **As above,** *with alarm.*
      140.00   160.00   (150.00)

- **Plush No. 8,** *silk, height 7¼", c. 1888, 1 Day, spring, lever (K-29).*
      120.00   145.00   (132.00)
- **As above,** *with alarm.*
      146.00   165.00   (155.00)

- **Plush House No. 3,** *silk, decorated bisque figures, height 6½", dial 2", c. 1888, 1 Day, spring, lever (E-80).*
      290.00   340.00   (315.00)

F. KROEBER / 327

Plush No. 2

Plush House No. 3

Plush Plaque No. 1

Plush No. 8

☐ **Plush Plaque No. 1,** *red, blue and olive silk, porcelain dial, alarm, height 10½", c. 1888, 1 Day, spring lever (E3-81).*
       150.00   175.00   (163.00)

☐ **Pug's House No. 1,** *silk, height 6½", dial 2", c. 1888, 1 Day, spring, lever (K-29).*
       275.00   310.00   (293.00)

☐ **Satchel,** *silk, height 6", dial 2", c. 1888, 1 Day, spring, lever (K-29).*
       140.00   165.00   (152.00)

☐ **Souvenir,** *silk with metal trimmings, height 5¼", dial 2", c. 1888, 1 Day, spring, lever (K-29).*
       90.00   110.00   (97.00)

☐ **Toilet No. 1,** *drawer with jewelry tray.*
       200.00   225.00   (212.00)

Pug's House No. 1

Satchel

Souvenier

Toilet No. 2

Toilet No. 3

Toilet No. 4

F. KROEBER / 329

☐ **Toilet No. 2,** *drawer with lady's work box tools, silk, cut glass bottles, height 7½", spring, lever (K-29).*
        280.00   310.00   **(295.00)**

☐ **Toilet No. 3,** *silk, cut glass bottles, drawer with manicure set, height 10¼", dial 2", c. 1888, spring, lever (K-29).*
        200.00   240.00   **(220.00)**

☐ **Toilet No. 4,** *silk, cut glass bottles, beveled plate glass doors, height 9½", dial 2", c. 1888, spring, lever (K-28).*
        265.00   290.00   **(288.00)**

☐ **Toilet No. 5,** *silk, cut glass bottles, height 4¾", dial 2", c. 1888, spring, lever (K-29).*
        160.00   195.00   **(177.00)**

NOVELTY/WINDOW

☐ **Window Clock,** *beveled edge, plate glass, gilt figures and hands, diameter 14", 30 hour, spring lever (K-14).*
        450.00   550.00   **(500.00)**

NOVELTY/MISCELLANEOUS

☐ **Baseball,** *real baseball with polished wooded bats, height 5¾", dial 2", c. 1888, spring (K-29).*
        140.00   160.00   **(150.00)**

☐ **Gypsy Kettle,** *nickel, height 8", dial 2", c. 1888, spring (K-26).*
        100.00   125.00   **(112.00)**

☐ **Grandfather,** *nickel, chronograph, sweep center seconds, quarter seconds, stopper, case 4½", dial 3", c. 1888, spring (K-25).*
        300.00   350.00   **(325.00)**

☐ **Sleigh,** *nickel, height 8", dial 3", c. 1888, spring (K-26).*
        130.00   150.00   **(140.00)**

Window Clock

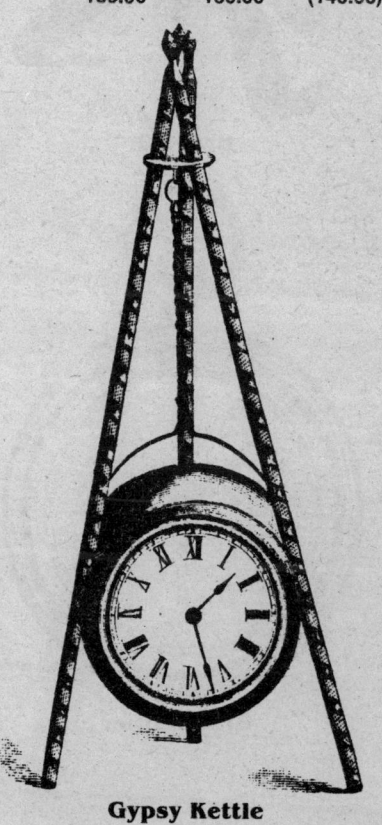

Gypsy Kettle

330 / F. KROEBER

Baseball

Grandfather

Sleigh

PORCELAIN

Enameled iron clocks made in six colors: white, green, blue, red, pink, and black, with gold and silver ornaments. Patented by F. Kroeber, no. 506450, October 3, 1893. They were available with the following dials: black or white paper American, French porcelain, brass, and French fancy gilt.

☐ **Antoinette,** *height 8¼", dial 3", c. 1893, spring, lever (K-36).*
      215.00   250.00   (233.00)

☐ **Charlotte,** *height 9", dial 3", c. 1893, 1 Day, spring, lever (K-35).*
      175.00   200.00   (188.00)

F. KROEBER / 331

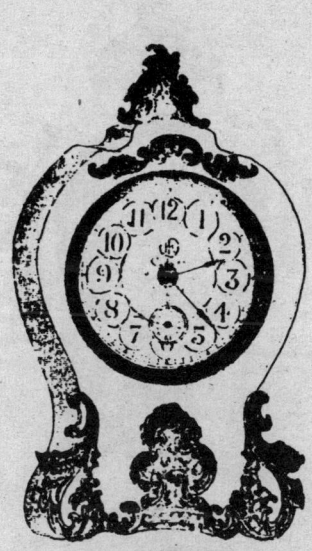

Antoinette

Conde

Charlotte

☐ **Conde**, *height 14¾", dial 5", c. 1893, 8 Day, strike, spring (K-35).*
    325.00   375.00   (350.00)

☐ **Hortense**, *height 13", dial 3", c. 1893, spring, lever (K-36).*
    200.00   250.00   (225.00)

☐ **India**, *height 14", dial 5", c. 1893, 8 Day, strike, spring (K-35).*
    385.00   435.00   (410.00)

☐ **Josephine**, *height 8¼", dial 3", c. 1893, spring, lever (K-35).*
    185.00   220.00   (203.00)

☐ **Louis XIV**, *height 16", dial 5", c. 1893, 8 Day, strike, spring (K-35).*
    300.00   365.00   (332.00)

☐ **Pompadour**, *height 18¼", dial 5", c. 1893, 8 Day, strike, spring (K-36).*
    525.00   575.00   (550.00).

☐ **Richelieu**, *height 11½", dial 5", c. 1893, 8 Day, strike, spring (K-35).*
    325.00   375.00   (350.00)

☐ **Turenne**, *height 12", dial 5", c. 1893, 8 Day, strike, spring (K-36).*
    325.00   375.00   (350.00)

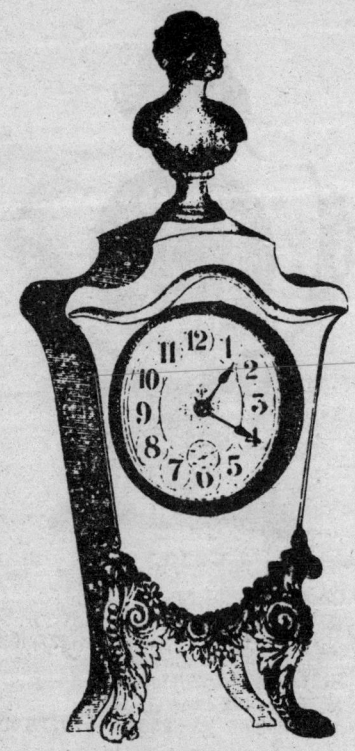

Hortense

Josephine

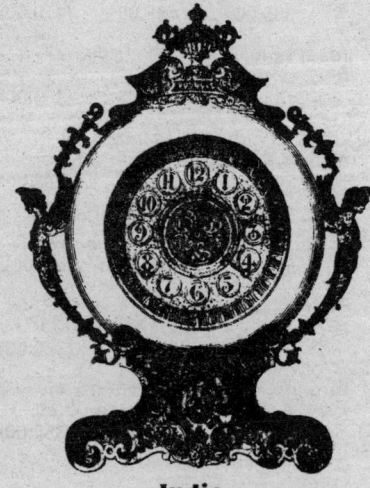

India

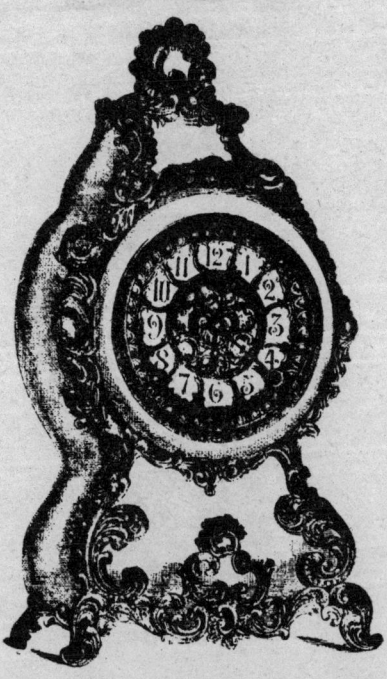

Louis XIV

Pompadour

Versailles

Turenne

Voltaire

334 / F. KROEBER

- **Versailles,** *height 15", dial 5", c. 1893, 8 Day, strike, spring (K-36).*
  400.00   475.00   (437.00)

- **Voltaire,** *height 13¾", dial 5", c. 1893, 8 Day, strike, spring (K-36).*
  300.00   360.00   330.00

REGULATOR/ASTRONOMICAL

- **English Regulator,** *walnut, engraved and silvered, jeweled pallets, mercurial pendulum, length 7', dials 16" and 18", c. 1888, weight, mercury pendulum (K-14).*
  12500.00   15000.00   (13750.00)

REGULATOR/DROP OCTAGON

- **Drop Octagon,** *rounded corners, oak, height 24", dial 12", c. 1888, 8 Day, spring (E3-78).*
  250.00   300.00   (275.00)
- **As above,** *8 Day, strike.*
  275.00   325.00   (300.00)
- **As above,** *8 Day, calendar.*
  275.00   325.00   (300.00)
- **As above,** *8 Day, strike, calendar.*
  300.00   350.00   325.00

Drop Octagon

REGULATOR/ROUND TOP LONG DROP

- **Regulator,** *height 32", dial 12", c. 1888, 8 Day, spring (E3-78).*
  350.00   400.00   (375.00)
- **As above,** *8 Day, strike.*
  400.00   450.00   (425.00)
- **As above,** *8 Day, calendar.*
  450.00   500.00   (475.00)
- **As above,** *8 Day, strike, calendar.*
  500.00   550.00   (525.00)

English Regulator

F. KROEBER / 335

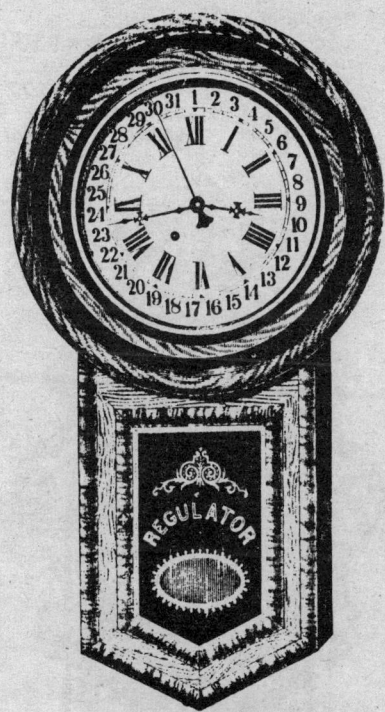

Regulator

Reflector

REGULATOR/IONIC

- **Reflecter,** *height 29½", dial 12", c. 1888, 8 Day, spring (K-15).*
    450.00   550.00   (500.00)
- **As above,** *8 Day, strike.*
    500.00   600.00   (550.00)

- **Saxon,** *walnut or oak, height 22", dial 10", c. 1888, 8 Day, spring (K-15).*
    350.00   400.00   (325.00)
- **As above,** *8 Day, strike.*
    375.00   425.00   (400.00)
- **As above,** *8 Day, calendar.*
    375.00   425.00   (400.00)
- **As above,** *8 Day, strike, calendar.*
    400.00   450.00   (425.00)

REGULATOR/PARLOR WALL

- **Regulator No. 31,** *walnut or mahogany, height 34", dial 6", c. 1888, 8 Day, spring (E3-79).*
    500.00   550.00   (525.00)
- **As above,** *8 Day, strike.*
    550.00   600.00   (575.00)

- **Regulator No. 41,** *walnut, height 44½", dial 14", c. 1888, 8 Day, spring (E3-78).*
    1250.00   1350.00   (1300.00)
- **As above,** *8 Day, strike.*
    1350.00   1450.00   (1400.00)

- **Regulator No. 42,** *walnut, height 50½", dial 12", c. 1888, 8 Day, spring (E3-78).*
    1300.00   1400.00   (1350.00)
- **As above,** *8 Day, strike.*
    1400.00   1500.00   (1450.00)

336 / F. KROEBER

Regulator No. 41

Regulator No. 42

☐ **Regulator No. 46,** *walnut, ash or mahogany, height 33½", dial 6", c. 1888, 8 Day, spring (E3-79).*
    880.00   850.00   (825.00)
☐ **As above,** *8 Day, strike.*
    850.00   900.00   (875.00)

☐ **Regulator No. 44,** *walnut or ash, height 30", dial 6", c. 1888, 8 Day, spring (E3-79).*
    450.00   500.00   (475.00)
☐ **As above,** *8 Day, strike.*
    500.00   550.00   (525.00)

☐ **Regulator No. 45,** *walnut, ash or mahogany, height 33", dial 6", c. 1888, 8 Day, spring (E3-79).*
    450.00   500.00   (475.00)
☐ **As above,** *8 Day, strike.*
    500.00   550.00   (525.00)

Regulator No. 44

Regulator No. 45

Regulator No. 47

338 / F. KROEBER

Regulator No. 46

- **Regulator No. 47,** *walnut, ash or mahogany, height 48", dial 8", c. 1888, 8 Day, spring (K-12).*
  900.00   950.00   (925.00)
- **As above,** *8 Day, strike.*
  950.00   1000.00   (975.00)

- **Regulator No. 48,** *mahogany or walnut, length 44", dial 8", c. 1888, 8 Day, spring (K-12).*
  900.00   1000.00   (950.00)
- **As above,** *8 Day, strike.*
  1000.00   1100.00   (1050.00)

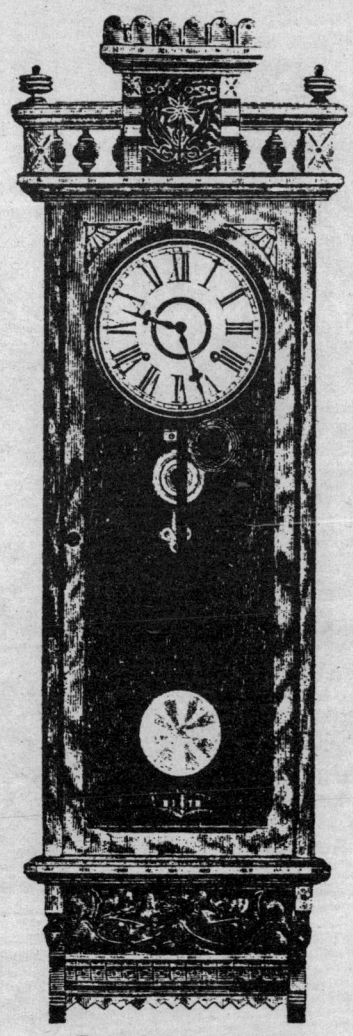

Regulator No. 48

REGULATOR/SECONDS BIT

- **Vienna Regulator No. 19,** *polished ebony, length 6', dial 10", c. 1888, 8 Day, weight (E3-79).*
  2300.00   2500.00   (2400.00)

Regulator No. 19

Regulator No. 33

Regulator No. 47

340 / F. KROEBER

☐ **Vienna Regulator No. 33,** *polished walnut, with ebony trimmings, porcelain dial, length 50", dial 7", c. 1888, 8 Day, weight.*
    1400.00   1500.00   (1450.00)

☐ **Vinenna Regulator No. 47,** *polished ebony, porcelain dial, length 47", dial 7", c. 1888, 8 Day, weight (K-13).*
    1400.00   1500.00   (1450.00)

☐ **Vienna Regulator No. 51,** *polished walnut with ebony trimmings, porcelain dial, length 47", dial 7", 8 Day, weight (E3-79).*
    1200.00   1300.00   (1250.00)

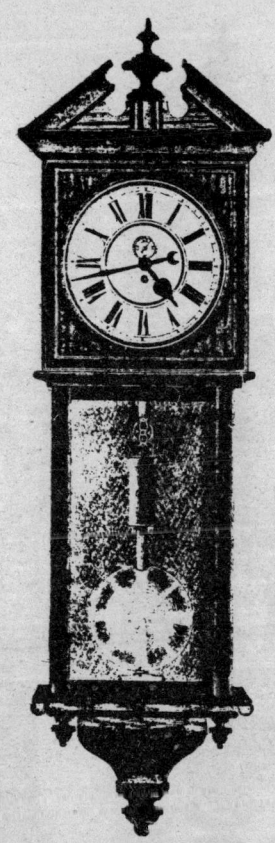

Vienna Regulator No. 84

☐ **Vienna Regulator No. 84,** *polished walnut with ebony trimmings, porcelain dial, length 47", dial 9", c. 1888, 8 Day, weight (E3-79).*
    1400.00   1500.00   (1450.00)

REGULATOR/SWEEP SECOND

☐ **Swiss Regulator No. 21,** *walnut, best quality movement, porcelain dial, length 6', dial 12", c. 1888, weight (E3-78).*
    4000.00   4500.00   (4250.00)

☐ **Swiss Regulator No. 22,** *walnut, best quality movement, length 7', dial 12", c. 1888, weight (K-13).*
    4500.00   5000.00   (4750.00)

Vienna Regulator No. 51

Swiss Regulator No. 21

Swiss Regulator No. 22

Swiss Regulator No. 24

Swiss Standing

Swiss Wall

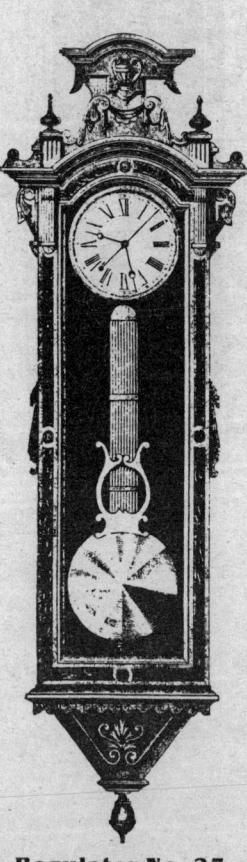

Regulator No. 27

F. KROEBER / 343

☐ **Swiss Regulator No. 28,** *walnut, porcelain dial, length 7'6", dial 12", c. 1888, weight (K-12).*
      7500.00   8000.00   (7750.00)

ROTARY

☐ **Noiseless Rotary No. 1,** *with glass shade, height 20½", dial 6", c. 1888, 8 Day, strike, spring (E3-80).*
      2100.00   2300.00   (2200.00)

☐ **Noiseless Rotary No. 2,** *ebony, porcelain dial, height 22", dial 5", 8 Day, strike, spring (K-19).*
      1500.00   1700.00   (1600.00)

☐ **Noiseless Rotary No. 3,** *ebony, porcelain, height 22½", dial 5", c. 1888, 8 Day, strike, spring (K-19).*
      1500.00   1700.00   (1600.00)

Swiss Regulator No. 28

☐ **Swiss Regulator No. 24,** *walnut, best quality movement, length 7'5", dial 12", c. 1888, weight (E3-78).*
      6500.00   7000.00   (6750.00)

☐ **Swiss Regulator,** *standing, walnut, best quality movement, height 9', dial 12", c. 1888, weight (K-14).*
      7000.00   7500.00   (7250.00)

☐ **Swiss Regulator No. 26,** *walnut, best quality movement, length 7'5", dial 12", weight (K-14).*
      7000.00   7500.00   (7250.00)

☐ **Swiss Regulator No. 27,** *walnut, porcelain dial, length 7'6", dial 12", c. 1888, weight (K-14).*
      6000.00   6500.00   (6250.00)

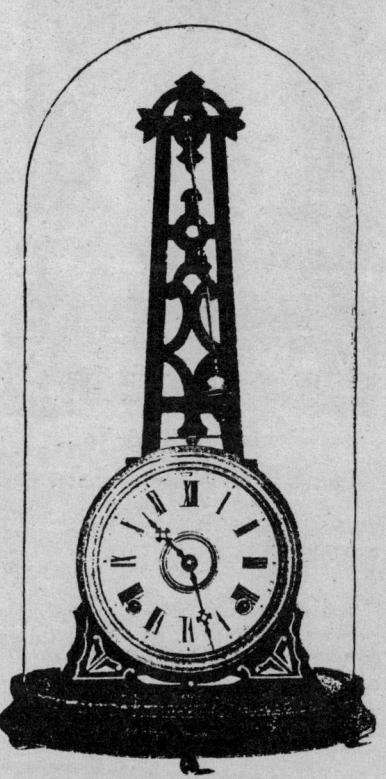

Noiseless Rotary No. 1

344 / F. KROEBER

Noiseless Rotary No. 2

Noiseless Rotary No. 3

Noiseless Rotary No. 4

- **Noiseless Rotary No. 4,** *enameled iron, porcelain dial, height 22", dial 4½", c. 1888, 8 Day, strike, spring (K-19).*
  1500.00   1700.00   (1600.00)

- **Noiseless Rotary No. 6,** *walnut, American black or white dial, height 21", dial 5", c. 1888, 8 Day, strike, spring (K-19).*
  1600.00   1800.00   (1700.00)

F. KROEBER / 345

Noiseless Rotary No. 6

Santa Barbara

Sonoma

Ventura

STATUE

☐ **Santa Barbara,** *bronze, porcelain dial, height 18", dial 5", 8 Day, strike (K-24).*
        400.00   565.00   (432.00)

☐ **Sonoma,** *bronze, porcelain dial, height 14", dial 5", 8 Day, strike (K-24).*
        450.00   500.00   (475.00)

☐ **Ventura,** *bronze, porcelain dial, height 13¼", dial 5", 8 Day, strike (K-24).*
        400.00   450.00   (425.00)

LUX AND KEEBLER

LUX AND KEEBLER PENDULETTES FUN AND FANTASY

Reprinted from an
Article in the *NAWCC Bulletin*,
by Jo Burt, Bloomfield Hills, MI:
August 1981
Whole #213
Vol. XXIII No. 4 Page 335 to 359

Resurgence of interest in the Lux and Keebler Pendulettes during recent years has led me to share seven years of fun and fantasy in collecting pendulettes with you. A seemingly endless variety, 200 fascinating beats per minute, and colorful topics make this particular type of clock collecting an interesting hobby most everyone can afford ... even in today's high-priced economy.

The Lux Company was founded by Paul Lux in 1912 after he had worked at the Waterbury Clock Company in Connecticut for 28 years. Paul Lux enlisted the aid of his wife and two sons, Fred and Herman, in this venture, Long hours and hard work demanded much of everyone's time, but after several years of persistent effort, their endeavors paid of and the company seemed to have been established. Unfortunately, at a time when anyone least expected it, tragedy struck and the company was demolished by a fire which destroyed most of its equipment, supplies and records.

The same diligence and perseverance which motivated and sustained Paul Lux in the past persisted, and he began to rebuild his dream. Since his sons were now in the Army, he was unable to utilize their services and relied on the help of close freinds. By the time Fred and Herman had returned from the war, the company was again an enterprising concern living up to their motto, "our clocks must go — or we go."

August C. Keebler was the founder of the Keebler Company of Chicago in 1931. Keebler was not a manufacturer of the pendulettes but a distributor, who also had a sales office in the Philadelphia area.

It is special interest to note that both companies, at times, marketed the same clock, but under separate names. Keebler had Lux make clocks for him and the Lux Company would, in turn, market the same clock for themselves. The efforts on the part of these two men gave us the Lux and Keebler pendulettes as we know them today. The companies took advantage of events and ideas which were pertinent during that time and incorporated these into clocks which had special meaning — such as interest in the Shmoo, Sally Rand, the Boy Scouts, Franklin Delano Roosevelt, etc. During these early times, the cloks ranged in price from $1.00 to $4.00 with the majority being priced at about $2.00. They were also used in incentive programs; whereby if enough coupons or tokens were collected, a clock was given in exchange.

NOTE: Numbers denoted with asterisk (*) in the following section are catalog numbers assigned by the author.

ALARM

☐ **Alarm No. 206,** *plain dial, ring on top, screw in legs, polished copper, nickel or brass finish, 5⁵⁄₁₆" X 4⁵⁄₈", c. 1969, 30 hour.*
        2.00   4.00   (3.00)

☐ **As above,** *No. 206-1, luminous dial.*
        2.00   4.00   (3.00)

☐ **Apollo No. 240-6-2,** *plain dial, ivory finish, metal, rectangular with case forming base, 4½" 4¹⁄₁₆" x 2⁵⁄₁₆", c. 1963, 30 hour.*
        4.00   6.00   (5.00)

☐ **As above,** *No. 240-7-2, luminous dial.*

☐ **Apollo No. 250-01,** *plastic moulded ivory finish, plastic case, square but smaller at the top, integral base, height 4¾", c. 1971, 30 hour.*
        3.00   5.00   (4.00)

☐ **Art Alarm,** *unbreakable molded wood product, finished in gold on green background, height 5", c. 1928, 30 hour, alarm.*
        35.00   55.00   (40.00)

LUX AND KEEBLER / 347

☐ **Chilton Alarm,** *round head, pedestal, stamped metal, height 5⅛", c. 1951, 48 hour, lever.*
    4.00   5.00   (4.50)

☐ **China, Dresden Type,** *two models, authentic reproductions, hand painted, gilded, fine glaze, height 7", c. 1950, 40 hour, alarm.*
    15.00   25.00   (20.00)

☐ **Conqueror Alarm,** *square metal case with rounded corners, ivory case, c. 1956.*
    4.00   5.00   (4.50)

☐ **As above,** *luminous dial.*
    4.00   5.00   (4.50)

☐ **Deluxe No. 243,** *plain dial, top heavy square, ivory colored metal case, recessed dial, has shadow box effect, gold bezel, height 4½", c. 1969, 30 hour.*
    2.00   4.00   (3.00)

☐ **As above,** *No. 2434, luminous dial.*
    2.00   4.00   (3.00)

☐ **Fairview Alarm,** *square case, red color with rural scene on dial, height 5", c. 1951, 48 hour.*
    10.00   12.00   (11.00)

☐ **Gabriel No. 280-2,** *copper, plain dial, round alarm with two bells and a handle on the top, 5¾", c. 1971, 30 hour, alarm.*
    6.00   8.00   (7.00)

☐ **As above,** *No. 280-03, copper, luminous dial.*
    6.00   8.00   (7.00)

☐ **As Above,** *No. 282-01, brass, plain dial.*
    6.00   8.00   (7.00)

☐ **As Above,** *No. 282-03, brass, luminous dial.*
    6.00   8.00   (7.00)

☐ **Harvester Alarm,** *square metal case, pearl gray hammered metal, 5" x 4¼", c. 1951, 48 hour, lever.*
    4.00   5.00   (4.50)

☐ **Hawthorne No. 207,** *baked ivory finish, round metal case, pedestal base, height 4¾", c. 1969, 30 hour.*
    2.00   4.00   (3.00)

☐ **Hexagon,** *styrene case, molded feet, provincial.*

☐ **Hexagon No. 255-01,** *plain dial, styrene case, molded feet, provincial style, ring on top, back set, dial 3½", c. 1966, 30 hour, alarm.*
    3.00   5.00   (4.00)

☐ **As above,** *No. 255-02, luminous.*
    3.00   5.00   (4.00)

☐ **Hummer Alarm,** *crackle finish, round metal case, ivory and green, concealed loud alarm, side shut off, pedestal base, height 5¼", c. 1927, 30 hour.*
    30.00   40.00   (35.00)

☐ **Hytone No. 763,** *rectangular ribbed dome top, metal case, short feet, assorted colors, back set, height 7¾", c. 1950, 30 hour, alarm.*
    3.00   5.00   (4.00)

☐ **Lebanon Alarm,** *round metal case, pedestal base, ivory case, c. 1956, 30 hour.*
    4.00   5.00   (4.50)

☐ **Luxette No. 205,** *round dial with seriated gold color bezel, has a shadow box appearance, back set, diameter 4", c. 1955, 30 hour.*
    4.00   6.00   (5.00)

☐ **As above,** *205-R, luminous.*
    4.00   6.00   (5.00)

☐ **Page Alarm,** *round, hammered gray metal case, height 4½", c. 1951.*
    4.00   5.00   (4.50)

☐ **Patriotic No. 282-09,** *red, white, and blue stars and stripes, two bell alarm, handle on top, back set, height 5¾", c. 1973, 30 hour.*
    6.00   10.00   (7.00)

☐ **As above,** *No. 284-02, five colors with eagle on face.*
    5.00   7.00   (6.00)

☐ **As above,** *No. 283-01, red, open face gears.*
    6.00   10.00   (7.00)

☐ **As above,** *No. 282-10, happy face.*
    5.00   7.00   (6.00)

☐ **Petit Alarm,** *round ivory case, dial 2⅞", c. 1951, 40 hour.*
    4.00   6.00   (5.00)

☐ **As above,** *with luminous dial.*
    4.00   6.00   (5.00)

348 / LUX AND KEEBLER

- [ ] **Slumberminder,** *round gunmetal case, gilt hands, c. 1951.*
  4.00   6.00   (5.00)
- [ ] **As above,** *ivory case.*
  4.00   6.00   (5.00)
- [ ] **Sphinx Alarm,** *unbreakable wood product, round head with pedestal base, height 5¼", c. 1928, 30 hour.*
  30.00   40.00   (35.00)
- [ ] **Spur,** *round with bell and ring on top, screw in legs, back set, 30 hour.*
  25.00   35.00   (30.00)
- [ ] **Symphony Alarm,** *molded walnut plastic case, bowed glass, height 4½", c. 1951, 48 hour.*
  4.00   6.00   (5.00)
- [ ] **Town and Country No. 523,** *plain dial, soled mahogany, square case, rounded corners, height 3¾", c. 1950.*
  2.00   4.00   (3.00)
- [ ] **As above,** *No. 522, luminous.*
  2.00   4.00   (3.00)
- [ ] **Travel Alarm,** *Riviera pull out, arabian ostrich covered metal, pull apart case, 4" x 2½", c. 1960, 30 hour.*
  4.00   6.00   (5.00)
- [ ] **Travel Alarm,** *jeweled and non-jeweled model, simulated tan pigskin, brown cordobe, grain lizard or plain, covered metal, folding case, 3¼" x 3⅞", c. 1960, 30 hour.*
  3.00   5.00   (4.00)
- [ ] **Vendome No. 761,** *rectangular art deco design, step top, metal case with integral base, assorted colors, backset, height 5¼", c. 1950, 30 hour.*
  6.00   7.00   (8.00)
- [ ] **Venus No. 247,** *Mark Two, all metal with square dial, case forms base, height 4½", c. 1956, 30 hour.*
  4.00   6.00   (5.00)
- [ ] **Vulcan No. 236,** *metal case, corners, pedestal base, assorted colors, height 4¾", c. 1950.*
  4.00   6.00   (5.00)
- [ ] **Wren No. 249,** *plain dial, top heavy square metal case, ivory, case forms base, height 4_{3/16}", c. 1969.*
  2.00   4.00   (3.00)

ALARM/ANIMATED

- [ ] **Butcher Animated,** *arm chops meat with pussy cat watching, square black metal case on pedestal base, height 4½", 30 hour, alarm.*
  100.00   125.00   (110.00)
- [ ] **Church Steeple,** *rural church with bell swinging back and forth, assorted colors, height 3¾", c. 1934, 30 hour.*
  100.00   125.00   (110.00)
- [ ] **Grist Mill Alarm,** *animated power wheel, square metal case with rounded corners, hammered gray, mill scene on dial, c. 1956, 30 hour.*
  75.00   85.00   (80.00)
- [ ] **Happy Day's Animated Clock,** *two drinkers over beer barrel, height 3¾", c. 1934.*
  100.00   125.00   (110.00)
- [ ] **Organ Grinder Dancing Bar,** *arm turns organ bear dancing with a stick, height 3⅞", 30 hour, alarm.*
  125.00   150.00   (130.00)
- [ ] **Organ Grinder And Monkey,** *arm turns organ and monkey climbing fence, black metal case, height 4½", 30 hour.*
  125.00   150.00   (130.00)
- [ ] **Spinning Wheel,** *with turning wheel or dial with homey scene, wine red, height 4", c. 1951, 48 hour.*
  75.00   85.00   (80.00)
- [ ] **Watermill,** *set in rose gold plated metal frame, octagon shape, dial shows country home and watermill, height 4¾", c. 1930, 30 hour.*
  75.00   85.00   (80.00)
- [ ] **Watermill,** *picture of a working windmill on a beautiful metal dial, height 5⅝", c. 1933, 30 hour.*
  100.00   125.00   (110.00)

LUX ART

☐ **Adelphia Art,** *boudoir clock, unbreakable molded wood product, carved and decorated in colors, oval shape, easel back, c. 1933, 30 hour.*
    65.00   85.00   (70.00)

☐ **Art Delo Modernistic,** *molded synthetic wood, square case supported by two triangles, height 8¼", c. 1930, 8 Day.*
    65.00   85.00   (70.00)

☐ **Blossom Time,** *table clock unbreakable molded wood product, green, Japanese design, decorated oval on a pedestal base, height 15¾", c. 1928, 8 Day.*
    90.00   115.00   (100.00)

☐ **Boucher,** *mantel clock, unbreakable molded wood product, red, gold, green, or walnut finish, bordered retangular frame on a platform base, height 12½", c. 1928, 8 Day.*
    80.00   100.00   (90.00)

☐ **Cambridge,** *table clock, unbreakable molded wood product, parliament finish, round with small feet, easel back, height 4", c. 1928, 30 hour, heart beat movement.*
    55.00   75.00   (60.00)

☐ **Du Barry,** *table clock, unbreakable molded wood product, green finish, round with feet, height 6", 30 hour.*
    40.00   60.00   (50.00)

☐ **Flamingo,** *boudoir clock, molded synthetic wood, octagon shape, easel back, height 5¾", c. 1930.*
    65.00   75.00   (70.00)

☐ **Hexagon Art Clock,** *molded wood product, orange and gold, design consists of raised semi circular balls and scallops in a petaled flower, diameter 4½", 30 hour.*
    35.00   50.00   (40.00)

Lans Down

☐ **Lans Down,** *table clock, unbreakable molded wood product, oval shaped, footed base, made in six colors, height 9", c. 1928, 30 hour.*
    65.00   85.00   (75.00)

☐ **Louis Fifteenth,** *Boudoir Clock, unbreakable molded wood product, flower wreaths in relief, height c. 1930, 30 hour.*
    40.00   60.00   (50.00)

☐ **Louis Fourteenth,** *wall hanging clock, unbreakable molded wood product, octagon case suspended by grained silk ribbon, height 12", c. 1933, 30 hour.*
    60.00   80.00   (70.00)

☐ **Louis Sixteenth,** *Boudoir Clock, unbreakable molded wood product, carved and decorated, richly hand colored, walnut finish, octagonal shape, height 7¼", c. 1933, 30 hour.*
    35.00   45.00   (40.00)

Louis XVI

Pendant

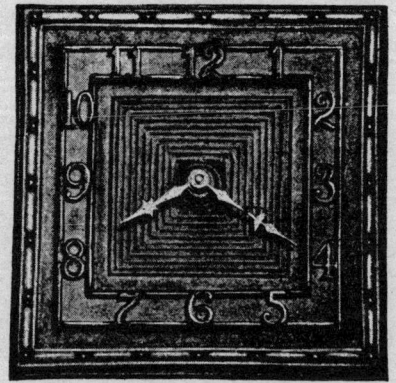

Times Square

☐ **Mignard,** *Boudoir Clock, unbreakable molded wood product, carved and decorated, walnut finish, octagonal, height 6", c. 1933, 30 hour.*
        40.00   50.00   (45.00)

☐ **Modernistic Wall Clock,** *square dial, thermometer, electric, height 13", c. 1938.*
        40.00   50.00   (45.00)

☐ **Oxford,** *Boudoir Clock, unbreakable molded wood product, decorated in relief colors, easel back, c. 1933, 30 hour.*
        45.00   55.00   (50.00)

☐ **Pendant,** *wall clock, molded synthetic wood, hand decorated, assorted colors, round case, diameter 3", c. 1930, 30 hour.*
        40.00   60.00   (50.00)

☐ **Pendant,** *wall clock, molded synthetic wood product embossed oval case, suspended on tangerine silk grosgrain ribbon, height 11", c. 1927, 30 hour.*
        60.00   80.00   (70.00)

LUX AND KEEBLER / 351

☐ **Rose Wreath,** *boudoir clock, tinted and embossed, molded synthetic wood product, with floral wreath decoration, dial 2", c. 1927, 30 hour.*
        25.00   35.00   (30.00)

☐ **Times Square,** *boudoir clock, molded wood product, ivory and blue, height 3", c. 1933, 30 hour.*
        20.00   30.00   (25.00)
☐ **As above,** *height 4".*
        25.00   35.00   (30.00)
☐ **As above,** *height 5".*
        30.00   40.00   (35.00)

CUCKOO/CHAIN AND WEIGHT

☐ **Bobbing Bird And Swiss Chalet,** *wall clock, bird's head bobs up and down with tick of the clock, molded wood product, c. 1942, 30 hour, chain and weight.*
       100.00   125.00   (115.00)

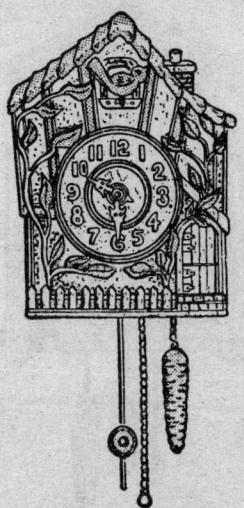
Bobbing Bird

☐ **Cuckoo,** *hunting scene, synthetic carved wood, deer head with glass eyes, ½ hour and 1 hour cuckoo, dial 4", c. 1942, chain and weights.*
       175.00   200.00   (190.00)
☐ **As above,** *quail design.*
       100.00   125.00   (110.00)
☐ **As above,** *bird design.*
       100.00   125.00   (110.00)

☐ **Swiss Chalet,** *synthetic carved wood, bobbing bird, height 8⅝", c. 1942, 1 Day, double weight and chain.*
       200.00   250.00   (225.00)

☐ **Swiss Chalet,** *old style molded wood product, bobbing bird, c. 1950, single chain and weight.*
       200.00   250.00   (225.00)

☐ **Town Hall,** *carved wood, ½ hour and 1 hour cuckoo, bell tolls, height 12", c. 1942, 1 Day, double chain and weights (E3-179).*
       250.00   300.00   (225.00)

Cuckoo

352 / LUX AND KEEBLER

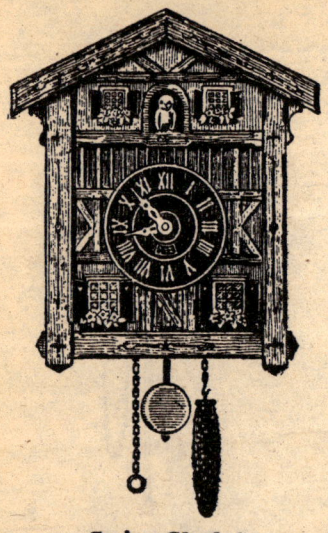

Swiss Chalet

Quail

ELECTRIC

☐ **Colonial No. 2004-01,** *broken arch with columns, square molded styrene in American walnut finish, height 16¾", c. 1971.*
      3.00   7.00   (4.00)

☐ **Calendar Clock,** *with date minder, sweep second, three apertures at bottom show day of the week, month and day of the month, assorted colors, c. 1956.*
     25.00   35.00   (30.00)

☐ **Electric Alarm No. 500-04,** *plain dial, white molded styrene, rectangular case, with small feet, height 4⅝".*
      2.00   5.00   (3.00)
☐ **As above,** *No. 5000-05, luminous.*
      2.00   5.00   (3.00)

☐ **Shadow Box No. 2009-01,** *square molded styrene, walnut grain, cordless battery, height 14", c. 1971.*
      3.00   7.00   (4.00)

☐ **Sunburst No. 200-19,** *rich walnut spears with golden trim, and scalloped clock case, cordless battery, diameter 27", c. 1971.*
      3.00   7.00   (4.00)

☐ **Wall Clock No. 5171-20,** *smile, yellow styrene, round case, height 6⅞", c. 1970.*
      6.00   8.00   (7.00)
☐ **As above,** *No. 5171, plain.*
      5.00   7.00   (6.00)
☐ **As above,** *No. 5171-22.*
      5.00   7.00   (6.00)

HEARTBEAT

☐ **Banjo Heartbeat Clock,** *unbreakable wood product with yellow finish, reproduction of Colonial banjo clock, dial 3½", length 18¾", c. 1928, 30 hour (C3-170).*
     75.00   100.00   (80.00)

☐ **Cupids Beating Heart,** *plastic heart shaped case, in assorted colors, height 3½", c. 1928, 30 hour, pendulum (E3-172).*
     40.00   50.00   (45.00)

☐ **Heartbeat,** *pink and blue on amber Ivorith, round top on legs, easel back, dial 2", c. 1927, 30 hour.*
    40.00   50.00   (45.00)

☐ **Lamp Heartbeat Clock,** *unbreakable wood product in three finishes, hand painted parchment shade with silk braid-binding, height 20", c. 1928, 30 hour (E3-170).*
    125.00   150.00   (130.00)

PENDULUM AND PENDULETTE

☐ **Baseball No. 18,** *metal ball supported by two wood posts, rectangular base, height 9½", c. 1940, 30 hour.*
    50.00   75.00   (55.00)

☐ **Bird's Nest No. 219,** *no animation, bird facing right on cuckoo house with nest and eggs at bottom, green and brown, height 6½", 30 hour, Keebler and Lux.*
    30.00   50.00   (40.00)

☐ **Black Cat Pendulette No. 325,** *pressed wood, cat's tail swings back and forth, eyes move from side to side, height 7⅑", c. 1937, 30 hour.*
    140.00   165.00   (155.00)

☐ **Bobbing Bird No. 240,** *bird facing right, molded wood product, animated, walnut, with bright trim, height 7", 30 hour.*
    25.00   30.00   (37.50)

☐ **As above,** *No. 312, bird faces left, height 7¼".*
    25.00   30.00   (27.50)

☐ **As above,** *No. 311, old cuckoo style, height 7".*
    25.00   30.00   (27.50)

☐ **As above,** *No. 18, hunting scene, stag head and crossed rifles, height 10".*
    35.00   60.00   (45.00)

☐ **Bobbing Bird,** *mantel clock, molded wood product, house with exposed pendulum, height 7½", 30 hour, Lux-Keebler.*
    25.00   40.00   (30.00)

Black Cat

Bobbing Bird

354 / LUX AND KEEBLER

- **Boy Scout Pendulette No. 304,** molded wood product, boy scout signals in front of campfire, height 6¾", 30 hour.
  275.00   325.00   (300.00)

- **Brass Faced No. 19,** made of finely stamped brass, no animation, 30 hour.
  350.00   400.00   (375.00)

- **Bulldog Pendulette No. 31*,** molded wood product, white and black face with blue collar, animated with moving eyes, height 4", 30 hour.
  400.00   500.00   (450.00)
- **As above,** not animated.
  500.00   600.00   (550.00)

- **Bulldog With Bone Pendulette No. 32*,** molded wood product, with animated swinging bone, 30 hour.
  60.00   70.00   (65.00)

- **Bulldog With Kittens No. 33*,** molded wood product, with animated swinging kittens, 30 hour.
  60.00   75.00   (65.00)

- **Bungalow Miniature No. 34*,** molded synthetic wood product, imitation chain and weights, deluxe key wind movement, assorted colors, c. 1931, 30 hour.
  50.00   75.00   (60.00)

- **Bunny And Floral Pendulette,** wall clock, octagon shape, tinted and embossed wood product, floral spray decoration with four rabbits, dial 4", c. 1927, 8 Day.
  125.00   150.00   (135.00)

- **Checkered Borders Pendulette No. 210,** no animation, octagon shape, painted enamel over metal, imitation chains and weights, long pendulum, 30 hour.
  125.00   150.00   (135.00)

- **Circus Clown Pendulette No. 36*,** swinging tie and goo goo eyes, metal, height 8½", c. 1937, 30 hour.
  275.00   325.00   (300.00)

- **Clown With Seals Pendulette No. 303,** molded wood product, height 7", 30 hour.
  200.00   250.00   (215.00)

- **Cocker Spaniel Pendulette No. 336,** molded synthetic wood product, a cocker spaniel overlooks a fence with glass eyes, c. 1940, 30 hour.
  200.00   250.00   (225.00)

- **Country Scene Pendulette No. 37*,** oval shaped metal, blue tinted scene of farm house and covered wagon, pendulum visible through diamond shape hole, height 6¾", 30 hour.
  250.00   300.00   (275.00)

- **Country Scene Wall Pendulette No. 275,** hard enamel metal front ornamental weights and chains, height 3½", c. 1930, 30 hour.
  130.00   150.00   (135.00)

- **Cuckoo Style Bobbing Bird Pendulette,** molded wood, walnut finish, red bird bobs in and out of window, keywind, height 7½", c. 1951, 30 hour.
  25.00   35.00   (27.50)
- **As above,** old style.
  30.00   40.00   (35.00)

- **Cuckoo,** old style pendulette, bird bobbing in and out, molded wood product, height 7", 30 hour, Keebler & Lux.
  30.00   35.00   (32.50)

- **Dog House Pendulette No. 333,** molded wood product, animated metal dog head moving side to side, 30 hour.
  200.00   250.00   (225.00)

- **Dixie Boy Pendulette No. 304,** necktie swings back and forth, eyes roll from side to side, c. 1937, 30 hour.
  325.00   375.00   (350.00)

- **Dutch Mill Wall Pendulette,** hard enamelled delft blue, ornamental weights and chains, height 3¼", c. 1930, 30 hour.
  200.00   250.00   (225.00)

LUX AND KEEBLER / 355

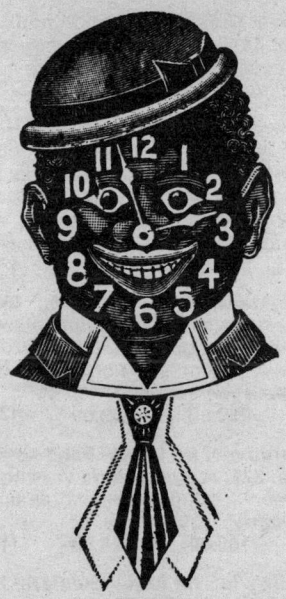

Dixie Boy

Enchanted Cottage

☐ **Dutch Boy And Girl Pendulette No. 40***, *table or wall clock, wood painted in blue, green and turquoise tints, Dutch boy and girl facing each other over an octagon clock on legs, height 9", c. 1940's, 30 hour.*
 75.00 100.00 (90.00)

☐ **Dutch Farm Scene Wall Pendulette No. 305**, *octagon metal front, ornamental weights and chains, height 2¾", c. 1930, 30 hour.*
 100.00 135.00 (120.00)

☐ **Dutch Cottage Bobbing Bird Pendulette No. 380**, *synthetic wood product, red, green, blue, brown on white background, height 7½", c. 1942, 30 hour.*
 65.00 90.00 (75.00)

☐ **Enchanted Forest Pendulette No. 225**, *metal dwarf holding an ax swings back and forth, molded wood product finished in lifelike tones with seven dwarfs, 5¼" x 4", 30 hour, Keebler.*
 100.00 125.00 (115.00)

☐ **Enchanted Cottage No. 380**, *synthetic carved wood, white with tan trim, red or green roof, bobbing bird, height 7½", 30 hour.*
 75.00 100.00 (80.00)

☐ **Fan Dancer Pendulette No. 307**, *fan wiggles back and forth, height 6¼", c. 1937, 30 hour.*
 225.00 275.00 (250.00)

☐ **Fire Chief Petunia Pendulette No. 322**, *brilliant red with green stalk and leaves, 30 hour.*
 115.00 135.00 (120.00)

☐ **Fort Dearborn On Pendulum No. 211**, *molded wood product, height 6", c. 1933, 30 hour, Keebler.*
 200.00 250.00 (225.00)

☐ **Four Post Iron Case Pendulette**, *height 6½", 30 hour.*
 75.00 90.00 (85.00)

☐ **Golfers No. 41***, *made of tin, finely painted green with a golfing scene, exposed pendulum, 30 hour.*
 250.00 300.00 (275.00)

356 / LUX AND KEEBLER

- **Happy Days Pendulette No. 42***, molded wood product, two beer drinkers facing each other over beer barrel, height 7½", 30 hour.
  325.00   375.00   (350.00)

- **Harvest Time Pendulette**, molded and pressed wood product, green background with farm scene at bottom, flowers along both sides and two horns of plenty emptying upwards on the top of the case, height 16½", 30 hour, De Luxe Clock Company (E3-Cover).
  200.00   250.00   (225.00)

- **Jack And Jill Pendulette No. 310**, molded wood product, height 7½"; 30 hour.
  400.00   450.00   (425.00)

- **Kiddy Clock Or ABC Clock Pendulette No. 43***, no animation, c. 1934, 30 hour, Westclox for Keebler.
  275.00   300.00   (285.00)

- **Kitty Kat Pendulette No. 335**, ivory molded synthetic wood, head and paws of cat resting on top of clock, height 7", 30 hour.
  200.00   250.00   (225.00)
- As above, grey.
  200.00   250.00   (225.00)
- As above, orange.
  250.00   300.00   (275.00)

- **Liberty Bell Pendulette No. 385**, molded wood product, replica of the National Liberty Bell in Philadelphia, height 5¾", 30 hour.
  175.00   225.00   (185.00)

- **Little Boy Blue Pendulette No. 43***, molded wood product, various shades of blue, head and neck with animated eyes, height 7¾", 30 hour.
  400.00   450.00   (425.00)

- **Love Birds No. 250**, birds kiss when clock runs, molded wood product, height 6", 30 hour, Keebler.
  75.00   100.00   (85.00)

- **Loyal Order Of Moose Pendulette No. 44***, molded wood products, broken arch top with moose head, height 5⅜", 30 hour.
  250.00   300.00   (275.00)

- **Mary Had A Little Lamb No. 45***, molded wood product, details in five relief, near natural colors of Mary and her lamb with barn, no animation, height 7¾", 30 hour.
  400.00   450.00   (425.00)

- **Nigara Or Horse Coach No. 46***, metal, exposed pendulum, coach and tavern scene finished in brown, green and light blue, no animation, height 7", 30 hour.
  250.00   300.00   (275.00)

- **Petunia "Fire Chief" Pendulette No. 322**, red plastic flower and green stem, bee on pendulum, height 7", 30 hour.
  100.00   125.00   (115.00)

- **Pussy In The Well Pendulette No. 47***, molded wood product, assorted colors, four children looking in a wishing well, height 7¾", 30 hour.
  400.00   450.00   (425.00)

- **Roosevelt In The White House No. 49***, white molded wood product, Roosevelt cameo in dome of White House, no animation, 30 hour.
  200.00   250.00   (225.00)

- **Rudolph The Red Nosed Reindeer No. 302**, cottage front of molded wood, animated, c. 1951, 30 hour.
  80.00   100.00   (90.00)

- **Schmoo Pendulette No. 320**, white, smooth molded plastic, height 7", c. 1951, 30 hour.
  100.00   125.00   (115.00)
- As above, pink.
  100.00   125.00   (115.00)
- As above, blue.
  100.00   125.00   (115.00)
- As above, black.
  150.00   200.00   (115.00)

LUX AND KEEBLER / 357

☐ **Scotty Dog No. 50*,** *black with green collar, molded wood product, red metal tounge moves as clock runs, height 7¼", 30 hour, Lux-Keebler.*
    175.00   225.00   (200.00)

☐ **Stand Clock-Pendulette No. 51*,** *metal base, blue and green carved effect, chains and weights, height 6½", c. 1933, 30 hour.*
    100.00   150.00   (135.00)

☐ **Sunburst Pendulette No. 52*,** *petals around face, metal, various colors, blue, brown and green, height 3", 30 hour.*
    100.00   125.00   (115.00)

☐ **Sunflower Pendulette No. 53*,** *scrolls around face, molded wood product, height 5¾", 30 hour.*
    75.00   100.00   (85.00)

☐ **Sunflower Pendulette No. 329,** *molded wood product, height 6½", 30 hour.*
    150.00   200.00   (175.00)

☐ **Swinging Bird No. 300,** *narrow type, animated bird rocks side to side, feeding babies in nest, cottage with chimney, height 6½", 30 hour.*
    25.00   35.00   (28.00)

☐ **As above,** *No. 301, wide type, height 7".*
    25.00   35.00   (28.00)

☐ **As above,** *No. 326, large type, height 8".*
    25.00   35.00   (28.00)

☐ **Swinging Bird No. 204,** *dove with oak leaf, animated bird faces right, rocks back and forth on pendulum, height 6", 30 hour, Lux/Keebler.*
    25.00   35.00   (30.00)

☐ **As above,** *No. 370, dove and flowers.*
    25.00   35.00   (30.00)

☐ **As above,** *No. 206, six crossed logs.*
    35.00   45.00   (40.00)

☐ **As above,** *No. 207, log cabin.*
    35.00   45.00   (30.00)

☐ **As above,** *No. 240, log cabin with maple leaves.*
    25.00   35.00   (30.00)

☐ **Tree House Mantle No. 223,** *molded wood product, with leaves decorating the sides, bobbing bird animation, exposed pendulum, height 7½", c. 1933, 30 hour.*
    150.00   175.00   (160.00)

☐ **Woody Woodpecker No. 535,** *plastic in various colors, stirrup pendulum, height 7", c. 1959, 30 hour, Westclox for Columbia Time.*
    200.00   250.00   (225.00)

MISCELLANEOUS

☐ **Bakelite Miniature,** *square gilt dial, assorted red, blue and green case with floral decoration, height 2½", c. 1927, 30 hour.*
    15.00   25.00   (20.00)

☐ **Bank,** *metal, brown crackle finish, two slots for dimes and quarters, key to open, height 4½", 30 hour.*
    50.00   75.00   (60.00)

☐ **Baseball Pendulum Clock No. 18*,** *metal ball supported by two wood posts, on rectangular base, height 9½", c. 1940, 30 hour.*
    50.00   75.00   (55.00)

☐ **Bunny On Fence Clock,** *tinted and enameled synthetic wood product, rustic fence with flowers and rabbit, height 7", c. 1927, 30 hour.*
    125.00   150.00   (135.00)

☐ **Cat,** *molded wood product, height 5½", 30 hour.*
    65.00   75.00   (70.00)

☐ **Camel,** *molded wood product, kneeling with an Arabian chair can on his back, height 2", 30 hour.*
    60.00   80.00   (70.00)

☐ **Chrome,** *flat base with two curved arms holding round clock, dial 3", 30 hour.*
    35.00   50.00   (40.00)

☐ **Crackle Boudoir,** *crackle finish metal front in six assorted colors, height 4", c. 1928, 30 hour.*
    10.00   25.00   (15.00)

358 / LUX AND KEEBLER

- **Clown,** *molded wood product, finished in bright colors, clown is smiling with hands at his chest, height 8", 30 hour.*
  75.00   100.00   (80.00)

- **Cut Glass,** *square cut patter, round, footed, height 3", 30 hour.*
  50.00   75.00   (60.00)

- **Elephant,** *gold plated metal, with rider, height 9½", c. 1933, 30 hour.*
  125.00   150.00   (130.00)

- **Elephant Boudoir Clock,** *synthetic marble, waxed finish, round clock supports front legs of elephant, height 7½", c. 1928, 30 hour.*
  100.00   125.00   (110.00)

- **Empire State Building,** *molded and carved elf's push wheel barrow, lighted windows, height 11", c. 1933, 30 hour.*
  100.00   125.00   (110.00)

- **Enamel Miniature,** *octagon shape, tinted floral spray, mahogany frame, silver embossed rim, dial 2½", c. 1927, 30 hour.*
  40.00   60.00   (45.00)

- **Flower Stand,** *molded wood product, pendulum mounted on flower stem, height 2", 30 hour.*
  40.00   60.00   (50.00)

- **Fountain Pen And Desk Set,** *octagonal shape with pencil rest, jade plastic, height 8", c. 1928, 30 hour.*
  50.00   70.00   (60.00)

- **Hall Clock Miniature,** *gilt dial with visible pendulum, made in mahogany, walnut, natural and red, blue, green, brown and black crackle finish, height 12½", c. 1928, 30 hour.*
  100.00   125.00   (110.00)

- **Homestead,** *molded synthetic wood product, tan and brown toned English cottage with green lawn and garden, height 9¾", c. 1927, 30 hour.*
  35.00   45.00   (40.00)

- **Lute Player Pendant Clock,** *bright red finish on composition white metal, octagonal upper clock case, c. 1933, 30 hour.*
  70.00   80.00   (75.00)

- **Monk,** *molded wood product, hatless with hands holding clock, height 6¼", 30 hour.*
  60.00   80.00   (70.00)

- **Owl,** *molded wood product, brown owl sitting on a branch with clock in stomach, height 5½", 30 hour.*
  75.00   100.00   (95.00)

- **Pedestal Pendulum Clock,** *dome shape, pedestal base, height 6½", c. 1928, 30 hour.*
  75.00   100.00   (95.00)

- **Pirate,** *cast metal case, fancy dial, pirate holding jewels facing right toward treasure chest, width 4½", c. 1937.*
  50.00   75.00   (60.00)

- **Rotary Calendar Alarm,** *molded plastic case, height, 5½", c. 1941, 30 hour.*
  45.00   65.00   (55.00)

- **Rotary Electric Tape Clock,** *height 5", c. 1941.*
  35.00   55.00   (45.00)

- **Rotary Mystery Tape Clock,** *metal drum with AM and PM on a circular tape, blue, red and black, height 5", c. 1941, 30 hour.*
  35.00   55.00   (45.00)

Pirate

MONARCH CALENDAR CLOCK COMPANY / 359

Watermill

☐ **Tambour Miniature,** *assorted blue, pink and white gilt, crackled finish, wood case shaped like Napeolon's hat, dial 2", 30 hour.*
15.00   25.00   (20.00)

☐ **Telephone,** *iron or pot metal, height 4", 30 hour.*
40.00   65.00   (45.00)

☐ **Telephone,** *white plastic, dial 2", 30 hour.*
40.00   60.00   (50.00)

☐ **Watch Holder,** *iron, 4¼" x 4⅛".*
25.00   35.00   (30.00)

☐ **Watermill DeLuxe,** *synthetic molded wood, reproduction of a country village mill, height 9¼", c. 1933, 30 hour.*
70.00   90.00   (80.00)

☐ **Windmill,** *molded wood product, in natural colors, height 10½", c. 1933, 1 Day.*
40.00   60.00   (50.00)
☐ **As above,** *8 Day.*
60.00   80.00   (65.00)
☐ **As above,** *8 Day, alarm.*
80.00   100.00   (90.00)

☐ **World Time Clock,** *two tone crackle finish, metal front, gold dial, height 4", c. 1928, 30 hour.*
25.00   35.00   (30.00)

MACOMB CALENDAR COMPANY

CALENDAR

☐ **Shelf Model,** *spring, 30" x 15½", time dial 6", moon phase dial 6½", 8 Day, strike (M323-105).*
2250.00   2700.00   (2750.00)

☐ **Shelf Model,** *spring, 30" x 15½", time dial 6", moon phase dial 6½", 8 Day, strike (M325-105).*
2350.00   2900.00   (3000.00)

☐ **Wall Model,** *spring, 30" x 14½", time dial 6", moon phase dial 6½", 8 Day, strike, (M324-105).*
2500.00   3000.00   (2700.00)

G. MARANVILLE

CALENDAR

☐ **Octagon Drop Wall,** *spring, 24" x 17", dial 11½", 8 Day, strike (M417-130).*
700.00   800.00   (750.00)

☐ **Octagon Drop Wall,** *spring, 23½" x 16¼", dial 11", 8 Day, strike (M420-131).*
750.00   850.00   (800.00)

☐ **Round Drop Wall,** *weight, 34" x 16", dial 11", 8 Day (M421-132).*
1500.00   1700.00   (1600.00)

MONARCH CALENDAR CLOCK COMPANY

CALENDAR

☐ **Shelf Clock,** *spring, made by New Haven Clock Co., 32" x 17½", dials 7", 8 Day, strike (M383-121).*
900.00   1100.00   (1100.00)

MOZART, BEACH AND HUBBELL

CALENDAR

☐ **Wall Clock,** 25" x 13", time with seconds bit 7", day of week dial 2¾", month and date dial 5¼", 1 year (M150-54).
    4250.00   5250.00   (5500.00)

MUELLER AND SON

CHARACTER

☐ **Guardian,** *cast iron front, height 15½", 8 Day, strike (E1-15).*
    175.00   200.00   (187.00)

Scotchman

Guardian

Shepherd Children

Old Man

☐ **Old Man,** *cast iron front, visible pendulum, height 13", 1 Day, strike (E1-10).*
    140.00   165.00   (152.00)

☐ **Scotchman,** *cast iron front, visible pendulum, height 18", 8 Day, strike (E1-10).*
    195.00   225.00   (210.00)

☐ **Shepherd Children,** *cast iron front, visible pendulum, height 17½", 8 Day, strike (E1-10).*
    160.00   185.00   (172.00)

ETRUSCAN

- **Doric,** *iron, height 14½", 1 Day, strike.*
  115.00   120.00   (117.50)

- **Etruscan,** *solid cast iron, height 18", 8 Day, strike (E1-14).*
  175.00   200.00   (187.00)

- **Etruscan,** *solid cast iron, height 18½", 8 Day, strike (E1-11).*
  165.00   190.00   (178.00)

- **Grisi,** *iron, height 18", 8 Day, strike.*
  179.00   190.00   (189.50)

- **Lattice,** *iron, height 18½", strike.*
  150.00   200.00   (175.00)

- **Pompeii,** *solid cast iron, height 18½", 8 Day, strike (E1-10).*
  165.00   190.00   (178.00)

- **Temple,** *solid cast iron, visible pendulum, height 18¾", 1 Day, strike (E1-13).*
  125.00   150.00   (137.00)
- **As above,** *8 Day, strike.*
  175.00   200.00   (187.00)

Etruscan

Etruscan

Grisi

Lattice

Washington

Temple

- **Washington,** iron, height 20", 8 Day, strike.
  150.00   215.00   (182.00)
- **As above,** height 17", 1 Day, strike.
  135.00   150.00   (142.00)

FLORA AND FAUNA

- **Arbor,** cast iron fronts, visible pendulum, height 17½", 1 Day, strike (E1-13).
  125.00   150.00   (137.00)
- **As above,** height 20", 8 Day, strike.
  175.00   200.00   (187.00)

- **Bouquet,** cast iron front, visible pendulum, height 16", 1 Day, strike (E1-15).
  125.00   150.00   (137.00)
- **As above,** height 19", 8 Day, strike.
  175.00   200.00   (187.00)

- **Cupid,** iron front, visible pendulum, three cherubs, floral pattern, height 18½", 8 Day, strike (E1-15).
  145.00   170.00   (159.00)
- **As above,** height 16", 8 Day, strike.
  135.00   160.00   (148.00)
- **As above,** height 16", 1 Day, strike.
  110.00   135.00   (122.50)

- **Doric,** cast iron front, visible pendulum, height 14½", 1 Day, strike (E1-14).
  95.00   115.00   (105.00)

- **Dragon,** cast iron front, visible pendulum, height 15½", 1 Day, strike (E1-15).
  110.00   135.00   (122.00)

Arbor

Renaissance

Ruin

☐ **Eagle,** cast iron front, visible pendulum, height 15", 1 Day, strike (E1-15).
    220.00   250.00   (235.00)

☐ **Eagle,** cast iron front, visible pendulum, height 18½", 8 Day, strike (E1-11).
    220.00   250.00   (235.00)

☐ **Fox And Hare,** cast iron front, visible pendulum, height 19¾", 8 Day, strike (E1-11).
    195.00   225.00   (210.00)

☐ **Grisi,** cast iron front, visible pendulum, height 16½", 1 Day, strike (E1-15).
    150.00   175.00   (162.00)
☐ **As above,** height 18", 8 Day, strike.
    175.00   200.00   (187.00)

☐ **Juno,** cast iron front, visible pendulum, height 16½", 1 Day, strike (E1-14).
    150.00   175.00   (162.00)
☐ **As above,** height 19½", 8 Day, strike.
    195.00   225.00   (210.00)

☐ **Lattice,** cast iron front, visible pendulum, height 18½", 1 Day, strike (E1-12).
    125.00   150.00   (137.00)
☐ **As above,** 8 Day, strike.
    175.00   200.00   (188.00)

☐ **Lion Head,** cast iron front, visible pendulum, height 15", 1 Day, strike (E1-11).
    125.00   150.00   (135.00)

☐ **Renaissance,** cast iron front, visible pendulum, height 16", 1 Day, strike (E1-10).
    160.00   185.00   (172.00)

364 / MUELLER AND SON

☐ **Ruin,** *cast iron front, floral pattern, height 12½", 8 Day, strike (E1-10).*
    140.00   165.00   (153.00)

☐ **Washington,** *cast iron front, visible pendulum, height 17", 1 Day, strike (E1-12).*
    125.00   150.00   (137.50)

☐ **As above,** *height 20", 8 Day, strike.*
    185.00   215.00   (200.00)

FLORAL PAINTED

☐ **Franklin,** *cast iron front, extra pearl, height 16", 1 Day, strike (E1-15).*
    80.00   100.00   (90.00)

Urn

Franklin

Wide Awake

☐ **Rococo,** *cast iron front, height 14½", 8 Day, strike (E1-10).*
    135.00   160.00   (122.50)

☐ **Urn,** *cast iron front, height 13", 1 Day, strike (E1-10).*
    110.00   135.00   (122.15)

☐ **Wide Awake,** *large, cast iron front, height 16¼", 1 Day, strike (E1-11).*
    100.00   120.00   (110.00)

☐ **Wide Awake,** *small, cast iron front, height 11", 1 Day, strike (E1-15).*
    95.00   105.00   (100.00)

Rococo

GOTHIC

☐ **Evangelist,** *gothic cast iron front, height 17", 1 Day, strike.*
　　150.00　　175.00　　(162.00)

Gilt Gothic

Peter And Paul

Oak Leaf

Vine Gothic

☐ **Evangelist,** *gothic cast iron front, height 20", 8 Day, strike (E1-11).*
　　195.00　　225.00　　(210.00)

☐ **Gilt Gothic,** *cast iron front, height 16½", 1 Day, strike.*
　　125.00　　150.00　　(137.00)

☐ **Gilt Gothic,** *cast iron front, height 19½", 8 Day, strike (E1-9).*
　　175.00　　200.00　　(187.50)

☐ **Gothic,** *cast iron front, height 16¼", 1 Day, strike.*
　　125.00　　150.00　　(137.00)

366 / MUELLER AND SON

- **Gothic,** cast iron front, height 18½", 8 Day, strike (E1-11).
  175.00   200.00   (187.50)
- **Oak Leaf,** cast iron front, height 20", 8 Day, strike (E1-12).
  150.00   175.00   (167.00)
- **Opera,** gothic cast iron front, height 18", 8 Day, strike (E1-12).
  175.00   200.00   (188.00)
- **Peter And Paul,** gothic cast iron front, height 20", 8 Day, strike (E1-12).
  195.00   225.00   (210.00)
- **Vine Gothic,** cast iron front, height 16½", 1 Day, strike (E1-9).
  105.00   125.00   (115.00)

IRON AND BRONZE

- **Birds,** bronze, height 21", 8 Day, strike.
  180.00   225.00   (202.50)
- **Dragon,** bronze, height 15½", 1 Day, strike.
  120.00   135.00   (127.00)

Dragon

Eagle

- **Eagle,** bronze, height 18½", 8 Day, strike.
  205.00   250.00   (227.00)
- **Eagle,** iron, height 15", 1 Day, strike.
  205.00   250.00   (250.00)
- **Fox And Hare,** bronze, height 19¾", 8 Day, strike.
  210.00   225.00   (217.00)

Birds

☐ **Juno,** *bronze, height 19½", 8 Day, strike.*
210.00   225.00   (217.00)
☐ **As above,** *height 16½", 1 Day, strike.*
160.00   175.00   (167.00)
☐ **Lion Head,** *bronze, height 15", 1 Day, strike.*
135.00   150.00   (143.00)

Lion Head

NOVELTY/ANIMATED

☐ **Continental,** *iron, winker, height 16", 1 Day (E1-9).*
800.00   900.00   (850.00)

☐ **Organ Grinder,** *iron, winker, height 17½", 1 Day (E1-9).*
850.00   950.00   (900.00)

☐ **Sambo,** *iron, winker, height 16", 1 Day (E1-9).*
800.00   900.00   (850.00)

☐ **Topsey,** *iron, winker, height 16", 1 Day (E1-9).*
800.00   900.00   (850.00)

Fox And Hare

Juno

Continental

368 / MUELLER AND SON

Topsey

Borne

Parlor

Webster

PARLOR

☐ **Borne,** *iron parlor, height 10", 8 Day, strike (E1-12).*
    110.00   135.00   (122.50

☐ **Fluted Column,** *iron parlor, height 16", 8 Day, strike (E1-14).*
    125.00   150.00   (137.00)

☐ **Parlor,** *iron, black, marbleized and ornamental, height 12" to 14", 1 Day, strike (E1-12).*
    80.00   100.00   (90.00)

☐ **Parlor,** *iron, plain or ornamented, height 10", 8 Day, strike (E1-15).*
    80.00   100.00   (90.00)

☐ **Parlor,** *iron, plain or ornamented, height 10½", 8 Day, strike (E1-12).*
    70.00   95.00   (82.00)

☐ **Parlor,** *iron, plain, or ornamented, height 10½", 8 Day, strike (E1-15).*
    80.00   100.00   (90.00)

☐ **Parlor,** *iron, plain or ornamented, height 10½", 8 Day, strike (E1-15).*
    85.00   105.00   (95.00)

☐ **Webster,** *iron parlor, visible pendulum, height 15", 8 Day, strike (E1-13).*
    105.00   125.00   (115.00)

STATUE

☐ **Amor,** *bronze front, height 20", 8 Day, strike (E1-11).*
195.00   225.00   (210.00)

☐ **Armorer,** *bronze front, height 18", 8 Day, strike (E1-15).*
145.00   170.00   (157.00)

☐ **Boy And Dog,** *bronze front, lever, height 11", 1 Day, strike (E1-10).*
60.00   75.00   (67.00)

Boy And Dog

Amor

Dolphin

☐ **Chase And Figure,** *bronze front, height 21", 8 Day, strike (E1-13).*
175.00   200.00   (187.00)

☐ **Dolphin,** *bronze front, height 20", 8 Day, strike (E1-13).*
195.00   225.00   (210.00)

☐ **Drama,** *bronze front, height 16", 1 Day, strike (E1-12).*
125.00   150.00   (137.00)
☐ **As above,** *8 Day, strike.*
175.00   200.00   (187.00)

☐ **Drummer,** *bronze front, height 18½", 8 Day, strike (E1-15).*
150.00   175.00   (162.00)

Armorer

370 / MUELLER AND SON

Drummer

Evangeline

French

Gleaner

☐ **Gleaner,** *bronze front, height 18½", 8 Day, strike (E1-14).*
　　175.00　　200.00　　(187.00)

☐ **Globe,** *bronze front, height 19½", 8 Day, strike (E1-11).*
　　195.00　　225.00　　(210.00)

☐ **Highlander,** *bronze front, height 19½", 8 Day, strike (E1-14).*
　　175.00　　200.00　　(187.00)

☐ **Evangeline,** *bronze front, height 19", 8 Day, strike (E1-9).*
　　155.00　　180.00　　(167.00)

☐ **Fisher Boy And Dog,** *bronze front, height 18", 8 Day, strike (E1-14).*
　　140.00　　165.00　　(152.00)

☐ **French,** *bronze front, height 20", 8 Day, strike (E1-9).*
　　155.00　　180.00　　(167.00)

☐ **Horse,** *bronze front, height 21", 8 Day, strike (E1-14).*
        155.00   180.00   (167.00)

☐ **Horse,** *(small) bronze front, height 14", 8 Day, strike (E1-9).*
        110.00   135.00   (122.50)

☐ **Lady Lever,** *bronze front, height 13", 1 Day (E1-15).*
        110.00   135.00   (122.50)

Lady Lever

Highlander

Louis XV

Horse

☐ **Louis XV,** *bronze front, height 18", 8 Day, strike (E1-13).*
        175.00   200.00   (187.00)

☐ **Lovers,** *bronze front, height 17", 8 Day, strike (E1-12).*
        175.00   200.00   (187.00)

☐ **Mermaid,** *bronze front, height 14¾", 1 Day (E1-14).*
        105.00   130.00   (117.00)

☐ **Mountaineer,** *bronze front, height 20", 8 Day, strike (E1-14).*
        175.00   200.00   (187.00)

372 / MUELLER AND SON

Mermaid

Mountaineer

☐ **Mustang,** *bronze front, height 15",
8 Day, strike (E1-12).*
    175.00   200.00   (187.00)

☐ **Neptune,** *bronze front, height 19",
8 Day, strike (E1-13).*
    175.00   200.00   (187.00)

☐ **Patchen,** *bronze front, height 19",
8 Day, strike (E1-13).*
    175.00   200.00   (187.00)

☐ **Pleasant Girl,** *bronze front, height 19", 8 Day, strike (E1-9).*
    155.00   180.00   (167.00)

☐ **Reaper,** *bronze front, height 18½", 8 Day, strike (E1-11).*
    150.00   175.00   (160.00)

Patchen

Pleasant Girl

MUELLER AND SON / 373

- **Savoyard,** *bronze front, height 18½", 8 Day, strike (E1-10).*
  140.00   165.00   (152.00)

- **Setter,** *bronze front, height 17", 8 Day, strike (E1-10).*
  125.00   150.00   (137.00)

- **Trophy,** *bronze front, height 18½", 8 Day, strike (E1-10).*
  195.00   225.00   (210.00)

Trophy

Savoyard

Vinter

- **Vintner,** *bronze front, height 19", 8 Day, strike (E1-15).*
  150.00   175.00   (162.00)

- **Wine Drinker,** *bronze front, height 20", 8 Day, strike (E1-14).*
  175.00   200.00   (187.00)

Setter

NICHOLAS MULLER'S SONS

ALARM/FANCY

☐ **Neptune,** *nickel and bronze, height 9", c. 1888, 8 Day, spring.*
    200.00   225.00   (215.00)
☐ **As above,** *simple calendar.*
    300.00   350.00   (325.00)
☐ **As above,** *with alarm.*
    225.00   250.00   (235.00)

☐ **Zulu,** *bronze with imitation marble base, height 7½", dial 4", c. 1888, 1 Day, spring (E-65).*
    85.00   110.00   (90.00)
☐ **As above,** *simple calendar.*
    125.00   150.00   (135.00)
☐ **As above,** *with alarm.*
    110.00   135.00   (125.00)

Neptune

Zulu

CABINET

☐ **Cabinet,** *imitation marble visible escapement, French sash, height 14½", c. 1888, 8 Day, spring.*
    180.00   210.00   (200.00)
☐ **As above,** *bronze.*
    200.00   225.00   (215.00)

Cabinet

MANTLE/BRONZE

☐ **Antique,** *cast iron or bronze, with honeycomb pattern with dragon, snake and leaves, porcelain dial and French sash, height 11¼". c. 1888, 8 Day, spring (E3-62).*
    200.00   240.00   (225.00)

☐ **Augar,** *with seated figure, cast bronze case with ornate birds, flowers and putti, height 10½", c. 1886, 8 Day, spring (E3-65).*
    200.00   230.00   (215.00)
☐ **As above,** *without top figure.*
    150.00   180.00   (160.00)

NICHOLAS MULLER'S SONS / 375

☐ **Bee,** *cast bronze case with bees and lizards, height 11½", c. 1888, 8 Day, spring (E3-65).*
225.00   250.00   (230.00)

☐ **Chapel,** *cast bronze, black or white dial, height 13", c. 1884, 8 Day, spring (E3-63).*
150.00   175.00   (160.00)

Bee

Antique

Chapel

Augar

☐ **Dexter,** *with horse figural on top, cast bronze, black or white American dial, height 19¼", c. 1880, 8 Day, spring (E3-65).*
165.00   185.00   (170.00)

☐ **Elephant,** *with indian on horse, cast bronze with two elephant heads and foliage decoration, height 10½", c. 1887, 8 Day, spring (E3-64).*
150.00   185.00   (160.00)

☐ **As above,** *without top figure.*
100.00   135.00   (120.00)

☐ **As above,** *with brass finish.*
190.00   225.00   (200.00)

Dexter

Alexandria

Elephant

Athens

Cairo

MANTLE/MARBLE

☐ **Alexandria,** *imitation marble, visible escapement, porcelain dial, French sash, 11½", c. 1886, 8 Day, spring (E3-63).*
      150.00   175.00   (160.00)

☐ **Athens,** *imitation marble, black, height 10½", c. 1887, 8 Day (E3-63).*
      125.00   150.00   (135.00)

Carthage

Nubia

Corinth

Crete

- **Cairo,** *imitation marble, French sash and dial, height 12", c. 1888, 8 Day, spring (E3-63).*
  125.00   150.00   (135.00)

- **Carthage,** *imitation marble, porcelain dial, French sash, height 12", c. 1887, 8 Day, spring (E3-62).*
  200.00   225.00   (210.00)

- **Corinth,** *imitation marble, French sash and dial, height 11½", c. 1888, 8 Day, spring (E3-62).*
  150.00   175.00   (165.00)

- **Crete,** *marble, black, French sash and dial, width 18", c. 1887, 8 Day, spring (E3-62).*
  160.00   185.00   (170.00)

- **Nubia,** *imitation marble, porcelain dial, French sash, height 12", c. 1885, 8 Day, spring (E3-63).*
  125.00   150.00   (130.00)

Pallas

378 / NICHOLAS MULLER'S SONS

Pyramid

Sparta

Royal

Soudan

- [ ] **Pallas**, *bronze metal case, imitation marble, height 11¾", c. 1888, 8 Day, spring (E3-63).*
  200.00   225.00   (215.00)
- [ ] **As above,** *with plush body.*
  225.00   250.00   (230.00)
- [ ] **Pyramid,** *imitation marble, French sash and dial, height 13½", c. 1888, 8 Day (E3-63).*
  125.00   150.00   (135.00)

- [ ] **Royal,** *cast decorated bronze case, imitation marble body, height 12½", c. 1888, 8 Day, spring.*
  200.00   225.00   (210.00)
- [ ] **As above,** *with plush body.*
  225.00   250.00   (235.00)
- [ ] **Sparta,** *imitation marble, porcelain dial, French sash, height 11", c. 1888, 8 Day, spring (E3-63).*
  150.00   175.00   (165.00)
- [ ] **Soudan,** *imitation marble case, porcelain dial, French sash, height 15", c. 1888, 8 Day, spring (E3-62).*
  165.00   190.00   (175.00)
- [ ] **Suez,** *imitation marble, height 11", c. 1887, 8 Day, spring (E3-62).*
  150.00   175.00   (160.00)

☐ **Syria,** *imitation, marble, black and red, porcelain dial, French sash, height 11", c. 1887, 8 Day, spring (E3-63).*
        130.00   165.00   (140.00)

☐ **Thebes,** *imitation marble, visible escapement, porcelain dial, French sash, width 18", c. 1888, 8 Day, spring (E3-62).*
        165.00   190.00   (170.00)

☐ **Tunis,** *imitation marble, red and black, height 10¾", c. 1888, 8 Day, spring (E3-62).*
        175.00   200.00   (180.00)

NOVELTY

☐ **Autumn,** *hammered plaque on plush panel, hangs or stands, height 10", c. 1888, 1 Day, spring (E3-65).*
        85.00   110.00   (95.00)

☐ **Cherub,** *five point plush star, diameter 9", c. 1886, 1 Day, spring (E3-65).*
        100.00   125.00   (115.00)

☐ **Wheelbarrow,** *small movement, height 6½", c. 1885, 1 Day, spring (E3-64).*
        100.00   125.00   (115.00)

Cherub

Wheelbarrow

Autumn

OFFICE/INK

☐ **Jupiter,** *nickel and bronze, cut glass ink bottles, height 8½", c. 1885, 1 Day, spring (E3-65).*
        175.00   200.00   (180.00)
☐ **As above,** *with simple calendar.*
        225.00   250.00   (230.00)

☐ **Mars,** *with call bell, bronze, cut glass ink bottles, height 10", c. 1886, 1 Day, spring (E3-64).*
        160.00   180.00   (175.00)
☐ **As above,** *with simple calendar.*
        250.00   275.00   (260.00)
☐ **As above,** *with alarm.*
        180.00   200.00   (190.00)

☐ **Phantom,** *bronze thermometer clock, height 10", c. 1885, 1 Day, spring.*
        150.00   175.00   (160.00)

380 / NATIONAL CALENDAR CLOCK COMPANY

Jupiter

☐ **Vesta,** *with call bell, calendar inkstand, height 10", c. 1885, 1 Day, spring (E3-64).*
    225.00   250.00   (230.00)
☐ **As above,** *with simple calendar.*
    225.00   250.00   (230.00)

STATUE

☐ **Harvest,** *with visible escapement, porcelain dial, French sash, height 17", c. 1887, 8 Day, spring (E3-65).*
    350.00   400.00   (375.00)

☐ **Pandora,** *brass or bronze finish, porcelain dial and French sash, height 12½", c. 1887, 8 Day, spring (E3-65).*
    325.00   350.00   (335.00)

Mars

Harvest

☐ **Uranus,** *nickel and bronze, cut glass ink bottles, height 6½", c. 1887, 1 Day, spring (E3-65).*
    180.00   200.00   (190.00)
☐ **As above,** *with simple calendar.*
    225.00   250.00   (235.00)

NATIONAL CALENDAR CLOCK COMPANY

CALENDAR

☐ **Column Shelf,** *spring, dials 7", 8 Day, strike, simple calendar (M381-120).*
    575.00   725.00   (650.00)

☐ **Fashion Styled Shelf,** *spring, dials 7", 8 Day, strike, simple calendar (M375-119).*
    1300.00   1475.00   (1385.00)

☐ **O.G.,** *spring, cathedral gong, 26" x 15½", dials 7", 8 Day, strike, simple calendar (M380-120).*
    525.00   675.00   (600.00)

NEW HAVEN CLOCK COMPANY

Hiram Camp was the president of the New Haven Clock Company during the time it was reputed to be one of the largest American clock manufacturing dealers. They produced a very wide range of clocks, scorning solely American models and traditional designs.

The New Haven Company managed to purchase the bankrupt Jerome Clock Company after the ill-fated Terry, Barnum, and Jerome partnership dissolved. Before this time New Haven had only produced movements; now they had the facilities necessary to manufacture whole clocks. From the existing records of the Company's sales performance, it seems they had some difficulty in turning a profit. Colleagues suggested that this was due to the tremendous variety New Haven offered rather than any lack of quality or endurance as far as the reputation of the company was concerned.

Like so many other clock companies of the times, New Haven put out a cheap pocket watch of the non-jeweled variety, as a means of staying afloat in troubled financial waters. Early in the 20th century they added wristwatches to their inventory.

The New Haven Clock Company lasted until well into the mid 1960's, when the entire plant was sold at a public auction.

ALARM

☐ **Bullfight,** *nickel, dial 4", c. 1900, 1 Day, alarm (E2-127).*
      175.00   200.00   (187.00)

☐ **Mandolin,** *nickel, dial 4", c. 1900, 1 Day, alarm (E2-127).*
      150.00   175.00   (162.00)

☐ **Pet,** *nickel, dial 4", c. 1900, 1 Day (E2-127).*
      195.00   225.00   (210.00)

☐ **Puff,** *nickel, dial 4", c. 1900, 1 Day (E2-127).*
      175.00   200.00   (187.00)

☐ **Shaver,** *nickel, dial 4", c. 1900, 1 Day, alarm (E2-127).*
      175.00   200.00   (187.00)

Pet

ALARM/FANCY

☐ **Herald,** *wood case, nickel or brass front, height 6½", dial 4", c. 1900, 1 Day, alarm (E2-111).*
      45.00   65.00   (55.00)

Little Duke

382 / NEW HAVEN CLOCK COMPANY

☐ **Little Duke,** *height 6¼", c. 1890, 1 Day (E2-88).*
  80.00   90.00   (85.00)
☐ **As above,** *1 Day, alarm.*
  90.00   110.00   (100.00)

ALARM/ROUND

☐ **Acorn,** *dial 2½", c. 1890, 1 Day (E2-88).*
  35.00   45.00   (40.00)
☐ **As above,** *1 Day, alarm.*
  40.00   50.00   (45.00)
☐ **Beacon,** *dial 4", c. 1890, 1 Day, alarm (E2-88).*
  35.00   45.00   (40.00)
☐ **Champion,** *seamless case 4½", dial 4", c. 1890, 1 Day, alarm (E2-88).*
  25.00   35.00   (30.00)
☐ **Elfin,** *nickel, plain or fancy dial 6", c. 1890, 1 Day, alarm (E2-88).*
  30.00   40.00   (35.00)
☐ **As above,** *1 Day, strike.*
  25.00   35.00   (30.00)
☐ **Flash,** *luminous dial 4", c. 1890 1 Day (E2-88).*
  25.00   35.00   (30.00)
☐ **As above,** *1 Day, alarm.*
  25.00   35.00   (30.00)
☐ **The Fly,** *nickel, dial 4", c. 1890, 1 Day (E2-88).*
  20.00   30.00   (25.00)
☐ **As above,** *1 Day, alarm.*
  25.00   35.00   (30.00)
☐ **Globe Calendar,** *height 6", dial 4", c. 1890, 1 Day, calendar (E2-88).*
  70.00   90.00   (80.00)
☐ **Kelpie,** *height 7", dial 4½", c. 1890, 1 Day, strike (E2-88).*
  30.00   40.00   (35.00)
☐ **Sprite,** *nickel, dial 4½", c. 1890, 1 Day, alarm (E2-88).*
  35.00   45.00   (40.00)
☐ **As above,** *1 Day, alarm, calendar.*
  60.00   85.00   (72.50)
☐ **Start,** *nickel, dial 4", c. 1890, 1 Day, alarm (E2-88).*
  25.00   35.00   (30.00)

Beacon

☐ **Sting,** *dial 2", c. 1890, 1 Day (E2-88).*
  35.00   45.00   (40.00)
☐ **Sting Alarm,** *nickel, or gilt, dial 2", c. 1890, 1 Day, alarm (E2-88).*
  40.00   50.00   (45.00)
☐ **Sting Repeating Strike,** *nickel, dial 2", 1 Day*
  195.00   220.00   (207.00)
☐ **Tattoo Alarm Luminous,** *international alarm movement, seamless case 4½", black dial 4", c. 1890, 1 Day, alarm (E2-88).*
  25.00   35.00   (30.00)
☐ **Tattoo,** *intermittent alarm, dial 4½", c. 1890, 1 Day, alarm (E2-88).*
  35.00   45.00   (40.00)
☐ **The Beacon,** *nickel or enamel, 6½" x 4¼", dial 4", c. 1890, 1 Day (E2-88).*
  25.00   35.00   (30.00)
☐ **As above,** *1 Day, calendar.*
  65.00   80.00   (72.00)
☐ **As above,** *1 Day, alarm.*
  60.00   75.00   (67.00)
☐ **As above,** *1 Day, alarm, calendar.*
  70.00   85.00   (77.00)

NEW HAVEN CLOCK COMPANY / 383

Tocsin

☐ **Tocsin,** *nickel, dial 4½", c. 1900, 1 Day, alarm (E1-44).*
20.00   30.00   (25.00)

AUTOMOBILE CLOCK

☐ **Cowl-NH,** *most accurate keywinding cowl clock made, black and nickel case, dial 2¼", 8 Day.*
30.00   50.00   (40.00)

☐ **Frisco 1,** *stem wind, matching screw, winding stem concealed, dial 2½", 1 Day.*
25.00   30.00   (27.50)

☐ **Frisco Cowl 2,** *stem wind, concealed winding stem, dial 2½", 1 Day.*
25.00   30.00   (27.50)

BANJO

☐ **Willis No. 2,** *mahogany, porcelain or silver dial, 17¾" x 5", c. 1917, 8 Day (E1-173).*
115.00   140.00   (127.00)

CABINET

☐ **Albatross,** *richly modeled, cast brass frame, panels of Chelsea tiles, cathedral gong, height 12", breadth 9", dial 4½", c. 1900, 8 Day, strike (E2-91).*
195.00   220.00   (207.00)

☐ **Amphion,** *oak, cathedral gong, height 18½", dial 5", c. 1900, 8 Day, strike (E2-91).*
140.00   165.00   (152.00)

☐ **Angela,** *oak, richly ornamented with cast brass trimmings, in antique finish, cathedral gong, height 21¾", dial 4½", c. 1900, 8 Day, strike (E2-93).*
270.00   300.00   (285.00)

☐ **Anita,** *mahogany, richly ornamented with cast brass trimmings, in antique finish, height 16", dial 4", c. 1900, 15 Day, strike (E2-93).*
195.00   220.00   (207.00)

☐ **Arab,** *antique oak, ivorized dial, height 18½", dial 4", c. 1900, 15 Day, strike (E2-93).*
220.00   250.00   (235.00)

Albatross

384 / NEW HAVEN CLOCK COMPANY

Amphion

Angela

☐ **Argyle Time,** *wood, height 13", c. 1894, 1 Day (E2-125).*
　　115.00　　135.00　　(137.00)

☐ **Argyle,** *wood, height 17", c. 1894, 1 Day, strike (E2-125).*
　　115.00　　135.00　　(137.00)

☐ **As above,** *8 Day, strike.*
　　140.00　　165.00　　(187.00)

☐ **Arrow,** *walnut, brass trimmings, height 16¼", dial 5", c. 1900, 8 Day, strike (E2-92).*
　　130.00　　150.00　　(152.00)

☐ **Aurania,** *antique oak, heavily gilt ornaments, cathedral gong, height 19¼", dial 5", c. 1900, 8 Day, strike (E2-92).*
　　150.00　　175.00　　(172.00)

☐ **As above,** *walnut.*
　　175.00　　200.00　　(197.50)

☐ **Bahama,** *wood, height 12", silver dial 0½", c. 1094, 8 Day, strike (E2-125).*
　　75.00　　95.00　　(90.00)

☐ **Banshee,** *cherry, brass ornaments, height 13½", dial 5", c. 1900, 1 Day, strike, alarm (E2-92).*
　　155.00　　180.00　　(177.00)

☐ **Bermuda,** *oak, height 12", dial 4", c. 1894, 8 Day, strike (E2-124).*
　　80.00　　100.00　　(95.00)

☐ **Cabinet No. 2,** *mahogany, height 17½", dial 5", c. 1900, 8 Day, strike (E2-92).*
　　150.00　　175.00　　(177.00)

☐ **Caliban,** *oak, cathedral gong, 14¾" x 11", white, gilt or ivorine dial 6", c. 1910, 8 Day, strike (E2-90).*
　　120.00　　145.00　　(142.50)

☐ **Cato,** *polished oak, 15" x 12", c. 1900 (E2-128).*
　　110.00　　135.00　　(132.00)

NEW HAVEN CLOCK COMPANY / 385

- **Cato,** oak, cathedral gong, 15" x 11½", fancy gilt or ivorine dial 5", c. 1910, 8 Day, strike (E2-90).
  140.00   165.00   (172.00)

- **Clifton,** oak, cathedral gong, 11½" x 13¼", white, gilt or ivorine dial 6", c. 1910, 8 Day, strike (E2-90).
  115.00   140.00   (142.00)

- **Etruria,** antique oak, heavily gilt ornaments, cathedral gong, height 18", base 21", dial 5", c. 1900, 8 Day, strike (E2-92).
  175.00   200.00   (207.00)
- **As above,** walnut, 8 Day, strike.
  195.00   225.00   (232.00)

- **Funston,** oak cabinet, barometer, thermometer and spirit level, cathedral gong, 15½" x 11¾", white, gilt or ivorine dial 6", c. 1910, 8 Day, strike (E2-90).
  140.00   165.00   (177.00)

Cato, oak

Cato, polished oak

Clifton

Etruria

386 / NEW HAVEN CLOCK COMPANY

Funston

☐ **Gallia,** antique oak, heavily gilt ornaments, cathedral gong, height 19", dial 5", c. 1900, 8 Day, strike (E2-92).
        140.00   165.00   (172.00)

☐ **As above,** walnut, 8 Day, strike.
        165.00   185.00   (197.00)

☐ **Granada,** wood, height 12", silver dial 8½", c. 1894, 8 Day, strike (E2-125).
        75.00   95.00   (90.00)

☐ **Harlequin,** bronze or silver trimmings, visible escapement, French sash, height 16", porcelain dial 4½", c. 1900, 8 Day, strike (E2-91).
        190.00   220.00   (205.00)

☐ **Hidalgo,** mahogany, solid wood, dead finish, height 17¾", dial 5", c. 1900, 8 Day, strike (E2-91).
        140.00   165.00   (162.50)

☐ **Martinique,** oak, height 12", dial 4", c. 1894, 8 Day, strike (E2-124).
        75.00   95.00   (95.00)

☐ **Medea,** oak, cathedral gong, 15¼" x 11¾", fancy gilt or ivorine dial 5", c. 1910, 8 Day, strike (E2-90).
        135.00   170.00   (172.00)

☐ **Melita,** oak, cathedral gong, 15¼" x 11¾", fancy gilt or ivorine dial 5", c. 1910, 8 Day, strike (E2-90).
        135.00   170.00   (172.00)

☐ **Mendon,** oak, cathedral gong, 15¼" x 11¾", fancy gilt or ivorine dial 5", c. 1910, 8 Day, strike (E2-90).
        135.00   170.00   (172.00)

☐ **Nero,** polished oak, 16" x 12", c. 1900, 8 Day, strike (E-92).
        115.00   140.00   (137.00)

☐ **Nero,** oak, cathedral gong, 16" x 12", fancy gilt or ivorine dial 5", c. 1910, 8 Day, strike (E2-90).
        150.00   175.00   (172.00)

☐ **Olga,** oak, height 13¼", dial 5", c. 1900, 8 Day, strike (E2-92).
        125.00   150.00   (147.00)

☐ **As above,** mahogany.
        140.00   175.00   (172.00)

☐ **Penobscot,** mahogany, solid wood, dead finish, height 16¼", dial 5", c. 1900, 8 Day, strike (E2-92).
        145.00   180.00   (177.00)

☐ **Russia,** antique oak, heavily gilt ornaments, cathedral gong, height 18½", dial 5", c. 1900, 8 Day, strike (E2-92).
        140.00   165.00   (162.00)

☐ **As above,** walnut, 8 Day, strike.
        165.00   180.00   (187.00)

Gallia

NEW HAVEN CLOCK COMPANY / 387

☐ **Scipio,** *oak, cathedral gong, 16" x 11¾", fancy gilt or ivorine dial 5", c. 1910, 8 Day, strike (E2-90).*
150.00   175.00   (172.00)

☐ **Servia,** *antique oak, heavily gilt ornaments, cathedral gong, height 19", dial 5", c. 1900, 8 Day, strike (E2-92).*
140.00   165.00   (162.00)

☐ **As above,** *walnut, 8 Day, strike.*
160.00   180.00   (187.00)

☐ **Trinidad,** *oak, height 12", dial 4", c. 1894, 8 Day, strike (E2-124).*
75.00   95.00   (90.00)

☐ **Umbria,** *oak, heavily gilt ornaments, cathedral gong, 18" x 22½", dial 5", c. 1900, 8 Day, strike (E2-92).*
175.00   200.00   (207.00)

☐ **Vreda,** *polished antique oak, cathedral gong, height 20½", dial 8", c. 1900, 8 Day, strike (E2-91).*
130.00   150.00   (152.00)

Penobscot

CABINET/WESTMINSTER CHIMES

☐ **The "Abbey" Chime Clock,** *oak, cast Rococo sash, 17¼" x 12⅝", pearl dial 6", c. 1900 (E1-41).*
165.00   195.00   (195.00)

☐ **Eight-Bell Chime No. 1,** *mahogany, French satin gilt trimmings, height 18", metal dial 7", c. 1890, 8 Day, strike (E2-89).*
565.00   625.00   (595.00)

☐ **Four-Bell Westminster Chime No. 3,** *wood, 18½" x 12", c. 1890, 8 Day, strike (E2-89).*
230.00   260.00   (245.00)

☐ **Four-Bell Westminster Chime No. 5,** *light oak, oxidized silver or bronze trimmings, 22¼" x 12¼", metal dial 6", c. 1890, 8 Day, strike (E2-89).*
230.00   260.00   (245.00)

☐ **Westminster Chime No. 4,** *mahogany, richly ornamented metal dial, 20" x 11", dial 5½", c. 1900, 8 Day, strike (E1-41).*
220.00   250.00   (235.00)

Medea

388 / NEW HAVEN CLOCK COMPANY

Westminister Chime No. 5

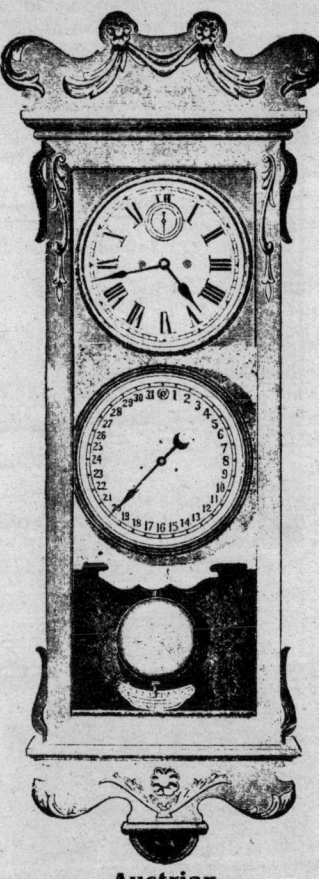

Austrian

CALENDAR

☐ **Austrian,** *49" x 19", dial 10", 30 Day, simple calendar, double dial (E2-125).*
    900.00   950.00   (925.00)

☐ **Austrian,** *wall regulator, 49" x 19", dial 10", 8 Day, strike, simple calendar (E2-125).*
    500.00   575.00   (537.00)

☐ **Bank Regulator,** *long drop, spring, 33" x 18", dial 12", 8 Day, simple calendar (M411-128).*
    350.00   400.00   (375.00)

☐ **Barbara,** *47" x 18½", dial 10", 30 Day, simple calendar, double dial (E2-125).*
    900.00   975.00   (937.00)

☐ **Barbara,** *wall regulator, 47" x 18½", dial 10", 8 Day, strike, simple calendar (E2-125).*
    500.00   600.00   (550.00)

☐ **Columbia Regulator,** *spring 48½" x 14½", dial 8", 8 Day, simple calendar (E1-164).*
    750.00   850.00   (800.00)

☐ **Conroy Victorian Shelf,** *spring, thermometer and barometer, 25" x 15½", dial 6", 8 Day, strike, simple calendar (E1-167).*
    200.00   215.00   (207.00)

☐ **Dneister,** *double dial wall or shelf, spring, also with Jerome label, height 31", dials 8", 8 Day (E1-103).*
    1000.00   1100.00   (1050.00)

NEW HAVEN CLOCK COMPANY / 389

Barbara wall regulator

Conroy Victorian Shelf

Dneister

☐ **12" Drop Octagon,** *height 24", dial 12", 8 Day, strike, simple calendar (E2-122).*
        300.00   350.00   (325.00)

☐ **8" Drop Octagon,** *short, brass bands, height 19" (E2-122).*
        225.00   275.00   (250.00)

☐ **10" Drop Octagon,** *short, brass bands, height 21" (E2-122).*
        350.00   400.00   (375.00)

☐ **12" Drop Octagon,** *short, brass bands, height 23" (E2-122).*
        275.00   325.00   (300.00)

☐ **Elfrida,** *double dial wall, double spring, New Haven calendar mechanism, retaining power, seconds bit, 58" x 21", dials 10", 30 Day, simple calendar (E2-123, M410-128).*
        900.00   1100.00   (1000.00)

390 / NEW HAVEN CLOCK COMPANY

☐ **Erie Standard Time,** *octagon top long drop, wall, spring, 33½" x 18½", dial 12", 8 Day, simple calendar (E1-183).*
  350.00   400.00   (375.00)

☐ **10" Gilt Octagon Top,** *height 21", dial 10", 8 Day, strike, simple calendar (E2-122).*
  275.00   350.00   (312.00)

☐ **12" Gilt Octagon Top,** *height 24", dial 12", 8 Day, strike, simple calendar (E2-122).*
  300.00   325.00   (312.00)

☐ **Globe,** *round nickel, dial 4", 1 Day, alarm, simple calendar (E2-88).*
  70.00   90.00   (80.00)

12" Drop Octagon

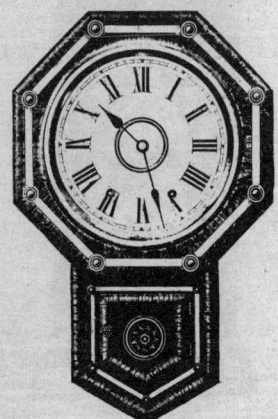

10" Drop Octagon

☐ **Emperor,** *Square Top Short Drop, oak, height 25½", dial 12", 8 Day, strike, simple calendar (E2-122).*
  250.00   300.00   (275.00)

☐ **Emperor,** *Square Top Short Drop, brass bands, height 25½", dial 12", 8 Day, strike, simple calendar (E2-122).*
  275.00   325.00   (300.00)

Elfrida

NEW HAVEN CLOCK COMPANY / 391

Emperor oak

Erie Standard Time

Emperor brass bands

10" Gilt Octagon Top

392 / NEW HAVEN CLOCK COMPANY

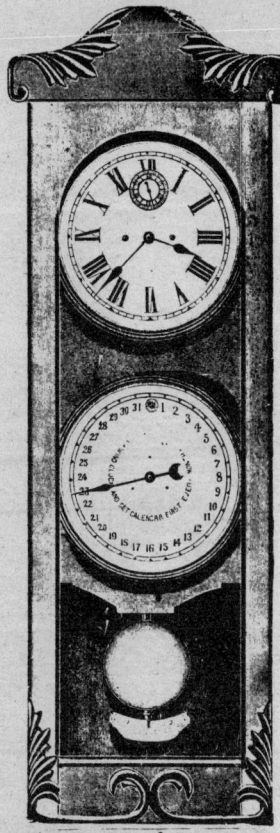

Gloriana

☐ **Gloriana,** *42" x 15½", 30 Day, simple calendar, double dial (E2-125).*
   800.00   900.00   (850.00)

☐ **Gloriana,** *wall regulator, 42" x 15½", dial 10", 8 Day, strike, simple calendar (E2-125).*
   525.00   575.00   (550.00)

☐ **Hebe,** *49" x 15½", dial 10", 30 Day, simple calendar, double dial (E2-125).*
   900.00   950.00   (925.00)

☐ **Hebe,** *wall regulator, 49" x 15½", dial 10", 8 Day, strike, simple calendar (E2-125).*
   500.00   575.00   (537.00)

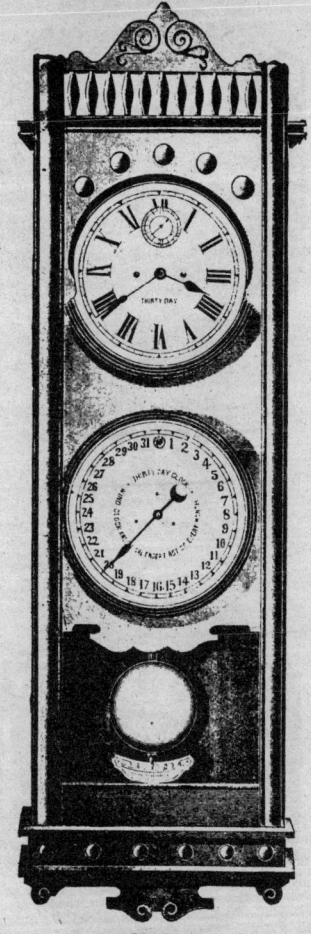

Hebe

☐ **Heron Figure 8,** *double dial wall, spring, some have labels, height 31", time dial 12", calendar dial 8", 8 Day (E1-103).*
   1100.00   1200.00   (1150.00)

☐ **Indicator D. R.,** *figure 8 wall regulator, spring, height 30½", dial 12", 8 Day, simple calendar (E1-46).*
   450.00   500.00   (475.00)

☐ **Intrepid,** *49" x 17", dial 10", 30 Day, simple calendar, double dial (E2-125).*
   900.00   1000.00   (950.00)

NEW HAVEN CLOCK COMPANY / 393

☐ **Intrepid,** *wall regulator, 49" x 17", dial 10", 8 Day, strike, simple calendar (E2-125).*
500.00   600.00   (550.00)

☐ **Ionic Figure 8,** *double dial wall, spring, height 29½", time dial 12", calendar dial 10", 8 Day (E1-101).*
1000.00   1100.00   (1050.00)

☐ **Louis Inkstand,** *brass, height 11½", dial 4", 1 Day, simple calendar (E2-112).*
225.00   275.00   (325.00)

Heron Figure 8

Louis Inkstand

Ionic Figure 8

12" Mosaic Octagon Top

394 / NEW HAVEN CLOCK COMPANY

- **Maintenon Inkstand,** *brass, 12" x 11", dial 4", 1 Day, simple calendar (E2-112).*
  250.00   300.00   (350.00)

- **Maywood Wall Regulator,** *spring, 43½" x 17", dial 8", 8 Day, simple calendar (E1-164).*
  650.00   750.00   (700.00)

- **12" Mosaic Octagon Top Short Drop,** *height 24", 8 Day, strike, simple calendar (E2-122).*
  250.00   300.00   (275.00)

- **Octagon Lever Wall,** *spring, Mother-of-Pearl inlaid on wood dial 9¼", diameter 13", 1 Day, strike, simple calendar (M405-127).*
  250.00   275.00   (262.00)

- **Octagon R.C. Lever,** *width 12", dial 8", 1 Day, simple calendar (E2-95).*
  175.00   200.00   (187.00)

- **Octagon R.C. Lever,** *width 14", dial 10", 8 Day, simple calendar (E2-95).*
  225.00   275.00   (250.00)

- **10" Octagon Top Short Drop,** *gilt buttons, height 21", dial 10", 8 Day, strike, simple calendar (E2-122).*
  300.00   350.00   (325.00)

- **Octagon Top Short Drop,** *height 24", dial 11", 8 Day, strike, simple calendar (M414-129).*
  275.00   300.00   (287.00)

- **Octagon Top Short Drop,** *spring, height 24", dial 12", 8 Day, strike, simple calendar (M413-129).*
  300.00   350.00   (325.00)

12" R.C. Drop Octagon

Referee Standard Time Wall

Regulator D.R.

NEW HAVEN CLOCK COMPANY / 395

Regulator

Regulator, with spring

Rokeby

Rutland

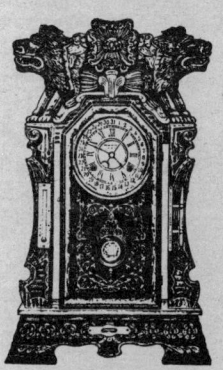

Sampson Victorian Shelf

396 / NEW HAVEN CLOCK COMPANY

- **Octagon Top Short Drop,** *spring, height 27", dial 12", 8 Day, strike, simple calendar (M412-129).*
  325.00   375.00   (350.00)

- **Plush Manual,** *height 7", dial 2", 1 Day, simple calendar (E2-103).*
  125.00   175.00   (150.00)

- **8" R.C. Drop Octagon,** *short, height 19" (E2-122).*
  225.00   250.00   (237.00)

- **10" R.C. Drop Octagon,** *short, height 21", simple calendar (E2-122).*
  250.00   275.00   (262.00)

- **12" R.C. Drop Octagon,** *short, height 24", simple calendar (E2-122).*
  275.00   300.00   (287.00)

- **Referee Standard Time Wall,** *spring, square cornered rectangle with trim, 35½" x 16", dial 12", 8 Day, simple calendar (E1-183).*
  350.00   400.00   (375.00)

- **Register,** *double dial wall, spring, also with Jerome label, height 31", dials 8", 8 Day (E1-104).*
  1200.00   1300.00   (1250.00)

- **Regulator D.R.,** *figure 8 type, height 31", dial 12", 8 Day, strike, simple calendar (E2-93).*
  350.00   400.00   (375.00)

- **Regulator Round Top Long Drop,** *height 32", dial 12", 8 Day, strike, simple calendar (E2-94).*
  325.00   375.00   (350.00)

- **Regulator Round Top Long Drop,** *spring, 32¼" x 17¾", dial 12", 8 Day, simple calendar (E1-183).*
  325.00   375.00   (350.00)

- **Rokeby,** *double dial wall, spring, also with Jerome label, height 63", dials 12", 8 Day (E1-104).*
  1450.00   1650.00   (1550.00)

- **Round Lever,** *wall, spring, dial 8", 8 Day, simple calendar (E1-45).*
  175.00   200.00   (187.00)

- **Rutland,** *wall Regulator, spring, 48" x 19½", dial 10", 8 Day, strike, simple calendar (E2-123).*
  500.00   600.00   (550.00)

- **Rutland,** *wall Regulator, spring, 48" x 19½", dial 10, 30 Day, double dial (E2-123).*
  800.00   900.00   (850.00)

- **Sampson Victorian Shelf,** *spring, with thermometer and barometer, 23½" x 15", dial 6", 8 Day, strike, simple calendar (E2-88).*
  200.00   215.00   (207.00)

Saxon

Sprite

NEW HAVEN CLOCK COMPANY / 397

☐ **Sampson Victorian Shelf,** *spring, with thermometer and barometer, 25" x 14½", dial 6", 8 Day, strike, simple calendar (M407-127).*
    200.00   215.00   (207.00)

☐ **Sampson Victorian Shelf,** *spring, with thermometer and barometer, 25" x 15½", dial 6", 8 Day, strike, simple calendar (E1-167).*
    200.00   215.00   (207.00)

☐ **8" Saxon,** *figure 8, height 20" (E2-122).*
    300.00   350.00   (325.00)

☐ **10" Saxon,** *figure 8, height 22" (E2-122).*
    325.00   375.00   (350.00)

☐ **12" Saxon,** *figure 8, height 24" (E2-122).*
    350.00   400.00   (375.00)

☐ **8" Saxon Mosaic,** *figure 8, height 20", 8 Day, strike, simple calendar (E2-122).*
    325.00   350.00   (337.00)

☐ **10" Saxon Mosaic,** *figure 8, height 22", 8 Day, strike, simple calendar (E2-122).*
    325.00   375.00   (350.00)

☐ **12" Saxon Mosaic,** *figure 8, height 24", 8 Day, strike, simple calendar (E2-122).*
    350.00   400.00   (375.00)

The Beacon

Vamoose Wall Regulator

Start

398 / NEW HAVEN CLOCK COMPANY

☐ **Scribe Inkstand,** plated, 12" x 14", dial 3", 1 Day, simple calendar (E2-112).
225.00   275.00   (325.00)

☐ **Sprite,** round nickel, dial 4½", 1 Day, alarm, simple calendar (E2-88).
65.00   85.00   (75.00)

☐ **Start,** round nickel, dial 4", 1 Day, alarm, simple calendar (E2-88).
60.00   80.00   (70.00)

☐ **The Beacon,** round nickel, dial 4¼", 1 Day, alarm, simple calendar (E2-88).
60.00   85.00   (72.00)

☐ **Trojan Wall Regulator,** spring, 44" x 13½", dial 8", 8 Day, simple calendar (E1-164).
650.00   700.00   (725.00)

☐ **Vamoose Wall Regulator,** spring, 45" x 15½", dial 10", 8 Day, simple calendar (E1-164).
400.00   450.00   (425.00)

☐ **Wall,** double dial, double spring, New Haven calendar mechanism, retaining power, seconds bit, 54" x 19", dials 10", 30 Day, simple calendar (M409-128).
850.00   950.00   (900.00)

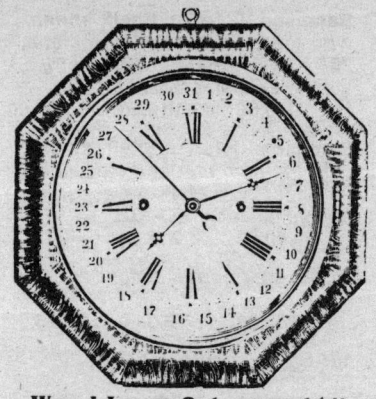

Wood Lever Octagon, 14"

☐ **Wood Lever Octagon,** veneered, width 12", dial 8", 1 Day, simple calendar (E2-118).
150.00   175.00   (162.00)

☐ **Wood Lever Octagon,** veneered, width 14", dial 10", 1 Day, simple calendar (E2-118).
175.00   200.00   (187.00)

CARRIAGE

☐ **Adela,** solid cast brass, hand finished, height 8¾", dial 2½", c. 1900, 8 Day (E2-111).
225.00   275.00   (187.00)

☐ **Alert,** nickel, height 6½", c. 1890, 1 Day, alarm (E2-88).
90.00   120.00   (157.00)

☐ **Alert,** nickel, height 7", dial 3", c. 1900, 1 Day, alarm (E1-44).
100.00   125.00   (162.00)

☐ **Badger,** nickel, single spring movement, with spring in barrel, height 7¼", c. 1900, 1 Day, alarm (E2-126).
140.00   165.00   (187.00)

☐ **Cavalier,** height 6", c. 1890, 1 Day, alarm (E2-88).
105.00   125.00   (115.00)

Wood Lever Octagon, 12"

NEW HAVEN CLOCK COMPANY / 399

Adela

Badger

Puck

☐ **Lantern Night Clock,** *brass hall lantern, studded with jewels, containing translucent dial clock, finished in antique brass and antique silver, opal dial 5", c. 1900, 1 Day (E2-111).*
      135.00   165.00   (137.00)

☐ **Messenger,** *nickel with gilt mat, height 7¼", dial 2¾", c. 1900, 1 Day, alarm (E2-126).*
      105.00   125.00   (115.00)

☐ **As above,** *1 Day, strike.*
      110.00   135.00   (122.00)

☐ **Peacock,** *extra gold plated, height 6½", dial 2½", c. 1900, 8 Day (E2-111).*
      150.00   175.00   (152.00)

400 / NEW HAVEN CLOCK COMPANY

☐ **Pilgrim,** *nickel, two-spring movement, c. 1900, 1 Day, alarm (E2-126).*
115.00   140.00   (115.00)

☐ **As above,** *1 Day, strike.*
120.00   145.00   (122.00)

☐ **As above,** *1 Day, strike, alarm.*
130.00   150.00   (132.00)

☐ **Pilgrim,** *height 6", c. 1890, 1 Day, alarm (E2-88).*
105.00   125.00   (115.00)

☐ **Puck,** *gilt, height 9", dial 3", c. 1900, 1 Day, strike (E2-126).*
125.00   150.00   (122.00)

☐ **As above,** *1 Day, strike, alarm.*
130.00   155.00   (132.00)

☐ **As above,** *1 Day, alarm.*
140.00   165.00   (142.00)

☐ **Toulon,** *French gilt case, 5" x 2⅝", porcelain dial, c. 1900, 1 Day (E1-44).*
195.00   225.00   (210.00)

☐ **Truro,** *5" x 2¾", c. 1900, 8 Day (E2-112).*
125.00   150.00   (137.00)

CHINA/LARGE

☐ **Gerald,** *decorated porcelain, visible escapement, 13" x 14¾", dial 5", c. 1900, 8 Day, strike (E1-42).*
310.00   350.00   (330.00)

☐ **Hamilton,** *decorated porcelain, visible escapement, 12⅛" x 8½", dial 5", c. 1900, 8 Day, strike (E1-42).*
145.00   170.00   (157.00)

☐ **Haverford,** *decorated porcelain, visible escapement, 13¼" x 13⅞", dial 5", c. 1900, 8 Day, strike (E1-43).*
290.00   330.00   (310.00)

☐ **Herbert,** *decorated porcelain, 12" x 9¼", dial 5", c. 1900, 8 Day, strike (E1-42).*
145.00   170.00   (157.00)

☐ **Holly,** *decorated porcelain, visible escapement, 14⅝" x 13¼", porcelain dial 5", c. 1900, 8 Day, strike (E1-43).*
320.00   360.00   (340.00)

Tancred

☐ **Horicon,** *decorated porcelain, visible escapement, 13⅞" x 12⅜", c. 1900, 8 Day, strike (E1-42).*
300.00   340.00   (320.00)

☐ **Hyperion,** *decorated porcelain, 11¾" x 8⅝", porcelain dial 5", c. 1900, 8 Day, strike (E1-43).*
145.00   170.00   (157.00)

☐ **Malabar,** *decorated porcelain, 10⅝" x 12¼", porcelain dial 5", c. 1900, 8 Day, strike (E1-43).*
145.00   170.00   (157.00)

☐ **Nivian,** *porcelain, 11¾" x 10¾", dial 5", c. 1900, 8 Day, strike (E2-121).*
190.00   220.00   (205.00)

☐ **Rockland,** *decorated porcelain, 10¾" x 11⅝", porcelain dial 5", c. 1900, 8 Day, strike (E1-43).*
155.00   180.00   (167.00)

☐ **Rosendale,** *decorated porcelain, 10¼" x 12", porcelain dial 5", c. 1900, 8 Day, strike (E1-43).*
155.00   180.00   (167.00)

☐ **Tancred,** *porcelain, 12" x 10½", dial 5", c. 1900, 8 Day, strike (E2-121).*
190.00   220.00   (205.00)

CHINA/SMALL

☐ **Achilles,** *decorated porcelain, 10¼" x 10", dial 4", c. 1900, 8 Day, strike (E1-42).*
140.00   165.00   (152.00)

☐ **Audubon,** *decorated porcelain, 10½" x 7⅞", dial 4", c. 1900, 8 Day, strike (E1-42).*
115.00   140.00   (127.00)

☐ **Bayard,** *decorated porcelain, 8" x 3⅞", dial 2", c. 1900, 1 Day (E1-37).*
45.00   60.00   (52.50)

☐ **Clinton,** *decorated porcelain, 12" x 6¾", dial 4", c. 1900, 8 Day, strike (E1-43).*
120.00   145.00   (132.00)

☐ **Creighton,** *decorated porcelain, 5½" x 6⅞", dial 2", c. 1900, 1 Day (E1-42).*
40.00   55.00   (47.50)

☐ **Fleetwood,** *decorated porcelain, 5½" x 3¼", dial 2", c. 1900, 1 Day (E1-43).*
30.00   40.00   (35.00)

☐ **Lionel,** *decorated porcelain, 5" x 4¼", dial 2", c. 1900, 1 Day (E1-42).*
30.00   40.00   (35.00)

☐ **Mabel,** *decorated porcelain, 11" x 11¼", dial 5", c. 1900, 8 Day, strike (E1-42).*
155.00   180.00   (167.00)

Mabel

San Remo

☐ **Morton,** *decorated porcelain, 5⅛" x 4½", dial 2", c. 1900, 1 Day (E1-43).*
30.00   40.00   (35.00)

☐ **Parry,** *decorated porcelain, 5⅞" x 7", dial 2", c. 1900, 1 Day (E1-43).*
40.00   55.00   (47.50)

☐ **Richmond,** *decorated porcelain, 6½" x 3½", dial 2", c. 1900, 1 Day (E1-37).*
40.00   50.00   (45.00)

☐ **Rupert,** *decorated porcelain, 4¾" x 6⅜", dial 2", c. 1900, 1 Day (E1-43).*
40.00   55.00   (47.50)

☐ **San Remo,** *porcelain, 10½" x 9", c. 1900, 1 Day (E2-121).*
105.00   125.00   (115.00)

☐ **St. Cloud,** *porcelain, height 7½", dial 2", c. 1900, 1 Day (E2-121).*
80.00   100.00   (90.00)

402 / NEW HAVEN CLOCK COMPANY

☐ **St. Louis,** *porcelain, height 7", dial 2", c. 1900, 1 Day (E2-121).*
  80.00   100.00   (90.00)

☐ **Turenne,** *porcelain, 9¾" x 7¾", dial 3", c. 1900, 8 Day, strike (E2-121).*
  150.00   175.00   (162.00)

☐ **Wakefield,** *decorated porcelain, 4⅝" x 5⅛", dial 2", c. 1900, 1 Day (E1-42).*
  30.00   40.00   (35.00)

☐ **Waldorf,** *porcelain, fancy etched silver, 8¼" x 7½", dial 3", c. 1900, 1 Day, alarm (E2-121).*
  90.00   110.00   (100.00)

☐ **Windsor,** *porcelain, fancy etched silver, 8¼" x 7½", dial 3", c. 1900, 1 Day, alarm (E2-121).*
  110.00   135.00   (122.50)

CONNECTICUT SHELF
ARCH TOP

☐ **Arch Top,** *wood, c. 1900, 8 Day, strike (E2-94).*
  160.00   185.00   (172.00)
☐ **As above,** *8 Day, strike, alarm*
  175.00   200.00   (187.00)

CONNECTICUT SHELF
BEE HIVE

☐ **Gothic,** *wood, height 19¼", c. 1900, 1 Day, strike (E2-94).*
  110.00   125.00   (100.00)
☐ **As above,** *8 Day, strike*
  125.00   150.00   (122.00)

Waldorf

Windsor

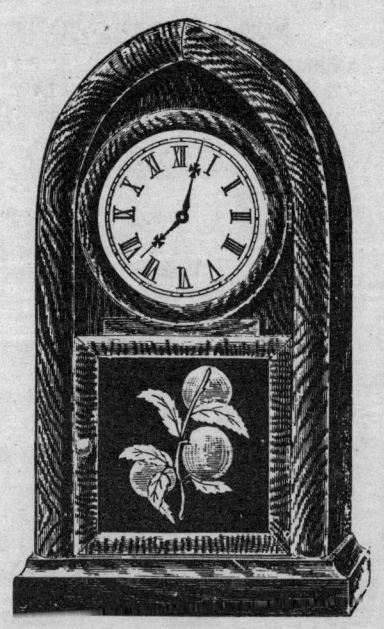

Gothic

- Round Gothic, *wood, height 19", c. 1900, 1 Day, simple spring (E1-45).*
  110.00   130.00   (100.00)
- As above, *8 Day, simple spring*
  120.00   150.00   (122.00)

CONNECTICUT SHELF
COTTAGE

- Auburn, *wood, height 14", c. 1900, 1 Day, strike (E2-94).*
  75.00   90.00   (82.50)
- Cottage, *wood, height 12", c. 1900, 1 Day, strike (E1-45).*
  55.00   70.00   (62.50)
- As above, *1 Day, simple spring*
  75.00   95.00   (85.00)
- Cottage Extra, *wood, height 12", c. 1900, 1 Day (E2-94).*
  65.00   80.00   (72.50)
- As above, *height 13", 1 Day, strike*
  75.00   95.00   (85.00)
- As above, *height 13", 8 Day, strike*
  100.00   120.00   (110.00)
- Cottage Extra, *zebra, height 14", dial 6", c. 1900, 1 Day, strike (E2-94).*
  110.00   125.00   (117.00)
- As above, *zebra, 8 Day, strike*
  120.00   140.00   (130.00)
- As above, *mahogany, 1 Day, strike*
  75.00   90.00   (82.50)
- As above, *mahogany, 8 Day, strike*
  85.00   105.00   95.00
- Cottage No. 2, *wood, height 12", c. 1900, 1 Day, (E2-94).*
  55.00   70.00   (62.50)
- As above, *1 Day, strike*
  70.00   85.00   (77.50)
- Cottage No. 2, *zebra, height 12", dial 6", c. 1900 1 Day (E2-94).*
  100.00   115.00   (107.00)
- As above, *zebra, 1 Day, strike*
  115.00   130.00   (117.00)
- As above, *mahogany, 1 Day.*
  65.00   80.00   (72.00)
- As above, *mahogany, 1 Day, strike*
  80.00   95.00   (87.50)
- Gem Cottage, *wood, height 9", c. 1900, 1 Day (E2-94).*
  55.00   70.00   (62.00)
- As above, *1 Day, alarm*
  70.00   85.00   (77.50)

- Prize, *wood, height 14", c. 1900, 1 Day, simple spring (E1-46).*
  65.00   80.00   (72.00)
- As above, *8 Day, simple spring*
  85.00   105.00   (95.00)
- Rattler, *wood, height 10¾", c. 1900, 1 Day (E2-95).*
  70.00   85.00   (77.50)
- Rose Gilt, *wood, height 9½", c. 1900, 1 Day, strike.*
  50.00   65.00   (57.00)

CONNECTICUT SHELF
OCTAGON TOP

- Alps, *wood, height 17", c. 1900, 1 Day, strike (E2-94).*
  80.00   100.00   (90.00)
- As above, *8 Day, strike*
  105.00   125.00   (115.00)
- Dreadnaught, *mahogany, height 14", dial 5", c. 1900, 1 Day, strike (E2-94).*
  80.00   100.00   (90.00)
- As above, *rosewood, 1 Day, strike*
  105.00   125.00   (115.00)
- As above, *zebra, 1 Day, strike*
  115.00   135.00   (125.00)
- Duchess, *mahogany, height 18", dial 6", c. 1900, 8 Day, strike (E2-94).*
  105.00   125.00   (115.00)
- As above, *zebra, 8 Day, strike*
  140.00   160.00   (150.00)
- Gem, *wood, height 15", c. 1900, 1 Day, simple spring (E1-46).*
  65.00   80.00   (72.50)
- As above, *8 Day, simple spring*
  85.00   105.00   (95.00)
- Octagon Prize, *wood, height 14½", c. 1900, 1 Day (E2-94).*
  70.00   85.00   (77.00)
- As above, *1 Day, alarm*
  75.00   90.00   (82.00)
- Octagon Prize, *V.P. wood, height 18", c. 1900, 1 Day, simple spring (E1-46).*
  75.00   90.00   (82.00)
- As above, *8 Day, simple spring*
  95.00   115.00   (105.00)

NEW HAVEN CLOCK COMPANY

Octagon Prize

☐ **Octagon Prize,** wood, height 17¼", c. 1900, 1 Day, strike (E2-94).
 75.00   90.00   (82.00)
☐ **As above,** 8 Day, strike
 95.00   115.00   (105.00)

☐ **Octagon Prize,** V.P., rosewood, height 17¾", dial 6", c. 1900, 1 Day, strike (E2-94).
 80.00   100.00   (90.00)
☐ **As above,** rosewood, 8 Day, strike
 105.00   125.00   (115.00)
☐ **As above,** zebra, 1 Day, strike
 115.00   135.00   (125.00)
☐ **As above,** zebra, 8 Day, strike
 140.00   155.00   (147.00)

☐ **Octagon Rocket,** imitation zebra, height 13", dial 4", c. 1900, 1 Day (E2-94).
 75.00   90.00   (82.00)

☐ **Small Octagon Prize Extra,** rosewood, height 16", dial 5", c. 1900, 1 Day, strike (E2-94).
 75.00   90.00   (82.00)
☐ **As above,** 8 Day, strike
 95.00   115.00   (105.00)

CONNECTICUT SHELF
O.G. AND O.O.G.

☐ **O.G. (Weight No. 1 or No. 2),** mahogany, height 26", dial 8", c. 1900, 1 Day, strike, weight (E2-93).
 140.00   165.00   (147.00)
☐ **As above,** zebra, 1 Day, strike, weight
 150.00   175.00   (162.00)

☐ **O.O.G.,** mahogany, height 30", c. 1900, 1 Day, strike, weight (E2-93).
 125.00   150.00   (187.00)
☐ **As above,** mahogany, 8 Day, strike, weight
 160.00   200.00   (152.00)
☐ **As above,** zebra, 1 Day, strike, weight
 125.00   150.00   (197.00)
☐ **As above,** zebra, 8 Day, strike, weight
 160.00   200.00   (162.00)

☐ **O.O.G.,** wood, height 26", c. 1900, 1 Day, strike, weight (E1-46).
 110.00   135.00   (115.00)

CONNECTICUT SHELF
ROUND TOP

☐ **Guide,** wood, height 17¼", c. 1900, 1 Day, strike (E2-94).
 80.00   100.00   (90.00)
☐ **As above,** 8 Day, strike
 105.00   125.00   (115.00)

☐ **Guide, Full Gilt,** finished with full gilt columns and mouldings, height 17¼", dial 6", c. 1900, 1 Day, strike (E2-94).
 75.00   90.00   (82.00)
☐ **As above,** 8 Day, strike
 95.00   115.00   (105.00)

☐ **Guide,** V.P., wood, height 17", c. 1900, 1 Day, simple spring (E1-4).
 90.00   110.00   (100.00)
☐ **As above,** 8 Day, simple spring
 110.00   135.00   (122.00)

☐ **Round Gothic Extra,** wood, height 17¼", c. 1900, 1 Day, strike (E2-94).
 95.00   115.00   (105.00)
☐ **As above,** 8 Day, strike
 115.00   140.00   (127.00)

Guide, Full Gilt

- [ ] **Round Gothic,** V.P., *rosewood, height 17¼", dial 6", c. 1900, 1 Day, strike (E2-94).*
  95.00   115.00   (105.00)
- [ ] **As above,** *rosewood, 8 Day, strike*
  115.00   140.00   (127.00)
- [ ] **As above,** *zebra, 1 Day, strike*
  105.00   125.00   (115.00)
- [ ] **As above,** *zebra, 8 Day, strike*
  125.00   150.00   (137.00)

CONNECTICUT SHELF
SPLIT TOP

- [ ] **Andes,** *wood, height 17", c. 1900, 1 Day, strike (E2-95).*
  75.00   90.00   (82.00)
- [ ] **As above,** *8 Day, strike*
  95.00   115.00   (105.00)
- [ ] **Coupon Preferred,** *wood, height 15½", c. 1900, 1 Day, strike (E2-95).*
  70.00   85.00   (77.00)
- [ ] **As above,** *8 Day, strike*
  90.00   110.00   (100.00)
- [ ] **Eclipse,** *rosewood, height 17", dial 6", c. 1900, 1 Day, strike (E2-95).*
  90.00   110.00   (100.00)
- [ ] **As above,** *8 Day, strike*
  110.00   135.00   (122.00)

Andes

- [ ] **Gem Cottage,** *wood, height 14", c. 1900, 1 Day, strike (E2-95).*
  105.00   125.00   (115.00)
- [ ] **As above,** *8 Day, strike*
  125.00   150.00   (137.00)
- [ ] **Gothic Gem,** *wood, height 17¾", c. 1900, 1 Day, strike (E2-95).*
  80.00   100.00   (90.00)
- [ ] **Mottled Tuscan,** *wood, height 16", dial 5", c. 1900, 1 Day, strike (E2-95).*
  80.00   100.00   (90. 00)
- [ ] **As above,** *8 Day, strike*
  105.00   125.00   (115.00)
- [ ] **Pyramid,** *wood, height 17", c. 1900, 1 Day, strike (E2-95).*
  75.00   90.00   (77.00)
- [ ] **As above,** *8 Day, strike*
  95.00   115.00   (105.00)
- [ ] **Reliable,** *wood, height 9¼", c. 1900, 1 Day (E2-95).*
  60.00   75.00   (67.00)
- [ ] **Rocket,** *chestnut or imitation zebra, height 10¾", dial 4", c. 1900, 1 Day (E2-95).*
  60.00   75.00   (67.00)
- [ ] **Small Tuscan Extra,** *rosewood, height 16", c. 1900, 1 Day, strike (E2-95).*
  65.00   80.00   (72.00)
- [ ] **As above,** *8 Day, strike*
  95.00   115.00   (105.00)

Small Tuscan Extra

- ☐ **Solo,** *wood, height 9¼", c. 1900, 1 Day (E2-95).*
  60.00   75.00   (67.00)
- ☐ **As above,** *1 Day, alarm*
  80.00   100.00   (90.00)
- ☐ **Tuscan,** *V.P., wood, height 17¾", c. 1900, 1 Day, strike (E2-95).*
  75.00   90.00   (82.00)
- ☐ **As above,** *8 Day, strike*
  95.00   115.00   (105.00)
- ☐ **Tuscan,** *wood, height 17¾", c. 1900, 1 Day, strike (E2-95).*
  75.00   90.00   (82.00)
- ☐ **As above,** *8 Day, strike*
  95.00   115.00   (105.00)
- ☐ **As above,** *height 14½", 1 Day.*
  70.00   85.00   (77.00)

CONNECTICUT SHELF
STEEPLE

- ☐ **Derby,** *T.P., wood, height 17", dial 5", c. 1900, 1 Day (E2-96).*
  105.00   125.00   (115.00)
- ☐ **Derby,** *wood, height 10½", dial 5½", c. 1900, 1 Day, strike (E2-96).*
  105.00   125.00   (115.00)

Derby

- ☐ **Diadem,** *zebra, veneered, height 18", dial 5", c. 1900, 1 Day (E2-96).*
  105.00   125.00   (115.00)
- ☐ **As above,** *1 Day, strike*
  115.00   140.00   (127.00)
- ☐ **Dolphin,** *zebra, veneered, height 17¾", dial 5", c. 1900, 1 Day (E2-96).*
  105.00   125.00   (115.00)
- ☐ **As above,** *1 Day, strike*
  115.00   140.00   (127.00)
- ☐ **As above,** *8 Day, strike*
  125.00   150.00   (137.00)
- ☐ **Large Gothic,** *V.P., wood, height 21", c. 1900, 1 Day, simple spring (E1-46).*
  90.00   110.00   (100.00)
- ☐ **As above,** *8 Day, simple spring*
  110.00   135.00   (122.00)
- ☐ **Sharp Gothic,** *rosewood, height 20½", dial 6", c. 1900, 1 Day, strike (E2-96).*
  105.00   125.00   (115.00)
- ☐ **As above,** *rosewood, 8 Day, strike*
  160.00   185.00   (172.00)
- ☐ **As above,** *mahogany, 1 Day, strike*
  105.00   125.00   (125.00)
- ☐ **As above,** *mahogany, 8 Day, strike*
  160.00   185.00   (172.00)
- ☐ **As above,** *zebra, 1 Day, strike*
  115.00   135.00   (125.00)
- ☐ **As above,** *zebra, 8 Day, strike*
  170.00   195.00   (182.00)

NEW HAVEN CLOCK COMPANY / 407

Sharp Gothic

☐ **Sharp Gothic,** V.P., mahogany, height 21", dial 6", c. 1900, 1 Day, strike (E2-96).
105.00   125.00   (115.00)
☐ **As above,** mahogany, 8 Day, strike
160.00   185.00   (172.00)
☐ **As above,** rosewood, 1 Day, strike
105.00   125.00   (115.00)
☐ **As above,** rosewood, 8 Day, strike
160.00   185.00   (172.00)
☐ **As above,** zebra, 1 Day, strike
115.00   135.00   (125.00)

☐ **Small Gothic,** V.P., rosewood, height 16", c. 1900, 1 Day (E2-96).
105.00   125.00   (115.00)
☐ **As above,** rosewood, 1 Day, strike
110.00   135.00   (122.00)
☐ **As above,** zebra, 1 Day.
115.00   135.00   (122.00)
☐ **As above,** zebra, 1 Day, strike
120.00   145.00   (132.00)

☐ **Small Gothic,** rosewood, height 15½", dial 5", c. 1900, 1 Day (E2-96).
105.00   125.00   (115.00)
☐ **As above,** rosewood, 8 Day.
125.00   150.00   (137.00)
☐ **As above,** zebra, 1 Day.
115.00   135.00   (127.00)
☐ **As above,** zebra, 8 Day.
135.00   160.00   (147.00)

Thoreau
CRYSTAL REGULATOR

☐ **Thieta,** mahogany, 13" x 9", dial 7", c. 1917, 8 Day, strike (E1-173).
265.00   305.00   (285.00)
☐ **Thoreau,** ormolu gold plate or antique Verde case, with beveled French plate glass sides, back and front, 15" x 8½", porcelain dial 4", c. 1900, 8 Day, strike (E2-119).
425.00   475.00   (450.00)
☐ **Tuxford,** mahogany, 10½" x 6", dial 4", c. 1917, 8 Day, strike (E1-173).
245.00   275.00   (265.00)

GALLERY

- ☐ **Canton,** nickel or brass, lever, c. 1900, 6", 1 Day (E2-118).
  105.00   125.00   (115.00)
- ☐ As above, 6", 1 Day, alarm
  110.00   135.00   (122.00)
- ☐ As above, 6", 1 Day, strike
  115.00   140.00   (127.00)
- ☐ As above, 8", 1 Day.
  125.00   150.00   (137.00)
- ☐ As above, 8", 1 Day, strike
  135.00   160.00   (147.00)
- ☐ As above, 6", 8 Day.
  125.00   150.00   (137.00)
- ☐ As above, 8", 8 Day.
  140.00   165.00   (152.00)
- ☐ As above, 8", 8 Day, strike
  150.00   175.00   (162.00)

- ☐ **Eagle,** carved oak, height 40", dial 17", c. 1900, 8 Day (E1-101).
  360.00   400.00   (380.00)
- ☐ As above, cherry
  410.00   450.00   (430.00)

- ☐ **R.C. Calendar Lever,** wood, dial 10", c. 1900, 1 Day, strike (E2-95).
  175.00   200.00   (187.00)
- ☐ As above, dial 8", 8 Day.
  245.00   275.00   (260.00)

- ☐ **Wood Lever,** polished veneered, c. 1900, 4", 1 Day (E2-118).
  90.00   110.00   (100.00)
- ☐ As above, 6", 1 Day.
  100.00   120.00   (110.00)
- ☐ As above, 6", 1 Day, alarm
  105.00   130.00   (117.00)
- ☐ As above, 6", 1 Day, strike
  115.00   140.00   (127.00)
- ☐ As above, 8", 1 Day.
  115.00   140.00   (127.00)
- ☐ As above, 8", 1 Day, alarm
  125.00   150.00   (137.00)
- ☐ As above, 8", 1 Day, strike
  135.00   160.00   (147.00)
- ☐ As above, 10", 1 Day.
  135.00   160.00   (147.00)
- ☐ As above, 10", 1 Day, strike
  145.00   170.00   (157.00)
- ☐ As above, 6", 8 Day.
  125.00   150.00   (137.00)
- ☐ As above, 8", 8 Day.
  135.00   160.00   (147.00)
- ☐ As above, 8", 8 Day, strike
  145.00   170.00   (157.00)
- ☐ As above, 10", 8 Day, strike
  145.00   170.00   (159.00)

Wood Lever

- ☐ **Wood Lever,** calendar, polished veneered, c. 1900, 8", 1 Day, calendar (E2-118).
  150.00   175.00   (162.00)
- ☐ As above, 10", 1 Day, calendar
  175.00   200.00   (187.00)

- ☐ **Round Calendar Lever,** wood, 8", c. 1900, 8 Day (E1-45).
  105.00   125.00   (115.00)

GALLERY/MARBLE

- ☐ **No. 1,** marble, 20" diameter, dial 17", c. 1910, 15 Day (E2-128).
  245.00   275.00   (260.00)
- ☐ **No. 2,** marble, diameter 27½", dial 23", c. 1910, 15 Day (E2-128).
  245.00   275.00   (260.00)
- ☐ **No. 3,** marble, Graham dead-beat escapement 27½" x 23", dial 17", c. 1910, 15 Day (E2-128).
  270.00   300.00   (285.00)
- ☐ **No. 4,** marble, Graham dead-beat escapement, 36" x 30", dial 23", c. 1910, 15 Day (E2-128).
  270.00   300.00   (285.00)
- ☐ **No. 5,** marble, Graham dead-beat escapement, 24" x 24", dial 17", c. 1910, 15 Day (E2-128).
  270.00   300.00   (285.00)

Mantel-Marble No. 5

☐ **No. 6**, marble, Graham dead-beat escapement, 32" x 32", dial 23", c. 1910, 15 Day (E2-128).
270.00   300.00   (285.00)

☐ **No. 7**, marble, Graham dead-beat escapement, 29½" x 16", dial 13", c. 1910, 15 Day (E2-128).
360.00   400.00   (380.00)

☐ **As above**, 15 Day, strike
375.00   425.00   (400.00)

GRANDFATHER

☐ **Chippendale**, oak, weights, pendulum, dial and movement polished and lacquered, solid brass dial with black numerals on a raised silver circle, 8' x 22½", dial 12", c. 1900, 8 Day, strike (E1-35).
1800.00   2200.00   (2000.00)

☐ **As above**, mahogany
1875.00   2275.00   (2075.00)

☐ **Hall Clock, No. 1**, oak, hand carved, cabinet finished, height 84", dial 12", c. 1900, 8 Day, strike (E1-104).
2000.00   2500.00   (2250.00)

☐ **As above**, mahogany
2075.00   2575.00   (2300.00)

KITCHEN

☐ **Alderman**, oak, interchangeable tops, "Hustler Series", dial 6", c. 1896, 8 Day, strike, spring wound (E2-106).
145.00   170.00   (157.00)

NEW HAVEN CLOCK COMPANY / 409

☐ **Ambassador**, oak, height 23", c. 1894, 1 Day, strike, spring wound (E2-103).
120.00   145.00   (132.00)

☐ **As above**, oak, 8 Day, strike, spring wound
1 45.00   170.00   (157.00)

☐ **As above**, walnut, 1 Day, strike, spring wound
145.00   170.00   (157.00)

☐ **As above**, walnut, 8 Day, strike, spring wound
170.00   195.00   (182.00)

☐ **Aral**, wood, height 20¼", dial 5", c. 1900, 1 Day, strike, spring wound (E2-98).
145.00   170.00   (157.00)

☐ **Avon**, wood, height 21", dial 5", c. 1900, 8 Day, strike, spring wound (E2-98).
145.00   170.00   (157.00)

☐ **Ayr**, wood, height 20¼", dial 5", c. 1900, 8 Day, strike, spring wound (E2-98).
145.00   170.00   (157.00)

☐ **Bobolink**, wood, height 17½", dial 6", c. 1900, 1 Day, strike, spring wound (E2-98).
140.00   165.00   (152.00)

☐ **Bonita**, wood, height 17¾", dial 6", c. 1900, 1 Day, strike, spring wound (E2-98).
135.00   160.00   (147.00)

☐ **Boreas**, wood, height 21½", dial 6", c. 1900, 1 Day, strike, spring wound (E2-98).
145.00   170.00   (157.00)

☐ **Calumet**, height 20¾", dial 6", 1 Day, strike, spring wound (E2-98).
140.00   165.00   (152.00)

☐ **Captain**, oak, "Great Military Series", 22" x 14", dial 6", spring wound (E2-103).
140.00   165.00   (152.00)

☐ **As above**, walnut, spring wound
165.00   185.00   (175.00)

☐ **Calumet**, height 20¾", dial 6", 1 Day, strike, spring wound.
165.00   185.00   (175.00)

410 / NEW HAVEN CLOCK COMPANY

Boreas

Calumet

Christine

☐ **Celeste**, wood, height 21", dial 5", c. 1900, 8 Day, strike, spring wound (E2-98).
      140.00   165.00   (152.00)

☐ **Charmer**, wood, height 22½", dial 5", c. 1900, 8 Day, strike, spring wound (E2-98).
      140.00   165.00   (152.00)

☐ **Christine**, wood, height 20¾", dial 5", c. 1900, 1 Day, strike, spring wound (E2-98).
      135.00   160.00   (147.00)

☐ **Clarita**, wood, height 22", dial 5", c. 1900, 8 Day, strike, spring wound (E2-97).
      145.00   170.00   (157.00)

☐ **Cinderella**, wood, height 25", dial 6", c. 1900, 8 Day, strike, spring wound (E2-97).
      150.00   175.00   (162.00)

☐ **Clochette**, wood, height 18", dial 6", c. 1900, 1 Day, strike spring wound (E2-97).
      135.00   160.00   (147.00)

☐ **Clyde**, wood, height 23", dial 5½", c. 1900, 8 Day, strike spring wound (E297).
      150.00   175.00   (162.00)

☐ **Carmen**, wood, height 21½", dial 6", c. 1900, 8 Day, strike, spring wound (E2-98).
      140.00   165.00   (152.00)

☐ **Cecile**, wood, height 22", dial 6", 8 Day, strike, spring wound (E2-98).
      145.00   170.00   (157.00)

NEW HAVEN CLOCK COMPANY / 411

Cinderella

- **Colonel**, oak, "Great Military Series" 22" x 14", dial 6", c. 1894, 8 Day, strike, spring wound (E2-103).
  140.00   165.00   (152.00)
- **As above**, walnut, spring wound.
  165.00   190.00   (177.00)
- **Conroy**, oak, "Norwich series", 25" x 15½", dial 6", c. 1900, 8 Day, strike, spring wound (E2-104).
  160.00   185.00   (172.00)
- **As above**, walnutm spring wound.
  185.00   210.00   (197.00)
- **Coquette**, wood, height 22", dial 6", c. 1900, 8 Day, strike, spring wound (E2-97).
  150.00   175.00   (162.00)
- **Councilman**, oak, interchangeable tops, "Hustler Series", dial 6", c. 1896, 8 Day, strike, spring wound (E2-106).
- *As above*, oak, spring wound
  145.00   170.00   (157.00)
- **As above**, walnut, spring wound
  170.00   195.00   (182.00)

- **Cygnet**, wood, height 23½", dial 6", c. 1900, 8 Day, strike, spring wound (E2-97).
  155.00   180.00   (167.00)
- **Danube**, wood, height 24", dial 6", c. 1900, 8 Day, strike, spring wound (E2-97).
  155.00   180.00   (167.00)
- **Dee**, oak, "D Series", 24⅜" x 15⅝", dial 6", c. 1900, 8 Day, strike, spring wound (E2-104).
  150.00   175.00   (162.00)
- **As above**, walnut, spring wound
  175.00   195.00   (185.00)
- **Dee**, wood, height 21", dial 5", c. 1900, 8 Day, strike, spring wound (E2-97),
  150.00   175.00   (162.00)
- **Don**, oak, "D Series", 24⅜" x 15⅝", dial 6", c. 1900, 8 Day, strike, spring wound (E2-104).
  150.00   175.00   (162.00)
- **As above**, walnuts, spring wound
  175.00   200.00   (187.00)
- **Don**, wood, height 18", dial 5½", c. 1900, 1 Day, strike, spring wound (E2-97).
  130.00   155.00   (142.00)

Don

412 / NEW HAVEN CLOCK COMPANY

☐ **Doon**, oak, "D Series", 24⅜" x 15⅝", dial 6", c. 1900, 8 Day, strike, spring wound (E2-104).
    150.00   175.00   (162.00)
☐ **As above**, walnut, spring wound
    175.00   200.00   (187.00)

☐ **Dora**, wood, height 20", dial 5", c. 1900, 8 Day, strike, spring wound (E2-97).
    145.00   170.00   (157.00)

☐ **Douro**, wood, height 21½", dial 5", c. 1900, 8 Day, strike, spring wound (E2-97).
    140.00   165.00   (152.00)

☐ **Drave**, wood, height 20", dial 5", c. 1900, 8 Day, strike, spring wound (E2-97).
    145.00   170.00   (157.00)

☐ **Duna**, wood, height 22", dial 6", c. 1900, 8 Day, strike, spring wound (E2-97).
    140.00   165.00   (152.00)

☐ **Electra**, walnut or mahogany veneered, brass ornaments, height 19½", dial 5", c. 1890, 8 Day, strike, spring wound (E2-89).
    150.00   175.00   (162.00)

☐ **Elma**, wood, height 21", dial 6", c. 1900, 8 Day, strike, spring wound (E2-100).
    150.00   175.00   (162.00)

☐ **Estelle**, walnut or mahogany veneered, brass ornaments, height 19½", dial 5", c. 1890, 8 Day, strike, spring wound (E2-89).
    150.00   175.00   (162.00)

☐ **Felix**, oak, height 22", rococo dial 6", c. 1917, 8 Day, strike, spring wound(E1-174).
    115.00   140.00   (127.00)

☐ **Festus**, oak, height 22", rococo dial 6", c. 1917, 8 Day, strike, spring wound(E1-174).
    115.00   140.00   (127.00)

☐ **Forum**, oak, height 22", rococo dial 6", c. 1917, 8 Day, strike, spring wound(E1-174).
    115.00   140.00   (127.00)

☐ **General**, oak, "Great Military Series", 22" x 14", dial 6", c. 1894, 8 Day, strike, spring wound (E2-103).
    140.00   165.00   (152.00)
☐ **As above**, walnut, spring wound
    165.00   190.00   (177.00)

☐ **Governor**, oak, height 23", dial 16", c. 1894, spring wound (E2-103).
    145.00   170.00   (157.00)
☐ **As above**, walnut, spring wound
    170.00   195.00   (182.00)

☐ **Grayling**, wood, height 19½", dial 5", c. 1900, 8 Day, strike, spring wound(E2-100).
    135.00   160.00   (147.00)

☐ **Humber**, wood, height 21", dial 6", c. 1900, 8 Day, strike, spring wound (E2-100).
    165.00   190.00   (177.00)

☐ **Imitation Walnut Or Chestnut**, height 19", dial 5", c. 1900, 1 Day, strike, spring wound (E2-100).
    105.00   125.00   (115.00)
☐ **As above**, height 21", 8 Day, strike, spring wound
    150.00   175.00   (162.00)

Grayling

- **Irex**, *wood, height 23½", dial 6", c. 1900, 8 Day, strike, spring wound (E2-100).*
  150.00   175.00   (162.00)

- **Janitor**, *oak, interchangeable tops, "Hustler Series", dial 6", c. 1896, 8 Day, strike, spring wound (E2-106).*
  145.00   170.00   (157.00)
- **As above**, *walnut, spring wound*
  170.00   195.00   (182.00)

- **Lieutenant**, *oak, "Great Military Series", 22" x 14", dial 6", c. 1894, 8 Day, strike, spring wound (E2-103).*
  140.00   165.00   (152.00)
- **As above**, *walnut, spring wound*
  165.00   190.00   (177.00)

- **Liris**, *wood, height 22½", dial 5", c. 1900, 1 Day, strike, spring wound (E2-100).*
  105.00   130.00   (117.00)

- **Lobbyist**, *oak, height 23", dial 16", c. 1894, 1 Day, strike, spring wound (E2-103).*
  120.00   145.00   (132.00)
- **As above**, *oak, 8 Day, strike, spring wound*
  145.00   170.00   (157.00)
- **As above**, *walnut, 1 Day, strike, spring wound*
  145.00   170.00   (157.00)
- **As above**, *walnut, 8 Day, strike, spring wound*
  170.00   195.00   (182.00)

- **Mail**, *wood, height 16", dial 5", c. 1900, 1 Day, strike, spring wound (E2-100, 105).*
  105.00   130.00   (117.00)

- **Major**, *oak, "Great Military Series", 22" x 14", dial 6", c. 1894, 8 Day, strike, spring wound (E2-103).*
  140.00   165.00   (152.00)
- **As above**, *walnut, spring wound*
  165.00   190.00   (177.00)

- **Marshall**, *oak, interchangeable tops, "Hustler Series", dial 6", c. 1896, 8 Day, strike, spring wound (E2-106).*
  145.00   170.00   (157.00)
- **As above**, *walnut, spring wound*
  170.00   195.00   (182.00)

- **Mayflower**, *wood, height 20½", dial 6", c. 1900, 8 Day, strike, spring wound (E2-100).*
  150.00   175.00   (162.00)

- **Mayor**, *oak, interchangeable tops, "Hustler Series", dial 6", c. 1896, 8 Day, strike, spring wound (E2-106).*
  145.00   170.00   (157.00)
- **As above**, *walnut, spring wound*
  170.00   195.00   (182.00)

- **Mersey**, *wood, height 21", dial 5", c. 1900, 1 Day, strike, spring wound (E2-100).*
  105.00   130.00   (117.00)

- **Morgath**, *oak, "Norwich Series", 25" x 15½", dial 6", c. 1900, 8 Day, strike, spring wound (E2-104).*
  160.00   185.00   (172.00)
- **As above**, *walnut, spring wound*
  185.00   210.00   (197.00)

- **Moselle**, *wood, height 26", dial 6", c. 1900, 8 Day, strike, spring wound (E2-99).*
  190.00   220.00   (205.00)

- **Nectar**, *wood, height 24", dial 6", c. 1900, 8 Day, strike, spring wound (E2-99).*
  160.00   185.00   (172.00)

- **Nereid**, *wood, height 23½", dial 6", c. 1900, 8 Day, strike, spring wound (E2-99).*
  145.00   170.00   (157.00)

- **Neva**, *wood, height 19", dial 5½", c. 1900, 8 Day, strike, spring wound (E2-99).*
  145.00   170.00   (157.00)

- **Oder**, *wood, height 20½", dial 6", c. 1900, 8 Day, strike, spring wound (E2-99).*
  145.00   170.00   (157.00)

- **Orient**, *wood veneer, 18¾" x 10½", c. 1900, 1 Day, spring wound (E2-96).*
  115.00   140.00   (127.00)
- **As above**, *1 Day, strike, spring wound.*
  135.00   160.00   (147.00)

414 / NEW HAVEN CLOCK COMPANY

☐ **Orphic,** *wood veneer,*
17½" x 10½", c. 1900, 1 Day,
spring wound (E2-96).
    115.00   140.00   (127.00)
☐ **As above,** *1 Day, strike,*
spring wound.
    135.00   160.00   (147.00)

☐ **Orphir,** *wood veneer, 18" x 10½",*
c. 1900, 1 Day, spring wound
(E2-96).
    115.00   140.00   (127.00)
☐ **As above,** *1 Day, strike,*
spring wound.
    135.00   160.00   (147.00)

☐ **Oruba,** *wood veneer, 19½" x 10½",*
c. 1900, 1 Day, spring wound
(E2-96).
    115.00   140.00   (127.00)
☐ **As above,** *1 Day, strike,*
spring wound.
    135.00   160.00   (147.00)

☐ **Osage,** *wood, height 21", dial 6", c.*
1900, 8 Day, strike, spring wound
(E2-99).
    175.00   200.00   (187.00)

☐ **Ouse,** *wood, height 19", dial 5", c.*
1900, 1 Day, strike, spring wound
(E2-99).
    135.00   160.00   (147.00)

☐ **President,** *walnut, height 23", dial*
16", c. 1894, 1 Day, strike, spring
wound (E2-103).
    145.00   170.00   (157.00)
☐ **As above,** *8 Day, strike,*
spring wound.
    170.00   195.00   (182.00)
☐ **As above,** *oak, 1 Day, strike,*
spring wound.
    120.00   145.00   (132.00)
☐ **As above,** *8 Day, strike,*
spring wound.
    145.00   170.00   (157.00)

☐ **Rambler,** *wood, height 19½", dial*
5", c. 1900, 8 Day, strike, spring
wound (E2-99).
    150.00   175.00   (162.00)

☐ **Rarus, T.P.,** *wood, height 15½",*
dial 5", c. 1900, 1 Day, spring
wound (E2-99).
    105.00   130.00   (117.00)

Rarus

☐ **Rarus,** *wood, height 17½", dial*
5½", c. 1900, 1 Day, strike, spring
wound (E2-99).
    105.00   130.00   (117.00)

☐ **Recorder,** *oak, interchangeable*
tops, "Hustler Series," dial 6", c.
1896, 8 Day, strike, spring wound
(E2-106).
    145.00   170.00   (157.00)

☐ **Rhine,** *wood, height 21", dial 6", c.*
1900, 8 Day, strike, spring wound
(E2-99).
    135.00   160.00   (147.00)

☐ **Saline,** *wood, height 21½", dial 6",*
c. 1900, 1 Day, strike, spring wound
(E2-101).
    105.00   130.00   (117.00)

☐ **Sampson,** *wood, thermometer,*
barometer, and spirit level,
23¾" x 15", dial 6", c. 1910,
8 Day, simple calendar, spring
wound (E-90).
    160.00   185.00   (172.00)

☐ **Sampson,** *oak, "Norwich Series,"*
25" x 15½", dial 6", c. 1900, 8 Day,
strike, spring wound (E2-104).
    160.00   185.00   (172.00)
☐ **As above,** *walnut, 8 Day, strike,*
spring wound.
    185.00   210.00   (197.00)

NEW HAVEN CLOCK COMPANY / 415

Sampson

Sanches

☐ **Sanches,** *solid oak, flemish finish, "Sancho Series," 22½" x 13", dial 6", c. 1900, 8 Day, strike, spring wound (E2-104).*
　　135.00　　160.00　　(147.00)

☐ **Secretary,** *walnut, height 23", dial 16", c. 1894, 1 Day, strike, spring wound (E2-103).*
　　145.00　　170.00　　(157.00)
☐ **As above,** *8 Day, strike, spring wound.*
　　170.00　　195.00　　(182.00)

☐ **Segura,** *solid oak, flemish finish, "Sancho Series," 22½" x 13", dial 6", c. 1900, 8 Day, strike, spring wound (E2-104).*
　　135.00　　160.00　　(147.00)

☐ **Seine,** *wood, height 23", dial 6", c. 1900, 1 Day, strike, spring wound (E2-101).*
　　105.00　　130.00　　(117.00)

☐ **Seminole,** *wood, height 22¾", dial 6", c. 1900, 8 Day, strike, spring wound (E2-101).*
　　160.00　　185.00　　(172.00)

☐ **Senator,** *walnut, height 23", dial 16", c. 1894, 1 Day, strike, spring wound (E2-103).*
　　145.00　　170.00　　(157.00)
☐ **As above,** *8 Day, strike, spring wound.*
　　170.00　　195.00　　(182.00)
☐ **As above,** *oak, 1 Day, strike, spring wound.*
　　120.00　　145.00　　(132.00)
☐ **As above,** *oak, 8 Day, strike, spring wound.*
　　145.00　　170.00　　(157.00)

☐ **Sergeant,** *walnut, 22" x 14", dial 6", "Great Military Series," c. 1894, 8 Day, strike, spring wound (E2-103).*
　　165.00　　190.00　　(177.00)
☐ **As above,** *oak, 8 Day, strike, spring wound.*
　　140.00　　165.00　　(152.00)

☐ **Severn,** *wood, height 19", dial 5½", c. 1900, 1 Day, strike, spring wound (E2-101).*
　　105.00　　125.00　　(115.00)

☐ **Shamrock,** *wood, height 23½", dial 6", c. 1900, 8 Day, strike, spring wound (E2-101).*
　　155.00　　180.00　　(167.00)

☐ **Shannon,** *wood, height 18", dial 5½", c. 1900, 1 Day, strike, spring wound (E2-101).*
　　105.00　　125.00　　(115.00)

☐ **Sorry,** *solid oak, flemish finish, "Sancho Series," 22½" x 13", dial 6", c. 1900, 8 Day, strike, spring wound (E2-104).*
　　135.00　　160.00　　(147.00)

Severn

Tiber

Tagus

☐ **Tagus**, wood, height 19", dial 5½", c. 1900, 1 Day, strike, spring wound (E2-101).
        105.00   125.00   (115.00)

☐ **Tamar**, wood, height 21¼", dial 6", c. 1900, 8 Day, strike, spring wound (E2-101).
        145.00   170.00   (157.00)

☐ **Thames**, wood, height 23", dial 6", c. 1900, 8 Day, strike, spring wound (E2-101).
        160.00   185.00   (172.00)

☐ **Theiss**, wood, height 19½", dial 5", c. 1900, 1 Day, strike, spring wound (E2-101).
        105.00   130.00   (117.00)

☐ **Tiber**, wood, height 19", dial 5½", c. 1900, 1 Day, strike, spring wound (E2-101).
        105.00   130.00   (117.00)

☐ **Titania**, wood, height 24", dial 6", c. 1900, 8 Day, strike, spring wound (E2-101).
        160.00   185.00   (172.00)

☐ **Tomahawk**, wood, height 23", dial 6", c. 1900, 8 Day, strike, spring wound (E2-102).
        150.00   175.00   (162.00)

☐ **Vampire**, wood, height 21½", dial 6", c. 1900, 8 Day, strike, spring wound (E2-102).
        145.00   170.00   (157.00)

☐ **Vindex**, wood, height 21½", dial 6", c. 1900, 8 Day, strike, spring wound (E2-102).
        150.00   175.00   (162.00)

NEW HAVEN CLOCK COMPANY / 417

KITCHEN/SERIES

Weser

- [ ] **Volga**, wood, height 21½", dial 6", c. 1900, 8 Day, strike, spring wound (E2-102).
  140.00   165.00   (152.00)
- [ ] **Walnut**, wood, height 20½", dial 5", c. 1900, 8 Day, strike, spring wound (E2-102).
  145.00   170.00   (157.00)
- [ ] **As above**, height 21½", 8 Day, strike, spring wound.
  150.00   175.00   (162.00)
- [ ] **Weser**, wood, height 20½", dial 6", c. 1900, 8 Day, strike, spring wound (E2-102).
  140.00   165.00   (152.00)
- [ ] **Yarana**, wood, height 21¼", dial 6", c. 1900, 8 Day, strike, spring wound (E2-102).
  145.00   170.00   (157.00)
- [ ] **Zingara**, wood, height 21", dial 6", c. 1900, 8 Day, strike, spring wound (E2-102).
  150.00   175.00   (162.00)

- [ ] **Assortment 7-18**, oak, height 22½", dial 6", c. 1900, 8 Day, strike, spring wound (E1-38).
  each 100.00   120.00   (110.00)
- [ ] **As above**, walnut, 8 Day, strike, spring wound.
  each 125.00   150.00   (137.00)
- [ ] **Brazilian Line**, oak or with metal trimmings, packed assorted six in a case, no individual names, three clocks shown, 22¼" x 15", dial 6", c. 1900, 8 Day, strike, spring wound (E2-105).
  each 155.00   180.00   (167.00)
- [ ] **Camden Series**, oak, assorted patterns, three patterns, no individual names, 22" x 14", dial 6", c. 1900, 8 Day, strike, spring wound (E2-107).
  each 145.00   170.00   (157.00)
- [ ] **Camden Series Hanging**, oak, three clocks shown, no names, 25" x 14", dial 6", c. 1900, 8 Day, strike, spring wound (E2-107).
  each 210.00   240.00   (225.00)
- [ ] **As above**, walnut.
  each 235.00   275.00   (255.00)
- [ ] **Colonial Series**, cherry, wire bell, assortment of six clocks, three cherry and three oak, height 18", dial 6", c. 1910, 8 Day, strike, spring wound (E2-128).
  each 155.00   180.00   (167.00)
- [ ] **As above**, oak.
  each 130.00   155.00   (142.00)
- [ ] **"D" Series**, walnut, Dee, Don, Doon, 24⅜" x 15⅜", dial 6", c. 1900, 8 Day, strike, spring wound (E2-104).
  each 150.00   175.00   (162.00)
- [ ] **Dandy Series**, wood, six different patterns, Dandy No. 1, Dandy No. 2, Dandy No. 3, Dandy No. 4, Dandy No. 5 and Dandy No. 6, height 22", dial 6", c. 1896, 8 Day, strike, spring wound (E2-106).
  each 145.00   170.00   (157.00)

418 / NEW HAVEN CLOCK COMPANY

Camden Series

Dandy Series

Camden Series Hanging

☐ **Great Military Series,** *oak, Sergeant, Colonel, Lieutenant, Captain, General, Major, 22" x 14", dial 6", c. 1894, 8 Day, strike, spring wound (E2-103).*
each 120.00   145.00   (132.00)
☐ **As above,** *walnut.*
each 140.00   165.00   (152.00)

☐ **Hustler Series,** *oak, interchangeable tops, Recorder, Alderman, Councilman, Marshall, Janitor, Mayor, dial 6", c. 1896, 8 Day, strike, spring wound (E2-106).*
each 125.00   150.00   (137.00)
☐ **As above,** *walnut.*
each 145.00   170.00   (157.00)

☐ **Maine Series,** *oak, packed assorted six in a case, two clocks shown, no individual names, 23½" x 15", dial 6", c. 1900, 8 Day, strike, spring wound (E2-105).*
each 130.00   155.00   (142.00)

☐ **Merchants Series,** *oak, comes two each pattern in case, two clocks shown, no names, 22" x 15", dial 6", c. 1917, 8 Day, strike, spring wound (E1-174).*
each 140.00   165.00   (152.00)

☐ **Mersey Series,** *oak, assorted patterns, three patterns, no individual names, 23" x 14", dial 6", c. 1900, 8 Day, strike, spring wound (E2-107).*
each 150.00   175.00   (162.00)
☐ **As above,** *walnut.*
each 175.00   200.00   (187.00)

NEW HAVEN CLOCK COMPANY / 419

Maine Series No. 2

- **Norwich Series,** oak, Sampson, Conroy, Morgath, Mantel, 25" x 15½", dial 6", c. 1900, 8 Day, strike, spring wound (E2-104).
  each 160.00   185.00   (172.00)
- **As above,** walnut.
  each 185.00   210.00   (197.00)

- **Patrol Series,** oak, packed assorted six in a case, three clocks shown, no individual names, 22¾" x 14¼", dial 6", c. 1900, 8 Day, strike, spring wound (E2-105).
  each 150.00   175.00   (162.00)
- **As above,** walnut.
  each 175.00   200.00   (187.00)

- **Picket Series,** oak, three patterns, no individual names, 22" x 13½", dial 6", c. 1900, 8 Day, strike, spring wound (E2-107).
  each 145.00   170.00   (157.00)
- **As above,** walnut.
  each 170.00   195.00   (182.00)

- **Sancho Series,** solid oak, flemish finish, Segura, Sanches, Sorry, 22½" x 13", dial 6", c. 1900, 8 Day, strike, spring wound (E2-104).
  each 135.00   160.00   (147.00)

- **Government Series,** oak, Lobbyist, Governor, Senator, Ambassador, Secretary, President, c. 1894, 8 Day, strike, spring wound (E2-103).
  each 125.00   150.00   (137.00)
- **As above,** walnut.
  each 145.00   170.00   (157.00)

KITCHEN/TEAR DROP

- **Elbe,** wood, height 24", dial 6", c. 1900, 8 Day, strike, spring wound (E2-100).
  250.00   280.00   (265.00)

- **Parisan,** wood, height 24", dial 6", c. 1900, 8 Day, strike, spring wound (E2-99).
  250.00   280.00   (265.00)

- **Salem,** oak, 26½" x 12¾", dial 6", c. 1900, 8 Day, strike, spring wound (E2-105).
  230.00   260.00   (245.00)

KITCHEN/WALL

- **Hudson,** cherry or walnut, height 26½", dial 5", c. 1900, 8 Day, strike, spring wound (E2-102).
  230.00   260.00   (245.00)

- **Matanzas,** oak, 27½" x 14¾", dial 6", c. 1921, 8 Day, strike, spring wound (E1-183).
  245.00   275.00   (260.00)

Matanzas

420 / NEW HAVEN CLOCK COMPANY

- **Standish**, *oak, 26¼" x 13", dial 6", c. 1900, 8 Day, strike, spring wound (E2-105).*
  210.00   240.00   (225.00)

- **Stanton**, *oak, 28" x 14¼", dial 6", c. 1900, 8 Day, strike, spring wound (E2-105).*
  210.00   240.00   ·(225.00)

MANTEL/BLACK IRON

- **Ailene**, *solid case brass frame, richly ornamented silver panels, hand modeled, height 9", dial 3¼", c. 1900, 8 Day, strike (E1-101).*
  625.00   700.00   (662.00)

- **Arno**, *enameled iron, Empire sash with porcelain or pearl dial, visible escapement, c. 1900, 8 Day, strike (E1-40).*
  120.00   145.00   (132.00)

- **Charlemont**, *enameled iron, French gilt trimmings, black or green marble finish, cast French sash, 11⅝" x 8⅜", porcelain dial 3", c. 1900, 8 Day, strike (E1-37).*
  105.00   130.00   (117.00)

- **Charlton**, *enameled iron, French gilt trimmings, black or green marble finish, cast French sash, 14⅝" x 9", porcelain dial 4", c. 1900, 8 Day, strike (E1-37).*
  125.00   150.00   (137.00)

Charlemont

Charlton

- **Chateau**, *enameled iron, black or green marble, bronze or gilt trimmings, 9½" x 11½", dial 4", c. 1900, 8 Day, strike (E1-39).*
  100.00   120.00   (110.00)

- **Chistlehurst**, *enameled iron, black or green marble, bronze or gilt trimmings, 10¾" x 10", dial 4", c. 1900, 8 Day, strike (E1-39).*
  100.00   120.00   (110.00)

- **Clarendon**, *black enameled wood, 10¼" x 13", white, gilt or pearl dial 6", c. 1900, 8 Day, strike (E1-40).*
  55.00   70.00   (62.50)

- **Florence**, *enameled iron, Empire sash with porcelain or pearl dial, visible escapement, c. 1900, 8 Day, strike (E1-39).*
  75.00   90.00   (82.50)

- **Fortuna**, *enameled iron, Empire sash with porcelain or pearl dial, visible escapement, c. 1900, 8 Day, strike (E1-39).*
  100.00   120.00   (110.00)

- **Galatea**, *enameled iron, Empire sash with porcelain or pearl dial, visible escapement, c. 1900, 8 Day, strike (E1-39).*
  105.00   130.00   (117.00)

NEW HAVEN CLOCK COMPANY / 421

Montrose

☐ **Harcourt,** *enameled iron, Empire sash with porcelain or pearl dial, visible escapement, c. 1900, 8 Day, strike (E1-39).*
  105.00   130.00   (117.00)

☐ **Leland,** *black enameled iron with gilt ornamentation, Empire sash with porcelain dial, 12⅛" x 9¾", dial 6", c. 1900, 8 Day, strike, (E1-39).*
  100.00   120.00   (110.00)

☐ **Mona,** *enameled iron, Empire sash, with porcelain or pearl dial, visible escapement, c. 1900, 8 Day, strike (E1-39).*
  80.00   100.00   (90.00)

☐ **Montrose,** *enameled iron, Empire sash with porcelain or pearl dial, visible escapement, c. 1900, 8 Day, strike (E1-40).*
  105.00   125.00   (115.00)

☐ **New Monaco,** *enameled iron, Empire sash with porcelain or pearl dial, visible escapement, c. 1900, 8 Day, strike (E1-39).*
  100.00   120.00   (110.00)

☐ **Olinda,** *black enameled iron, bronze or gilt trimmings, Empire sash, visible escapement, plain white or mother-of-pearl dial, 12¼" x 11½", dial 6", c. 1900, 8 Day, strike (E1-39).*
  95.00   115.00   (105.00)

☐ **Pocahontas,** *enameled iron, Empire sash, porcelain or pearl dial, visible escapement, c. 1900, 8 Day, strike (E1-39).*
  115.00   140.00   (127.00)

☐ **Rosalind,** *enameled iron, Empire sash with porcelain or pearl dial, visible escapement, c. 1900, 8 Day, strike (E1-40).*
  105.00   125.00   (115.00)

☐ **Thetis,** *enameled iron, Empire sash with porcelain or pearl dial, visible escapement, c. 1900, 8 Day, strike (E1-39).*
  90.00   110.00   (100.00)

☐ **Triad,** *dark blue or dark green porcelain bowl with best gold finish trimmings, cathedral gong, ivorized porcelain dial, fancy gilt center or decorated porcelain dial, Empire sash and heavy beveled glass, 21½" x 9", dial 4", c. 1900, 8 Day, strike (E2-110).*
  190.00   220.00   (205.00)

MANTLE/BLACK WOOD

☐ **Alexander,** *black enameled wood, white, gilt or pearl dial, 11¾" x 16", dial 6", c. 1900, 8 Day, strike (E1-40).*
  75.00   90.00   (82.40)

☐ **Bancroft,** *black enameled wood, white, gilt or pearl dial, bronze or gilt trimmings, 11" x 16", dial 6", c. 1900, 8 Day, strike (E1-39).*
  80.00   95.00   (87.50)

☐ **Brandon,** *black enameled wood, white, gilt or pearl dial, bronze or gilt trimmings, 11" x 16", dial 6", c. 1900, 8 Day, strike (E1-40).*
  75.00   90.00   (82.50)

Brandon

422 / NEW HAVEN CLOCK COMPANY

- **Burlington,** black enameled wood, white, gilt or pearl dial, bronze or gilt trimmings, 11" x 16", dial 6", c. 1900, 8 Day, strike (E1-40).
  75.00   90.00   (82.50)

- **Numa,** black enameled wood, white, gilt or pearl dial, 11" x 16", dial 6", c. 1900, 8 Day, strike (E1-40).
  75.00   90.00   (82.50)

- **Pembroke,** black enameled wood, white, gilt or pearl dial, 10⅞" x 16", dial 6", c. 1900, 8 Day, strike (E1-40).
  70.00   85.00   (77.50)

- **Seneca,** black enameled wood, white, gilt or pearl dial, 11" x 16", dial 6", c. 1900, 8 Day, strike (E1-40).
  80.00   95.00   (87.50)

- **Winifred,** black enameled wood, white, gilt or pearl dial, 10½" x 14⅜", dial 6", c. 1900, 8 Day, strike (E1-40).
  65.00   80.00   (72.50)

MANTLE/BRASS FINISH

- **Antique Brass No. 2,** visible escapement, height 13½", dial 4", c. 1900, 8 Day, strike (E2-126).
  220.00   250.00   (235.00)

- **Czar,** brass finish, cathedral gong, visible escapement, height 13½", base 15", dial 5½", c. 1900, 8 Day, strike (E2-93).
  210.00   230.00   (235.00)

Czar

- **Iroquois,** brass finish, visible escapement, French sash, porcelain dial, height 18¼", dial 5½", c. 1900, 8 Day, strike (E2-93).
  230.00   260.00   (245.00)

MANTLE/MAHOGANY CASE

- **Auris,** mahogany, bowed glass, 10⅛" x 8⅞", dial 6", 8 Day, strike (E1-172).
  30.00   40.00   (35.00)

- **Ausprey,** mahogany, bowed glass, 8⅞" x 15¾", dial 6", c. 1911, 8 Day, strike (E1-172).
  30.00   40.00   (35.00)

- **Auston,** mahogany, 10¼" x 8¼", dial 6", c. 1911, 8 Day, strike (E1-172).
  20.00   35.00   (27.50)

- **Austro,** mahogany, bowed glass, 9¾" x 8¼", dial 6", 8 Day, strike (E1-172).
  20.00   35.00   (27.50)

- **Author,** mahogany, 9" x 14¾", dial 6", c. 1911, 8 Day, strike (E1-172).
  35.00   45.00   (40.00)

- **Garcia,** mahogany, 6¼" x 13", dial 4½", c. 1911, 1 Day, alarm (E1-172).
  20.00   30.00   (25.00)

- **Green,** mahogany, 6¾" x 7¼", dial 4½", c. 1911, 1 Day, alarm (E1-172).
  15.00   25.00   (20.00)

- **Oval No. 52,** mahogany, 6¼" x 7½", dial 3½", c. 1917, 8 Day (E1-173).
  15.00   25.00   (20.00)

- **Oval No. 53,** mahogany, 6¼" x 12", dial 3½", c. 1917, 8 Day (E1-173).
  20.00   30.00   (25.00)

- **Wager,** mahogany, 6" x 5⅞", dial 3½", c. 1917, 8 Day, strike (E1-173).
  20.00   30.00   25.00

MANTLE/ONYX

- **Malcolm,** Brazilian onyx, ivorized porcelain dial, gilt center, Empire sash, heavy beveled glass, cathedral gong, 11¼" x 15¾", dial 4", c. 1900, 8 Day, strike (E2-110).
  140.00   165.00   (152.00)

- **Mandan,** Brazilian onyx, ivorized porcelain dial, gilt center, Empire sash, heavy beveled glass, cathedral gong, 18½" x 9¾", dial 4", c. 1900, 8 Day, strike (E2-110).
  190.00   220.00   (205.00)

- **Marston,** Brazilian onyx, ivorized porcelain dial, gilt center, Empire sash, heavy beveled glass, cathedral gong, 16½" x 9½", dial 4", c. 1900, 8 Day, strike (E2-110).
  190.00   220.00   (205.00)

- **Mercy,** Brazilian onyx, ivorized porcelain dial, gilt center, Empire sash, heavy beveled glass, cathedral gong, 10" x 12", dial 4", c. 1900, 8 Day, strike (E2-110).
  135.00   160.00   (147.00)

- **Monroe,** Brazilian onyx, ivorized porcelain dial, gilt center, Empire sash, heavy beveled glass, cathedral gong, 10¼" x 10¼", dial 4", c. 1900, 8 Day, strike (E2-110).
  125.00   150.00   (137.00)

- **Myrtle,** Brazilian onyx, ivorized porcelain dial, gilt center, Empire sash, heavy beveled glass, cathedral gong, 11" x 11¾", dial 4", c. 1900, 8 Day, strike (E2-110).
  135.00   160.00   (148.00)

MANTLE/TAMBOUR

- **Garfield,** mahogany, 6½" x 13", dial 4½", c. 1911, 1 Day, alarm (E1-172).
  20.00   30.00   (25.00)

- **Jacobean No. 55,** mahogany, porcelain or silver dial, 6½" x 13½", dial 3½", c. 1917, 8 Day (E1-173).
  20.00   30.00   (25.00)

- **Quayle,** mahogany, porcelain or silver dial, 6½" x 12¼", dial 3½", c. 1917, 8 Day (E1-173).
  15.00   25.00   (20.00)

- **Tambour No. 1,** mahogany, porcelain or silver dial, 10¼" x 21½", dial 6", c. 1917, 8 Day, strike (E1-173).
  60.00   75.00   (67.00)

- **Tambour No. 2,** mahogany, porcelain or silver dial, 11½" x 24", dial 7", c. 1917, 8 Day, strike (E1-173).
  75.00   95.00   (85.00)

- **Tambour No. 6,** mahogany, porcelain or silver dial, 11½" x 24½", dial 7", c. 1917, 8 Day, strike (E1-173).
  65.00   80.00   (72.00)

- **Tambour No. 13,** mahogany, 10" x 22", dial 6", c. 1911, 8 Day, strike (E1-172).
  40.00   50.00   (45.00)

- **Tambour No. 15,** mahogany, 12¼" x 29½", dial 7½", c. 1917, 8 Day, strike (E1-173).
  80.00   100.00   (90.00)

- **Tambour No. 16,** mahogany, bowed glass, 9" x 18", dial 6", c. 1911, 8 Day, strike (E1-172).
  25.00   35.00   (30.00)

- **Tambour No. 17,** mahogany, bowed glass, 9⅞" x 15⅞", dial 6", c. 1911, 8 Day, strike (E1-172).
  30.00   40.00   (35.00)

MIRROR SIDES

- **Apollo,** wood, height 20", dial 5½", c. 1890, 8 Day, strike (E2-89).
  260.00   280.00   (270.00)

- **As above,** 8 Day, alarm.
  275.00   300.00   (287.00)

- **Countess,** black walnut, 12 mirrors and solid metal head, height 26", dial 6", c. 1890, 8 Day, strike (E2-89).
  285.00   325.00   (305.00)

- **Oakdale,** oak, silver ornaments, 24" x 15¼", dial 6", c. 1910, 8 Day, strike (E2-90).
  285.00   325.00   (305.00)
- **As above,** walnut, gilt ornaments.
  315.00   355.00   (335.00)

- **Occidental,** oak, silver ornaments, height 24", dial 6", c. 1910, 8 Day, strike (E2-90).
  285.00   325.00   (305.00)
- **As above,** walnut, gilt ornaments.
  315.00   355.00   (335.00)

424 / NEW HAVEN CLOCK COMPANY

Apollo

MISSION

☐ **San Jose,** oak, cast numerals, polished brass hands and pendulum ball, 24½" x 13", dial 12", c. 1920, 8 Day, strike (E1-183).
65.00   80.00   (72.50)

MISSION/CABINET

☐ **Alva,** solid oak, Flemish finish, wood dial with white figures painted on a dark blue background, pendulum movement, brass hands, 13" x 6½", dial 4", 1 Day (E2-108).
70.00   85.00   (77.50)

☐ **Arco,** solid oak, Flemish finish, wood dial with white figures painted on a dark blue background, lever movement, 13" x 4½", dial 2", 1 Day (E2-108).
80.00   95.00   (87.50)

☐ **Los Alamos,** solid oak, Flemish finish, wood dial with brass hands and numerals, 14½" x 11¾", dial 6", c. 1910, 8 Day, strike (E2-109).
100.00   120.00   (110.00)

☐ **Los Barrios,** solid oak, Flemish finish, wood dial with brass hands and numerals, 13½" x 11½", dial 6", c. 1910, 8 Day, strike (E2-109).
100.00   120.00   (110.00)

☐ **Los Santos,** solid oak, Flemish finish, wood dial with brass hands and numerals, 13¼" x 12¼", dial 6", c. 1910, 8 Day, strike (E2-109).
100.00   120.00   (110.00)

☐ **Moro,** solid oak, Flemish finish, wood dial with white figures painted on a dark blue background, pendulum movement, brass hands, 13" x 6½", dial 4", 1 Day.
70.00   85.00   (77.50)

☐ **Pasco,** solid oak, Flemish finish, wood dial with white figures painted on a dark blue background, lever movement, brass hands, 13" x 5½", dial 3", 1 Day.
70.00   85.00   (77.50)

☐ **San Carlos,** weathered oak, wooden dial with white figures on a background of dark brown, fancy brass hands, 20" x 9", dial 6", c. 1910, 8 Day, strike (E2-108).
80.00   100.00   (90.00)

☐ **San Juan,** weathered oak, wooden dial with white figures on a background of dark brown, fancy brass hands, 20½" x 9½", dial 6", c. 1910, 8 Day, strike (E2-108).
80.00   100.00   (90.00)

☐ **Tosca,** solid oak, Flemish finish, wood dial with white Arabic figures painted on a dark blue background, brass hands, pendulum movement, 12½" x 6½", dial 4", c. 1910, 8 Day, strike (E2-108).
95.00   115.00   (105.00)

☐ **Vega,** solid oak, Flemish finish, wood dial with white Arabic figures painted on a dark blue background, brass hands, pendulum movement, 13" x 6", dial 4", c. 1910, 8 Day, strike (E2-108).
95.00   115.00   (105.00)

NEW HAVEN CLOCK COMPANY / 425

MISSION/GRANDFATHER

☐ **Dutch No. 40,** *solid oak, Flemish finish, cast brass hands and numerals, 77½" x 17½", c. 1910, 8 Day, strike, spring (E2-108).*
    210.00   240.00   (225.00)

☐ **Dutch No. 45,** *solid oak, Flemish finish, stamped brass hands and numerals, 68½" x 15½", c. 1910, 8 Day, strike, spring (E2-108).*
    210.00   240.00   (225.00)

MISSION/KITCHEN

☐ **La Lanza,** *weathered oak, brass numerals and hands, 22" x 13½", c. 1910, 8 Day, strike (E2-108).*
    110.00   135.00   (117.00)

☐ **La Plata,** *weathered oak, brass numerals and hands, 22¾" x 13¾", c. 1910, 8 Day, strike (E2-108).*
    110.00   135.00   (117.00)

☐ **Minas,** *solid oak, Flemish finish, fitted with pendulum movement with brass hands and numerals, 12" x 4½", dial 3", c. 1910, 1 Day (E2-109).*
    55.00   70.00   (62.50)

☐ **Minch,** *solid oak, Flemish finish, fitted with pendulum movement with brass hands and numerals, 12" x 4½", dial 3", c. 1910, 1 Day (E2-109).*
    55.00   70.00   (62.50)

☐ **Minho,** *solid oak, Flemish finish, fitted with pendulum movement, with brass hands and numerals, 12" x 4½", dial 3", c. 1910, 1 Day (E2-109).*
    55.00   70.00   (62.50)

☐ **San Benito,** *weathered oak, 21" x 13½", dial 6", c. 1910, 8 Day, strike (E2-109).*
    110.00   135.00   (117.00)

☐ **Santa Clara,** *weathered oak, six-inch dial with brass numerals and hands, 20¼" x 11¼", c. 1910, 8 Day, strike (E2-109).*
    105.00   130.00   (117.00)

☐ **San Mateo,** *weathered oak, six-inch dial with brass numerals and hands, 20½" x 9½", c. 1910, 8 Day, strike (E2-109).*
    105.00   130.00   (117.00)

☐ **San Pedro,** *weathered oak, six-inch dial with brass numerals and hands, 19" x 12½", c. 1910, 8 Day, strike (E2-109).*
    105.00   130.00   (117.00)

MISSION/KITCHEN, HANGING

☐ **Durance Hanging,** *solid oak, Flemish finish, cast brass hands and numerals, 37½" x 15¾", c. 1910, 8 Day (E2-109).*
    140.00   165.00   (152.00)

☐ **As above,** *8 Day, strike*
    190.00   220.00   (205.00)

☐ **As above,** *30 Day*
    210.00   240.00   (225.00)

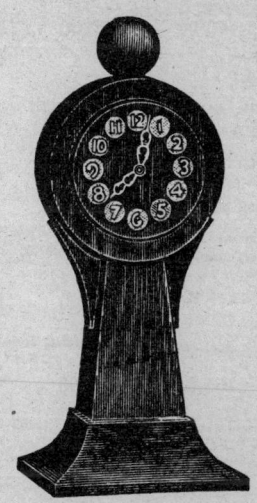

Loma

MISSION/NOVELTY

☐ **Liso,** *solid oak, Flemish finish, wood dial with white figures painted on a dark blue background, lever movement, 8½" x 4½", dial 2", c. 1910, 1 Day (E2-109).*
    40.00   55.00   (47.50)

426 / NEW HAVEN CLOCK COMPANY

☐ **Loma,** solid oak, Flemish finish, wood dial with white figures painted on a dark blue background, lever movement, 8½" x 4", dial 2", c. 1910, 1 Day (E2-109).
        40.00   55.00   (47.50)

☐ **Lute,** solid oak, Flemish finish, wood dial with white figures painted on a dark blue background, lever movement, 9" x 4½", dial 2", c. 1910, 1 Day (E2-109).
        40.00   55.00   (47.50)

MISSION/OCTAGON, DROP

☐ **Dulce,** solid oak, Flemish finish, cast brass hands and numerals, 24" x 16", wood dial 12", c. 1910, 8 Day (E2-109).
        165.00   190.00   (177.00)
☐ **As above,** 8 Day, strike
        190.00   220.00   (205.00)

NOVELTY/FANCY

☐ **Acme,** solid cast brass, hand finished, 2½" enamel dial, c. 1900, 1 Day (E2-111).
        80.00   95.00   (87.50)

☐ **Acrobat,** cast in brass, barbadienne finish, silver and gold finish, bell, height 16¼", dial 4", c. 1900, 8 Day, strike (E2-112).
        175.00   200.00   (187.00)

☐ **Aida,** antique brass, height 12¾", dial 6", c. 1900, 15 Day (E2-112).
        105.00   125.00   (115.00)

☐ **Andorra,** ormolu gold plated case, 10¼" x 3¾", porcelain dial 2", c. 1900 1 Day (E2 113).
        60.00   75.00   (67.50)

☐ **Bamboo,** height 8¾", c. 1900, 1 Day (E2-112).
        80.00   100.00   (90.00)
☐ **As above,** 1 Day, calendar
        125.00   150.00   (137.00)

☐ **Banjo,** silver plated and oxidized, height 7", dial 2", c. 1900, 1 Day (E2-112).
        70.00   85.00   (77.50)

Andorra

Bouquet

NEW HAVEN CLOCK COMPANY / 427

- **Barrel On Skids,** *oak with brass hoops, height 6¾", dial 2½", c. 1900, 1 Day (E2-111).*
  40.00   55.00   (47.50)

- **Bouquet,** *gold or silver plated, beveled glass, mirror and cut glass scent bottle, height 8", c. 1900, 1 Day (E2-111).*
  125.00   150.00   (137.00)

- **Buffalo Ink,** *polished horn, brass trimmings, cut glass inks, front glass of best crystal lens, ½" thick, and of high magnifying power, c. 1900, 1 Day (E2-112).*
  75.00   90.00   (82.50)

- **Calendar,** *plush, assorted colors, c. 1900, 1 Day, calendar (E2-112).*
  125.00   150.00   (137.00)

- **Chatelaine,** *antique brass finish, height 14", dial 6", length over all 21", c. 1900, 15 Day (E2-112).*
  175.00   200.00   (187.00)

- **Cigar Lighter,** *c. 1900, 1 Day (E2-111).*
  150.00   175.00   (162.00)

- **Egyptian,** *height 8", c. 1900, 1 Day (E2-112).*
  75.00   90.00   (82.50)
- **As above,** *1 Day, calendar*
  105.00   125.00   (115.00)

- **Etruscan,** *pottery case, c. 1900, 1 Day (E2-112).*
  60.00   75.00   (67.50)
- **As above,** *1 Day, alarm*
  80.00   95.00   (87.50)

- **Flush,** *ormolu gold plated case, 5" x 5", dial 2", c. 1900, 1 Day (E2-113).*
  55.00   70.00   (62.50)

- **Lighthouse,** *oxidized silver and gilt, cut pinion movement, revolving lanterns, height 12½", dial 2", c. 1900, 1 Day (E2-111).*
  175.00   200.00   (187.00)

- **Lisbon,** *ormolu gold plated case, 6" x 6½", dial 2", c. 1900, 1 Day (E2-113).*
  55.00   70.00   (62.50)

Lighthouse

- **Mace,** *silver body with gold spikes, c. 1900, 1 Day (E2-112).*
  105.00   125.00   (115.00)

- **Mandolin,** *black and silver finish, length 23", dial 5", c. 1900, 8 Day (E2-112).*
  110.00   135.00   (122.00)

- **Paper Weight,** *watch movement, width 3", c. 1900, 1 Day (E2-112).*
  45.00   60.00   (52.00)

428 / NEW HAVEN CLOCK COMPANY

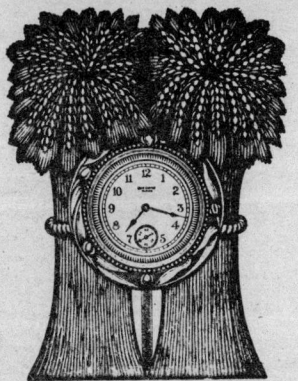

Sheaf

☐ **Parasol,** finished in black and gold, height 15", c. 1900, 15 Day (E2-111).
150.00   175.00   (162.00)

☐ **Racquet,** gold finish, c. 1900, 1 Day (E2-112).
95.00   115.00   (105.00)

☐ **Sheaf,** ormolu gold plated case, 7½" x 6", dial 2", c. 1900, 1 Day (E2-113).
75.00   90.00   (82.50)

☐ **Stirrup,** gold and silver finish, height 17", dial 2", c. 1900, 1 Day (E2-112).
70.00   85.00   (77.50)

NOVELTY/GILT

☐ **Aire,** ormolu gold plated case, 6" x 5", dial 2", c. 1900, 1 Day (E2-113).
83.00   100.00   (67.50)

☐ **Allier,** ormolu gold plated case, 11½" x 6", porcelain dial 2", c. 1900, 1 Day (E2-114).
95.00   110.00   (77.50)

☐ **Altair,** ormolu gold plated case, cast sash, decorated porcelain panel, 12½" x 7", porcelain dial 3", c. 1900, 8 Day (E2-119).
400.00   460.00   (380.00)

☐ **Alvord,** French satin gold or bronze finish, 6" x 4¼", ivorized dial 2", c. 1900, 1 Day (E2-117).
85.00   100.00   (77.50)

Allier

☐ **Amanda,** ormolu gold plate or antique verde case, 19¼" x 11", porcelain dial 4", c. 1900, 8 Day, strike (E2-119).
225.00   250.00   (225.00)

☐ **Amoret,** ormolu gold plated case, 6¾" x 3½", porcelain dial 2", c. 1900, 1 Day (E2-116).
75.00   95.00   (47.50)

☐ **Annecy,** ormolu gold plated case, 10¾" x 6¼", porcelain dial 2", c. 1910, 8 Day (E2-119).
100.00   120.00   (110.00)

☐ **Arcot,** ormolu gold plated case, 6¾" x 5", porcelain dial 2", c. 1900, 1 Day (E2-116).
75.00   95.00   (77.50)

☐ **Arden,** French satin gold or bronze finish, 8½" x 4¾", ivorized dial 2", c. 1900, 1 Day (E2-117).
75.00   95.00   (72.50)

☐ **Ardennes,** ormolu gold plated case, 11½" x 4¼", porcelain dial 2", c. 1900, 1 Day (E2-115).
75.00   95.00   (72.50)

☐ **Ariel,** ormolu gold plated case, 8" x 4½", porcelain dial 2", c. 1900, 1 Day (E2-114).
80.00   95.00   (82.50)

NEW HAVEN CLOCK COMPANY / 429

☐ **Arverne,** *French satin gold finish, 10½" x 7½", ivorized dial 2", c. 1900, 1 Day (E2-115).*
      80.00   100.00   (77.50)
☐ **As above,** *8 Day*
      120.00   145.00   (130.00)

☐ **Astoria (Jeweled Watch),** *14K gold plate finish, stem wind and stem set, jeweled front, fitted with folding back as desk ornament, 3¼" x 2¾", white porcelain dial 1¾", c. 1900, 1 Day (E2-119).*
      100.00   125.00   (72.50)

☐ **Atlas,** *French satin gold or bronze finish, height 9¼", porcelain dial 1¾", c. 1900, 1 Day (E2-117).*
      75.00   90.00   (82.50)

☐ **Baroda,** *ormolu gold plate, 9¾" x 7", porcelain dial 2", c. 1911, 1 Day (E1-172).*
      80.00   100.00   (87.00)

☐ **Bellona,** *ormolu gold plated case, 9¾" x 6½", porcelain dial 2", c. 1900, 1 Day (E2-116).*
      80.00   100.00   (77.50)

☐ **Bellona,** *French satin gold or bronze finish, 9¾" x 6½", ivorized dial 2", c. 1910, 1 Day (E2-120).*
      80.00   100.00   (62.50)
☐ **As above,** *8 Day*
      120.00   145.00   (135.00)

Corolan

☐ **Bermuda,** *ormolu gold plate, 9¾" x 6½", ivorized dial 2", c. 1911, 1 Day (E1-172).*
      80.00   100.00   (87.00)

☐ **Bucknell,** *ormolu gold plated case, 6½" x 4¼", dial 2", c. 1900, 1 Day (E2-113).*
      60.00   75.00   (67.50)

☐ **Capel,** *ormolu gold plated case, 6¼" x 5", dial 2", c. 1900, 1 Day (E2-113).*
      60.00   75.00   (57.50)

☐ **Celeste,** *ormolu gold plated case, 8¼" x 4", porcelain dial 2", c. 1900, 1 Day (E2-116).*
      60.00   75.00   (57.50)

☐ **Clovelly,** *French satin gold or bronze finish, 4¼" x 4¼", ivorized dial 2", c. 1900, 1 Day (E2-117).*
      50.00   70.00   (52.00)

☐ **Corolan,** *French satin gold or bronze finish, 8½" x 5", ivorized dial 2", c. 1900, 1 Day (E2-117).*
      125.00   150.00   (137.00)
☐ **As above,** *8 Day*
      155.00   180.00   (167.00)

Bucknell

430 / NEW HAVEN CLOCK COMPANY

☐ **Crescent Stand,** *bronze, nickel or gilt finish, either the Jasper or Astoria will fit this, 7¾" x 6½", base 3½", c. 1900 (E2-119).*
  40.00   55.00   (47.50)

☐ **Criterion,** *French satin gold or bronze finish, 14¾" x 6½", ivorized dial 2", c. 1910, 8 Day (E2-120).*
  150.00   175.00   (162.00)

☐ **Cupid,** *French satin gold or bronze finish, 12½" x 6", ivorized dial 2", c. 1910, 1 Day (E2-120).*
  70.00   85.00   (77.50)

☐ **As above,** *8 Day*
  115.00   140.00   (127.00)

☐ **Dalton,** *French satin gold or bronze finish, 10" x 3½", ivorized dial 2", c. 1900, 1 Day (E2-117).*
  55.00   70.00   (62.00)

☐ **Daphne,** *ormolu gold plate, 5⅜" x 3¼", white dial 2", c. 1911, 1 Day (E1-172).*
  40.00   50.00   (35.00)

☐ **Darien,** *ormolu gold plate, 8½" x 6¾", porcelain dial 2", c. 1920, 1 Day (E1-176).*
  60.00   75.00   (57.50)

☐ **Delano,** *ormolu gold plated case, 8" x 4¾", porcelain dial 2", c. 1910, 1 Day (E2-118).*
  65.00   80.00   (72.50)

☐ **Delong,** *ormolu gold plate, 5½" x 4½", white dial 2", c. 1911, 1 Day (E1-172).*
  40.00   50.00   (30.00)

☐ **Devon,** *ormolu gold plate, 5¾" x 4½", porcelain dial 2", c. 1911, 1 Day (E1-172).*
  60.00   75.00   (67.50)

☐ **Dixon,** *ormolu gold plated case, 9" x 6¾", porcelain dial 2", c. 1900, 1 Day (E2-115).*
  60.00   75.00   (67.50)

☐ **Dixon,** *ormolu gold plated case, 9" x 6¾", porcelain dial 3", c. 1900, 8 Day (E2-115).*
  75.00   90.00   (82.00)

Dixon

☐ **Drew,** *ormolu gold plated case, 7" x 5", porcelain dial 2", c. 1910, 1 Day (E2-118).*
  75.00   90.00   (82.00)

☐ **Dunstan,** *ormolu gold plate, 10½" x 5¾", porcelain dial 2", c. 1920, 1 Day (E1-176).*
  80.00   100.00   (90.00)

☐ **Eberle,** *ormolu gold plate, 7¾" x 4½", porcelain dial 2", c. 1920, 1 Day (E1-176).*
  65.00   80.00   (72.50)

☐ **Eldon,** *ormolu gold plated case, 5½" x 3½", porcelain dial 2", c. 1900, 1 Day (E2-116).*
  60.00   75.00   (67.50)

☐ **Eldora,** *ormolu gold plated case, 6¾" x 4¾", porcelain dial 2", c. 1900, 1 Day (E2-115).*
  50.00   70.00   (52.50)

☐ **Falmouth,** *ormolu gold plate, 11½" x 8½", porcelain dial 3", c. 1920, 8 Day (E1-176).*
  70.00   85.00   (77.50)

☐ **Fenwick,** *ormolu gold plated case, 6¼" x 6", porcelain dial 2", c. 1900, 1 Day (E2-115).*
  50.00   70.00   (52.50)

NEW HAVEN CLOCK COMPANY / 431

☐ **Ferney,** *ormolu gold plated case, 5¾" x 5¾", porcelain dial 2", c. 1900, 1 Day (E2-114).*
      80.00   95.00   (87.50)

☐ **Fleury,** *French satin gold or bronze finish, 5" x 4", ivorized dial 2", c. 1900, 1 Day (E2-117).*
      45.00   65.00   (55.00)

☐ **Flores,** *ormolu gold plated case, gilt hands, 15" x 8", porcelain dial 4", c. 1900, 8 Day, strike (E2-119).*
      155.00   180.00   (167.00)

☐ **Follen,** *ormolu gold plated case, 11½" x 7", porcelain dial 3", c. 1900, 8 Day (E2-116).*
      105.00   125.00   (115.00)

☐ **Forli,** *ormolu gold plated case, 7½" x 6½", porcelain dial 2", c. 1900, 1 Day (E2-115).*
      45.00   60.00   (52.50)

☐ **Furness,** *ormolu gold plated case, 11½" x 7", porcelain dial 3", c. 1900, 8 Day (E2-116).*
      95.00   115.00   (105.00)

☐ **Galva,** *ormolu gold plated case, 9" x 5½", porcelain dial 2", c. 1900, 1 Day (E2-114).*
      110.00   135.00   (117.00)

☐ **Garland,** *ormolu gold plated case, 9" x 6½", porcelain dial 2", c. 1900, 1 Day (E2-116).*
      50.00   65.00   (57.50)

☐ **Garnet,** *ormolu gold plated case, 6½" x 4½", porcelain dial 2", c. 1900, 1 Day (E2-114).*
      55.00   70.00   (62.50)

☐ **Gaudin,** *ormolu gold plated case, 9" x 6", porcelain dial 2", c. 1900, 1 Day (E2-114).*
      75.00   90.00   (82.00)

☐ **Hazel,** *ormolu gold plate, 4⅜" x 3¼", white dial 2", c. 1911, 1 Day (E1-172).*
      40.00   55.00   (30.00)

Ferney

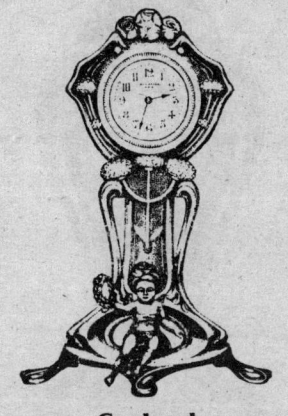

Garland

432 / NEW HAVEN CLOCK COMPANY

Heath

Laveta

☐ **Heath,** *ormolu gold plated case, 6¾" x 5¾", porcelain dial 2", c. 1900, 1 Day (E2-114).*
      75.00   90.00   (82.00)

☐ **Isere,** *ormolu gold plated case, visible pendulum, 18¼" x 19¼", porcelain dial with beveled glass 4", c. 1900, 8 Day, strike (E2-119).*
      270.00   300.00   (285.00)

☐ **Jasper,** *finished in nickel, bronze or gilt with best French magnifying lens back and front, stem wind and stem set, made with beveled bottom for use as paper weight or may be combined with Dolphin or Crescent stand, 3¼" x 2¾", white porcelain dial 1¾", and 2½" lens, c. 1900, 1 Day (E2-119).*
      125.00   150.00   (137.00)

☐ **Kazan,** *ormolu gold plated case, 6¼" x 5½", dial 2", c. 1900, 1 Day (E2-113).*
      50.00   70.00   (52.50)

☐ **Lachute,** *ormolu gold plated case, 7" x 4", porcelain dial 2", c. 1900, 1 Day (E2-116).*
      50.00   70.00   (52.50)

☐ **Lantier,** *ormolu gold plated case, 6½" x 5¾", porcelain dial 2", c. 1900, 1 Day (E2-116).*
      60.00   75.00   (67.50)

☐ **Laveta,** *ormolu gold plated case, 9¾" x 5", porcelain dial 3", c. 1900, 1 Day (E2-114).*
      85.00   105.00   (95.00)

☐ **Lannes,** *ormolu gold plated case, 6" x 3½", porcelain dial 2", c. 1900, 1 Day (E2-116).*
      50.00   65.00   (57.50)

☐ **Larissa,** *ormolu gold plated case, 7" x 6½", porcelain dial 2", c. 1900, 1 Day (E2-114).*
      75.00   90.00   (82.00)

NEW HAVEN CLOCK COMPANY / 433

- **Lascar,** French satin gold or bronze finish, 5½" x 4½", ivorized dial 2", c. 1900, 1 Day (E2-117).
  50.00   65.00   (52.50)

- **Le Fuel,** ormolu gold plated case, 12¼" x 7", porcelain dial 3", c. 1900, 8 Day (E2-115).
  105.00   125.00   (115.00)

- **Leroy,** French satin gold or bronze, 3¾" x 2½", ivorized dial 2", c. 1900, 1 Day (E2-117).
  125.00   150.00   (137.00)

- **Lescot,** ormolu gold plated case, 6" x 4¼", porcelain dial 2", c. 1900, 1 Day (E2-114).
  55.00   70.00   (62.50)

- **Lescure,** ormolu gold plated case, 6" x 5¼", dial 2", c. 1900, 1 Day (E2-113).
  50.00   65.00   (57.50)

- **Levan,** ormolu gold plated case, 8¾" x 3½", porcelain dial 2", c. 1900, 1 Day (E2-117).
  50.00   75.00   (52.50)

- **Libitina,** ormolu gold plated case, cathedral gong, 17¼" x 9¼", porcelain dial with beveled glass 4", c. 1900, 8 Day, strike (E2-119).
  230.00   260.00   (245.00)

- **Libourne,** ormolu gold plated case, 10½" x 5¼", porcelain dial 3", c. 1900, 8 Day (E2-115).
  95.00   115.00   (105.00)

- **Lillian,** ormolu gold plated case, 6¼" x 7", porcelain dial 3", c. 1900, 1 Day (E2-114).
  105.00   125.00   (115.00)

- **Limoges,** ormolu gold plated case, 5½" x 4¼", dial 2", c. 1900, 1 Day (E2-113).
  50.00   70.00   (52.50)

- **Loire,** ormolu gold plated case, 6½" x 7", porcelain dial 2", c. 1900, 1 Day (E2-114).
  75.00   90.00   (82.50)

Nana

- **Lucile,** ormolu gold plated case, 9¼" x 5½", porcelain dial 3", c. 1900, 1 Day (E2-114).
  130.00   155.00   (142.00)

- **Maintenon,** French satin gold or bronze finish, 3½" x 8", ivorized dial 2", c. 1900, 1 Day (E2-117).
  50.00   65.00   (57.50)
- **As above,** 8 Day
  90.00   110.00   (100.00)

- **Mangrove,** French satin gold finish, 10¼" x 5¼", ivorized dial 2", c. 1900, 1 Day (E2-115).
  55.00   70.00   (62.50)
- **As above,** 8 Day
  90.00   110.00   (100.00)

- **Manila,** French satin gold or bronze finish, 4" x 3¼", ivorized dial 2", c. 1900, 1 Day (E2-117).
  40.00   55.00   (47.50)

- **Minot,** ormolu gold plated case, 9¾" x 6¾", porcelain dial 2", c. 1900, 1 Day (E2-114).
  85.00   105.00   (95.00)

- **Mistral,** French satin gold or bronze finish, height 10¼", porcelain dial 1¾".
  60.00   80.00   (70.00)

434 / NEW HAVEN CLOCK COMPANY

Trianon

☐ **Nana,** ormolu gold plated case, 5½" x 3½", porcelain dial 2", c. 1900, 1 Day (E2-117).
    90.00   110.00   (100.00)

☐ **Napier,** ormolu gold plated case, 7" x 4½", porcelain dial 2", c. 1910, 1 Day (E2-118).
    55.00   70.00   (62.00)

☐ **Naruna,** ormolu gold plated case, 6¾" x 5¾", porcelain dial 2", c. 1910, 1 Day (E2-118).
    75.00   90.00   (82.00)

☐ **Nashoba,** ormolu gold plate, 7" x 4½", dial 2", c. 1920, 1 Day (E1-176).
    50.00   70.00   (45.00)

☐ **Paran,** ormolu gold plated case, 5½" x 4½", porcelain dial 2", c. 1900, 1 Day (E2-114).
    55.00   70.00   (62.00)

☐ **Pavia,** French satin gold or bronze finish, 10¼" x 5¼", ivorized dial 2", c. 1910, 1 Day (E2-120).
    70.00   85.00   (77.00)
☐ **As above,** 8 Day
    115.00   140.00   (127.00)

☐ **Pelham,** ormolu gold plated case, 6½" x 4½", porcelain dial 2", c. 1900, 1 Day (E2-116).
    60.00   75.00   (67.00)

☐ **Perley,** ormolu gold plated case, 8½" x 5", porcelain dial 2", c. 1900, 1 Day (E2-115).
    50.00   65.00   (57.50)

☐ **Phillipina,** French satin gold or bronze finish, 4¼" x 3¼", ivorized dial 2", c. 1900, 1 Day (E2-117).
    50.00   65.00   (57.50)

☐ **Picton,** ormolu gold plated case, 7" x 4½", porcelain dial 2", c. 1900, 1 Day (E2-116).
    50.00   70.00   (52.50)

☐ **Plevna,** French satin gold finish, 11¾" x 8½", ivorized dial 2", c. 1900, 1 Day (E2-115).
    70.00   85.00   (77.00)
☐ **As above,** 8 Day
    115.00   140.00   (127.00)

☐ **Reita,** ormolu gold plated case, 7" x 4½", porcelain dial 2", c. 1900, 1 Day (E2-115).
    50.00   65.00   (57.00)

☐ **Reno,** ormolu gold plated case, 8" x 4½", porcelain dial 2", c. 1900, 1 Day (E2-116).
    50.00   70.00   (52.50)

☐ **Rochelle,** *French satin gold or bronze finish, 11" x 6½", ivorized dial 2", c. 1910, 1 Day (E2-120).*
  65.00 80.00 (72.00)
☐ **As above,** *8 Day*
  105.00 135.00 (120.00)

☐ **Samoa,** *French satin gold or bronze finish, 7¼" x 4", ivorized dial 2", c. 1900, 1 Day (E2-117).*
  105.00 135.00 (120.00)
☐ **As above,** *8 Day*
  140.00 165.00 (152.00)

☐ **Toltec,** *ormolu gold plated case, 6¼" x 5¼", dial 2", c. 1900, 1 Day (E2-113).*
  50.00 70.00 (45.00)

☐ **Tralee,** *French satin gold or bronze finish, 4½" x 3", ivorized dial 2", c. 1900, 1 Day (E2-117).*
  45.00 60.00 (52.50)

☐ **Trianon,** *ormolu gold plated case, 7½" x 3¾", porcelain dial 2", c. 1900, 1 Day (E2-113).*
  65.00 80.00 (72.00)

☐ **Trianon,** *French satin gold or bronze finish, 7½" x 3¾", ivorized dial 2", c. 1900, 1 Day (E2-117).*
  65.00 80.00 (72.00)

☐ **Tulle,** *ormolu gold plated case, 8" x 3", porcelain dial 2", c. 1900, 1 Day (E2-116).*
  65.00 80.00 (72.00)

☐ **Tyrone,** *French satin gold or bronze finish, 5¼" x 3¾", ivorized dial 2", c. 1900, 1 Day (E2-117).*
  50.00 65.00 (57.50)

☐ **Valetta,** *ormolu gold plated case, 10¾" x 4¾", porcelain dial 2", c. 1910, 1 Day (E2-119).*
  90.00 110.00 (100.00)

Yesner

☐ **Vendome,** *ormolu gold plated case, 6" x 3½", porcelain dial 2", c. 1900, 1 Day (E2-113).*
  55.00 70.00 (62.00)

☐ **Vieta,** *ormolu gold plated case, 6" x 5½", porcelain dial 2", c. 1900, 1 Day (E2-117).*
  65.00 80.00 (72.00)

☐ **Yantus,** *ormolu gold plated case, 6½" x 6¾", porcelain dial 2", c. 1910, 1 Day (E2-118).*
  55.00 70.00 (62.00)

☐ **Yesner,** *ormolu gold plated case, 9¼" x 6", porcelain dial 2", c. 1910, 1 Day (E2-118).*
  80.00 100.00 (90.00)

☐ **Yuma,** *ormolu gold plated case, 6¼" x 5¼", dial 2", c. 1900, 1 Day (E2-113).*
  50.00 65.00 (57.50)

436 / NEW HAVEN CLOCK COMPANY

NOVELTY/FRENCH GILT

☐ **Arnold,** French satin gold finish with decorated porcelain panels, 14" x 9", decorated porcelain dial 3", c. 1900, 8 Day, strike (E2-120).
375.00   450.00   (305.00)

☐ **Lakeside,** French satin gold finish with decorated porcelain panels, 18½" x 10¾", decorated porcelain dial 3", c. 1900, 8 Day, strike (E2-120).
675.00   750.00   (712.00)

☐ **Larchmont,** French satin gold finish with decorated porcelain panels, 16" x 9", decorated porcelain dial 3", c. 1900, 8 Day, strike (E2-120).
490.00   550.00   (520.00)

☐ **Lenore,** French satin gold finish with decorated porcelain panels, 15" x 9", decorated porcelain dial 3", c. 1900, 8 Day, strike (E2-120).
400.00   500.00   (355.00)

☐ **Lyons,** French satin gold finish with decorated porcelain panels, 16½" x 9", decorated porcelain dial 3", c. 1900, 8 Day, strike (E2-120).
500.00   600.00   (475.00)

☐ **Sicilian,** French satin gold finish with decorated porcelain panels, 16½" x 8", decorated porcelain dial 3", c. 1900, 8 Day, strike (E2-120).
450.00   550.00   (425.00)

OFFICE INK

☐ **Louis Ink,** solid brass, c. 1900, 1 Day (E2-111).
225.00   275.00   (330.00)

☐ **Maintenon Ink,** solid brass, c. 1900, 1 Day (E2-111).
250.00   300.00   (355.00)

☐ **Secretary Ink,** hand chased cast brass stand, with cut glass inks, c. 1900, 1 Day (E2-111).
105.00   125.00   (115.00)

Maintenon Ink

REGULATOR/FIGURE EIGHT

☐ **Indicator,** D.R. wood, height 30½", dial 12", c. 1900, 8 Day, strike (E1-46).
310.00   350.00   (330.00)
☐ **As above,** 8 Day, simple spring
360.00   400.00   (380.00)

Larchmont

- ☐ **8" Saxon,** *rosewood, height 20",*
  dial 8", c. 1900, 8 Day (E2-122).
  245.00   275.00   (255.00)
- ☐ **As above,** *8 Day, strike*
  270.00   300.00   (285.00)
- ☐ **As above,** *8 Day, calendar*
  285.00   325.00   (305.00)
- ☐ **As above,** *8 Day, stirke, calendar*
  310.00   350.00   (330.00)
- ☐ **8" Saxon Mosaic,** *wood, height 20", dial 8", c. 1900, 8 Day (E2-122).*
  245.00   275.00   (260.00)
- ☐ **As above,** *8 Day, strike*
  270.00   300.00   (285.00)
- ☐ **As above,** *8 Day, calendar*
  285.00   325.00   (305.00)
- ☐ **As above,** *8 Day, strike, calendar*
  310.00   350.00   (330.00)
- ☐ **10" Saxon,** *rosewood, height 22", dial 10", c. 1900, 8 Day (E2-122).*
  270.00   300.00   (285.00)
- ☐ **As above,** *8 Day, strike*
  285.00   325.00   (305.00)
- ☐ **As above,** *8 Day, calendar*
  310.00   350.00   (330.00)
- ☐ **10" Saxon Mosaic,** *wood, height 22", dial 10", c. 1900, 8 Day (E2-122).*
  270.00   300.00   (285.00)
- ☐ **As above,** *8 Day, stirke*
  285.00   325.00   (305.00)
- ☐ **As above,** *8 Day, calendar*
  310.00   350.00   (330.00)
- ☐ **As above,** *8 Day, strike, calendar*
  335.00   375.00   (355.00)
- ☐ **Regulator D.R., Calendar,** *wood, height 31", dial 12", c. 1900, 8 Day (E2-93).*
  270.00   300.00   (285.00)
- ☐ **As above,** *8 Day, strike*
  285.00   325.00   (305.00)
- ☐ **As above,** *8 Day, calendar*
  310.00   350.00   (330.00)
- ☐ **As above,** *8 Day, strike, calendar*
  335.00   375.00   (355.00)

REGULATOR/OCTAGON TOP, LONG DROP

- ☐ **Erie,** *oak, 33½" x 18½", dial 12", c. 1920, 8 Day (E1-183).*
  245.00   275.00   (260.00)
- ☐ **As above,** *8 Day, strike*
  270.00   300.00   (285.00)

8" Saxon

Erie

REGULATOR/OCTAGON TOP, SHORT DROP

☐ **Blake,** oak, height 27", dial 12", c. 1900, 8 Day (E1-37).
   195.00   225.00   (210.00)

☐ **Drop Octagon No. 2,** wood, height 24", dial 12", c. 1900, 8 Day (E2-122).
   220.00   250.00   (235.00)
☐ **As above,** 8 Day, strike
   245.00   275.00   (260.00)

☐ **Ventura,** light or dark wood, height 24¾", dial 12", c. 1900, 8 Day (E1-37).
   195.00   225.00   (210.00)

☐ **10" Small Drop Octagon,** rosewood and zebra, gilt and gilt buttons, height 21", dial 10", c. 1900, 8 Day (E2-122).
   195.00   225.00   (210.00)
☐ **As above,** 8 Day, strike
   220.00   250.00   (235.00)
☐ **As above,** 8 Day, calendar
   245.00   275.00   (260.00)
☐ **As above,** 8 Day, strike, calendar
   270.00   300.00   (285.00)

☐ **10" Small Drop Octagon Gilt,** rosewood or zebra, c. 1900, 8 Day (E2-122).
   195.00   225.00   (210.00)
☐ **As above,** 8 Day, strike
   220.00   250.00   (235.00)
☐ **As above,** 8 Day, calendar
   245.00   275.00   (260.00)
☐ **As above,** 8 Day, strike, calendar
   270.00   300.00   (285.00)

☐ **12" Drop Octagon,** R.C. rosewood or zebra, height 24", dial 12", c. 1900, 8 Day (E2-122).
   195.00   225.00   (210.00)
☐ **As above,** 8 Day, strike
   220.00   250.00   (235.00)
☐ **As above,** 8 Day, calendar
   245.00   275.00   (260.00)
☐ **As above,** 8 Day, strike, calendar
   270.00   300.00   (285.00)

☐ **12" Drop Octagon, Calendar,** rosewood or zebra, height 24", dial 12", c. 1900, 8 Day (E2-122).
   195.00   225.00   (210.00)
☐ **As above,** 8 Day, strike
   220.00   250.00   (235.00)
☐ **As above,** 8 Day, calendar
   245.00   275.00   (260.00)
☐ **As above,** 8 Day, strike, calendar
   270.00   300.00   (285.00)

☐ **12" Mosaic Drop,** wood, height 24", dial 12", c. 1900, 8 Day (E2-122).
   195.00   225.00   (210.00)
☐ **As above,** 8 Day, strike
   220.00   250.00   (235.00)
☐ **As above,** 8 Day, calendar
   245.00   275.00   (260.00)
☐ **As above,** 8 Day, strike, calendar
   270.00   300.00   (285.00)

12" Drop Octagon Calendar

NEW HAVEN CLOCK COMPANY / 439

REGULATOR/OPEN SWINGING

- **Ros Study No. 1,** oak height 35", silver dial and trimmings, c. 1894, 8 Day, strike (E2-124).
  425.00   475.00   (450.00)

- **Ros Study No. 2,** oak, height 26", gilt dial and trimmings, c. 1894, 8 Day, strike (E2-124).
  325.00   375.00   (330.00)

REGULATOR/PARLOR SHELF

- **Champion,** black walnut, height 25", dial 6", c. 1890, 8 Day, strike (E2-89).
  300.00   340.00   (320.00)
- **As above,** 8 Day, strike, alarm
  300.00   350.00   (325.00)

- **Corsair,** black walnut, metal ornaments, height 24", dial 6¾", c. 1890, 8 Day, strike (E2-89).
  250.00   280.00   (265.00)

- **Vistula,** wood, height 23½", dial 6", c. 1900, 8 Day, strike (E2-102).
  190.00   220.00   (205.00)

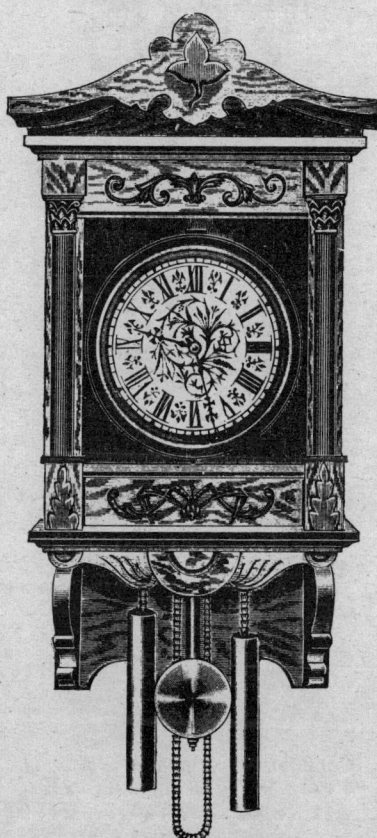

Ros Study No. 2

Champion

440 / NEW HAVEN CLOCK COMPANY

REGULATOR
PARLOR TEAR DROP
☐ **Cuba,** *oak, 25⅞″ x 12¾″, dial 6″, c. 1920, 8 Day, strike (E1-183).*
  270.00   300.00   (285.00)

REGULATOR/PARLOR WALL
☐ **Cambria,** *walnut, height 42, dial 8″, c. 1900, 8 Daytime (E1-101).*
  540.00   600.00   (570.00)
☐ **As above,** *8 Day, strike*
  575.00   650.00   (610.00)

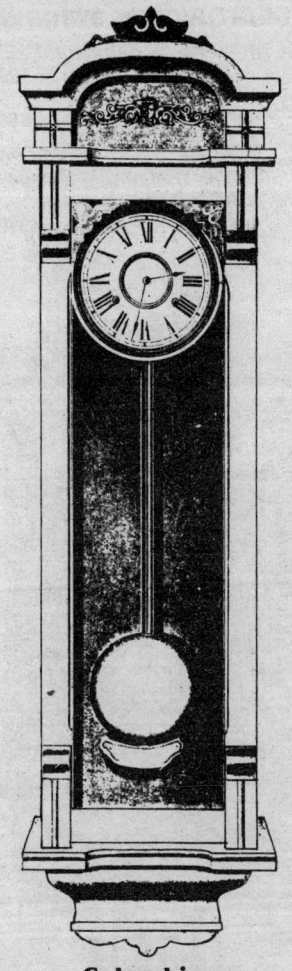

Columbian

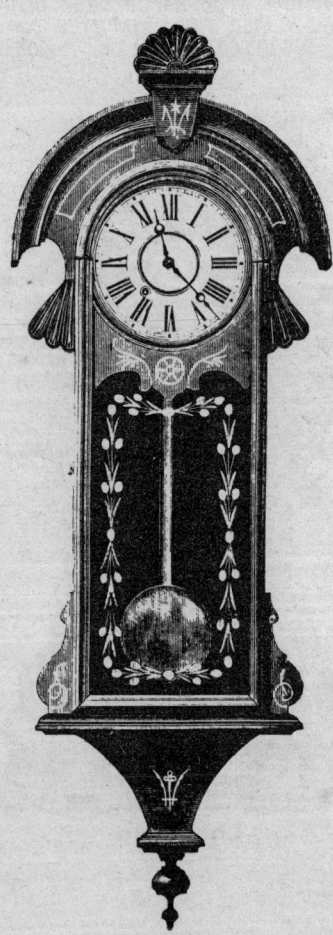

Cambria

☐ **Columbian,** *oak height 48½″, dial 8″, c. 1894, 30 Daytime (E2-124).*
  750.00   850.00   (800.00)
☐ **Fatinitza, Gilt,** *walnut, veneered, ebony and gilt trimmings, height 33″, dial 6″, c. 1900, 8 Daytime (E1-101).*
  490.00   550.00   (520.00)
☐ **As above,** *8 Day, strike*
  540.00   600.00   (570.00)

NEW HAVEN CLOCK COMPANY / 441

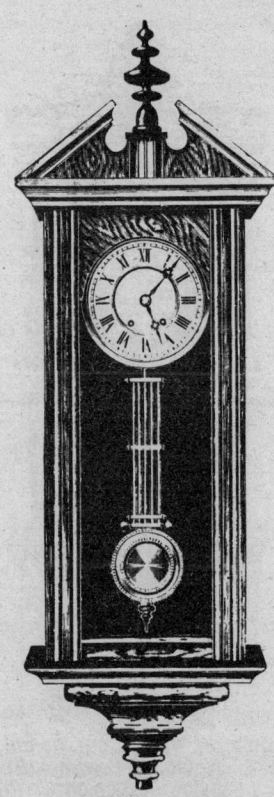

Fatinitza, Gilt

- ☐ **Faustina, Gilt,** *walnut, veneered, ebony and gilt trimmings, height 33", dial 6", c. 1900, 8 Daytime (E1-101).*
  540.00   600.00   (570.00)
- ☐ **As above,** *8 Day, strike*
  575.00   650.00   (610.00)

- ☐ **Jestla,** *mahogany, 17¾" x 7", dial 5", c. 1920, 8 Day, strike (E1-184).*
  85.00   105.00   (95.00)

- ☐ **Madero,** *oak or mahogany, 28¾" x 13", dial 8", c. 1920, 8 Day, strike (E1-184).*
- ☐ **As above,** *oak*

- ☐ **Maywood,** *oak, 44½" x 17", dial 8", c. 1900, 8 Daytime (E1-36).*
  450.00   500.00   (475.00)

- ☐ **Mimosa,** *oak or mahogany, 26¾" x 10¾", dial 8", c. 1920, 8 Day, strike (E1-184).*
- ☐ **As above,** *oak*
  145.00   175.00   (147.00)
- ☐ **As above,** *mahogany*
  150.00   185.00   (165.00)

- ☐ **Mirada,** *oak or mahogany, 28¼" x 12", dial 8", c. 1920, 8 Day, strike (E1-184).*
- ☐ **As above,** *oak*
  145.00   175.00   (147.00)
- ☐ **As above,** *mahogany*
  210.00   235.00   (222.00)

- ☐ **Norseman,** *oak and walnut, height 47½", dial 10", c. 1900, 8 Daytime (E1-102).*
- ☐ **As above,** *oak*
  575.00   650.00   (610.00)
- ☐ **As above,** *oak*
  625.00   700.00   (662.00)
- ☐ **As above,** *walnut*
  675.00   750.00   (715.00)
- ☐ **As above,** *walnut*
  725.00   800.00   (762.00)

Mirada

442 / NEW HAVEN CLOCK COMPANY

- ☐ **Referee**, *oak or mahogany, 35½" x 16", dial 12", c. 1920 (E1-183).*
- ☐ **As above**, *oak, 8 Daytime*
  270.00   300.00   (285.00)
- ☐ **As above**, *oak, 8 Daytime, strike*
  285.00   325.00   (305.00)
- ☐ **As above**, *oak, 8 Daytime, calendar*
  310.00   350.00   (330.00)
- ☐ **As above**, *oak, 8 Daytime, strike, calendar*
  335.00   375.00   (355.00)
- ☐ **As above**, *mahogany, 8 Daytime*
  345.00   375.00   (360.00)
- ☐ **As above**, *mahogany, 8 Daytime, strike*
  360.00   400.00   (380.00)
- ☐ **As above**, *mahogany, 8 Daytime, strike, calendar*
  410.00   450.00   (430.00)

Regulator, B.B.

- ☐ **Regulator**, *B.B. walnut, height 41", dial 8", c. 1900, 8 Daytime (E1-103).*
  540.00   600.00   (570.00)
- ☐ **Regulator**, *C.C. walnut, 37½", dial 8", c. 1900, 8 Daytime (E1-101).*
  540.00   600.00   (570.00)
- ☐ **Riverton**, *oak 34½" x 15¾", dial 12", c. 1920, 8 Daytime (E1-184).*
  150.00   175.00   (162.00)
- ☐ **As above**, *8 Daytime, strike*
  175.00   200.00   (187.00)
- ☐ **As above**, *30 Daytime*
  220.00   250.00   (235.00)
- ☐ **Saracen**, *mahogany, height 49", dial 10", c. 1900, 8 Daytime (E1-102).*
  540.00   600.00   (570.00)
- ☐ **As above**, *8 Day, strike*
  575.00   650.00   (610.00)
- ☐ **Solent**, *oak, antique finish, 36¾" x 13½", dial 8", c. 1914, 8 Daytime (E2-123).*
  310.00   350.00   (330.00)

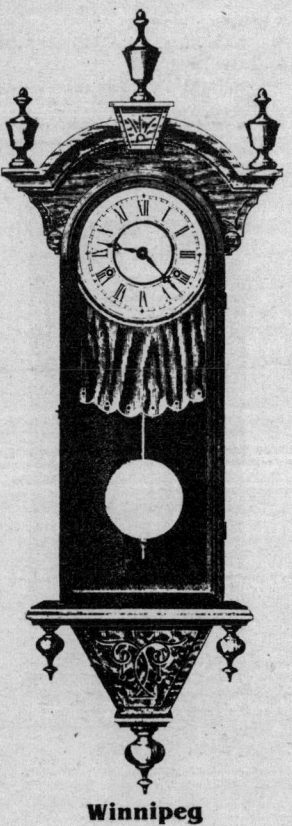

Winnipeg

NEW HAVEN CLOCK COMPANY / 443

REGULATOR/ROUND TOP

Viking

☐ **Barometer Regulator,** *wood, height 37", dial 12", c. 1900, 8 Daytime (E2-93).*
    360.00   400.00   (380.00)
☐ **As above,** *8 Daytime, strike*
    400.00   450.00   (425.00)

☐ **Glenor,** *mahogany or oak, antique finish, 36½" x 15¼", dial 12, c. 1914, 8 Daytime, weight (E2-123).*
    600.00   675.00   (637.00)

☐ **Imperial,** *rosewood, height 32½", dial 12", c. 1900, 8 Daytime (E2-93).*
    310.00   350.00   (330.00)

☐ **Regulator,** *oak, 32¼" x 17¾", dial 12", c. 1920, 8 Daytime (E1-183).*
    235.00   265.00   (250.00)
☐ **As above,** *8 Daytime, strike*
    290.00   330.00   (310.00)
☐ **As above,** *8 Daytime, strike, calendar*
    335.00   375.00   (355.00)

☐ **Regulator,** *walnut veneer, solid walnut circle, height 32", dial 12", c. 1900, 8 Daytime (E1-37).*
    270.00   300.00   (285.00)
☐ **As above,** *8 Daytime, strike*
    285.00   325.00   (305.00)

☐ **Vidette,** *oak and walnut, height 42", dial 10", c. 1900 (E1-102).*
☐ **As above,** *oak, 8 Daytime*
    540.00   600.00   (570.00)

☐ **Viking,** *oak and walnuit, height 44", dial 8", c. 1900 (E1-102).*
☐ **As above,** *oak, 8 Daytime*
    540.00   600.00   (570.00)
☐ **As above,** *oak, 8 Day, strike*
    575.00   650.00   (610.00)
☐ **As above,** *walnut, 8 Daytime*
    640.00   700.00   (670.00)
☐ **As above,** *walnut, 8 Day, strike*
    675.00   750.00   (710.00)

☐ **Winnipeg,** *walnut, height 35", dial 6", c. 1900, 8 Daytime (E1-102).*
    540.00   600.00   (570.00)
☐ **As above,** *8 Day, strike*
    575.00   650.00   (610.00)

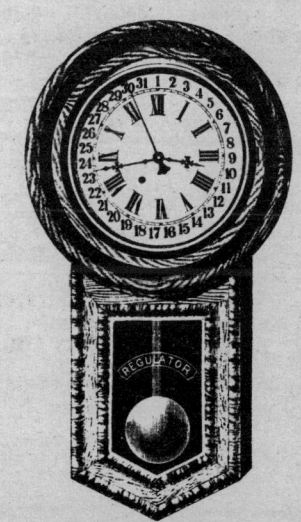

Regulator - Calendar

444 / NEW HAVEN CLOCK COMPANY

☐ **Regulator — Calendar,** *walnut veneer, solid walnut circle, height 32", c. 1900, 8 Daytime, calendar (E1-37).*
      310.00   350.00   (330.00)
☐ **As above,** *8Day, strike, calendar*
      335.00   375.00   (355.00)

☐ **Regulator — Calendar,** *wood, height 32", dial 12, c. 1900, 8 Daytime (E2-93).*
      270.00   300.00   (285.00)
☐ **As above,** *8 Daytime, strike*
      285.00   325.00   (305.00)
☐ **As above,** *8 Daytime, calendar*
      310.00   350.00   (330.00)
☐ **As above,** *8 Day, strike, calendar*
      335.00   375.00   (355.00)

REGULATOR/SECONDS BIT

☐ **Austrian,** *oak or cherry, 48¾" x 19", dial 10", c. 1900 (E1-36).*
☐ **As above,** *oak, 8 Daytime*
      360.00   400.00   (380.00)
☐ **As above,** *oak, 8 Day, strike*
      400.00   450.00   (425.00)
☐ **As above,** *oak, 30 Daytime*
      450.00   500.00   (475.00)
☐ **As above,** *oak, 8 Daytime, weight*
      575.00   650.00   (610.00)
☐ **As above,** *cherry, 8 Daytime*
      610.00   650.00   (630.00)
☐ **As above,** *cherry, 8 Day, strike*
      650.00   700.00   (675.00)
☐ **As above,** *cherry, 30 Daytime*
      700.00   750.00   (725.00)
☐ **As above,** *cherry, 8 Daytime, weight*
      825.00   900.00   (860.00)

☐ **Cimbrian,** *oak, 44" x 17¾", dial 10", c. 1896, 30 Daytime (E2-123).*
      575.00   650.00   (615.00)
☐ **As above,** *8 Daytime*
      540.00   600.00   (570.00)
☐ **As above,** *8 Daytime, strike*
      490.00   550.00   (520.00)

Elfrida

- **Elfrida,** *wood, 49" x 19", dial 10", c. 1896, 8 Daytime (E2-123).*
  650.00   750.00   (700.00)
- **As above,** *8 Daytime, strike*
  700.00   800.00   (750.00)
- **As above,** *8 Daytime, weight*
  900.00   1000.00   (950.00)
- **As above,** *30 Day*
  800.00   900.00   (850.00)

- **Enquirer,** *wood, 50½" x 19", dial 10", c. 1896, 8 Daytime (E2-123).*
  900.00   1000.00   (950.00)
- **As above,** *8 Daytime, strike*
  950.00   1050.00   (1000.00)
- **As above,** *8 Daytime, weight*
  1100.00   1200.00   (1150.00)

- **Gloriana,** *oak, height 42", dial 10", c. 1894, 30 Daytime (E2-124).*
  575.00   650.00   (610.00)

- **Grecian,** *oak, 51" x 20", dial 10", c. 1900, 8 Daytime, weight (E1-36).*
  750.00   850.00   (800.00)

- **Hebe,** *oak, height 49", dial 10", c. 1894, 30 Daytime (E2-124).*
  600.00   700.00   (650.00)

- **Office No. 2,** *walnut or mahogany, height 41", dial 12", c. 1900 (E1-102).*
- **As above,** *mahogany, 8 Daytime, weight*
  700.00   800.00   (750.00)
- **As above,** *walnut, 8 daytime, weight*
  750.00   850.00   (800.00)

- **Prussian,** *oak, 51½" x 19", dial 10", c. 1896, 30 Daytime (E2-123).*
  575.00   650.00   (610.00)
- **As above,** *8 Daytime*
  490.00   550.00   (520.00)

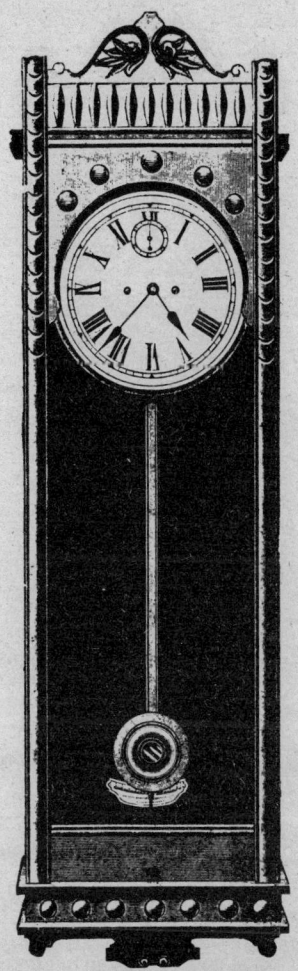

Hebe

446 / NEW HAVEN CLOCK COMPANY

Rutland

- ☐ **Rutland,** *oak, 48" x 19½", dial 10", c. 1914, 8 Daytime (E2-123).*
  450.00   500.00   (475.00)
- ☐ **As above,** *8 Daytime, strike*
  490.00   550.00   (520.00)
- ☐ **As above,** *8 Daytime, calendar*
  540.00   600.00   (570.00)
- ☐ **As above,** *8 Daytime, strike, calendar*
  575.00   650.00   (610.00)
- ☐ **As above,** *30 Daytime*
  540.00   600.00   (570.00)
- ☐ **As above,** *30 Day, calendar*
  800.00   900.00   (850.00)

- ☐ **Standing Regulator No. 10,** *oak, walnut, mahogany, height 90", dial 12", c. 1900 (E1-104).*
- ☐ **As above,** *mahogany, 8 Daytime*
  2000.00   2400.00   (2200.00)
- ☐ **As above,** *oak, 8 Daytime*
  1850.00   2250.00   (2050.00)
- ☐ **As above,** *walnut, 8 Daytime*
  2050.00   2450.00   (2250.00)

- ☐ **Tampico,** *oak, 43" x 15½", dial 12", c. 1914, 8 Daytime (E2-123).*
  360.00   400.00   (380.00)
- ☐ **As above,** *30 Daytime*
  400.00   450.00   (425.00)

- ☐ **Vamoose,** *light wood, height 45", dial 10", c. 1900, 8 Daytime (E1-36).*
  285.00   325.00   (305.00)
- ☐ **As above,** *8 Day, strike*
  310.00   350.00   (330.00)
- ☐ **As above,** *8 Daytime, calendar*
  360.00   400.00   (380.00)

- ☐ **Watchman's Electric Clock,** *walnut, height 64", dial 12", c. 1900, 8 Daytime (E1-102).*
  1000.00   1100.00   (1050.00)

- ☐ **Watchman's Electric Clock,** *walnut, height 64", dial 12", register 8", c. 1900 (E2-93).*
- ☐ **As above,** *Battery*
  900.00   1000.00   (950.00)
- ☐ **As above,** *weight*
  1200.00   1300.00   (1250.00)

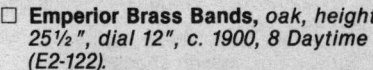

REGULATOR/SQUARE TOP

☐ **Emperor,** *oak, height 25½", dial 12", c. 1900, 8 Daytime (E2-122).*
   220.00   250.00   (235.00)
☐ **As above,** *8 Daytime, strike*
   245.00   275.00   (260.00)
☐ **As above,** *8 Daytime, calendar*
   270.00   300.00   (285.00)
☐ **As above,** *8 Daytime, strike, calendar*
   285.00   325.00   (305.00)

☐ **Emperior Brass Bands,** *oak, height 25½", dial 12", c. 1900, 8 Daytime (E2-122).*
   245.00   275.00   (260.00)
☐ **As above,** *8 Daytime, strike*
   270.00   300.00   (285.00)
☐ **As above,** *8 Daytime, calendar*
   285.00   325.00   (305.00)
☐ **As above,** *8 Daytime, strike, calendar*
   310.00   350.00   (330.00)

Emperor

Emperior Brass Bands

REGULATOR/SWEEP SECOND

- ☐ **Giant,** *solid oak, Swiss regulator movement, sweep second, 10'3" x 3', dial 12", c. 1900, 8 Day (E1-35).*
  2200.00 2400.00 (2300.00)

- ☐ **New York,** *oak, Swiss regulator movement, sweep second, height 7'2", dial 12", c. 1900, 8 Day (E1-35).*
  2200.00 2400.00 (2300.00)

- ☐ **Regulator No. O,** *black walnut, oak mahogany, 84" x 31", c. 1900 (E1-104).*
- ☐ **As above,** *blackwalnut, 8 Daytime, weight*
  3200.00 3700.00 (3410.00)
- ☐ **As above,** *black walnut, 8 Daytime, strike, weight*
  3450.00 3950.00 (3700.00)
- ☐ **As above,** *oak, 8 Daytime, weight*
  3000.00 3500.00 (3250.00)
- ☐ **As above,** *oak, 8 Daytime, strike, weight*
  3250.00 3750.00 (3500.00)
- ☐ **As above,** *mahogany, 8 Daytime, weight*
  3150.00 3650.00 (3400.00)
- ☐ **As above,** *mahogany, 8 Daytime, strike, weight*
  3400.00 3900.00 (3650.00)

- ☐ **Regulator No. 00,** *oak or mahogany, wood pendulum rod, polished brass weights, height 63", dial 10", c. 1900 (E1-104).*
- ☐ **As above,** *oak, 8 Daytime, weight*
  2000.00 2200.00 (2100.00)
- ☐ **As above,** *oak, 8 Daytime, sweep seconds*
  2250.00 2500.00 (2375.00)
- ☐ **As above,** *mahogany, 8 Daytime, weight*
  2150.00 2350.00 (2250.00)
- ☐ **As above,** *mahogany, 8 Daytime, sweep seconds*
  2400.00 2650.00 (2525.00)

- ☐ **Regulator No. 2,** *walnut, glass sides, dead beat pin escapement, height 7'4", c. 1900, 8 Daytime (E1-103).*
  3350.00 3850.00 (3600.00)

Regulator No. 00

NEW HAVEN CLOCK COMPANY / 449

☐ **Regulator No. 4,** walnut, glass sides, dead-beat pin escapement, height 10'2½", c. 1900, 8 Daytime (E1-103).
    5000.00   5500.00   (3750.00)

Regulator No. 3

Regulator No. 4

☐ **Regulator No. 3,** walnut, mahogany, ash, glass sides, dead-beat pin escapement, height 7'2", c. 1900 (E1-103).
☐ **As above,** mahogany, 8 Daytime
    3350.00   3900.00   (3625.00)
☐ **As above,** walnut, 8 Daytime
    3400.00   3950.00   (3675.00)
☐ **As above,** ash, 8 Daytime
    3450.00   4000.00   (3725.00)

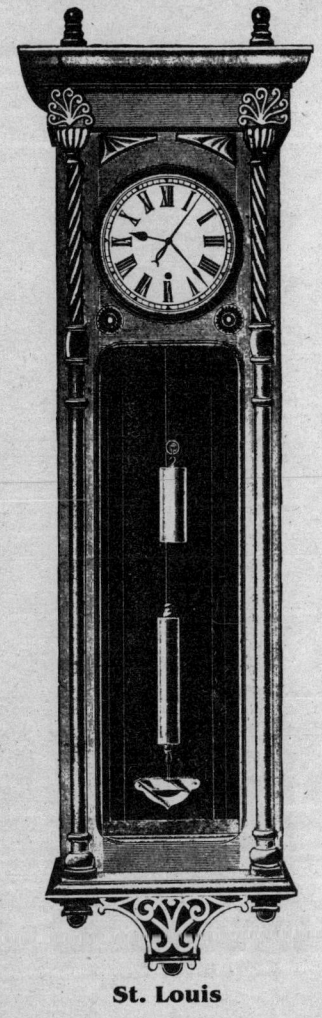

St. Louis

☐ **Regulator No. 6,** *ebony finish, hardwood polished case, white carvings, finished in gold leaf, glass sides, dead-beat, escapement, height 78", c. 1900, sweep second (E1-104).*
  2250.00   2750.00   (2150.00)
☐ **As above,** *sweep second, Swiss*
  2750.00   3000.00   (1500.00)

☐ **Regulator No.8,** *walnut, glass sides, dead-beat escapement, height 10'6", c. 1900, 8 Day (E1-104).*
  3000.00   3500.00   (3250.00)
☐ **As above,** *8 Daytime, sweep*
  3500.00   4000.00   (3750.00)

☐ **Regulator No. 9,** *walnut, glass sides, dead-beat pin escapement, c. 1900, 8 Daytime (E1-103).*
  3000.00   3500.00   (3250.00)

☐ **Regulator No 10,** *oak, walnut, mahogany, height 77½", dial 12", c. 1900 (E1-103).*
☐ **As above,** *walnut, 8 Daytime*
  3750.00   4250.00   (2675.00)
☐ **As above,** *oak, 8 Daytime*
  3500.00   4000.00   (2500.00)
☐ **As above,** *mahogany, 8 Daytime*
  3750.00   4250.00   (2650.00)

☐ **St. Louis,** *oak or cherry, Swiss regulator movement, sweep second, height 6'6", dial 12", c. 1900, 8 Day (E1-35).*
☐ **As above,** *oak*
  3500.00   4000.00   (2050.00)
☐ **As above,** *cherry*
  3750.00   4250.00   (2300.00)

☐ **Thornton,** *hanging, oak or cherry, Swiss regulator movement, sweep second, 74" x 22", c. 1900, 8 Day (E1-36).*
☐ **As above,** *oak*
  2250.00   2750.00   (1750.00)
☐ **As above,** *cherry*
  2550.00   3100.00   (1950.00)

STATUE/LARGE

- **Aegean,** black enamel or Malachite finish, French gilt or bronze trimmings, cathedral gong, ivorized porcelain dial, fancy gilt center or decorated porcelain dial, Empire sash and heavy beveled glass, 20" x 12¼", dial 4", c. 1900, 8 Day, strike (E2-110).
  210.00   240.00   (225.00)

- **Carthage,** gilt or bronze, empire sash, ivorized porcelain dial, visible escapement, 20" x 20", dial 6", c. 1900, 8 Day, strike (E2-127).
  275.00   315.00   (295.00)

- **Don Juan,** bronze and silver, visible escapement, height 21", c. 1900, 8 Day, strike (E1-112).
  450.00   500.00   (475.00)

- **Lulli,** bronze and silver, visible escapement, height 21", base 17¼", c. 1900, 8 Day, strike (E1-112).
  375.00   425.00   (400.00)

- **Norman,** gilt or bronze, empire sash, ivorized porcelain dial, visible escapement, 20½" x 20", dial 6", c. 1900, 8 Day, strike (E2-127).
  285.00   325.00   (305.00)

- **Philip,** bronze and silver, visible escapement, height 23", c. 1900, 8 Day, strike (E1-112).
  375.00   425.00   (400.00)

- **Roman,** gilt or bronze, empire sash, ivorized porcelain dial, visible escapement, 20" x 20", dial 6", c. 1900, 8 Day, strike (E2-127).
  275.00   315.00   (295.00)

Aegean

Norman

452 / NEW HAVEN CLOCK COMPANY

Roman

☐ **Saxon,** gilt or bronze, empire sash, ivorized porcelain dial, visible escapement, 20" x 20", dial 6", c. 1900, 8 Day, strike (E2-127).
275.00   315.00   (295.00)

☐ **Spartan,** antique brass or barbadiene, ivorized dial, height 24", dial 4½", c. 1900, 15 Day, strike (E1-101).
750.00   850.00   (800.00)

STATUE/SMALL

☐ **Benvenuto Cellini,** gilt or bronze, empire sash, ivorized porcelain dial, visible escapement, 16" x 20", dial 6", c. 1900, 8 Day, strike (E2-127).
255.00   285.00   (270.00)

☐ **Bernard Palissy,** gilt or bronze, empire sash, ivorized porcelain dial, visible escapement, 16" x 20", dial 6", c. 1900, 8 Day, strike (E2-127).
255.00   285.00   (270.00)

☐ **Brennus,** bronze or gold finish, with black or colored marbleized base, empire sash, porcelain dial, visible escapement, 16" x 26", dial 6", c. 1900, 8 Day, strike (E1-41).
255.00   285.00   (270.00)

☐ **Carthage,** bronze and silver, visible escapement, height 19¼", base 17", c. 1900, 8 Day, strike (E1-112).
400.00   450.00   (425.00)

☐ **Clotho,** gilt or bronze, empire sash, ivorized porcelain dial, visible escapement, 16" x 20", dial 6", c. 1900, 8 Day, strike (E2-126).
245.00   275.00   (260.00)

☐ **Fame,** gilt or bronze, empire sash, ivorized porcelain dial, visible escapement, 16" x 20", dial 6", c. 1900, 8 Day, strike (E2-127).
255.00   285.00   (270.00)

☐ **Fisher Boy,** bronze and silver, visible escapement, height 28", base 17", c. 1900, 8 Day, strike (E1-112).
490.00   550.00   (520.00)

Carthage

NEW HAVEN CLOCK COMPANY / 453

☐ **Flower Girl,** *gilt or bronze, empire sash, ivorized porcelain dial, visible escapement, 16" x 20", dial 6", c. 1900, 8 Day, strike (E2-126).*
225.00   285.00   (255.00)

☐ **Flute Player,** *gilt or bronze, empire sash, ivorized porcelain dial, visible escapement, 16" x 20", dial 6", c. 1900, 8 Day, strike (E2-126).*
255.00   285.00   (270.00)

☐ **Horse,** *gilt or bronze, empire sash, ivorized porcelain dial, visible escapement, 16" x 20", dial 6", c. 1900, 8 Day, strike (E2-126).*
255.00   285.00   (270.00)

Flute Player

☐ **Hunter And Dog,** *bronze and silver, visible escapement, height 15½", c. 1900, 8 Day, strike (E1-112).*
425.00   475.00   (450.00)

☐ **Infantry,** *bronze and silver, visible escapement, height 20", base 17", c. 1900, 8 Day, strike (E1-112).*
360.00   400.00   (380.00)

☐ **Ivanhoe,** *gilt or bronze, empire sash, ivorized porcelain dial, visible escapement, 16" x 20", dial 6", c. 1900, 8 Day, strike (E2-127).*
255.00   285.00   (270.00)

☐ **Knight,** *gilt or bronze, empire sash, ivorized porcelain dial, visible escapement, 17" x 20", dial 6", c. 1900, 8 Day, strike (E2-127).*
270.00   300.00   (285.00)

☐ **Mignon,** *bronze and silver, visible escapement, height 19¼", base 17", c. 1900, 8 Day, strike (E1-112).*
335.00   375.00   (355.00)

☐ **Octavius,** *gilt or bronze, empire sash, ivorized porcelain dial, visible escapement, 16" x 20", dial 6", c. 1900, 8 Day, strike (E2-128).*
255.00   285.00   (270.00)

Orpheus

454 / NEW HAVEN CLOCK COMPANY

☐ **Orpheus,** *satin gold or bronze, with black or green enameled iron base, cathedral gong, empire sash, heavy beveled glass, ivorized porcelain dial with gilt center, or decorated porcelain dial, 16" x 12½", dial 3", c. 1900, 8 Day, strike (E2-110).*
    210.00   240.00   (225.00)

☐ **Poetry,** *gilt or bronze, empire sash, ivorized porcelain dial, visible escapement, 16" x 20", dial 6", c. 1900, 8 Day, strike (E2-126).*
    265.00   295.00   (280.00)

☐ **Rebecca,** *bronze and silver, visible escapement, height 19", base 17", c. 1900, 8 Day, strike (E1-112).*
    375.00   425.00   (400.00)

☐ **Roman,** *bronze or gold finish, with black or colored marbleized base, empire sash, porcelain dial, visible escapement, 16" x 20", dial 6", c. 1900, 8 Day, strike (E1-41).*
    275.00   315.00   (295.00)

☐ **Sir Christopher,** *bronze and silver, visible escapement, height 15⅝", base 16¼", c. 1900, 8 Day, strike (E1-112).*
    360.00   400.00   (380.00)

☐ **Tempest,** *satin gold or bronze, cathedral gong, empire sash, heavy beveled glass, ivorized porcelain dial with gilt center, or decorated porcelain dial, 19¼" x 11¼", dial 3", c. 1900, 8 Day, ½ hour strike (E2-110).*
    210.00   240.00   (225.00)

WATCH

☐ **Sting,** *nickel or silver, size 3", c. 1900 (E2-111).*
    100.00   125.00   (77.50)

Sting

G.B. OWEN

George B. Owen worked for the Gilbert Clock Company in Winsted as a business manager for many years. A case stylist in his own right, Owen maintained a private business in Connecticut and New York.

CALENDAR

☐ **Round Top Shelf,** *13½" x 10", dial 4½", 8 Day, strike (M429-134).*
    800.00   900.00   (850.00)

J.I. PEATFIELD

CALENDAR

☐ **Calendar Clock,** *(M519-159).*
    2500.00   2800.00   (2650.00)

PRENTISS IMPROVEMENT CLOCK COMPANY

A small eastern firm, Prentiss manufactured calendar clocks. It was one of several companies begun with the idea of producing a new calendar design, distinctive of the particular company. Their movements were usually bought in Connecticut.

CALENDAR

☐ **Empire,** *dial 10", 2 spring, 80 beat pendulum, 8 Day, (E2-87, M513-157).*
    1350.00   1800.00   (1575.00)
☐ **As above,** *15 Day.*
    1440.00   1890.00   (1665.00)
☐ **As above,** *30 Day.*
    1485.00   1935.00   (1705.00)
☐ **As above,** *60 Day.*
    1530.00   1980.00   (1755.00)
☐ **As above,** *90 Day.*
    1620.00   2070.00   (1835.00)
☐ **Office Gallery,** *28" x 37", dial 14", 2 spring, 120 beat pendulum, rare, 8 Day (E2-87, M515-157).*
    1800.00   1980.00   (1890.00)
☐ **As above,** *15 Day.*
    1890.00   2070.00   (1980.00)
☐ **As above,** *60 Day.*
    1980.00   2160.00   (2070.00)

Empire

☐ **Standard,** *47" x 16", dial 12", 2 spring, 72 beat pendulum, 15 Day (E2-87, M514-157).*
    1800.00   2160.00   (1985.00)
☐ **As above,** *30 Day.*
    1800.00   2160.00   (1985.00)
☐ **As above,** *60 Day.*
    1890.00   2250.00   (2065.00)
☐ **As above,** *90 Day.*
    1980.00   2430.00   (2200.00)
☐ **Regulator,** *62" x 18", dial 14", 2 spring, 60 beat pendulum, 15 Day (E2-87, M512-156).*
    1890.00   2520.00   (2200.00)
☐ **As above,** *30 Day.*
    2250.00   2500.00   (2375.00)
☐ **As above,** *60 Day.*
    2520.00   2880.00   (2725.00)
☐ **As above,** *90 Day.*
    2700.00   3150.00   (2925.00)
☐ **Regulator,** *62" x 18", dial 14", 2 spring, beats seconds, 60 Day (E2-86).*
    2250.00   2700.00   (2475.00)
☐ **As above,** *90 Day.*
    2430.00   2880.00   (2675.00)

RUSSELLL & JONES CLOCK COMPANY

The Russell & Jones Clock Company, bought out the Massachusetts business of the famous Terry family. It lasted from 1888, (the time of their takeover) until it failed seven years before the turn of the century.

CALENDAR

- **Beacon,** *round nickel, lever, dial 4", 1 Day, alarm, simple calendar (E1-84).*
  100.00   125.00   (112.00)

- **Beacon,** *round nickel, lever, dial 4", 1 Day, simple calendar (E1-84).*
  110.00   135.00   (122.00)

- **8" Octagon Top,** *short drop, height 19", spring, 8 Day, simple calendar (E1-88).*
  300.00   400.00   (350.00)

- **10" Octagon Top,** *short drop, height 21", spring, 8 Day, simple calendar (E1-88).*
  350.00   450.00   (400.00)

- **12" Octagon Top,** *long drop, height 31", spring, 8 Day, simple calendar (E1-89).*
  400.00   500.00   (450.00)

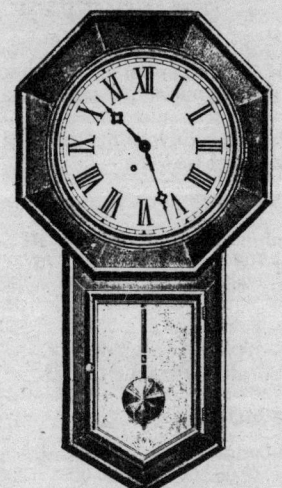

12" Octagon Top

JOSEPH K. SEEM DIAL COMPANY

CALENDAR

- **Steeple Shelf,** *E. Ingraham Clock, 20" x 11", spring, 8 Day (M312-102).*
  400.00   425.00   (412.00)

- **Cottage Shelf,** *Ansonia Clock, 13½" x 10½", dial 5", spring, 1 Day, strike (M313-102).*
  450.00   500.00   (475.00)

SEEM CALENDAR

CALENDAR

- **Seem Mechanism,** *fitted to Seth Thomas, column flat, top clock, 30 hour strike, weight (M321-104).*
  2250.00   2500.00   (2375.00)

10" Octagon Top

SESSIONS CLOCK COMPANY

Originally the E.N. Welch Manufacturing Company, William Sessions acquired the firm by buying up stock at a gradual rate, and waiting until the financial difficulties of the former owners became so great they were forced to sell.

A father and son operation, the Sessions Clock Company began manufacturing around the turn of the century. They continued to put out many of the Welch classics, such as the black mantel and oak cased kitchen clock. During the depression the firm suffered difficulties, but succeeded in switching over to a line of popular electric clocks. The company prospered until the end of the 1950's when it was sold to an electronics corporation and subsequently to a metal goods company.

Meanwhile, a descendant of the original Sessions pair succeeded in opening a clock company in legendary Bristol, although he eventually relocated in Farmington.

CALENDAR

- ☐ **Eclipse Regulator,** *square cornered rectangle with trim, 38" x 17", dial 11", spring, 8 Day, simple calendar (M230-79).*
    325.00   400.00   (362.00)

- ☐ **Gentry Octagon Top,** *short drop, height 24", dial 12", spring, 8 Day, simple calendar (E1-175).*
    325.00   475.00   (400.00)

- ☐ **Regulator "E",** *square cornered rectangle with trim, 38½" x 17", dial 12", spring, 8 Day, simple calendar (E1-175).*
    400.00   550.00   (475.00)

- ☐ **Star Pointer Regulator Octagon Top,** *long drop, height 32", dial 12", spring, 8 Day, simple calendar (E1-176).*
    350.00   500.00   (425.00)

Gentry Octagon Top

SETH THOMAS CLOCK COMPANY

In the early 1800's Seth Thomas was thought to be conservative and C. Jerome wrote that he did not change his clocks until forced to do so to keep his customers. This probably helped the company weather some of the depressions of the 1800's and resulted in very long runs of production for many models of Seth Thomas clocks. He produced wood works clocks until 1844 or 45, and was probably one of the last major makers to abandon the wood works.

During this period all his labels were of the Plymouth Hollow, Connecticut location, except for the clocks sold through southern outlets that had the following labels: Couch, Stowe and Company, Rocksprings, Tennessee; Reeves and Huson, Fayetteville, North Carolina; Case, Dye, Wadsworth and Company, Savannah, Georgia. These are rare labels much desired by collectors.

Probably prompted by lagging sales after the panic of 1837 and the extensive crop failures of 1835, 1837 and 1838, Chauncey Jerome had his brother, Noble, develop and patent the 30 hour brass movement that could be made much cheaper than wood works, and after 1845 Seth Thomas switched to the brass works.

458 / SETH THOMAS CLOCK COMPANY

In 1850 the Seth Thomas factory was reported to have a production of 24,000 clocks annually, with a total value that averaged about $2.50 each.

In 1852 Seth Thomas built a brass rolling mill, which he then incorporated in 1853 as a "joint stock company." That same year, because (or so an old article reported) he was beginning to feel the effects of old age, he incorporated his clock company. His death followed six years later in 1859. Up to this time his company had produced only weight movements in about a half dozen styles, although they had sold a very few of their clocks with brass spring movements purchased from Terry and Andrews. Immediately after his death the company began to put many new models into production.

In 1860 they started the production of small spring driven clocks, and in that year they were reported to have an annual production of 40,000 clocks, with a total value that averaged about $3.00 each. That year they also started the production of some regulators, including the No. 2, which saw a production run of 90 years and is being extensively reproduced at the present time. The production of calendars was started in 1862, and the 1876 Andrews improvement made the Perpetual Calendar such a popular item that by 1888 15 different styles of calendar clocks were offered. The No. 3 Parlor Calendar, introduced in 1868, was produced until 1917, giving it a production run of about 49 years.

In 1865 the Connecticut city name of Plymouth Hollow was changed to Thomaston, and although it was not officially incorporated as such until 1875, all Seth Thomas clock labels immediately showed Thomaston, giving collectors an immediate quick and easy division point in determining the age of all Seth Thomas clocks. In 1865 Seth Thomas became associated with the sales agency, American Clock Company, as was E.N. Welch, Welch Spring and Company, New Haven Clock Company, and Seth Thomas' Sons and Company. Seth Thomas' Sons and Company was incorporated in 1865 to make Marine or Lever movements, and by 1870 was producing 15,887 Marine movements annually, with a total value that averaged about $4.25 each. In 1879 this company was consolidated with Seth Thomas Clock Company. In its 14 years of existence this company made high quality movements and clocks, and the statue clocks made by this company are prized by collectors today.

By 1870 Seth Thomas Company had an annual production of 135,000 clocks, with a total value that averaged about $3.50 each. In 1931 the Seth Thomas Company became a division of General Time Instruments Corporation, later known as General Time Corporation.

By 1932 leadership of Seth Thomas passed out of the Thomas family for the first time, ending a long reign of producing clocks that are probably more prized today than at that time. Few of the clocks produced after this time are desired by collectors. The name "Seth Thomas" is still seen on clocks today, keeping the public aware of the name and perhaps being a part of the reason why some very common clocks with the name Seth Thomas are prized by collectors, and thus command good prices.

This account gives information that allows the general determining of the age of Seth Thomas clocks. Very specific dating of the early models can be accomplished by checking the address of the printer, Elihu Geer of Hartford. This name and the address is usually found in the lower righthand corner of the label. Unfortunately, this part of the label is usually one of the first parts to wear off. The addresses, and dates at each, for Elihu Greer are:

26½ State Street	1839-1844
26 State Street	1845-1846
1 State Street	1847-1849
10 State Street	1850-1855
16 State Street	1856-1864
18 State Street	1865-?

This printer was used by Seth Thomas until 1863, after which their labels were printed by Francis and Loutrel of New York City. Since Elihu Geer also printed labels for other companies, this table is useful in dating many clocks. The approximate years of production of various case styles of clocks are as follows:

SETH THOMAS CLOCK COMPANY / 459

MAJOR YEARS OF PRODUCTION

Steeple	1879-1917
Regulators	1860-1950
No. 1	1860-1890 Tablet dropped 1879
No. 2	1860-1950 Seconds Bit adopted 1879, Tablet dropped 1880, being extensively reproduced today.
No. 3	1863-1879 Original model as 8D Reg. 1879-1917 As No. 3 1928-1930 As No. 3
No. 10	1879-1909
No. 12	1880-1911 Mercury pendulum.
No. 14	1880-1911 Mercury pendulum.
No. 15	1880-1911 Mercury pendulum.
Ships Bell Brass Movement	1884-1941
Hall Clocks	1888-1911 (in 1902 had 26 models)
Walnut Kitchen	1884-1909
Oak Kitchen	1890-1915
Marble	1887-1895
Black Iron	1892-1895
Black Wood	1890-1917
Porcelain	1898-1917
Tambours	1904-Present (Became popular 1914, and was most popular model 1920's-30's).
Sonora Chimes	After 1914
Banjos	1924-probably late 40's.
Electric	1928-Present
Calendars	1862-1917
No. 1 Office	1863-1884
No. 2 Office	1863-1879
No. 3 Office	1866-1870 or 72
No. 4 Office	1868-1879
No. 1 Parlor	1866-1887
No. 3 Parlor	1868-1917

Seth Thomas Clocks normally have just that on the label, "Seth Thomas," even though the company name was Seth Thomas Company until the incorporation in 1863, and Seth Thomas Clock Company afterwards. Therefore, the other information on the label and the production information above must be used to estimate the age of these clocks.

ALARM/FANCY

☐ **Advance,** *black adamantine finish, green marbleized top and base mouldings, gold plated feet and ornaments, height 11", dial 4½", c. 1904, 8 Day, alarm (E1-124).*
    45.00   60.00   (52.50)

☐ **As above,** *8 Day, strike, alarm.*
    60.00   75.00   (67.50)

☐ **Elk Lever Alarm,** *nickel dial 4½", c. 1888, 1 Day, alarm (E1-33).*
    65.00   80.00   (72.50)

☐ **Grand,** *metal case and dial, verde antique base, gun metal top and hands, gold dial, silver center and raised black numerals and minute dots, height 10", base 7½", gold dial 7", c. 1904, 8 Day, alarm (E1-124).*
    60.00   75.00   (67.50)

Elk Lever Alarm

Student Lever

Bee

- ☐ **Lodge Lever,** *nickel frame and sides, metal case, gold gilt front, height 7", dial 3", c. 1888, 1 Day (E1-33).*
  65.00 80.00 (72.50)
- ☐ **As above,** *1 Day, strike.*
  85.00 105.00 (105.00)
- ☐ **As above,** *1 Day, alarm.*
  80.00 95.00 (87.00)
- ☐ **"Nutmeg" Lever,** *brass or nickel, c. 1880 (E1-55).*
  40.00 50.00 (45.00)
- ☐ **Progress,** *quartered oak and mahogany, highly finished and polished, height 12½", dial 4½", c. 1904, 8 Day, alarm (E1-124).*
  40.00 50.00 (45.00)
- ☐ **As above,** *8 Day, strike, alarm.*
  50.00 65.00 (57.50)
- ☐ **Student Lever,** *nickel plated frame, sides and bell, c. 1888, 1 Day, alarm (E1-33).*
  75.00 90.00 (82.00)

ALARM/ROUND

- ☐ **Anvil Lever,** *nickel, c. 1888, 1 Day, alarm (E1-33).*
  150.00 175.00 (162.00)
- ☐ **Bee,** *nickel, dial 2", c. 1888, 1 Day (E1-33).*
  40.00 50.00 (45.00)
- ☐ **As above,** *1 Day, alarm.*
  50.00 65.00 (57.00)

Echo

- ☐ **Echo,** *nickel, dial 4½", c. 1888, 1 Day, alarm (E1-33).*
  25.00 35.00 (30.00)
- ☐ **As above,** *1 Day.*
  20.00 30.00 (25.00)
- ☐ **No. 1,** *nickel or gilt, width 2", c. 1888, 30 hour (E1-33).*
  35.00 45.00 (40.00)
- ☐ **No. 2,** *nickel or gilt, width 2", c. 1888, 30 hour, calendar (E1-33).*
  60.00 75.00 (67.50)

CABINET

- **Austin,** oak, metal ornaments at head and base, porcelain dial, height 15½", dial 4½", c. 1890, 8 Day, strike, spring (E1-50).
  165.00   190.00   (187.00)
- **As above,** walnut, 8 Day, strike, spring.
  180.00   200.00   (212.00)
- **As above,** cherry, 8 Day, strike, spring.
  175.00   200.00   (212.00)

- **Bee,** oak, marqueterie panel, height 14", c. 1880, 15 Day, strike (E1-56).
  140.00   165.00   (162.00)
- **As above,** mahogany, 15 Day, strike.
  165.00   190.00   (187.00)
- **As above,** walnut, 15 Day, strike.
  165.00   190.00   (187.00)

- **Carson,** sheet brass case, nickeled body, gold gilt ornaments at head and base, bronzed alligator panel, porcelain dial, French sash with beveled glass, height 14½", dial 4½", c. 1920, 8 Day, strike (E1-139).
  125.00   150.00   (137.00)

- **Cordova,** mahogany, metal ornaments, old brass finish, porcelain dial, French sash, beveled glass, height 10¾", base 9¾", dial 4", c. 1900, 8 Day, strike (E2-129).
  120.00   145.00   (142.00)
- **As above,** golden oak.
  145.00   170.00   (167.00)

- **Dallas,** oak, metal ornaments at base, porcelain dial, height 13", dial 4½", c. 1880, 8 Day, strike, spring (E1-56).
  165.00   180.00   (187.00)
- **As above,** walnut, 8 Day, strike, spring.
  180.00   200.00   (212.00)
- **As above,** cherry, 8 Day, strike, spring.
  180.00   200.00   (212.00)

- **Hotel,** mahogany, height 18", dial 8", c. 1900, 8 Day, strike (E2-129).
  140.00   165.00   (167.00)
- **As above,** old oak, 8 Day, strike.
  115.00   140.00   (137.00)

Cordova

Kent

- **Kent,** dark oak, solid sash with beveled glass, height 14½", dial 5", c. 1900, 8 Day, strike (E2-129).
  125.00   150.00   (147.00)

- **Mentone,** oak, metal ornaments in bronze finish, cream porcelain dial, French sash with beveled glass, height 11¼", base 10", dial 4", 8 Day, strike (E2-136).
  125.00   150.00   (147.00)

462 / SETH THOMAS CLOCK COMPANY

☐ **Milan,** oak, cream porcelain dial, French sash, beveled glass, height 10¼", base 9½", dial 4", c. 1900, 8 Day, strike (E2-129).
    125.00   150.00   (147.00)
☐ **As above,** mahogany, 8 Day, strike.
    150.00   175.00   (172.00)

☐ **Minster,** oak, height 15½", c. 1880, 15 Day, strike (E1-56).
    150.00   175.00   (172.00)
☐ **As above,** mahogany, 15 Day, strike.
    175.00   200.00   (197.00)
☐ **As above,** walnut, 15 Day, strike.
    175.00   200.00   (197.00)

☐ **No. 800,** walnut case with ash beryl veneers, height 11½", base 13", c. 1920, 8 Day, strike (E1-139).
    115.00   135.00   (135.00)
☐ **As above,** oak case with French walnut veneers, old oak finish, 8 Day, strike.
    90.00   110.00   (110.00)

☐ **Normandy,** walnut, height 15", c. 1880, 15 Day, strike (E1-56).
    140.00   165.00   (162.00)
☐ **As above,** ash, 15 Day, strike.
    165.00   185.00   (187.00)

☐ **Portland,** walnut, height 17", dial 5", dial 5", c. 1920, 8 Day, strike (E1-139).
    105.00   115.00   (117.50)
☐ **As above,** oak.
    80.00   100.00   (95.00)

☐ **Selma,** walnut, height 16½", dial 5", c. 1920, 8 Day, strike (E1-130).
    100.00   115.00   (117.50)
☐ **As above,** old oak.
    80.00   100.00   (95.00)

☐ **Seville,** mahogany, metal ornaments in bronze finish, cream porcelain dial, French sash with beveled glass, height 11¼", base 10", dial 4", c. 1910, 8 Day, strike (E2-136).
    150.00   175.00   (172.00)
☐ **As above,** oak, 8 Day, strike.
    125.00   150.00   (147.00)

CALENDAR

☐ **Dixie Victorian Shelf,** height 28", dial 8", 8 Day, strike, simple calendar (E2-142).
    350.00   385.00   (612.00)

☐ **Drop Octagon,** spring, 24" x 16", dial 12", 8 Day, simple calendar (M58-24).
    325.00   425.00   (375.00)

☐ **Empire Parlor Calendar,** Plymouth Hollow label, 30" x 16½", 8 Day, strike (E1-61, M19-12).
    1000.00   1200.00   (850.00)

☐ **Office No. 1,** 40" x 19½", time dial 12", calendar dial 14", 8 Day (E1-51, M11-10).
    1600.00   1800.00   (1700.00)

☐ **Office No. 2,** 42½" x 20½", dials 14", 8 Day (E1-52, M14-10).
    1200.00   1500.00   (1350.00)

☐ **Office No. 3,** peanut, two springs, 23½" x 11", time dial 5", calendar dial 7", 8 Day (E1-61, M21-13).
    3050.00   3650.00   (3350.00)

Empire Parlor Calendar

SETH THOMAS CLOCK COMPANY / 463

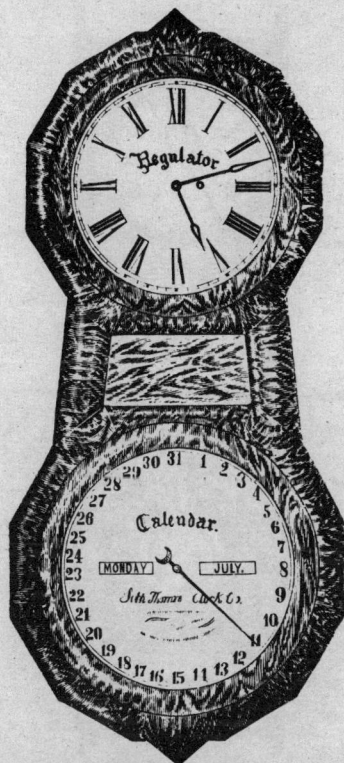

Office No. 1

Office No. 3

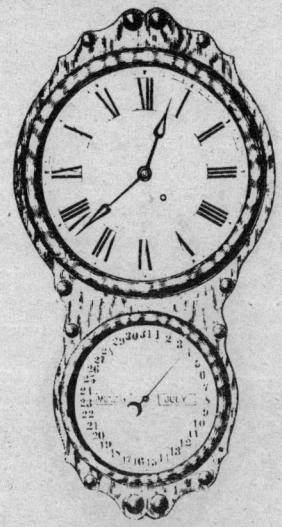

Office No. 4

☐ **Office No. 4,** spring, 28" x 15", time dial 12", calendar dial 7", 8 Day (E1-51, M23-13).
    1050.00   1250.00   (1000.00)

☐ **Office Calendar No. 5,** 50" x 21", dials 14", 8 Day (E1-51, M47-21).
    3000.00   3500.00   (3250.00)

☐ **Office Calendar No. 6,** spring, height 32", 12" time dial 10", calendar dial, 8 Day, (E1-49)
    2200.00   2900.00   (2550.00)

☐ **Office Calendar No. 8,** height 66", dials 14", 8 Day (E1-49, M51-22).
    3250.00   3750.00   (3500.00)

☐ **Office Calendar No. 9,** height 68", dials 14", 8 Day (E1-49, M52-22).
    2000.00   2500.00   (2250.00)

☐ **Office Calendar No. 10,** height 49", dials 10", 8 Day (E1-49, M53-22).
    1800.00   2450.00   (2125.00)

☐ **Office Calendar No. 11,** 68½" x 25", dials 14", 8 Day (E1-49, M54-23).
    4000.00   5000.00   (4500.00)

☐ **Office Calendar No. 12,** 48" x 20", dials 10", 8 Day (E1-49, M56-24).
    1800.00   2000.00   (1900.00)

Office Calendar No. 6

Office Calendar No. 8

Office Calendar No. 9

- ☐ **Office Calendar No. 13,** *height 49",
  dials 12", 8 Day (E1-49, M57-24).*
      1800.00   2200.00   (2000.00)

- ☐ **12" Octagon Top Short Drop,**
  *height 23½", 8 Day, strike, simple
  calendar (E1-143).*
      300.00   375.00   (337.00)

- ☐ **12" Octagon Top Short Drop,**
  *height 23½", 8 Day, strike, simple
  calendar (E1-32).*
      325.00   400.00   (362.00)

- ☐ **Parlor Calendar No. 6,** *spring, 27"
  x 15", dials 7½", 8 Day, strike
  (E1-49, M39-19).*
      900.00   1000.00   (950.00)

SETH THOMAS CLOCK COMPANY / 465

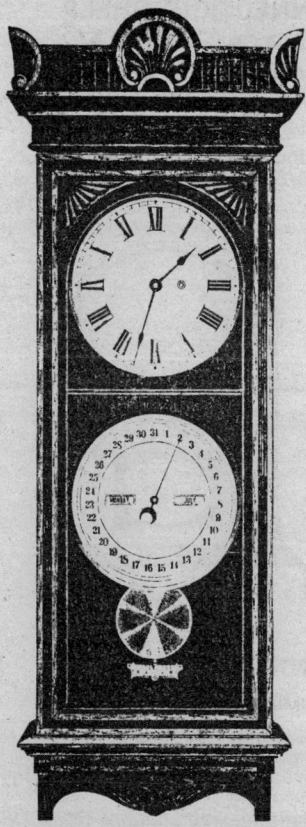

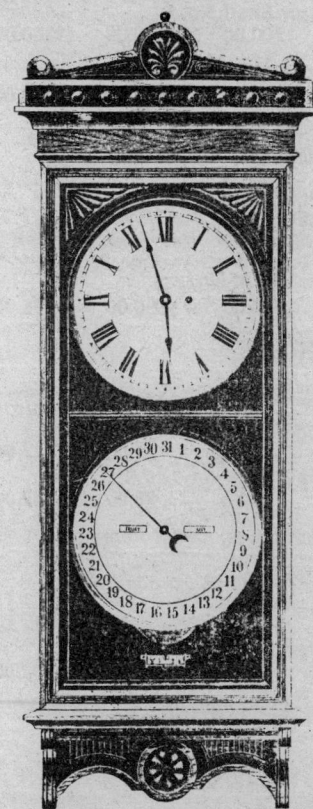

Office Calendar No. 12

Office Calendar No. 13

☐ **Parlor Calendar No. 10,** *36" x 24",
dials 10", 8 Day, strike (E1-49,
M43-20).*
2100.00   2500.00   (2300.00)

☐ **Parlor Calendar No. 11,** *spring, 30"
x 16", dials 7½", 8 Day, strike
(E1-49, M45-20).*
1450.00   1600.00   (1525.00)

☐ **Parlor No. 1,** *new, 33" x 15", dials
10", 8 Day, strike (M28-15).*
950.00   1050.00   (1000.00)

☐ **Parlor No. 2.**
1000.00   1100.00   (1050.00)

☐ **Parlor No. 3,** *spring, 27" x 14",
dials 7½", 8 Day, strike (E1-51,
M31-16).*
800.00   975.00   (887.00)

☐ **Parlor No. 4,** *spring, 24" x 15½",
dials 7½", 8 Day, strike (E1-51,
M33-16).*
900.00   1175.00   (1037.00)

☐ **Parlor No. 5,** *spring, 20" x 12¾",
dials 7½", 8 Day, strike (E1-54,
M36-18).*
700.00   800.00   (750.00)

☐ **Parlor Shelf,** *spring, 29½" x 18",
dials 7½", 8 Day, strike (M42-19).*
1750.00   2000.00   (1875.00)

466 / SETH THOMAS CLOCK COMPANY

- **Parlor Shelf No. 8.**
  1200.00 1400.00 (1300.00)
- **Parlor Shelf No. 9.**
  1400.00 1600.00 (1500.00)
- **8" Round Top Long Drop,** 8 Day, strike, simple calendar.
  300.00 375.00 (337.00)
- **Shelf Double Dial,** Plymouth Hollow label, rosewood, octagon dial, openings in door, 30" x 18½", 8 Day, strike (M7-9).
  1500.00 1650.00 (1575.00)

CARRIAGE

- **Artist Lever,** nickel plated frame and glass sides, gold gilt handle, c. 1888, 1 Day, alarm (E1-33).
  70.00 85.00 (77.50)
- **As above,** 1 Day, strike.
  75.00 90.00 (82.00)
- **Joker Lever,** nickel frame and glass sides, gold gilt front and handle, dial 3", c. 1888, 1 Day, alarm (E1-33).
  70.00 85.00 (77.50)
- **As above,** 1 Day, strike.
  75.00 90.00 (82.00)

Joker Lever

CONNECTICUT SHELF
ARCH TOP

- **Arch top,** wood, height 16", c. 1875, 8 Day, strike, spring (E1-54).
  160.00 185.00 (172.00)
- **Cincinnati,** wood, height 17", c. 1875, 8 Day, strike, spring (E1-53).
  175.00 200.00 (187.00)

Cincinnati

CONNECTICUT SHELF
COLUMN

- **Chicago,** wood, height 17", c. 1875, 8 Day, strike, spring (E1-53).
  120.00 145.00 (132.00)
- **Column,** wood, height 16", c. 1875, 30 hour, strike, spring (E1-53).
  115.00 140.00 (127.00)
- **As above,** 8 Day, strike, spring
  150.00 175.00 (162.00)
- **Column,** walnut veneer, height 25", c. 1888, 1 Day, strike, weight (E1-27).
  130.00 155.00 (142.00)
- **As above,** 8 Day, strike, weight
  195.00 225.00 (210.00)
- **As above,** rosewood, 1 Day, strike, weight
  155.00 180.00 (167.00)
- **As above,** rosewood, 8 Day, strike, weight
  210.00 250.00 (230.00)

SETH THOMAS CLOCK COMPANY / 467

- ☐ **Column,** *walnut veneer, polished rosewood shell or gilt columns, height 25", dial 7½", c. 1920, 1 Day, strike, weight (E1-139).*
      105.00   125.00   (115.00)
- ☐ **As above,** *8 Day, strike, weight*
      170.00   195.00   (182.00)
- ☐ **As above,** *rosewood, 1 Day, strike, weight*
      125.00   150.00   (137.00)
- ☐ **As above,** *rosewood, 8 Day, strike, weight*
      195.00   220.00   (208.00)
- ☐ **Rosewood,** *gilt column, rosewood, height 25", c. 1875, 30 hour, strike, weight).*
      140.00   165.00   (152.00)
- ☐ **As above,** *8 Day, strike, weight*
      195.00   225.00   (210.00)
- ☐ **Rosewood,** *shell column, wood, height 25", c. 1875, 30 hour, strike, weight (E1-53).*
      195.00   225.00   (210.00)
- ☐ **As above,** *8 Day, strike, weight*
      220.00   250.00   (235.00)
- ☐ **St. Louis,** *wood, height 15½", c. 1875, 30 hour, strike, spring (E1-53).*
      150.00   175.00   (162.00)
- ☐ **As above,** *8 Day, strike, spring*
      185.00   215.00   (200.00)

Rosewood, shell column

CONNECTICUT SHELF COTTAGE

- ☐ **Cottage,** *wood, height 9", c. 1880, 8 Day (E1-55).*
      125.00   150.00   (137.00)
- ☐ **As above,** *30 hour,*
      105.00   125.00   (115.00)
- ☐ **Cottage,** *wood, height 14½", c. 1894, 1 Day, strike, spring (E1-143).*
      70.00   85.00   (77.00)

Rosewood, gilt column

Cottage

468 / SETH THOMAS CLOCK COMPANY

Cottage, extra

- Large Rosewood, *gilt column, rosewood, height 32", c. 1875, 8 Day, strike, weight (E1-53).*
  310.00   350.00   (330.00)
- Large Rosewood, *shell column, rosewood, height 32", c. 1875, 8 Day, strike, weight (E1-53).*
  310.00   350.00   (330.00)

CONNECTICUT SHELF
OCTAGON TOP

- Nashville, *V.P., wood, height 16", c. 1875, 8 Day, strike, spring (E1-54).*
  125.00   150.00   (137.00)
- As above, *30 hour, simple spring*
  100.00   120.00   (110.00)
- Octagon Top, *wood, height 9", c. 1880, 1 Day (E1-55) (E1-147).*
  105.00   125.00   (115.00)

CONNECTICUT SHELF
EMPIRE

- Franklin, *mahogany, gold gilt columns, hand carved scroll at head, cathedral bell, dial 10", c. 1912, 8 Day, strike, weight (E2-143).*
  400.00   450.00   (425.00)

Rosewood, gilt column

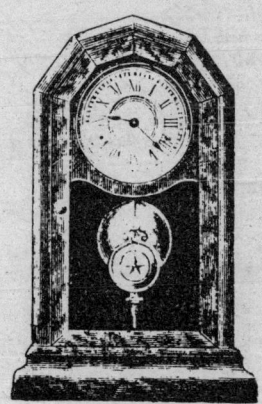

Nashville

CONNECTICUT SHELF
O.G. AND O.O.G.

- O.G., *wood, height 25" and 29½", c. 1894, 1 Day, strike, weight (E1-143).*
  130.00   155.00   (142.00)
- O.G., *wood, height 25", c. 1875, 30 hour, strike, weight, Plymouth Hollow (E1-53).*
  135.00   160.00   (147.00)
- O.O.G., *wood, height 25", c. 1875, 8 Day, strike, weight, Thomaston (E1-53).*
  105.00   130.00   (117.00)

CONNECTICUT SHELF
REPRODUCTIONS OF EARLY MODELS

- ☐ **Continental,** *mahogany case, brass or wood tips, 32" x 17½", dial 10", c. 1910, 8 Day, strike, spring (E2-142).*
  220.00   250.00   (235.00)

- ☐ **Plymouth,** *mahogany, 17" x 9¼", decorated dial 5", c. 1926, 8 Day, strike (E2-141).*
  210.00   240.00   (225.00)

- ☐ **Salem,** *mahogany, 13" x 9¼", decorated dial 5", c. 1926, 8 Day, strike (E2-141).*
  105.00   125.00   (115.00)

- ☐ **Sharon,** *mahogany, 14¼" x 9¼", decorated dial 5", c. 1926, 8 Day, strike (E2-141).*
  140.00   165.00   (152.00)

CONNECTICUT SHELF
ROUND TOP

- ☐ **Cabinet,** *wood, height 9½", c. 1880, 8 Day (E1-55).*
  125.00   150.00   (137.00)

- ☐ **As above,** *30 hour, strike*
  105.00   130.00   (117.00)

- ☐ **Chicago,** *V.P., wood, height 17", c. 1875, 8 Day, strike, spring (E1-54).*
  105.00   130.00   (117.00)

- ☐ **Louisville,** *V.P., wood, height 22", c. 1875, 8 Day, strike, spring (E1-54).*
  195.00   225.00   (210.00)

- ☐ **Tudor No. 1,** *wood, height 16", c. 1880, 8 Day, strike, spring (E1-55).*
  125.00   150.00   (137.00)

- ☐ **Tudor No. 3,** *wood, height 12", c. 1880, 8 Day, strike, spring (E1-55).*
  125.00   150.00   (137.00)

CONNECTICUT SHELF
SPLIT TOP

- ☐ **Albert,** *wood, height 16½", c. 1894, 1 Day, strike, spring (E1-143).*
  70.00   85.00   (77.00)

- ☐ **As above,** *8 Day, strike, spring*
  85.00   105.00   (95.00)

CONNECTICUT SHELF
STEEPLE

- ☐ **Sharp Gothic,** *wood, height 21", c. 1894, 1 Day, strike, spring (E1-143).*
  90.00   110.00   (100.00)

- ☐ **As above,** *8 Day, strike, spring*
  120.00   145.00   (132.00)

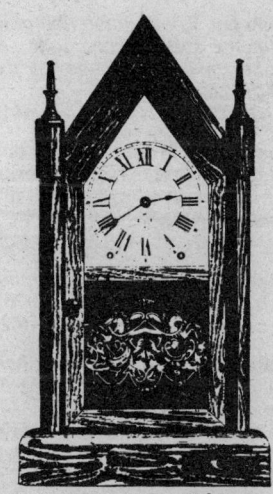

Sharp Gothic

CRYSTAL REGULATOR

- ☐ **Empire No. 0,** *polished gold finish, height 10¾", base 6½", c. 1920 (E1-129).*
  220.00   250.00   (235.00)

- ☐ **Empire No. 1,** *polished gold finish, height 11", c. 1920 (E1-127).*
  220.00   250.00   (235.00)

- ☐ **Empire No. 2,** *rich gold finish, height 11¾", base 7", c. 1920 (E1-127).*
  310.00   350.00   (330.00)

- ☐ **Empire No. 3,** *mahogany and old oak base and top, height 12¼", base 7", c. 1920 (E1-129).*
  325.00   365.00   (345.00)

- ☐ **Empire No. 4,** *bronze top and base, gold body and trimmings, raised gold ornaments, height 11", base 6¼", c. 1920 (E1-127).*
  245.00   275.00   (260.00)

470 / SETH THOMAS CLOCK COMPANY

☐ **Empire No. 5,** bronze top and base, gold body and trimmings, height 14", c. 1920, 8 Day, strike (E1-126).
400.00   450.00   (425.00)

☐ **Empire No. 6,** rich gold finish, height 10½", base 6½", c. 1920 (E1-128).
220.00   250.00   (235.00)

☐ **Empire No. 7,** with bust, rich gold ornaments and polished gold uprights, height 17", base 8½", c. 1920 (E1-128).
390.00   440.00   (415.00)

☐ **Empire No. 8,** bronze top and base, gold body and trimmings, convex front, height 12½", dial 4", c. 1920, 8 Day, strike (E1-128).
400.00   450.00   (425.00)

☐ **Empire No. 9,** rich gold finish, height 13", c. 1920, 8 Day, strike (E1-126).
400.00   450.00   (425.00)

☐ **Empire No. 11,** rich gold with hand burnighing, height 14", c. 1920, 8 Day (E1-127).
380.00   435.00   (407.00)

☐ **Empire No. 14,** ormolu gold (E1-127).
490.00   550.00   (520.00)

☐ **Empire No. 15,** rich gold finish, height 15½", base 8", c. 1920 (E1-127).
360.00   400.00   (380.00)

☐ **Empire No. 16,** rich gold ornaments and polished gold uprights, height 16", base 8", c. 1920 (E1-126).
625.00   700.00   (662.00)

☐ **Empire No. 19,** rich gold and burnished finish, height 15½", c. 1920, 8 Day (E1-129).
360.00   400.00   (380.00)

☐ **Empire No. 20,** rich gold finish, height 14", base 8", c. 1920 (E1-126).
280.00   320.00   (300.00)

☐ **Empire No. 22,** rich gold finish, height 13½", base 7¾", c. 1920 (E1-128).
250.00   280.00   (265.00)

☐ **Empire No. 23,** rich gold finish, porcelain dial, height 11½", concave base 7¼", c. 1920 (E1-126).
310.00   350.00   (330.00)

Empire No. 27

☐ **Empire No. 27,** rich gold and bronze art nouveau finish, cathedral bell, height 21½", base 11", porcelain dial 3", c. 1910, 15 Day, strike (E2-140).
775.00   875.00   (825.00)

☐ **Empire No. 28,** bronze top and base, gold body and trimmings, height 16½", base 10", c. 1920 (E1-129).
625.00   700.00   (662.00)

☐ **Empire No. 29,** bronze top and base, gold body and trimmings, height 17", base 8½", decorated dial 3½", c. 1920, 15 Day (E1-126).
575.00   650.00   (612.00)

SETH THOMAS CLOCK COMPANY / 471

☐ **Empire No. 30,** *polished gold, steel cut pinions and springs in barrels, cut glass top, sides, columns and and base, height 12¾", base 8", decorated porcelain dial 4", c. 1920, 15 Day (E1-129).*
900.00   1000.00   (950.00)

☐ **Empire No. 31,** *figure and base bronze, barbedienne finish, body and trimmings rich gold, burnished, cut glass columns, height 25", base 14½", c. 1920 (E1-128).*
725.00   800.00   (762.00)

☐ **Empire No. 32,** *figure bronze art nouveau, base barbedienne finish, body and trimmings rich gold, burnished, cut glass columns, height 20", base 14½", c. 1920 (E1-128).*
725.00   800.00   (762.00)

☐ **Empire No. 35,** *rich gold finish, height 10", base 6", c. 1920 (E1-129).*
245.00   275.00   (260.00)

☐ **Empire No. 41,** *rich gold finish, decorated dial, height 13½", base 6", c. 1920 (E1-129).*
425.00   475.00   (450.00)

☐ **Empire No. 42,** *rich gold finish, height 8¾", c. 1920, 15 Day, strike (E1-128).*
310.00   350.00   (330.00)

☐ **Empire No. 43,** *polished top and base, rich gold columns, height 9½", c. 1920, 15 Day (E1-127).*
310.00   350.00   (330.00)

☐ **Empire No. 44,** *polished gold body, rich gold pillars and top, height 12¼", c. 1920 (E1-129).*
600.00   675.00   (637.00)

☐ **Empire No. 45,** *polished top and base, rich gold columns, height 9½", c. 1920, 15 Day.*
310.00   350.00   (330.00)

☐ **Empire No. 46,** *polished gold body, gold pillars and top, sharp square corners on base and top, height 12¼", c. 1920 (E1-129).*
600.00   675.00   (637.00)

☐ **Empire No. 47,** *rich gold ornaments and polished gold uprights, height 10", base 6", c. 1920 (E1-129).*
335.00   375.00   (355.00)

☐ **Empire No. 48,** *polished gold finish, convex front, height 8¾", c. 1920 (E1-126).*
360.00   400.00   (380.00)

☐ **Empire No. 48, extra,** *rich gold finish, convex front, height 8¾", c. 1920 (E1-126).*
360.00   400.00   (380.00)

☐ **Empire No. 49,** *rich gold finish, convex front, metal columns, height 9½", base 7", c. 1920 (E1-127).*
400.00   450.00   (425.00)
☐ **As above,** *cut glass columns*
470.00   530.00   (500.00)

☐ **Empire No. 60,** *polished gold finish, convex front, height 11", c. 1920 (E1-126).*
360.00   400.00   (380.00)

☐ **Empire No. 60, extra,** *rich gold finish, convex front, height 11", c. 1920 (E1-126).*
360.00   400.00   (380.00)

☐ **Empire No. 63,** *rich gold finish, porcelain dial, height 11", base 7½", c. 1920 (E1-127).*
400.00   450.00   (425.00)

☐ **Empire No. 64,** *rich gold finish, decorated dial, height 11½", base 9", c. 1920 (E1-126).*
450.00   500.00   (475.00)

☐ **Empire No. 65,** *polished gold finish, convex front, metal columns, height 11", base 9½", c. 1920 (E1-128).*
575.00   650.00   (612.00)
☐ **As above,** *cut glass columns*
725.00   800.00   (762.00)
☐ **As above,** *gold decorated columns*
750.00   850.00   (800.00)

☐ **Empire No. 67,** *rich gold finish, height 12½", base 9½", c. 1920 (E1-128).*
370.00   420.00   (395.00)

472 / SETH THOMAS CLOCK COMPANY

☐ **Empire No. 100,** *onyx top and base, polished gold body, convex front, height 11", dial 4", c. 1920, 8 Day (E1-128).*
200.00   230.00   (215.00)

☐ **Empire No. 140,** *onyx top and base, polished gold body, convex front, height 9", c. 1920 (E1-129).*
360.00   400.00   (380.00)

☐ **Empire No. 148,** *onyx top and base, polished gold body, convex front, height 9", c. 1920, (E1-126).*
425.00   475.00   (450.00)

☐ **Empire No. 160,** *onyx top and base, polished gold body, convex front, height 11", c. 1920 (E1-126).*
425.00   475.00   (450.00)

☐ **Empire No. 201,** *polished gold finish, height 10", c. 1920, 8 Day (E1-129).*
190.00   220.00   (205.00)

☐ **Orchid No. 3,** *polished gold finish, height 10¼", base 6¾", c. 1920 (E1-128).*
270.00   300.00   (285.00)

☐ **Orchid No. 4,** *polished gold finish, height 10¾", base 6¾", c. 1920 (E1-126).*
280.00   320.00   (300.00)

☐ **Orchid No. 5,** *c. 1920 (E1-127).*
280.00   320.00   (300.00)

☐ **Orchid No. 8,** *brass case, gold plated and lacquered, cased in a cylinder cup bell, French sash, convex beveled glass, height 11", base 8", porcelain dial 3½", c. 1920, 15 Day, movement (E1-127).*
220.00   250.00   (235.00)

☐ **Orchid No. 10,** *metal case, gold plated, burnished and lacquered, rich gold trimmings, cased in a cylinder cup bell, French sash, convex beveled glass, height 18", base 11", porcelain dial 3½", c. 1920, 15 Day, movement (E1-127).*
575.00   650.00   (612.00)

GALLERY/WALL LEVER

☐ **Banner Lever,** *brass, dial 4", c. 1880 (E1-55).*
105.00   125.00   (115.00)
☐ **As above,** *dial 6"*
125.00   150.00   (137.00)
☐ **As above,** *dial 8"*
150.00   175.00   (162.00)

☐ **Brass Lever,** *for locomotives, 6", c. 1880, 1 Day (E1-55).*
105.00   125.00   (115.00)
☐ **As above,** *8 Day*
125.00   150.00   (137.00)

☐ **Chronometer Lever,** *brass or nickel plate, dial 3½", c. 1880, 1 Day (E1-55).*
195.00   225.00   (210.00)
☐ **As above,** *dial 4½", 1 Day*
245.00   275.00   (260.00)

☐ **Engine Lever,** *brass or nickel, dial 6", c. 1888, 1 Day (E1-33).*
105.00   125.00   (110.00)
☐ **As above,** *8 Day*
125.00   150.00   (137.00)

☐ **French Lever,** *rosewood or walnut, jeweled balance, dial 8", c. 1880 (E1-55).*
150.00   175.00   (162.00)

French Lever

SETH THOMAS CLOCK COMPANY / 473

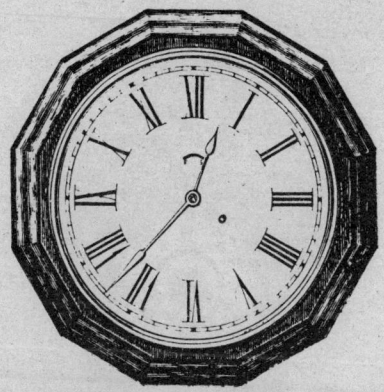

Lever

- **Lever,** *wood, dial 10", c. 1880 (E1-55).*
  150.00   175.00   (162.00)
- **As above,** *dial 12"*
  175.00   200.00   (187.00)
- **Ship's Bell Lever,** *nickel, height 10½", dial 6", c. 1888, 1 Day, strike (E1-33).*
  310.00   350.00   (330.00)

GRANDFATHER

- **Hall Clock No. 21,** *oak or old oak veneer, height 94", metal dial 12", c. 1890, 8 Day, strike, weight (E1-47).*
  1600.00   1800.00   (1700.00)
- **As above,** *mahogany, 8 Day, strike, weight*
  1700.00   1900.00   (1800.00)
- **Hall Clock No. 22,** *oak, height 98", painted moon face dial 12", c. 1890, 8 Day, strike, weight (E1-47).*
  2250.00   2700.00   (2525.00)
- **As above,** *old oak or mahogany, 8 Day, strike, weight*
  2350.00   2800.00   (2575.00)

Hall Clock No. 22

KITCHEN

- **Albany,** *walnut, spring wound, height 20", dial 6", c. 1888, 8 Day, strike (E1-29).*
  160.00   185.00   (172.00)
- **Alton,** *walnut, spring wound, height 19", dial 5", c. 1888, 1 Day, strike (E1-29).*
  150.00   175.00   (162.00)
- **Athens,** *walnut, spring wound, height 17", dial 6", c. 1888, 1 Day, strike (E1-29).*
  100.00   125.00   (112.00)

474 / SETH THOMAS CLOCK COMPANY

☐ **Atlanta,** V.P., wood, spring wound, height 19½", c. 1894, 1 Day, strike (E1-143).
    135.00   160.00   (147.00)
☐ **As above,** 8 Day, strike
    105.00   130.00   (117.00)

☐ **Atlas,** walnut, spring wound, height 22½", c. 1894, 8 Day, strike, weight, calendar (E1-143).
    245.00   275.00   (260.00)
☐ **As above,** cherry
    245.00   275.00   (260.00)
☐ **As above,** oak
    220.00   250.00   (235.00)

☐ **Bangor,** walnut, spring wound, height 20", dial 6", c. 1894, 8 Day, strike (E1-142).
    120.00   145.00   (137.00)
☐ **As above,** oak
    100.00   120.00   (110.00)

☐ **Boston,** walnut, spring wound, height 21", dial 6", c. 1890, 8 Day, strike (E1-50).
    195.00   225.00   (210.00)

☐ **Buffalo,** walnut, brass pillars, spring wound, height 20½", dial 6", c. 1880, 8 Day, strike (E1-56).
    175.00   200.00   (187.00)

☐ **Cairo,** walnut, spring wound, height 18½", dial 5", c. 1888, 1 Day, strike (E1-29).
    150.00   175.00   (162.00)

☐ **Cambridge,** old oak, cathedral bell, packed and sold in "assortments" consisting of six clocks, one of each of the six different patterns, Cambridge, New York, Oxford, Yale, Harvard, Cornell, spring wound, height 23", dial 6", c. 1910, 8 Day, strike (E2-131).
    155.00   180.00   (167.00)

☐ **Camden,** walnut, spring wound, height 22½", dial 6", c. 1888, 8 Day, strike (E1-29).
    150.00   175.00   (162.00)

☐ **Columbus,** walnut, spring wound, height 24½", dial 6", c. 1880, 8 Day, strike (E1-56).
    195.00   225.00   (210.00)

Cambridge

☐ **Concord,** walnut, spring wound, height 22½", dial 6", c. 1888, 8 Day, strike (E1-29).
    175.00   200.00   (187.00)

☐ **Cornell,** old oak, cathedral bell, packed and sold in "assortments" consisting of six clocks, one of each of the six different patterns, college series, spring wound, height 23", dial 6", c. 1910, 8 Day, strike (E2-131).
    155.00   180.00   (167.00)

☐ **Derby,** walnut, spring wound, height 20", dial 6", c. 1894, 8 Day, strike (E1-142).
    120.00   145.00   (132.00)

☐ **Detroit,** walnut, spring wound, height 19½", dial 6", c. 1880, 1 Day, strike (E1-56).
    150.00   175.00   (162.00)
☐ **As above,** 8 Day, strike
    175.00   200.00   (187.00)

SETH THOMAS CLOCK COMPANY / 475

☐ **Dover,** *oak, spring wound, height 20", dial 6", c. 1894, 8 Day, strike (E1-142).*
      100.00   120.00   (110.00)

☐ **As above,** *walnut*
      120.00   145.00   (132.00)

☐ **Erie,** *walnut, spring wound, height 19", dial 6", c. 1880, 8 Day, strike (E1-56).*
      195.00   225.00   (210.00)

☐ **Harvard,** *old oak, cathedral bell, packed and sold in "assortments" consisting of six clocks, one of each of the six different patterns, college series, spring wound, height 23", dial 6", c. 1910, 8 Day, strike (E2-131).*
      155.00   180.00   (167.00)

☐ **Hecla,** *walnut, spring wound, height 22½", dial 6", c. 1894, 8 Day, strike (E1-142).*
      145.00   170.00   (157.00)

☐ **As above,** *cherry*
      145.00   170.00   (157.00)

☐ **As above,** *oak*
      125.00   150.00   (137.00)

☐ **Lafayette,** *walnut, spring wound, height 25½", dial 6", c. 1880, 8 Day, strike (E1-56).*
      245.00   275.00   (260.00)

☐ **Lyons,** *walnut, rosewood veneer, spring wound, height 21½", dial 6", c. 1894, 8 Day, strike (E1-143).*
      135.00   160.00   (147.00)

☐ **Midland,** *walnut, spring wound, height 22", dial 6", c. 1920, 8 Day, strike (E1-139).*
      145.00   170.00   (157.00)

☐ **Newark,** *walnut, spring wound, height 22", dial 6", c. 1888, 8 Day, strike (E1-29).*
      175.00   200.00   (187.00)

☐ **New York,** *old oak, cathedral bell, packed and sold in "assortments" consisting of six clocks, one of each of the six different patterns, college series, spring wound, height 23", dial 6", c. 1910, 8 Day, strike (E2-131).*
      155.00   180.00   (167.00)

New York

☐ **Norfolk,** *walnut, spring wound, height 19½", dial 6", c. 1880, 1 Day, strike (E1-56).*
      125.00   150.00   (137.00)

☐ **As above,** *8 Day, strike*
      150.00   175.00   (162.00)

☐ **Ogden,** *walnut, spring wound, height 21½", dial 6", c. 1888, 8 Day, strike (E1-29).*
      175.00   200.00   (187.00)

☐ **Omaha,** *walnut, spring wound, height 19", dial 6", c. 1888, 8 Day, strike (E1-29).*
      155.00   19.00   (165.00)

☐ **As above,** *oak*
      105.00   130.00   (117.00)

☐ **Oregon,** *cocobola finish, marqueterie top, spring wound, height 19½", dial 6", c. 1880, 8 Day, strike (E1-56).*
      160.00   185.00   (172.00)

476 / SETH THOMAS CLOCK COMPANY

☐ **Peoria,** walnut, spring wound, height 20", dial 6", c. 1888, 8 Day, strike (E1-29).
130.00   155.00   (142.00)

☐ **Pittsburgh,** V.P., wood, spring wound, height 23", c. 1875, 8 Day, strike (E1-54).
220.00   250.00   (235.00)

☐ **Princeton,** walnut, spring wound, height 23½", dial 6", c. 1888, 8 Day, strike (E1-29).
165.00   190.00   (177.00)

☐ **Reno,** walnut, spring wound, height 19½", dial 6", c. 1888, 8 Day, strike (E1-29).
175.00   200.00   (187.00)

☐ **Santa Fe,** walnut, spring wound, height 22½", dial 6", c. 1888, 8 Day, strike (E1-29).
220.00   250.00   (235.00)

☐ **St. Paul,** V.P., wood, spring wound, height 21", c. 1875, 8 Day, strike (E1-54).
310.00   350.00   (330.00)

☐ **Summit,** walnut, spring wound, height 18½", dial 6", c. 1888, 8 Day, strike (E1-29).
120.00   145.00   (132.00)

☐ **Tacoma,** oak, spring wound, dial 6", c. 1920, 8 Day, strike (E1-139).
105.00   130.00   (117.00)

☐ **Topeka,** walnut, spring wound, height 20", dial 6", c. 1888, 8 Day, strike (E1-29).
130.00   155.00   (142.00)

☐ **Utica,** walnut, spring wound, height 22", dial 6", c. 1888, 8 Day, strike (E1-29).
150.00   175.00   (162.00)

☐ **Yale,** old oak, cathedral bell, packed and sold in "assortments" consisting of six clocks, one of each of the six different patterns, college series, spring wound, height 23", dial 6", c. 1910, 8 Day, strike (E2-131).
155.00   180.00   (167.00)

KITCHEN/SERIES

☐ **Capitol Series,** The glass tablets on this line show three pictures of the Capitol at Washington, D.C., also three pictures of the White House. The buildings are an exact reproduction of color scheme and the grounds show the green lawns, etc. Cathedral bell, oak only, packed and sold only in assortments, consisting of six clocks, one of each of the six different patterns. Capital no. 1 — 6 shown, spring wound, height 23", dial 6", c. 1910, 8 Day, ½ hour strike (E2-130).
each 170.00   195.00   (182.00)

☐ **College Series,** old oak, cathedral bell, packed and sold in "assortments" consisting of six clocks, one of each of the six different patterns, Cambridge, New York, Oxford, Yale, Harvard, Cornell, spring wound, height 23", dial 6", c. 1910, 8 Day, strike (E2-131).
each 155.00   180.00   (167.00)

☐ **Exposition Series,** golden oak finish, highly embossed, embossed wood, sold in "assortments" of six clocks, two of each of the three different patterns, 6 clocks shown (no names), spring wound, height 25", dial 6", c. 1904, 8 Day, strike (E2-129).
each 170.00   195.00   (182.00)

☐ **Fleet Series,** oak, tablets show picture of four of the celebrated battleships that took part in the famous peace cruise around the work in 1907-08-09, packed and sold in assortments, six clocks, two of each of the three different patterns, spring wound, height 23", dial 6", c. 1910, 8 Day, strike (E2-130).
each 175.00   200.00   (187.00)

SETH THOMAS CLOCK COMPANY / 477

Fleet No. 1

Fleet No. 3

Fleet No. 2

☐ **The Metal Series,** *old oak, metal ornaments, cathedral bell, packed and sold in "assortments" consisting of six clocks, one of each of the six different patterns, metal no. 1 through no. 6, spring wound, height 23", dial 6", c. 1910, 8 Day, strike (E2-131).*
each 150.00   175.00   (162.00)

KITCHEN/TEAR DROP

☐ **Concord,** *walnut, spring wound, height 22½", dial 6", c. 1894, 8 Day, strike, spring (E1-143).*
    145.00   170.00   (157.00)

☐ **Tampa,** *walnut, spring wound, height 22", dial 6", c. 1894, 8 Day, strike, spring (E1-143).*
    165.00   190.00   (177.00)

MANTEL/BRASS FINISH

☐ **Paris,** Dull gold plated brass base and feet, verde antique top, gold plated sash and mat and beveled glass, height 8½", base 9", porcelain 3½", c. 1910, 15 Day, strike (E2-138).
  155.00   180.00   (167.00)

MANTEL/BRONZE

☐ **Duchess,** bronze finish, height 9¾", dial 4½", c. 1910 (E2-137).
  150.00   175.00   (162.00)

Duke

☐ **Duke,** bronze and verde finishes, five gold plated top ornaments, height 13", dial 4½", c. 1910 (E2-137).
  160.00   185.00   (172.00)

MANTEL/DECORATED METAL

☐ **La Reine,** bronze finish, French sash and beveled glass, height 13½", decorated dial 3½", c. 1910, 8 Day, strike (E2-137).
  150.00   175.00   (157.00)

☐ **Louvre,** metal, porcelain dial, height 11½", base 7½", c. 1910, 8 Day, strike (E2-136).
  270.00   300.00   (245.00)

☐ **Marseilles,** etched metal on art glass, verde antique and bronze finishes, cathedral bell, French sash and beveled glass, height 12½", base 7½", porcelain dial 4", c. 1910, 8 Day, strike (E2-137).
  300.00   350.00   (380.00)

☐ **Rex,** brass antique and bronze finish, height 12½", porcelain dial 4½", c. 1910, 8 Day, strike (E2-136).
  160.00   180.00   (187.00)

☐ **Versailles,** metal, porcelain dial, height 12½", base 8", c. 1910, 8 Day, strike (E2-136).
  450.00   500.00   (305.00)

MANTEL/MAHOGANY

☐ **Dundee,** mahogany, silvered dial, 10¼" x 8¾", minute circle 4½", c. 1912, 8 Day, strike (E2-133).
  65.00   80.00   (72.50)

☐ **Gothic,** real bronze case and finish, bronze dial silvered with cut raised numerals and minute dots fastened back of dial, convex beveled glass, height 11¾", base 7¾", dial 5", c. 1904, 15 Day, strike (E1-124).
  95.00   115.00   (105.00)

☐ **As above,** height 14", base 9½", dial 6"
  110.00   135.00   (122.00)

☐ **As above,** height 18", base 12", dial 8"
  140.00   165.00   (152.00)

☐ **Leader,** mahogany, height 10", convex and glass dial 5", c. 1912, 8 Day, strike (E2-133).
  35.00   45.00   (40.00)

☐ **Perth,** mahogany, silvered dial, 11¼" x 8¾", minute circle 4½", c. 1912, 8 Day, strike (E2-133).
  65.00   80.00   (72.50)

☐ **Priscilla,** mahogany, colored tablet, 13" x 8½", dial 5", c. 1912, Day (E2-133).
  105.00   125.00   (115.00)

SETH THOMAS CLOCK COMPANY / 479

MANTEL/METAL REGENCY

☐ **Blossom,** rich gold finish, height 13", base 6½", c. 1910, 8 Day, strike (E2-136).
    210.00   240.00   (225.00)

☐ **Cluny,** rich gold and bronze art nouveau finish, cathedral bell, height 15½", base 8", porcelain dial 3", c. 1910, 15 Day, strike (E2-140).
    140.00   165.00   (152.00)

☐ **Dauphin,** rich gold and bronze art nouveau finish, cathedral bell, height 21", base 12", porcelain dial 3", c. 1910, 15 Day, strike (E2-140).
    170.00   195.00   (182.00)

☐ **Garnish,** rich gold and bronze art nouveau finish, cathedral bell, height 12½", base 9", porcelain dial 3", c. 1910, 15 Day, strike (E2-140).
    160.00   185.00   (172.00)

☐ **Imperial,** rich gold and bronze art nouveau finish, cathedral bell, height 21", base 12", porcelain dial 3", c. 1910, 15 Day, strike (E2-140).
    375.00   425.00   (400.00)

☐ **La Fleur,** rich gold finish, height 14", base 7½", c. 1910, 8 Day, strike (E2-136).
    195.00   220.00   (207.00)

☐ **La Norma,** rich gold finish, height 12", base 7", c. 1910, 8 Day, strike (E2-136).
    195.00   220.00   (207.00)

☐ **Piper,** rich gold finish, height 9¾", c. 1910, 8 Day, strike (E2-136).
    80.00   95.00   (87.00)

☐ **Royal,** rich gold and bronze art nouveau finish, cathedral bell, height 16", base 10", porcelain dial 3", c. 1910, 15 Day, strike (E2-140).
    210.00   240.00   (225.00)

☐ **Vista,** rich gold finish, height 12¾", base 8", c. 1910, 8 Day, strike (E2-136).
    310.00   350.00   (330.00)

MANTEL/ROUND TOP

☐ **Elect,** metal case and dial, verde antique base, gun metal top and hands, silver center and raised black numerals and minute dots, height 10", base 7½", gold dial 7", c. 1910, 8 Day, strike (E2-138).
    70.00   85.00   (77.00)

MANTEL/WESTMINSTER CHIMES

☐ **Chime Clock No. 71,** mahogany, silvered dial, 13⅜" x 10½", depth 7¼", c. 1912 (E2-133).
    210.00   240.00   (225.00)

☐ **Chime Clock No. 72,** mahogany, silvered dial, 14¾" x 10¼", depth 7¼", c. 1912 (E2-133).
    210.00   240.00   (225.00)

Chime No. 75

☐ **Chime Clock No. 73,** mahogany, silvered dial, 13⅞" x 10¾", depth 7⅛", c. 1912 (E2-133).
    270.00   300.00   (285.00)

☐ **Chime Clock No. 74 (Tambour),** mahogany, silvered dial, 10" x 20¼", depth 6¾", convex beveled glass dial, cast sash, 6", c. 1912 (E2-133).
    220.00   250.00   (235.00)

☐ **Chime Clock No. 75,** mahogany, cast sash, silvered mat and convex beveled glass, 9¾" x 22½", depth 6⅞", convex silvered dial 6", c. 1912 (E2-133).
    220.00   250.00   (235.00)

MISSION

- **Aztec**, *panel birdseye maple, body dark red oak, visible pendulum, height 17", base 11¾", metal dial 6", c. 1910, 8 Day, strike (E2-130).*
  125.00   150.00   (137.00)

Aztec

Zuni

- **Onava**, *panel dark olive green oak, body silver gray oak, visible pendulum, height 15¾", base 11½", metal dial 6", c. 1910, 8 Day, strike (E2-130).*
  125.00   150.00   (137.00)

- **Zuni**, *panel dark red oak, body weathered oak, height 14½", base 12", metal dial 6", c. 1910, 8 Day, strike (E2-130).*
  125.00   150.00   (137.00)

NOVELTY/ART NOUVEAU

- **Abe**, *rich gold, and art nouveau bronze, height 8½", porcelain dial 2", c. 1910, 1 Day (E2-135).*
  70.00   85.00   (77.00)

- **Alice**, *rich gold, and art nouveau bronze, height 10", porcelain dial 2", c. 1910, 1 Day (E2-135).*
  55.00   70.00   (62.50)

- **Artful**, *rich gold and bronze art nouveau finish, cathedral bell, height 16", base 8", porcelain dial 3", c. 1910, 15 Day, strike (E2-139).*
  140.00   165.00   (152.00)

- **Beth**, *rich gold, also art nouveau bronze, height 9½", porcelain dial 2", c. 1910, 1 Day (E2-134).*
  60.00   75.00   (67.00)

- **Bungalow**, *rich gold, also art nouveau bronze, height 7¼", porcelain dial 2", c. 1910, 1 Day (E2-134).*
  55.00   70.00   (62.50)

- **Cis**, *rich gold, and art nouveau bronze, height 8", porcelain dial 2", c. 1910, 1 Day (E2-135).*
  50.00   65.00   (57.50)

- **Colin**, *rich gold, also art nouveau bronze, height 6", porcelain dial 2", c. 1910, 1 Day (E2-134).*
  50.00   65.00   (57.50)

- **Colonial**, *rich gold, and art nouveau bronze, height 8¾", porcelain dial 2", c. 1910, 1 Day (E2-135).*
  40.00   55.00   (47.50)

SETH THOMAS CLOCK COMPANY / 481

☐ **Corinna,** *rich gold finish, height 5¼", porcelain dial 2", c. 1910, 1 Day (E2-134).*
    35.00   45.00   (40.00)

☐ **Cyril,** *rich gold finish, height 9½", porcelain dial 2", c. 1910, 1 Day (E2-134).*
    60.00   75.00   (67.00)

☐ **Dimple,** *rich gold finish, height 8¾", porcelain dial 2", c. 1910, 1 Day (E2-135).*
    70.00   85.00   (77.00)

☐ **Dorothy,** *rich gold and bronze art nouveau finish, cathedral bell, height 16", base 9", porcelain dial 3", c. 1910, 15 Day, strike (E2-139).*
    135.00   160.00   (147.00)

☐ **Flora,** *rich gold and bronze art nouveau finish, cathedral bell, height 14", base 7", porcelain dial 3", c. 1910, 15 Day, strike (E2-139).*
    135.00   160.00   (147.00)

☐ **Florizel,** *rich gold finish, height 8¾", porcelain dial 2", c. 1910, 1 Day (E2-135).*
    50.00   65.00   (57.00)

☐ **Floss,** *rich gold, and art nouveau bronze, height 8½", porcelain dial 2", c. 1910, 1 Day (E2-135).*
    50.00   65.00   (57.00)

☐ **Fountain,** *rich gold finish, height 8½", porcelain dial 2", c. 1910, 1 Day (E2-135).*
    70.00   85.00   (77.00)

☐ **Holly,** *rich gold, porcelain dial 2", height 7½", c. 1910, 1 Day (E2-134).*
    50.00   65.00   (57.00)

☐ **Irma,** *rich gold and bronze art nouveau finish, decorated dial, French sash and beveled glass, height 18", base 11", dial 4½", c. 1910, 8 Day, strike (E2-138).*
    175.00   200.00   (187.00)

☐ **Isabel,** *rich gold and bronze art nouveau finish, cathedral bell, porcelain dial 3", height 18", base 11", c. 1910, 15 Day, strike (E2-140).*
    190.00   220.00   (205.00)

Corinna

☐ **Jen,** *rich gold, and art nouveau bronze, porcelain dial, height 11", dial 2", c. 1910, 1 Day (E2-135).*
    60.00   75.00   (67.00)

☐ **Jess,** *rich gold, also art nouveau bronze, porcelain dial, height 9", dial 2", c. 1910, 1 Day (E2-134).*
    60.00   75.00   (67.00)

☐ **Lily,** *Jap bronze with gold panel, imitation porcelain dial, plain beaded sash and plain glass, height 11½" x 8½", c. 1904, 8 Day, strike (E1-124).*
    80.00   95.00   (87.00)

☐ **Lola,** *rich gold finish, porcelain dial, height 7¼", dial 2", c. 1910, 1 Day (E2-134).*
    45.00   60.00   (52.50)

☐ **Lucerne,** *rich gold and bronze art nouveau finish, cathedral bell, porcelain dial, height 15½", base 9", dial 3", c. 1910, 15 Day, strike (E2-139).*
    145.00   170.00   (157.00)

☐ **Lucrece,** *rich gold and bronze art nouveau finish, cathedral bell, porcelain dial, height 15½", base 9", dial 3", c. 1910, 15 Day, strike (E2-139).*
    135.00   160.00   (147.00)

482 / SETH THOMAS CLOCK COMPANY

Serenade

☐ **Mignon,** *rich gold and bronze art nouveau finish, cathedral bell, porcelain dial, height 15" x 8", dial 3", c. 1910, 15 Day, strike (E2-139).*
    135.00   160.00   (147.00)

☐ **Nan,** *rich gold finish, porcelain dial, height 7¼", dial 2", c. 1910, 1 Day (E2-134).*
    45.00   60.00   (52.50)

☐ **Natty,** *rich gold finish, porcelain dial, height 6½", dial 2", c. 1910, 1 Day (E2-134).*
    35.00   45.00   (40.00)

☐ **Orleans,** *rich gold and bronze art nouveau finish, cathedral bell, porcelain dial, height 14½", base 9½", dial 3", c. 1910, 15 Day, strike (E2-139).*
    125.00   150.00   (137.00)

☐ **Paddock,** *rich gold, also art nouveau bronze, porcelain dial, height 7½", dial 2", c. 1910, 1 Day (E2-134).*
    50.00   65.00   (57.00)

☐ **Poppy,** *rich gold and bronze art nouveau finish, cathedral bell, porcelain dial, height 19", base 9", c. 1910, 15 Day, strike (E2-139).*
    140.00   165.00   (152.00)

☐ **Roselle,** *rich gold and bronze art nouveau finish, cathedral bell, porcelain dial, height 15", base 9", dial 3", c. 1910, 15 Day, strike (E2-139).*
    175.00   200.00   (187.00)

☐ **Serenade,** *rich gold and nart nouveau bronze, porcelain dial, height 8½", dial 2", c. 1910, 1 Day (E2-135).*
    60.00   75.00   (67.00)

☐ **Thistle,** *rich gold, cathedral bell, decorated porcelain dial, French sash and beveled glass, height 14½", base 7", dial 3½", c. 1910, 8 Day, strike (E2-138).*
    145.00   170.00   (157.00)

☐ **Tick Tick,** *rich gold and art nouveau bronze, porcelain dial, height 6½", dial 2", c. 1910, 1 Day (E2-135).*
    50.00   65.00   (57.00)

☐ **Tristan,** *rich gold and bronze art nouveau finish, cathedral bell, porcelain dial, height 12", base 8½", dial 3", c. 1910, 15 Day, strike (E2-139).*
    150.00   175.00   (162.00)

☐ **Vanity,** *rich gold, and art nouveau bronze, porcelain dial, height 12½", dial 2", c. 1910, 1 Day (E2-135).*
    60.00   75.00   (67.00)

NOVELTY/CHINA

☐ **Tile Clock,** *art tile in dark olive, brown, light blue and canary, gilt hands, lever, 6" square, c. 1904, 1 Day (E1-124).*
    70.00   85.00   (77.00)

SETH THOMAS CLOCK COMPANY / 483

Tile Clock

NOVELTY/GILT

☐ **Ada,** Rich gold finish, porcelain dial, height 4", dial 2", c. 1910, 1 Day (E2-134).
55.00   70.00   (62.00)

☐ **Bona,** rich gold finish, porcelain dial, height 5¾", dial 2", c. 1910, 1 Day (E2-134).
80.00   100.00   (90.00)

☐ **Bouquet,** rich gold finish, porcelain dial, height 7", dial 2", c. 1910, 1 Day (E2-135).
40.00   50.00   (45.00)

☐ **Cherubs,** rich gold finish, porcelain dial, height 5¾", dial 2", c. 1910, 1 Day (E2-134).
70.00   85.00   (77.00)

☐ **Elephant,** rich gold finish, porcelain dial, height 5", dial 2", c. 1910, 1 Day (E2-135).
45.00   60.00   (52.50)

☐ **Dido,** rich gold finish, porcelain dial, height 5¾", dial 2", c. 1910, 1 Day (E2-134).
35.00   45.00   (40.00)

☐ **Dorrit,** rich gold finish, porcelain dial, height 5", dial 2", c. 1910, 1 Day (E2-135).
70.00   85.00   (77.00)

☐ **Eagle,** rich gold finish, porcelain dial, height 7", dial 2", c. 1910, 1 Day (E2-135).
40.00   55.00   (47.50)

☐ **Goethe,** bronze top and base, rich gold pillars and center, porcelain dial, height 8", dial 2", c. 1910, 1 Day (E2-134).
90.00   110.00   (87.00)

☐ **Jacket,** bronze, also yellow, porcelain dial, height 3", dial 2", c. 1910, 1 Day (E2-135).
45.00   60.00   (52.50)

☐ **Mozart,** bronze top and base, rich gold pillars and center, porcelain dial, height 8", dial 2", c. 1910, 1 Day (E2-134).
90.00   110.00   (87.00)

☐ **Schiller,** bronze top and base, rich gold pillars and center, porcelain dial, height 8", dial 2", c. 1910, 1 Day (E2-134).
90.00   110.00   (87.00)

☐ **School Days,** rich gold, also gold clock with bronze girl, porcelain dial, height 7½", dial 2", c. 1910, 1 Day (E2-135).
55.00   70.00   (52.50)

☐ **School Girl,** rich gold, also gold clock with bronze girl, porcelain dial, height 5", dial 2", c. 1910, 1 Day (E2-135).
45.00   55.00   (45.00)

Shakespeare

Veva

☐ **Shakespeare,** *bronze top and base, rich gold pillars and center, porcelain dial, height 8", dial 2", c. 1910, 1 Day (E2-134).*
      90.00   110.00   (87.00)

☐ **Veva,** *rich gold finish, porcelain dial, height 8½", dial 2", c. 1910, 1 Day (E2-135).*
      75.00   95.00   (57.50)

☐ **Wagner,** *bronze top and base, rich gold pillars and center, porcelain dial, height 8", dial 2", c. 1910, 1 Day (E2-134).*
      90.00   110.00   (87.00)

NOVELTY/IRON

☐ **Arab,** *metal, light blue or pink, enameled and gilt case, lever, height 6½", base 5¼", c. 1904, 1 Day (E1-124).*
      40.00   50.00   (45.00)

☐ **Kaffir,** *metal, light blue or pink, enameled and gilt case, lever, height 8", base 5", c. 1904, 1 Day (E1-124).*
      60.00   75.00   (67.00)

☐ **Turk,** *metal, light blue or pink, enameled and gilt case, height 7", base 4¼", c. 1904, 1 Day (E1-124).*
      40.00   50.00   (45.00)

NOVELTY/WALL

☐ **Lusitania Hanging Clock,** *rich gold highly burnished, fitted with a fine lever time movement, 11 jewels, compensating balance, porcelain dial, French sash and convex beveled glass, 20" x 9½", dial 4¼", c. 1904, 8 Day (E1-124).*
      125.00   150.00   (137.00)

REGULATOR/FIGURE EIGHT

☐ **Signet,** *walnut, height 23", dial 10", c. 1890, 8 Day (E1-52).*

REGULATOR/OCTAGON TOP, LONG DROP

☐ **Globe,** *old oak, veneer polished, height 31", dial 12", c. 1890, Day (E1-50).*
      285.00   325.00   (305.00)
☐ **As above,** *8 Day, strike.*
      310.00   350.00   (330.00)
☐ **As above,** *walnut, 8 Day.*
      335.00   375.00   (355.00)
☐ **As above,** *walnut, 8 Day, strike.*
      360.00   400.00   (380.00)
☐ **As above,** *rosewood, 8 Day.*
      335.00   375.00   (355.00)
☐ **As above,** *rosewood, 8 Day, strike.*
      360.00   400.00   (380.00)

REGULATOR/OCTAGON TOP, SHORT DROP

☐ **Office No. 2,** *walnut, height 26", dial 12", c. 1890, 8 Day, strike, spring, (E1-50).*
      270.00   300.00   (285.00)
☐ **As above,** *8 Day, strike, spring.*
      285.00   325.00   (305.00)

☐ **Office No. 3,** *walnut veneer or rosewood, height 21½", dial 10", c. 1890, 8 Day, strike, spring (E1-50).*
      345.00   375.00   (355.00)

☐ **10" Drop Octagon,** *gilt, wood, height 21½", dial 10", c. 1888, 8 Day, spring (E1-32).*
☐ **As above,** *8 Day, strike, spring.*
      220.00   250.00   (207.00)

SETH THOMAS CLOCK COMPANY / 485

REGULATOR/OPEN SWINGING

☐ **Jupiter,** *oak, moon face, height 59", dial 12", c. 1890, 8 Day, strike (E1-52).*
    1350.00   1500.00   (1425.00)
☐ **As above,** *mahogany, 8 Day, strike.*
    1500.00   1650.00   (1575.00)

☐ **Lunar,** *oak, moon face, height 41", dial 12", c. 1890, 8 Day, strike (E1-52).*
    2250.00   2500.00   (2375.00)
☐ **As above,** *mahogany, 8 Day, strike.*
    2400.00   2650.00   (2525.00)

REGULATOR/PARLOR SHELF

☐ **Dixie,** *oak with bronze metal trimmings, 28" x 17½", dial 8", c. 1910, 8 Day (E2-142).*
    300.00   350.00   (375.00)
☐ **As above,** *8 Day, strike.*
    325.00   375.00   (400.00)
☐ **As above,** *8 Day, simple calendar.*
    350.00   385.00   (450.00)

☐ **Garfield,** *oak, brass weights, wooden rod, height 29", dial 8", c. 1920, 8 Day, strike, weight (E1-139).*
    700.00   800.00   (700.00)
☐ **As above,** *cherry, 8 Day, strike, weight.*
    800.00   900.00   (800.00)
☐ **As above,** *walnut, 8 Day, strike, weight.*
    800.00   900.00   (775.00)

☐ **Greek,** *oak, height 24", dial 6", c. 1890, 8 Day, strike, spring (E1-50).*
    220.00   250.00   (235.00)
☐ **As above,** *mahogany, 8 Day, strike, spring.*
    270.00   300.00   (285.00)
☐ **As above,** *walnut, 8 Day, strike, spring.*
    295.00   325.00   (310.00)

☐ **Lincoln,** *V.P. walnut, height 27", dial 8", c. 1920, 8 Day, strike, weight (E1-139).*
    650.00   750.00   (575.00)
☐ **As above,** *oak, 8 Day, strike, weight.*
    600.00   700.00   (550.00)

☐ **Rome,** *walnut, height 20½", dial 6", c. 1920, 8 Day, strike (E1-139).*
    135.00   160.00   (147.00)

Dixie

☐ **Yorktown,** *mahogany case, hand carved columns, feet and ornament, cathedral bell, height 36", base 18", dial 10", c. 1910, 8 Day (E2-128).*
    335.00   375.00   (355.00)

REGULATOR/PARLOR WALL

☐ **Flora,** *mahogany, case hand carved, height 38", dial 8", c. 1890, 8 Day, strike, weight (E1-52).*
    875.00   975.00   (925.00)
☐ **As above,** *oak, 8 Day, strike, weight.*
    800.00   900.00   (850.00)
☐ **As above,** *cherry, 8 Day, strike, weight.*
    950.00   1050.00   (1000.00)
☐ **As above,** *walnut, 8 Day, strike, weight.*
    900.00   1000.00   (950.00)

☐ **March,** *oak, height 46", dial 8½", 1890, 8 Day, strike, spring (E1-47).*
    1050.00   1300.00   (1175.00)

486 / SETH THOMAS CLOCK COMPANY

Panama

☐ **Panama**, oak, height 30", dial 6", c. 1912, 8 Day, strike, spring (E2-143).
      575.00   650.00   (612.00)
☐ As above, walnut.
      675.00   750.00   (712.00)
☐ As above, cherry.
      750.00   800.00   (775.00)

REGULATOR/PARLOR WALL CHIME

☐ **Chime Clock No. 101**, mahogany, silvered dial, 28" x 13", depth 7½", dial 8½", c. 1912 (E2-133).
      190.00   220.00   (205.00)

☐ **Chime Clock No. 103**, mahogany, dull rubbed finish, hand-painted dial in antique finish with ornamental corners in colors, fine crotch mahogany panel in lower door, 31" x 12", depth 8", dial 8", c. 1912 (E2-133).
      310.00   350.00   (330.00)

☐ **Chime Clock No. 102**, mahogany, silvered dial, 31" x 13", depth 7½", dial 8", c. 1912 (E2-133).
      240.00   270.00   (255.00)

REGULATOR/PRECISION

☐ **Precision Clock**, metal case, dead beat escapement, height 62", dial 14", c. 1890, 32 Day (E1-47).
      7500.00   10000.00   (8750.00)
☐ As above, 8 Day, gravity.
      7500.00   10000.00   (8750.00)

REGULATOR/ROUND TOP

☐ **Brighton**, mahogany, height 22¼", dial 12", c. 1910, 8 Day, strike, spring (E2-142).
      210.00   240.00   (225.00)

Rio

SETH THOMAS CLOCK COMPANY / 487

- ☐ **Office No. 1,** *walnut, height 25",
dial 12", c. 1890, 8 Day, spring
(E1-50).*
270.00   300.00   (285.00)
- ☐ **As above,** *8 Day, strike, spring.*
285.00   325.00   (305.00)
- ☐ **Rio,** *mahogany veneer, polished,
height 25¼", dial 12", c. 1910, 8
Day, strike, spring, (E2-142).*
245.00   275.00   (260.00)

REGULATOR/SECONDS BIT

- ☐ **Queene Anne,** *walnut, height 36",
dial 8½", c. 1890, 8 Day, spring
(E1-52).*
600.00   650.00   (625.00)
- ☐ **As above,** *walnut, 8 Day, strike,
spring.*
650.00   700.00   (675.00)
- ☐ **As above,** *oak, 8 Day, spring.*
400.00   450.00   (425.00)
- ☐ **As above,** *oak, 8 Day, strike,
spring.*
450.00   500.00   (475.00)
- ☐ **As above,** *cherry, 8 Day, spring.*
650.00   700.00   (675.00)
- ☐ **As above,** *cherry, 8 Day, strike,
spring.*
700.00   750.00   (725.00)

- ☐ **Regulator No. 2,** *walnut and oak
veneer, polished movement 2½" x
4½", lantern pinions Graham
pallets, brass covered zinc ball
and wood rod, 80 beats to the
minute, movement has retaining
power, height 24", dial 12", c. 1888,
8 Day, weight (E1-26).*
540.00   600.00   (570.00)

- ☐ **Regulator No. 3,** *walnut, height
14", dial 14", c. 1890, 8 Day, weight
(E1-52).*
900.00   1150.00   (1025.00)
- ☐ **As above,** *8 Day, strike, weight.*
1000.00   1250.00   (1125.00)

- ☐ **Regulator No. 4,** *walnut, height
47", dial 7", c. 1890, 8 Day, weight
(E1-50).*
1250.00   1500.00   (1375.00)

- ☐ **Regulator No. 5,** *walnut, height
50", porcelain dial 7½", c. 1890, 8
Day, weight (E1-50).*
1250.00   1500.00   (1375.00)

Regulator No. 7

- ☐ **Regulator No. 6,** *oak, 80 beats to
the minute, retaining power,
Graham pallets, lantern pinions,
brass covered zinc ball, wood rods,
height 49", dial 10", c. 1888, 8 Day,
weight (E1-24).*
1000.00   1200.00   (1100.00)
- ☐ **As above,** *cherry, 8 Day, weight.*
1250.00   1450.00   (1350.00)
- ☐ **As above,** *walnut, 8 Day, weight.*
1200.00   1400.00   (1300.00)

488 / SETH THOMAS CLOCK COMPANY

☐ **Regulator No. 7,** *oak, height 45",
dial 12", 8 Day, weight.*
    1250.00   1500.00   (1375.00)
☐ **As above,** *cherry.*
    1500.00   1750.00   (1625.00)
☐ **As above,** *walnut.*
    1450.00   1700.00   (1675.00)

☐ **Regulator No. 11,** *golden oak,
Graham dead-beat escapement
and maintaining power, beats
seconds, height 56", dial 12", c.
1900, 8 Day, weight (E2-144).*
    1250.00   1450.00   (1350.00)
☐ **As above,** *mahogany, 8 Day,
weight.*
    1350.00   1550.00   (1450.00)

☐ **Regulator No. 15,** *walnut, mercury
pendulum, independent second,
beats seconds, height 100", dial
14", c. 1890, 8 Day, weight (E1-47).*
    3000.00   3500.00   (3250.00)

☐ **Regulator No. 17,** *oak or old oak,
beats seconds, height 68", dial
14", c. 1890, 8 Day, weight.*
    1400.00   1600.00   (1500.00)
☐ **As above,** *cherry.*
    1550.00   1750.00   (1650.00)
☐ **As above,** *walnut.*
    1500.00   1700.00   (1600.00)

☐ **Regulator No. 18,** *walnut veneer,
beats seconds, brass weights,
wood rod, Graham pallets, lantern
pinions and retaining power,
height 54", dial 14", c. 1888, 8 Day,
weight (E1-24).*
    1600.00   1800.00   (1700.00)

☐ **Regulator No. 19,** *old oak, height
48½", dial 14", c. 1912, 8 Day,
weight (E2-143).*
    1300.00   1500.00   (1400.00)
☐ **As above,** *mahogany.*
    1400.00   1600.00   (1500.00)

☐ **Regulator No. 20,** *cherry,
mahogany and old oak, large
movement, wood rod, brass
covered zinc ball, Graham dead-
beat escapement and maintaining
power, the round top and two side
pieces can be removed if a plain
top case is desired, beats
seconds, height 62", dial 14", c.
1900, 8 Day, weight (E2-144).*
    1500.00   1750.00   (1625.00)

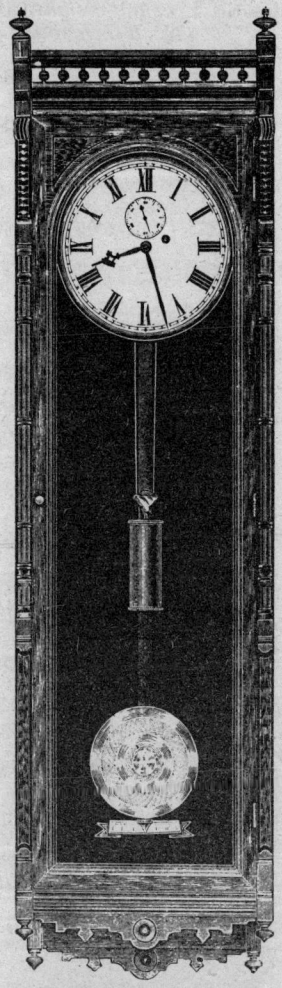

Regulator No. 32

☐ **Regulator No. 31,** *walnut, cherry,
oak or old oak, beats seconds,
height 68", dial 18", c. 1890, 8 Day,
weight (E1-47).*
    1600.00   1800.00   (1700.00)

☐ **Regulator No. 32,** *old oak, Graham
dead-beat escapement and
maintaining power, beats seconds,
height 68", dial 12", c. 1900, 8 Day,
weight (E2-144).*
    1800.00   2000.00   (1900.00)

SETH THOMAS CLOCK COMPANY / 489

☐ **Regulator No. 63,** *mahogany or golden oak, Graham dead-beat escapement, brass covered zinc ball, wood rod, beats seconds, height 76", dial 14", c. 1900, 8 Day, weight (E2-143).*
    2000.00   2250.00   (2125.00)

☐ **As above,** *8 Day, spring.*
    225.00   275.00   (250.00)

REGULATOR/SQUARE TOP

☐ **Litchfield,** *mahogany finish, Graham dead-beat escapement, gold leaf border on upper and lower glasses, height 31", dial 12", c. 1910, 30 Day (E2-142).*
    400.00   450.00   (425.00)

☐ **Regulator No. 25,** *Flemish oak, height 32", dial 12", c. 1910, 8 Day, weight (E2-142).*
    750.00   850.00   (800.00)

REGULATOR/STORE

☐ **Office No. 6,** *old oak finish, height 36", dial 12", c. 1910, 8 Day, spring (E2-142).*
    245.00   275.00   (260.00)

☐ **30 Day Office,** *large double spring time movement, with Graham dead-beat escapement, oak, height 42", dial 12", c. 1910 (E2-142).*
    270.00   300.00   (285.00)

Litchfield

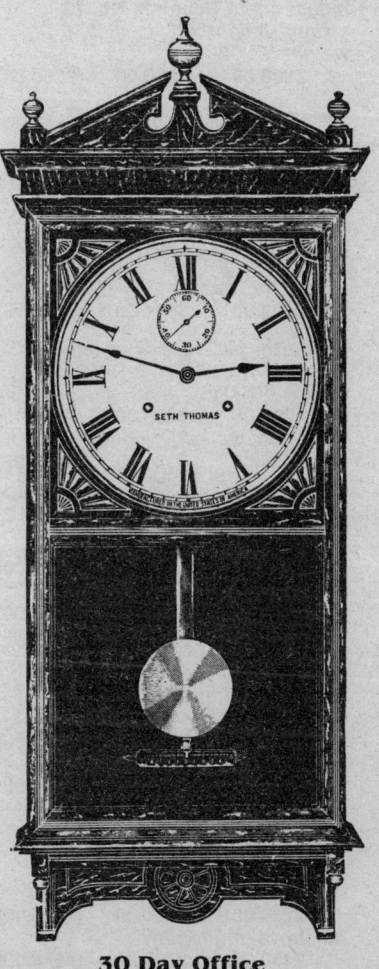

30 Day Office

REGULATOR/SWEEP SECONDS

- **Sweep Second No. 10,** *walnut, height 72", c. 1890, 8 Day, weight (E1-52).*
  2500.00   3000.00   (2750.00)

- **Sweep Second No. 11,** *walnut, beats seconds, height 96", c. 1890, 8 Day, weight (E1-52).*
  2500.00   3000.00   (2750.00)

- **Independent Seconds No. 12,** *walnut, height 72", c. 1890, 8 Day, weight (E1-52).*
  2000.00   2500.00   (2250.00)

- **Independent Seconds No. 13,** *walnut, beats seconds, height 96", c. 1890, 8 Day, weight (E1-52).*
  2100.00   2300.00   (2200.00)

- **Regulator No. 14,** *walnut, mercury pendulum, beats seconds, sweep second, height 100", dial 14", c. 1890, 8 Day, weight (E1-47).*
  3000.00   3500.00   (3250.00)

- **Regulator No. 16,** *oak or old oak, height 75", dial 12", c. 1890, 8 Day, weight (E1-47).*
  2500.00   2800.00   (2650.00)
- **As above,** *walnut*
  2700.00   3000.00   (2850.00)

- **Regulator No. 19,** *oak or old oak, beats seconds, height 75", dial 12", c. 1890, 8 Day, weight (E1-47).*
  2600.00   2900.00   (2250.00)
- **As above,** *walnut*
  2800.00   3100.00   (2950.00)

- **Regulator No. 60,** *oak, Graham escapement, beats seconds, height 58½", dial 14", c. 1912, 8 Day, weight (E2-143).*
  2600.00   3000.00   (2800.00)
- **As above,** *mahogany*
  2800.00   3200.00   (3000.00)

- **Regulator No. 62,** *oak, Graham pallets, retaining power, beats seconds, height 60", dial 14", c. 1912, 8 Day, weight (E2-143).*
  2250.00   2500.00   (2375.00)
- **As above,** *mahogany*
  2450.00   2700.00   (2575.00)

Regulator No. 60

STATUE/OVER 18"

- **Frolic,** *bronze and verde antique finishes, height 23", base 9¼", porcelain dial 4½", c. 1910, 8 Day, strike (E2-137).*
  150.00   175.00   (162.00)

- **Huntress,** *Seth Thomas' Sons And Company 20" strikes hour and half hour, French bronze, verde antique, light verde, c. 1875, 15 Day (E1-59).*
  375.00   425.00   (400.00)

SETH THOMAS CLOCK COMPANY / 491

Frolic

Toiler

☐ **Toiler,** *bronze and brass antique finishes, height 27", base 9¼", porcelain dial 4¼", c. 1910, 8 Day, strike (E2-137).*
    140.00   165.00   (152.00)

☐ **Victory,** *Syrian bronze finish, French sash and beveled glass, height 22", decorated porcelain dial 4", c. 1904, 8 Day, strike (E1-124).*
    220.00   250.00   (235.00)

☐ **Whistling Boy,** *Syrian bronze finish, French sash and beveled glass, height 21", decorated porcelain dial 4", c. 1904, 8 Day, strike (E1-124).*
    220.00   250.00   (235.00)

STATUE/ART NOUVEAU, OVER 18"

☐ **Creation,** *rich gold and bronze art nouveau finish, cathedral bell, height 18", base 14", porcelain dial 3", c. 1910, 15 Day, strike (E2-139).*
    270.00   300.00   (285.00)

☐ **Folly,** *bronze art nouveau finish, French sash and beveled glass, height 21½", base 9", porcelain dial 4", c. 1910, 15 Day, strike (E2-138).*
    210.00   240.00   (225.00)

492 / SETH THOMAS CLOCK COMPANY

☐ **Gaiety,** *rich gold and bronze art nouveau finishes, cathedral bell, height 22½", base 14", porcelain dial 3", c. 1910, 15 Day, strike (E2-139).*
230.00   260.00   (245.00)

☐ **Innocence,** *bronze art nouveau finish, cathedral bell, French sash and beveled glass, height 21", base 21", porcelain dial 4", c. 1910, 8 Day, strike (E2-137).*
310.00   350.00   (330.00)

☐ **Inspiration,** *bronze art nouveau finish, cathedral bell, French sash and beveled glass, height 21", base 21", porcelain dial 4", c. 1910, 8 Day, strike (E2-137).*
285.00   325.00   (305.00)

☐ **Inspiration And Innocence,** *bronze art nouveau finish, cathedral bell, French sash and beveled glass, height 21", base 26", porcelain dial 4", c. 1910, 8 Day, strike (E2-137).*
360.00   400.00   (380.00)

☐ **Jeannette,** *rich gold and bronze art nouveau finish, cathedral bell, height 20", base 8½", porcelain dial 3", c. 1910, 15 Day, strike (E2-140).*
175.00   200.00   (187.00)

☐ **Josephine,** *bronze art nouveau finish, French sash and beveled glass, height 21", base 12½", porcelain dial 4", c. 1910, 8 Day, strike (E2-138).*
190.00   220.00   (205.00)

☐ **Mercedes,** *bronze art nouveau finish, French sash and beveled glass, height 26", base 15", porcelain dial 4", c. 1910, 8 Day, strike (E2-138).*
210.00   240.00   (225.00)

☐ **Tanya,** *bronze art nouveau finish, French sash, beveled glass, height 25", base 10", porcelain dial 4", c. 1910, 8 Day, strike (E2-138).*
210.00   240.00   (225.00)

☐ **Valentine,** *bronze finish with verde ball, French sash, beveled glass, height 22½", base 14", porcelain dial 4", c. 1910, 15 Day, strike (E2-138).*
210.00   240.00   (225.00)

☐ **Vivien,** *rich gold and bronze art nouveau finish, cathedral bell, height 27½", base 16½", porcelain dial 3", c. 1910, 15 Day, strike (E2-140).*
490.00   550.00   (520.00)

STATUE/UNDER 18"

☐ **Leisure,** *Seth Thomas' Sons And Company 18" strikes, quarter and half hours, French bronze, verde antique, light verde, c. 1875, 15 Day (E1-59).*
285.00   325.00   (305.00)

☐ **Rebecca At The Well,** *bronze art nouveau finish, cathedral bell, French sash and beveled glass, height 15½", base 15", porcelain dial 4", c. 1910, 8 Day, strike (E2-137).*
335.00   375.00   (355.00)

STATUE/ART NOUVEAU, UNDER 18"

☐ **Nymph,** *rich gold and bronze art nouveau finish, cathedral bell, height 18", base 9½", porcelain dial 3", c. 1910, 15 Day, strike (E2-140).*
140.00   165.00   (152.00)

STREET

☐ **Two Dial Post Clock,** *iron column and iron head, height 13', dial 10", 40", c. 1910 (E2-128).*
1500.00   2000.00   (1550.00)

☐ **Four Dial Post Clock,** *iron dials with black or gilt numerals, height to center of dial 13', base of column 36", 24" square, dial 3", c. 1910 (E2-128).*
2500.00   3000.00   (2750.00)

NOTE: These two clocks represent typical examples of street clocks which were made in many styles and decorations. Most of the eight day movements have been replaced by electric movements and for a collector the electric movement decreases the value. Because they are rare and varied each clock must be judged on its merits and a guide to value is hard to determine.

SOUTHERN CALENDAR CLOCK COMPANY

One of the better known calendar clock manufacturing outfits, the Southern Calendar Clock Company was based in St. Louis, Missouri, although they bought their clock movements from Connecticut firms.

CALENDAR

☐ **Fashion Model 1,** *28½" x 15½", dials 7", spring, 8 Day, strike, alarm (M330-107).*
    950.00   1100.00   (987.00)

☐ **Fashion Model 2,** *short pendulum, 21" x 15", dials 7½", spring, 8 Day, strike (M331-107).*
    1250.00   1450.00   (1450.00)

☐ **Fashion Model 3,** *short pendulum, 32" x 16", dials 7½", spring, 8 Day, strike (M342-110).*
    1650.00   1975.00   (1812.00)

☐ **Fashion Model 4,** *short pendulum, 32" x 16", dials 7½", spring, 8 Day, strike (M343-110).*
    1600.00   2000.00   (1875.00)

☐ **Fashion Model 5,** *long pendulum, 32" x 16½", dials 7½", spring, 8 Day, strike (M353-133).*
    1850.00   2250.00   (2050.00)

☐ **Fashion Model 6,** *long pendulum, 32" x 16½", dials 7½", spring, 8 Day, strike (M354-113).*
    2000.00   2450.00   (2225.00)

☐ **Fashion Model 7,** *long pendulum, 32½" x 16½", dials 7½", spring, 8 Day, strike (M359-115).*
    1900.00   2325.00   (2112.00)

☐ **Fashion Model 8,** *long pendulum, 32½" x 16½", dials 7½", spring, 8 Day, strike (M360-115).*
    1850.00   2375.00   (2125.00)

☐ **Fashion Model 9,** *short pendulum, 32" x 17", dials 7", spring, 8 Day, strike (M364-116).*
    1500.00   1675.00   (1587.00)

SOUTHERN CLOCK COMPANY

CALENDAR

☐ **O.G.,** *25¾" x 15¼", dials 8", spring, 8 Day, strike, simple calendar (M468-144).*
    350.00   425.00   (387.00)

STANDARD CALENDAR CLOCK COMPANY
O.G. CLOCK COMPANY

CALENDAR

☐ **O.G. Standard Calendar Clock Co.,** *made by New Haven Clock Co., 25¾" x 15½", spring, 8 Day, strike, simple calendar (M385-122).*
    245.00   275.00   (260.00)

☐ **O.G. Clock Co.,** *made by New Haven Clock Co., 26" x 15½", spring, 8 Day, strike (M387-122).*
    300.00   400.00   (350.00)

TERRY CLOCK COMPANY

Eli Terry, born at East Windsor in Connecticut, showed a mechanical inclination early in life. Inspired by Eli Whitney, inventor of the cotton gin, Terry is credited as the father of mass clock mechanization. Seth Thomas was his assistant at one time, as was Silas Hoadley.

In a mill by the Naugatuck river, he created a shelf clock design, that virtually displaced the longcase model and was more popular than either the wall or standing clock variations. Terry is also responsible for the start of Bristol's reputation as a clock making center of the state of Connecticut. Terry's patent, was of course widely imitated, and Terry despite his efforts was not successful in inhibiting patent reproductions. Seth Thomas, his former partner, discontinued licensing and fee paying for the privilege of the original design. A lawsuit followed where the issue was not resolved in Terry's favor, further opening the doors for shelf clock imitators to proceed without censor.

Terry's sons Eli Jr., Silas and Samuel followed him into the business, as did his grandsons, Cornelius, Solon, and Simeon. As mentioned earlier the firm passed into the hands of Russell & Jones, near the end of the century, ending the Terry family's tradition of almost a century's worth of expertise, pioneering, and enterprise within the horological field.

CALENDAR

- **Octagon Wall**, *short drop, reverse O.G. moulding on case, 22¼" x 16", dial 11", spring, 8 Day, simple calendar (M233-80).*
  500.00   750.00   (625.00)

- **Octagon Wall**, *short drop, height 22¾", dial 9", spring, 8 Day, simple calendar (M235-80).*
  400.00   475.00   (437.00)

CONNECTICUT SHELF CHAPEL

- **No.160**, *bronze, height 13", dial 4", spring, pendulum, 8 Day, strike.*
  200.00   250.00   (225.00)

Chapel No. 120

- **No.120**, *bronze, height 9½", dial 3½", 1 Day, spring, pendulum.*
  125.00   150.00   (137.00)

- **No.121**, *bronze, height 9½", dial 3½", 1 Day, spring, pendulum, alarm.*
  135.00   160.00   (147.00)

- **No.22**, *walnut, height 10½", dial 4", 1 Day, spring, pendulum.*
  180.00   200.00   (190.00)

- **No.23**, *walnut, height 10½", dial 4", 1 Day, spring, pendulum, alarm.*
  200.00   220.00   (210.00)

- **No.24**, *walnut, height 10½", dial 4", 1 Day, spring, pendulum, strike.*
  230.00   250.00   (240.00)

- **No.25**, *walnut, height 10½", dial 4", 8 Day, spring, pendulum.*
  230.00   250.00   (240.00)

- **No.26**, *walnut, height 10½", dial 4", 8 Day, spring, pendulum, strike.*
  270.00   290.00   (280.00)

CONNECTICUT SHELF COLUMN

- **Rose Column**, *wood, 22½" x 15", dial 8", 1 Day, weight, pendulum, strike.*
  150.00   165.00   (157.00)

Chapel No. 160

Rose Column

No. 43 Gothic

- **Rose Column,** *wood, 22½" x 15", dial 8", 8 Day, weight, pendulum, strike.*
  200.00   225.00   (212.00)

CONNECTICUT SHELF
COTTAGE

- **Cottage,** *wood, height 11", dial 5", 1 Day, spring, pendulum.*
  120.00   150.00   (135.00)

- **Cottage,** *wood, height 11", dial 5", 1 Day, spring pendulum, alarm.*
  130.00   160.00   (145.00)

CONNECTICUT SHELF
GOTHIC AND MANTEL

- **No.43,** *Gothic black and gilt iron, height 13", dial 5", 1 Day, spring, pendulum.*
  180.00   200.00   (190.00)

- **No.44,** *Gothic black and gilt iron, height 13", dial 5", 1 Day, spring, pendulum, alarm.*
  200.00   225.00   (212.00)

- **No.45,** *Gothic black and gilt iron, height 13", dial 5", 8 Day, spring, pendulum.*
  180.00   200.00   (190.00)

- **No.46,** *Gothic black and gilt iron, height 13", dial 5", 8 Day, spring, pendulum, alarm.*
  200.00   225.00   (212.00)

- **No.47,** *Gothic black and gilt iron, height 13", dial 5", 8 Day, pendulum, strike.*
  240.00   260.00   (250.00)

- **No.48,** *Gothic black and gilt iron, height 13", dial 5", 8 Day, pendulum, strike, alarm.*
  250.00   275.00   (262.00)

- **No.110,** *Mantel bronze, height 7½", dial 2½", 1 Day, spring, pendulum.*
  130.00   150.00   (140.00)

- **No.111,** *Mantel bronze, height 7½", dial 2½", 1 Day, spring, pendulum, alarm.*
  130.00   150.00   (140.00)

CONNECTICUT SHELF
NOVELTY

- **No.140, Boy and Dog,** *bronze, height 11½", dial 3", 1 Day, spring, pendulum.*
  130.00   150.00   (140.00)

496 / TERRY CLOCK COMPANY

No. 150 Alhambra

☐ **No.141, Boy and Dog,** *bronze, height 11½", dial 3", 1 Day, spring, pendulum, alarm.*
    140.00   160.00   (150.00)

☐ **No.150, Alhambra,** *bronze, height 10", dial 4", 1 Day, spring, pendulum, strike.*
    255.00   275.00   (265.00)

CONNECTICUT SHELF
O.G., O.O.G. AND REVERSED O.G.

☐ **Reversed O.G.,** *wood, 1 Day, spring pendulum.*
    110.00   120.00   (115.00)

☐ **As above,** *spring pendulum, alarm.*
    120.00   130.00   (125.00)

☐ **As above,** *spring pendulum, strike.*
    130.00   150.00   (140.00)

☐ **As above,** *8 Day, spring pendulum, strike.*
    130.00   150.00   (140.00)

☐ **O.G. No.2,** *wood, 18" x 11½", dial 6", 1 Day, weight, pendulum strike.*
    400.00   500.00   (450.00)

☐ **O.G.,** *wood, 18" x 11½", dial 6", 8 Day, weight, pendulum strike.*
    500.00   600.00   (550.00)

☐ **O.O.G.,** *wood, 18" x 11½", dial 6", 1 Day, weight, pendulum strike.*
    400.00   500.00   (450.00)

☐ **As above,** *8 Day, weight, pendulum strike.*
    500.00   600.00   (550.00)

O.G. No. 2

CONNECTICUT SHELF
ROUND TOP

☐ **No.1,** *plain black iron, height 6", dial 2½", c. 1873, 1 Day, spring pendulum.*
    100.00   120.00   (110.00)

☐ **No.2,** *black and gilt iron, height 6", dial 2½", c. 1873, 1 Day, spring pendulum.*
    110.00   130.00   (120.00)

☐ **No.7,** *plain black iron, height 8", dial 3½", c. 1873, 1 Day, spring pendulum.*
    100.00   120.00   (115.00)

☐ **No.8,** *black and gilt iron, height 8", dial 3½", c. 1873, 1 Day, spring pendulum.*
    110.00   130.00   (120.00)

☐ **No.10,** *plain black iron, height 8", dial 3½", c. 1873, 1 Day, spring pendulum, strike.*
    110.00   130.00   (120.00)

☐ **No.11,** *black and gilt iron, height 8", dial 3½", c. 1873, 1 Day, spring pendulum, strike.*
    120.00   140.00   (130.00)

☐ **No.13,** *plain black iron, height 8", dial 3½", c. 1873, 1 Day, spring pendulum, alarm.*
    110.00   130.00   (120.00)

TERRY CLOCK COMPANY / 497

- ☐ **No.14,** *black and gilt iron, height 8", dial 3½", c. 1873, 1 Day, spring pendulum, alarm.*
  120.00   130.00   (125.00)

- ☐ **No.16,** *plain black iron, height 8", dial 3½", c. 1873, 1 Day, spring alarm, strike.*
  130.00   150.00   (127.00)

- ☐ **No.17,** *black and gilt iron, height 8", dial 3½", c. 1873, 1 Day, spring pendulum, strike, alarm.*
  140.00   160.00   (150.00)

- ☐ **No.20,** *plain black iron, height 6", dial 2½", c. 1873, 1 Day, spring pendulum, alarm.*
  110.00   130.00   (120.00)

- ☐ **No.21,** *black and gilt iron, height 6", dial 2½", c. 1873, 1 Day, spring pendulum, alarm.*
  120.00   140.00   (130.00)

- ☐ **No.27,** *plain black iron, height 9", dial 4", c. 1873, 8 Day, spring pendulum.*
  110.00   130.00   (120.00)

- ☐ **No.28,** *black and gilt iron, height 9", dial 4", c. 1873, 8 Day, spring pendulum*
  120.00   140.00   (130.00)

- ☐ **No.30,** *plain black iron, height 9", dial 4", c. 1873, 8 Day, spring pendulum, strike.*
  120.00   140.00   (130.00)

No. 27 Round Top

- ☐ **No.31,** *black and gilt iron, height 9", dial 4", c. 1873, 8 Day, spring pendulum, strike.*
  130.00   150.00   (140.00)

- ☐ **No.33,** *plain black iron, height 9", dial 4", c. 1873, 8 Day, spring, alarm.*
  110.00   130.00   (120.00)

- ☐ **No.34,** *black and gilt iron, height 9", dial 4", c. 1873, 8 Day, spring pendulum, strike, alarm.*
  120.00   140.00   (130.00)

- ☐ **No.36,** *plain black iron, height 9", dial 4", c. 1873, 8 Day, spring, alarm, strike.*
  130.00   150.00   (140.00)

- ☐ **No.37,** *black and gilt iron, height 9", dial 4", c. 1873, 8 Day, spring pendulum, alarm, strike.*
  140.00   160.00   (150.00)

- ☐ **No.130,** *plain black iron, height 11", dial 5", c. 1873, 8 Day, spring pendulum, strike.*
  180.00   200.00   (190.00)

- ☐ **No.131,** *black and gilt iron, height 11", dial 5", c. 1873, 8 Day, spring pendulum, strike.*
  200.00   220.00   (210.00)

No. 7 Round Top

498 / TERRY CLOCK COMPANY

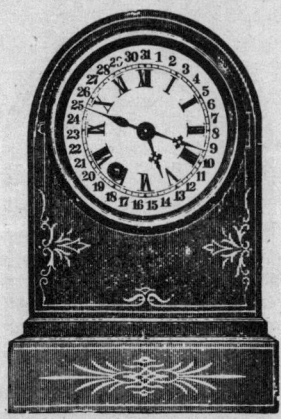

No. 130 Round Top

☐ **No.133,** plain black iron, height 11", dial 5", c. 1873, 8 Day, spring pendulum, calendar.
    350.00   400.00   (375.00)

☐ **No.134,** black and gilt iron, height 11", dial 5", c. 1873, 8 Day, spring pendulum, calendar.
    350.00   400.00   (375.00)

☐ **No.136,** plain black iron, height 11", dial 5", c. 1873, 8 Day, spring pendulum, strike, calendar.
    500.00   600.00   (550.00)

☐ **No.137,** black and gilt iron, height 11", dial 5", c. 1873, 8 Day, spring pendulum, strike, calendar.
    500.00   600.00   (550.00)

REGULATOR

☐ **O.G. Octagon Top,** wood, 23" x 15½", dial 12", 1 Day, spring pendulum.
    325.00   350.00   (337.00)

☐ **As above,** 1 Day, spring pendulum, strike.
    350.00   375.00   (362.00)

☐ **As above,** 1 Day, spring pendulum, calendar.
    375.00   400.00   (387.00)

☐ **As above,** 1 Day, spring pendulum, strike, calendar.
    400.00   425.00   (412.00)

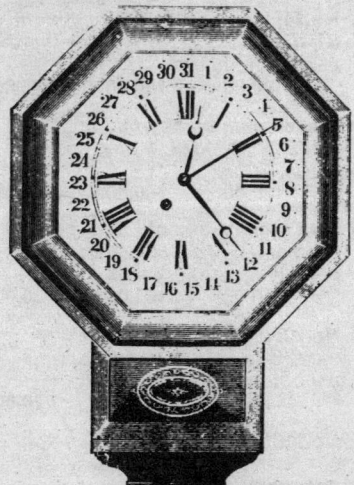

O.G. Octagon Top

Octagon Top

☐ **Octagon Top,** black and gilt iron, height 21", dial 12", 8 Day, spring, ½ second, pendulum.
    450.00   500.00   (475.00)

☐ **As above,** 8 Day, spring, ½ second, pendulum, strike.
    500.00   550.00   (525.00)

WALTHAM / 499

☐ **No.50,** *round top drop, black and gilt iron, height 19", dial 8", 8 Day, spring pendulum.*
    450.00   500.00   (475.00)

☐ **No.51,** *round top drop, black and gilt iron, height 19", dial 8", 8 Day, spring pendulum, strike.*
    475.00   525.00   (500.00)

☐ **No.60,** *octagon top drop, black and gilt iron, height 19", dial 8", 8 Day, spring pendulum that beats ½ seconds.*
    450.00   500.00   (475.00)

☐ **No.61,** *Octagon top drop, black and gilt iron, height 19", dial 8", 8 Day, spring pendulum that beats ½ seconds, strike.*
    475.00   525.00   (500.00)

☐ **No.70,** *round top mantel, black and gilt iron, height 19", dial 8", 8 Day, spring pendulum that beats ½ seconds.*
    450.00   500.00   (475.00)

☐ **No.71,** *Round Top Mantle, black and gilt iron, height 19", dial 8", spring pendulum that beats ½ seconds, strike.*
    475.00   525.00   (500.00)

WALTHAM

These clocks are priced according to the definition of "retail value" as given in the front of this book. However, in this case, there have been many transactions ABOVE this so-called top price. The reasons are simple. The seller may not always make it very clear that these are 1900's production clocks. Waltham and many other manufacturers produced both weight and spring banjos that more or less resembled Willard and Howard banjos. "Willard Clock" and "Banjo Clock" were used as synonyms in some of the advertising, and some sellers today use these terms in the same way but do not always so indicate to an eager buyer.

Some buyers will pay well above the retail value of these banjos because they intend to resell at a much higher price after some modifications. These modifications usually consist of a nameless dial, usually appearing quite old, and marriages with other movements if the clock has a lever or electric movement.

Some buyers are so eager to add a banjo to their collection that the seller of a 1934 Waltham, or other modern versions, has only to imply that it is old, and while maintaining an air of ignorance as to its origin, let the dreams of the buyer persuade him to pay an exorbitant price.

Some sellers have found great profit in replacing electric movements in modern banjos with old pendulum movements. The same has been done with some lever movements. Weight movements have been and are today being reproduced, and sometimes appear in the larger banjos.

"Caveat Emptor" — let the buyer beware. Remember that between the two World Wars, almost all major producers had in their lines banjo clocks.

No. 60 Octagon Top

500 / WALTHAM

Waltham stated in their advertising that, while they reproduced the Willard Clock "in its general lines", they "added much to the symmetry and beauty of design". All of these banjos are collectible and will add to any collection if original and identifiable. Approach an unmarked, unidentifiable banjo with caution, especially if the seller "believes it could be by a well-known maker". The results of a "May and December marriage" of a modern case to an old works will not add greatly to your collection. For further discussion of the fakes who misrepresent these fine clocks, read the section in this book on Replicas, Reproductions and Fakes.

BANJO

☐ **No.1500,** *antique mahogany, torus molding, ornament, 41" x 10½", deep 4", 8 Day, weight.*
    2000.00   2500.00   (2750.00)

☐ **As above,** *walnut.*
    2000.00   2500.00   (2950.00)

☐ **No.1505,** *antique mahogany, carved top and side ornaments, Waltham design glasses, 41½" x 10½", deep 4", 8 Day, weight.*
    3500.00   4000.00   (4000.00)

☐ **No.1525,** *mahogany, gold leaf front, acorn base, Waltham design glasses, 40½" x 10½", deep 4", 8 Day, weight.*
    4000.00   5000.00   (4500.00)

☐ **No.1540,** *mahogany or walnut ivory, red or green crackle flat moulding, brass eagle and side rails, 40½" x 10½", deep 4", 8 Day, weight.*
    2250.00   2750.00   (3000.00)

☐ **No.1543,** *mahogany or walnut carved, gilded rope and balls, 40½" x 10½", deep 4", 8 Day, weight.*
    2250.00   2750.00   (2750.00)

☐ **No.1546,** *mahogany or walnut inlay, 40½" x 10½", deep 4", 8 Day, weight.*
    2000.00   2500.00   (3000.00)

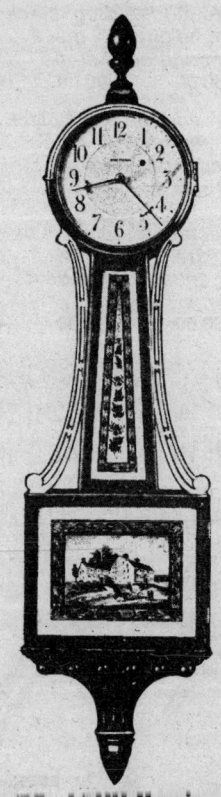

No. 1500 Banjo

☐ **No.1550,** *mahogany, walnut or crackle, 21" x 5¼", deep 2", 7 jewel spring, 8 Day.*
    250.00   350.00   (300.00)

☐ **No.1553,** *mahogany or walnut, torus molding, 21" x 5½", deep 2", 8 Day, spring.*
    250.00   350.00   (300.00)

☐ **No.1554,** *mahogany or walnut, torus molding, 21" x 5¼", deep 2", 8 Day, spring.*
    300.00   375.00   (300.00)

☐ **No.1555,** *mahogany, gold leaf front, 21" x 5¼", deep 2", 8 Day, spring.*
    2250.00   2500.00   (2375.00)

WALTHAM / 501

LIBRARY

This unusually attractive clock is available in mahogany, walnut or black finish.

☐ **No.1425,** *7 jewel, mahogany, 13¼" x 9¾", deep 1⅛".*
    75.00   100.00   (62.00)

☐ **No.1426,** *7 jewel, walnut, 13¼" x 9¾", deep 1⅛".*
    75.00   100.00   (62.00)

☐ **No.1427,** *7 jewel, black finish, 13¼" x 9¾", deep 1⅛".*
    75.00   100.00   (62.00)

☐ **No.1428,** *17 jewel, mahogany, 13¼" x 9¾", deep 1⅛".*
    75.00   100.00   (137.00)

☐ **No.1429,** *15 jewel, walnut, 13¼" x 9¾", deep 1⅛".*
    75.00   100.00   (137.00)

☐ **No.1430,** *15 jewel, black finish, 13¼" x 9¾", deep 1⅛".*
    75.00   100.00   (137.00)

☐ **No.1467,** *antique gilt modernistic type, 15½" x 13", deep 1½", 7 jewel.*
    60.00   90.00   (75.00)
☐ **As above,** *No.1468, 15 jewel.*
    120.00   150.00   (137.00)

☐ **No.1470,** *an adaptation of the quaint colonial clock, exclusive Waltham design, gilded eagle, hand painted glasses, carved base reminiscent of the early American period. Brass ornaments, gilt rope, solid mahogany, ivory dial with black figures, 14½"x 5¼", 7 jewel.*
    650.00   900.00   (775.00)
☐ **As above,** *No.1471, 15 jewel.*
    800.00   1000.00   (900.00)

☐ **No.8514,** *mahogany only, brass trimmings, hand painted panel glasses, 12" x 5¾", 7 jewel.*
    850.00   925.00   (800.00)

No. 1470 Library

No. 1467 Library

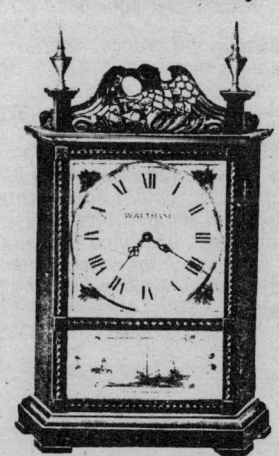

No. 8514 Library

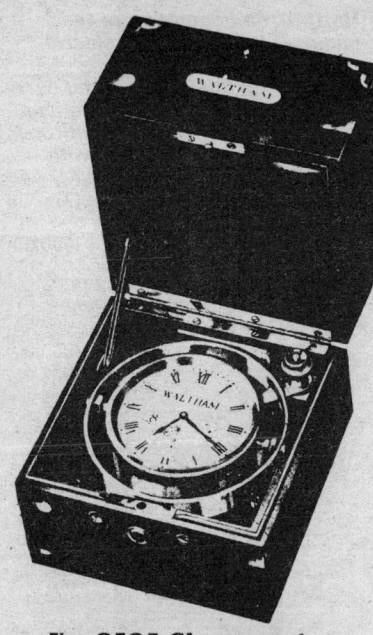

No. 8525 Chronometer

- **No.8516,** *solid bronze, natural finish, art deco, 11¾" x 13½", deep 1½", 15 jewel.*
  350.00   400.00   (375.00)
- **As above,** *No.8517, 15 jewel, verde finish*
  350.00   400.00   (375.00)
- **No.8518,** *solid bronze, natural finish, art deco, 11" x 11½", deep 1⅝", 15 jewel.*
  350.00   400.00   (375.00)
- **No.8525,** *Waltham Chronometer, lever escapement, winding indicator movement adjusted to changes in temperature and isochronism, enclosed in a dust and weather proof case suspended on gimbals in solid mahogany box, 15 jewel.*
  300.00   350.00   (325.00)

W. A. TERRY — ANSONIA
CALENDAR

- **Round Wall,** *short drop, 25½" x 16", dial 11", 8 Day, strike (M243-84).*
  750.00   850.00   (800.00)
- **Shelf Clock,** *Ansonia Brass and Copper Co., Ansonia, Ct., 32¾" x 16", dial 11", 8 Day, strike (M242-83).*
  1000.00   1100.00   (1050.00)

W. A. TERRY — ATKINS
CALENDAR

- **Italian Type Shelf,** *18" x 11", spring, 8 Day, strike (M237-81).*
  1000.00   1200.00   (1100.00)

WATERBURY CLOCK COMPANY

A major producer of clocks in its time, Waterbury began production of a cheap watch towards the end of the 19th century, and continued up until the present.

The company originated through a brass producing firm, and was connected with Chauncey Jerome for a time. There was a place for brass in the clock manufacturing world, and Waterbury was quick to make that lucrative connection.

The company styled its own clocks, the most notable examples being the round top, and octagon drop regulators. The company also sold substantial numbers of its own movements.

Waterbury and all other clock companies for that matter, issued a catalogue to their dealers every year or so. It pictured and described the clocks they offered, along with prices, terms, etc. The dealers or wholesalers, depending on their size and other factors, selected the clocks they wanted to offer for sale from the Waterbury line. These clocks were usually combined with clocks from

WATERBURY CLOCK COMPANY / 503

other companies and then pictured in their general catalogue. This is why some old catalogues show many pictures of several clocks of different manufacturers. Waterbury clocks are relatively easy to distinguish, as some were made only for a short time, although others ran as long as ten to forty years.

ALARM/CALENDAR

- ☐ **Index Nickel,** *lever, dial 3¾", 1 Day, simple calendar (E1-34).*
  75.00   120.00   (97.00)

- ☐ **Kremlin Nickel,** *lever, dial 3¾", 1 Day, simple calendar (E1-34).*
  75.00   120.00   (97.00)

- ☐ **Monitor Nickel,** *lever, dial 3¾", 1 Day simple calendar (E1-34).*
  75.00   120.00   (97.00)

- ☐ **Moslem Nickel,** *lever, dial 3¾", 1 Day, simple calendar (E1-34).*
  75.00   120.00   (97.00)

- ☐ **Sentry,** *lever, dial 5", 1 Day, simple calendar (E1-34).*
  80.00   125.00   (102.00)

NOTE: The above alarm type calendars were avaliable in hammered or fancy ornamented, or brass or nickel cases.

Sentry

ALARM/ROUND

- ☐ **Caliph,** *nickel, brass recessed backs, brass winding and setting parts, dial 3¾", c. 1888, 1 Day (E1-34).*
  25.00   35.00   (30.00)

- ☐ **Envoy,** *nickel, brass recessed backs, brass winding and setting parts, dial 3¾", c. 1888, 1 Day, (E1-34).*
  25.00   35.00   (30.00)

- ☐ **Index,** *calendar, nickel, brass recessed backs, brass winding and setting parts, dial 3¾", c. 1888, 1 Day, calendar (E1-34).*
  60.00   75.00   (67.00)

- ☐ **Knight,** *nickel, dial 5", c. 1888, 1 Day, alarm (E1-34).*
  30.00   40.00   (35.00)

- ☐ **Kremlin,** *nickel, brass recessed backs, brass winding and setting parts, dial 3¾", c. 1888, 1 Day, calendar, alarm (E1-34).*
  60.00   75.00   (67.00)

- ☐ **Monitor,** *calendar, nickel, brass recessed backs, brass winding and setting parts, dial 3¾", c. 1888, 1 Day, calendar, alarm (E1-34).*
  60.00   75.00   (67.00)

Moslem Nickel

504 / WATERBURY CLOCK COMPANY

Knight

☐ **Sunrise**, *nickel, brass recessed backs, brass winding and setting parts, dial 3¾", 1 Day, c. 1888, alarm (E1-34).*
  30.00 40.00 (35.00)

☐ **Turk**, *nickel, dial 4½", c. 1888, 1 Day, alarm (E1-34).*
  40.00 55.00 (47.00)

CABINET

☐ **Cabinet E**, *walnut, height 16", porcelain dial, c. 1888, 8 Day, strike(E1-32).*
  110.00 135.00 (122.00)
☐ **As above**, *ash.*
  135.00 160.00 (147.00)
☐ **As above**, *cherry.*
  110.00 135.00 (117.00)

☐ **Cabinet F**, *walnut, height 19½", porcelain dial, c. 1888, 8 Day, strike (E1-23).*
  125.00 150.00 (137.00)
☐ **As above**, *ash.*
  150.00 175.00 (162.00)
☐ **As above**, *cherry.*
  125.00 150.00 (137.00)

Turk

Cabinet E

☐ **Moslem**, *nickel, brass recessed backs, brass winding and setting parts, dial 3¾", c. 1888, 1 Day, calendar (E1-34).*
  60.00 75.00 (67.00)

☐ **Sentry**, *nickel, dial 5", c. 1888, 1 Day, calendar, alarm (E1-34).*
  40.00 50.00 (45.00)

WATERBURY CLOCK COMPANY / 505

CALENDAR

- **Andes Figure 8,** *height 24", dial 12", 8 Day, strike, simple calendar (E1-183).*
  300.00   400.00   (350.00)

- **Antique Drop, Octagon Top,** *short drop, spring, 22½" x 14½", dial 10", spring, 8 Day, strike, simple calendar (E1-25, M301-99).*
  375.00   450.00   (412.00)

- **Arion Octagon Top 10",** *short drop, 22½" x 15", spring, 8 Day, strike, simple calendar (E1-183, M300-99).*
  275.00   325.00   (300.00)

- **Arion Octagon Top 12",** *short drop, height 24", 8 Day, strike, simple calendar (E1-183).*
  300.00   375.00   (337.00)

- **Bahia Mosaic Figure 8,** *height 22", dial 10", spring, 8 Day, strike, simple calendar (E1-149).*
  375.00   425.00   (400.00)

- **Belden Victorian Shelf,** *22" x 15", dial 5", spring, 8 Day, strike, simple calendar (M295-98).*
  225.00   275.00   (250.00)

Double Dial Shelf No. 40

- **Box Regulator No.2,** *oak, height 38½", dial 12", 8 Day, strike, simple calendar (E1-184).*
  350.00   450.00   (400.00)

- **Box Regulator No.4,** *mahogany, height 38½", dial 12", 8 Day, strike, simple calendar (E1-184).*
  350.00   450.00   (400.00)

- **Dabney Shelf,** *height 22", dial 6", with thermometer and barometer, 8 Day, strike, simple calendar (M306-100).*
  225.00   275.00   (250.00)

- **Double Dial Shelf No.40,** *23½" x 14½", dials 6", spring, 8 Day (M279-94).*
  750.00   850.00   (800.00)

- **Double Dial Shelf No.40,** *24" x 14½", dials 6", spring, 8 Day, strike (E1-151, M285-95).*
  750.00   850.00   (800.00)

- **Double Dial Shelf No.43,** *height 28¼", dials 8", spring, 8 Day, strike (E1-98, M283-95).*
  700.00   900.00   (800.00)

- **Double Dial Shelf No.44,** *24" x 14½", dials 6", spring, 8 Day, strike (E1-151, M284-95).*
  650.00   750.00   (700.00)

Arion Octagon Top 12"

506 / WATERBURY CLOCK COMPANY

Double Dial Shelf No. 43

Double Dial Shelf No. 44

Double Dial Wall No. 25

☐ **Double Dial Wall No.25,** *double weight dead beat, retaining power, 49½" x 19¼", dials 10", seconds bit, 8 Day (E1-98, M270-92).*
    1900.00   2100.00   (2000.00)

☐ **Double Dial Wall No.26,** *double weight dead beat, retaining power, height 46", dials 9", seconds bit, 8 Day (E1-153).*
    1900.00   2150.00   (2025.00)

☐ **Double Dial Wall No.27,** *44¾" x 14½", dials 10", spring, 8 Day (E1-150, M271-92).*
    1400.00   1600.00   (1500.00)

☐ **Double Dial Wall No.28,** *41" x 15", dials 8", spring, 8 Day (E1-151, M272-92).*
    1800.00   2000.00   (1900.00)

WATERBURY CLOCK COMPANY / 507

Double Dial Wall No. 28

Double Dial Wall No. 30

- **Double Dial Wall No.30,** *height 40¼", dials 9", spring, 8 Day (E1-151).*
   1900.00   2100.00   (1900.00)

- **Double Dial Shelf No.33,** *39" x 15", dials 8", spring, 8 Day (E1-98, M274-93).*
   900.00   1100.00   (1000.00)

- **Double Dial Shelf No.34,** *29" x 15¾", spring, 11" time and 10" calendar dials, 8 Day (M277-93).*
   1100.00   1250.00   (1175.00)

- **Double Dial Shelf No. 36,** *28" x 15", dials 6", spring, 8 Day (E1-151, M275-93).*
   900.00   1000.00   (950.00)

- **Double Dial Shelf No.38,** *height 28", dials 6", spring, 8 Day (E1-151).*
   1800.00   2000.00   (1900.00)

- **No.39,** *not pictured.*
   1700.00   1900.00   (1800.00)

- **Felix Shelf,** *height 22", dial 6", spring, 8 Day, simple calendar (M304-100).*
   225.00   275.00   (250.00)

- **Gibson Victorian Shelf,** *24" x 15", dial 5", with thermometer and barometer, spring, 8 Day, strike, simple calendar (M296-98).*
   225.00   250.00   (237.00)

- **Glenwood Figure 8,** *height 25½", dial 12", 8 Day, strike, simple calendar (E1-100).*
   450.00   550.00   (500.00)

- **Heron Octagon Top,** *long drop, height 32", dial 12", 8 Day, strike, simple calendar (E1-183).*
   350.00   425.00   (387. 00)

- **Joliet Roller Type Wall,** *spring, 8 Day (M309-101).*
   1500.00   1750.00   (1625.00)

- **Natchez Wall,** *40" x 13¾", dial 8", spring, 8 Day, simple calendar (E1-97, M303-100).*
   600.00   675.00   (637.00)

508 / WATERBURY CLOCK COMPANY

Double Dial Wall No. 31

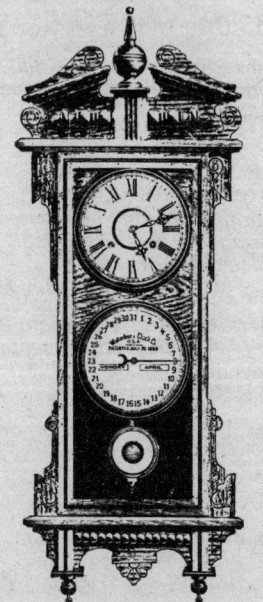

Double Dial Shelf No. 33

Double Dial Shelf No. 36

☐ **Octagon Lever Wall 8"**, *spring, 8 Day, simple calendar (E1-27).*
    250.00   300.00   (275.00)

☐ **Octagon Lever Wall 8"**, *spring, 1 Day, simple calendar (M307-101).*
    225.00   275.00   (250.00)

☐ **Octagon Lever Wall 10"**, *spring, 1 Day, simple calendar (E1-27).*
    250.00   300.00   (275.00)

☐ **Octagon Lever Wall 10"**, *spring, 8 Day, simple calendar (E1-27).*
    275.00   350.00   (312.00)

☐ **Octagon Lever Wall 12"**, *spring, 8 Day, simple calendar (E1-27).*
    300.00   375.00   (337.00)

☐ **Octagon Top 12"**, *short drop, height 24", spring, 8 Day, strike, simple calendar (E1-183).*
    300.00   375.00   (337.00)

☐ **Octagon Top 8"**, *short drop, height 19", spring, 8 Day, strike, simple calendar (E1-25).*
    250.00   300.00   (275.00)

☐ **Octagon Top 10"**, *short drop, 22½" x 15", spring, 8 Day, strike, simple calendar (E1-149).*
    275.00   325.00   (300.00)

WATERBURY CLOCK COMPANY / 509

- ☐ **Octagon Top 10"**, *"Zebra Case" short drop, height 21", spring, 8 Day, strike, simple calendar (E1-32).*
  275.00   325.00   (300.00)

- ☐ **Octagon Top 10"**, *gilt case, short drop, height 21", spring, 8 Day, strike, simple calendar (E1-32).*
  275.00   325.00   (300.00)

- ☐ **Octagon Top 12"**, *short drop, height 24", spring, 8 Day, strike, simple calendar (M299-99).*
  325.00   375.00   (350.00)

- ☐ **Ontario Victorian Shelf,** *28½" x 17½", dials 7", spring, 8 Day, strike, simple calendar (M293-97).*
  325.00   375.00   (350.00)

- ☐ **Oswego Double Dial Shelf,** *28" x 17½", dials 7", spring, 8 Day, strike (M287-96).*
  550.00   650.00   (600.00)

- ☐ **Paris Parlor Shelf,** *23" x 13", dial 5", spring, 8 Day, strike, simple calendar (M297-98).*
  300.00   400.00   (350.00)

- ☐ **Pelican Box Regulator,** *height 37½", dial 12", 8 Day, strike, simple calendar (E1-184).*
  350.00   450.00   (400.00)

Octagon Top 8"

- ☐ **Peoria Roller Type Wall,** *spring, 8 Day, not pictured.*
  1600.00   1850.00   (1725.00)

- ☐ **Regent Octagon Top,** *long drop, height 32", dial 12", spring, 8 Day, strike, simple calendar (E1-100).*
  400.00   500.00   (450.00)

- ☐ **Rochester Victorian Shelf,** *27" x 17½", dial 7", spring, 8 Day, strike, simple calendar (M289-96).*
  300.00   375.00   (337.00)

- ☐ **Selborne Victorian Shelf,** *height 23", dial 6", 8 Day, strike, simple calendar (E1-28).*
  200.00   300.00   (250.00)

- ☐ **Springfield Wall Regulator,** *40½" x 13¾", dial 8", spring, 8 Day, strike, simple calendar (E1-96, M302-100).*
  600.00   675.00   (637.00)

- ☐ **Victorian Kitchen Shelf,** *spring, dial 5", with thermometer and barometer, 8 Day, strike, simple calendar (M294-97).*
  225.00   250.00   (237.00)

- ☐ **Walton Wall Regulator,** *41" x 15¼", dial 10", 8 Day, strike, simple calendar (E1-96).*
  500.00   600.00   (550.00)

CARRIAGE

- ☐ **Compass,** *nickel, dial 3½", c. 1888, 1 Day, strike (E1-34).*
  105.00   125.00   (115.00)

- ☐ **Magnet,** *nickel, dial 3½", c. 1888, 1 Day, alarm (E1-34).*
  95.00   115.00   (105.00)
- ☐ **As above** *1 Day, alarm, sweep sec.*
  105.00   130.00   (117.00)

- ☐ **Passenger,** *nickel, dial 3½", c. 1888, 1 Day, alarm (E1-34).*
  80.00   95.00   (87.00)

- ☐ **Tourist,** *nickel, dial 3½", c. 1888, 1 Day, alarm (E1-34).*
  80.00   95.00   (87.00)
- ☐ **As above,** *1 Day, strike.*
  85.00   105.00   (95.00)

510 / WATERBURY CLOCK COMPANY

Magnet

Passenger

☐ **Traveler,** *nickel, dial 2¼",
c. 1888, 1 Day, alarm (E1-34).*
      100.00   120.00   (110.00)
☐ **As above,** *1 Day, alarm, sweep
sec.*
      110.00   135.00   (122.00)
☐ **Voyager,** *nickel, dial 2¼",
c. 1888, 1 Day, strike (E1-34).*
      105.00   130.00   (122.00)

CONNECTICUT SHELF
COTTAGE

☐ **Cottage Extra,** *polished wood,
height 12¾", c. 1888, 1 Day, strike,
spring (E1-27).*
      70.00   85.00   (77.00)
☐ **As above,** *8 Day, strike, spring*
      100.00   120.00   (110.00)

☐ **Cottage No. 2,** *polished wood,
height 12", c. 1888, 1 Day, spring
(E1-27).*
      60.00   75.00   (67.00)
☐ **As above,** *1 Day, strike, spring*
      80.00   100.00   (90.00)

☐ **Tick Tack,** *imitation mahogany,
height 11", c. 1888, 1 Day, spring
(E1-27).*
      55.00   70.00   (62.00)

Cottage No. 2

CONNECTICUIT SHELF/O.G.

☐ **O.G.,** *weight, polished wood,
height 26", dial 8", c. 1888, 1 Day,
strike (E1-27).*
      130.00   155.00   (142.00)
☐ **As above,** *8 Day, strike*
      175.00   200.00   (187.00)

CRYSTAL REGULATOR

☐ **Aubert,** *rich gold plated or Syrian
bronze, visible escapement, cast
gilt bezel, beveled glass front,
sides and back, 13³⁄₈" x 6¼", ivory
dial 4½", c. 1910, 8 Day, strike
(E1-130).*
      270.00   310.00   (290.00)

WATERBURY CLOCK COMPANY / 511

Aude

☐ **Aude,** *rich gold plated, ivory center, visible escapament, cast gilt bezel, beveled glass front, sides and back, 10⅛" x 7¾", ivory dial 4¼", c. 1910, 8 Day, strike (E1-130).*
    270.00   315.00   (292.00)

☐ **Bordeaux,** *rich gold plated, ivory center, visible escapement, cast gilt bezel, beveled glass front, sides and back, 18¼" x 8⅝", ivory dial 4½", c. 1910, 8 Day, strike (E1-131).*
    515.00   575.00   (540.00)

☐ **Brest,** *rich gold plated, ivory center, visible escapement, cast gilt bezel, beveled glass front, sides and back, 9¼" x 5¾", ivory dial 3½", c. 1910, 8 Day, strike (E1-132).*
    145.00   170.00   (157.00)

☐ **Brittany,** *rich gold plated, ivory center, visible escapement, cast gilt bezel, beveled glass front, sides and back, 11⅞" x 7", ivory dial 4½", c. 1910, 8 Day, strike (E1-130).*
    335.00   375.00   (355.00)

☐ **Caen,** *rich gold plated, ivory center, visible escapement, cast gilt bezel, beveled glass front, sides and back, 9⅞" x 7", ivory dial 4¼", c. 1910, 8 Day, strike (E1-132).*
    205.00   235.00   (225.00)

☐ **Calais,** *rich gold plated, ivory center, visible escapement, cast gilt bezel, beveled glass front, sides and back, 11⅞" x 7", ivory dial 4¼", c. 1910, 8 Day, strike (E1-131).*
    400.00   450.00   (425.00)

☐ **Cantal,** *rich gold plated, ivory center, visible escapement, cast gilt bezel, beveled glass front, sides and back, 10⅜" x 6⅝", ivory dial 4¼", c. 1910, 8 Day, strike (E1-131).*
    310.00   350.00   (330.00)

☐ **Charente,** *rich gold plated, ivory center, visible escapement, cast gilt bezel, beveled glass front, sides and back, 11⅜" x 8⅛", ivory dial 4½", c. 1910, 8 Day, strike (E1-130).*
    340.00   380.00   (360.00)

☐ **Dieppe,** *rich gold plated, ivory center, visible escapement, cast gilt bezel, beveled glass front, sides and back, 10⅝" x 7⅝", ivory dial 4½", c. 1910, 8 Day, strike (E1-132).*
    255.00   285.00   (270.00)

☐ **Dijon,** *rich gold plated, ivory center, visible escapement, cast gilt bezel, beveled glass front, sides and back, 13⅛" x 9", ivory dial 3½", c. 1910, 8 Day, strike (E1-131).*
    490.00   550.00   (520.00)

☐ **Flanders,** *rich gold plated, polished mahogany lower part of base and lower part of top, ivory center, visible escapement, cast gilt bezel, beveled glass front, sides and back, 12⅛" x 6⅝", ivory dial 4¼", c. 1910, 8 Day, strike (E1-132).*
    270.00   310.00   (290.00)

☐ **Gard,** *rich gold plated, green onyx base and top, ivory center, visible escapement, cast gilt bezel, beveled glass front, sides and back, 16" x 7½", ivory dial 4½", c. 1910, 8 Day, strike (E1-131).*
    540.00   600.00   (570.00)

512 / WATERBURY CLOCK COMPANY

Marseilles

☐ **Gers,** rich gold plated, green onyx base and top, ivory center, visible escapement, cast gilt bezel, beveled glass front, sides and back, 11¼" x 7⅞", ivory dial 4½", c. 1910, 8 Day, strike (E1-131).
450.00   500.00   (475.00)

☐ **Gironde,** rich gold plated, green onyx base and top, ivory center, visible escapement, cast gilt bezel, beveled glass front, sides and back, 12¾" x 7¾", ivory dial 4½", c. 1910, 8 Day, strike (E1-131).
500.00   560.00   (530.00)

☐ **Granville,** rich gold plated, ivory center, visible escapament, cast gilt bezel, beveled glass front, sides and back, 10⅞" x 6¾", ivory dial 4½", c. 1910, 8 Day, strike (E1-132).
205.00   235.00   (220.00)

☐ **Landes,** rich gold plated, polished mahogany columns, ivory center, visible escapement, cast gilt bezel, beveled glass front, sides and back, 10⅝" x 7⅞", ivory dial 4¼", c. 1910, 8 Day, strike (E1-130).
285.00   325.00   (305.00)

☐ **Marseilles,** rich gold plated, ivory center, visible escapement, cast gilt bezel, beveled glass front, sides and back, 16" x 6¼", ivory dial 4½", c. 1910, 8 Day, strike (E1-130).
275.00   315.00   (295.00)

☐ **Mogul,** rich gold plated, ivory center, visible escapement, cast gilt bezel, beveled glass front, sides and back, 15⅛" x 7", ivory dial 3½", c. 1910, 8 Day, strike (E1-130).
460.00   520.00   (490.00)

☐ **Morlaix,** rich gold plated, ivory center, visible escapement, cast gilt bezel, beveled glass front, sides and back, 9⅛" x 5¾", ivory dial 3½", c. 1910, 8 Day, strike (E1-132).
165.00   190.00   (177.00)

☐ **Navaree,** rich gold plated, ivory center, visible escapement, cast gilt bezel, beveled glass front, sides and back, 8⅞" x 6½", ivory dial 3½", c. 1910, 8 Day, strike (E1-132).
195.00   225.00   (207.00)

☐ **Orleans,** rich gold plated or Syrian bronze, ivory center, visible escapement, cast gilt bezel, beveled glass front, sides and back, 14¾" x 7", ivory dial 3½", c. 1910, 8 Day, strike (E1-130).
450.00   500.00   (477.00)

☐ **Orne,** rich gold plated, cut glass columns, ivory center, visible escapement, cast gilt bezel, beveled glass front, sides and back, 13⅛" x 9", ivory dial 3½", c. 1910, 8 Day, strike (E1-131).
750.00   850.00   (800.00)

☐ **Ostend,** rich gold plated, ivory center, visible escapement, cast gilt bezel, beveled glass front, sides and back, 9⅞" x 6⅛", ivory dial 4¼", c. 1910, 8 Day, strike (E1-132).
155.00   180.00   (167.00)

WATERBURY CLOCK COMPANY / 513

Rennes

☐ **Paris,** *rich gold plated, polished mahogany base and top, ivory center, visible escapement, cast gilt bezel, beveled glass front, sides and back, 19" x 13¼", ivory dial 4½", c. 1910, 8 Day, strike (E1-131).*
    875.00   975.00   (925.00)

☐ **Rennes,** *rich gold plated, ivory center, visible escapement, cast gilt bezel, beveled glass front, sides and back, 13½" x 8¼", ivory dial 3½", c. 1910, 8 Day, strike (E1-132).*
    540.00   600.00   (570.00)

☐ **Riviera,** *rich gold plated or Syrian bronze, ivory center, visible escapement, cast gilt bezel, beveled glass front, sides and back, 11½" x 7½", ivory dial 4½", c. 1910, 8 Day, strike (E1-130).*
    310.00   350.00   (330.00)

☐ **Savoy,** *rich gold plated, ivory center, visible escapement, cast gilt bezel, beveled glass front, sides and back, 10⅝" x 7", ivory dial 3½", c. 1910, 8 Day, strike (E1-132).*
    295.00   335.00   (315.00)

☐ **Sevres,** *rich gold plated, ivory center, visible escapement, cast gilt bezel, beveled glass front, sides and back, 14½" x 10", ivory dial 4½", c. 1910, 8 Day, strike (E1-131).*
    575.00   650.00   (615.00)

☐ **Tarn,** *rich gold plated, ivory center, visible escapement, cast gilt bezel, beveled glass front, sides and back, 10⅜" x 7", ivory dial 4¼", c. 1910, 8 Day, strike (E1-130).*
    285.00   325.00   (305.00)

☐ **Toulon,** *rich gold plated, ivory center, visible escapement, cast gilt bezel, beveled glass front, sides and back, 10⅝" x 7", ivory dial 4½", c. 1910, 8 Day, strike (E1-132).*
    170.00   195.00   (182.00)

☐ **Vannes,** *rich gold plated, ivory center, visible escapement, cast gilt bezel, beveled glass front, sides and back, 10⅝" x 6⅛", ivory dial 4¼", c. 1910, 8 Day, strike (E1-132).*
    160.00   185.00   (172.00)

☐ **Vendee,** *rich gold plated, polished mahogany columns, base and top, ivory center, visible escapement, cast gilt bezel, beveled glass front, sides and back, 11¾" x 8¼", ivory dial 4¼", c. 1910, 8 Day, strike (E1-130).*
    285.00   325.00   (305.00)

GALLERY/WALL LEVER

☐ **R.C. Octagon Lever,** *mahogany, spring, c. 1888, 1 Day, 4" (E1-27).*
    80.00   95.00   (87.00)
☐ **As above,** *1 Day, 6".*
    90.00   110.00   (100.00)
☐ **As above,** *1 Day, 8".*
    105.00   125.00   (115.00)
☐ **As above,** *1 Day, 10".*
    115.00   140.00   (127.00)
☐ **As above,** *8 Day, 6".*
    125.00   150.00   (137.00)
☐ **As above,** *8 Day, 8".*
    135.00   160.00   (149.00)

☐ **R.C. Octagon Lever,** *rosewood, spring, c. 1888, 1 Day, 4" (E1-27).*
    100.00   115.00   (107.00)
☐ **As above,** *1 Day, 6".*
    110.00   130.00   (120.00)
☐ **As above,** *1 Day, 8".*
    125.00   150.00   (137.00)
☐ **As above,** *1 Day, 10".*
    135.00   160.00   (149.00)
☐ **As above,** *8 Day, 6".*
    145.00   170.00   (157.00)
☐ **As above,** *8 Day, 8".*
    155.00   180.00   (167.00)

GRANDFATHER

☐ **Hall Clock,** *mahogany case, 7'7½" x 23½", 12" gilt and silver plated dial, 8 Day, strike (E2-174).*
    2000.00   2250.00   (2125.00)

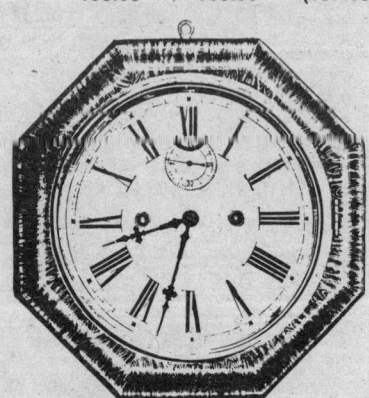

R.C. Octagon Lever

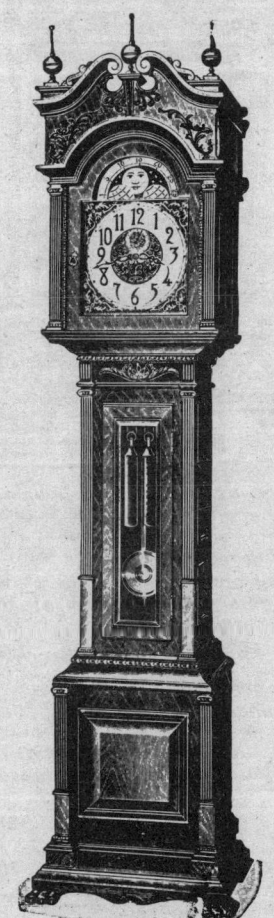

Hall Clock No. 72

WATERBURY CLOCK COMPANY / 515

☐ **Hall Clock No.72,** *quartered oak, beveled plate glass panel, moon's phases, brass weights, beats seconds, dead-beat escapement, retaining power, solid polished movement frames, 99" x 25", dial 12", c. 1915, 8 Day, strike, weight (E1-96).*
　　1980.00　　2200.00　　(2090.00)
☐ **As above,** *mahogany.*
　　2080.00　　2300.00　　(2190.00)

☐ **Hall Clock No.77,** *quartered oak, gilt ornaments, beveled plate glass panel, moon's phases, brass weights, beats seconds, dead-beat escapement, retaining power, solid polished movement frames, 96" x 29½", dial 12", c. 1915, 8 Day, weight (E1-96).*
　　3375.00　　3750.00　　(3575.00)

KITCHEN

☐ **Albany,** *walnut, height 24", dial 6", c. 1888, 8 Day, strike (E1-28).*
　　135.00　　160.00　　(147.00)
☐ **Antrim,** *walnut, height 20¾", dial 6", c. 1888, 1 Day, strike (E1-27).*
　　115.00　　140.00　　(127.00)
☐ **Arcade,** *walnut, height 24", dial 6", c. 1888, 8 Day, strike (E1-31).*
　　125.00　　150.00　　(137.00)
☐ **Auburn,** *ash, height 19½", dial 6", c. 1888, 8 Day, strike (E1-31).*
　　130.00　　155.00　　(142.00)
☐ **Belmont,** *walnut, height 22¼", dial 6", c. 1888, 1 Day, strike (E1-27).*
　　115.00　　140.00　　(127.00)

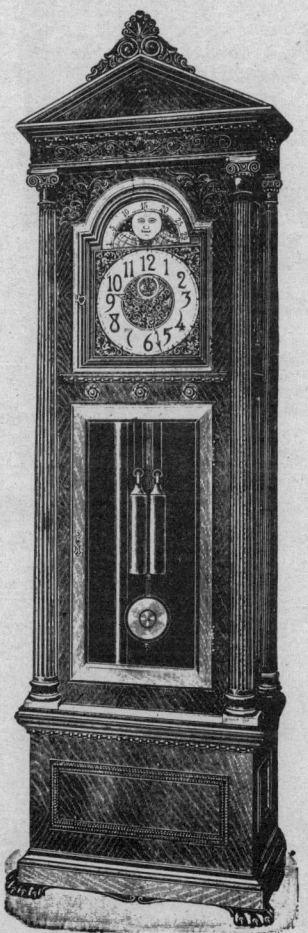

Hall Clock No. 77

Belmont

516 / WATERBURY CLOCK COMPANY

- **Borden,** *walnut, height 21½", dial 6", c. 1888, 8 Day, strike (E1-31).*
  125.00   150.00   (137.00)

- **Branford,** *oak, height 17¼", dial 6", c. 1888, 8 Day, strike (E1-31).*
  100.00   120.00   (110.00)

- **Clyde,** *walnut, height 21¾", dial 6", c. 1888, 1 Day, strike (E1-27).*
  115.00   140.00   (127.00)

- **Corona,** *walnut, height 17¼", dial 5", c. 1888, 1 Day, strike (E1-27).*
  110.00   135.00   (117.00)

- **Corning,** *walnut, height 22", dial 6", c. 1888, 8 Day, strike (E1-28).*
  130.00   155.00   (142.00)

- **Dayton,** *walnut, height 21", dial 6", c. 1888, 8 Day, strike (E1-31).*
  130.00   155.00   (142.00)

- **Delhi,** *walnut, height 22¼", dial 6", c. 1888, 8 Day, strike (E1-28).*
  125.00   150.00   (137.00)

- **Dunbar,** *walnut, height 21", dial 6", c. 1888, 8 Day, strike (E1-28).*
  130.00   155.00   (142.00)

- **Dunkirk,** *walnut, height 22⅞", dial 6", c. 1888, 8 Day, strike (E1-28).*
  130.00   155.00   (142.00)

- **Elmira,** *walnut, height 22⅜", dial 6", c. 1888, 8 Day, strike (E1-28).*
  130.00   155.00   (142.00)

- **Essex,** *ash with walnut trimmings, height 19", dial 6", c. 1888, 8 Day, strike (E1-31).*
  125.00   150.00   (137.00)

- **Fonda,** *walnut, height 21¾", dial 6", c. 1888, 8 Day, strike (E1-28).*
  125.00   150.00   (137.00)

- **Foster,** *walnut, height 25", dial 6", c. 1888, 8 Day, strike (E1-28).*
  130.00   155.00   (142.00)

- **Gibson Calendar,** *oak, with thermometer and barometer, height 24", dial 6", 8 Day, strike (E2-160).*
  200.00   225.00   (212.00)
- **As above,** *8 Day, gong.*
  225.00   250.00   (237.00)

- **Gibson Calendar,** *walnut, with thermometer and barometer, height 24", dial 6", 8 Day, strike (E2-160).*
  225.00   250.00   (237.00)
- **As above,** *8 Day, gong.*
  250.00   275.00   (262.00)

- **Gilford,** *walnut, height 20", dial 6", c. 1888, 1 Day, strike (E1-27).*
  110.00   135.00   (117.00)

- **Graham,** *walnut, height 21⅝", dial 6", c. 1888, 8 Day, strike (E1-31).*
  130.00   155.00   (142.00)

- **Granville,** *walnut, height 22½", dial 6", c. 1888, 8 Day, strike (E1-31).*
  120.00   145.00   (132.00)

- **Harding,** *walnut, height 21½", dial 6", c. 1888, 1 Day, strike (E1-27).*
  115.00   140.00   (127.00)

- **Highland,** *walnut, height 24½", dial 6", c. 1888, 8 Day, strike (E1-31).*
  125.00   150.00   (137.00)

Gibson Calendar

WATERBURY CLOCK COMPANY / 517

- **Homer,** *walnut, height 22", dial 6", c. 1888, 8 Day, strike (E1-31).*
  125.00   150.00   (137.00)

- **Jenner,** *walnut, height 21¾", dial 6", c. 1888, 8 Day, strike (E1-28).*
  125.00   150.00   (137.00)

- **Kimble,** *walnut, height 20¾", dial 6", c. 1888, 8 Day, strike (E1-31).*
  125.00   150.00   (137.00)

- **Knox,** *walnut, height 22¼", dial 6", c. 1888, 1 Day, strike (E1-27).*
  115.00   140.00   (127.00)

- **Lodi,** *walnut, height 21⅜", dial 6", c. 1888, 8 Day, strike (E1-28).*
  110.00   135.00   (117.00)

- **Lyons,** *walnut, height 21⅞", dial 6", c. 1888, 8 Day, strike (E1-28).*
  110.00   135.00   (117.00)

- **Malvern,** *walnut, height 19½", dial 6", c. 1888, 1 Day, strike (E1-27).*
  115.00   140.00   (127.00)

- **Medina,** *walnut, height 22", dial 6", c. 1888, 8 Day, strike (E1-28).*
  125.00   150.00   (137.00)

- **Merwin,** *walnut, height 24", dial 6", c. 1888, 8 Day, strike (E1-31).*
  125.00   150.00   (137.00)

- **Middlesex,** *ash with walnut trimmings, height 21", dial 6", c. 1888, 8 Day, strike (E1-31).*
  135.00   160.00   (147.00)

- **Morris,** *walnut, height 20⅛", dial 6", c. 1888, 8 Day, strike (E1-31).*
  115.00   140.00   (127.00)

- **Napier Extra,** *oak, with thermometer and barometer, height 24", dial 6", c. 1888, 8 Day, strike (E1-31).*
  150.00   175.00   (162.00)
- **As above,** *walnut*
  175.00   200.00   (187.00)

- **Paris,** *walnut, height 24", dial 6", c. 1888, 8 Day, strike (E1-28).*
  195.00   225.00   (210.00)

- **Rondo,** *walnut, height 24", dial 6", c. 1888, 8 Day, strike (E1-31).*
  125.00   150.00   (137.00)

Knox

- **Seaford,** *walnut, height 21⅛", dial 6", c. 1888, 8 Day, strike (E1-28).*
  130.00   155.00   (142.00)

- **Selborne,** *walnut, height 22⅞", dial 6", c. 1888, 8 Day, strike (E1-28).*
  120.00   145.00   (132.00)

- **Sussex,** *walnut, height 22¼", dial 6", c. 1888, 8 Day, strike (E1-31).*
  125.00   150.00   (137.00)

- **Ventnor,** *walnut, height 21¾", dial 6", c. 1888, 8 Day, strike (E1-28).*
  130.00   155.00   (142.00)

- **Vernon,** *walnut, height 17⅜", dial 6", c. 1888, 1 Day, strike, (E1-27).*
  110.00   135.00   (117.00)

KITCHEN/WALL

- **Cato,** *walnut, with thermometer and barometer, height 27", dial 6", 8 Day, strike (E2-163).*
  335.00   375.00   (355.00)
- **As above,** *8 Day, strike, calendar.*
  385.00   425.00   (405.00)
- **As above,** *8 Day, strike, calendar.*
  285.00   325.00   (305.00)
- **As above,** *8 Day, strike, calendar.*
  335.00   375.00   (355.00)

518 / WATERBURY CLOCK COMPANY

Cato

- [ ] **Climax,** *walnut, with thermometer and barometer, height 26⅝", dial (rococo) 6", 8 Day, strike (E2-163).*
  320.00   350.00   (335.00)
- [ ] **As above,** *8 Day, strike, calendar.*
  360.00   400.00   (380.00)

- [ ] **Climax,** *oak, with thermometer and barometer, height 26⅝", dial (rococo) 6", 8 Day, strike (E2-163).*
  270.00   300.00   (285.00)
- [ ] **As above,** *8 Day, strike, calendar.*
  310.00   350.00   (330.00)

- [ ] **Havana,** *walnut, height 29¾", dial (rococo) 6", 8 Day, strike (E2-163).*
  320.00   350.00   (335.00)
- [ ] **As above,** *oak.*
  270.00   300.00   (285.00)

Havanna

- [ ] **Lawrence,** *walnut, height 29", dial 6", c. 1888, 8 Day (E1-32).*
  310.00   350.00   (330.00)

- [ ] **Olive,** *walnut, height 18¼", dial 6", c. 1915, 8 Day, strike (E2-163).*
  155.00   175.00   (165.00)
- [ ] **As above,** *oak.*
  105.00   125.00   (165.00)

- [ ] **Orange,** *walnut, height 18¼", dial 6", c. 1915, 8 Day, strike (E2-163).*
  155.00   175.00   (165.00)

- [ ] **Orrin,** *walnut, height 18¼", dial 6", c. 1915, 8 Day, strike (E2-163).*
  155.00   175.00   (165.00)
- [ ] **As above,** *oak.*
  105.00   125.00   (115.00)

MANTEL/METAL REGENCY

☐ **Cadosia,** rich Roman gold plated, ivory center, visible escapement, rococo cast gilt sash and bezel, beveled glass, 12" x 7⅞", ivory dial 4½", c. 1900, 8 Day, strike (E1-110).
    110.00   135.00   (122.00)

☐ **Carlisle,** rich Roman gold plated, ivory center, visible escapement, rococo cast gilt sash and bezel, beveled glass, 13" x 8⅞", ivory dial, c. 1900, 8 Day, strike (E1-110).
    230.00   260.00   (245.00)

☐ **Nantes,** rich Roman gold plated, ivory center, visible escapement, rococo cast gilt sash and bezel, beveled glass, 15½" x 9⅜", ivory dial, c. 1900, 8 Day, strike (E1-110).
    360.00   400.00   (380.00)

☐ **Sartoris,** rich Roman gold plated, decorated porcelain panel, ivory center, visible escapement, rococo cast gilt sash and bezel, beveled glass, 14" x 7¼", ivory dial, c. 1900, 8 Day, strike (E1-117).
    310.00   350.00   (330.00)

☐ **Seine,** rich Roman gold plated or golden bronze, ivory center, visible escapement, rococo cast gilt sash and bezel, beveled glass, 13½" x 9⅛", ivory dial, c. 1900, 8 Day, strike (E1-117).
    105.00   130.00   (117.00)

☐ **Valhalla,** Japanese or Syrian Bronze, ivory center, visible escapement, rococo cast gilt sash and bezel, beveled glass, 12¼" x 8⅛", ivory dial, c. 1900, 8 Day, strike (E1-117).
    200.00   250.00   (90.00)

☐ **Valiant,** Japanese or Syrian bronze, ivory center, rococo cast gilt sash and bezel, beveled glass, 18" x 10⅞", ivory dial, c. 1900, 8 Day, strike (E1-117).
    245.00   275.00   (260.00)

☐ **Vancouver,** Japanese or Syrian bronze, ivory center, visible escapement, rococo cast gilt sash and bezel, beveled glass, 17¼" x 11¼", ivory dial, c. 1900, 8 Day, strike (E1-117).
    195.00   225.00   (210.00)

Cadosia

Nantes

520 / WATERBURY CLOCK COMPANY

☐ **Varick,** Japanese or Syrian bronze, ivory center, visible escapement, rococo cast gilt sash and bezel, beveled glass, 14⅝" x 11½", ivory dial 4½", c. 1900, 8 Day, strike (E1-109).
    135.00   160.00   (147.00)

☐ **Vicksburg,** Japanese or Syrian bronze, ivory center, rococo cast gilt sash and bezel, beveled glass, 12½" x 8½", ivory dial, c. 1900, 8 Day, strike (E1-117).
    105.00   130.00   (117.00)

☐ **Winner,** bronze or nickel, 9" x 6⅜", c. 1900, 1 Day, alarm (E1-117).
    40.00   55.00   (47.50)

MISSION

☐ **Den No.3,** dark oak, height 26⅞" x 13", dial 10", 8 Day (E2-163).
    95.00   115.00   (105.00)
☐ **As above,** 8 Day, strike.
    110.00   135.00   (117.00)

Den No. 4

☐ **Den No.4,** dark oak, height 17½" x 12", dial 12, c. 1900, 8 Day (E2-163).
    105.00   125.00   (115.00)
☐ **As above,** 8 Day, strike.
    125.00   150.00   (137.00)

☐ **Den No.5,** dark oak, height 27½" x 14½", dial 12", 8 Day (E2-163).
    125.00   150.00   (137.00)
☐ **As above,** 8 Day, strike.
    150.00   175.00   (162.00)

NOVELTY/ART NOUVEAU

☐ **Acme,** rich Roman gold plated, ivory center, rococo cast gilt sash and bezel, beveled glass, 7½" x 6⅝", ivory dial 4½", c. 1900, 8 Day, strike (E1-110).
    60.00   75.00   (67.50)

☐ **Art,** rich Roman gold plated, ivory center, rococo cast gilt sash and bezel, beveled glass, ivory dial, c. 1900, 1 Day (E1-110).
    70.00   95.00   (75.00)

☐ **Canoga,** rich Roman gold plated or Syrian bronze, ivory center, visible escapement, rococo cast gilt sash and bezel, beveled glass, 13½" x 9", ivory dial 4½", c. 1900, 8 Day, strike (E1-110).
    125.00   150.00   (137.00)

Den No. 3

WATERBURY CLOCK COMPANY / 521

Art

Surprise

☐ **Castalia,** *rich Roman gold plated, ivory center, visible escapement, rococo cast gilt sash and bezel, beveled glass, 12" x 7¾", ivory dial 4½", c. 1900, 8 Day, strike (E1-110).*
    145.00   160.00   (152.00)

☐ **Ino,** *rich Roman gold plated, ivory center, rococo cast gilt sash and bezel, beveled glass, 11" x 6½", ivory dial, c. 1900, 8 Day, strike (E1-110).*
    125.00   150.00   (137.00)

☐ **Mercury,** *rich Roman gold plated, ivory center, rococo cast gilt sash and bezel, beveled glass, 8" x 7", ivory dial, c. 1900, 8 Day, strike (E1-110).*
    90.00   110.00   (100.00)

☐ **Rajah,** *rich Roman gold plated or Syrian bronze, ivory center, rococo cast gilt sash and bezel, beveled glass, 12⅜" x 8½", ivory dial, c. 1900, 8 Day, strike (E1-110).*
    145.00   160.00   (152.00)

☐ **Sardis,** *rich Roman gold plated, ivory center, rococo cast gilt sash and bezel, beveled glass, 11" x 6½", ivory dial 4½", c. 1900, 8 Day, strike (E1-110).*
    125.00   150.00   (137.00)

☐ **Surprise,** *rich Roman gold plated, ivory center, visible escapement, rococo cast gilt sash and bezel, beveled glass, 7½" x 6⅝", ivory dial 4½", c. 1900, 8 Day, strike (E1-110).*
    60.00   75.00   (67.00)

NOVELTY/IRON

☐ **Stunner,** *bronze, long alarm with intermissions, height 9¾", dial 4½", c. 1900, 1 Day, alarm (E1-117).*
    40.00   55.00   (47.50)

Stunner

Bahia, mosaic

Bahia, rosewood

REGULATOR/FIGURE EIGHT

- **Bahia,** *mosaic, height 22", dial 10", 8 Day (E2-163).*
  270.00   300.00   (285.00)
- **As above,** *8 Day, strike.*
  285.00   325.00   (305.00)
- **As above,** *8 Day, calendar.*
  310.00   350.00   (330.00)
- **As above,** *8 Day, strike, calendar.*
  335.00   375.00   (355.00)

- **Bahia,** *rosewood veneered, height 22", dial 10", 8 Day (E2-163).*
  270.00   300.00   (285.00)
- **As above,** *8 Day, strike.*
  285.00   325.00   (305.00)
- **As above,** *8 Day, calendar.*
  310.00   350.00   (330.00)
- **As above,** *8 Day, strike, calendar.*
  335.00   375.00   (355.00)

REGULATOR/OCTAGON TOP, LONG DROP

- **Regent Calendar,** *rosewood, height 32", dial 12", c. 1910, 8 Day (E1-100).*
  335.00   375.00   (355.00)
- **As above,** *8 Day, strike.*
  360.00   400.00   (380.00)

WATERBURY CLOCK COMPANY / 523

☐ **Regent**, wood, height 32", dial 12, c. 1888, 8 Day, sp. (E1-23).
285.00   325.00   (305.00)
☐ **As above**, 8 Day, strike, sp.
310.00   350.00   (330.00)
☐ **As above**, 8 Day, calendar, sp.
335.00   375.00   (355.00)
☐ **As above**, 8 Day, strike, calendar, sp.
360.00   400.00   (380.00)

☐ **Regent**, rosewood, height 32", dial 12", c. 1910, 8 Day (E1-100).
335.00   375.00   (355.00)*
☐ **As above**, 8 Day, strike.
375.00   425.00   (400.00)

☐ **10 Inch Heron**, oak, height 30", dial 10", 8 Day (E2-162).
220.00   250.00   (235.00)
☐ **As above**, 8 Day, strike.
245.00   275.00   (260.00)
☐ **As above**, 8 Day, calendar.
270.00   300.00   (285.00)

REGULATOR/OCTAGON TOP, SHORT DROP

☐ **Digby**, oak, height 27", dial 12", 8 Day (E2-162).
220.00   250.00   (235.00)
☐ **As above**, 8 Day, strike.
245.00   275.00   (260.00)
☐ **As above**, 8 Day, calendar.
270.00   300.00   (285.00)
☐ **As above**, 8 Day, strike, calendar.
285.00   325.00   (305.00)

☐ **8 Inch Drop Octagon**, oak, height 19", dial 8", 8 Day (E2-162).
150.00   175.00   (162.00)
☐ **As above**, 8 Day, strike.
175.00   200.00   (187.00)
☐ **As above**, 8 Day, calendar.
195.00   225.00   (210.00)
☐ **As above**, 8 Day, strike, calendar.
220.00   250.00   (235.00)
☐ **As above**, rosewood, 8 Day.
200.00   225.00   (212.00)
☐ **As above**, 8 Day, strike.
225.00   250.00   (237.00)

Heron

Digby

524 / WATERBURY CLOCK COMPANY

- [ ] **8 Inch Yeddo,** *rosewood veneered, brass trimmings, height 19", dial 8", 8 Day (E2-162).*
  150.00   175.00   (162.00)
- [ ] **As above,** *8 Day, strike.*
  175.00   200.00   (187.00)
- [ ] **As above,** *8 Day, calendar.*
  195.00   225.00   (207.00)
- [ ] **As above,** *8 Day, strike, calendar.*
  220.00   250.00   (235.00)

- [ ] **10 Inch Arion,** *oak, height 22", dial 10", 8 Day (E2-162).*
  175.00   200.00   (187.00)
- [ ] **As above,** *8 Day, strike.*
  195.00   225.00   (207.00)
- [ ] **As above,** *8 Day, calendar.*
  220.00   250.00   (235.00)
- [ ] **As above,** *8 Day, strike, calendar.*
  245.00   275.00   (260.00)

- [ ] **10 Inch Drop Octagon,** *oak, height 22", dial 10", 8 Day (E2-162).*
  175.00   200.00   (187.00)
- [ ] **As above,** *8 Day, strike.*
  195.00   225.00   (210.00)
- [ ] **As above,** *8 Day, calendar.*
  220.00   250.00   (235.00)
- [ ] **As above,** *8 Day, strike, calendar.*
  245.00   275.00   (260.00)
- [ ] **As above,** *rosewood, 8 Day.*
  225.00   250.00   (237.00)
- [ ] **As above,** *8 Day, strike.*
  245.00   275.00   (260.00)
- [ ] **As above,** *8 Day, calendar.*
  270.00   300.00   (285.00)
- [ ] **As above,** *8 Day, strike, calendar.*
  295.00   325.00   (310.00)

- [ ] **10 Inch Yeddo,** *rosewood veneered, brass trimmings, height 22", dial 10", 8 Day (E2-162).*
  175.00   200.00   (187.00)
- [ ] **As above,** *8 Day, strike.*
  195.00   225.00   (210.00)
- [ ] **As above,** *8 Day, calendar.*
  220.00   250.00   (235.00)
- [ ] **As above,** *8 Day, strike, calendar.*
  245.00   275.00   (260.00)

- [ ] **12 Inch Arion,** *oak, height 24", dial 12", 8 Day (E2-162).*
  195.00   225.00   (210.00)
- [ ] **As above,** *8 Day, strike.*
  220.00   250.00   (235.00)
- [ ] **As above,** *8 Day, calendar.*
  245.00   275.00   (260.00)
- [ ] **As above,** *8 Day, strike, calendar.*
  270.00   300.00   (285.00)
- [ ] **As above,** *mahogany finish, 8 Day.*
  225.00   255.00   (240.00)
- [ ] **As above,** *8 Day, strike.*
  250.00   280.00   (265.00)
- [ ] **As above,** *8 Day, calendar.*
  275.00   305.00   (290.00)
- [ ] **As above,** *8 Day, strike, calendar.*
  300.00   330.00   (315.00)

- [ ] **12 Inch Drop Octagon,** *oak, height 24", dial 12", 8 Day (E2-162).*
  195.00   225.00   (210.00)
- [ ] **As above,** *8 Day, strike.*
  220.00   250.00   (235.00)
- [ ] **As above,** *8 Day, calendar.*
  245.00   275.00   (260.00)
- [ ] **As above,** *8 Day, strike, calendar.*
  270.00   300.00   (285.00)
- [ ] **As above,** *rosewood veneered, 8 Day.*
  245.00   275.00   (260.00)
- [ ] **As above,** *8 Day, strike.*
  270.00   300.00   (285.00)
- [ ] **As above,** *8 Day, calendar.*
  295.00   325.00   (310.00)
- [ ] **As above,** *8 Day, strike, calendar.*
  320.00   350.00   (335.00)

- [ ] **12 Inch Yeddo,** *rosewood veneered, brass trimmings, height 24", dial 12", 8 Day (E2-162).*
  195.00   225.00   (210.00)
- [ ] **As above,** *8 Day, strike.*
  220.00   250.00   (235.00)
- [ ] **As above,** *8 Day, calendar.*
  245.00   275.00   (260.00)
- [ ] **As above,** *8 Day, strike, calendar.*
  270.00   300.00   (285.00)

REGULATOR/OPEN SWINGING

- [ ] **Alabama,** *oak, 38¾" x 17¼", dial 8" porcelain, c. 1915, 8 Day, strike, weight (E1-99).*
  800.00   900.00   (850.00)
- [ ] **As above,** *mahogany.*
  900.00   1000.00   (950.00)

WATERBURY CLOCK COMPANY / 525

Study No. 3

Buffalo Calendar

- **Study No.3,** oak, 27¼" x 14", dial 8" porcelain, 8 Day, strike, weight (E1-99).
  490.00   550.00   (520.00)

- **Study No.4,** oak, 35¼" x 15¼", dial 8" porcelain, c. 1915, 8 Day, strike, weight (E1-99).
  675.00   750.00   (712.00)

- **Study No.10,** oak, glass sides, cast bell, height 26⅝", dial 8", 8 Day, weight (E2-163).
  450.00   550.00   (500.00)
- **As above,** cherry.
  550.00   650.00   (600.00)

REGULATOR/PARLOR SHELF

- **Buffalo Calendar,** walnut, height 26⅞", dial 8", 8 Day (E2-160).
  270.00   300.00   (285.00)
- **As above,** 8 Day, strike.
  285.00   325.00   (305.00)
- **As above,** 8 Day, calendar.
  310.00   350.00   (330.00)
- **As above,** 8 Day, strike, calendar.
  335.00   375.00   (355.00)

- **Elberon,** walnut, height 32¾", dial 8", c. 1888, 8 Day, strike (E1-32).
  310.00   350.00   (330.00)

REGULATOR/PARLOR WALL

- **Aurora,** oak, 42¼" x 17¼", dial 8", 8 Day (E2-161).
  490.00   550.00   (520.00)
- **As above,** 8 Day, strike.
  540.00   600.00   (570.00)

- **Berlin,** walnut, height 46", dial 10", c. 1910, 8 Day, weight (E1-98).
  800.00   1050.00   (925.00)

- **Breton,** oak, glass sides, 44¼" x 14⅛", dial 8", c. 1915, 8 Day (E1-97).
  540.00   600.00   (570.00)
- **As above,** 8 Day, strike
  625.00   700.00   (662.00)
- **As above,** mahogany, 8 Day
  615.00   675.00   (645.00)
- **As above,** mahogany, 8 Day, strike
  700.00   775.00   (737.00)

- **Cairo,** oak, 43" x 17⅛", dial 10", c. 1915, 8 Day (E1-96).
  450.00   500.00   (475.00)
- **As above,** 8 Day, strike
  490.00   550.00   (520.00)
- **As above,** walnut, 8 Day
  550.00   600.00   (575.00)
- **As above,** walnut, 8 Day, strike
  590.00   650.00   (620.00)

526 / WATERBURY CLOCK COMPANY

☐ **Cambridge**, *oak, 50⅝" x 20¼", dial 12", c. 1915, 8 Day (E1-99).*
   490.00   550.00   (520.00)
☐ **As above**, *8 Day, strike*
   540.00   600.00   (570.00)
☐ **As above**, *30 Day*
   575.00   650.00   (612.00)
☐ **As above**, *walnut, 8 Day*
   590.00   650.00   (620.00)
☐ **As above**, *walnut, 8 Day, strike*
   640.00   700.00   (670.00)
☐ **As above**, *walnut, 30 Day*
   675.00   750.00   (717.00)

☐ **Camden**, *walnut, height 46", dial 10", c. 1910, 8 Day, weight (E1-100).*
   900.00   1000.00   (950.00)

☐ **Carleton**, *walnut, height 42", dial 8", 8 Day (E1-26).*
   450.00   500.00   (475.00)
☐ **As above**, *8 Day, strike*
   490.00   550.00   (520.00)

☐ **Eton**, *oak, 39¼" x 15", dial 8", c. 1915, 8 Day (E1-97).*
   400.00   450.00   (425.00)
☐ **As above**, *8 Day, strike*
   490.00   550.00   (520.00)
☐ **As above**, *walnut, 8 Day*
   500.00   550.00   (525.00)
☐ **As above**, *walnut, 8 Day, strike*
   590.00   650.00   (520.00)

☐ **Fostoria**, *oak, 40¾" x 16¼", dial 12", c. 1893, 8 Day (E2-163).*
   360.00   400.00   (380.00)
☐ **As above**, *8 Day, strike.*
   400.00   450.00   (425.00)
☐ **As above**, *30 Day, sec. hand.*
   450.00   500.00   (475.00)
☐ **As above**, *8 Day*
   460.00   500.00   (480.00)
☐ **As above**, *8 Day, strike.*
   500.00   550.00   (525.00)
☐ **As above**, *30 Day, sec. hand.*
   550.00   600.00   (575.00)

☐ **Freeport**, *oak, 45" x 18⅛", dial 10", 8 Day, (E2-161).*
   490.00   550.00   (520.00)
☐ **As above**, *8 Day, strike.*
   515.00   575.00   (545.00)
☐ **As above**, *30 Day, sec. hand.*
   540.00   600.00   (570.00)
☐ **As above**, *walnut, 8 Day.*
   590.00   650.00   (620.00)
☐ **As above**, *8 Day, strike.*
   615.00   675.00   (645.00)

☐ **Kingston**, *walnut, height 37", dial 8", c. 1910, 8 Day (E1-100).*
   490.00   550.00   (475.00)
☐ **As above**, *8 Day, strike.*
   490.00   550.00   (520.00)

Perth

WATERBURY CLOCK COMPANY / 527

☐ **Leipsic,** *oak, 48" x 17¾", dial 8" porcelain, c. 1915, 8 Day, strike (E1-99).*
540.00 600.00 (570.00)
☐ **As above,** *30 Day.*
625.00 700.00 (662.00)
☐ **As above,** *walnut, 8 Day, strike.*
640.00 700.00 (670.00)
☐ **As above,** *30 Day.*
725.00 800.00 (762.00)

☐ **Nassau,** *oak, 45" x 18¹/₈₀, dial 10₀, c. 1915, 8 Day. strike spring.(E1-96).*
360.00 400.00 (380.00)
☐ **As above,** *30 Day.*
400.00 450.00 (425.00)

☐ **Natchez,** *oak, 40⅛" x 13¾", dial 8", c. 1915, 8 Day (E1-97).*
400.00 450.00 (425.00)
☐ **As above,** *8 Day, strike.*
450.00 500.00 (475.00)
☐ **As above,** *8 Day, calendar.*
540.00 600.00 (570.00)
☐ **As above,** *8 Day, strike, calendar.*
575.00 650.00 (615.00)
☐ **As above,** *mahogany, 8 Day.*
475.00 525.00 (500.00)
☐ **As above,** *8 Day, strike.*
525.00 575.00 (550.00)
☐ **As above,** *8 Day, calendar.*
615.00 675.00 (645.00)
☐ **As above,** *8 Day, strike, calendar.*
650.00 725.00 (687.00)

☐ **Nelson,** *oak, 50⅝" x 14¾", dial 8", c. 1915, 8 Day (E1-99).*
490.00 550.00 (520.00)
☐ **As above,** *8 Day, strike.*
575.00 650.00 (615.00)
☐ **As above,** *mahogany, 8 Day.*
565.00 625.00 (595.00)
☐ **As above,** *8 Day, strike.*
650.00 725.00 (687.00)

☐ **Montreal,** *walnut, height 37½", c. 1910, dial 8", 8 Day (E1-100).*
725.00 800.00 (762.00)
☐ **As above,** *8 Day, strike.*
750.00 850.00 (800.00)

☐ **Ontario,** *walnut, height 40", dial 8", c. 1910, 8 Day (E1-100).*
540.00 600.00 (570.00)
☐ **As above,** *8 Day, strike*
575.00 650.00 (615.00)

☐ **Ottawa,** *walnut, height 32", dial 6", c. 1888, 8 Day (E1-32).*
360.00 400.00 (380.00)

☐ **Perth,** *walnut, height 41½", dial 8", 8 Day (E2-161).*
825.00 900.00 (862.00)
☐ **As above,** *8 Day, strike.*
850.00 950.00 (900.00)
☐ **As above,** *cherry, 8 Day.*
875.00 950.00 (915.00)
☐ **As above,** *oak, 8 Day*
725.00 800.00 (762.00)
☐ **As above,** *oak, 8 Day, strtike*
750.00 850.00 (800.00)

☐ **Pictou,** *oak, 50¾" x 16⅜", dial 10", c. 1915, 8 Day (E1-99).*
490.00 550.00 (520.00)
☐ **As above,** *8 Day, strike.*
540.00 600.00 (570.00)
☐ **As above,** *mahogany, 8 Day.*
565.00 625.00 (595.00)
☐ **As above,** *8 Day, strike.*
615.00 675.00 (645.00)

☐ **Pontiac,** *walnut, height 43", dial 8", 8 Day (E1-26).*
540.00 600.00 (570.00)
☐ **As above,** *8 Day, strike.*
575.00 650.00 (615.00)

☐ **Prescott,** *walnut, height 32", dial 6", c. 1888, 8 Day (E1-32).*
360.00 400.00 (380.00)

☐ **Quebec,** *walnut, height 42", dial 8", c. 1910, 8 Day, weight (E1-98).*
725.00 800.00 (762.00)
☐ **As above,** *8 Day, strike, weight.*
800.00 900.00 (850.00)

☐ **Regulator No.4,** *walnut, height 51", dial 10", dead beat escapement, retaining power, c. 1888, 8 Day, weight (E1-23).*
975.00 1225.00 (1100.00)
☐ **As above,** *ash.*
1025.00 1275.00 (1150.00)
☐ **As above,** *mahogany.*
950.00 1200.00 (1075.00)

☐ **Springfield,** *oak, 39⅜" x 16½", dial 8", c. 1915, 8 Day (E1-96).*
360.00 400.00 (380.00)
☐ **As above,** *8 Day, strike.*
400.00 450.00 (425.00)

528 / WATERBURY CLOCK COMPANY

☐ **Stafford,** *ash, height 35", dial 8", c. 1888, 8 Day, sp. (E1-23).*
435.00   475.00   (455.00)
☐ **As above,** *8 Day, strike, sp.*
475.00   525.00   (500.00)
☐ **As above,** *walnut, 8 Day, sp.*
360.00   400.00   (380.00)
☐ **As above,** *8 Day, strike, sp.*
400.00   450.00   (425.00)

☐ **Toronto,** *walnut, height 45", dial 8", c. 1910, 8 Day, sp. (E1-98).*
800.00   900.00   (850.00)
☐ **As above,** *8 Day, strike, sp.*
900.00   1000.00   (950.00)

☐ **Walton,** *oak, 41" x 15¼", dial 10", c. 1915, 8 Day (E1-96).*
310.00   350.00   (330.00)
☐ **As above,** *8 Day, strike.*
360.00   400.00   (380.00)
☐ **As above,** *8 Day, calendar.*
400.00   450.00   (425.00)

☐ **Yarmouth,** *oack, height 30", dial 6", rococo, c. 1915, 8 Day (E1-97).*
400.00   450.00   (425.00)
☐ **As above,** *8 Day, strike.*
450.00   500.00   (475.00)

REGULATOR/ROUND TOP, LONG DROP

☐ **Regulator,** *oak, dead beat escapement, retaining power, solid movement frame, height 41", dial 18", 8 Day, weight (E2-163).*
1000.00   1250.00   (1125.00)

☐ **Regulator No.2,** *wood, height 36½", dial 12", dead beat escapement, retaining power, c. 1888, 8 Day, weight (E1-23).*
725.00   800.00   (762.00)

REGULATOR/ROUND TOP, SHORT DROP

☐ **Andes,** *oak, height 24", dial 12", 8 Day (E1-162).*
175.00   200.00   (187.00)
☐ **As above,** *8 Day, strike.*
195.00   225.00   (210.00)
☐ **As above,** *8 Day, calendar.*
220.00   250.00   (235.00)
☐ **As above,** *8 Day, strike, calendar.*
245.00   275.00   (260.00)

Regulator, Round Top

☐ **English Drop No.2,** *veneered, inlaid, height 27¾", dial 12", 8 Day (E2-161).*
310.00   350.00   (330.00)
☐ **As above,** *8 Day, strike.*
335.00   375.00   (355.00)
☐ **As above,** *8 Day, calendar.*
360.00   400.00   (380.00)
☐ **As above,** *8 Day, strike, calendar.*
375.00   425.00   (400.00)

☐ **Glenwood, Calendar,** *rosewood, height 25½", dial 12", c. 1910, 8 Day (E1-100).*
360.00   400.00   (380.00)
☐ **As above,** *8 Day, strike.*
400.00   450.00   (425.00)

WATERBURY CLOCK COMPANY / 529

Andes

- ☐ **Round Head Drop,** *oak, height 24", dial 12", 8 Day (E2-162).*
  195.00   225.00   (210.00)
- ☐ **As above,** *8 Day, strike.*
  220.00   250.00   (235.00)
- ☐ **As above,** *8 Day, calendar.*
  245.00   275.00   (255.00)
- ☐ **As above,** *8 Day, strike, calendar.*
  270.00   300.00   (285.00)

REGULATOR/SECONDS BIT

- ☐ **Regulator No.3,** *walnut, brass weights, dead beat escapement, retaining power, solid movement frames, height 46", dial 9", (E2-161).*
  1050.00   1250.00   (1150.00)
- ☐ **Kendall,** *oak, height 52", dial 10", 30 Day (E2-161).*
  800.00   900.00   (850.00)
- ☐ **As above,** *walnut.*
  1000.00   1200.00   (1100.00)
- ☐ **Regulator,** *walnut, cabinet finish, glass sides, dead beat escapement, retaining power, beats seconds, height 87", silver dial 10", c. 1890, 8 Day, weight (E2-173).*
  2025.00   2250.00   (2137.00)
- ☐ **As above,** *8 Day, weight, strike.*
  2070.00   2300.00   (2210.00)
- ☐ **Regulator No.3,** *walnut, height 46", dial 9", dead beat escapement, c. 1888, 8 Day, weight (E1-23).*
  950.00   1050.00   (1000.00)
- ☐ **As above,** *ash.*
  1000.00   1100.00   (1050.00)
- ☐ **As above,** *mahogany.*
  900.00   1000.00   (950.00)
- ☐ **Regulator No.6,** *walnut, height 87", dial 10", beats seconds, dead beat escapement, retaining power, c. 1888, 8 Day, weight (E1-23).*
  2025.00   2250.00   (2137.00)

Round Head Drop

Regulator No. 19

☐ **Regulator No.19,** oak, dead beat escapement, retaining power, solid polished movement frames, 50" x 19½", dial 12", 8 Day, weight (E2-161).
    850.00   950.00   (900.00)

☐ **Waterbury Regulator No.2,** rosewood, height 36½", dial 12", c. 1910, 8 Day, weight (E1-100).
    675.00   750.00   (712.00)

REGULATOR/SWEEP SECONDS

☐ **Jewelers' Regulator No.60,** quartered oak, cabinet finish, glass sides, brass weights, sweep seconds, dead beat escapement, retaining power, 79½" x 26", porcelain dial 12", 8 Day, weight (E2-175).
    3375.00   3750.00   (3565.00)
☐ **As above,** walnut.
    3575.00   3975.00   (3775.00)

☐ **Jewelers' Standing Regulator No.61,** quartered oak, dead beat pin escapement, sweep second, retaining power, brass weight, Swiss pattern movement, 96¼" x 28⅝", porcelain dial 12", 8 Day, weight (E2-175).
    3600.00   4000.00   (3800.00)
☐ **As above,** walnut.
    3800.00   4200.00   (4000.00)

☐ **Jewelers' Regulator No.65,** fine quartered oak, sweep seconds, dead beat escapement, retaining power, 81" x 24", dial 12", 8 Day, weight (E2-175).
    3375.00   3750.00   (3565.00)
☐ **As above,** walnut.
    3575.00   3950.00   (3775.00)

☐ **Regulator No.7,** walnut, glass sides, sweep seconds, dead beat escapement, retaining power, height 82", porcelain dial 12", 8 Day, weight (E1-23).
    3600.00   4000.00   (3800.00)
☐ **As above,** cherry.
    3700.00   4100.00   (3900.00)

☐ **Regulator No.11,** oak, glass sides, brass weights, dead beat escapement, retaining power, solid polished movement frames, height 52¼", dial 10", 8 Day, weight (E2-161).
    900.00   1150.00   (1025.00)
☐ **As above,** cherry.
    1150.00   1400.00   (1275.00)
☐ **As above,** walnut.
    1100.00   1350.00   (1225.00)

☐ **Regulator No.14,** walnut, beats seconds, dead beat escapement, retaining power, height 72", dial 12", c. 1888, 8 Day, weight (E1-23).
    1300.00   1600.00   (1450.00)

WATERBURY CLOCK COMPANY / 531

Jewelers' Standing No. 61

☐ **Regulator No.7,** *quartered oak, brass weights, dead beat escapement, sweep second, retaining power, glass sides, 82" x 25½", porcelain dial 12", c. 1915, 8 Day, weight (E1-97).*
    3600.00   4000.00   (3800.00)

☐ **Regulator No.15,** *walnut, glass sides, dead beat pin escapement, sweep second, retaining power, height 91", porcelain dial 12", c. 1888, 8 Day, weight (E1-23).*
    3700.00   4100.00   (3900.00)
☐ **As above,** *cherry.*
    3850.00   4250.00   (4050.00)
☐ **As above,** *antique oak.*
    3600.00   4000.00   (3800.00)

☐ **Regulator No.61,** *quartered oak, brass weights, dead beat escapement, sweep second, retaining power, 96¼" x 28⅝", porcelain dial 12", c. 1915, 8 Day, weight (E1-97).*
    3600.00   4000.00   (3800.00)
☐ **As above,** *walnut.*
    3800.00   4200.00   (4000.00)

☐ **Regulator No.70,** *quartered oak, polished finish, dead beat escapement, sweep second, retaining power, 82" x 26¼", porcelain dial 12", 8 Day, weight (E2-175).*
    3375.00   3750.00   (3565.00)
☐ **As above,** *mahogany.*
    3525.00   3900.00   (3715.00)

☐ **Regulator No.71,** *quartered oak, brass weights, dead beat escapement, sweep seconds, retaining power, 96¼" x 28", porcelain dial 12", c. 1915, 8 Day, weight (E1-97).*
    3600.00   4000.00   (3800.00)
☐ **As above,** *mahogany.*
    3750.00   4150.00   (3950.00)

☐ **Walnut, Regulator No.9,** *walnut, pin escapement, sweep second, height 88", dial 12", 8 Day, c. 1910, weight (E1-98).*
    3600.00   4000.00   (3800.00)

☐ **Walnut Regulator No.10,** *walnut, pin escapement, sweep second, height 85", dial 12", c. 1910, 8 Day, weight (E1-98).*
    3375.00   3750.00   (3565.00)

STATUE/OVER 18"

☐ **Cavalier**, *rich Roman gold plated, ivory center, visible escapement, rococo cast gilt sash and bezel, beveled glass, 22¼" x 17¼", ivory dial 4½", c. 1900, 8 Day, strike (E1-109).*
    375.00   425.00   (400.00)

☐ **Crusader**, *rich Roman gold plated, ivory center, visible escapement, rococo cast gilt sash and bezel, beveled glass, 27¼" x 17¾", ivory dial 4½", c. 1900, 8 Day, strike (E1-109).*
    450.00   500.00   (475.00)

☐ **Verndale**, *Japanese or Syrian bronze, ivory center, rococo cast gilt sash and bezel, beveled glass, 21" x 23", ivory dial, c. 1900, 8 Day, strike (E1-117).*
    490.00   550.00   (520.00)

STATUE/UNDER 18"

☐ **Valencia**, *Japanese or Syrian bronze, ivory center, visible escapement, rococo cast gilt sash and bezel, beveled glass, 12½" x 12½", ivory dial, c. 1900, 8 Day, strike (E1-117).*
    175.00   200.00   (187.00)

☐ **Vassar**, *Japanese or Syrian bronze, ivory center, visible escapement, rococo cast gilt sash and bezel, beveled glass, 16⅞" x 16¼", ivory dial 4½", c. 1900, 8 Day, strike (E1-109).*
    310.00   350.00   (330.00)

☐ **Venango**, *Japanese or Syrian bronze, ivory center, visible escapement, rococo cast gilt sash and bezel, beveled glass, 15½" x 19¾", ivory dial 4½", c. 1900, 8 Day, strike (E1-109).*
    450.00   500.00   (475.00)

☐ **Verona**, *Japanese or Syrian bronze, ivory center, visible escapement, rococo cast gilt sash and bezel, beveled glass, 13½" x 12", ivory dial, c. 1900, 8 Day, strike (E1-110).*
    310.00   350.00   (330.00)

☐ **Viborg**, *Japanese or Syrian bronze, ivory center, visible escapement, rococo cast gilt sash and bezel, beveled glass, 12½" x 14", ivory dial 4½", c. 1900, 8 Day, strike (E1-109).*
    190.00   220.00   (205.00)

☐ **Vilna**, *Japanese or Syrian bronze, ivory center, visible escapement, rococo cast gilt sash and bezel, beveled glass, 19⅜" x 19¾", ivory dial 4½", c. 1900, 8 Day, strike (E1-109).*
    285.00   325.00   (305.00)

☐ **Vineland**, *Japanese or Syrian bronze, ivory center, visible escapement, rococo cast gilt sash and bezel, beveled glass, 16⅞" x 20", ivory dial 4½", c. 1900, 8 Day, strike (E1-109).*
    450.00   500.00   (475.00)

Crusader

THE E.N. WELCH MANUFACTURING COMPANY / 533

Vassar

☐ **Volga,** *Japanese or Syrian bronze, ivory center, visible escapement, rococo cast gilt sash and bezel, beveled glass, 19³⁄₈" x 19³⁄₄", ivory dial 4½", c. 1900, 8 Day, strike (E1-109).*
    270.00   300.00   **(285.00)**

☐ **Voltaire,** *Japanese or Syrian bronze, ivory center, visible escapement, rococo cast gilt sash and bezel, beveled glass, 12¼" x 14¾", ivory dial, c. 1900, 8 Day, strike (E1-117).*
    190.00   220.00   **(205.00)**

THE E.N. WELCH MANUFACTURING COMPANY

Elisha Niles Welch is the founding father of this famous company, which continues today under the name of *The Sessions Clock Company*. With his father, Elisha ran an iron foundry in Bristol, selling the valuable weights and sometimes bells, to clock makers. By 1834 Welch was in the clock business himself, with partner Thomas Barnes.

The partnership changed hands a few times with Welch emerging on top. It is important to note that Welch's business was primarily concerned with the manufacture of metals for clocks and clock movements.

The company subsidized Welch, Spring and Company, producing a high quality grade of clocks even for Bristol. Eventually E.N. Welch Manufacturing Company absorbed the entire firm. Elisha's son James suffered financial difficulties, and the firm was taken over by Sessions, as has been previously noted.

ALARM/FANCY

☐ **Fairy Queen,** *nickel, height 4¾", dial 2½", c. 1875, 1 Day, lever (E1-62).*
    25.00   35.00   **(30.00)**

☐ **Fairy Queen,** *nickel, height 5", dial 2½", c. 1875, 1 Day, Alarm, lever (E1-62).*
    30.00   40.00   **(35.00)**

Fairy Queen

ALARM/ROUND

☐ **Boom,** *nickel, height 5¾", dial 3", c. 1875, 1 Day, Lever (E1-62).*
    20.00   30.00   **(25.00)**

☐ **Brilliant,** *nickel, height 5¾", dial 3½", c. 1890, 1 Day, alarm (E1-66).*
    30.00   40.00   **(35.00)**

☐ **Charmer,** *nickel, height 5¼", dial 4", 8 Day, calendar, lever (E1-62).*
    60.00   75.00   **(67.00)**

☐ **Daybreak,** *hammered brass, height 5¾", dial 3½", c. 1890, 1 Day, alarm (E1-66).*
    30.00   40.00   **(35.00)**

534 / THE E.N. WELCH MANUFACTURING COMPANY

Nelson

- **The Little Chick,** *nickel, dial 2½",
  c. 1890, 1 Day, strike (E1-67).*
    45.00   60.00   (47.50)
- **As above,** *1 Day, alarm*
    45.00   60.00   (47.50)
- **As above,** *1 Day*
    40.00   50.00   (45.00)
- **Morning Glory,** *nickel, height 7",
  dial 5", c. 1890, 1 Day, alarm
  (E1-67).*
    35.00   45.00   (40.00)
- **Nelson,** *nickel, height 5¾", dial
  4", c. 1890, 1 Day (E1-66).*
    20.00   30.00   (25.00)
- **As above,** *1 Day, alarm*
    25.00   35.00   (30.00)

CABINET

- **Cabinets No. 1 Series,** *oak, (6) 3
  different patterns, 2 of each
  pattern, turnback movement, height
  16½", dial 5", c. 1890, 8 Day, strike
  (E1-72).*
    each 85.00   105.00   (95.00)
- **Cabinet K (61 to 65),** *wood, height
  17", dial 5", c. 1900, 8 Day, strike
  (E1-68).*
    each 115.00   140.00   (127.00)
- **Martini,** *oak, turnback movement,
  height 16½", dial 5", c. 1890, 8 Day,
  strike (E1-72).*
    85.00   105.00   (95.00)

Rubini

Spotini

- **Rubini,** *oak, turnback movement,
  height 16½", dial 5", c. 1890, 8 Day,
  strike (E1-72).*
    85.00   105.00   (95.00)
- **Spontini,** *oak, turnback movement,
  height 16½", dial 5", c. 1890, 8 Day,
  strike (E1-72).*
    85.00   105.00   (95.00)

CALENDAR

- **Axtell Octagon,** *short drop, 25" x
  18", dial 12", 8 Day, strike, simple
  calendar (E1-72).*
    300.00   350.00   (325.00)

THE E.N. WELCH MANUFACTURING COMPANY / 535

☐ **Dodecagon (12 Sided),** *lever, seconds bit, gallery clock, dial 10", 1 Day, strike, simple calendar (E1-22, M214-73).*
    175.00   250.00   (212.00)

☐ **No. 1 Drop Octagon,** *spring 24½", dial 12", 8 Day, simple calendar (E1-72).*
    300.00   350.00   (325.00)

☐ **Eclipse Regulator,** *spring, 35" x 15", dial 7", 8 Day, simple calendar (M207-72).*
    500.00   600.00   (550.00)

☐ **Eclipse Regulator,** *spring, 39" x 15", dial 7", 8 Day, strike, simple calendar (M206-72).*
    500.00   600.00   (550.00)

☐ **Eclipse Regulator,** *long drop octagon, spring, 33" x 17", dial 11", 8 Day, simple calendar (M210-73).*
    425.00   475.00   (450.00)

☐ **Gentry Octagon Top,** *short drop, 26", dial 12", 8 Day, strike, simple calendar (E1-69).*
    325.00   375.00   (350.00)

☐ **Globe Kitchen,** *spring, 23" x 15", dial 6", 8 Day, strike, simple calendar (E1-142).*
    200.00   250.00   (225.00)

Octagon

☐ **8" Miniature Octagon Top,** *short drop, 18½", dial 8", 8 Day, simple calendar (E1-72).*
    300.00   350.00   (325.00)

☐ **Octagon,** *short drop, spring 24" x 16½", dial 12", 8 Day, strike, simple calendar (E1-21, M212-73).*
    350.00   375.00   (362.00)

☐ **Octagon,** *short drop, spring, 24" x 17", dial 11", 8 Day, strike, simple calendar (M208-72).*
    350.00   425.00   (387.00)

☐ **Patchen Octagon Top,** *short drop, 26", dial 12", 8 Day, strike, simple calendar (E1-69).*
    300.00   350.00   (325.00)

☐ **Press Kitchen Extra,** *spring, thermometer and barometer, 23" x 15", dial 6", 8 Day, strike, simple calendar (E1-142).*
    225.00   275.00   (250.00)

☐ **Press Kitchen,** *spring, 23" x 15", dial 6", 8 Day, strike, simple calendar (E1-142).*
    200.00   250.00   (225.00)

☐ **Ruddygore Victorian Kitchen,** *spring 24", dial 6", 8 Day, strike, simple calendar (E1-163).*
    450.00   500.00   (475.00)

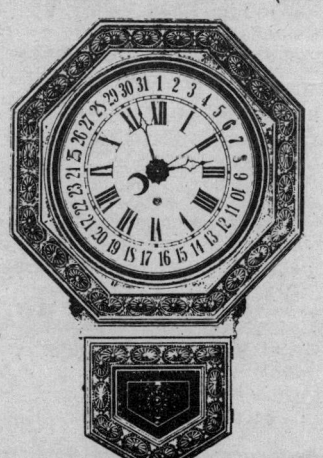

Gentry Octagon Top

536 / THE E.N. WELCH MANUFACTURING COMPANY

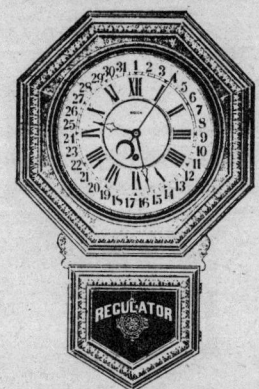

Patchen Octagon Top

Star Pointer Octagon Top

- [ ] **Star Pointer Octagon Top,** *long drop, 32½", dial 12", 8 Day, simple calendar (E1-69).*
  400.00   450.00   (425.00)

- [ ] **St. Clair Octagon Top,** *long drop, spring 32½", dial 12", 8 Day, simple calendar (E1-69).*
  400.00   450.00   (425.00)

- [ ] **Victorian Kitchen,** *spring, 24" x 13", dial 5", 8 Day, strike, simple calendar (M213-73).*
  300.00   375.00   (337.00)

CALENDAR
WELCH, SPRING AND COMPANY

- [ ] **Arditi Shelf DD,** *height 27", dial 8", 8 Day, strike (E1-163).*
  1250.00   1500.00   (350.00)

- [ ] **Auber,** *spring, height 36½", dials 10", 8 Day, strike (E1-21, M196A-69).*
  2100.00   2350.00   (2221.00)

- [ ] **Auber,** *strap brass movement, V calendar mechanism, height 42", dials 12", 8 Day, strike (E1-21, M196-69).*
  2000.00   2350.00   (2225.00)

- [ ] **Damrosch Double Dial Wall Regulator,** *height 41", dials 8" (E1-163).*
  2500.00   3000.00   (2750.00)

- [ ] **Double Dial Shelf,** *spring, 30" x 20", dial 7", 8 Day, strike (M192-68).*
  2050.00   2500.00   (2275.00)

- [ ] **Italian Shelf No. 1,** *spring, dials 7", 8 Day (M190A-67).*
  700.00   800.00   (750.00)

- [ ] **Italian-Type Shelf,** *spring, V calendar mechanism, 17" x 19½", 4½" time and 5" calendar dial, 8 Day, strike (M185-66).*
  800.00   1000.00   (900.00)

- [ ] **Italian-Type Shelf,** *spring, V Calendar Mechanism, 19½" x 12", dial 6½", 8 Day, strike (M186-66).*
  700.00   800.00   (750.00)

- [ ] **Italian-Type Shelf,** *spring, Y calendar, 21" x 11½", dial 5", 8 Day, strike (M184-66).*
  900.00   1050.00   (975.00)

- [ ] **Regulator Calendar No. 3,** *double weight retaining power, V calendar mechanism, 52", dial 10", 8 Day (E1-22, M200-70).*
  4200.00   4750.00   (4475.00)

- [ ] **Regulator Calendar No. 3 Mantel,** *double weight, 45", dial 10", 8 Day (M202-71).*
  3400.00   3800.00   (3600.00)

- [ ] **Regulator Calendar No. 5,** *spring, 41", 8" time and 8½" calendar dial, 30 Day (E1-22, M204-71).*
  2900.00   3150.00   (3025.00)

THE E.N. WELCH MANUFACTURING COMPANY / 537

☐ **Round Head Calendar No. 4,** *spring, 32" x 16", 11½" time and 7" calendar dial, 8 Day (E1-22, M203-71).*
    1100.00   1450.00   (1275.00)

☐ **Round Head Regulator No. 1,** *double weight retaining power, V calendar mechanism, 1 second pendulum, 18" time and 12" calendar dial, 8 Day (E1-22, M198-70).*
    2000.00   2400.00   (2200.00)

☐ **Round Head Regulator No. 2,** *double weight retaining power, V calendar mechanism, 34", 12" time and 8" calendar dial, 8 Day (E1-22, M199-70).*
    1800.00   2000.00   (1900.00)

☐ **Shelf No. 1,** *spring, 32" x 20", dial 7" 8 Day, strike (M191-68).*
    2000.00   2575.00   (2287.00)

☐ **Wagner Hanging,** *spring, height 32½", dial 7", 8 Day, strike (E1-21, M194-69).*
    2100.00   2550.00   (2325.00)

☐ **Wagner Mantel,** *spring, height 26", dial 7", 8 Day, strike (E1-21, M195-69).*
    1900.00   2100.00   (2000.00)

CARRIAGE

☐ **Furore,** *nickel, height 3½", c. 1890, 1 Day (E1-67).*
    35.00   45.00   (40.00)

☐ **Little Lord Fauntleroy,** *nickel, height 2½", c. 1890, 1 Day (E1-67).*
    35.00   45.00   (40.00)

☐ **The Lurline,** *nickel frame, sides and top glass, height 5½", dial 2½", c. 1890, 1 Day, alarm (E1-67).*
    100.00   120.00   (110.00)

☐ **The Outing,** *nickel, front and sides glass, 5", c. 1890, 1 Day (E1-67).*
    80.00   100.00   (90.00)

The Outing

CONNECTICUT SHELF
BEEHIVE

☐ **Round Gothic,** *wood, height 19", c. 1875, 1 Day, strike, spring (E1-16).*
    100.00   120.00   (110.00)

Round Head Regulator No. 1

538 / THE E.N. WELCH MANUFACTURING COMPANY

Round Gothic

☐ **Column,** *mahogany case, shell/gilt column, height 25", dial 8", c. 1875, 1 Day, strike, weight (E1-63).*
    105.00   125.00   (115.00

☐ **As above,** *rosewood, height 2", dial 8", 1 Day, strike, weight*
    105.00   125.00   (115.00)

☐ **As above,** *rosewood, 8 Day, strike, weight*
    105.00   125.00   (115.00)

CONNECTICUT SHELF
COTTAGE

☐ **Cottage,** *wood, height 11" to 13", c. 1875, 1 Day, spring (E1-16).*
    65.00   80.00   (72.50)

☐ **As above,** *1 Day, strike*
    80.00   100.00   (90.00)

CONNECTICUT SHELF
COLUMN

☐ **Arch Column,** *rosewood, rose and gilt pillars, height 17", c. 1875, 8 Day, strike, spring (E1-20).*
    170.00   195.00   (182.00)

Cottage

Column 1362

Cottage-Extra

THE E.N. WELCH MANUFACTURING COMPANY / 539

- ☐ **Cottage-Extra,** *height 11", c. 1875, 1 Day, spring (E1-16).*
  65.00　　80.00　　(72.50)
- ☐ **As above,** *height 13", 8 Day, strike*
  110.00　　135.00　　(122.00)
- ☐ **Cottage No. 1,** *wood, height 13", dial 6", c. 1875 1 Day (E1-63).*
  55.00　　70.00　　(62.50)
- ☐ **Cottage No. 2,** *wood, height 12", dial 6", c. 1875 1 Day, spring (E1-63).*
  60.00　　75.00　　(67.50)

CONNECTICUT SHELF
EMPIRE

- ☐ **Extra Column,** *wood, height 33", c. 1875, 8 Day, strike, weight (E1-20).*
  310.00　　350.00　　(330.00)

Extra Column

CONNECTICUT SHELF
OCTAGON TOP

- ☐ **Aimee,** *wood, height 10¾", c. 1875, 1 Day, spring (E1-16).*
  80.00　　95.00　　(87.00)
- ☐ **Empress,** *wood, height 16", c. 1875, 1 Day, strike, spring (E1-16).*
  75.00　　90.00　　(82.00)
- ☐ **As above,** *8 Day, strike*
  105.00　　125.00　　(115.00)
- ☐ **Empress, V.P.,** *wood, height 17", c. 1875, 1 Day, strike, spring (E1-16).*
  80.00　　100.00　　(90.00)
- ☐ **As above,** *8 Day, strike*
  125.00　　150.00　　(137.00)
- ☐ **Seguin,** *wood, height 10¾", c. 1875, 1 Day, spring (E1-16).*
  80.00　　95.00　　(87.00)

Empress, V.P.

CONNECTICUT SHELF
O.G. AND O.O.G.

- ☐ **O.G. Nos. 1 And 2,** *wood, height 26", dial 8", c. 1875, 1 Day, strike (E1-63).*
  130.00　　155.00　　(142.00)
- ☐ **O.G. And O.O.G.,** *mahogany, height 29", c. 1875, 8 Day, strike, weight (E1-20).*
  195.00　　225.00　　(210.00)
- ☐ **As above,** *rosewood, 8 Day, strike, weight*
  195.00　　225.00　　(210.00)

Connecticut Shelf O.O.G.

☐ **O.O.G.**, *wood, height 18", c. 1875, 1 Day, strike, spring (E1-20).*
130.00   155.00   (142.00)
☐ **As above,** *8 Day, strike, spring*
145.00   170.00   (157.00)

☐ **O.O.G.**, *wood, height 18", dial 6", c. 1875, 1 Day, strike, spring (E1-63).*
140.00   165.00   (152.00)
☐ **As above,** *8 Day, strike, spring*
195.00   225.00   (210.00)

☐ **O.O.G.**, *wood, height 26", dial 8", c. 1875, 1 Day, strike, weight (E1-63).*
135.00   160.00   (147.00)

CONNECTICUT SHELF
ROUND TOP

☐ **Italian No. 1,** *wood, height 18½", c. 1875, 8 Day, strike, spring (E1-16).*
150.00   175.00   (162.00)

☐ **Italian No. 2, V.P.,** *wood, height 16", c. 1875, 8 Day, strike, spring (E1-16).*
115.00   145.00   (130.00)

☐ **Italian No. 2,** *wood, height 16", c. 1875, 8 Day, strike, spring (E1-16).*
140.00   165.00   (152.00)

Italian No. 3, V.P.

☐ **Italian No. 3, V.P.,** *wood, height 14", c. 1875, 1 Day, strike, spring (E1-16).*
110.00   135.00   (122.00)

CONNECTICUT SHELF
SPLIT TOP

☐ **Peerless, V.P.,** *wood, height 17½", dial 6", c. 1875, 1 Day, strike, spring (E1-62).*
75.00   90.00   (82.00)
☐ **As above,** *8 Day, strike, spring*
105.00   125.00   (115.00)

Peerless V.P.

CONNECTICUT SHELF
STEEPLE

☐ **Sharp Gothic, V.P.,** *wood, height 20", dial 6", c. 1875, 1 Day, strike, spring (E1-62).*
80.00   100.00   (90.00)
☐ **As above,** *8 Day, strike*
110.00   135.00   (122.00)

THE E.N. WELCH MANUFACTURING COMPANY / 541

Small Gothic

- Sharp Gothic, wood, height 20", c. 1875, 1 Day, strike, spring, (E1-16).
  100.00 120.00 (110.00)
- Small Gothic, wood, height 14½", c. 1875, 1 Day, spring (E1-16).
  90.00 110.00 (100.00)
- As above, 8 Day, strike
  100.00 120.00 (110.00)

GALLERY/WALL LEVER

- Carved And Gilt Gallery, metal, height 12", c. 1875, 8 Day (E1-20).
  245.00 275.00 (260.00)
- Nickel Lever, 3", c. 1875 1 Day, strike (E1-16).
  45.00 60.00 (52.50)
- As above, 3", 8 Day, strike
  60.00 75.00 (65.50)
- As above, 6", 1 Day, strike
  75.00 90.00 (82.00)
- As above, 6", 8 Day, strike
  90.00 110.00 (100.00)
- As above, 8", 1 Day, strike
  90.00 110.00 (100.00)
- As above, 8", 8 Day, strike
  110.00 135.00 (122.00)
- Round Corner Octagon Lever, wood, 4", c. 1875, 8 Day, strike (E1-16).
  40.00 50.00 (45.00)
- As above, 6"
  55.00 70.00 (62.00)
- As above, 8"
  75.00 90.00 (82.00)
- As above, 12"
  80.00 100.00 (90.00)

Round Corner Octagon Lever

KITCHEN

- Agnesi, oak, the Bassos series, height 23", dial 6", spring wound, 8 Day, strike, c. 1890 (E1-73).
  150.00 170.00 (160.00)
- As above, walnut
  175.00 195.00 (185.00)
- Albani, oak, the Contraltos series, height 22", dial 6", spring wound, 8 Day, strike, c. 1890 (E1-73).
  140.00 160.00 (150.00)
- As above, walnut
  165.00 185.00 (175.00)
- Booth, oak, Actors series, height 23", dial 6", spring wound, 8 Day, strike, c. 1890 (E1-72).
  150.00 170.00 (160.00)
- Cary, oak, the Contraltos series, height 22", dial 6", spring wound, 8 Day, strike, c. 1890 (E1-73).
  140.00 160.00 (150.00)
- As above, walnut
  165.00 185.00 (175.00)
- Dewey, oak, height 24", dial 6", spring wound, 8 Day, strike, c. 1900 (E1-69).
  250.00 275.00 (262.00)
- Dolaro, walnut, height 23", dial 6", spring wound, 8 Day, strike, c. 1890 (E1-65).
  185.00 205.00 (195.00)
- Falka, walnut, height 23¼", dial 6", spring wound, 8 Day, strike, c. 1890 (E1-65).
  200.00 225.00 (212.00)

542 / THE E.N. WELCH MANUFACTURING COMPANY

Dewey

☐ **Fannie Rice,** oak, Prima Donnas series, height 23", dial 6", spring wound, 8 Day, strike, c. 1890 (E1-73).
150.00   170.00   (160.00)
☐ As above, walnut
175.00   195.00   (185.00)

☐ **Foli,** oak, the Bassos series, height 23", dial 6", spring wound, 8 Day, strike, c. 1890 (E1-73).
150.00   170.00   (170.00)
☐ As above, walnut
175.00   195.00   (185.00)

☐ **Hal Pointer,** oak, height 23", dial 6", spring wound, 8 Day, strike, c. 1890 (E1-72).
150.00   170.00   (160.00)

☐ **Hatton,** walnut, height 23", dial 6", spring wound, 8 Day, strike, c. 1890 (E1-65).
185.00   205.00   (195.00)

☐ **Irving,** oak, Actors series, height 23", dial 6", spring wound, 8 Day, strike, c. 1890 (E1-72).
150.00   170.00   (160.00)

☐ **Jansen,** walnut, height 22", dial 6", spring wound, 1 Day, strike, c. 1890 (E1-65).
200.00   225.00   (212.00)

☐ **Lee,** oak, height 24", dial 6", spring wound, 8 Day, strike, c. 1900 (E1-69).
250.00   275.00   (262.00)

☐ **Lillian Russell,** oak, Prima Donnas series, height 23", dial 6", spring wound, 8 Day, strike, c. 1890 (E1-72).
150.00   170.00   (160.00)
☐ As above, walnut
175.00   195.00   (185.00)

☐ **Litta,** walnut, height 23", dial 6", spring wound, 8 Day, strike, c. 1890 (E1-65).
185.00   205.00   (195.00)

☐ **Louise Montague,** oak, Prima Donnas series, height 23", dial 6", spring wound, 8 Day, strike, c. 1890 (E1-72).
150.00   170.00   (160.00)
☐ Above, walnut
175.00   195.00   (185.00)

☐ **The Maine,** oak, height 24", dial 6", spring wound, 8 Day, strike, c. 1900 (E1-69).
250.00   275.00   (262.00)

☐ **Marie Tempest,** oak, Prima Donnas series, height 23", dial 6", spring wound, 8 Day, strike, c. 1890 (E1 73).
150.00   170.00   (160.00)
☐ As above, walnut.
175.00   195.00   (185.00)

☐ **Marion Manola,** oak, Prima Donnas series, height 23", spring wound, dial 6", 8 Day, strike, c. 1890 (E1-72).
150.00   170.00   (160.00)
☐ As above, walnut
175.00   195.00   (185.00)

☐ **Materna,** walnut, height 23", dial 6", spring wound, 8 Day, strike, c. 1890 (E1-65).
185.00   205.00   (195.00)

☐ **Nanon,** walnut, height 21½", dial 6", spring wound, 8 Day, strike, c. 1890 (E1-65).
200.00   225.00   (212.00)

THE E.N. WELCH MANUFACTURING COMPANY / 543

☐ **Pauline Hall,** oak, Prima Donnas series, height 23", dial 6", spring wound, 8 Day, strike, c. 1890 (E1-73).
    150.00   170.00   (160.00)
☐ **As above,** walnut
    175.00   195.00   (185.00)

☐ **Roze,** walnut, height 21", dial 6", spring wound, 8 Day, strike, c. 1890 (E1-65).
    175.00   200.00   (187.00)

☐ **Sampson,** oak, height 24", dial 6", spring wound, 8 Day, strike, c. 1900 (E1-69).
    250.00   275.00   (262.00)

☐ **Scalchi,** oak, the Contraltos series, height 22", dial 6", spring wound, 8 Day, strike, c. 1890 (E1-73).
    140.00   160.00   (150.00)
☐ **As above,** walnut
    165.00   185.00   (175.00)

☐ **Schley,** oak, height 24", dial 6", spring wound, 8 Day, strike, c. 1900 (E1-69).
    250.00   270.00   (260.00)

☐ **Thursby,** walnut, height 23", dial 6", spring wound, 1 Day, strike, c. 1890 (E1-65).
    175.00   200.00   (187.00)

☐ **Wheeler,** oak, height 24", dial 6", spring wound, 8 Day, strike, c. 1900 (E1-69).
    250.00   275.00   (262.00)

☐ **Whitney,** oak, the Bassos series, height 23", dial 6", spring wound, 8 Day, strike, c. 1890 (E1-73).
    150.00   175.00   (162.00)
☐ **As above,** walnut
    175.00   195.00   (185.00)

KITCHEN/SERIES

☐ **The Actors Series (6),** oak, 2 patterns, 3 of each pattern, turnback movement, Booth, Irving, height 23", dial 6", c. 1890, 8 Day, strike (E1-72).
    150.00   170.00   (160.00)

☐ **Assortment A. (1 to 6),** oak, height 22¾", dial 6", 8 Day, strike, c. 1900 (E1-68).
    140.00   160.00   (150.00)

Actor No. 2

☐ **Assortment B. (7 to 12),** oak, height 23", dial 6", 8 Day, strike, c. 1900 (E1-68).
    150.00   170.00   (160.00)
☐ **As above,** walnut
    175.00   195.00   (185.00)

☐ **Assortment C. (13 to 18),** oak, height 23", dial 6", 8 Day, strike, c. 1900 (E1-68).
    150.00   170.00   (160.00)
☐ **As above,** walnut
    175.00   195.00   (185.00)

☐ **Assortment D. (19 to 24),** oak, height 23¼", dial 6", 8 Day, strike, c. 1900 (E1-69).
    140.00   170.00   (155.00)

☐ **The Bassos Series,** oak, 3 different patterns, 1 walnut and 1 oak of each pattern, Whitney, Foll, Agnesi, turnback movement, height 23", dial 6", 8 Day, strike, c. 1890 (E1-73).
    150.00   170.00   (160.00)
☐ **As above,** walnut
    175.00   195.00   (185.00)

☐ **The Contraltos Series,** oak, 3 different patterns, 1 walnut and 1 oak of each pattern, Cary, Scalchi, Albani, turnback movement, height 22", dial 6", 8 Day, strike, c. 1890 (E1-73).
    140.00   160.00   (150.00)
☐ **As above,** walnut
    165.00   185.00   (175.00)

544 / THE E.N. WELCH MANUFACTURING COMPANY

☐ **The Prima Donnas Series,** *oak, 6 different patterns, 3 walnut and 3 oak, Marie Tempest, Pauline Hall, Fannie Rice, Marion Manola, Louise Montague, Lillian Russell, turnback movement, height 23", dial 6", 8 Day, strike, c. 1890 (E1-73).*
    150.00   170.00   (160.00)

☐ **As above,** *walnut*
    175.00   195.00   (185.00)

KITCHEN/TEAR DROP

☐ **Parepa, V.P.,** *spring, height 22", dial 6", 8 Day, strike, c. 1890 (E1-65).*
    350.00   450.00   (400.00)

☐ **Parisian,** *walnut, height 24", dial 6", 8 Day, strike, c. 1890 (E1-65).*
    275.00   325.00   (300.00)

☐ **Texas,** *walnut, height 23", dial 6", 8 Day, strike, c. 1890 (E1-65).*
    275.00   325.00   (300.00)

MANTEL/BLACK IRON

☐ **Cremona,** *black enameled iron, bronze feet and side ornaments, mouldings marbleized, gilt or white dials, regular sash and glass, 10¾" x 16½", dial 5", c. 1890 (E1-71).*
    105.00   125.00   (115.00)

☐ **Maritana,** *black enameled iron, bronze feet and side ornaments, gilt mouldings, gilt or white dials, with regular sash and glass, 12½" x 11", dial 5", c. 1890 (E1-70).*
    175.00   200.00   (187.00)

☐ **Oberon,** *black enameled iron, bronze feet and side ornaments, mouldings marbleized, gilt or white dials, regular sash and glass, 12½" x 11", dial 5", c. 1890, 8 Day, strike (E1-70).*
    175.00   200.00   (187.00)

☐ **Tuba,** *black enameled iron, bronzed columns, gilt or white dials, with regular sash and glass, 10½" x 12", dial 5", c. 1890, 8 Day, strike (E1-71).*
    90.00   110.00   (100.00)

Oberon

MANTEL/BLACK WOOD

☐ **Bellini,** *black enameled wood, bronze feet and side ornaments, panels marbleized, white or gilt dials, regular sash and glass, 11" x 16", dial 5", c. 1890, 8 Day, strike (E1-71).*
    75.00   90.00   (82.00)

☐ **Camilla Urso,** *black enameled wood, bronze feet and side ornaments, mouldings and panels marbleized, white or gilt dials, regular sash and glass, 11" x 16½", dial 5", c. 1890, 8 Day, strike (E1-70).*
    85.00   105.00   (95.00)

☐ **Del Puente,** *black enameled wood, bronze feet and side ornaments, mouldings marbleized, white, black or gilt dials, regular sash and glass, c. 1890, 8 Day, strike (E1-73).*
    85.00   105.00   (95.00)

☐ **De Murska,** *black enameled wood, bronze feet and side ornaments, mouldings marbleized, white, black or gilt dials, regular sash and glass, 11" x 17", dial 5", c. 1890, 8 Day, strike (E1-73).*
    90.00   110.00   (100.00)

THE E.N. WELCH MANUFACTURING COMPANY / 545

Kodak

☐ **Kodak,** *black enameled wood, bronze feet and side ornaments, mouldings marbleized, white, black or gilt dials, regular sash and glass, 11" x 16½", dial 5", c. 1890, 8 Day, strike (E1-71).*
85.00   105.00   (95.00)

☐ **La Favorita,** *black enameled wood, bronze feet and side ornaments, columns marbleized, white or gilt dials, with regular sash and glass, 11" x 15½", dial 5", c. 1890, 8 Day, strike (E1-70).*
85.00   105.00   (95.00)

NOVELTY/FANCY

☐ **The Escalop,** *nickel, height 4", c. 1890, 1 Day (E1-67).*
20.00   30.00   (25.00)

☐ **The Jewel,** *cut glass case in crystal (white), amber and sapphire, height 3½", porcelain dial 2½", c. 1890, 1 Day (E1-67).*
30.00   40.00   (35.00)

NOVELTY/IRON

☐ **Chalet,** *gilt or nickel, diamond pin escapement, solid steel pinion movement, height 9", dial 3", c. 1875, 8 Day, pendulum (E1-62).*
65.00   80.00   (72.00)

☐ **Egypt,** *gilt or nickel, height 7¾", dial 3", c. 1875, 1 Day, lever (E1-62).*
60.00   75.00   (67.50)

☐ **Fire Bug,** *nickel, lamp lights automatically at the hour for alarm, height 8", dial 3", c. 1875, 1 Day, alarm, lever (E1-62).*
80.00   100.00   (90.00)

☐ **Galaxy,** *gilt or nickel, height 7¾", dial 3", c. 1875, 1 Day, lever (E1-62).*
50.00   65.00   (57.00)

☐ **Good Luck,** *gilt or nickel, height 6", dial 3", c. 1875, 1 Day, lever (E1-62).*
40.00   50.00   (45.00)

☐ **La Banniere,** *gilt or nickel, height 9", dial 3", c. 1875, 1 Day, lever (E1-62).*
80.00   100.00   (90.00)

☐ **La Belle,** *gilt or nickel, height 6", dial 3", c. 1875, 1 Day, lever (E1-62).*
45.00   60.00   (52.50)

☐ **La Reine,** *gilt or nickel, height 8¼", dial 3", c. 1875, 1 Day, lever (E1-62).*
80.00   95.00   (87.00)

☐ **As above,** *8 Day, pendulum*
85.00   105.00   (95.00)

☐ **Le Prince,** *gilt or nickel, height 8", dial 3", c. 1875, 1 Day, lever (E1-62).*
65.00   80.00   (72.50)

☐ **Le Roi,** *gilt or nickel, height 6½", dial 3", c. 1875, 1 Day, lever (E1-62).*
50.00   65.00   (57.50)

☐ **L'Imperial,** *gilt or nickel, height 9¼", dial 3", c. 1875, 1 Day, lever (E1-62).*
80.00   100.00   (90.00)

☐ **As above,** *8 Day, pendulum*
90.00   110.00   (100.00)

La Reine

PATTI MOVEMENTS

- **Cary, V.P.**, *height 20", wood dial 5", c. 1875, 8 Day, strike, spring (E1-63).*
  750.00   850.00   (800.00)

- **Eveline**, *oak, height 17½", dial 5", c. 1890, 8 Day, strike (E1-65).*
  675.00   750.00   (715.00)
- **As above**, *mahogany*
  725.00   800.00   (762.00)

- **Gerster, V.P.**, *wood, height 18½", dial 5", c. 1875, 8 Day, strike, spring (E1-63).*
  750.00   850.00   (800.00)

- **Nilsson**, *polished mahogany, cathedral bell, height 22", dial 6", c. 1890, 8 Day, strike (E1-65).*
  800.00   900.00   (850.00)
- **As above**, *walnut*
  850.00   950.00   (900.00)

- **Parepa, V.P.**, *height 22", wood dial 6", c. 1875, 8 Day, strike, spring (E1-63).*
  360.00   400.00   (380.00)

- **Patti, V.P.**, *wood, height 18½", dial 5", c. 1875, 8 Day, strike, spring (E1-63).*
  725.00   800.00   (762.00)

- **Patti No. 2, V.P.**, *wood, height 10¼", dial 3", c. 1875, 8 Day, spring (E1-63).*
  1665.00   1850.00   (1755.00)

Scaichi

- **Scalchi**, *walnut, height 19½", dial 5", c. 1890, 8 Day, strike (E1-65).*
  725.00   800.00   (762.00)

- **Victoria**, *ebony, plain or gilded front, hand painted, height 13½", dial 4", c. 1890, 8 Day, strike (E1-65).*
  725.00   800.00   (762.00)

REGULATOR/FIGURE EIGHT

- **Alexis No. 1**, *wood, height 26", dial 12", c. 1875, 8 Day, spring (E1-63).*
  270.00   300.00   (285.00)
- **As above**, *8 Day, strike, spring*
  285.00   325.00   (305.00)
- **As above**, *30 Day, duplex*
  310.00   350.00   (330.00)

- **Alexis No. 2**, *wood, height 22", dial 10", c. 1875, 8 Day, spring (E1-63).*
  270.00   300.00   (285.00)
- **As above**, *8 Day, strike, spring*
  285.00   325.00   (305.00)

- **Ionic**, *wood, height 22", c. 1875, 8 Day, spring (E1-20).*
  270.00   300.00   (285.00)
- **As above**, *8 Day, strike, spring*
  285.00   325.00   (305.00)

- **Regulator**, *wood, height 2'9", dial 12", c. 1875 (E1-20).*
  1125.00   1250.00   (1187.00)

REGULATOR
OCTAGON TOP, LONG DROP

- **St. Clair Calendar**, *oak, height 32½", dial 12", c. 1900, 8 Day (E1-69).*
  270.00   300.00   (285.00)
- **As above**, *8 Day, strike*
  285.00   325.00   (305.00)
- **As above**, *8 Day, calendar*
  310.00   350.00   (330.00)
- **As above**, *8 Day, strike, calendar*
  335.00   375.00   (355.00)

- **Star Pointer Calendar**, *oak, height 32½", dial 12", c. 1900, 8 Day (E1-69).*
  270.00   300.00   (285.00)
- **As above**, *8 Day, strike*
  285.00   325.00   (305.00)
- **As above**, *8 Day, calendar*
  310.00   350.00   (330.00)
- **As above**, *8 Day, strike, calendar*
  335.00   375.00   (355.00)

THE E.N. WELCH MANUFACTURING COMPANY / 547

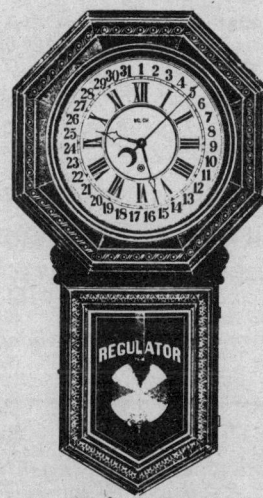

St. Clair Calendar

REGULATOR/OCTAGON TOP SHORT DROP

☐ **Axtell,** drop octagon, rosewood finish, height 25", dial 12", c. 1890, 8 Day, spring (E1-72).
195.00   225.00   (210.00)
☐ **As above,** 8 Day, strike, spring
220.00   250.00   (235.00)
☐ **As above,** 8 Day, calendar, spring
245.00   275.00   (260.00)
☐ **As above,** 8 Day, strike, calendar, spring
270.00   300.00   (285.00)

☐ **8" Inch Drop Octagon,** rosewood, height 18¾", dial 8", c. 1890, 8 Day (E1-72).
150.00   175.00   (162.00)
☐ **As above,** 8 Day, strike
175.00   200.00   (187.00)
☐ **As above,** 8 Day, calendar
195.00   225.00   (210.00)
☐ **As above,** 8 Day, strike, calendar
270.00   300.00   (285.00)
☐ **As above,** zebra, 8 Day
170.00   195.00   (182.00)
☐ **As above,** zebra, 8 Day, strike
195.00   220.00   (207.00)
☐ **As above,** zebra, 8 Day, calendar
205.00   245.00   (227.00)
☐ **As above,** zebra, 8 Day, strike, calendar
290.00   320.00   (305.00)

☐ **Drop Octagon,** wood, height 25", dial 12", c. 1875, 8 Day, spring (E1-20).
310.00   350.00   (330.00)
☐ **As above,** 8 Day, strike, spring
360.00   400.00   (380.00)
☐ **Drop Octagon, R.C.,** wood, height 25", dial 12", c. 1875, 8 Day, spring (E1-63).
195.00   225.00   (210.00)
☐ **As above,** 8 Day, strike, spring
220.00   250.00   (235.00)
☐ **Drop Octagon No. 1,** rosewood, spring, height 24½", dial 12", c. 1890, 8 Day (E1-72).
195.00   225.00   (210.00)
☐ **As above,** 8 Day, strike
220.00   250.00   (235.00)
☐ **Drop Octagon No. 2,** wood, height 25", dial 12", c. 1875, 8 Day, spring (E1-63).
220.00   250.00   (235.00)
☐ **As above,** 8 Day, strike, spring
245.00   275.00   (260.00)
☐ **Gentry Calendar,** oak, height 26", dial 12", c. 1900, 8 Day (E1-69).
195.00   225.00   (210.00)
☐ **As above,** 8 Day, strike
220.00   250.00   (235.00)
☐ **As above,** 8 Day, calendar
245.00   275.00   (260.00)
☐ **As above,** 8 Day, strike, calendar
270.00   300.00   (285.00)

REGULATOR/PARLOR SHELF

☐ **Lucca, V.P.,** wood, height 24", dial 6", c. 1890, 8 Day, strike (E1-65).
540.00   600.00   (570.00)

REGULATOR/PARLOR WALL

☐ **Italian Hanging, V.P.,** wood, height 28", dial 7", c. 1875, 8 Day, strike (E1-63).
1260.00   1400.00   (1330.00)

☐ **Meyerbeer,** walnut, height 40", dial 8", c. 1890, 8 Day, spring (E1-66).
640.00   700.00   (670.00)
☐ **As above,** 8 Day, calendar, spring
725.00   800.00   (762.00)
☐ **As above,** 8 Day, strike, spring
825.00   900.00   (862.00)
☐ **As above,** 8 Day, strike, spring
725.00   800.00   (762.00)

548 / THE E.N. WELCH MANUFACTURING COMPANY

☐ **Regulator G.,** *mahogany, hanging, height 51½", dial 10", c. 1890, 8 Day, weight.*
  1215.00   1350.00   (1280.00)
☐ **As above,** *walnut*
  1240.00   1375.00   (1315.00)

☐ **Regulator H.,** *mahogany, hanging, height 38", dial 8", c. 1890, 8 Day, spring (E1-64).*
  490.00   550.00   (520.00)
☐ **As above,** *8 Day, strike, spring*
  540.00   600.00   (570.00)

☐ **Regulator No. 6,** *wood, height 41", dial 8", c. 1875, 8 Day, weight (E1-63.*
  360.00   400.00   (380.00)

REGULATOR/ROUND TOP LONG DROP

☐ **Regulator No. 3,** *wood, height 35", dial 12", c. 1890, 8 Day, weight (E1-65).*
  575.00   650.00   (615.00)

REGULATOR/ROUND TOP, SHORT DROP

☐ **Round Head,** *wood, height 26", dial 12", c. 1875, 8 Day, spring (E1-63).*
  270.00   300.00   (285.00)
☐ **As above,** *8 Day, strike, spring*
  310.00   350.00   (330.00)
☐ **Round Top Drop,** *wood, height 24", c. 1875, 8 Day, spring.*
  270.00   300.00   (285.00)

REGULATOR/SECONDS BIT

☐ **Regulator No. 2,** *wood, height 53", dial 18", c. 1890, 8 Day, weight (E1-64).*
  900.00   1000.00   (950.00)

☐ **Regulator No. 11,** *oak, seconds pendulum, 60" x 18", dial 10", c. 1890, 30 Day (E1-67).*
  1000.00   1175.00   (1085.00)

☐ **Regulator No. 12,** *oak, seconds pendulum, 66" x 22½", dial 12", c. 1890, 30 Day (E1-67).*
  1530.00   1700.00   (1615.00)
☐ **As above,** *mahogany*
  1680.00   1850.00   (1765.00)

☐ **Regulator E.,** *mahogany, hanging, height 56", dial 10", c. 1890, 8 Day, weight (E1-64).*
  1350.00   1500.00   (1425.00)

☐ **Regulator F.,** *mahogany, hanging, height 56", dial 10", c. 1890, 8 Day, weight (E1-64).*
  1250.00   1500.00   (1375.00)

REGULATOR/SWEEP SECOND

☐ **Regulator A.,** *oak, three cell mercurial compensating pendulum, dead beat pin escapement, jeweled movement, 108" x 32½", depth 12½", porcelain dial with sweep seconds 12", c. 1890, 8 Day, weight (E1-67).*
  3375.00   3750.00   3562.00)

☐ **Regulator C.,** *oak, three cell mercurial compensating pendulum, dead beat pin escapement, jeweled movement, sweep second, 90" x 26", depth 10", c. 1890, 8 Day, weight (E1-67).*
  3150.00   3500.00   (3300.00)

☐ **Regulator (I) Eye,** *hanging, mahogany, sweep second, 62" x 16¾", dial 10", c. 1890, 8 Day, weight (E1-64).*
  1000.00   1700.00   (1350.00)

☐ **Regulator (J) Jay,** *hanging, mahogany, sweep second, 62" x 14", dial 10", c. 1890, 8 Day, weight (E1-64).*
  1100.00   1800.00   (1450.00)

☐ **Regulator No. 7,** *wood, sweep secondhand, height 47", dial 8", c. 1890, 8 Day, weight (E1-64).*
  2250.00   2500.00   (2375.00)

ROTARY

☐ **Brown's Rotary,** *brass or nickel, c. 1875, 1 Day, spring (E1-16).*
  325.00   375.00   (350.00)

WATCHES

☐ **Bicycle,** *nickel, luminous dial, watch and holder, c. 1890 (E1-66).*
  125.00   150.00   (135.00)

☐ **The Columbian,** *nickel or gilt, height 4½", length 4", c. 1890, 1 Day (E1-66).*
  310.00   350.00   (330.00)

ABOUT THE AUTHOR

The author is a long-time member of the National Association of Watch and Clock collectors, attending many Regional and Chapter meetings in order to keep in close contact with the "heartbeat" of clock and watch collectors and dealers. He travels extensively each year attending NAWCC Marts, antique shows, gun shows, flea markets, etc., buying, selling and trading clocks and watches.

He was awarded an NAWCC Fellowship in 1977 in recognition of his contribution to his fellow collectors, and in 1981 was elected a Director of that Association. He receives many requests from various Regionals and Chapters to participate in their meetings as a guest speaker, and is internationally known as an authority in the field of clocks and watches.

[E1-]

When **(E1—)** followed by a page number appears at the end of the clock description, it means more information (including an illustration) is available in the book described on this page. Example:
(E1—121 = Ehrhardt's Clock Book 1, page 121).

CLOCK
IDENTIFICATION & PRICE GUIDE
BOOK 1

by
Roy Ehrhardt
&
Malvern "Red" Rabeneck

First Printing — 1977

198, 8½ x 11 pages, Plastic Bound to lay flat.
Beautiful Color Cover.

4,000 CLOCKS PICTURED OR DESCRIBED.

[E2-]

When **(E2—)** followed by a page number appears at the end of the clock description, it means more information (including an illustration) is available in the book described on this page. Example:
(E2—140) = Ehrhardt's Clock Book 2, page 140.

CLOCK
IDENTIFICATION & PRICE GUIDE
BOOK 2

by
Roy Ehrhardt
&
Malvern "Red" Rabeneck

First Printing — 1979

198, 8½ x 11 pages, Perfect Bound.
Beautiful Color Cover.

3,257 CLOCKS PICTURED OR DESCRIBED.

[E3-]

When (E3—) followed by a page number appears at the end of the clock description, it means more information (including an illustration) is available in the book described on this page. Example:

(E2—140) = Ehrhardt's Clock Book 3, page 140)

CLOCK
IDENTIFICATION & PRICE GUIDE
BOOK 3

by
Roy Ehrhardt
&
Malvern "Red" Rabeneck

First Printing — 1983

208, 8½x11 pages. Perfect Bound.
Beautiful Color Cover.

1,966 Clocks Pictured or Described.

[K-]

When (K—) followed by a page number appears at the end of the clock description, it means more information (including an illustration) is available in the book described on this page. Example:

(K—30) = F. Kroeber Clock Co. book, page 30)

F. KROEBER CLOCK CO.
IDENTIFICATION & PRICE GUIDE

by
Roy Ehrhardt
&
Malvern "Red" Rabeneck

36, 8½x11 pages, Perfect Bound — 1983
292 CLOCK ILLUSTRATIONS

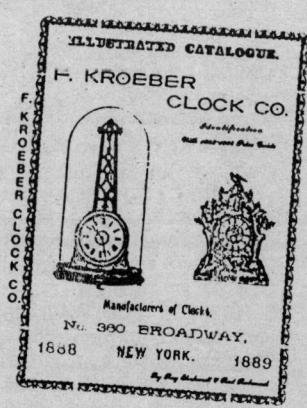

Ordering Information: Clock Book 1, 2 and 3 are each $15.00. The F. Kroeber book is $8.00. Send $1.00 postage for first book, 30 cents each add'l.
Heart of America Press
P.O. Box 9808, Kansas City, MO 64134

for more information...

POCKET WATCH BOOKS

AMERICAN POCKET WATCH IDENTIFICATION & PRICE GUIDE, BOOK 2. Ehrhardt, 1974 (Prices revised in 1980). 192, 8½x11 pages. 1 lb. 10 oz $15.00

FOREIGN & AMERICAN POCKET WATCH IDENTIFICATION & PRICE GUIDE, BOOK 3. Ehrhardt, 1976. 172, 8½x11 pages. 1 lb. 8 oz $10.00

1976 POCKET WATCH PRICE INDICATOR. Ehrhardt, 1975. 64, 8½x11 pages. 14 oz $5.00

1977 POCKET WATCH PRICE INDICATOR. Ehrhardt, 1976. 110, 8½x11 pages. 1 lb $7.00

1978 POCKET WATCH PRICE INDICATOR. Ehrhardt, 1978. 110, 8½x11 pages. 1 lb. 2 oz $10.00

1979 POCKET WATCH PRICE INDICATOR. Ehrhardt, 1979. 110, 8½x11 pages. 1 lb. 2 oz $10.00

1980 POCKET WATCH PRICE INDICATOR. Ehrhardt, 1980. 110, 8½x11 pages. 1 lb. 2 oz $12.00

AMERICAN POCKET WATCH COMPANIES. (Pocket book with 50 inventory pages). Ehrhardt, 1979. 96, 3½x5½ pages. 2 oz $3.00

MASTER INDEX TO 13 WATCH BOOKS. (Books published before 1980). Ehrhardt, 1979. 16, 8½x11 pages. 6 oz $4.00

ELGIN POCKET WATCH IDENTIFICATION & PRICE GUIDE. Ehrhardt, 1976. 120, 8½x11 pages. 1 lb. 2 oz $10.00

ILLINOIS SPRINGFIELD WATCHES ID. & PRICE GUIDE. Ehrhardt, 1976. 136, 8½x11 pages. 1 lb. 4 oz $10.00

WALTHAM POCKET WATCH ID. & PRICE GUIDE. Ehrhardt, 1976. 172, 8½x11 pages. 1 lb. 4 oz $10.00

HAMILTON POCKET WATCH ID. & PRICE GUIDE. Ehrhardt, 1976. (Revised 1981). 53, 8½x11 pages. 1 lb. 4 oz $10.00

ROCKFORD GRADE & SERIAL NUMBERS WITH PRODUCTION FIGURES. Ehrhardt, 1976. 44, 8½x11 pages. 12 oz $10.00

TRADEMARKS. Ehrhardt, 1976. 128, 8½x 11 pages. 1 lb. 2 oz $10.00

THE PRICELESS POSSESSIONS OF A FEW. A brief history of the Gruen Watch Company, their 50th Anniversary Watch, and contemporary prestige watches: Edward Howard — Premier Maximus — C. H. Hurlburd — Lord Elgin — Hamilton Masterpiece. Eugene T. Fuller, 1974. 64 perfect bound pages. 10 oz. $10.00

AMERICAN POCKET WATCH ENCYCLOPEDIA & PRICE GUIDE. Ehrhardt, 1982. 216, 8½x11 pages. 1 lb. 10 oz. **Volume 1, June 1982.** $25.00
Volume 2, Tentative— $25.00
Volume 3, Tentative— $25.00
Volume 4, Tentative— $25.00

(Price of Volume 1, 2, 3 & 4 subject to change after April 1, 1983).

EVERYTHING YOU WANTED TO KNOW ABOUT AMERICAN WATCHES & DIDN'T KNOW WHO TO ASK. Col. George E. Townsend, 1971. (With **1983** Price Guide by Roy Ehrhardt). 88, 6x0 pages. 0 oz $8.00

AMERICAN RAILROAD WATCHES. Col. George E. Townsend, 1977. (With **1983** Price Guide by Roy Ehrhardt). 44, 6x9 pages. 8 oz. $8.00

THE WATCH THAT MADE THE DOLLAR FAMOUS. Col. George E. Townsend, 1974. (With **1983** Price Guide by Ralph Whitmer). 45, 6x9 pages. 8 oz $8.00

SET OF 3 PRICE GUIDES TO TOWNSEND BOOKS $9.00

E. HOWARD & CO. WATCHES 1858-1903. The last word on Howard watches: Identification — Production — Price Guide. Col. George E. Townsend, Author. **(With Price Guide by Roy Ehrhardt).** 1983. This manuscript was ready for publication when Col. Townsend died. The Price Guide was written by Roy Ehrhardt after his death. 48, 8½x11 paperback. 6 oz. $8.00

THE TIMEKEEPER (Hamilton Reprint). 31, 5x7 pages. 2 oz $3.00

AMERICAN WALTHAM WATCH CO. MOVEMENT PRODUCTION.
Vernon Hawkins, 1982. 33, 8½x11 pages. 8 oz $7.50
E. HOWARD & CO. 1858 (Reprint). 23, 5½x8½ pages. 2 oz $3.00

THE PERFECTED AMERICAN WATCH by The Waltham Watch Co., Waltham, Mass. 1907 Reprint (London Edition). 44, 5½x8½ pages. 4 oz $3.00
VINTAGE AMERICAN & EUROPEAN WRIST WATCH PRICE GUIDE.
Ehrhardt & Planes, 1984. 336, 6x9 pages. 1 lb. $9.95

CLOCK BOOKS

CLOCK IDENTIFICATION & PRICE GUIDE, BOOK 1. Ehrhardt & Rabeneck, 1977. (Prices revised in 1979). 198, 8½x11 pages.
1 lb. 12 oz $15.00
CLOCK IDENTIFICATION & PRICE GUIDE, BOOK 2. Ehrhardt & Rabeneck, 1979. 192, 8½x11 pages. 1 lb. 10 oz $15.00
CLOCK IDENTIFICATION & PRICE GUIDE, BOOK 3. Ehrhardt & Rabeneck, 1983. 203, 8½x11, perfect bound pages. 1 lb. 8 oz $15.00
(All three clock books contain different clocks. You need all three to have a complete library.)
THE OFFICIAL 1983 PRICE GUIDE TO ANTIQUE CLOCKS. Ehrhardt. 1983. 561, 6x9 paperback. 1 lb. 8 oz. $9.95
F. KROEBER CLOCK CO. ID. & PRICE GUIDE. Ehrhardt & Rabeneck, 1983. 36, 8½x11 pages. 8 oz $8.00
1979 CLOCK PRICE UP-DATE & INDEX TO BOOK 1. Ehrhardt, 1979. 18, 8½x11 pages. 6 oz $4.00

VIOLIN BOOKS

VIOLIN IDENTIFICATION & PRICE GUIDE, BOOK 1. Ehrhardt & Atchley, 1977. 192, 8½x11 pages. 1 lb. 10 oz $25.00
VIOLIN IDENTIFICATION & PRICE GUIDE, BOOK 2. Ehrhardt & Atchley, 1978. 206, 8½x11 pages. 1 lb. 10 oz $25.00
VIOLIN IDENTIFICATION & PRICE GUIDE, BOOK 3. Ehrhardt & Atchley, 1978. 152, 8½x11 pages. 1 lb. 5 oz. $15.00

MISCELLANEOUS BOOKS

AMERICAN COLLECTOR DOLLS PRICE GUIDE, BOOK 1. S. Ehrhardt & D. Westbook, 1975. 128, 8½x11 pages. 1 lb. 2 oz $9.00
AMERICAN CUT GLASS PRICE GUIDE, (Revised 1977). Alpha Ehrhardt. 120, 8½x11 pages. 1 lb. 2 oz $7.00
POCKET KNIFE BOOK 1 & 2 PRICE GUIDE (Revised 1977). J. Ferrell & R. Ehrhardt. 128, 8½x11 pages. 1 lb. 2 oz. $7.00

The books listed above are sold on a satisfaction guarantee. If you are not sure about the books you want, send a self-addressed, stamped envelope and we will send you detailed brochures on all of the publications. For orders in the U.S. and Canada, send the price of the book plus $1.00 postage and handling for the first book and 30 cents for each additional. Foreign countries — Check with your post office for rate, your choice, Air or Sea Mail, Book Rate. Book and carton weights listed. Send orders to:

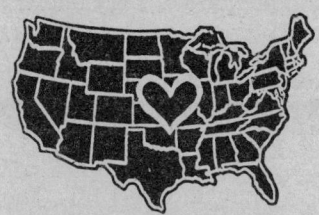

HEART OF AMERICA PRESS
P. O. Box 9808
Kansas City, Missouri 64134
(816) 761-0080

We sell reliable information.

TEMPUS VITAM REGIT

THE NATIONAL ASSOCIATION OF WATCH AND CLOCK COLLECTORS, INC.
BOX 33, 514 POPLAR STREET, COLUMBIA, PA 17512

This non-profit, scientific and educational corporation was founded in 1943 to bring together people who are interested in timekeeping in any form or phase. More than 33,000 members now enjoy its benefits. The Headquarters, Museum and Library are located in the Borough of Columbia on the eastern bank of the Susquehanna River within historic Lancaster County, Pennsylvania, where a continuing heritage of clock and watch-making spans two and one-quarter centuries.

Some of the tangible benefits of membership are the Association's publications. The bi-monthly **Bulletin** is the world's leading publication devoted to timekeeping. It contains papers written by members on technical and historic aspects of horology. Through its "Answer Box" column it also provides the member with an opportunity to direct his "knotty" horological problems to a panel of fifty volunteer authorities from around the world, many of whom are authors of definitive works in their respective areas of interest. Reviews help the collector keep abreast with the ever growing number of horological publications. Activities of the more than 100 Chapters located around the world are also included as are listings of stolen items. The **Mart,** also bi-monthly, is an informal medium in which members may list items that they wish to buy, trade, or sell. Like the **Bulletin,** its circulation exceeds 33,000. Other publications include the **Roster of Members,** a listing of books available through the Association's Lending Library, and occasional papers meriting separate publication.

Another benefit of membership is the use of the Nation's largest collection of books devoted to timekeeping. A number of the titles are duplicated in the Lending Library and may be borrowed through the mail for merely the cost of postage and, on occasion, insurance. The Library is under the supervision of a professional librarian who will also help a member in his research. A visitor can study the various horological periodicals of many sister horological associations around the world. The serious researcher may also examine rare and early works concerning horology. The Nation's only computerized Horological Data Bank is at the member's disposal as are thousands of American patents dealing with timekeeping.

Free admission to the NAWCC Museum in Columbia for both the member and his immediate family is yet another benefit. The Museum offers a rare opportunity to examine a collection of watches, clocks, tools, and other related items which range from the primitive to the modern. The "how and why" of timekeeping is emphasized throughout whether the display be of early non-mechanical timepieces or of the highly sophisticated "Atomic Clock." Movements of wood, iron, and brass are displayed for study. Many of the items exhibited are becoming increasingly rare and beyond the reach of many private collectors. Two special exhibitions are mounted each year: a three-month winter exhibition and a six-month summer exhibition. Items included in the special exhibitions are drawn from the collections of members, friends, and other museums.

Membership in the National Association also makes one eligible for membership in one or more of the more than 100 Chapters located in the United States, Australia, Canada, England, and Japan. It also makes one eligible to register for the regularly scheduled regional and national meetings each year. Chapter, regional, and national meetings usually consist of seminars, exhibits, and an opportunity to improve the member's own collection through trading, buying, or selling to other members. Finally, membership can enable a person to form lasting friendships with some of the finest people in the world: timekeeper enthusiasts!

For a brochure and membership application write to the Administrator, N.A.W.C.C., Box 033, Columbia, PA 17512.

WAY'S WATCH and CLOCK REPAIR

C.R. WAY
CLOCKMAKER • WATCHMAKER

A master craftsman for more than 24 years specializing in the repair and restoration of

- **ANTIQUE CLOCKS**
- **ANTIQUE AND CONTEMPORARY WATCHES**
- **JEWELRY**
- **MUSIC BOXES**

6296 Silver Star Rd.
Orlando, FL 32809

(305) 295-7127

A member in good standing N.A.W.C.C. 33586

SPECIAL LIMITED OFFER

40% Discount on

...an indispensible book for every collector, hobbyist, dealer and investor!

THE MOST VALUABLE BOOK YOU'LL EVER OWN...

Successful collectors know —
What they have... What they paid... and What it's worth... at a moments notice!

- The ultimate collection organizer.
- Your complete inventory at a glance.
- An indisputable insurance & tax record.
- Track price trends.

PLUS...

- A directory for Clubs, Dealers, and Fellow Collectors.
- List of recommended Museums and Publications.
- Special advice on — Appraisals — Insurance — Taxes — Buying & Selling — Care & Storage — Restoration and Detecting Fakes & Reproductions.

(256 pp., paperback, 5¼" x 7⅞")

...A GUIDE TO CATALOGING & IDENTIFYING Your Antiques & Collectibles

A Regular $4.95 Value...
Now Only $2.50 (plus 50¢ postage)

ORDERING INSTRUCTIONS

To be eligible for this special limited offer **you must fill out completely,** the reader survey questionaire on the back of this order form.

SEND ORDERS TO: *THE HOUSE OF COLLECTIBLES,* DEPARTMENT RS
1900 PREMIER ROW, ORLANDO, FLORIDA 32809

☐ Please send one copy of "The Official Collector's Journal" at my special discount price of $2.50 + $.50 postage = $3.00
☐ Check or money order enclosed $_____ (include postage)
☐ Please charge $_____ to my: ☐ MASTERCARD ☐ VISA

Account No. (All Digits)_____ Expiration Date _____

Signature _____

NAME (please print)_____ PHONE _____
ADDRESS _____ APT. # _____
CITY _____ STATE _____ ZIP _____ (50)

Note: This offer is limited to one copy per customer. Additional copies may be ordered at the regular price. See order blank at back of book.

READER SURVEY

The House of Collectibles continually seeks to improve, expand and update the material in *The Official Price Guide Series*. The assistance and cooperation of numerous collectors and dealers have added immeasurably to the success of the books in this series. Please take a few seconds and give us your help so we can provide you with information needed to become a successful collector.

Name _____ Phone (____) _____
Address _____
City _____ State _____ Zip _____
Age Group: ☐ under 18 ☐ 18-24 ☐ 25-34 ☐ 35-44 ☐ 45-54 ☐ 55 & over
Title of book purchased _____
Date of purchase _____
Name & address of bookshop _____
_____

Reason for purchase:
[ ] I had the previous edition.
[ ] I saw it in a public library.
☐ I was looking for a book about this subject.
☐ I saw it advertised.
☐ It was recommended to me.

Do you plan to buy the new revised
edition of this book when it's published? ☐ Definitely ☐ Probably ☐ No

Did you have difficulty locating a bookshop
that carries The House of Collectibles titles? ☐ Yes ☐ No

Is this the first House of
Collectibles book that you've purchased? ☐ Yes ☐ No

Is there any way you feel this book could be improved? _____
_____

How do you feel this book compares with other books about the same subject?
_____

Check the publisher's catalogue at the back of this book, then tell us:
are there any titles you'd like to see added to our series? _____
_____

Would you consider yourself primarily a:
[ ] Collector [ ] Dealer [ ] Investor [ ] Home Decorator [ ] General Reader

Do you have any information not included
in the book but which you think should be? [ ] Yes [ ] No

If you do, would you be interested
in becoming a contributor to a future edition? [ ] Yes [ ] No
(If your answer is yes, we'll be contacting you with full details on how you can become an "Official Member" of the world's largest hobby publishing team!)

How did your plates do?

Reco's "Little Boy Blue" by John McClelland

UP 214% in 1 Year

Some limited edition plates gained more in the same year, some less, and some not at all...But *Plate Collector* readers were able to follow the price changes, step by step, in Plate Price Trends, a copyrighted feature appearing in each issue of the magazine.

Because *The Plate Collector* is your best source guide...has more on limited editions than all other publications combined...and gives you insight into every facet of your collecting...you too will rate it

Your No. 1 Investment In Limited Editions

Plate Collector, established in 1972, was the first publication to feature limited editions only. Since then it's expanded, adding figurines, bells and prints, earning such reader raves as "Objective and impartial," "...has great research," "...a major guide to the plates I buy," and "It is the best collector magazine on the market."

To bring you the latest, most valuable information every month, our editors travel the world. Sometimes stories lead them to the smaller Hawaiian islands, or to the porcelain manufactories of Europe.

Their personal contact with artisans, hobby leaders, collectors, artists and dealers lets you share an intimate view of limited editions.

Each fat, colorful, monthly issue brings you new insight, helps you enjoy collecting more.

You'll find *Plate Collector* a complete source guide. Consider new issue information and new issue announcements. Use the ratings of new releases and wide array of dealer ads to help you pick and choose the best.

Read regular columns and check current market values in Plate Price Trends to add to your storehouse of knowledge.

Learn about clubs (perhaps there's one meeting near you) and the growing number of collector conventions and shows. Profit from tips on insurance, decorating with limited editions, safeguarding your collectables...just a sample of recurring feature subjects.

Read *Plate Collector* magazine to become a true limited edition art insider. Order now. See new and old plates in sparkling color.

And now there's FIGURINE COLLECTOR... Providing the same kind of objective reporting about the world of figurine collecting, this quarterly publication is the first in its field.

Figurine Collector lets you in on what's new in this rapidly growing area. A veritable feast of information, it will instruct and entertain you with valuable information on a wide range of topics from how figurines are made to how they're doing on the secondary market.

To help you stay on top of what's happening in plate and figurine collecting, subscribe to both publications from Collector's Media, Inc., at the special combined rate.

16 issues (12 issues Plate Collector + 4 issues Figurine Collector) $30
Plate Collector only...12 issues (1 year) $24.95
Figurine Collector only...4 issues (1 year) $9.95

Collector's Media, Inc.

P.O. Box 1729-HS   San Marcos, TX 78667-1729

To use VISA and MasterCard, include all raised information on your card

There is only one...
THE OFFICIAL®
PRICE GUIDE

THE MULTIPURPOSE REFERENCE GUIDE!!

THE OFFICIAL PRICE GUIDE SERIES has gained the reputation as the standard barometer of values on collectors' items. When you need to check the market price of a collectible, turn first to the OFFICIAL PRICE GUIDES ... for impartial, unbiased, current information that is presented in an easy-to-follow format.

- **CURRENT VALUES FOR BUYING AND SELLING.** ACTUAL SALES that have occurred in all parts of the country are CAREFULLY EVALUATED and COMPUTERIZED to arrive at the most ACCURATE PRICES AVAILABLE.

- **CONCISE REFERENCES.** Each OFFICIAL PRICE GUIDE is designed primarily as a *guide to current market values.* They also include a useful summary of the information most readers are seeking: a history of the item; how it's manufactured; how to begin and maintain a collection; how and where to sell; addresses of periodicals and clubs.

- **INDEXED FORMAT.** The novice as well as the seasoned collector will appreciate the unique alphabetically *indexed format* that provides *fast retrieval* of information and prices.

- **FULLY ILLUSTRATED.** All the OFFICIAL PRICE GUIDES are richly illustrated. Many feature COLOR SECTIONS as well as black and white photos.

Over 21 years of experience has made
THE HOUSE OF COLLECTIBLES
the most respected price guide authority!

TRADE PRICE GUIDE SERIES

■ **American Silver & Silver Plate** — Due to recent **skyrocketing** demand, **American Silverware** has become the most profitable collectible field in the nation. • Over **16,000 current market values** *for all types of American antique and modern silverware and holloware.* • *A handy pattern reference guide.* • *Valuable advice on starting and building a collection.* • *Silversmiths.' marks.* • *Care and storage tips.* • *ILLUSTRATED.*
3rd Edition, 608 pgs., 5⅜" x 8", Paperback, ISBN: 402-X, $9.95.

■ **Anheuser Busch Collectibles** — The official guide endorsed by Anheuser Busch • *Thousands of values are given for every known product of this prestigious brewery.* • *Includes steins, glasses, umbrellas, T-shirts, pool cues, aprons, trays, beer cans, key rings, insulators, playing cards, tie tacks, belt buckles, hats, caps, coolers, dart games, light fixtures, towels, and more.* • *ILLUSTRATED.*
1st Edition, 576 pgs., 5⅜" x 8", Paperback, ISBN: 417-8, $9.95.

■ **Antique Clocks** — Acclaimed by clock enthusiasts as the most **comprehensive** guide to antique American clocks in print today! • Over **10,000 current market values.** • Over *1,000 line drawings from actual manufacturers' catalogs dating back to the 19th century.* • *Advice on displaying, cleaning, and storing your collection.* • *Complete list of clock suppliers, museums, libraries, periodicals, and books.* • *ILLUSTRATED.*
2nd Edition, 576 pgs., 5⅜" x 8", Paperback, ISBN: 420-8, $9.95

■ **Antique & Modern Dolls** — Historically a **favorite hobby**, antique and modern dolls are a **hot investment.** • More than **6,000 current retail selling prices** *for dolls in all price ranges.* • *Antique dolls in wax, carved wood, china, and bisque.* • *Modern and semi-modern dolls in celluloid, chalk, plastic, composition, and cloth.* • *Shirley Temples, Barbie, G.I. Joe, Peanuts, Kewpies, and more.* • *ILLUSTRATED.*
1st Edition, 576 pgs., 5⅜" x 8", Paperback, ISBN: 381-3, $9.95.

■ **Antique & Modern Firearms** — Serious gun enthusiasts have long **recognized** this work to be the **official definitive source for pricing collector firearms.** • Over **20,500 current market values** *for pistols, rifles, and shotguns made by more than 1,300 manufacturers!* • *Colonial muzzle-loaders, semi and automatic handguns, sub-machine guns, revolvers, shotguns, and bolt and lever action rifles.* • *ILLUSTRATED.*
4th Edition, 576 pgs., 5⅜" x 8", Paperback, ISBN: 421-6, $9.95.

■ **Antiques and Other Collectibles** — • Over **100,000 current market values** and detailed listings *for more than* **200 categories** *of antiques and collectibles.* • *A special price column indicates which items have increased in value offering the best investment potential.* • **Learn expert tactics for successful collecting** *from how to build a collection to understanding market trends.* • **Fully Indexed.** • *ILLUSTRATED.*
4th Edition, 832 pgs., 5⅜" x 8", Paperback, ISBN: 374-0, $9.95

■ **Antique Jewelry** — Acclaimed by critics, jewelers, appraisers, and collectors, this is the **most respected** and **extensive guide** to antique and collectible jewelry ever **published.** • Over **8,300 current prices,** *organized for easy reference by category, all cross-referenced in a complete index.* • *A history lesson in Georgian, Victorian, Art Nouveau, and Art Deco jewelry designs.* • *ILLUSTRATED.*
3rd Edition, 672 pgs., 5⅜" x 8", Paperback, ISBN: 401-1, $9.95.

■ **Bottles Old & New** — Long recognized by the experts as the most **comprehensive and reliable value guide** in the antique and collectible bottle field! • Over **22,000 current collector values** *for antique, figural, and current production collectible bottles.* • *Ale, Bitters, Flasks, Medicine, Poison, Soda, Avon, Jim Beam, and more.* • *Complete glossary.* • *ILLUSTRATED.*
7th Edition, 672 pgs., 5⅜" x 8", Paperback, ISBN: 399-6, $9.95.

For your convenience use the handy order form.

TRADE PRICE GUIDE SERIES

■ **Collectible Cameras** — Today **astonishing prices** are being paid for many **fine antique, classic,** and even **secondhand cameras.** • More than **5,000 selling prices** *for all types of popular collector cameras.* • *Information on manufacturer, model name, model number, specifications, and date.* • *Advice on buying and building a collection.* • *A step-by-step guide through the hobby.* • *ILLUSTRATED.*
1st Edition, 320 pgs., 5⅜" x 8", Paperback, ISBN: 383-X, $9.95.

■ **Collectibles of the Third Reich** — **Phenomenal** is the only word to describe the **rising interest** in **Nazi militaria.** *Perhaps our desire never to forget the horror of Hitler is the root cause of this astonishing collectible field.* • *Included in this extensive guide are firearms, badges, insignia, flags, standards, banners, uniforms, bayonets, daggers, swords, and much more.* • *ILLUSTRATED.*
1st Edition, 320 pgs., 5⅜" x 8", Paperback, ISBN: 422-4, $9.95.

■ **Military Collectibles** — The **definitive guide** to war memorabilia containing military objects from all over the world, 15th century to date: armor, weapons, uniforms, bayonets, rare, and unusual objects. • *Over* **12,000 totally revised prices** *assembled from actual nationwide sales results!* • *Advice on buying and selling from auction houses, mail order, and retail dealers.* • *Museums.* • *Glossary.* • *ILLUSTRATED.*
3rd Edition, 608 pgs., 5⅜" x 8", Paperback, ISBN: 398-8, $9.95.

■ **Music Collectibles** — This revised and expanded edition is the **best selling reference guide** in the music memorabilia field. • *Over* **11,000 current market values.** • *Detailed descriptions, historical backgrounds, and values for all types of American and foreign made music machines from the 15th century to the present.* • *Expert advice on grading condition, restoration, and buying and selling.* • *ILLUSTRATED.*
3rd Edition, 576 pgs., 5⅜" x 8", Paperback, ISBN: 406-2, $9.95.

■ **Old Books & Autographs** — Fully revised and updated, this is the **most comprehensive** guide to vintage books and autographs **in print today.** • *Over* **11,000 current market values** *for children's books, the old West, novels, detective fiction, book sets, Bibles, and collectible autographs.* • *Glossary of collector terminology.* • *Biographies of the great printers and bibliophiles.* • *Care and repair of old books.* • *ILLUSTRATED.*
5th Edition, 576 pgs., 5⅜" x 8", Paperback, ISBN: 410-0, $9.95.

■ **Oriental Collectibles** — **Unravel the mystique** of the **Orient** with this fascinating guide **documented in detail.** • *Over* **10,000 current market values** *compiled from actual sales records from auctions and private sales throughout the U.S.* • *Detailed listings for Chinese, Japanese, and Asian collectors' items including pottery, Japanese weapons, jade carvings, ivories, netsuke, rugs and more.* • *ILLUSTRATED.*
1st Edition, 512 pgs., 5⅜" x 8", Paperback, ISBN: 375-9, $9.95.

■ **Paper Collectibles** — Tour the **fabulous** world of paper collectibles. • *Over* **27,000 prices** *for paper items of every description dating from medieval times to the present including books, posters, checks, documents, photographs, newspapers, celebrity autographs, and much more!* • *Sections on buying, selling, and caring for paper collectibles.* • *Find the bargains and enjoy the hobby like never before!* • *ILLUSTRATED.*
3rd Edition, 608 pgs., 5⅜" x 8", Paperback, ISBN: 394-5, $9.95.

■ **Pottery & Porcelain** — This comprehensive guide has *over* **12,000 current market values** for American pottery and porcelain of **all types** and **all periods** from the 18th to the 20th century! • *Art pottery, tableware, functional pieces, and novelties.* • *Backgrounds for all the major manufacturers including Rookwood, Roseville, Weller, Hull, and more.* • *Trademark reference guide.* • *Tips on building a collection.* • *ILLUSTRATED.*
3rd Edition, 576 pgs., 5⅜" x 8", Paperback, ISBN: 403-8, $9.95.

For your convenience use the handy order form.

TRADE PRICE GUIDE SERIES

■ **Collector Knives** — Endorsed by the American Blade Collectors. • Over **14,000 current collector values.** • *1,250 worldwide knife manufacturers.* • *Special section for Case, Ka-Bar, and limited edition knives.* • *Valuable collector information.* • *Exclusive identification guide for pocket knife shields, knife nomenclature, and blade and knife patterns.* • *Up-to-date list of knife organizations and trade publications.* • *ILLUSTRATED.*
6th Edition, 736 pgs., 5⅜" x 8", Paperback, ISBN: 389-9, $9.95.

■ **Collector Plates** — The plate collector's bible! Contains the **most complete listing** of all U.S. and foreign plate manufacturers and distributors **in print!** • *Over 18,000 current collectors values.* • *Includes thousands of collector plates from 1895 to date.* • *Tips on cleaning, shipping, storing, and displaying.* • *A glossary and complete list of plate publications and clubs.* • *How to buy and an investment review.* • *ILLUSTRATED.*
2nd Edition, 672 pgs., 5⅜" x 8", Paperback, ISBN: 393-7, $9.95.

■ **Collector Prints** — The **most accurate** and **authoritative work** on limited edition prints in publication today. • *Over 14,750 listings of collector prints for more than* **400 of the world's leading artists.** • *A list of galleries, agents and publishers.* • *Information on buying, selling, storing, and caring for prints.* • *A glossary of printmaking and print collecting terminology.* • *Artists' biographies.* • *ILLUSTRATED.*
5th Edition, 576 pgs., 5⅜" x 8", Paperback, ISBN: 395-3, $9.95.

■ **Comic Books and Collectibles** — America's **indispensable guide** to comic books and related collectibles. • *Over 50,000 current values compiled from marketplace transactions.* • *Exclusive sections on Big Little Books, Comic Character Memorabilia, Original Art, and Newspaper Comic Art.* • *Advice on buying, selling, investing, and swapping.* • *An in-depth glossary.* • *ILLUSTRATED.*
7th Edition, 672 pgs., 5⅜" x 8", Paperback, ISBN: 411-9, $9.95.

■ **Depression Glass** — The largest price guide devoted exclusively to depression glass in print today! *Thousands of items listed, every known pattern and manufacturer included.* • *Clear and concise line drawings illustrate each pattern.* • *Valuable collector tips on buying and selling, care and display, fakes, reproductions, and much more.* • *Complete list of collector publications, museums, and clubs.* • *ILLUSTRATED.*
1st Edition, 576 pgs., 5⅜" x 8", Paperback, ISBN: 433-X, $9.95.

■ **Glassware** — For the first time in print, the **most comprehensive** price guide to collectible glassware **ever produced!** • *Over 60,000 current market values for all of the major types of collectible glass including Art, Carnival, Cut, Depression, and Pattern.* • *Collecting advice and informative background histories.* • *Includes museums, clubs, and manufacturers' marks.* • *ILLUSTRATED.*
1st Edition, 672 pgs., 5⅜" x 8", Paperback, ISBN: 125-X, $9.95.

■ **Hummel Figurines & Plates** — Hummel collectors are **unanimous** in their **praise** of this **comprehensive** guide! • *Over 18,000 current market values for every known Hummel.* • *Complete guide to trademarks and variations.* • *A detailed history of Berta Hummel and the Goebel factory.* • *Tips on collecting, care, and repair.* • *Information on clubs, exhibits, publications, and contests.* • *ILLUSTRATED.*
4th Edition, 480 pgs., 5⅜" x 8", Paperback, ISBN: 390-2, $9.95.

■ **Kitchen Collectibles** — This is the only value guide in print today devoted **exclusively** to collectible kitchenware. • *More than 28,000 current selling prices.* • *China, glassware, silver, copper, iron, and wood.* • *Historical backgrounds.* • *Comprehensive descriptions of every item, including use, manufacturer, material, style, date, and size.* • *Hints on buying, selling, care, and storage.* • *ILLUSTRATED.*
1st Edition, 544 pgs., 5⅜" x 8", Paperback, ISBN: 371-6, $9.95.

For your convenience use the handy order form.

TRADE PRICE GUIDE SERIES

■ **Radio, TV, and Movie Memorabilia** — **For the first time ever,** a comprehensive value guide is devoted **exclusively** to these collectibles. • Includes thousands of actual selling prices gathered from across the country on animated cels, autographs and autographed articles, books, buttons, pins, rings, costumes, design sketches, fanzines, figurines, games, magazines, posters, press kits, and much more. • ILLUSTRATED.
1st Edition, 576 pgs., 5⅜" x 8", Paperback, ISBN: 416-X, $9.95.

■ **Records** — Find out if your **"golden oldies"** are worth a small fortune. • More than **32,000 current collector prices** for all categories of old, rare, and modern records from 1953 to date! • Exclusive photos and biographies of nearly 200 recording stars. • Collecting advice on condition, care, and storage. • Complete discographies for Motown and Philles records • Inventory checklist. • ILLUSTRATED.
5th Edition, 576 pgs., 5⅜" x 8", Paperback, ISBN: 409-7, $9.95.

■ **Royal Doulton** — Acclaimed by critics as the **definitive value guide** to the delightful world of **Royal Doulton figurines.** • Over **5,500 current collector market values.** • Features market trends, areas of collector interest, and the investment potential. • A handy "quick" reference numerical index for all HN and M model numbers. • Includes the Kate Greenaway series, Gilbert and Sullivan, and more. • ILLUSTRATED.
3rd Edition, 576 pgs., 5⅜" x 8", Paperback, ISBN: 407-0, $9.95.

■ **Science Fiction and Fantasy Collectibles** — **The interest has never been greater** for a guide devoted exclusively to this fascinating field. • Thousands of values given for "sci-fi" autographs, original art, posters, paperbacks, novels, Big Little books, games, fanzines, lobby cards, comics, toys, and much more. • Advice on buying and selling, care, display, and condition. • ILLUSTRATED.
1st Edition, 576 pgs., 5⅜" x 8", Paperback, ISBN: 418-6, $9.95.

■ **Wicker** — The most detailed guide to the fabulous world of vintage wicker on the market today! • All types of American made wicker furniture and accessories from the Victorian, Turn of the Century, and Art Deco eras. • Over **600 photos** • **Detailed descriptions** for positive identification. • **Current collector values.** • A guide to restoring wicker with professional repair methods. • ILLUSTRATED.
2nd Edition, 480 pgs., 5⅜" x 8", Paperback, ISBN: 380-5, $9.95.

■ **Collectible Toys** — This is the book no toy collector can afford to be **without!** • Over 25,000 current values for trains, windups, autos, soldiers, boats, banks, guns, musical toys, Disneyana, comic characters, Star Trek, Star Wars, and more. • Major manufacturers from the Civil War to the present. • Valuable collecting tips. • Toy manufacturing in America. • The Evolution of toy collecting. • ILLUSTRATED.
1st Edition, 576 pgs., 5⅜" x 8", Paperback, ISBN: 384-8, $9.95.

■ **Collector Cars** — The worldwide love affair with the automobile has **resulted in unprecedented profits.** • Over 37,000 actual current prices for 4,100 models of U.S. and Foreign antique and classic automobiles. • United States production figures — 1897 to date. • A list of reference publications, museums, and collector clubs. • Advice on how to buy and sell successfully at auctions, to dealers, and individuals. • ILLUSTRATED.
5th Edition, 576 pgs., 5⅜" x 8", Paperback, ISBN: 408-9, $9.95.

■ **Collector Handguns** — **No other book** on the subject **comes close** to supplying the **concise** and **comprehensive** information found here. • More than 5,000 current retail prices for handguns of all styles and all calibers. • Every gun identified by manufacturer, model name, action, caliber, length, date, type of stock, weight, serial number, and markings. • Extensive ammo section. • Advice on buying and selling. • ILLUSTRATED.
1st Edition, 544 pgs., 5⅜" x 8", Paperback, ISBN: 367-8, $9.95.

For your convenience use the handy order form.

MINI PRICE GUIDE SERIES

■ **Antiques & Flea Markets** — Do your antique browsing with the experts... take along this **super compact guide** to more than **15,000** old, rare, and unusual collectors' items! • **Spot the bargains ... avoid the fakes ... make the best deals** *when you buy or sell at antique shops, auctions, flea markets, and garage sales.* • **Current market values** *for thousands of collectors' items in all categories.* • *Learn the professional approach to grading, storage, and restoration.* • *ILLUSTRATED.*
2nd Edition, 320 pgs., 4" x 5½", Paperback, ISBN: 392-9, $3.95.

■ **Antique Jewelry** — The indispensable guide to **valuable, but affordable jewelry** — for collecting, wearing, and investing. • **Over 2,500 current values** *for jewelry from 1750 to 1930.* • **Complete descriptions** *of styles, patterns, and identifying features.* • *Date of manufacture.* • **Important collector's advice** — *buying, selling, cleaning, storing, and displaying.* • **Grading information** *for diamonds, gold, and silver.* • **Historical background** *of jewelry.* • *ILLUSTRATED.*
2nd Edition, 288 pgs., 4" x 5½", Paperback, ISBN: 442-9, $3.95.

■ **Baseball Cards** — For thousands of fans, young and old, baseball card collecting is **a year round hobby.** This newly revised edition is the collector's standard reference. • *Over* **100,000 current market values.** • **Valuable collecting information** — *The history of card manufacturing in the U.S., tips on buying and selling, and how to grade condition to determine the value of your collection.* • *A special price column indicates which items have increased in value.* • **Exclusive checklist "grading" system.** • *ILLUSTRATED.*
4th Edition, 352 pgs., 4" x 5½", Paperback, ISBN: 438-0, $3.95.

■ **Beer Cans** — **Collectors agree** this handy carry along guide contains everything you will ever need to know about one of America's fastest growing hobbies! • *Over* **6,000 actual selling prices** *for old, modern, rare, and common beer cans.* • **All brands** *and all types of cans. Includes all label design variations, with information for identifying every variation.* • **History of brewing** *through 6,000 years!* • **Tips** *on how to find valuable cans and how to buy, sell, and trade* • *ILLUSTRATED.*
2nd Edition, 288 pgs., 4" x 5½", Paperback, ISBN: 440-2, $3.95.

■ **Bottles** — Never before in pocket size! Here is the **most convenient** guide to collectible **bottles** in print! *Thousands of values given for all types of old and new bottles.* • *Includes ale & gin, beer, bitters, cure, flasks, fruit jars, Hutchinson, ink, medicine, mineral, poison, Pontil, soda, spirits, Avon, Jim Beam, Brooks, Old Fitzgerald, and many more.* • *Also valuable collecting tips on buying and selling, grading condition, conducting a dig, background histories, bottle clubs, basic bottle shapes, trademarks, and investment advice.* • *ILLUSTRATED.*
1st Edition, 288 pgs., 4" x 5½", Paperback, ISBN: 431-3, $3.95.

■ **Cars and Trucks** — You could have a fortune parked in your own garage! *Over* **10,000 current auction and dealer prices** *for all popular U.S. and foreign made antique, classic, and collector cars.* • **Each detailed listing includes:** *the model name and year of production, engine specifications, body style, and a price range value from fair to excellent condition.* • **Learn how to evaluate** *the condition of a collector car the way the professionals do!* • *ILLUSTRATED.*
1st Edition, 240 pgs., 4" x 5½", Paperback, ISBN: 391-0, $2.95.

For your convenience use the handy order form.

MINI PRICE GUIDE SERIES

■ **Collectible Records** — One of the **most enjoyable and profitable hobbies** today. • Over **11,000 current market prices for** Rock and Country recordings. A chronological listing of discs from 1953 to date. • Listed by their original label and issue number. • **Collecting tips** — How to begin a collection, buying, selling, and grading the condition of records and jackets. • A handy guide to "Golden Oldie" shops, conventions, flea markets, and garage sales. • ILLUSTRATED.
1st Edition, 240 pgs., 4" x 5½", Paperback, ISBN: 400-3, $2.95.

■ **Collector Guns** — This **handy pocket guide** contains over **9,000 dealer prices** compiled from nationwide sales records for handguns, rifles, and shotguns. Covers American and foreign manufacturers. • **Complete data** on model names, barrel lengths, calibers, and sight types. • Information on the history of firearms, biographies of famous gunmakers, and collecting techniques! • ILLUSTRATED.
1st Edition, 240 pgs., 4" x 5½", Paperback, ISBN: 396-1, $2.95.

■ **Comic Books** — Join the **thousands** who have discovered the fascinating world of comic collecting, one of the nation's fastest-growing hobbies. • **Current market values for over 5,000 old and new comics.** • **Learn how** to start a comic collection and watch it grow into a **profitable investment.** • **Tips on** buying, selling, and swapping your comics. Start a comic collection with purchases from the newsstand. • ILLUSTRATED.
2nd Edition, 288 pgs., 4" x 5½", Paperback, ISBN: 382-1, $3.95.

■ **Dolls** — Reap pleasure and profit! • Over 3,000 current market prices for dolls of all types and all manufacturers. • **Positive identification** by maker, name of doll, markings, hair color, eye color, type of eye, date of manufacture, and size. • **Valuable collector information** on buying and selling, fakes, repairs, and how to care for your dolls. • **Extensive glossary** of doll making and collecting terms. • ILLUSTRATED.
2nd Edition, 288 pgs., 4" x 5½", Paperback, ISBN: 434-8, $3.95.

■ **Football Cards** — Call the right signals every time with the most **authoritative** guide to football cards **in print today!** This revised edition features all the latest cards and price changes. • Over 50,000 current market values for collectible football cards. • **Valuable collector information** — tips on trading, buying and selling, and how to grade condition to determine the value of your collection. • **Exclusive checklist system.** • ILLUSTRATED.
3rd Edition, 288 pgs., 4" x 5½", Paperback, ISBN: 388-0, $2.95.

■ **Glassware** — The handiest guide to collectible glassware on the market today! Contains thousands of values for the five major types of collectible glass — art, carnival, cut, depression, and pattern. • Includes history of each period, manufacturer's marks, pattern and motif identification guide, extensive glossary, and much more. • Plus valuable collector advice on buying, selling, care, display, collector publications, clubs, organizations, and museums. • ILLUSTRATED.
1st Edition, 288 pgs., 4" x 5½", Paperback, ISBN: 432-1, $3.95.

■ **Hummels** — Handy pocket guide with over 2,000 current collector prices for the most common and most popular Hummels. All the latest releases are included. • **A Hummel encyclopedia** — from Berta Hummel's beginnings to the growth of the Goebel firm, plus a collector's glossary. • **Valuable collector information** on buying, selling, storage, and display. • Pictures for each listing from 1923 to date. • ILLUSTRATED.
2nd Edition, 288 pgs., 4" x 5½", Paperback, ISBN: 435-6, $3.95.

For your convenience use the handy order form.

MINI PRICE GUIDE SERIES

■ **Military Collectibles** — The **indispensable carry along guide** to the fascinating and historical world of **war souvenirs.** • *Over* **4,000 current prices** *for a wide assortment of military objects from all over the world* — *19th century to World War II.* • **Positive identification** *with dates, markings, country of origin, army, and thorough descriptions.* • **Valuable collecting tips** — *How to build a collection, grading condition, displaying your collection, and glossary of collectors' terms.* • *ILLUSTRATED.*
1st Edition, 240 pgs., 4" x 5½", Paperback, ISBN: 378-3, $2.95.

■ **Paperbacks & Magazines** — Your **old paperbacks and magazines** could be worth a **fortune** today! • Over **10,000 values** are given on paperbacks and magazines dating from the 1800's through the 1980's compiled from actual sales between dealers and collectors. • *Learn what makes them valuable and why!* • *ILLUSTRATED.*
2nd Edition, 288 pgs., 4" x 5½", Paperback, ISBN: 405-4, $3.95.

■ **Pocket Knives** — A **complete price listing** of all **Case and Kabar pocket knives** plus **thousands of current values** *for all popular collector knives.* • **Complete identification** of **every knife** *by manufacturer, pattern, stamping, year of manufacture, length, and handle type.* • **Helpful advice** *on buying, selling, and caring for your knife collection.* • *Pocket knife terminology, grading condition, blade patterns, knife collector organizations, counterfeit specimens, and much more.* • *ILLUSTRATED.*
2nd Edition, 288 pgs., 4" x 5½", Paperback, ISBN: 443-7, $3.95.

■ **Scouting Collectibles** — **Attention, Scouts!** *Here's your* **"field guide"** *to the profitable hobby of scouting memorabilia.* • **Price listings for thousands of scouting items** *in all categories.* • *You'll learn about the fascinating history of scouting and the accessories that were in use over the past years including tools, gadgets, badges, and medals.* • *ILLUSTRATED.*
2nd Edition, 288 pgs., 4" x 5½", Paperback, ISBN: 397-X, $3.95.

■ **Sports Collectibles** — Whatever your sport, you will **find it here!** All the popular collectibles of baseball, football, basketball, hockey, boxing, hunting, fishing, horse racing, and other top sports. • **Over 12,000 current prices** *that collectors are actually paying for a host of sports memorabilia.* • **Old and modern sports collectibles** *from the 17th to the 20th century.* • **The inside facts** *on buying from dealers and selling your sports collectibles for maximum prices!* • *ILLUSTRATED.*
1st Edition, 240 pgs., 4" x 5½", Paperback, ISBN: 379-1, $2.95.

■ **Star Trek/Star Wars Collectibles** — The **phenomenal popularity** of these space age collectibles continues to **skyrocket!** • *Over* **6,000 current values** *for every category of Star Trek and Star Wars collector's items.* • **Fascinating information** *on the history of the television show and the making of the movies. Tips on building and caring for a collection to buying and selling.* • **Special sections** *on the conventions with a complete calendar of events.*
2nd Edition, 288 pgs., 4" x 5½", Paperback, ISBN: 437-2, $3.95.

■ **Toys** — Whether eight to eighty, you are **never too old** to seriously enjoy toy collections. • *Over* **8,000 current values** *for every category of toys* **from animal-drawn vehicles to rocketships.** • **A toy encyclopedia** — *histories of the manufacturers, valuable collector information on buying, selling, and grading condition.* • *ILLUSTRATED.*
2nd Edition, 288 pgs., 4" x 5½", Paperback, ISBN: 436-4, $3.95.

For your convenience use the handy order form.

OFFICIAL PRICE GUIDE SERIES

■ **Collector's Journal** — This is the most **valuable** book any collector could own! Use it to record dealers, collectors, clubs, museums, and reference materials. • Special inventory forms allow the recording of individual collectibles in minute detail. • Value development chart provides space for keeping track of investment value. • Vital information is provided on appraisal, insurance, taxes, and buying and selling.
1st Edition, 256 pgs., 5¼" x 7⅜", Paperback, ISBN: 445-3, $4.95.

■ **The Official Encyclopedia of Antiques and Collectibles** — More than 10,000 definitions. • Plus - U.S. automobile production figures. • bottle trademarks. • clock chronology. • collector plate backstamps. • pottery and porcelain marks. • U.S. firearm trademarks. • precious metal purity and weight conversion tables. • silversmith's marks. • pewter backstamps. • furniture style charts.
1st Edition, 704 pgs., 5⅜" x 8" Paperback, ISBN: 365-1, $9.95.

■ **The Official Guide to Buying and Selling Antiques and Collectibles** — covers every phase of collecting from beginning a collection to its ultimate sale • Examines IN DETAIL the collecting potential of approximately **200 different categories IN ALL PRICE RANGES.** • Learn how the collectible market operates and what makes an item valuable. Every possible source of collector's items is explored IN DEPTH.
1st Edition, 608 pgs., 5⅜" x 8", Paperback, ISBN: 369-4, $9.95.

■ **Identification Guide to Early American Furniture** — A comprehensive guide to identifying antique American furniture dating from 1603 to the 1840's. • Provides instant access to hundreds of pieces with superb line drawings. • Includes Jacobean, Pilgrim, William and Mary, Queen Anne, Chippendale, and Neo-Classical Revival. • Features the famous cabinetmakers Adam, Hepplewhite, Sheraton, and others. • ILLUSTRATED.
1st Edition, 320 pgs., 4" x 8", Paperback, ISBN: 414-3, $9.95.

IDENTIFICATION GUIDE SERIES

■ **Identification Guide to Glassware** — Over **100 types** of glass are completely described. • Hundreds of illustrated marks and line drawings. • Includes Agata, Amberina, Blown, Burmese, Cameo, Carnival, Cranberry, Crown Milano, Custard, Cut, Depression, Durand, Fry, Galle, Kew Blas, Lalique, Loetz, Mercury, Milk, Napoli, Nash, Paperweights, Peach Blow, Pressed, Ruby, Silveria, and dozens more. • ILLUSTRATED.
1st Edition, 320 pgs., 4" x 8", Paperback, ISBN: 413-5, $9.95.

■ **Identification Guide to Gunmarks** — An important "companion" identification guide to both The Antique and Modern Firearms and the Collector Handguns Price Guides. • Over **1,500** of the most commonly encountered trademarks on modern and antique guns. • Learn which marks are valuable and how to spot fakes and forgeries. • An alphabetical listing of trade names and codes for firearms without trademarks.
1st Edition, 256 pgs., 5⅜" x 8", Paperback, ISBN: 346-5, $6.95.

■ **Identification Guide to Pottery and Porcelain** — Absolutely the most comprehensive guide to identifying pottery and porcelain in print today! • Includes manufacturers in the United States, Austria, Belgium, Denmark, Holland, England, France, Germany, Ireland, Italy, Prussia, Russia, Scotland, Spain, Sweden, and Switzerland. • Complete descriptions of characteristics and all known marks are given for each of the hundreds of individual types listed.
1st Edition, 320 pgs., 4" x 8", Paperback, ISBN: 412-7, $9.95.

■ **Identification Guide to Victorian Furniture** — There is a **tremendous surge of interest** in the ornate furniture of the **Victorian Period.** • Complete descriptions of every piece and hundreds of line drawings make identification quick and easy. • Also contains manufacturers' histories and an extensive furniture glossary. • Includes Victorian, Renaissance Revival, Rococo Revival (Belter), Spool-turned, Cottage, Louis XVI Revival, Arts and Crafts, Wicker, Cast Iron, and Indian Teak.
1st Edition, 320 pgs., 4" x 8", Paperback, ISBN: 415-1, $9.95.

For your convenience use the handy order form.

NUMISMATIC SERIES

■ **1984 Blackbook Price Guide of United States Coins** — A coin collector's guide to current market values for all U.S. coins from 1616 to date — over **16,500 prices.** THE OFFICIAL BLACKBOOK OF COINS has gained the reputation as the most reliable, up-to-date guide to U.S. Coin values. This new edition features, an exclusive gold and silver identification guide. Learn how to test, weigh and calculate the value of any item made of gold or silver. Proven professional techniques revealed for the first time. Detecting altered coins section. Take advantage of the current "BUYERS' MARKET" in gold and silver. *ILLUSTRATED.*
$2.95-22nd Edition, 288 pgs., 4" x 5½", Paperback, Order #: 385-6

■ **1984 Blackbook Price Guide of United States Paper Money** — Over **9,000 buying and selling prices** covering U.S. currency from 1861 to date. Every note issued by the U.S. government is listed and priced including many Confederate States notes. Error Notes are described and priced, and there are detailed articles on many phases of the hobby for beginner and advanced collector alike. Comprehensive grading section. *ILLUSTRATED.*
$2.95-16th Edition, 240 pgs., 4" x 5½", Paperback, Order #: 387-2

■ **1984 Blackbook Price Guide of United States Postage Stamps** — *Featuring all U.S. stamps from 1847 to date pictured in full color.* Over **19,000** current selling prices. General issues, airmails and special delivery. United Nations, first day covers, and more. New listings for the most current commemorative and regular issue stamps, a feature not offered in any other price guide, at any price! Numerous important developments in the fast moving stamp market during the past year are all included in this *NEW REVISED EDITION. ILLUSTRATED.*
$2.95-6th Edition, 240 pgs., 4" x 5½", Paperback, Order #: 386-4

INVESTORS SERIES

■ **Investors Guide to Gold, Silver, Diamonds** — *All you need to know* about making money trading in the precious metals and diamonds markets. This practical, easy-to-read investment guide is for everyone in all income brackets. How to determine authenticity and value of gold, silver, and diamonds. *ILLUSTRATED.*
$6.95-1st Edition, 208 pgs., 5⅜" x 8½", Paperback, Order #: 171-3

■ **Investors Guide to Gold Coins** — *The first complete book* on investing in gold coins. Eclusive price performance charts trace all U.S. gold coins values from **1955 to date.** Forecast price trends and best bets. *ILLUSTRATED.*
$6.95-1st Edition, 288 pgs., 5⅜" x 8½", Paperback, Order #: 300-7

■ **Investors Guide to Silver Coins** — *The most extensive listing* of all U.S. Silver coins. Detailed price performance charts trace actual sales figures from **1955 to date.** Learn how to figure investment profit. *ILLUSTRATED.*
$6.95-1st Edition, 288 pgs., 5⅜" x 8½", Paperback, Order #: 301-5

■ **Investors Guide to Silver Dollars** — Regardless of your income, you can *become a successful silver dollar investor.* Actual sales figures for every U.S. silver dollar **1955 to date.** Comprehensive grading section. *ILLUSTRATED.*
$6.95-1st Edition, 192 pgs., 5⅜" x 8½", Paperback, Order #: 302-3

For your convenience use the handy order form.

FOR IMMEDIATE DELIVERY
VISA & MASTER CARD CUSTOMERS
ORDER TOLL FREE!
1-800-327-1384

This number is for orders only, it is not tied into the customer service or business office. Customers not using charge cards must use mail for ordering since payment is required with the order — sorry no C.O.D.'s. Florida residents call (305) 857-9095 — ask for order department.

OR SEND ORDERS TO

THE HOUSE OF COLLECTIBLES, ORLANDO CENTRAL PARK
1900 PREMIER ROW, ORLANDO, FL 32809   (305) 857-9095

☐ *Please send me the following price guides—*
☐ *I would like the most current edition of the books listed below.*

☐ 402-X @ 9.95	☐ 393-7 @ 9.95	☐ 409-7 @ 9.95	☐ 388-0 @ 2.95	☐ 413-5 @ 9.95
☐ 417-8 @ 9.95	☐ 395-3 @ 9.95	☐ 407-0 @ 9.95	☐ 432-1 @ 3.95	☐ 346-5 @ 6.95
☐ 420-8 @ 9.95	☐ 411-9 @ 9.95	☐ 418-6 @ 9.95	☐ 435-6 @ 3.95	☐ 412-7 @ 9.95
☐ 381-3 @ 9.95	☐ 433-X @ 9.95	☐ 380-5 @ 9.95	☐ 378-3 @ 2.95	☐ 415-1 @ 9.95
☐ 421-6 @ 9.95	☐ 125-X @ 9.95	☐ 392-9 @ 3.95	☐ 405-4 @ 3.95	☐ 385-6 @ 2.95
☐ 374-0 @ 9.95	☐ 390-2 @ 9.95	☐ 442-9 @ 3.95	☐ 443-7 @ 3.95	☐ 387-2 @ 2.95
☐ 401-1 @ 9.95	☐ 371-6 @ 9.95	☐ 438-0 @ 3.95	☐ 397-X @ 3.95	☐ 386-4 @ 2.95
☐ 399-6 @ 9.95	☐ 398-8 @ 9.95	☐ 440-2 @ 3.95	☐ 379-1 @ 2.95	☐ 171-3 @ 6.95
☐ 383-X @ 9.95	☐ 406-2 @ 9.95	☐ 431-3 @ 3.95	☐ 437-2 @ 3.95	☐ 300-7 @ 6.95
☐ 422-4 @ 9.95	☐ 410-0 @ 9.95	☐ 391-0 @ 2.95	☐ 436-4 @ 3.95	☐ 301-5 @ 6.95
☐ 384-8 @ 9.95	☐ 375-9 @ 9.95	☐ 400-3 @ 2.95	☐ 445-3 @ 4.95	☐ 302-3 @ 6.95
☐ 408-9 @ 9.95	☐ 394-5 @ 9.95	☐ 396-1 @ 2.95	☐ 365-1 @ 9.95	
☐ 367-8 @ 9.95	☐ 403-8 @ 9.95	☐ 382-1 @ 3.95	☐ 369-4 @ 9.95	
☐ 389-9 @ 9.95	☐ 416-X @ 9.95	☐ 434-8 @ 3.95	☐ 414-3 @ 9.95	

POSTAGE & HANDLING RATE CHART

TOTAL ORDER/POSTAGE	TOTAL ORDER/POSTAGE	
0 to $10.00 - **$1.25**	$20.01 to $30.00 - **$2.00**	$50.01 & Over -
$10.01 to $20.00 - **$1.60**	$30.01 to $40.00 - **$2.75**	**Add 10% of your total order**
	$40.01 to $50.00 - **$3.50**	(Ex. $75.00 x .10 = $7.50)

☐ Check or money order enclosed $_____ (include postage and handling)

☐ Please charge $_____ to my: ☐ MASTERCARD ☐ VISA

Charge Card Customers Not Using Our Toll Free Number Please Fill Out The Information Below.

Account No. (All Digits)_____ Expiration Date_____

Signature_____

NAME (please print)_____ PHONE_____

ADDRESS_____ APT. #_____ ⑩

CITY_____ STATE_____ ZIP_____